Beginning C# Objects: From Concepts to Code

JACQUIE BARKER AND GRANT PALMER

Apress™

Beginning C# Objects: From Concepts to Code
Copyright ©2004 by Jacquie Barker and Grant Palmer

ISBN (pbk): 1-59059-360-X

Printed and bound in the United States of America 10987654321

Trademarked names may appear in this book. Rather than use a trademark symbol with every occurrence of a trademarked name, we use the names only in an editorial fashion and to the benefit of the trademark owner, with no intention of infringement of the trademark.

Lead Editor: Dominic Shakeshaft

Technical Reviewer: James Huddleston

Editorial Board: Steve Anglin, Dan Appleman, Ewan Buckingham, Gary Cornell, Tony Davis, John Franklin, Jason Gilmore, Chris Mills, Steve Rycroft, Dominic Shakeshaft, Jim Sumser, Karen Watterson, Gavin Wray, John Zukowski

Project Manager: Kylie Johnston

Copy Edit Manager: Nicole LeClerc

Copy Editor: Ami Knox

Production Manager: Kari Brooks

Production Editor: Laura Cheu

Compositor: Kinetic Publishing Services, LLC

Proofreader: Liz Welch

Indexer: Michael Brinkman

Artist: Kinetic Publishing Services, LLC

Cover Designer: Kurt Krames

Manufacturing Manager: Tom Debolski

Distributed to the book trade in the United States by Springer-Verlag New York, Inc., 175 Fifth Avenue, New York, NY 10010 and outside the United States by Springer-Verlag GmbH & Co. KG, Tiergartenstr. 17, 69112 Heidelberg, Germany.

In the United States: phone 1-800-SPRINGER, e-mail orders@springer-ny.com, or visit http://www.springer-ny.com. Outside the United States: fax +49 6221 345229, e-mail orders@springer.de, or visit http://www.springer.de.

For information on translations, please contact Apress directly at 2560 Ninth Street, Suite 219, Berkeley, CA 94710. Phone 510-549-5930, fax 510-549-5939, e-mail info@apress.com, or visit http://www.apress.com.

The source code for this book is available to readers at http://www.apress.com in the Downloads section.

In loving memory of my wonderful parents, Bill and Dorothy Jost.

—Jacquie Barker

I would like to dedicate this book to my dog Bailey, who is a good, old dog.

—Grant Palmer

Contents at a Glance

Contents

Chapter 14 Transforming Our UML Model into C# Code 547

Chapter 15 Rounding Out Our Application, Part 1: Adding File Persistence 611

Chapter 16 Rounding Out Our Application, Part 2: Adding a Graphical User Interface 667

About the Authors

Jacquie Barker is a professional software engineer, author, and adjunct faculty member at George Washington University in Washington, DC. With over 25 years of experience as a hands-on software developer and project manager, Jacquie has spent the past 12 years focusing on object technology, becoming proficient as an object modeler and Sun Microsystems–certified Java programmer. She is currently employed as a senior member of the technical staff at Technology Associates, Inc. in Herndon, Virginia, and is also the founder of ObjectStart LLC, an object technology mentorship and training firm.

Jacquie earned a bachelor of science degree in computer engineering with highest honors from Case Western Reserve University in Cleveland, Ohio. She later received a master of science degree in computer science, focusing on software systems engineering, from UCLA, and has subsequently pursued post-graduate studies in information technology at George Mason University in Fairfax, Virginia.

Beginning C# Objects was adapted from Jacquie's bestselling book, *Beginning Java Objects: From Concepts to Code,* published originally by the former Wrox Press, Ltd. and now by Apress. Jacquie's "winning formula" for teaching object fundamentals continues to receive praise from readers around the world, and *Beginning Java Objects* has been adopted by many universities as a key textbook in their core IT curricula.

Please visit her web site, http://objectstart.com, for more information on her various publications and service offerings.

On a personal note, Jacquie's passions include her husband, Steve; pet rats; chocolate; and programming in Java. When not engaged in computer-related pursuits, Jacquie and Steve enjoy motorcycle road trips through the Virginia countryside, tandem bicycling, vacations at the beach, and spending quality time with family and friends.

For the past 20 years, **Grant Palmer** has worked in the Space Technology Division at NASA Ames Research Center in Moffett Field, CA. Grant was a NASA engineer for 15 years and currently works as a scientific programmer with the ELORET Corporation, developing computer applications that help design the thermal protection systems of spacecraft reentering the Earth's atmosphere.

Grant earned a bachelor of science degree in mechanical engineering from the University of California, Berkeley. He later received a master of science degree in aerospace engineering from Stanford University. Grant is an expert in FORTRAN, C, C++, and Perl, but these days does most of his programming in the more modern languages of Java and C#. He has authored or coauthored seven books on computer programming, including *C# Programmer's Reference*.

Grant lives in Phoenix, Arizona, with his wife, Lisa; his two sons, Jackson and Zachary; and a good, old dog named Bailey.

Acknowledgments

I'D LIKE TO OFFER my sincere, heartfelt thanks to everyone who helped Grant and me to produce this book:

- To James Huddleston, a true Renaissance man and reviewer extraordinaire for the tremendous job he did in assisting us with sorting out the "finer points" of C# as our primary technical reviewer.

- To Dominic Shakeshaft, our editor, for his dedication to ensuring the clarity of our book's message.

- To Gary Cornell, Apress publisher, for suggesting a Java-to-C# "port" of *Beginning Java Objects*.

- To *all* the folks at Apress—especially Kylie Johnston, Ami Knox, Laura Cheu, and Glenn Munlawin—for their superb editorial/production/ marketing support.

- To my coauthor, Grant Palmer, for keeping the best of humor throughout even the "darkest days"!

- To my husband, Steve, for *once again* being patient as I became temporarily *consumed* with the "writing biz." I love you tons!!!

—Jacquie Barker

To my coauthor, Jacquie Barker, for being fun to work with and for teaching me a lot about writing and object-oriented principles.

To the technical reviewers—Jim Huddleston and Dominic Shakeshaft—for the wonderful comments and insights they provided us on our book. Jim is a true computer guru who has probably forgotten more about programming than I will ever know.

To the editorial/production staff at Apress—Kylie Johnston, Ami Knox, Laura Cheu, and Glenn Munlawin—for their tireless efforts in keeping this project on time and on target.

Finally, to my beautiful wife, Lisa, and my wonderful boys, Jackson and Zachary, who make life worth living.

—Grant Palmer

Preface

As a Java developer and instructor, I wrote my first book, *Beginning Java Objects*, to communicate my passionate belief that learning objects thoroughly is an essential first step in mastering an object-oriented programming language. Since *B.J.O.* was first published in November 2000, I've heard from countless readers who agree wholeheartedly!

I've been extremely pleased with the wonderful response that I've gotten to *B.J.O.*, and was therefore delighted when Gary Cornell, the publisher of Apress and Dominic Shakeshaft, Apress editorial director, approached me about producing a C# version of my book. It's indeed true that basic object concepts are "language neutral." What you'll learn conceptually about objects in Part One of this book, and about object modeling in Part Two, could apply equally well to C#, or Java, or Visual Basic .NET , or C++, or Ada, or Smalltalk, or an as-yet-to-be-invented object-oriented (OO) language.

But, our goal for this book is twofold: not only do we want to teach you about objects and object modeling, but we also want to get you properly jump-started with the C# programming language by showing you how such concepts translate into C# syntax specifically. Hence, *Beginning C# Objects* was born!

Because I'm focused wholly on Java technologies in my career as a software engineer, Apress sought professionals experienced with C# to help me in translating my book from Java into C#. Grant Palmer, my coauthor, and James Huddleston, our primary technical reviewer, were the perfect collaborators, and I'm pleased to have had the opportunity to work with them both in producing this book.

—Jacquie Barker

Introduction

THIS IS A BOOK, first and foremost, about software objects: what they are, why they are so "magical" and yet so straightforward, and how one goes about structuring a software application to use objects appropriately.

This is also a book about C#: not a hard-core, "everything there is to know about C#" book, but rather a gentle yet comprehensive introduction to the language, with special emphasis on how to transition from an object model to a fully functional C# application—something that few, if any, other books provide.

Goals for this Book

Our goals in writing this book (and, hopefully, yours for buying it) are to

- *Make you comfortable with fundamental object-oriented (OO) terminology and concepts.*

- *Give you hands-on, practical experience with object modeling:* that is, with developing a "blueprint" that can be used as the basis for subsequently building an object-oriented software system.

- *Illustrate the basics of how such an object model is translated into a working software application—a C# application, to be specific,* although the techniques that you'll learn for object modeling apply equally well to any OO language.

If you're already experienced with the C# language (but not with object fundamentals), it's critical to your successful use of the language that you learn about its object-oriented roots. On the other hand, if you're a newcomer to C#, then this book will get you properly "jump-started." *Either way, this book is a "must-read" for anyone who wishes to become proficient with an OO programming language like C#.*

Just as importantly, this book is ***not*** meant to

- ***Turn you into an overnight "pro" in object modeling:*** Like all advanced skills, becoming totally comfortable with object modeling takes two things: a good theoretical foundation and a lot of practice! We give you the foundation in this book, along with suggestions for projects and exercises that will enable you to apply and practice your newfound knowledge. But the only way you'll really get to be proficient with object modeling is by participating in OO modeling and development projects over time. This book will give you the skills, and hopefully the confidence, to begin to apply object techniques in a professional setting, which is where your real learning will take place, particularly if you have an OO-experienced mentor to guide you through your first "industrial-strength" project.

- ***Make you an expert in any particular OO methodology:*** There are dozens of different formal methods for OO software development, new variations continue to emerge, and no one methodology is necessarily better than another. For example, UML (which stands for the "Unified Modeling Language") notation is the newest, OMT (which stands for "Object Modeling Technique") notation is one of the oldest, yet the two are remarkably similar because the UML is based to a great extent on OMT. By making sure that you understand the generic ***process*** of object modeling along with the specifics of the UML, you'll be armed with the knowledge you need to read about, evaluate, and select a specific methodology (or to craft your own—who knows, maybe someday you'll even write a book yourself on the methodology that you invent!).

- ***Teach you everything you'll ever need to know about C#:*** C# is a very rich language, consisting of dozens of core classes, hundreds of classes available from the Framework Class Library, and literally thousands of operations that can be performed with and by these classes. If C# provides a dozen alternative ways to do something in particular, we'll explain the one or two ways that we feel best suit the problem at hand, to give you an appreciation for how things are done. Nonetheless, you'll definitely see enough of the C# language in this book to be able to build a complete application.

Armed with the foundation you gain from this book, you'll be poised and ready to appreciate a more thorough treatment of C# such as that offered by one of the many other C# references that are presently on the market, or an in-depth UML reference.

Why Is Understanding Objects So Critical to Being a Successful OO Programmer?

Time and again, we meet software developers—at our places of employment, at clients' offices, at professional conferences, on college campuses—who have attempted to master an OO programming language like C# by taking a course in C#, reading a book about C#, or installing and using a C# integrated development environment (IDE) such as Visual Studio .NET. However, there is something fundamentally missing: a basic understanding of what objects are all about, and more importantly, knowledge of how to structure a software application from the ground up to make the most of objects.

Imagine that you've been asked to build a house, and that you know the basics of home construction. In fact, you're a world-renowned home builder whose services are in high demand! Your client tells you that all of the materials you'll need for building this home are going to be delivered to you. On the day construction is to begin, a truck pulls up at the building site and unloads a large pile of strange, blue, star-shaped blocks with holes in the middle. You're totally baffled! You've built countless homes using materials like lumber, brick, and stone, and know how to approach a building project using these familiar materials; but you haven't got a clue about how to assemble a house using blue stars.

Scratching your head, you pull out a hammer and some nails and try to nail the blue stars together as if you were working with lumber, but the stars don't fit together very well. You then try to fill in the gaps with the same mortar that you would use to adhere bricks to one another, but the mortar doesn't stick to these blue stars very well. Because you're working under tight cost and schedule constraints for building this home for your client, however (and because you're too embarrassed to admit that you, as an "expert" builder, don't know how to work with these modern materials), you press on. Eventually, you wind up with something that looks (on the outside, at least) like a house.

Your client comes to inspect the work, and is terribly disappointed. One of the reasons he had selected blue stars as a construction material was that they are extremely energy efficient; but, because you have used nails and mortar to assemble the stars, they have lost a great deal of their inherent ability to insulate the home. To compensate, your client asks you to replace all of the windows in the home with thermal glass windows so that they will allow less heat to escape. You're panicking at this point! Swapping out the windows will take as long, if not longer, than it has taken to build the house in the first place, not to mention the cost of replacing stars that will be damaged in the renovation process. When you tell your customer this, he goes ballistic! Another reason that he selected blue stars as the construction material was because of their recognized flexibility and ease of accommodating design changes; but, because of the ineffective way in which you assembled these stars, you're going to have to literally rip them apart and replace a great many of them.

This is, sad to say, the way many programmers wind up building an OO application when they don't have appropriate training in how to approach the project from the perspective of objects. Worse yet, the vast majority of would-be OO programmers are blissfully ignorant of the need to understand objects in order to program in an OO language. So, they take off programming with a language like C# and wind up with a far from ideal result: a program that lacks flexibility when an inevitable "mid-course correction" occurs in terms of a change in the requirements specification, as when new functionality needs to be introduced after an application has been deployed.

Who Is This Book Written For?

Anyone who wants to get the most out of an object-oriented programming language like C#! It has been written for

- Anyone who has yet to tackle C#, but wants to get off on the right foot with the language

- Anyone who has ever purchased a book on C#, and who has read it faithfully, who understands the "bits and bytes" of the language, but doesn't quite know how to structure an application to best take advantage of the OO features of the language

- Anyone who has purchased a C# integrated development environment (IDE) software tool, but really only knows how to drag and drop graphical user interface (GUI) components and to add a little bit of logic behind buttons, menus, etc., without any real sense of how to properly structure the core of the application around objects

- Anyone who has built a C# application, but was disappointed with how difficult it was to maintain or modify it when new requirements were presented later in the application's life cycle

- Anyone who has previously learned something about object modeling, but is "fuzzy" on how to transition from an object model to real, live code (C# or otherwise)

The bottom line is that anyone who really wants to master an OO language like C# **must** become an expert in objects ***first!***

In order to gain the most value from this book, you should have some programming experience under your belt; virtually any language will do. You should understand simple programming concepts such as

- Simple data types (integer, floating point, etc.)

- Variables and their scope (including the notion of global data)

- Control flow (if-then-else statements, for/do/while loops, etc.)

- What arrays are, and how to use them

- The notion of a function/subroutine/subprogram: how to pass data in and get results back out but, you needn't have had any prior exposure to C# (we'll give you a taste of the language at the beginning of Part One, and will go into the language in depth in Part Three). And, you needn't have ever been exposed to objects, either—in the software sense, at least! As you'll learn in Chapter 2, human beings naturally view the entire world from the perspective of objects.

Even if you've already developed a full-fledged C# application, it's certainly not too late to read this book if you still feel "fuzzy" when it comes to the object aspects of structuring an application. Universities often offer separate courses in object modeling and in C# programming. Although it's ideal for students to take both courses in sequence, students often arrive at an object modeling course having already taken a stab at learning C#. Even for such folks, who will see some familiar landmarks (in the form of C# code examples) in this book, many new insights will be gained as they learn the rationale for why we do many of the things that we do when programming in C# (or any other OO programming language for that matter).

It ultimately makes someone a better C# programmer to know the "whys" of object orientation rather than merely the mechanics of the language. If you have had prior experience with C#, you may find that you can quickly skim those chapters that provide an introduction to the language—namely, Chapter 1 in Part One and Chapter 13 in Part Three.

Because this book has its roots in courses that the authors teach, it's ideally suited for use as a textbook for a semester-long graduate or upper-division undergraduate course in either object modeling or C# programming. We've included some suggestions for how to use the book in that fashion in Appendix A.

What If You're Interested in Object Modeling, but Not Necessarily in C# Programming?

Will this book still be of value to you? Definitely! Even if you don't plan on making a career of programming (as is true of many of our object modeling students), we've found that being exposed to a smattering of code examples written in an OO language like C# really helps to cement object concepts. So, you're encouraged to read Part Three—at least through Chapter 14—even if you never intend to set your hands to the keyboard for purposes of C# programming.

How This Book Is Organized

The book is structured around three major topics, as follows:

Part One: The ABCs of Objects

Before we dive into the how-to's of object modeling and the details of OO programming in C#, it's important that we all speak the same language with respect to objects. Part One, consisting of Chapters 1–7, starts out slowly, by defining basic concepts that underlie all software development approaches, OO or otherwise. But, the chapters quickly ramp up to a discussion of advanced object concepts so that, by the end of Part One, you should be "object savvy."

Part Two: Object Modeling 101

In Part Two—Chapters 8–12 of the book—we focus on the underlying principles of how and, more importantly, why we do the things that we do when we develop an object model of an application—principles that are common to all object modeling techniques. It's important to be conversant in UML notation, as this is the industry standard and is most likely what the majority of your colleagues/clients will be using, and so we teach you the basics of the UML and use the UML for all of our concrete modeling examples. Using the modeling techniques presented in these chapters, we'll develop an object model "blueprint" for a Student Registration System (SRS), the requirements specification for which is presented at the end of this introduction.

Part Three: Translating an Object "Blueprint" into C# Code

In Part Three of the book—Chapters 13–17—we illustrate how to render the SRS object model that we've developed in Part Two into a fully functioning C# application, complete with a graphical user interface and a way to persist data from one user logon to the next. All of the code examples that we present in this section are available for download from the Apress web site—http://www.apress.com—and we strongly encourage you to download and experiment with this code. In fact, we provide exercises at the end of each chapter that encourage such experimentation. The requirements specification for the SRS is written in the narrative style with which software system requirements are often expressed. You may feel confident that you could build an application today to solve this problem, but by the end of this book you should feel much more confident in your ability to build it as an *object-oriented* application. Three additional case studies—for a Prescription Tracking System, a Conference Room Reservation System, and an Airline Ticketing System, respectively—are presented in Appendix B; these serve as the basis for many of the exercises presented at the end of each chapter.

To round out the book, we've included a final chapter titled "Next Steps," which provides suggestions for how you might wish to continue your object-oriented discovery process after finishing this book. We furnish you with a list of recommended books that will take you to the next level of proficiency, depending on what your intention is for applying what you've learned in this book.

Conventions

To help you get the most from the text and keep track of what's happening, we've used a number of conventions throughout the book.

For instance:

> *Note boxes reflect important background information.*

As for styles in the text

- When we introduce ***important words,*** we highlight them.

- We show filenames, URLs, and code within the text like so: `WriteObject()`

Example code is shown as follows:

```
// Bolding is used to call attention to new or significant code:
Student s = new Student();
// whereas unbolded code is code that's less important in the
// present context, or perhaps has been seen before.
int x = 3;
```

Which Version of C# Is This Book Based On?

As with any programming language, from time to time new versions of C# will be released by Microsoft. The good news is that, because we focus only on core C# language syntax in this book—language features that have been stable since C#'s inception—this book isn't version specific. The techniques and concepts you learn reading this book will serve you equally well when new versions of C# appear.

A Final Thought Before We Get Started

A lot of the material in this book—particularly at the beginning of Part One— may seem overly simplistic to experienced programmers. This is because much of object technology is founded on basic software engineering principles that have been in practice for many years, and, in many cases, just repackaged slightly differently! There are indeed a few new tricks that make OO languages extremely powerful and which were virtually impossible to achieve with non-OO languages—inheritance and polymorphism, for example, which you'll learn more about in Chapters 5 and 7, respectively. (Such techniques can be simulated by hand in a non-OO language, just as programmers could program their own database management system (DBMS) from scratch instead of using a commercial product like Oracle, Sybase, or MS SQL Server—but who'd want to?)

The biggest challenge for experienced programmers in becoming proficient with objects is in reorienting the manner in which they think about the problem they will be automating.

- Software engineers/programmers who have developed applications using non–object-oriented methods often have to "unlearn" certain approaches used in the traditional methods of software analysis and design.

- Paradoxically, people just starting out as programmers (or as OO modelers) sometimes have an easier time when learning the OO approach to software development as their only approach.

Fortunately, the way we need to think about objects when developing software turns out to be the natural way that people think about the world in general. So, learning to "think" objects—and to program them in C#—is as easy as 1, 2, 3!

Tell Us What You Think

We've worked hard to make this book as useful to you as possible, so we'd like to know what you think. We're always keen to know what it is you want and need to know.

We appreciate feedback on our efforts and take both criticism and praise to heart in our future editorial efforts. If you've anything to say, please let us know at info@apress.com or http://www.apress.com, or contact the authors at jacquie@objectstart.com, http://objectstart.com, or grantepalmer@msn.com.

Student Registration System Case Study: Student Registration System (SRS) Requirements Specification

We have been asked to develop an automated Student Registration System (SRS). This system will enable students to register online for courses each semester, as well as track a student's progress toward completion of his or her degree.

When a student first enrolls at the university, he or she uses the SRS to set forth a plan of study as to which courses he or she plans on taking to satisfy a particular degree program, and chooses a faculty advisor. The SRS will verify whether or not the proposed plan of study satisfies the requirements of the degree that the student is seeking. Once a plan of study has been established, then, during the registration period preceding each semester, students are able to view the schedule of classes online, and choose whichever classes they wish to attend, indicating the preferred section (day of the week and time of day) if the class is offered by more than one professor. The SRS will verify whether or not the student has satisfied the necessary prerequisites for each requested course by referring to the student's online transcript of courses completed and grades received (the student may review his or her transcript online at any time).

Assuming that (a) the prerequisites for the requested course(s) are satisfied, (b) the course(s) meets one of the student's plan of study requirements, and (c) there is room available in each of the class(es), the student is enrolled in the class(es).

If (a) and (b) are satisfied, but (c) is not, the student is placed on a first-come, first-served waiting list. If a class/section that he or she was previously waitlisted for becomes available (either because some other student has dropped the class or because the seating capacity for the class has been increased), the student is automatically enrolled in the waitlisted class, and an email message to that effect is sent to the student. It is his or her responsibility to drop the class if it is no longer desired; otherwise, he or she will be billed for the course.

Students may drop a class up to the end of the first week of the semester in which the class is being taught.

Part One

The ABCs of Objects

CHAPTER 1

A Little Taste of C#

IF THE FIRST PART OF this book is supposed to be about general object concepts, then why on earth are we starting out with an introductory chapter on C#?

- It's indeed true that objects are "language neutral," and so what you'll learn conceptually about objects in Part One of this book, and about object modeling in Part Two, could apply equally well to C#, or Java, or C++, or Ada, or Smalltalk, or an as-yet-to-be-invented object-oriented (OO) language.

- We've found that seeing a sprinkling of code examples helps to cement object concepts; but, we *could* have simply used language-neutral **pseudocode**—a natural-language way of expressing computer logic without worrying about the syntax of a specific language like C#—for all of our code examples in Parts One and Two.

This brings us back to our initial question: *why are we diving into C# syntax so soon?* Our reason for doing so is that we'd like you to become comfortable with C# syntax from the start, because our goal for this book is not only to teach you about objects and object modeling, but also to ultimately show you how objects translate into C# code. So, although we do indeed use a bit of pseudocode to hide some of the more complex logic of our code examples throughout Parts One and Two, we focus for the most part on real C# syntax. Just remember that the object concepts you'll learn in Parts One and Two of our book are equally applicable to other OO languages, unless otherwise noted.

In this chapter, you'll learn about

- The many strengths of the C# programming language

- Predefined C# types, operators on those types, and expressions formed with those types

- The anatomy of a simple C# program

- C#'s block structured nature

- Various types of C# expressions

- Loops and other control flow structures

- Printing messages to the screen, primarily for use in testing code as it evolves

- Elements of C# programming style

If you're a proficient C, C++, or Java programmer, you'll find much of C# syntax to be very familiar, and you should be able to breeze through this chapter fairly quickly.

If you've already been exposed to C# language basics, please feel free to skip to Chapter 2.

Getting "Hands On" with C#

You're probably eager to get started writing, compiling, and running C# programs. But we're purposely not going to get into the details of downloading and installing C# and the .NET Framework on your computer, the mechanics of compiling programs, or any of that just yet. Here is a little roadmap of how this book is organized:

- Part One of the book focuses on object concepts—in other words, the "what" of objects; we don't want you to be distracted from learning these basic concepts by the "bits and bytes" of getting the C# environment up and running on your machine.

- Part Two of the book focuses on object modeling—that is, the "how" of designing an application to make the best use of objects. We don't want you to be trying to program without an appropriate OO "blueprint" to work from.

- We'll then be ready for the "grand finale"—rendering our object model in C# code, in order to produce a working Student Registration System (SRS) application—in Part Three.

If you can remain patient, and resist the temptation to dive into C# programming until we get to Part Three, we promise that you'll have ample opportunity to get your hands dirty with C# code at the appropriate stage in your learning process.

Why C#?

We *could* walk you through building the SRS using any OO programming language: Java, or C++, or Ada, or Smalltalk, or Eiffel, or C#, or any of the OO flavors of conventional programming languages such as COBOL, Fortran, or Visual Basic. Why might we want to use C#? Read on, and you'll quickly see why!

Practice Makes Perfect

The designers of C# were able to draw upon the lessons learned from other OO programming languages that preceded it. They borrowed the best features of C++, Java, Eiffel, and Smalltalk, and then added some capabilities and features not found in those languages. Conversely, the features that had proven to be most troublesome in earlier languages were eliminated. As a result, C# is a powerful programming language that at the same time is an easy language to learn.

This isn't to say that C# is a "perfect" language—no language is!—but simply that it has made some significant improvements over many of the languages that have preceded it.

C# Is Part of an Integrated Application Development Framework

The C# language is integrated into Microsoft's **.NET Framework**—Microsoft's revolutionary new platform for developing applications and managing their runtime environment. The .NET Framework supports over 20 programming languages, including C#, C++, and Visual Basic .NET. A core element of the .NET Framework is the **common language runtime (CLR)** that is responsible for the runtime management of a C# program. The CLR takes care of loading, running, and providing support services for your C# program.

The .NET Framework provides a high degree of interoperability between the languages it supports—C#, C++, Visual Basic, JScript—through a **Common Language Specification (CLS)** that defines a common set of types and behaviors that every .NET language is guaranteed to recognize. The CLS allows developers to seamlessly integrate C# code with code written in any of the other .NET languages. For organizations that have standardized on Microsoft technology, C# provides a way to easily integrate with other Microsoft components.

The .NET Framework also contains a vast collection of libraries called the **.NET Framework Class Library (FCL)** that provides almost all of the common functionality needed to develop applications on the Windows platform. You'll find that with the FCL, a lot of programming work has already been done for you on topics ranging from file access to mathematical functions to database connectivity. The C# language, in effect, provides "one-stop shopping" for all your programming needs.

You can find out more about the .NET Framework at the following URL:
`http://msdn.microsoft.com/library/default.asp?url=/library/en-us/netstart/`
`html/cpframeworkref_start.asp`

C# Is Object-Oriented from the Ground Up

Before newer OO languages like C# and Java arrived on the scene, one of the most widely used OO languages was C++, which is actually an object-oriented extension of the non-OO language C. As such, C++ provides a lot of "back doors" that make it very easy to write decidedly "un-OO" code. In fact, many proficient C programmers transitioned to C++ as a "better" C without properly learning how to design an object-oriented application, and hence wound up using C++ for the most part as a procedural (non-OO) language.

In contrast, C# was built from the ground up to be a purely object-oriented programming language. As we'll discuss in more detail in the chapters that follow, *everything* in C# is an object:

- All of your data, even simple numerical types, are objects.

- All of the GUI building blocks—windows, buttons, text input fields, scroll bars, lists, menus, and so on—are objects.

- All functions are attached to objects, and are known as **methods**—there can be no "free-floating" functions as there were in C/C++.

- Even the main function (now called the **Main method**) no longer stands alone, but is instead bundled within a **class,** the reasons for which we'll explore in depth in chapters to come.

Because of this, C# lends itself particularly well to writing applications that uphold the object-oriented paradigm. Yet, as we pointed out in the Introduction to this book, merely using such an object-oriented language doesn't *guarantee* that the applications you produce will be *true* to this paradigm! You must be knowledgeable in *both* (a) how to design an application from the ground up to make the best use of objects and (b) how to apply the language correctly, our two primary intents of this book.

C# Is Free

One last valuable feature of C# that we'll mention is that it's *free!* You can download the C# compiler and all other libraries and utilities you'll need from the Microsoft Developer Network (MSDN) web site at no cost. We go into the details of setting up C# on your machine in Chapter 13 and Appendix C.

C# Language Basics

For those readers who have never seen C# code before, the rest of this chapter will present an introduction to the basic syntax of the C# programming language. Keep in mind that this is only a taste of C#, enough to help you understand the coding examples in Parts One and Two of this book. We'll revisit C# in substantially more depth in Part Three (Chapters 13 through 16), where we'll delve much more deeply into the language in building a fully functional Student Registration System (SRS) application.

> *If you haven't taken the time to read the Introduction to this book, now is a good time to do so! The SRS application requirements are introduced as a case study at the end of the Introduction.*

A Reminder Regarding "Pseudocode" vs. Real C# Code

As we mentioned in the beginning of this chapter, we occasionally use little bits of pseudocode in our code examples throughout Parts One and Two of the book to hide irrelevant logic details. To make it clear as to when we're using pseudocode vs. real code, we've used *italic* versus regular SansMono condensed font.

This is real C# syntax:

```
for (int i = 0; i <= 10; i++) {
```

This is pseudocode!

```
compute the grade for the ith Student
}
```

We'll remind you of this fact a few more times, so that you don't forget and accidentally try to type in and compile pseudocode somewhere along the way.

Anatomy of a Simple C# Program

One of the simplest of all C# applications is shown in Figure 1-1.

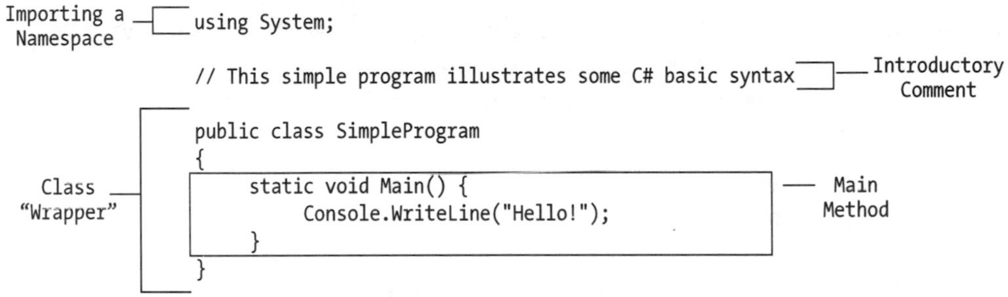

```
Importing a ───┐  using System;
Namespace      

                  // This simple program illustrates some C# basic syntax ──── Introductory
                                                                                Comment

                  public class SimpleProgram
                  {
Class ───             static void Main() {                          ── Main
"Wrapper"                 Console.WriteLine("Hello!");                   Method
                      }
                  }
```

Figure 1-1. Anatomy of a simple C# program

Let's go over the key elements of our simple program.

The "using System;" Statement

The first line of the program,

```
using System;
```

is required in order for our program to compile and run properly, by providing the compiler with knowledge of the types in the System **namespace;** a namespace is a logical grouping of predefined C# programming elements (in the case of C#, part of the FCL mentioned earlier). We'll defer a detailed explanation of namespaces until Chapter 13; for now, simply realize that the using System; statement is required for our program to compile properly (specifically, for the line Console.WriteLine("Hello!"); to compile properly).

using is a C# **keyword;** keywords, also known as **reserved words,** are tokens that have special meaning in a language, and which therefore may not be used by programmers as the names of variables, functions, or any of the other C# building blocks that you'll be learning about. We'll encounter many more C# keywords throughout the book; Appendix E presents the complete set of C# keywords.

Comments

The next line of our program is a comment:

```
// This simple program illustrates some basic C# syntax.
```

C# supports three different comment styles; we'll review two of them here.

The C language style of block comment begins with a forward slash followed by an asterisk (/*) and ends with an asterisk followed by a forward slash (*/). Everything enclosed between these delimiters is treated as a comment and is therefore ignored by the compiler, no matter how many lines the comment spans.

```
/* This is a single line C-style comment. */

/* This is a multiline C-style comment. This is a handy way to temporarily
   comment out entire sections of code without having to delete them.
   From the time that the compiler encounters the first 'slash asterisk'
   above, it doesn't care what we type here; even legitimate lines of code,
   as shown below, are treated as comment lines and thus ignored by the
   compiler until the first 'asterisk slash' combination is encountered.
x = y + z;
a = b / c;
j = s + c + f;
*/
```

The C++ single line form of comment uses a double slash (//) to comment just to the end of a line, as shown here:

```
x = y + z;    // text of comment continues through to the end of the line
a = b / c;
// Here is a BLOCK of sequential C++ style (single-line) comments.
// This serves as an alternative to using the C style
// of block comments (/* ... */).
m = n * p;
```

> There is also a third type of C# comment that is used within XML document files, but that topic is beyond the scope of this book.

Note that comments can't be nested: that is, the following will **not** compile:

```
/* This starts a comment ...
x = 3;
/* Whoops!  We are mistakenly trying to nest a SECOND comment
before terminating the FIRST!
This is going to cause us compilation problems, because the
compiler is going to IGNORE the start of this second/inner comment -- we're IN
a comment already, after all! -- and so as soon as we try to terminate
this SECOND/inner comment, the compiler will think that we've terminated the
FIRST/outer comment instead ... */
z = 2;
*/
```

When the compiler reaches what we intended to be the terminating */ of the "outer" comment in the last line of the preceding code example, the following compiler error will be reported:

```
error CS1525: Invalid expression term '/'
error CS1002: ; expected
```

Class Declaration/"Wrapper"

Next comes a class "wrapper"—more properly termed a **class declaration**—of the form

```
public class name
{ ... }
```

e.g.,

```
public class SimpleProgram
{ ... }
```

where braces, { ... }, enclose the main logic to be performed by the program, as well as enclosing other building blocks of a class; in later chapters, you'll learn all about classes, how to name them, and in particular why we even need a class wrapper in the first place. For now, simply note that the tokens public and class are two more of C#'s keywords, whereas SimpleProgram is a name that we've invented.

Main Method

Within the SimpleProgram class declaration, we find the starting function for the program, called the **Main method** in C#. The Main method serves as the entry point for a C# program. When the program executable is invoked, the system will call the Main method to launch our application.

> *With trivial applications such as this simple example, all logic can be contained within this single method. For more complex applications, on the other hand, the* Main *method can't possibly contain all of the logic for the entire system; you'll learn how to construct an application that transcends the boundaries of the* Main *method later in the book.*

The first line of the method, shown here:

```
static void Main() {
```

defines what is known as the Main method's **header,** and must appear exactly as shown (with one minor exception that we'll explain in Chapter 13 having to do with optionally receiving arguments from the command line).

Our Main **method body,** enclosed in braces, { ... }, consists of a single statement:

```
Console.WriteLine("Hello!");
```

which prints the message

```
Hello!
```

to the screen. We'll talk more about this statement's syntax in a bit, but for now, note the use of a semicolon at the end of the statement. As in C, C++, and Java, semicolons are placed at the end of individual C# statements. Braces, { ... }, delimit **blocks** of code, the significance of which we'll discuss in more detail later in this chapter in the section "Code Blocks and Variable Scope."

Other things that we'd typically do inside of the Main method of a more elaborate program include declaring variables, creating objects, and calling other methods.

Now that we've looked at a simple C# program, let's explore some of the basic syntax features of C# in more detail.

Predefined Types

C# is said to be a **strongly typed** programming language in that when a variable is declared, its type must also be declared. Among other things, declaring a variable's type tells the compiler how much memory to allocate for the variable.

The C# language and .NET Framework make use of the **Common Type System (CTS),** a specification that defines a set of types as well as the behavior of those types. The CTS defines a wide variety of types in two main families—**value types** and **reference types.** In this chapter, we'll focus on C#'s **predefined value types,** also known as **simple types,** along with the string type, which happens to be a reference type; we'll defer a discussion of reference types in general until Chapter 3.

The C# language supports a variety of simple types. The most commonly used types are as follows (all of these are C# keywords):

- bool: Boolean true or false value

- char: 16-bit Unicode character

- byte: 8-bit unsigned integer

- short: 16-bit signed integer

- int: 32-bit signed integer

- long: 64-bit signed integer

- float: 32-bit single-precision floating point

- double: 64-bit double-precision floating point

Each variable declared to be of a simple type represents a *single* integer, floating point, Boolean, byte, or character value.

Variables

As previously stated, before a variable can be used in a program, the type and name of the variable must be declared. An initial value can be supplied when a variable is first declared, or the variable can be assigned a value later in the program. For example, the following code snippet declares two simple type variables. The first variable, of type int, is given an initial value when the variable is declared. The second variable, of type double, is declared and then assigned a value on a subsequent line of code.

```
int count = 3;

double total;
// intervening code ... details omitted
total = 34.3;
```

A value can be assigned to a `bool` variable using the `true` or `false` keywords.

```
bool blah;
blah = true;
```

Boolean variables are often used as flags to signal whether or not some code should be conditionally performed. An example follows:

```
bool error = false;  // Initialize the flag.
// ...

// Later in the program (pseudocode):
if (some error situation arises) {
  // Set the flag to true to signal that an error has occurred.
  error = true;
}
// ...

// Still later in the program:
if (error) {
    // Pseudocode.
    take corrective action
}
```

> We'll talk specifically about the syntax of the `if` statement, one of several different kinds of C# flow control statements, a bit later.

A literal value may be assigned to a variable of type `char` by surrounding the value (a single Unicode character) in *single* quotes as follows:

```
char c = 'A';
```

Variable Naming Conventions

Most variable names use what is known as **Camel casing**, wherein the first letter of the name is in *lowercase,* the *first* letter of each subsequent concatenated word in the variable name is in *uppercase,* and the rest of the characters are in *lowercase.*

> In subsequent chapters, we'll refine the rules for naming variables as we introduce additional object concepts.

For example, the following variable names follow the C# variable naming conventions:

```
int grade;
double averageGrade;
string myPetRat;
bool weAreFinished;
```

Recall that, as mentioned earlier, a C# keyword can't be used as a variable name.

```
int float;  // this won't compile—"float" is a keyword
```

Variable Initialization

In C#, variables aren't automatically assigned an initial value when they are declared, and so we must explicitly assign a value to a variable before the variable's value is accessed in a statement. For example, in the following code snippet, two integer variables are declared named foo and bar. A value is assigned to the variable foo, but not to the variable bar, and an attempt is made to add the two variables together.

```
int foo;
int bar;

foo = 3; // We're initializing foo, but not bar.
foo = foo + bar;    // this line won't compile
```

If we were to try to compile this code snippet, we would get the following compilation error message regarding the last line of the preceding code example:

```
error CS0165: use of unassigned local variable 'bar'
```

The compiler is telling us that the variable bar has been declared, but that its value is undefined. To correct this error, we would need to assign an explicit value to bar before trying to add its value to foo:

```
int foo;
int bar;

foo = 3;
bar = 7;  // We're now initializing BOTH variables explicitly.

foo = foo + bar;  // This line will now compile properly.
```

> *As it turns out, the story with respect to variable initialization is a bit more complex than what we've discussed here. You'll learn in Chapter 13 that the rules of automatic initialization are somewhat different when dealing with the "inner workings" of objects.*

Strings

We'll discuss one more important predefined type in this chapter—the string type.

> *Just a reminder: unlike the other C# types that we've introduced in this chapter,* string *isn't a value type, but rather, is a reference type, as we mentioned earlier. For purposes of this introductory discussion of strings, this observation isn't important; the significance of the* string *type's being a reference type will be discussed in Chapter 13.*

A string represents a sequence of Unicode characters. There are several ways to create and initialize a string variable. The easiest and most commonly used way is to declare a variable of type string and to assign the variable a value using a **string literal.** A string literal is any text enclosed in double quotes:

```
string name = "Zachary";
```

Note that we use double quotes, not single quotes, to surround a string literal when assigning it to a string variable, even if it consists of only a single character:

```
string shortString = "A";        // Use DOUBLE quotes when assigning a literal
                                 // value to a string ...

string longString = "supercalifragilisticexpialadocious";   // (ditto)

char c = 'A';                     // ... and SINGLE quotes when assigning a literal
                                 // a value to a char.
```

Two commonly used approaches for assigning an initial value to a string variable as a placeholder are as follows:

- Setting it equal to an empty string, represented by two consecutive double quote marks:

  ```
  string s = "";
  ```

- Setting it equal to the reserved word null, which is the "zero equivalent" value for the string type (and, as you'll learn later on, for reference types/objects in general):

```
string s = null;
```

The plus sign (+) operator is normally used for addition, but when used with string variables, it represents **string concatenation.** Any number of string variables or string literals can be concatenated together with the + operator.

```
string x = "foo";
string y = "bar";
string z = x + y + "!";   // z now equals "foobar!"; x and y are unchanged
```

You'll learn about some of the many other operations that can be performed with or on strings, along with gaining insights into their object-oriented nature, in Chapter 13.

Case Sensitivity

C# is a **case-sensitive** language. That is, the use of uppercase vs. lowercase in C# is deliberate and mandatory. For example:

- Variable names that are spelled the same way but which differ in their use of case, e.g., x (lowercase) vs. X (uppercase), represent *different* variables.

- All keywords are expressed in all lowercase: public, class, int, bool, and so forth. Don't get "creative" about capitalizing these, as the compiler will violently object!

- Capitalization of the name of the Main method is mandatory.

C# Expressions

A **simple expression** in C# is either

- A constant: 7, false

- A char(acter) literal: 'A', '&'

- A string literal: "foo"

- The name of any variable declared to be of one of the predefined types that we've discussed so far: myString, x

- Any *two* of the preceding items that are combined with one of the C# **binary operators** (discussed in detail later in this chapter): x + 2

- Any *one* of the preceding items that is modified by one of the C# **unary operators** (discussed in detail later in this chapter): i++

- Any of the preceding simple expressions enclosed in parentheses: (x + 2)

plus a few more expression types having to do with objects that you'll learn about in Chapter 13.

Assignment Statements

Assigning a value to a variable is accomplished by using the assignment operator, =. An assignment statement consists of a (previously declared) variable name to the left of the =, and an expression that evaluates to the appropriate type to the right of the =. For example:

```
int count = 1;

total = total + 4.0;   // assuming that total was declared to be a double variable

price = cost + (a + b)/length;   // assuming all variables properly declared
```

Arithmetic Operators

The C# language provides a number of basic arithmetic operators, as follows:

+	Addition
-	Subtraction
*	Multiplication
/	Division
%	Modulus (The modulus is the remainder when the operand to the left of the % operator is divided by the operand to the right.)

The + and - operators can also be used in prefix fashion to indicate positive or negative numbers: -3.7, +42.

In addition to the simple assignment operator, =, there are a number of specialized **compound assignment operators,** which combine variable assignment with an operation. The compound assignment operators for arithmetic operations are as follows:

`+=`   `a += b` is equivalent to `a = a + b`.

`-=`   `a -= b` is equivalent to `a = a - b`.

`*=`   `a *= b` is equivalent to `a = a * b`.

`/=`   `a /= b` is equivalent to `a = a / b`.

`%=`   `a %= b` is equivalent to `a = a % b`.

> *The compound assignment operators don't add any new functionality; they are simply provided as a convenience to simplify code. For example, the statement*
>
> ```
> total = total + 4.0;
> ```
>
> *can be alternatively written as*
>
> ```
> total += 4.0;
> ```

The final two arithmetic operators that we'll introduce are the **increment** (++) and **decrement** (--) operators, which are used to increase or decrease the value of an integer variable by 1 or of a floating point value by 1.0. The increment and decrement operators can also be used on `char` variables. For example, consider the following code snippet:

```
char c = 'e';
c++;
```

When the code snippet is executed, the variable `c` will have the value `f`, which is the next character in the Unicode sorting sequence.

The increment and decrement operators can be used in either a **prefix** or **postfix** manner.

If the operator is placed *before* the variable it's operating on (*prefix* mode), the increment or decrement of that variable is performed *before* the variable's value is used in any assignments made via that statement.

If the operator is placed *after* the variable it's operating on (*postfix* mode), the increment or decrement occurs *after* the variable's value is used in any assignments made via that statement.

For example, consider the following code snippet, which uses the prefix increment (++) operator:

```
int a = 1;
int b = ++a;  // a will be incremented to 2, then b will be assigned the value 2
```

After both lines of code have executed, the value of variable a will be 2, as will the value of variable b. This is because, in the second line of code, the increment of variable a (from 1 to 2) occurs ***before*** the value of a is assigned to variable b. The preceding two lines of code are logically equivalent to the following three lines:

```
int a = 1;
a = a + 1;
int b = a;
```

Now let's look at the same code snippet with the increment operator written in a postfix manner:

```
int a = 1;
int b = a++;  // b will be assigned the value 1, then a will be incremented to 2
```

After both lines of code have executed, the value of variable b will be 1, whereas the value of variable a will be 2. This is because, in the second line of code, the increment of variable a (from 1 to 2) occurs ***after*** the (old) value of a is assigned to variable b. The preceding two lines of code are logically equivalent to the following three lines:

```
int a = 1;
int b = a;
a = a + 1;
```

Here is a slightly more complex example:

```
int y = 1;
int z = 2;
int x = y++ * ++z;  // x will be assigned the value 3, because z will be
                    // incremented from 2 to 3 before its value is used in the
                    // multiplication, whereas y will remain at 1 until AFTER its
                    // value is used.
```

As you'll see in a bit, the increment and decrement operators are commonly used in loops and other flow of control structures.

Evaluating Expressions and Operator Precedence

Expressions of arbitrary complexity can be built up around the various simple expression types by nesting parentheses—e.g., $((((4/x) + y) * 7) + z)$. The compiler evaluates such expressions from innermost to outermost parentheses, left to right. Assuming that x, y, and z are declared and initialized as shown here:

```
int x = 1;
int y = 2;
int z = 3;
```

then the expression on the right-hand side of the following assignment statement:

```
int answer = ((8 * (y + z)) + y) * x;
```

would be evaluated piece by piece as follows:

$$((8 * \underline{(y + z)}) + y) * x$$
$$(\underline{(8 * 5)} + y) * x$$
$$\underline{(40 + y)} * x$$
$$\underline{42 * x}$$
$$42$$

In the absence of parentheses, certain operators take precedence over others in terms of when they will be applied in evaluating an expression. For example, multiplication or division is by default performed before addition or subtraction. The automatic precedence of one operator over another can be explicitly altered through the use of parentheses; operations inside parentheses will be performed before operations outside of them. Consider the following code snippet:

```
int j = 2 + 3 * 4;   // j will be assigned the value 14
int k = (2 + 3) * 4;    // k will be assigned the value 20
```

In the first line of code, which uses no parentheses, the multiplication operation takes precedence over the addition operation, and so the overall expression evaluates to the value $2 + 12 = 14$; it's as if we've explicitly written "2 + (3 * 4)" without having to do so.

In the second line of code, parentheses are explicitly placed around the operation "2 + 3" so that the addition operation will be performed first, and the resultant sum will then be multiplied by 4 for an overall expression value of $5 * 4 = 20$.

Logical Operators

A logical expression compares two (simple or complex) expressions *exp1* and *exp2*, in a specified way, and evaluates to a Boolean value of `true` or `false`.

To create logical expressions, C# provides the following **relational operators:**

exp1 == *exp2*	`true` if *exp1* equals *exp2* (note use of a ***double*** equal sign).
exp1 > *exp2*	`true` if *exp1* is greater than *exp2*.
exp1 >= *exp2*	`true` if *exp1* is greater or equal to *exp2*.
exp1 < *exp2*	`true` if *exp1* is less than *exp2*.
exp1 <= *exp2*	`true` if *exp1* is less than or equal to *exp2*.
exp1 != *exp2*	`true` if *exp1* isn't equal to *exp2* (! is read as "not").
!*exp*	`true` if *exp* is `false`, and `false` if *exp* is true.

In addition to the relational operators, C# provides **logical operators** that can be used in combination with the relational operators to create complex logical expressions that involve more than one comparison.

&&	Logical "and"
||	Logical "or"
!	Logical "not" (The ! operator toggles the value of a logical expression from `true` to `false` and vice versa.)

The logical "and" and "or" operators are binary operators; their left and right operands must both be valid logical expressions so that they evaluate to Boolean values. If the && operator is used, both the left and right operands must be true for the compound logical expression to be true. With the || operator, the compound logical expression will be true if either the left or right operand is true.

Here is an example that uses the logical "and" operator to program the compound logical expression "if x is greater than 2.0 and y isn't equal to 4.0":

```
if (x > 2.0 && y != 4.0) {
  // Pseudocode.
  do some stuff ...
}
```

Note that, because the > and != operators take precedence over the && operator, we don't need to insert extra parentheses as shown here:

```
if ((x > 2.0) && (y != 4.0)) {
  // Pseudocode.
  do some stuff ...
}
```

but may wish to do so to enhance readability.

Logical expressions are most commonly seen in flow of control structures, discussed later in this chapter.

Implicit Type Conversions and Explicit Casting

C# supports **implicit type conversions.** This means that if we try to assign the value of some variable y to another variable x as shown here:

```
x = y;
```

and the two variables were originally declared to be of different types, then C# will attempt to perform the assignment, automatically converting the type of the value of y to the type of x, but *only if precision won't be lost in doing so.* (C# differs from C and C++ in this regard, as the latter two perform automatic type conversions even if precision is lost.) This is best understood by looking at an example:

```
int x;
double y;
y = 2.7;
x = y;  // Trying to assign a double value to an int variable; this line will
        // compile in C and C++, but not in C#.
```

In the preceding code snippet, we're attempting to copy the double value of y, 2.7, into x, which is declared to be an int. If this assignment were to take place, the fractional part of y would be truncated, and x would wind up with an integer value of 2. This represents a loss in precision, also known as a **narrowing conversion.** A C or C++ compiler will permit this assignment, thereby silently truncating the value; rather than assuming that this is what we intended to do, however, the C# compiler will generate an error on the last line.

```
Error: CS0029:  Cannot implicitly convert type 'double' to type 'int'
```

In order to signal to the C# compiler that we're willing to accept the loss of precision, we must perform an **explicit cast,** which involves preceding the expression whose value is to be converted with the desired target type enclosed in parentheses. In other words, we'd have to rewrite the last line of the preceding example as follows in order for the C# compiler to accept it:

```
int x;
double y;
y = 2.7;
x = (int) y;    // This will compile now. The C# compiler 'relaxes',
                // because we have explicitly told it that we WANT the
                // narrowing conversion to occur.
```

Of course, if we were to reverse the direction of the assignment:

```
int x;
double y;
x = 2;
y = x;                  // Assign an int value to a double variable; y will assume the
                        // value 2.0.
```

the C# compiler would have no problem with the last statement, because in this particular case, we're assigning a value of less precision—2—to a variable capable of more precision; y will wind up with the value of 2.0. This is known as a **widening conversion;** such conversions are performed automatically in C#, and need not be explicitly cast.

Note that there is an idiosyncrasy with regard to assigning constant values to floats in C#; the statement

```
  float y = 3.5;    // won't compile!
```

will generate a compiler error, because a numeric constant value with a fractional component like 3.5 is automatically treated by C# as a more precise double value, and so the compiler will once again refuse to make a transfer that causes precision to be lost. To make such an assignment, we must explicitly cast the floating point constant into a float:

```
  float y = (float) 3.5;    // OK; we're using a cast here.
```

or, alternatively, force the constant on the right-hand side of the assignment statement to be treated as a float by using the suffix "F", as shown here:

```
  float y = 3.5F;    // OK, because we're indicating that the constant is to be
                     // treated as a float, not as a double.
```

> *Yet another option would be to simply use* double *rather than* float *variables to represent floating point numeric values. We'll typically use* doubles *instead of* floats *whenever we need to declare floating point variables in our SRS application, just to avoid these hassles of type conversion.*

The only C# simple type that can't be cast, either implicitly or explicitly, into another type is the bool type.

You'll see other applications of casting, involving objects, later in the book.

Loops and Other Flow of Control Structures

Very rarely will a program execute sequentially, line-by-line from start to finish. Instead, the execution flow of the program will be conditional. It may be necessary to have the program execute a certain block of code if a condition is met, or another block of code if the condition isn't met. A program may have to repeatedly execute the same block of code. The C# language provides a number of different types of loops and other flow of control structures to take care of these situations.

if Statements

The if statement is a basic conditional branch statement that executes one or more lines of code if a condition, represented as a logical expression, is satisfied. Alternatively, one or more lines of code can be executed if the condition is *not* satisfied by placing that code after the keyword else. The use of an else clause with an if statement is optional.

The basic syntax of the if statement is as follows:

```
if (condition) {
  execute whatever code is contained within the braces if condition is met
}
```

or, adding an optional else clause:

```
if (condition) {
  execute whatever code is contained within the braces if condition is met
}
else {
  execute whatever code is contained within the braces if condition is NOT met
}
```

If only one executable statement follows either the if or (optional) else keyword, the braces can be omitted as shown here:

```
// Pseudocode.
if (condition) single statement to execute if true;
else single statement to execute if false;
```

but it's generally considered good practice to always use braces.

A single Boolean variable, as a simple form of Boolean expression, can of course serve as the logical expression/condition of an if statement. For example, it's perfectly acceptable to write the following:

```
// Use this bool variable as a 'flag' that gets set to true when
// some particular operation is completed.
bool finished;

// Initialize it to false.
finished = false;

// Intervening code, in which the flag may get set to true ... details omitted.

// Test the flag.
if (finished) { // equivalent to:   if (finished == true) {
    Console.WriteLine("we are finished");
}
```

In this case the logical expression serving as the condition for the if statement corresponds to "if finished" or, alternatively, "if finished equals true".

The ! operator can be used to negate a logical expression, so that the block of code associated with an if statement is executed when the expression is false.

```
if (!finished) { // equivalent to:   if (finished == false)
    // If the finished variable is set to false, this code will execute.
    Console.WriteLine("we are not finished");
}
```

In this case, the logical expression serving as the condition for the if statement corresponds to "if *not* finished" or, alternatively, "if finished equals false".

When testing for equality, remember that we must use *two consecutive* equal signs, not just one:

```
if (x == 3) { // Note use of double equal signs (==) to test for equality.
    y = x;
}
```

> *A common mistake made by beginning C# programmers is to try to use a **single** equal sign to test for equality as in this example:*
>
> ```
> if (x = 3) { ... }
> ```
>
> *In C#, an if test must be based on a valid **logical** expression; x = 3 isn't a logical expression, but rather, an **assignment** expression.*
>
> *The preceding if statement won't even compile in C#, whereas it **would** compile in the C and C++ programming languages, because in those languages, if tests are based on evaluating expressions to either the integer value 0 (equivalent to false) or nonzero (equivalent to true).*

It's possible to nest if-else constructs to test more than one condition. If nested, an inner if (plus optional else) statement is placed within the else part of an outer if.

A basic syntax for a two-level nested if-else construct is shown here:

```
if (condition1) {
  // execute this code
}
else {
  if (condition2) {
    // execute this alternate code
  }
  else {
    // execute this code if none of the conditions are met
  }
}
```

There is no limit (within reason!) to how many nested if-else constructs can be used.

The nested if statement shown in the preceding example may alternatively be written without using nesting as follows:

```
if (condition1) {
  // execute this code
}
else if (condition2) {
  // execute this alternate code
}
```

```
else {
    // execute this code if none of the conditions are met
}
```

The two forms are logically equivalent.

Here is an example that uses a nested if-else construct to determine the size of an employee's bonus based on the employee's sales and length of service:

```
using System;

public class IfDemo
{
    static void Main() {
        double sales = 40000.0;
        int lengthOfService = 12;
        double bonus;

        if (sales > 30000.0 && lengthOfService >= 10) {
            bonus = 2000.0;
        }
        else {
            if (sales > 20000.0) {
                bonus = 1000.0;
            }
            else {
                bonus = 0.0;
            }
        }

        Console.WriteLine("Bonus = " + bonus);
    }
}
```

Here's the output generated by this example code:

```
Bonus = 2000.0
```

switch Statements

A switch statement is similar to an if-else construct in that it allows the conditional execution of one or more lines of code. However, instead of evaluating a logical expression as an if-else construct does, a switch statement compares the value of an integer or string expression against values defined by one or more case labels. If a match is found, the code following the matching case label is executed. An optional default label can be included to define code that is to be executed if the integer or string expression matches none of the case labels.

The general syntax of a switch statement is as follows:

```
switch (int-or-string-expression) {
    case value1:
        // code to execute if expression matches value1
        break;
    case value2:
        // code to execute if expression matches value2
        break;
        // more case labels, as needed ...
        case valueN:
        // code to execute if expression matches valueN
        break;
    default:
        // default code if no case matches
        break;
}
```

For example:

```
int x;

// x is assigned a value somewhere along the line ... details omitted.

switch (x) {
    case 1:
        // Pseudocode.
        do something based on the fact that x equals 1
        break;
    case 2:
        // Pseudocode.
        do something based on the fact that x equals 2
        break;
    default:
        // Pseudocode.
        do something based on the fact that x equals something other than 1 or 2
        break;
}
```

Note the following:

- The expression in parentheses following the switch keyword must be an expression that evaluates to a string or integer value. (Note that the char, int, and long types are all considered to be forms of integer, and so any of these types of expression can be used.)

- The values following the case labels must be constant values (a "hardwired" integer constant, character literal, or a string literal).

- Colons, not semicolons, terminate the case and default labels.

- The statements following a given case label don't have to be enclosed in braces. They constitute a **statement list** rather than a code block.

Unlike an if statement, a switch statement isn't automatically terminated when a match is found and the code following the matching case label is executed. To exit a switch statement, a **jump statement** must be used—typically, a break statement. If a jump statement isn't included following a given case label, the execution will "fall through" to the next case or default label. This behavior can be used to our advantage: when the same logic is to be executed for more than one case label, two or more case labels can be stacked up back to back as shown here:

```
// x is assumed to have been previously declared as an int
switch (x) {
    case 1:
    case 2:
    case 3:
        // code to be executed if x equals 1, 2, or 3
        break;
    case 4:
        // code to be executed if x equals 4
}
```

A switch statement is useful for making a selection between a series of mutually exclusive choices. In the following example, a switch statement is used to assign a value to a variable named capital based on the value of a variable named country. If a match isn't found, the capital variable is assigned the value "not in the database".

```
using System;

public class SwitchDemo
{
    static void Main() {
```

```
string country;
string capital;
country = "India";

// A switch statement compares the value of the variable "country"
// against the value of three case labels. If no match is found,
// the code after the default label is executed.

switch (country) {
  case "England":
    capital = "London";
    break;
  case "India":
    capital = "New Delhi";
    break;
  case "USA":
    capital = "Washington";
    break;
  default:
    capital = "not in the database";
    break;
}

    Console.WriteLine("The capital of " + country + " is " + capital);
  }
}
```

Here's the output for the preceding code example:

```
The capital of India is New Delhi
```

for Statements

A for statement is a programming construct that is used to execute one or more statements a certain number of times. The general syntax of the for statement is as follows:

```
for (initializer; condition; iterator) {
  // code to execute while condition is true
}
```

A for statement defines three elements that are separated by semicolons and placed in parentheses after the for keyword.

The **initializer** is used to provide an initial value for a **loop control variable.** The variable can be declared as part of the initializer or it can be declared earlier in the code, ahead of the for statement. For example:

```
// The loop control variable 'i' is declared within the for statement:
   for (int i = 0; condition; iterator) {
     // code to execute while condition is true
}
// Note that i goes out of scope when the 'for' loop exits.
```

or:

```
// The loop control variable 'i' is declared earlier in the program:
int i;

for (i = 0; condition; iterator) {
     // code to execute while condition is true
}
// Note that because i is declared before the for loop begins in this case,
// i remains in scope when the 'for' loop exits.
```

The **condition** is a logical expression that typically involves the loop control variable:

```
for (int i = 0; i < 5; iterator) {
     // code to execute as long as i is less than 5
}
```

The **iterator** typically increments or decrements the loop control variable:

```
for (int i = 0; i < 5; i++) {
     // code to execute as long as i is less than 5
}
```

Again, note the use of a semicolon (;) after the initializer and condition, but *not* after the iterator.

Here's a breakdown of how a for loop operates:

- When program execution reaches a for statement, the initializer is executed first (and only once).

- The condition is then evaluated. If the condition evaluates to true, the block of code following the parentheses is executed.

- After the block of code finishes, the iterator is executed.

- The condition is then reevaluated. If the condition is still `true`, the block of code and update statement are executed again.

This process repeats until the condition becomes `false`, at which point the `for` loop exits.

Here is a simple example of using nested `for` statements to generate a simple multiplication table. The loop control variables, j and k, are declared inside their respective `for` statements. As long as the conditions in the respective `for` statements are met, the block of code following the `for` statement is executed. The ++ operator is used to increment the values of j and k each time the respective block of code is executed.

```
using System;

public class ForDemo
{
  static void Main() {
    // Compute a simple multiplication table.

    for (int j = 1; j <= 4; j++) {
      for (int k = 1; k <= 4; k++) {
        Console.WriteLine("" + j + " * " + k + " = " + (j * k));
      }
    }
  }
}
```

Here's the output:

```
1 * 1 = 1
1 * 2 = 2
1 * 3 = 3
1 * 4 = 4
2 * 1 = 2
2 * 2 = 4
2 * 3 = 6
2 * 4 = 8
```

etc.

Note the use of the string *concatenation operator, +, in the* ForDemo *example;* string *representations of the value of* int *variables* j *and* k *are concatenated to the* string *literals* "", " * ", *and* " = ".

Each of the three elements inside the parentheses of a for statement is optional (although the two separating semicolons are mandatory):

If the initializer is omitted, the loop control variable must have been declared and initialized before the for statement is encountered.

```
 int i = 0;
for (; i < 5; i++) {

     // do some stuff as long as i is less than 5
}
```

If the iterator is omitted, we must make sure to take care of explicitly updating the loop control variable within the body of the for loop to avoid an infinite loop:

```
for (int i = 0; i < 5; ) {
    // do some stuff as long as i is less than 5

  // Explicitly increment i.
  i++;
}
```

If the condition is omitted, the result is a potentially infinite loop:

```
for (;;) {
    // infinite loop!
}
```

> In the section titled "Jump Statements" later in this chapter, we'll see that jump statements can be used to break out of a loop.

As with other flow of control structures, if only one statement is specified after the for condition, the braces can be omitted:

```
for (int i = 0; i < 3; i++) sum = sum + i;
```

but it is considered good programming practice to use braces regardless.

while Statements

A while statement is similar in function to a for statement, in that both are used to repeatedly execute an associated block of code. However, if the number of times that the code is to be executed is unknown when the loop first begins, a while statement is the preferred choice, because a while statement continues to execute as long as a specified condition is met.

The general syntax for the while statement is as follows:

```
while (condition) {
  // code to execute while condition is true
}
```

The condition can be either a simple or complex logical expression that evaluates to a true or false value. For example:

```
int x = 1;
int y = 1;

while (x < 20 || y < 10) {
  // Pseudocode.
  presumably do something that affects the value of either x or y
}
```

When program execution reaches a while statement, the condition is evaluated first. If true, the block of code following the condition is executed. When the block of code is finished, the condition is evaluated again and if it's still true, the process repeats itself until the condition evaluates to false, at which point the while loop exits.

Here is a simple example illustrating the use of a while loop. A bool variable named finished is initially set to false. The finished variable is used as a flag: as long as finished is false, the block of code following the while loop will continue to execute. Presumably, there will be some condition inside the block of code that will eventually set finished to true, at which point the while loop will exit.

```
using System;

public class WhileDemo
{
  static void Main() {
    bool finished = false;
    int i = 0;

    while (!finished) {
      Console.WriteLine(i);
      i++;
      if (i == 3) finished = true; // toggle the flag value
    }
  }
}
```

Here's the output:

```
0
1
2
```

As with the other flow of control structures, if only one statement is specified after the condition, the braces can be omitted:

```
while (x < 20) x = x * 2;
```

but it is considered good programming practice to use braces regardless.

do Statements

With a while loop, the condition is evaluated before the code block following it is (conditionally) executed. Thus, it's possible that the code will never be run if the condition is false from the start. A do loop is similar to a while loop, except that the block of code is executed **before** the condition is evaluated. Therefore, we are guaranteed that the code block of the loop will be executed at least once.

The general syntax of a do statement is as follows:

```
do {
    // code to execute
} while (condition);
```

As was the case with the while statement, the condition of a do statement is a logical expression that evaluates to a Boolean value. A semicolon is placed after the parentheses surrounding the condition, to signal the end of the do statement. We typically use a do loop when we know that we need to perform at least one iteration of a loop for initialization purposes.

```
bool flag;

do {
    // perform some code regardless of initial setting of 'flag', then
    // evaluate whether the loop should iterate again based on the
    // value of 'flag'.  The value of 'flag' can be set to false within
    // the loop to signal that the loop is to terminate.
} while (flag);
```

Jump Statements

Some of the loops and flow of control structures we've discussed will exit automatically when a condition is met (or not met) and some of them will not. The C# language defines a number of **jump statements** that are used to redirect program execution to another statement elsewhere in the code. The two types of jump statement that we'll discuss in this section are the break and continue statements. Another jump statement, the return statement, is generally used to exit a method. We'll defer our discussion of the return statement until Chapter 4.

We've already seen break statements in action earlier in this chapter, when they were used in conjunction with a switch statement. A break statement can also be used to abruptly terminate a do, for, or while loop. When a break statement is encountered during loop execution, the loop immediately terminates, and program execution is transferred to the line of code immediately after the loop or flow of control structure.

```
// This loop is intended to execute four times ...
for (int j = 1; j <= 4; j++) {
    // ... but, as soon as j attains a value of 3, the following 'if'
    // test passes, the break statement that it controls executes, and we
    // 'break out of' the loop.
    if (j == 3) break;

    // If, on the other hand, the 'if' test fails, we skip over the
    // 'break' statement, print the value of j, and keep on looping
    Console.WriteLine(j);
}

// The break statement, if/when executed, takes us to this line of code
// immediately after the loop.
Console.WriteLine("Loop finished");
```

The output produced by the code in the preceding example would be as follows:

```
1
2
Loop finished
```

A continue statement, on the other hand, is used to exit from the current iteration of a loop without terminating overall loop execution. A continue statement transfers program execution back up to the top of the loop without finishing the particular iteration that is already in progress.

```
// This loop is intended to execute four times ...
for (int j = 1; j <= 4; j++) {
    // ... but, as soon as j attains a value of 3, the following 'if' test passes
    // and we 'jump' back to the beginning of the loop, with
    // j being incremented to 4 ...
    if (j == 3) continue;


    // ... and so the following line doesn't get executed when j equals 3,
    // but DOES get executed when j equals 1, 2, and 4.
    Console.WriteLine(j);
}
Console.WriteLine("Loop finished");
```

The output produced by this code would be as follows:

```
1
2
4
Loop finished
```

Code Blocks and Variable Scope

C# (like C, C++, and Java) is a **block structured language.** As mentioned earlier in the chapter, a "block" of code is a series of zero or more lines of code enclosed within braces, { ... }.

- A method declaration, like the Main method of our SimpleProgram, defines a block.

- A class declaration, like the SimpleProgram class as a whole, also defines a block.

- As we've seen, many **control flow statements** also involve defining blocks of code.

Blocks may be nested inside one another to any arbitrary depth.

```
public class SimpleProgram
{
    // We're inside of the 'class' block (one level deep).
    static void Main() {
        // We're inside of the 'main method' block (two levels deep).
```

```
    int x = 3;
    int y = 4;
    int z = 5;

    if (x > 2) {
        // We're now one level deeper (level 3), in a nested block.
        if (y > 3) {
            // We're one level deeper still (level 4), in yet another
            // nested block.
            // (We could go on and on!)
        } // We've just ended the level 4 block.
        // (We could have additional code here, at level 3.)
    } // Level 3 is done!
    // (We could have additional code here, at level 2.)
} // That's it for level 2!
// (We could have additional code here, at level 1.)
} // Adios, amigos! Level 1 has just ended.
```

The **scope** of a variable name is defined as that portion of code in which a name remains defined to the compiler: typically, from the point where it is first declared down to the closing (right) brace for the block of code that it was declared in. A variable is said to be **in scope** only inside the block of code in which it is declared. Once program execution exits a block of code, any variables that were declared inside that block go out of scope and will be inaccessible to the program.

As an example of the consequences of variable scope, let's write a program called ScopeDemo, shown next. The ScopeDemo class declares three nested code blocks: one for the ScopeDemo class declaration, one for the Main method, and one as part of an if statement inside the body of the Main method.

```
public class ScopeDemo
{
    static void Main() {
        double cost = 2.65;

        if (cost < 5.0) {
            double discount = 0.05;  // declare a variable inside the 'if' block
            // other details omitted ...
        }

        // When the 'if' block exits, the variable 'discount' goes out of scope, and
        // is no longer recognized by the compiler. If we try to use it in a
        // subsequent statement, the compiler will generate an error.
```

```
      double refund = cost * discount;    // this won't compile - discount is no
   }                                       // longer in scope
}
```

In the preceding example, a variable named cost is declared inside the block of code comprising the Main method body. Another variable named discount is declared inside the block of code associated with the if statement. When the if statement block of code exits, the discount variable goes out of scope. If we try to access it later in the program, as we do in the following line of code:

```
double refund = cost * discount;
```

the compiler will generate the following error:

```
error: CS0103: The name 'discount' does not exist in the class or namespace
'ScopeDemo'
```

Note that a variable declared in an **outer** code block *is* accessible to any **inner** code blocks that follow the declaration. For example, in the preceding ScopeDemo example, the variable cost is accessible inside the nested if statement code block that follows its declaration.

Printing to the Screen

Most applications communicate information to users by displaying messages via the application's GUI. However, it is also useful at times to be able to display simple text messages to the command line window from which we're running a program as a "quick and dirty" way of verifying that a program is working properly (you'll learn how to run C# programs from the command line in Chapter 13). Until we discuss how to craft a C# GUI in Chapter 16, this will be our program's primary way of communicating with the "outside world."

To print text messages to the screen, we use the following syntax:

```
Console.WriteLine(expression to be printed);
```

The Console.WriteLine method can accept very complex expressions, and does its best to ultimately turn these into a single string value, which then gets displayed on the screen. Here are a few examples:

```
Console.WriteLine("Hi!");   // Printing a string literal/constant.

string s = "Hi!";
Console.WriteLine(s);        // Printing the value of a string variable.
```

```
string s = "foo";
string t = "bar";
Console.WriteLine(s + t);    // Using the string concatenation operator (+) to
                             // print "foobar".


int x = 3;
int y = 4;

Console.WriteLine(x);        // Converts x's int value into a string and
                             // prints the value "3" to the screen.


Console.WriteLine(x + y);    // Computes the sum of x and y, then
                             // prints the value "7" to the screen.
```

Note in the last line of code that the plus sign (+) is interpreted as the ***integer*** addition operator, not as the string concatenation operator, because it separates two variables that are both declared to be of type int. So, the sum of 3 + 4 is computed to be 7, which is then printed. In the next example, however, we get different (and arguably undesired) behavior:

```
Console.WriteLine("The sum of x plus y is:   " + x + y);
```

The preceding line of code causes the following to be printed:

```
The sum of x plus y is:   34
```

Why is this?

We evaluate expressions from left to right, and so since the first of the two plus signs separates a string literal and an int, it is interpreted as a string concatenation operator, and the value of x is thus converted into a string, producing the intermediate string value "The sum of x plus y is: 3".

The second plus sign separates this intermediate string value from an int as well (y), so it, too, is interpreted as a string concatenation operator, and the value of y is thus converted into a string, producing the final string value "The sum of x plus y is: 34", which is what finally gets printed.

To print the correct sum of x and y, we must force the second plus sign to be interpreted as an integer addition operator by enclosing the addition expression in nested parentheses:

```
Console.WriteLine("The sum of x plus y is: " + (x + y));
```

The nested parentheses cause the innermost expression to be evaluated first; the second plus sign is now seen by the compiler as separating two int values, and will thus serve as the integer addition operator. Then, the first plus sign is seen as separating a string from an int, and is thus treated as a string concatenation operator, ultimately causing this print statement to display the correct message on the screen:

```
The sum of x plus y is: 7
```

When writing code that involves complex expressions, it is a good idea to use parentheses liberally to make our intentions clear to the compiler. Extra parentheses never hurt!

Write vs. WriteLine

When we use `Console.WriteLine(...)`, whatever expression is enclosed inside the parentheses will be printed, followed by a **line terminator.** The following code snippet:

```
Console.WriteLine("First line.");
Console.WriteLine("Second line.");
Console.WriteLine("Third line.");
```

produces as output:

```
First line.
Second line.
Third line.
```

By contrast, the statement

```
Console.Write(expression to be printed);
```

causes whatever expression is enclosed in parentheses to be printed *without* a line terminator. Using Write in combination with WriteLine allows us to build up a single line of output with a series of Write statements, as shown by the following example:

```
Console.Write("C");        // Using Write here.
Console.Write("SHA");       // Using Write here.
Console.WriteLine("RP");    // Note use of WriteLine as the last statement.
```

This code snippet produces the single line of output:

```
CSHARP
```

When a single print statement gets too long to fit on a single line, as in this example:

```
// Pseudocode.
statement;
```

```
another statement;
Console.WriteLine("Here is an example of a single print statement that
is very long ... SO long that it wraps around and makes the program
listing difficult to read.");
yet another statement;
```

we can make a program listing more readable by breaking up the contents of such a statement into multiple concatenated strings, and then breaking the statement along plus-sign boundaries:

```
statement;
another statement;
Console.WriteLine("Here is an example of how " +
                  "to break up a long print statement " +
                  "with plus signs.");

yet another statement;
```

Even though the preceding statement is broken across three lines of code, it will be printed as a single line of output:

```
Here is an example of how to break up a long print statement with plus signs.
```

Escape Sequences

C# defines a number of **escape sequences** so that we can represent special characters, such as newline and tab characters, in string expressions. The most commonly used escape sequences are listed here:

\n	Newline
\b	Backspace
\t	Tab
\v	Vertical tab
\\	Backslash
\'	Single quote
\"	Double quote

One or more escape sequences can be included in the expression that is passed to the Write and WriteLine methods. For example, consider the following code snippet:

```
Console.WriteLine("Presenting ...");
Console.WriteLine("\n... for a limited \"time\" only ...\n");
Console.WriteLine("\tBailey the Wonder Dog!");
```

When the preceding code is executed, the following output is displayed:

```
Presenting ...

... for a limited "time" only ...

  Bailey the Wonder Dog!
```

There is a blank line before and after the second line of output because we've inserted extra \n escape sequences in the second statement; the word "time" is quoted because of our use of the \" escape sequences in that same statement; and, the third line of output has been tabbed over one position to the right by virtue of our use of \t.

Elements of C# Style

One of the trademarks of a good programmer is that they produce readable code. Your professional life will probably not involve generating code by yourself on a mountaintop, and so your colleagues will need to be able to work with and modify your programs. Here are some guidelines and conventions that will help you to produce clear, readable C# programs.

Proper Use of Indentation

One of the best ways to make C# programs readable is through proper use of indentation to clearly delineate statement hierarchies. Statements within a block of code should be indented relative to the starting/end line of the enclosing block (i.e., indented relative to the lines carrying the braces). The examples in the MSDN web pages use four spaces, but some programmers use two spaces and others prefer three. The examples in this book use a two-space indentation convention.

To see how indentation can make a program readable, consider the following two programs. In the first program, no indentation is used:

```
using System;

public class StyleDemo
{
static void Main() {
```

```
string name = "cheryl";
for (int i = 0; i < 4; i++) {
if (i != 2) {
Console.WriteLine(name + " " + i);
}
}
Console.WriteLine("what's next");
}
}
```

It's easy to see how someone would have to go through this program very carefully in order to figure out what it's trying to accomplish; it's not very readable code.

Now let's look at the same program when proper indentation is applied. Each statement within a block is indented two spaces relative to its enclosing block. It's much easier now to see what the code is doing. It's clear, for example, that the if statement is inside of the for statement's code block. If the if statement condition is true, the WriteLine method is called. It's also obvious that the last WriteLine method call is outside of the for loop. Both versions of this program produce the same result when executed, but the second version is much more readable.

```
using System;

public class StyleDemo
{
  static void Main() {
    string name = "Cheryl";
    for (int i = 0; i < 4; i++) {
      if (i != 2) {
        Console.WriteLine(name + " " + i);
      }
    }
    Console.WriteLine("What's next");
  }
}
```

This code's output is shown here:

```
Cheryl 0
Cheryl 1
Cheryl 2
What's next
```

Failure to properly indent makes programs unreadable and hence harder to debug—if a compilation error arises due to imbalanced braces, for example, the error message often occurs much later in the program than where the problem exists. For example, the following program is missing an opening brace on line 12, but the compiler doesn't report an error until line 26!

```csharp
using System;
public class Indent2
{
   static void Main() {
      int x = 2;
      int y = 3;
      int z = 1;

      if (x >= 0) {
        if (y > x) {
          if (y > 2) // missing opening brace here on line 12, but ...
             Console.WriteLine("A");
             z = x + y;
          }
          else {
             Console.WriteLine("B");
             z = x - y;
          }
        }
        else {
          Console.WriteLine("C");
          z = y - x;
        }
      }
      else Console.WriteLine("D");  // compiler first complains here!   (line 26)
   }
}
```

The error message that the compiler generates in such a situation is rather cryptic; it points to line 26 as the problem:

```
IndentDemo.cs (26,5) error CS1519: Invalid token.
```

and doesn't really help us much in locating the real problem on line 12. However, at least we've properly indented, so it will likely be easier to hunt down the missing brace than it would be if our indentation were sloppy.

Sometimes, we have so many levels of nested indentation, or individual statements are so long, that lines "wrap" when viewed in an editor or printed as hardcopy:

```csharp
while (a < b) {
    while (c > d) {
```

```
    for (int j = 0; j < 29; j++) {
        x = y + z + a + b - 125
(c * (d / e) + f) - g + h + j - l - m - n + o +
p * q / r + s;
    }
  }
}
```

To avoid this, it is best to break the line in question along white space or punctuation boundaries:

```
while (a < b) {
  while (c > d) {
    for (int j = 0; j < 29; j++) {
      // This is cosmetically preferred.
      x = y + z + a + b - (c * (d / e) + f) - g +
          h + j - l - m - n + o + p * q / r + s;
    }
  }
}
```

Use Comments Wisely

Another important feature that makes code more readable is the liberal use of meaningful comments. Always keep in mind when writing code that you know what you're trying to do, but someone else trying to read your code may not. (We sometimes even need to remind *ourselves* of why we did what we did if we haven't looked at code that *we've* written in a while!)

If there can be any doubt as to what a section of code does, add a comment.

- Include enough detail in the comment to clearly explain what you mean.

- Make sure that the comment adds value; don't state the obvious. The following is a fairly useless comment because it states the obvious:

  ```
  // Declare x as an integer, and assign it an initial value of 3.
  int x = 3;
  ```

- Indent each comment to the same level as the block of code or statement to which it applies.

For an example of how comments are important in making code readable, let's revisit an example from earlier in the chapter:

```csharp
using System;

public class IfDemo
{
  static void Main() {
    double sales = 40000.0;
    int lengthOfService = 12;
    double bonus;

    if (sales > 30000.0 && lengthOfService >= 10) {
      bonus = 2000.0;
    }
    else {
      if (sales > 20000.0) {
        bonus = 1000.0;
      }
      else {
        bonus = 0.0;
      }
    }

    Console.WriteLine("Bonus = " + bonus);
  }
}
```

Because of the lack of comments, someone trying to read the code might have difficulty figuring out what business logic this program is trying to apply. Now let's look at the same program when clear, descriptive comments have been included in the code listing:

```csharp
using System;

// This program computes the size of an employee's bonus.
//
// Written on January 5, 2004 by Jacquie Barker and Grant Palmer.

public class IfDemo
{
  static void Main() {
```

```
// Quarterly sales in dollars.
double sales = 40000.0;

// Length of employment in months.
int lengthOfService = 12;

// Amount of bonus to be awarded in dollars.
double bonus;

// An employee gets a $2K bonus if (a) they have worked for the company
// for 10 months or more and (b) they've sold more than $30K this quarter.
if (sales > 30000.0 && lengthOfService >= 10) {
  bonus = 2000.0;
}
else {
  // Otherwise, ANY employee who has sold more than $20K this quarter earns a
  // bonus of $1K, regardless of how long they've worked for the company.
  if (sales > 20000.0) {
    bonus = 1000.0;
  }
  // Employees who have sold less than $20K earn no bonus.
  else {
    bonus = 0.0;
  }
}

Console.WriteLine("Bonus = " + bonus);
  }
}
```

The program is now much more understandable because the comments explain what each section of the code is intended to accomplish; i.e., the business logic of the application.

Placement of Braces

For block structured languages that use braces, { ... }, to delineate the start/end of blocks (e.g., C, C++, Java, C#), there are two general schools of thought as to where the left/opening brace of a code block should be placed.

The first style is to place the left brace at the end of the line of code that starts the block, and the matching right/closing brace on a line by itself.

Left brace is on the same line as the class declaration:

```
public class Test {
```

Ditto for method headers:

```
    static void Main() {
```

And ditto yet again for control flow statements:

```
        for (int i = 0; i < 3; i++) {
            Console.WriteLine(i);
```

Each closing brace goes on its own line:

```
        }
      }
    }
```

An alternative opening brace placement style is to place every opening brace on a line by itself:

```
public class Test
{
    static void Main()
    {
        for (int i = 0; i < 3; i++)
        {
            Console.WriteLine("i");
        }
    }
}
```

The C# convention is a hybrid of these two approaches: in C#, we typically use the second style (brace on a separate line) for class declarations, and the first style (brace on the same line) for virtually everything else:

```
public class Test
    {
    static void Main() {
        for (int i = 0; i < 3; i++) {
            Console.WriteLine(i);
        }
      }
    }
```

There is no absolute right or wrong style, in that the compiler doesn't care one way or the other. It is a good practice to maintain consistency in your code, however, so pick a brace placement style and stick with it.

Either way, it is important that the closing brace for a given block be indented the same number of spaces as the first line of code in the block so that they visually line up, as was discussed earlier.

Self-Documenting Variable Names

As with indentation and comments, the goal when choosing variable names is to make a program as readable, and hence self-documenting, as possible. Avoid using single letters as variable names, except for loop control variables. Abbreviations should be used sparingly, and only when the abbreviation is commonly used and widely understood by developers. Consider the following variable declaration:

```
int grd;
```

It's not completely clear what the variable name "grd" is supposed to represent. Is the variable supposed to represent a grid, a grade, or a gourd? A better practice would be to spell the entire word out:

```
int grade;
```

At the other end of the spectrum, names that are too long—such as perhaps

```
double averageThirdQuarterReturnOnInvestment;
```

can make a code listing overwhelming to anyone trying to read it. It can sometimes be challenging to reduce the size of a variable name and still keep it descriptive, but do try to keep the length of your variable names within reason.

We'll talk about naming conventions for other OO building blocks, such as methods and classes, as we introduce these topics later in the book.

The .NET Framework provides a series of naming guidelines to promote a uniform style across C# programs. If you'd like to read the complete details on the C# naming conventions, the guidelines can be found at the following URL: `http://msdn.microsoft.com/library/default.asp?url=/library/en-us/cpgenref/html/cpconnamingguidelines.asp`

Summary

In this chapter, we discussed some of the advantages of C#—namely, that

- C# is an intuitive OO programming language that improves upon many languages that preceded it.

- C# was designed from the ground up to be fully object-oriented.

- C# is part of, and hence has access to the power of, Microsoft's .NET Framework.

- C# can be downloaded for free from the MSDN web site.

> *Of course, we haven't sung* **all** *of C#'s praises in this chapter; there are many other features that make C# a powerful object-oriented programming language that we'll cover in subsequent chapters.*

In addition to exploring some of the advantages of C#, we also introduced you to some basic elements of C# syntax. In particular, we

- Presented the anatomy of a simple C# program

- Discussed the predefined simple types and the `string` type

- Examined how value type variables are declared and initialized

- Introduced how a value of one type can be cast into a different type

- Discussed arithmetic, assignment, and logical expressions

- Presented loops and other flow of control structures available with C#

- Explored how to define blocks of code and the concept of variable scope

- Learned how to print text messages to the console with the `Write` and `WriteLine` methods

- Discussed some basic elements of good C# programming style

There's a lot more to learn about C#—things we'll need to know in building the Student Registration System application in Part Three of the book—but we need to explain a number of basic object concepts first. So, on to Chapter 2!

Exercises

1. Research Microsoft's C# Language Tour web site at

   ```
   http://msdn.microsoft.com/library/default.asp?url=/library/
   en-us/cscon/html/vclrfgettingstarted_pg.asp
   ```

   Cite any advantages or features of C# not mentioned in this chapter.

2. Explore the Microsoft .NET Framework home page at

   ```
   http://msdn.microsoft.com/library/default.asp?url=/library/
   en-us/dnanchor/html/netfxanchor.asp
   ```

   Remember that C# can make use of all of the libraries and other capabilities provided by the .NET Framework.

3. Using a `for` loop and a `continue` statement, create a code snippet that will write the even numbers from 2 to 10 to the console.

4. Using what you know about defining blocks of code and proper indentation technique, make the following code snippet more readable:

   ```
   int count = 0;
   for (int j = 0; j < 2; j++) {
   count = j;
   for (int k = 0; k < 3; k++)
   count++;
   Console.WriteLine("count = " + count);
   }
   ```

5. Compare what you've learned about C# so far to another programming language that you are already familiar with. What is similar about the two languages? What is different?

6. Given these initial variable declarations and value assignments:

    ```
    int a = 1;
    int b = 1;
    int c = 1;
    ```

    evaluate the following expression:

    ```
    ((((c++ + --a) * b) != 2) && true)
    ```

Abstraction
and Modeling

As human beings, we're flooded with information every day of our lives. Even if we could temporarily turn off all of the sources of "e-information" that are constantly bombarding us—emails, voicemails, news broadcasts, and the like—our five senses alone collect millions of bits of information per day just from our surroundings. Yet, we manage to make sense out of all of this information, typically without getting overwhelmed. Our brains naturally simplify the details of all that we observe so that these details are manageable through a process known as **abstraction.**

In this chapter, you'll learn

- How abstraction serves to simplify our view of the world

- How we organize our knowledge hierarchically to minimize the amount of information that we have to mentally juggle at any given time

- The relevance of abstraction to software development

- The inherent challenges that we face as software developers when attempting to model a real-world situation in software

Simplification Through Abstraction

Take a moment to look around the room in which you're reading this book. At first, you may think that there really aren't that many things to observe: some furniture, light fixtures, perhaps some plants, artwork, even some other people, or pets. Maybe there is a window to gaze out of that opens up the outside world to observation.

Now, look again: for each thing that you see, there are a myriad of details to observe: its size, its color, its intended purpose, the components from which it's assembled (the legs on a table, the lightbulbs in a lamp), etc. In addition, each one of these components in turn has details associated with it: the type of material used to make the legs of the table (wood or metal), the wattage of the lightbulbs, etc. Now, factor in your other senses: the sound of someone snoring (we hope not while reading this book!), the smell of popcorn coming from the microwave oven down the hall, and so forth. Finally, think about all of the unseen details of these objects—who they were manufactured by, or what their chemical, molecular, or genetic composition is.

It's clear that the amount of information to be processed by our brains is truly overwhelming! For the vast majority of people, this doesn't pose a problem, however, because we're innately skilled at **abstraction:** a process that involves recognizing and focusing on the important characteristics of a situation or object, and filtering out or ignoring all of the unessential details.

One familiar example of an abstraction is a road map. As an abstraction, a road map represents those features of a given geographic area relevant to someone trying to navigate with the map, perhaps by car: major roads and places of interest, obstacles such as major bodies of water, etc. Of necessity, a road map can't include every building, tree, street sign, billboard, traffic light, fast food restaurant, etc. that physically exists in the real world. If it did, then it would be so cluttered as to be virtually unusable; none of the important features would stand out.

Compare a road map with a topographical map, a climatological map, and a population density map of the same region: each abstracts out different features of the real world—namely, those relevant to the intended user of the map in question.

As another example, consider a landscape. An artist may look at the landscape from the perspective of colors, textures, and shapes as a prospective subject for a painting. A homebuilder may look at the same landscape from the perspective of where the best building site may be on the property, assessing how many trees will need to be cleared to make way for a construction project. An ecologist may closely study the individual species of trees and other plant/animal life for their biodiversity, with an eye toward preserving and protecting them; a child may simply be looking at all of the trees in search of the best site for a tree house! Some elements are common to all of these four observers' abstractions of the landscape—the types, sizes, and locations of trees, for example—while others aren't relevant to all of the abstractions.

Generalization Through Abstraction

If we eliminate enough detail from an abstraction, it becomes generic enough to apply to a wide range of specific situations or instances. Such generic abstractions can often be quite useful. For example, a diagram of a generic cell in the human body, such as the one in Figure 2-1, might include only a few features of the structures that are found in an actual cell.

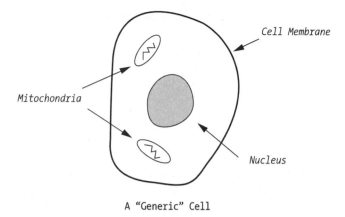

A "Generic" Cell

Figure 2-1. A generic abstraction of a cell

This overly simplified diagram doesn't look like a real nerve cell, or a real muscle cell, or a real blood cell; and yet, it can still be used in an educational setting to describe certain aspects of the structure and function of all of these cell types—namely, those features that the various cell types have in common.

The simpler an abstraction—that is, the fewer features it presents—the more general it is, and the more versatile it is in describing a variety of real-world situations. The more complex an abstraction, the more restrictive it is, and thus the fewer situations it is useful in describing.

Organizing Abstractions into Classification Hierarchies

Even though our brains are adept at abstracting concepts such as road maps and landscapes, that still leaves us with hundreds of thousands, if not millions, of separate abstractions to deal with over our lifetimes. To cope with this aspect of complexity, human beings systematically arrange information into categories according to established criteria; this process is known as **classification.**

For example, science categorizes all natural objects as belonging to either the animal, plant, or mineral kingdom. In order for a natural object to be classified as an animal, it must satisfy the following rules:

- It must be a living being.

- It must be capable of spontaneous movement.

- It must be capable of rapid motor response to stimulation.

The rules for what constitute a plant, on the other hand, are different:

- It must be a living being (same as for an animal).

- It must lack an obvious nervous system.

- It must possess cellulose cell walls.

Given clear-cut rules such as these, placing an object into the appropriate category, or **class,** is rather straightforward. We can then "drill down," specifying additional rules that differentiate various types of animal, for example, until we've built up a hierarchy of increasingly more complex abstractions from top to bottom. A simple example of an **abstraction hierarchy** is shown in Figure 2-2.

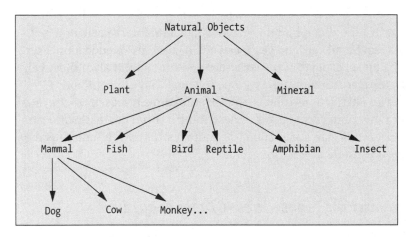

Figure 2-2. A simple abstraction hierarchy of natural objects

When thinking about an abstraction hierarchy such as the one shown in Figure 2-2, we mentally step up and down the hierarchy, automatically zeroing in on only the single layer or subset of the hierarchy (known as a **subtree**) that is important to us at a given point in time. For example, we may only be concerned with mammals, and so can focus on the mammalian subtree, shown in Figure 2-3, temporarily ignoring the rest of the hierarchy.

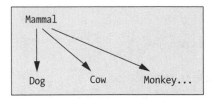

Figure 2-3. Focusing on a small subset of the hierarchy is less overwhelming.

By doing so, we automatically reduce the number of concepts that we mentally need to juggle at any one time to a manageable subset of the overall abstraction hierarchy; in our simplistic example, we're now dealing with only 4 concepts rather than the original 13. No matter how complex an abstraction hierarchy grows to be, it needn't overwhelm us if it's properly organized.

Coming up with precisely which rules are necessary to properly classify an object within an abstraction hierarchy isn't always easy. Take, for example, the rules we might define for what constitutes a bird: namely, something that

- Has feathers

- Has wings

- Lays eggs

- Is capable of flying

Given these rules, neither an ostrich nor a penguin could be classified as a bird, because neither can fly (see Figure 2-4).

Figure 2-4. Deriving the correct classification rules can be difficult.

If we attempt to make the rule set less restrictive by eliminating the "flight" rule, we're left with

- Has feathers

- Has wings

- Lays eggs

According to this rule set, we now may properly classify both the ostrich and the penguin as birds, as shown in Figure 2-5.

Figure 2-5. Proper classification rules have been established.

This rule set is still unnecessarily complicated, because as it turns out, the "lays eggs" rule is redundant: whether we keep it or eliminate it, it doesn't change our decision of what constitutes a bird versus a non-bird. Therefore, we simplify the rule set once again:

- Has feathers

- Has wings

Feeling particularly daring (!), we try to take our simplification process one step further, by eliminating yet another rule, defining a bird as something that

- Has wings

As Figure 2-6 shows, we've gone too far this time: the abstraction of a bird is now so general that we'd include airplanes, insects, and all sorts of other non-birds in the mix!

Figure 2-6. A rule set that is too relaxed is as much of a problem as an overly restrictive rule set.

The process of rule definition for purposes of categorization involves "dialing in" just the right set of rules—not too general, not too restrictive, and containing no redundancies—to define the correct membership in a particular class.

Abstraction As the Basis for Software Development

When pinning down the requirements for an information systems development project, we typically start by gathering details about the real-world situation on which the system is to be based. These details are usually a combination of

- Those that are explicitly offered to us as we interview the intended users of the system, plus

- Those that we otherwise observe

We must make a judgment call as to which of these details are relevant to the system's ultimate purpose. This is essential, as we can't automate them all! To include too much detail is to overly complicate the resultant system, making it that much more difficult to design, program, test, debug, document, maintain, and extend in the future.

As with all abstractions, all of our decisions of inclusion versus elimination when building a software system must be made within the context of the overall purpose and **domain,** or subject matter focus, of the future system. When representing a person in a software system, for example, is their eye color important? How about their genetic profile? Salary? Hobbies? The answer is, *any* of these features of a person may be relevant or irrelevant, depending on whether the system to be developed is a

- Payroll system

- Marketing demographics system

- Optometrist's patient database

- FBI's "most wanted" tracking system

- Public library

Once we've determined the essential aspects of a situation—something that we'll show you how to do in Part Two of this book—we can prepare a **model** of that situation. **Modeling** is the process by which we develop a pattern for something to be made. A blueprint for a custom home, a schematic diagram of a printed circuit, and a cookie cutter are all examples of such patterns. As we'll see in Parts Two and Three, an **object model** of a software system is such a pattern. Modeling and abstraction go hand in hand, because a model is essentially a physical or graphical portrayal of an abstraction; before we can model something effectively, we must have determined the essential details of the subject to be modeled.

Reuse of Abstractions

When learning about something new, we automatically search our mental archive for other abstractions/models that we've previously built and mastered, to look for similarities that we can build upon. When learning to ride a two-wheeled bicycle for the first time, for example, you may have drawn upon lessons that you learned about riding a tricycle as a child (see Figure 2-7). Both have handlebars that are used to steer; both have pedals that are used to propel the bike forward. Although the abstractions didn't match perfectly—a two-wheeled bicycle introduced the new challenge of having to balance oneself—there was enough of a similarity to allow you to draw upon the steering and pedaling expertise you already had mastered, and to focus on learning the new skill of how to balance on two wheels.

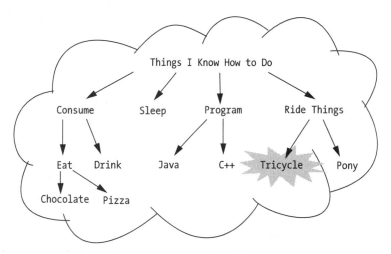

Figure 2-7. The human brain is adept at learning by building upon already-established abstractions.

This technique of comparing features to find an abstraction that is similar enough to be reused successfully is known as **pattern matching and reuse**. As we'll see in Chapter 12, pattern reuse is an important technique for object-oriented software development, as well, because it spares us from having to reinvent the wheel with each new project. If we can reuse an abstraction or model from a previous project, we can focus on those aspects of the new project that differ from the old, gaining a tremendous amount of productivity in the process.

Inherent Challenges

Despite the fact that abstraction is such a natural process for human beings, developing an appropriate model for a software system is perhaps the most difficult aspect of software engineering, because

- There are an unlimited number of possibilities. Abstraction is to a certain extent in the eye of the beholder: several different observers working independently are almost guaranteed to arrive at different models. Whose is the best? *Passionate* arguments have ensued!

- To further complicate matters, there is virtually never only one "best" or "correct" model, only "better" or "worse" models relative to the problem to be solved. The same situation can be modeled in a variety of different, equally valid ways. As you'll see when we get into actually doing some modeling in Part Two of this book, we'll look at a number of valid alternative abstractions for our Student Registration System (SRS) case study that was presented at the end of the Introduction.

- Note, however, that there *is* such a thing as an ***incorrect*** model: namely, one that misrepresents the real-world situation (for example, modeling a person as having two different blood types).

- There is no acid test to determine if a model has adequately captured all of a user's requirements. The ultimate evidence of whether or not an abstraction was appropriate is in how successful the resultant software system turns out to be. We don't want to wait until the end of a project before finding out that we've gone astray. Because of this, it's critical that we learn ways of communicating our model concisely and unambiguously to the following people:

  - The intended future users of our application, so that they may sanity check our understanding of the problem to be solved before we embark upon software development

  - Our fellow software engineers, so that team members can share a common vision of what we're to build collaboratively

Despite all of these challenges, it's critical to get the up-front abstraction "right" before beginning to build a system. Fixing mistakes in the abstraction once a system is modeled, designed, coded, documented, and undergoing acceptance testing is much more costly (by orders of magnitude) than correcting the abstraction when it's still a gleam in the project team's eye. This isn't to imply that an abstraction should be rigid—quite the contrary! The art and science of object modeling, when properly applied, yields a model that is flexible enough to withstand a wide variety of functional changes. In addition, the special properties of objects further lend themselves to flexible software solutions, as you'll learn throughout the rest of the book. However, all things being equal, we'd like to harness this flexibility in expanding a system's capabilities over time, rather than in repairing mistakes.

What Does It Take to Be a Successful Object Modeler?

Coming up with an appropriate abstraction as the basis for a software system model requires

- ***Insight into the problem domain:*** Ideally, you'll be able to draw upon your own real-world experience, such as your former or current experience as a student, which will come in handy when determining the requirements for the SRS.

- **Creativity:** We must be able to think "outside the box," in case the future users that we're interviewing have been immersed in the problem area for so long that they fail to see innovations that might be made.

- **Good listening skills:** These will come in handy as future users of the system describe how they do their jobs currently, or how they envision doing their jobs in the future, with the aid of the system that we're about to develop.

- **Good observational skills:** Actions often speak louder than words; just by observing users going about their daily business, we may pick up an essential detail that they have neglected to mention because they do it so routinely that it has become a habit.

But all this isn't enough; we also need

- An organized **process** for determining what the abstraction should be. If we follow a proven checklist of steps for producing a model, then we greatly reduce the probability that we'll omit some important feature or neglect a critical requirement.

- A way to **communicate** the resultant model concisely and unambiguously to our fellow software developers and to the intended users of our application. While it's certainly possible to describe an abstraction in narrative text, a picture is worth 1,000 words, and so the language with which we communicate a model is often a **graphical notation.** Throughout this book, we'll focus on the **Unified Modeling Language** (**UML**—see Figure 2-8) notation as our model communication language (you'll learn the basics of UML in Chapters 9, 10, and 11). Think of a graphical model as a blueprint of the software application to be built.

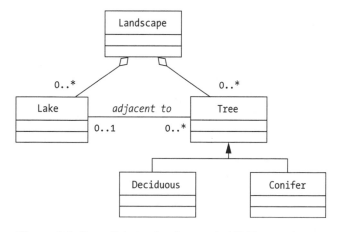

Figure 2-8. Describing a landscape in UML notation

> *You'll learn how to interpret UML diagrams in Part Two of the book.*

- Ideally, we'll also have a ***software tool*** to help us automate the process of producing such a blueprint.

Part Two of this book covers these three aspects of modeling—process, notation, and tool—in detail; for starters, however, we'll make sure that you understand the basics of objects, which is the focus of the remainder of Part One.

Summary

In this chapter, you've learned that

- Abstraction is a fundamental technique that people use to perceive the world, and is a necessary first step of all software development.

- We naturally organize information into classification hierarchies based upon rules that we carefully structure, so that they are neither too general nor too restrictive.

- We often reuse abstractions when attempting to model a new concept.

- Producing an abstraction of a system to be built, known as a model, is in some senses second nature to us, and yet paradoxically is one of the hardest things that software developers have to do in the life cycle of an information systems project. It's also one of the most important.

Exercises

1. Sketch a class hierarchy that relates all of the following classes in a reasonable manner:

   Apple

   Banana

   Beef

   Beverage

   Cheese

Consumable

Dairy Product

Food

Fruit

Green Bean

Meat

Milk

Pork

Spinach

Vegetable

Note any challenges you faced in doing so.

2. What aspects of a television set would be important to abstract from the perspective of

- A consumer wishing to buy one?

- An engineer responsible for designing one?

- A retailer who sells them?

- The manufacturer?

3. Select a problem area that you would like to model from an object-oriented perspective. Ideally, this will be a problem that you're actually going to be working on at your place of employment, or that you have a keen interest in. Assume that you're going to write a program to automate some aspect of this problem area. Write a one-page overview of the requirements for this program, patterned after the Student Registration System case study.

Make certain that your first paragraph summarizes the intent of the system, as the first paragraph in the SRS case study does. Also, emphasize the *functional requirements*—that is, those which a nontechnical end user might state as to how the system should behave—and avoid stating *technical requirements*—for example, "This system must run on a Windows NT platform, and must use the TCP/IP protocol to . . .".

4. Read the case study for a Conference Room Reservation System (CRRS) in Appendix B. In your opinion, how effective is this case study as an abstraction: are there details that you think could have been omitted, or missing details that you think would have been important to include? If you had an opportunity to interview the intended users of the CRRS, what additional questions might you ask them to better refine this abstraction?

CHAPTER 3

Objects and Classes

OBJECTS ARE THE FUNDAMENTAL building blocks of an object-oriented (OO) system. Just as you learned in Chapter 2 that abstraction involves producing a model of the real world, you'll see in this chapter that objects are "mini abstractions" of the various real-world components that comprise such a model.

In this chapter, you'll learn

- What makes up a software object

- How we use classes to specify an object's data and behavior

- How we create objects based on a class definition

- How objects keep track of one another

What Is an Object?

Before we talk about software objects, let's talk about real-world objects in general. According to Merriam-Webster's Collegiate Dictionary, an object is

(1) Something material that may be perceived by the senses; (2) something mental or physical toward which thought, feeling, or action is directed.

The first part of this definition refers to objects as we typically think of them: as physical "things" that we can see and touch, and which occupy space. Because we intend to use the Student Registration System (SRS) case study as the basis for learning about objects throughout this book, let's think of some examples of **physical objects** that make sense in the general context of an academic setting, namely

- The *students* who attend classes

- The *professors* who teach them

- The *classrooms* in which class meetings take place

- The *furniture* in these classrooms

- The *buildings* in which the classrooms are located

- The *textbooks* students use

and on and on. Of course, while all of these types of objects are commonly found on a typical college campus, not all of them are relevant to registering students for courses, nor are they all necessarily called out by the SRS case study, but we won't worry about that for the time being. In Part Two of this book, you'll learn a technique for using a requirements specification as the basis for identifying which types of objects are relevant to a particular abstraction.

Now, let's focus on the second half of the definition, particularly on the phrase ***"something mental . . . toward which thought, feeling, or action is directed."*** There are a great many **conceptual objects** that play important roles in an academic setting; some of these are

- The *courses* that students attend

- The *departments* that faculty work for

- The *degrees* that students receive

and, of course, many others. Even though we can't see, hear, touch, taste, or smell them, conceptual objects are every bit as important as physical objects are in describing an abstraction.

Let's now get a bit more formal, and define a **software object:**

- A (**software**) **object** is a software construct that bundles together **state** (**data**) and **behavior** (**operations**) that, taken together, represent an abstraction of a "real-world" (physical or conceptual) object.

Let's explore the two sides of objects—their **state** and **behavior**—separately, in more depth.

State/Attributes/Data

If we wish to record information about a student, what data might we require? Some examples might be

- The student's name

- His or her student ID number

- The student's birthdate

- His or her address

- The student's designated major field of study, if the student has declared one yet

- His or her cumulative grade point average (GPA)

- Who the student's faculty advisor is

- A list of the courses that the student is currently enrolled in this semester (i.e., the student's current course load)

- A history of all of the courses that the student has taken to date, the semester/year in which each was taken, and the grade that was earned for each: in other words, the student's transcript

and so on. Now, how about for an academic course? Perhaps we'd wish to record

- The course number (e.g., "ART 101")

- The course name (e.g., "Introductory Basketweaving")

- A list of all of the courses that must have been successfully completed by a student prior to allowing that student to register for *this* course (i.e., the course's prerequisites)

- The number of credit hours that the course is worth

- A list of the professors who have been approved to teach this course

and so on. In object nomenclature, the data elements used to describe an object are referred to as the object's **attributes.**

*Use of the term "attribute" in this fashion is a language-neutral object modeling and programming convention. But, all .NET languages (including C#) have a specific **programming construct** called an attribute, which has a more complex purpose than simply referring to a data element of an object. It's important not to confuse the two uses of the term "attribute" when talking specifically about one of the .NET languages. (.NET languages instead prefer to use the term "field" to refer to an object's data elements/attributes in the generic sense of the word.)*

We'll explain what an attribute in the C# (.NET) specific sense is all about in Chapter 13. For the time being, however (i.e., throughout the remainder of Parts One and Two of the book), whenever we use the term "attribute," we're using it in the generic OO sense.

An object's attribute values, when taken collectively, are said to define the **state,** or condition, of the object. For example, if we wanted to determine whether or not a student is "eligible to graduate" (a state), we might look at a combination of

- The student's transcript (an attribute), and

- The list of courses he or she is currently enrolled in (a second attribute)

to see if the student is indeed expected to have satisfied the course requirements for their chosen major field of study (a third attribute) by the end of the current academic year.

A given attribute may be simple—for example, "GPA", which can be represented as a simple floating point number—or complex—for example, "transcript", which represents a rather extensive collection of information with no simple representation (at least as far as C# simple types are concerned).

Behavior/Operations/Methods

Now, let's revisit the same two types of object—a student and a course—and talk about these objects' respective behaviors. A student's behaviors (relevant to academic matters, that is!) might include

- Enrolling in a course

- Dropping a course

- Choosing a major field of study

- Selecting a faculty advisor

- Telling you his or her GPA

- Telling you whether or not he or she has taken a particular course, and if so, when the course was taken, which professor taught it, and what grade the student received

It's a bit harder to think of an inanimate, conceptual object like a course as having behaviors, but if we were to imagine a course to be a living thing, then we can imagine that a course's behaviors might include

- Permitting a student to register

- Determining whether or not a given student is *already* registered

- Telling you how many students have registered so far, or conversely, how many seats remain before the course is full

- Telling you what its prerequisite courses are

- Telling you how many credit hours it's worth

- Telling you which professor is assigned to teach the course this semester

and so on.

When we talk about software objects specifically, we define an object's behaviors, also known as its **operations,** as both the things that an object does to **access** its attributes (data), and the things that an object does to **modify/maintain** its attribute values (data).

If we take a moment to reflect back on the behaviors we expect of a student as listed previously, we see that each operation involves one or more of the student's attributes. For example:

- Telling you his or her GPA involves *accessing* the value of the student's "GPA" attribute.

- Choosing a major field of study involves *modifying* the value of the student's "major" attribute.

- Enrolling in a course involves *modifying* the value of the student's "course load" attribute.

Since we recently learned that the collective set of attribute values for an object defines its state, we now can see that operations are capable of *changing an object's state.* Let's say that we define the state of a student who hasn't yet selected a major field of study as an "undeclared" student. Asking such a student object to perform its "choosing a major field of study" method will cause that object to update the value of its "major field of study" attribute to reflect the newly selected major field. This, then, changes the student's state from "undeclared" to "declared".

Yet another way to think of an object's operations are as **services** that can be requested of the object. For example, one service that we might call upon a course object to perform is to provide us with a list of all of the students who are currently registered for the course (i.e., a student roster).

When we actually get around to programming an object in a language like C#, we refer to the programming language representation of an operation as a **method,** whereas, strictly speaking, the term "operation" is typically used to refer to a behavior conceptually.

Classes

A **class** is an abstraction describing the common features of all objects in a group of similar objects. For example, a class called "Student" could be created to describe all student objects recognized by the Student Registration System.

A class defines the following:

- The data structure (names and types of attributes) needed to define an object belonging to that class

- The operations to be performed by such objects: specifically, what these operations are, how an object belonging to that class is formally called upon to perform them, and what "behind the scenes" things an object has to do to actually carry them out

For example, the Student class might be defined to have the nine attributes described in Table 3-1.

Table 3-1. Proposed Attributes of the Student Class

Attribute	Type
name	string
studentId	string
birthdate	DateTime
address	string

Table 3-1. Proposed Attributes of the Student Class (continued)

Attribute	Type
major	string
gpa	double
advisor	???
courseLoad	???
transcript	???

This means each and every Student object will have these *same* nine attributes. Note that many of the attributes can be represented by predefined C# types (e.g., string, double, and DateTime) but that a few of the attributes—advisor, courseLoad, and transcript—are too complex for predefined types to handle; you'll learn how to tackle such attributes a bit later on.

In terms of operations, the Student class might define five methods as follows:

- RegisterForCourse

- DropCourse

- ChooseMajor

- ChangeAdvisor

- PrintTranscript

Note that an object can only do those things for which methods have been defined by the object's class. In that respect, an object is like an appliance: it can do whatever it was designed to do (a DVD player provides buttons to play, pause, stop, and seek a particular movie scene), and nothing more (you can't ask a DVD to toast a bagel—at least not with much chance of success!). So, an important aspect of successfully designing an object is making sure to anticipate all of the behaviors it will need to be able to perform in order to carry out its "mission" within the system. We'll see how to determine what an object's mission, data structure, and behaviors should be, based on the requirements for a system, in Part Two of the book.

> *The terms **feature** and **member** are used interchangeably to refer to both attributes and methods of a class. That is, a class definition that includes three attribute declarations and five method declarations is said to have eight features/members. "Feature" is the generic OO term, "member" the C#-specific term. We'll use generic OO terminology in Parts One and Two of the book, switching to C#-specific terminology in Part Three.*

Features are the building blocks of a class: virtually everything found within a class definition is either an attribute or a method of the class.

> *In the C# language, several other types of things are included within the boundaries—i.e., are features—of a class definition, but we won't worry about these until we get to Part Three of the book. Conceptually, it's sufficient to think of an object as consisting only of attributes and methods at this point in time.*

A Note Regarding Naming Conventions

It's recommended practice to name classes starting with an ***uppercase*** letter, but to use mixed case for the name overall: Student, Course, Professor, and so on. When the name of a class would ideally be stated as a multiword phrase, such as "course catalog", start each word with a capital letter, and concatenate the words without using spaces, dashes, or underscores to separate them: for example, CourseCatalog. This style is known as **Pascal casing**.

For method names, the C# convention is to use Pascal casing as well. Typical method names might thus be Main, GetName, or RegisterForCourse.

In contrast, the C# convention for attribute names is to start with a ***lowercase*** letter, but to capitalize the first letter of any subsequent words in the attribute name. Typical attribute names might thus be name, studentId, or courseLoad. This style is known as **Camel casing.**

In subsequent chapters, we'll refine the rules for how Pascal and Camel casing are to be applied.

Instantiation

A class definition may be thought of as a template for creating software objects—a "pattern" used to

- Stamp out a prescribed data area in memory to house the attributes of a new object.

- Associate a certain set of behaviors with that object.

The term **instantiation** is used to refer to the process by which an object is created (constructed) based upon a class definition. From a single class definition—for example, Student—we can create many objects, in the same way that we use a single cookie cutter to make many cookies. Another way to refer to an object, then, is as an **instance** of a particular class—e.g., a Student object is an instance of the Student class. We'll talk about the physical process of **instantiating** objects as it occurs in C# in a bit more detail later in this chapter.

Classes may be differentiated from objects, then, as follows:

- A *class* defines the features—attributes, methods, etc.—that all objects belonging to the class possess, and can be thought of as serving as an object *template*, as illustrated in Figure 3-1.

- An *object*, on the other hand, is a unique instance of a *filled-in* template for which attribute values have been provided, and on which methods may be called, as illustrated in Figure 3-2.

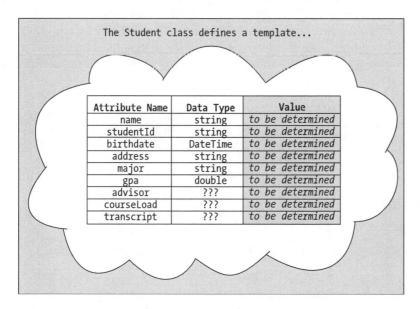

The Student class defines a template...

Attribute Name	Data Type	Value
name	string	to be determined
studentId	string	to be determined
birthdate	DateTime	to be determined
address	string	to be determined
major	string	to be determined
gpa	double	to be determined
advisor	???	to be determined
courseLoad	???	to be determined
transcript	???	to be determined

Figure 3-1. A class defines attribute names and types.

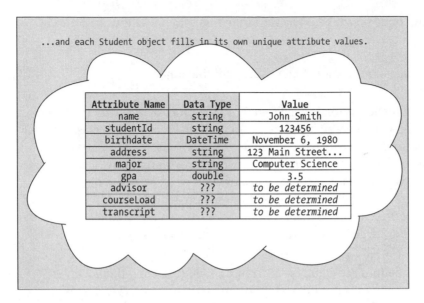

Figure 3-2. An object provides attribute values.

Encapsulation

Encapsulation is a formal term referring to the mechanism that bundles together the state and behavior of an object into a single logical unit. Everything that we need to know about a given student is, in theory, contained within the "walls" of the student object, either directly as a field of that object or indirectly as a method that can answer a question or make a determination about the object's state.

Encapsulation isn't unique to OO languages, but in some senses is perfected by them. For those of you familiar with C, you know that a C struct*(ure) encapsulates data:*

```
struct employee {
    char name[30];
    int age;
}
```

and a C function encapsulates logic—data is passed in, operated on, and an answer is optionally returned:

```
float average(float x, float y) {
    return (x + y)/2.0;
}
```

But only with OO programming languages is the notion of encapsulating data and behavior in a single construct, to represent an abstraction of a real-world entity, truly embraced.

User-Defined Types and Reference Variables

In a non-OO programming language such as C, the statement

```
int x;
```

is a **declaration** that variable x is an int(eger), one of several simple, **predefined types** defined to be part of the C language.

What does this *really* mean? It means that

- x is a symbolic name that represents an integer value.

- The "thing" that we've named x understands how to respond to a number of different operations, such as addition (+), subtraction (–), multiplication (*), division (/), logical comparisons (>, <, =), and so on that have been defined for the int type.

- Whenever we want to operate on this particular integer value in our program, we refer to it via its symbolic name x:

```
if (x > 17) x = x + 5;
```

In an object-oriented language like C#, we can define a class such as Student, and then declare a variable as follows:

```
Student y;
```

What does this mean? It means that

- y is a symbolic name that refers to a Student object (an instance of the Student class).

- The "thing" that we have named y understands how to respond to a number of different service requests—how to register for a course, drop a course, and so on—that have been defined by the Student class.

- Whenever we want to operate on this particular object, we refer to y:

```
// Pseudocode.
   if (y hasn't chosen an advisor yet) Console.WriteLine ("Uh oh ...");
```

Note the parallels between y as a Student in the preceding example and x as an int earlier. Just as int is a predefined type (in both C and C#), the Student class is a **user-defined type**. And, because y in the preceding example is a variable that *refers to* an instance (object) of class Student, y is informally known as a **reference variable.**

Names for (nonattribute) reference variables follow the same convention as method and attribute names: i.e., they use Pascal casing. Some sample reference variable declarations are as follows:

```
Student x;
Student aStudent;
Course prerequisiteOfThisCourse;
Professor myAdvisor;
```

Instantiating Objects: A Closer Look

Different OO languages differ in terms of when an object is actually instantiated (created). In C#, when we declare a variable to be of a user-defined type, like

```
Student y;
```

we haven't actually created an object in memory yet. Rather, we've simply declared a reference variable of type Student named y. This reference variable has the *potential* to refer to a Student object, but it doesn't refer to one just yet; rather, it's said to have the value null, which as we saw in Chapter 1 is the C# keyword used to represent a nonexistent object.

We have to take the distinct step of using a special C# operator, the new operator, to actually carve out a brand-new Student object in memory, and to then associate the new object with the reference variable y, as follows:

```
y = new Student();
```

> Behind the scenes, what we're actually doing is associating the value of the *physical memory address* at which this object was created—known as a *reference*—to variable y.
>
> Don't worry about the parentheses at the end of the preceding statement; we'll talk about their significance in Chapter 4, when we discuss the notion of *constructors*.

Think of the newly created object as a helium balloon, as shown in Figure 3-3, and a reference variable as the hand that holds a string tied to the balloon so that we may access the object whenever we'd like.

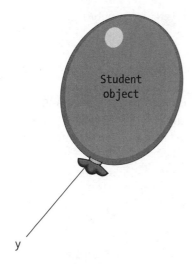

y

Figure 3-3. Using a reference variable to keep track of an object in memory

Because a reference variable is sometimes informally said to "hold onto" an object, we often use the informal term **handle,** as in the expression "reference variable y maintains a handle on a Student object."

We can also create a new object without immediately assigning it to a reference variable, as in the following line of code:

```
new Student();
```

but such an object would be like a helium balloon without a string tied to it: it would indeed exist, but we'd never be able to access this object in our program. It would, in essence, "float away" from us in memory.

Note that we can combine the two steps—declaring a reference variable and actually instantiating an object for that variable to refer to—into a single line of code:

```
Student y = new Student();
```

Another way to initialize a reference variable is to hand it a ***preexisting*** object: that is, an object ("helium balloon") that is already being referenced ("held onto") by a ***different*** reference variable ("hand"). Let's look at an example:

```
// We declare a reference variable, and instantiate our first Student object.
Student x = new Student();

// We declare a second reference variable, but do not instantiate a
// second object.
Student y;
```

```
// We pass y a "handle" on the same object that x is holding onto
// (x continues to hold onto it, too).  We now, in essence,
// have two "strings" tied to the same "balloon".
y = x;
```

The conceptual outcome of the preceding code is illustrated in Figure 3-4: two "strings", being held by two different "hands", tied to the same "balloon"—that is, two *different* reference variables referring to the *same* physical object in memory.

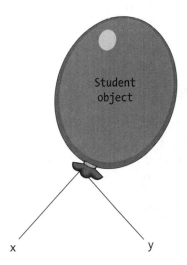

Figure 3-4. Maintaining multiple handles on the same object

We therefore see that the same object can have many reference variables simultaneously referring to it; but, as it turns out, any *one* reference variable can only hold onto/refer to *one* object at a time. To grab onto a new object handle means that a reference variable must let go of the object handle that it was previously holding onto, if any.

If there comes a time when *all* handles for a particular object have been let go of, then as we discussed earlier the object is no longer accessible to our program, like a helium balloon that has been let loose. Continuing with our previous example (note highlighted code below and Figures 3-5, 3-6, and 3-7):

```
// We instantiate our first Student object.
Student x = new Student();

// We declare a second reference variable, but do not instantiate a
// second object.
Student y;
```

```
// We pass y a "handle" on the same object that x is holding onto
// (x continues to hold onto it, too).  We now, in essence,
// have TWO "strings" tied to the same "balloon".
y = x;

// We now declare a third reference variable and instantiate a second
// Student object.
Student z = new Student();
```

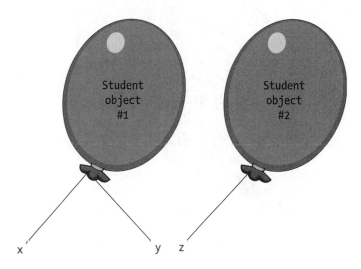

Figure 3-5. A second object comes into existence.

```
// y now lets go of the first Student object and grabs onto the second.
y = z;
```

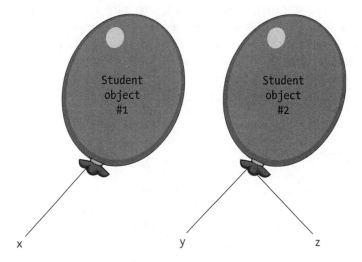

Figure 3-6. Transferring object handles

```
// Finally, x lets go of the first Student object, and grabs onto
// the second, as well; the first Student object is now lost to
// the program because we no longer have any reference variables
// maintaining a "handle" on it!
x = z;
```

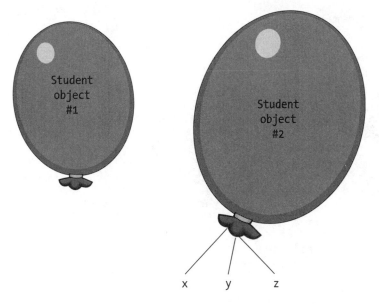

Figure 3-7. The first object is now lost to our program.

As it turns out, if all of an object's handles are lost, it might seem as though the memory that the object occupies is permanently wasted. (In a language like C++, this is indeed the case, and programmers have to explicitly take care to "reclaim" the memory of an object that is no longer needed before all of its handles are dropped. Failure to do so is a chronic source of problems in C++ programs.) In C# (and all other .NET languages) the **common language runtime (CLR)** periodically performs **garbage collection,** a process that automatically reclaims the memory of "lost" objects for us. We'll revisit this topic in Chapter 13.

Objects As Attributes

When we first discussed the attributes and methods associated with the Student class, we stated that some of the attributes could be represented by predefined types provided by the C# language, whereas the types of a few others (advisor, courseLoad, and transcript) were left undefined. Let's now put what we've learned about user-defined types to good use.

Rather than declaring the Student class's advisor attribute as simply a string representing the advisor's name, we'll declare it to be of user-defined type—namely, type Professor, another class that we've invented (see Table 3-2).

Table 3-2. Student Class Attributes, Revisited

Attribute	Type
name	string
studentID	string
birthdate	DateTime
address	string
major	string
gpa	double
advisor	Professor
courseLoad	???
transcript	???

By having declared the advisor attribute to be of type Professor—i.e., by making the advisor attribute a reference variable—we've just enabled a Student object to maintain a handle on the actual Professor object that is advising the student. We'll still leave the courseLoad and transcript types unspecified for the time being; we'll see how to handle these a bit later.

The Professor class, in turn, might be defined to have attributes as listed in Table 3-3.

Table 3-3. Student Class Attributes

Attribute	Type
name	string
employeeID	string
birthdate	DateTime
address	string
worksFor	string (or Department)
studentAdvisee	**Student**
teachingAssignments	???

Again, by having declared the `studentAdvisee` attribute of `Professor` to be of type `Student`—i.e., by making the `studentAdvisee` attribute a reference variable—we've just given a `Professor` object a way to hold onto/refer to the actual `Student` object that the professor is advising. We'll leave the type of `teachingAssignments` undefined for the time being.

The methods of the `Professor` class might be as follows:

- `TransferToDepartment`

- `AdviseStudent`

- `AgreeToTeachCourse`

- `AssignGrades`

A few noteworthy points about the `Professor` class:

- It's likely that a professor will be advising several students simultaneously, so having an attribute like `studentAdvisee` that can only reference a single `Student` object is not terribly useful. We'll discuss techniques for handling this in Chapter 6, when we talk about **collections,** which we'll also see as being useful for defining the `teachingAssignments` attribute of `Professor` and the `courseLoad` and `transcript` attributes of `Student`.

- The `worksFor` attribute represents the department to which a professor is assigned. We can choose to represent this as either a simple `string` representing the department name—for example, "MATH"—or as a reference variable that maintains a handle on a `Department` object—specifically, the `Department` object representing the "real-world" Math Department. Of course, to do so would require us to define the attributes and methods for a new class called `Department`. As we'll see in Part Two of this book, the decision of whether or not we need to invent a new user-defined type/class to represent a particular real-world concept/abstraction isn't always clear-cut.

Composition

Whenever we create a class, such as `Student` or `Professor`, in which one or more of the attributes are themselves handles on other objects, we are employing an OO technique known as **composition**. The number of levels to which objects can be conceptually bundled inside one another is endless, and so composition enables us to model very sophisticated real-world concepts. As it turns out, most "interesting" classes employ composition.

With composition, it may seem as though we're nesting objects one inside the other, as depicted in Figure 3-8.

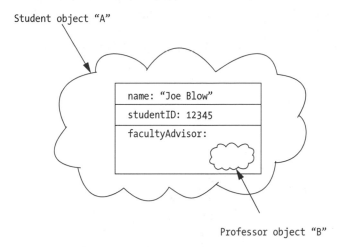

Figure 3-8. Conceptual object "nesting"

Actual object nesting (i.e., declaring one class inside of another) is possible in some OO programming languages, and does indeed sometimes make sense: namely, if an object **A** doesn't need to have a life of its own from the standpoint of an OO application, and only exists for the purpose of serving enclosing object **B.**

- Think of your brain, for example, as an object that exists only within the context of your body (another object).

- As an example of object nesting relevant to the SRS, let's consider a grade book used to track student performance in a particular course. If we were to define a GradeBook class, and then create GradeBook objects as attributes—one per Course object—then it might be reasonable for each GradeBook object to exist wholly within the context of its associated Course object. No other objects would need to communicate with the GradeBook directly; if a Student object wished to ask a Course object what grade the Student has earned, the Course object might internally consult its embedded GradeBook object, and simply hand a letter grade back to the Student.

However, we often encounter the situation—as with the sample Student and Professor classes—in which an object **A** needs to refer to an object **B**, object **B** needs to refer back to **A**, and ***both*** objects need to be able to respond to requests independently of each other as made by the application as a whole. In such a case, handles come to the rescue! In reality, we are ***not*** storing whole objects as attributes inside of other objects; rather, we are storing ***references*** to objects. When an attribute of an object **A** is defined in terms of an object reference **B,** the two objects exist separately in memory, and simply have a convenient way of finding one another whenever it's necessary for them to interact. Think of your-self as an object, and your cellular phone number as your reference. Other people—"objects"—can reach you to speak with you whenever they need to, even though they don't know where you're physically located, using your cell phone number.

Memory allocation using handles might look something like Figure 3-9 conceptually.

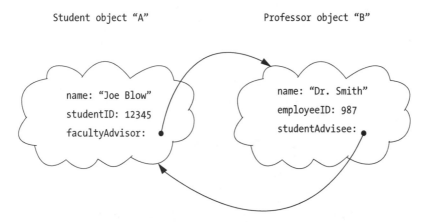

Figure 3-9. Objects exist separately in memory and maintain handles on one another.

With this approach, each object is allocated in memory only once; the Student object knows how to find and communicate with its advisor (Professor) object whenever it needs to through its handle/reference, and vice versa.

What do we gain by defining the Student's advisor attribute as a reference to a Professor object, instead of merely storing the name of the advisor as a string attribute of the Student object?

For one thing, we can ask the Professor object its name whenever we need it (through a technique that we'll discuss in Chapter 4). Why is this important? ***To avoid data redundancy and the potential for loss of data integrity.***

- If the Professor object's name changes for some reason, the name will only be stored in one place: encapsulated as an attribute within the Professor object that "owns" the name, which is precisely where it belongs.

- If we instead were to redundantly store the Professor's name both as a string attribute of the Professor object and as a string attribute of the Student object, we'd have to remember to update the name in two places any time the name changed (or three, or four, or however many places this Professor's name is referenced as an advisor of countless Students). If we were to for-get to do so, then the name of the Professor would be "out of synch" from one instance to another.

Just as importantly, by maintaining a handle on the Professor object via the advisor attribute of Student, the Student object can also ***request other services*** of this Professor object via whatever methods are defined for the Professor class. A Student object may, for example, ask its advisor (Professor) object where the Professor's office is located, or what classes the Professor is teaching so that the Student can sign up for one of them.

Another advantage of using object handles from an implementation standpoint is that they also reduce memory overhead. Storing a reference to (aka memory address of) an object only requires 4 bytes (on 32-bit machines) or 8 bytes (on 64-bit machines) of memory, instead of however many bytes of storage the referenced object as a whole occupies in memory. If we were to have to make a copy of an entire object every place we needed to refer to it in our application, we could quickly exhaust the total memory available to our application.

Three Distinguishing Features of an Object-Oriented Programming Language

In order to be considered truly object oriented, a programming language must provide support for three key mechanisms:

- (Programmer creation of) User-defined types

- Inheritance

- Polymorphism

We've just learned about the first of these mechanisms, and will discuss the other two in chapters to follow.

Summary

In this chapter, you've learned that

- An object is a software abstraction of a physical or conceptual real-world object.

- A class serves as a template for defining objects: specifically, a class defines the following:

  - What data the object will house, known as an object's attributes

  - What behaviors an object will be able to perform, known as an object's operations (methods)

- An object may then be thought of as a filled-in template.

- Just as we can declare variables to be of simple predefined types such as int, double, and bool, we can also declare variables to be of user-defined types such as Student and Professor.

- When we create a new object (a process known as instantiation), we typically store a reference to that object in a reference variable. We can then use that "handle" to communicate with the object.

- We can define attributes of a class A to serve as handles on objects belonging to another class B. In doing so, we allow each object to encapsulate the information that rightfully belongs to that object, but enable objects to share information by contacting one another whenever necessary.

Exercises

1. From the perspective of an academic setting (but not necessarily the SRS case study specifically), think about what the appropriate attributes and methods of the following classes might be:

   - Classroom

   - Department

   - Degree

   Which of the attributes of each of these classes should be declared using predefined C# types, and which should be declared using user-defined types? Explain your rationale.

2. For the problem area whose requirements you defined for exercise 3 in Chapter 2, list the classes that you might need to create in order to model it properly.

3. List the classes that you might need to create in order to model the Prescription Tracking System discussed in Appendix B.

4. Would Color be a good candidate for a user-defined type/class? Why or why not?

CHAPTER 4

Object Interactions

As you learned in Chapter 3, objects are the building blocks of an object-oriented software system. In such a system, objects collaborate with one another to accomplish common system goals, similar to the ants in an anthill, or the employees of a corporation, or the cells in your body. Each object has a specific structure and "mission"; these respective missions complement one another in accomplishing the mission of the system as a whole.

In this chapter, you'll learn

- How external events set the objects within an OO application in motion.

- How methods can be used to specify an object's behaviors. We'll talk about the various code elements that make up a method and how methods are invoked.

- How objects publicize their methods as services to one another.

- How objects communicate with one another to request one another's services.

- How objects maintain their data, and how they "guard" their data to ensure its integrity.

- About the power of encapsulation, and how it can be used to limit "ripple effects" when the private implementation details of a class change.

- How constructors can be used to initialize attribute values when an object is instantiated.

Events Drive Object Collaboration

At its simplest, the process of object-oriented software development involves

- Properly establishing the functional requirements for, and overall mission of, an application

- Designing the appropriate classes necessary to fulfill these requirements and mission

- Instantiating the classes to create objects

- Setting the objects in motion through external triggering events

Think of an anthill: at first glance, you may see no apparent activity taking place. But if you drop an ice cream cone nearby, a flurry of activity suddenly begins as ants rush around to gather up the "goodies," as well as to repair any damage that may have been caused if you dropped the ice cream cone ***too close*** to the anthill!

Within an OO application (the "anthill"), the objects ("ants") may be set in motion by an external event such as

- The click of a button on the Student Registration System (SRS) graphical user interface (GUI), indicating a student's desire to register for a particular course

- The receipt of information from some other automated system, such as when the SRS receives a list of all students who have paid their tuition from the university's billing system

As soon as such a triggering event has been noted by an OO system, the appropriate objects react, performing services themselves or requesting services of other objects in chain-reaction fashion, until some overall system goal has been accomplished. For example, the request to register for a course as made by a student user via the SRS application's GUI may involve the collaboration of many different objects (see also Figure 4-1):

- A Student object (an abstraction of the ***real*** student user)

- A DegreeProgram object, to ensure that the requested course is truly required for the student to graduate

- The appropriate Course object, to make sure that there is a seat available in the course for the student

- A Classroom object, representing the room in which the course will be meeting, to verify its seating capacity

- A Transcript object—specifically, the Transcript of the Student of interest—to ensure that the student has met all prerequisites for the course

An external event gets objects talking!

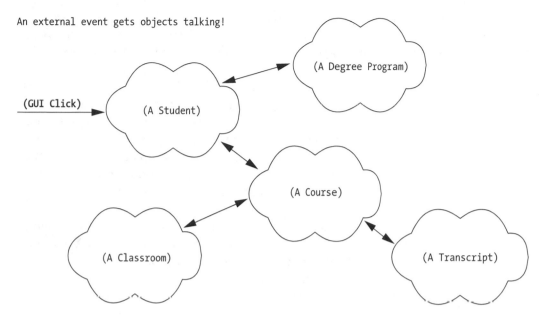

Figure 4-1. SRS objects must collaborate to accomplish the overall SRS mission.

Meanwhile, the user of the SRS is blissfully ignorant of all the objects that are "scurrying around" behind the scenes to accomplish the student's goal; the student merely fills in a few fields and clicks a button on the SRS GUI, and a few moments later sees a message that either confirms or rejects the student's registration request.

Once the ultimate goal of an event chain has been achieved (for example, registering a student for a course), an application's objects may effectively become idle, and may remain so until the next such triggering event occurs. An object-oriented application is in some ways similar to a game of billiards: hit the cue ball with your cue stick, and it (hopefully!) hits another ball, which might collide with three other balls, and so on. Eventually, however, all balls will come to a standstill until the cue ball is hit again.

Declaring Methods

Let's talk in a bit more detail about how we specify an object's behaviors. Recall from Chapter 3 that an object's methods may be thought of as services that the object can perform. In order for an object A to request some service of an object B, A needs to know the specific language with which to communicate with B. That is:

- ***Object** A needs to be clear as to exactly which of B's methods/services A wants B to perform.* **Think of yourself as object** A, and a pet dog as object B. Do you want your dog to sit? Stay? Heel? Fetch?

- ***Depending on the service request, object*** A *may need to give* B *some additional information so that* B *knows exactly how to proceed.* **If you tell your dog to fetch, the dog needs to know** *what* **to fetch: A ball? A stick? The neighbor's cat?**

- ***Object*** B *in turn needs to know whether object* A *expects* B *to report back the outcome of what it has been asked to do.* **In the case of a command to fetch something, your dog will hopefully bring the requested item to you as an outcome. However, if your dog is in another room and you call out the command "sit," you won't see the result of your command; you have to trust that the dog has done what you have asked it to do.**

We take care of communicating these three aspects of each method by defining a **method header.** We must then program the behind-the-scenes logic for *how* B will perform the requested service, aka the **method body.**

Let's look at method headers first.

Method Headers

A method header is a formal specification (from a programming standpoint) of how that method is to be invoked. A method header consists of

- A method's name

- An optional list of comma-separated **formal parameters** (specifying their names and types) to be passed to the method enclosed in parentheses

- A method's **return type**—that is, the data type of the information that is going to be passed back by object **B** to object **A**, if any, when the method is finished executing

As an example, here is a typical method header that we might define for the Student class:

```
            bool RegisterForCourse(string courseID, int secNo)
   return type      method name      comma-separated list of formal parameters,
                                      enclosed in parentheses
                                      (parentheses may be left empty)
```

> When casually referring to a method such as IsHonorsStudent *in narrative text, many authors attach an empty set of parentheses, (), to the method name, for example,* IsHonorsStudent(). *This doesn't necessarily imply that the formal header has no arguments, however.*

Passing Arguments to Methods

The purpose of passing arguments into a method is twofold:

- To provide the object receiving the request with the (optional) "fuel" necessary to do its job, or

- To (optionally) guide its behavior in some fashion

In the RegisterForCourse method shown previously, for example, it's necessary to tell the receiving Student object which course we want it to register for by passing in the course ID (for example, "MATH 101") and the section number (for example, 10, which happens to meet Monday nights from 8–10 p.m.).

Had we instead declared the RegisterForCourse method header with an *empty* parameter list:

```
bool RegisterForCourse()
```

the request would be ambiguous, because the receiving Student object would have no idea as to which course it's expected to register for.

Not all methods require such "fuel," however; some methods are able to produce results solely based on the information stored internally within an object, in which case no additional guidance is needed in the form of arguments. For example, the method

```
int GetAge()
```

is designed to be **parameterless** (i.e., takes no arguments) because a Student object can presumably tell us its age (based on its birthDate attribute, perhaps) without having to be given any qualifying information. Let's say, however, that we wanted a Student object to be able to report its age expressed either in years (rounded to the nearest year) or in months; in such a case, we might wish to declare the GetAge method as follows:

```
int GetAge(int ageType)
```

We would pass in an int(eger) argument to serve as a control flag for informing the Student object of how we want the answer to be returned; that is, we might program the GetAge method so that

- If we pass in a value of 1, it means that we want the answer to be returned in terms of years (for example, 30).

- If we pass in a value of 2, we want the answer to be returned in terms of months (for example, $30 \times 12 = 360$).

An alternative way of handling the requirement to retrieve the age of a Student *object in two different formats would be to define two separate methods, such as perhaps the following:*

```
int GetAgeInYears()
int GetAgeInMonths()
```

but in object-oriented programming, it's common practice to control a method's behavior through the values (and types) of arguments.

Method Return Types

The RegisterForCourse method as previously declared is shown to have a return type of bool, which implies that this method will return one of the following two values:

- A value of true, to signal "mission accomplished"—namely, that the Student object has successfully registered for the course that it was instructed to register for.

- A value of false, to signal that the mission has failed for some reason: perhaps the desired section was full, or the student didn't meet the prerequisites of the course, or the requested course/section has been cancelled, etc.

*In Part Three of the book, you'll learn techniques for communicating and determining precisely why the mission has failed when we discuss **exception handling**.*

Note that a method need not return anything—that is, it may go about its business silently, without reporting the outcome of its efforts. If so, it is declared to have a return type of void (another C# keyword).

Here are several additional examples of method headers that we might define for the Student class:

- void SetName(string newName)

This method requires one argument—a string representing the new name that we want this Student to assume—and performs "silently" by setting the Student's internal name attribute to whatever value is being passed into the method, returning no answer in response.

- void SwitchMajor(string newDepartment, Professor newAdvisor)

This method represents a request for a Student to change his or her major field of study, which involves designating both a new academic department (for example, "BIOLOGY") as well as a reference to the Professor object that is to serve as the student's advisor in this new department.

The preceding example demonstrates that we can declare parameters to be of any type, including user-defined types; the same is true for the **return type** of a method:

- Professor GetAdvisor()

This method is used to ask a Student object who its advisor is. Rather than merely returning the name of the advisor, the Student object returns a reference to the Professor object as a whole (as recorded in Student attribute facultyAdvisor).

We'll see a need for returning handles to objects in this fashion shortly, when we explore how objects interact.

Note that a method can return only one result or answer, which may seem limiting. What if, for example, we want to ask a Student object for a list of all of the courses that the student has ever taken: must we ask for these one-by-one through multiple method calls? Fortunately not: the result handed back by a method can actually be a reference to an object of arbitrary complexity, including a special type of object called a **collection** that can contain multiple other objects. We'll talk about collections in more depth in Chapter 6.

Method Bodies

When we design and program a class in an OO language, we must not only provide headers for all of its methods, but also program the internal details of how each method should behave when it's invoked. These internal programming details, known as the **method body,** are enclosed within braces { ... } immediately following the method header, as follows:

```
public class Student
{
  // Attributes.
  double gpa;
  // other attributes omitted from this snippet ...
```

```
// Here is a full-blown method, complete with a block of code to be executed
// when the method is invoked.
bool IsHonorsStudent() {
  // The programming details of what this method is to do
  // go between the braces ... this is the method body.

  // "gpa" is an attribute of the Student class, declared above.
  if (gpa >= 3.5) {
    return true;    // true means "yes, this is an honors student"
  }
  else {
    return false;  // false means "no, this isn't an honors student"
  }
} // end of the method body

// etc.
}
```

Methods Implement Business Rules

The logic contained within a method body defines the **business logic,** also known as **business rules,** for an abstraction. In the IsHonorsStudent method shown in the preceding code, for example, there is a single business rule for determining whether or not a student is an honors student:

> "If a student has a grade point average (GPA) of 3.5 or higher, then he/she is an honors student."

This rule is implemented in the preceding method through the use of a simple if test:

```
if (gpa >= 3.5) {
```

If the business rules underlying this method were more complex—say, if the rules were as follows:

> "In order for a student to be considered an honors student, the student must

(a) Have a grade point average (GPA) of 3.5 or higher;

(b) Have taken at least three courses;

(c) Have received no grade lower than 'B' in any of these courses."

then our method logic would of necessity be more complex:

```
bool IsHonorsStudent() {
    // Pseudocode.
    if ((gpa >= 3.5) &&
        (number of courses taken >= 3) &&
        (no grades lower than a B have been received)) {
      return true;
    }
    else {
      return false;
    }
  }
```

The return Statement

A return statement is a jump statement that is used to exit a method:

```
public void DoSomething() {
  // Pseudocode.
  do whatever ...

  return;
}
```

Whenever a return statement is executed, the method containing that return statement stops executing, and execution control returns to the code that invoked the method in the first place.

For methods with a return type of void, the return keyword can be used by itself, as a complete statement:

```
  return;
```

However, it turns out that for methods with a return type of void, use of a return statement is **optional.** If omitted, a return; statement is implied as the last line of the method. That is, the following two versions of method DoSomething are equivalent:

```
  public void DoSomething() {
    int x = 3;
    int y = 4;
    int z = x + y;
  }
```

and:

```
public void DoSomething() {
   int x = 3;
   int y = 4;
   int z = x + y;
   return;
}
```

The bodies of methods with a non-void return type ***must*** include at least one explicit return statement. The return keyword in such a case must be followed by an expression that evaluates to the proper type to match the method's return type:

```
return expression;
```

For example, if a method is defined to have a return type of int, any of the following return statements would be acceptable:

```
return 13;      // returning a constant integer value

return x;       // assuming x is declared to be an int

return x + y;   // assuming both x and y are declared to be ints
```

and so forth.

A method body is permitted to include more than one return statement if desired. For an example of a method containing multiple return statements, let's look once again at the IsHonorsStudent method discussed previously:

```
bool IsHonorsStudent() {
  if (gpa >= 3.5) {
    return true;    // first return statement
  }
  else {
    return false;   // second return statement
  }
}
```

Good programming practice, however, is to only have ***one*** return statement in a method, and to use a locally declared variable to capture the result that is to ultimately be returned. Here is an alternative version of the IsHonorsStudent method that observes this practice:

```
bool IsHonorsStudent() {
  // Declare a local variable to keep track of the outcome; arbitrarily
  // initialize it to false.
  bool result = false;

  if (gpa >= 3.5) {
    result = true;
  }
  else {
    result = false;
  }

  // We now have a single return statement at the end of our method.
  return result;
}
```

Naming Suggestions

Inventing descriptive names for both methods and parameters helps to make methods self-documenting. For example, the method header

```
void SwitchMajor(string newDepartment, Professor newAdvisor)
```

is much more self-explanatory than this alternative version:

```
void Switch(string d, Professor p)
```

In the latter case, we don't know what is being "switched," or what values for d and p would be relevant, without referring to the documentation for this method. Yet, to the compiler, both versions of the header are equally acceptable.

> *Of course, one could argue that we'd always want to look at the documentation of a method anyway to determine its intended purpose and proper usage; but making the header self-documenting is even better.*

C# method names are crafted using a style known as **Pascal casing,** wherein the first letter of the name is in ***uppercase;*** the ***first*** letter of each subsequent concatenated word in the variable name is in ***uppercase;*** and the remaining characters are in ***lowercase.*** As an example, SwitchMajor is an appropriate method name, whereas neither `Switchmajor` (lowercase "m") nor `switchMajor` (lowercase "s") would be appropriate.

> *Recall from Chapter 1 that most variable names use what is known as Camel casing, which is the same as Pascal casing except for the fact that with Camel casing, the first letter is in* **lowercase**, *whereas with Pascal casing, the first letter is* **capitalized**.

Method Invocation and Dot Notation

Now that we understand how methods are formally specified, how do we represent in code that a method is being invoked on an object? We create what is known as a **message.** A message is an expression formed by following the name of the reference variable representing the object that is to receive the message with a "dot" (period) followed by a method (function) call. For example:

```
// Instantiate a Student object.
Student x = new Student();

// Send a message to (call a method on) Student object x, asking it to
// register for course MATH 101, section 10.
x.RegisterForCourse("MATH 101", 10);  // This is a message!
```

Because we are using a "dot" to "glue" the reference variable to the method header, this is informally known as **dot notation**. And, in referring to the following logic:

```
x.RegisterForCourse("MATH 101", 10);
```

we can describe this as either "calling a method on object x" or as "sending a message to object x."

> *In C#, we formally refer to the use of dot notation as "qualifying a (method) name," but we'll stick with the informal, generally accepted OOP nomenclature of "dot notation" throughout this book.*

Arguments vs. Parameters

A bit of terminology: to make sure that everyone understands the difference between "parameters" and "arguments," both of which are generic programming language terms, let's define both terms here.

A **parameter** is a locally scoped variable, declared in a method header, that temporarily comes into existence while a method is executing. For example, when the method

```
public void Foo(int bar) { ... }
```

is invoked, a variable named bar of type int temporarily comes into existence and is initialized with the value of the **argument** that is passed in when the method is invoked from client code:

```
// Here, we're invoking the Foo method, passing in an argument value of 3.
x.Foo(3);
```

In this case, *parameter* bar assumes the *argument* value 3.

While the method is executing, it can then use the parameter as a variable as it sees fit:

```
public void Foo(int bar) {
  // Use the value of bar as appropriate.
  if (bar > 17) {
    // Pseudocode.
    Do something nifty!
  }
  // "bar" goes out of scope here ... it's only defined within the Foo method.
```

The parameter bar ceases to exist—i.e., goes out of scope (a concept we discussed in Chapter 1)—when the method exits.

Although the two terms "parameter" and "argument" are frequently and casually used interchangeably, the bottom line is that they are different concepts: namely, *arguments are values; parameters are variables.*

Objects As the Context for Method Invocation

In an object-oriented programming language, an object serves as the context for a method call. We can thus think of the notation "x.*method_call(...)*" as **"talking to object** x"; specifically, "talking to object x to request it to perform a particular method." Let's use a simple example to illustrate this point.

With respect to household chores, a person is capable of

- Taking out the trash

- Mowing the lawn

- Washing the dishes

Expressing this abstraction as C# code:

```
public class Person {
  // Attributes omitted from this example.

  // Methods:

  public void TakeOutTheTrash() {  ... }
  public void MowTheLawn() { ... }
  public void WashTheDishes()  { ... }
}
```

We decide that we want our teenaged sons Larry, Moe, and Curley to each do one of these three chores. How would we ask them to do this? If we were to say

- "Please wash the dishes."

- "Please take out the trash."

- "Please mow the lawn."

chances are that ***none*** of the chores would get done, because we haven't tasked a ***specific*** son with fulfilling any of these requests! Larry, Moe, and Curley will probably all stay glued to the TV, because none of them will acknowledge that a request has been directed toward them.

On the other hand, if we were to instead say

- "***Larry,*** please wash the dishes."

- "***Moe,*** please take out the trash."

- "***Curley,*** please mow the lawn."

we'd be assigning each task to a ***specific*** son; again, using C# syntax, this might be expressed as follows:

```
// We create three Person objects/instances:
Person larry = new Person();
Person moe = new Person();
Person curley = new Person();

// We send a message to each, indicating the service that we wish
// each of them to perform:
larry.WashTheDishes();
moe.TakeOutTheTrash();
curley.MowTheLawn();
```

By applying each method call to a different "son" (Person object reference), there is no ambiguity as to which object is being asked to perform which service.

> *We'll learn in Chapter 7 that a* **class** *as a whole can also be the target of a method call for a special type of method known as a* **static method.**

Assuming that WashTheDishes is a Person method as defined previously, the following code won't compile in C# (or, for that matter, in any OOPL):

```
public class BadCode
{
  static void Main() {
    // This next line won't compile -- where's the "dot"?
    WashTheDishes();
  }
}
```

because the compiler would expect the call to WashTheDishes(), as a Person method, to be associated with a particular Person object via dot notation; the following error message would result:

```
error CS0120: An object reference is required for the non-static field,
    method, or property 'Person.WashTheDishes()'
```

However, in a ***non***-OOPL language like C, there are no objects or classes, and so functions are ***always*** called "in a vacuum."

C# Expressions, Revisited

When we defined the term **simple expression** in Chapter 1, there was one form of expression that we omitted, because we hadn't yet talked about objects: namely, messages. We've repeated our list of what constitutes C# expressions here, adding messages to the mix:

- A constant: 7, false

- A char(acter) literal: 'A', '&'

- A string literal: "foo"

- The name of any variable declared to be of one of the predefined types that we've seen so far: `myString`, `x`

- **A message:** `z.length()`

- Any two of the preceding that are combined with one of the C# binary operators: `x + 2`

- Any one of the preceding that is modified by one of the C# unary operators: `i++`

- Any of the preceding simple expressions enclosed in parentheses: `(x + 2)`

> *In Chapter 13, you'll learn about one more type of expression: a "chain" of two or more messages, concatenated by dots (.): e.g.,* `x.GetAdvisor().GetName();`.

The type of a "message expression" is, by definition, the type of result that the method returns when executed. For example, if `RegisterForCourse` is a method with a return type of `bool`, then the expression `s.RegisterForCourse(...)` is said to be an expression of type `bool`.

Capturing the Return Value from a Method Call

In an earlier example, although we declared the `Student` class's `RegisterForCourse` method to have a return type of `bool`:

```
bool RegisterForCourse(string courseId, int sectionNumber)
```

we didn't capture the returned `bool` value when we invoked the method:

```
x.RegisterForCourse("MATH 101", 10);
```

Whenever we invoke a non-`void` method, it's up to us whether to ignore or respond to the value that it returns. If we wish to respond to the returned value, we can optionally capture the result in a specific variable:

```
boolean outcome;
outcome = x.registerForCourse("MATH 101", 10);

if (!outcome) {
  action to be taken if registration failed ...
}
```

If we only plan on using the returned value once, however, then going to the trouble of declaring an explicit variable such as outcome to capture the result is overkill. We can instead react to the result simply by "nesting" a ***message*** (which we learned a moment ago is considered to be a valid expression type) within a more complex statement. For example, we can rewrite the preceding code snippet to eliminate the variable outcome as follows:

```
// An if expression must evaluate to a Boolean result; the
// RegisterForCourse method does indeed return a Boolean value, however, and so
// the expression (message) enclosed within parentheses represents valid syntax.
if (!(x.RegisterForCourse("MATH 101", 10))) {
  action to be taken if registration failed ...
}
```

In fact, we use the "message-as-expression" syntax liberally when developing object-oriented applications; for example, when returning values from methods:

```
public string GetAdvisorName() {
   return advisor.GetName();
}
```

or printing to the console:

```
Console.WriteLine("The student's gpa is:  " + s.GetGPA());
```

etc. This is one of the aspects of OOP that seems to take the most getting used to for folks who are just getting started with learning the object-oriented paradigm.

Method Signatures

We've already learned that a method header consists of the method's return type, name, and formal parameter list:

```
void SwitchMajor(string newDepartment, Professor newAdvisor)
```

From the standpoint of the code used to ***invoke*** a method on an object, however, the return type and parameter names aren't immediately evident upon inspection:

```
Student s = new Student();
Professor p = new Professor();

// Details omitted ...

s.SwitchMajor("MATH", p);
```

We can infer from inspecting this code that

- SwitchMajor is a method defined for the Student class, because s is a Student and we're invoking SwitchMajor on s.

- The SwitchMajor method requires two arguments of type string and Professor, respectively, because that's what we're passing in.

However, we can't see how the formal parameters were named in the corresponding method header, nor can we tell whether the method returns a result or not and, if so, what type of result it returns, because it may be returning a result that we've simply chosen to ignore.

For this reason, we refer to a **method**'s **signature** as those aspects of a method header that are "discoverable" from the perspective of the code used to invoke the method: namely, the method's name, and the order, types, and number of arguments being passed into the method, but *excluding* the parameter names and method return type.

Let's introduce one more bit of terminology: we've coined the informal terminology **"argument signature"** to refer to that subset of a method's signature consisting of the order, types, and number of arguments comprising a method signature, but not their specific names.

Some examples of method headers and their corresponding method/argument signatures are shown here:

- **Method header:** int GetAge(bool ageType)

  - **Method signature:** GetAge(bool)

  - **Argument signature:** (bool)

- **Method header:** void SwitchMajor(string newDepartment, Professor newAdvisor)

  - **Method signature:** SwitchMajor(string, Professor)

  - **Argument signature:** (string, Professor)

- **Method header:** `string GetName()`

  - **Method signature:** `GetName()`

  - **Argument signature:** `()`

"Argument signature" isn't an industry standard term, but one that we nonetheless find very useful. We'll find the notion of argument signatures to be particularly handy when we discuss the concept of overloading in Chapter 5.%

Message Passing Between Objects

Let's now look at a message passing example involving two objects. Assume that we have two classes defined—`Student` and `Course`—and that the methods listed in Table 4-1 are defined on each.

Table 4-1. `Student` and `Course` class methods

Method	Description
Student Method:	
`bool SuccessfullyCompleted(Course c)`	Given a reference c to a particular Course object, we're asking the Student object receiving this message to confirm that they have indeed taken the course in question and received a passing grade.
Course Method:	
`bool Register(Student s)`	Given a reference s to a particular Student object, we are asking the Course object receiving this message to do whatever is necessary to register the student. In this case, we expect the Course to ultimately respond `true` or `false` to indicate success or failure of the registration request.

Figure 4-2 reflects one possible message interchange between a `Course` object c and a `Student` object s; each numbered step in the diagram is narrated in the text that follows.

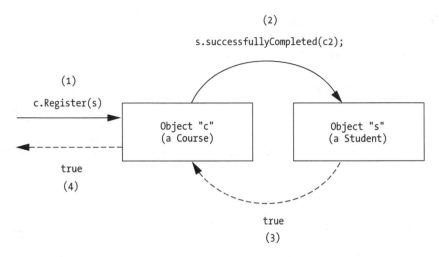

Figure 4-2. Message passing between a Student *and* Course *object*

(Please refer back to this diagram when reading through steps 1 through 4.)

1. A Course object c receives the message

    c.Register(s);

    where s represents a particular Student object. (For now, we won't worry about the origin of this message; it was most likely triggered by a user's interaction with the SRS GUI. We'll see the complete code context of how all of these messages are issued later in this chapter, in the section entitled "Objects As Clients and Suppliers.")

2. In order for Course object c to officially determine whether or not s should be permitted to register, c sends the message

    s.SuccessfullyCompleted(c2);

    to Student s, where c2 represents a reference to a ***different*** Course object that happens to be a prerequisite of Course c. (Don't worry about how Course c knows that c2 is one of its prerequisites; this involves interacting with c's internal prerequisites attribute, which we haven't talked about. Also, Course c2 isn't depicted in Figure 4-2 because, strictly speaking, c2 isn't engaged in this "discussion" between objects c and s; c2 is being talked about, but isn't doing any talking itself!)

3. Student object s replies with the value true to c, indicating that s has successfully completed the prerequisite course. (We will for the time being ignore the details as to how s determines this; it involves interacting with s's internal transcript attribute, which we haven't fully explained the structure of just yet.)

4. Convinced that the student has complied with the prerequisite requirements for the course, Course object c finishes the job of registering the student (internal details omitted for now) and confirms the registration by responding with a value of true to the originator of the service request.

This example was overly simplistic; in reality, Course c may have had to speak to numerous other objects:

- A Classroom object (the room in which the course is to be held, to make sure that it has sufficient room for another student)

- A DegreeProgram object (the degree sought by the student, to make sure that the requested course is indeed required for the degree that the student is pursuing)

and so forth—before sending a true response to indicate that the request to register Student s had been fulfilled. We'll see a slightly more complicated version of this message exchange later in the chapter.

Accessing Attributes via Dot Notation

Just as we use dot notation to formulate messages to be passed to objects, we can also use dot notation to refer to an object's attributes. For example, if we declare a reference variable x to be of type Student, we can refer to any of Student x's attributes via the following notation:

x.*attribute_name*

where the dot is used to **qualify** the name of the ***attribute*** of interest with the name of the reference variable representing the ***object*** of interest: x.name, x.gpa, and so forth.

Here are a few additional examples:

```
// Instantiate three objects.
Student x = new Student();
Student y = new Student();
Professor z = new Professor();
```

```
// We may use dot notation to access attributes as variables.

// Set student x's name ...
x.name = "John Smith";

// ... and student y's name.
y.name = "Joe Blow";

// Set professor z's name to be the same as student x's name.
z.name = x.name;

// Compute the total of the two students' ages.
int i = x.age + y.age;

// Set the professor's age to be 40.
z.age = 40;
```

However, we'll see later in this chapter that just because we ***can*** access attributes this way doesn't mean that we ***should.*** There are many reasons why we'll want to restrict access to an object's data so as to give the object complete control over when and how its data is altered, and several mechanisms for how we can do so.

Delegation

If a request is made of an object A and, in fulfilling the request, A in turn requests assistance from another object B, this is known as **delegation** by A to B. The concept of delegation among objects is exactly the same as delegation between people in the real world: if your "significant other" asks you to mow the lawn while he or she is out running errands, and you in turn hire a neighborhood teenager to mow the lawn, then, as far as your partner is concerned, the lawn has been mowed. The fact that you delegated the activity to someone else is (hopefully!) irrelevant.

The fact that delegation has occurred between objects is often transparent to the initiator of a message, as well. In our previous message passing example, Course c delegated part of the work of registering Student s ***back to*** s when c asked s to verify a prerequisite course. However, from the perspective of the ***originator*** of the registration request—c.Register(s);—this seems like a simple interaction: namely, the requestor asked c to register a student, and it did so! All of the "behind the scenes" details of what c had to do to accomplish this are hidden from the requestor (see Figure 4-3).

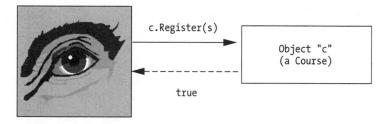

Figure 4-3. A requestor sees only the external details of a message exchange.

Access to Objects

The only way that an object A can pass a message to an object B is if A has access to a handle on B. This can happen in several different ways:

- **Object** A *might maintain a handle/reference to* B *as one of* A's *attributes;* **for example, here's the example from Chapter 3 of a** Student object having a Professor reference as an attribute:

      ```
      public class Student
      {
        // Attributes.
        string name;
        Professor facultyAdvisor;
        // etc.
      ```

- **Object** A *may be handed a reference to* B *as an argument of one of* A's *methods.* **This is how** Course object c obtained access to Student object s in the preceding message passing example, when c's Register method was called:

      ```
      c.Register(s);
      ```

- *A reference to object* B *may be made "globally available" to the entire application,* **such that all other objects can access it. We'll discuss techniques for doing so when we construct the SRS in Part Three of the book.**

- **Object** A *may have to explicitly request a handle/reference to* B *by calling a method on some third object* C. **Since this is potentially the most complex way for** A to obtain a handle on B, we'll illustrate this with an example.

Going back to the example interaction between Course object c and Student object s from a few pages ago, let's complicate the interaction a bit.

- First, we'll introduce a third object: a `Transcript` object t, which represents a record of all courses taken by `Student` object s.

- Furthermore, we'll assume that `Student` s maintains a handle on `Transcript` t as one of s's attributes (specifically, the `transcript` attribute), and conversely, that `Transcript` t maintains a handle on its "owner", `Student` s, as one of t's attributes (see Figure 4-4).

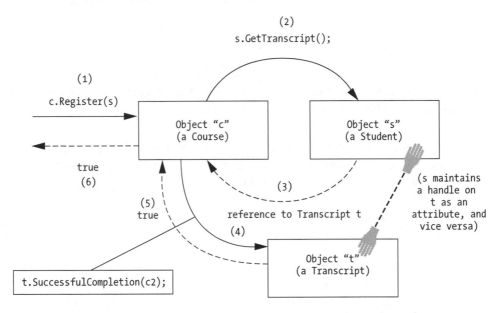

Figure 4-4. A more complex message passing example involving three objects

1. In this enhanced object interaction, the first step is exactly as previously described: namely, a `Course` object c receives the message

   ```
   c.Register(s);
   ```

   where s represents a `Student` object.

2. Now, instead of `Course` c sending the message s.`SuccessfullyCompleted(c2)` to `Student` s as before, where c2 represents a prerequisite `Course`, `Course` object c instead sends the message

   ```
   s.GetTranscript();
   ```

to the Student, because c wants to check s's transcript firsthand. This message corresponds to a method on the Student class whose header is defined as follows:

```
Transcript GetTranscript()
```

Note that this method is defined to return a Transcript object reference: specifically, a handle on the Transcript object t belonging to this student.

3. Because Student s maintains a handle on its Transcript object as an attribute, it's a snap for s to respond to this message by passing a handle on t back to Course object c.

4. Now that Course c has its ***own*** temporary handle on Transcript t, object c can talk directly to t. Object c proceeds to ask t whether t has any record of c's prerequisite course c2 having successfully been completed by Student s by passing the message

```
t.SuccessfulCompletion(c2);
```

This implies that there is a method defined for the Transcript class with the header

```
bool SuccessfulCompletion(Course c)
```

5. Transcript object t answers back with a response of true to Course c, indicating that Student s has indeed successfully completed the prerequisite course in question. (Note that Student s is unaware that c is talking to t; object s knows that it was asked by c to return a handle to t in an earlier message, but s has no insights as to ***why*** c asked for the handle.)

> *This is not unlike the real-world situation in which person A asks person B for person C's phone number, without telling B why he or she wants to call C.*

6. Satisfied that Student s has complied with its prerequisite requirements, Course object c finishes the job of registering the student (internal details omitted for now) and confirms the registration by responding with a value of true to the originator of the registration request that first arose in step 1. Now that c has finished with this transaction, it discards its (temporary) handle on t.

Note that, from the perspective of whoever sent the original message

```
c.Register(s);
```

to Course c, this more complicated interaction appears ***identical*** to the earlier, simpler interaction, as shown in Figure 4-5.

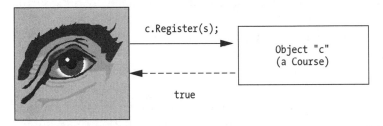

Figure 4-5. The external details of this more complex interaction appear identical from the requestor's standpoint.

All the sender of the original message knows is that Course c eventually responded with a value of true to the request.

Objects As Clients and Suppliers

In the preceding example of message passing between a Course object and a Student object, we can consider Course object c to be a **client** of Student object s, because c is requesting (by initiating a message) that s perform one of its methods—namely, GetTranscript—as a **service** to c. This is identical to the real-world concept of ***you***, as a client, requesting the services of an accountant, or an attorney, or an architect. Similarly, c is a client of Transcript t when c asks t to perform its SuccessfulCompletion method. We therefore refer to code that invokes a method on an object **A** as **client code** relative to **A** because the code benefits from the service(s) performed by **A**.

Let's look at a few examples of client code. The following code corresponds to the message passing example involving a Course, Student, and Transcript object from a few pages back, and as promised earlier, provides the context for the messages that were passed in that example.

The following code snippet, taken from the Main method of an application, instantiates two objects and invokes a method on one of them, which gets them "talking":

```
static void Main() {
    Course c = new Course();
    Student s = new Student();

    // Details omitted.

    // Invoke a method on Course object c.
    // (This is labeled as message (1) in the earlier figure; the returned
    // value, labeled as (6) in that figure, is being "ignored" in this
    // case.)
    c.Register(s);

    // etc.
}
```

In this example, the Main method is considered to be client code relative to Course object c because it calls upon c to perform its Register method as a service.

Let's now look at the code that implements the body of the Register method, inside of the Course class:

```
public class Course
{
    // details omitted ...

    public bool Register(Student s) {
        boolean outcome = false;

        // Request a handle on Student s's Transcript object.
        // (This is labeled as message (2) in the earlier figure.)
        Transcript t = s.GetTranscript();
        // (The return value from this method is labeled as (3) in
        // the earlier figure.)

        // Now, request a service on that Transcript object.
        // (Assume that c2 is a handle on some prerequisite Course ...)
        // (This is labeled as message (4) in the earlier figure.)
        if (t.SuccessfulCompletion(c2)) {
            // (This next return value is labeled as (5) in the earlier figure.)
            outcome = true;
        }
        else {
            outcome = false;
        }
```

```
        return outcome;
    }


    // etc.
}
```

We see that the `Register` method body is considered to be client code relative to **both** `Student` object s and `Transcript` object t because this code calls upon s and t to each perform a service.

Whenever an object `A` is a client of object `B`, object `B` in turn can be thought of as a **supplier** of `A`.

Note that the roles of client and supplier are not absolute between two objects; such roles are only relevant for the duration of a particular message passing event. If I ask you to pass me the bread, I am your client, and you are my supplier; and if a moment later you ask me to pass you the butter, then you are my client, and I am your supplier.

> *The notion of clients and suppliers is discussed further in* Object-Oriented Software Construction *by Bertrand Meyer (Prentice Hall).*

Information Hiding/Accessibility

As we discussed earlier in this chapter, dot notation can be used to access an object's attribute values, as in the following simple example:

```
Student x = new Student();

// Set the value of the name attribute of Student x.
x.name = "Fred Schnurd";

// Retrieve the value of x's name so as to print it.
Console.WriteLine(x.name);
```

In reality, however, objects often restrict access to some of their features (attributes in particular). Such restriction is known as **information hiding.** In a well-designed object-oriented application, an object publicizes *what* it can do—that is, the services it is capable of providing, or its method headers—but *hides* the internal details both of *how* it performs these services and of the data (attributes) that it maintains in order to *support* these services.

We use the term **accessibility** to refer to whether or not a particular feature of an object (attribute or method) can be accessed outside of the class in which it is declared. The accessibility of a feature is established by placing an **access modifier keyword** at the beginning of its declaration:

```
public class ClassName
{
    // Attribute declaration.
    access-modifier-keyword  attributeType attributeName;
    // etc.

    // Method declaration.
    access-modifier-keyword  returnType methodName(arguments) {
        ...
    }
    // etc.
}
```

Types of Accessibility

C# defines five different access modifier keywords: public, private, protected, internal, and protected internal.

When a feature is declared to have **public accessibility,** it's freely accessible by the method code in any other class; that is, we can access public attributes from client code using dot notation.

For example, if we were to declare that the name attribute of the Student class were public, which we do by placing the keyword public just ahead of the attribute's type declaration:

```
public class Student
{
  public string name;
 // etc.
```

then it would be perfectly acceptable to write client code as follows:

```
using System;

public class MyProgram
{
  static void Main() {
    Student x = new Student();

    // Because name is a public attribute, we may access it via dot
    // notation from client code.
    x.name = "Fred Schnurd";
    // or:
    Console.WriteLine(x.name);
```

```
        // etc.
    }
  }
```

> *Since we first introduced the notion of a class wrapper in Chapter 1, recall that we've also been using the* public *access modifier on all of our* **class** *declaration examples:*
>
> ```
> public class Student { ...
> public class SimpleProgram { ...
> ```
>
> *etc. We'll discuss what it means to define a* **class's** *accessibility, and in particular, what other accessibility modifiers make sense for a class besides* public, *in Chapter 13.*

Similarly, if we were to declare the IsHonorsStudent method of Student to be public, which we do by again inserting the keyword public into the method header:

```
public class Student
{
  // Attributes omitted.

  // Methods.
  public bool IsHonorsStudent() {
    // details omitted.
  }

  // etc.
}
```

it would then be perfectly acceptable to invoke the IsHonorsStudent method from client code as follows:

```
public class MyProgram
{
  static void Main() {
    Student x = new Student();

    // Because IsHonorsStudent() is a public method, we may access it
    // via dot notation from client code.
    if (x.IsHonorsStudent()) {
      // details omitted.
    }

    // etc.
```

When a feature is declared to have **private accessibility,** on the other hand, it's ***not*** accessible outside of the class in which it's declared.

For example, if we were to declare that the ssn attribute of the Student class were private:

```
public class Student
{
  public string name;
  private string ssn;
  // etc.
```

then we are ***not*** permitted to access it directly via dot notation from client code, as illustrated here:

```
public class MyProgram
{
  static void Main() {
    Student x = new Student();

    // Not permitted from client code!  ssn is private to the
    // Student class, and so this will not compile.
    x.ssn = "123-45-6789";
```

The following compilation error will result:

```
MyProgram.cs(8,3): error CS0122: Student.ssn is inaccessible due to
its protection level
```

The same is true for methods that are declared to be private: that is, they can't be invoked from client code. (We'll discuss ***why*** we'd ever want to declare a method as private a bit later in this chapter.) For example, if we were to declare the PrintInfo method of Student to be private:

```
public class Student
{
  // Attributes omitted.

  // Methods.
  private void PrintInfo() {
    // details omitted.
  }

  // etc.
}
```

121

then it would ***not*** be possible to invoke the `PrintInfo` method from client code:

```
public class MyProgram
{
  static void Main() {
    Student x = new Student();

    // Because PrintInfo() is a private method, we may not access it
    // via dot notation from client code; this won't compile:
    x.PrintInfo();

    // etc.
```

The following compiler error would result:

```
error CS0122: 'Student.PrintInfo()' is inaccessible due to its protection level
```

We'll defer a discussion of the other three C# access modifiers—**protected, internal**, and **protected internal**—until Chapter 13, because there are a few more object concepts that we have to cover first. For now, it's perfectly appropriate to think of accessibility as coming in only two "flavors"—public and private.

If we don't explicitly specify the accessibility of a feature when we declare it, it will be ***private*** by default:

```
public class Student
{
  private string age;
  string name;  // Since accessibility is not explicitly specified for
                // the "name" attribute, it will be private by default.

  // The same is true for this method.
  void DoSomething() {
    // details omitted
  }

  // etc.
}
```

Accessing Features of a Class from Within Its Own Methods

Note that we can access all of a given class's features, regardless of their accessibility, from ***within*** any of that class's ***own*** method bodies; that is, public/private designations only affect access to a feature *from outside the class itself*, i.e., *from client code*.

In the following example, the Student class's PrintAllAttributes method is accessing the private name and ssn attributes of the Student class:

```
using System;

public class Student
{
  private string name;
  private string ssn;
  // etc.

  public void PrintAllAttributes() {
    Console.WriteLine(name);
    Console.WriteLine(ssn);
    // etc.
  }

  // etc.
}
```

Furthermore, note that we needn't use dot notation to access a feature of a class when we're inside the body of one of the class's own methods; it's automatically understood that the class is accessing one of its own features when a **simple name**—that is, a name without a dot notation prefix (aka an **unqualified name**)—is used. This language feature is illustrated by the following (abbreviated) Student class code:

```
public class Student
{
  // A few private attributes.
  private double totalLoans;
  private double tuitionOwed;
  // other attributes omitted

  public bool AllBillsPaid() {
    // We can call upon another method that is defined within this
    // SAME class (see declaration of MoneyOwed() below) without using
    // dot notation.
    double amt = MoneyOwed();
    if (amt == 0.0) {
      return true;
```

```
        }
        else {
            return false;
        }
    }

    public double MoneyOwed() {
        // We can access attributes of this class (totalLoans and
        // tuitionOwed) -- even though they are declared to be private! --
        // without using dot notation.
        return totalLoans + tuitionOwed;
    }
}
```

> *Note that the order in which methods are declared within a C# class doesn't matter; that is, we're permitted to call a method* B *from within method* A *even though the definition of method* B *comes after/below* A *in the class declaration. In particular, in the preceding code example, we call* MoneyOwed *from within* AllBillsPaid *despite the fact that* MoneyOwed *is declared* **after** AllBillsPaid.

Publicizing Services

As it turns out, methods of a class are typically declared public because an object (class) needs to publicize its services (as in a Yellow Pages ad!) so that client code may request these services. By contrast, most attributes are typically declared private (and effectively "hidden"), so that an object can maintain ultimate control over its data; we'll go into significant detail later in this chapter about how an object does so.

> *The notion that a class is "guaranteed" to do what it advertises that it's going to do is often referred to as programming by contract; for more information, see* Object-Oriented Software Construction *by Bertrand Meyer (Prentice Hall).*

Although it isn't explicitly declared as such, the internal code that implements each method (that is, the method body) is also, in a sense, ***implicitly*** private. When a client object A asks another object B to perform one of its methods, A doesn't need to know the "behind the scenes" details of how B is doing what it's doing; A needs simply to trust that object B will perform the "advertised" service (see Figure 4-6).

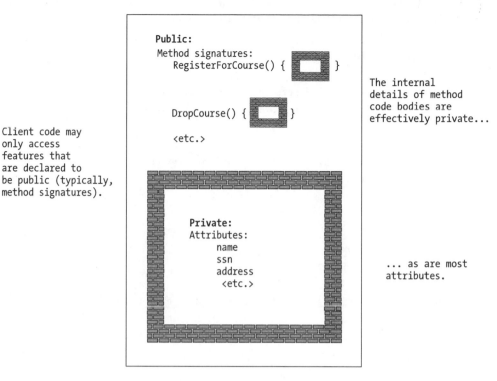

Figure 4-6. Attributes and the internal details of how methods work are "walled off" from client code.

Camel vs. Pascal Casing, Revisited

Previously in the book, we've introduced the Camel and Pascal capitalization styles and discussed how they are applied to C# programming elements. Now that we've touched on accessibility, let's refine our understanding of when to use these two alternate styles.

- *Pascal casing* (uppercase starting letter) is used for **all class and method names**, **regardless** of their accessibility. It's also used for the names of **public** attributes.

- *Camel casing* (lowercase starting letter) is used for the names of **nonpublic** attributes.

Here is an example class to illustrate these rules:

```
public class Student // uppercase S for class name
{
    private string name;   // lowercase n for private attribute
    public string Major;   // uppercase M for public attribute
    // etc.

    public void DoSomething() { // uppercase D for method name
        // A local variable; while not explicitly private, it is not accessible
        // from outside this method, and so begins with a lowercase letter.
        int x = 0;

        // details omitted ...
    }

    private void DoSomethingElse() { // Uppercase D, even though private, because
        // details omitted ...              ALL methods are named using Pascal casing.
    }                                  // regardless of their accessibility.

    // etc.
}
```

Method Headers, Revisited

Going back to our definition of method header from a bit earlier in the chapter, let's amend that definition to also include the accessibility modifier for a method. That is, a method header actually consists of the following:

- A method's return type—that is, the data type of the information that is going to be passed back by object B to object A, if any, when the method is finished executing.

- **A method's (accessibility) modifier(s).**

> *There are also other types of modifiers on methods besides accessibility modifiers. We'll talk about some of the other modifiers that can be applied to methods in Chapters 7 and 13.*

- A method's name

- An optional list of comma-separated formal parameters (specifying their names and types) to be passed to the method enclosed in parentheses

As an example, here is a typical method header that we might define for the Student class:

public	bool	RegisterForCourse	(string courseID, int secNo)
accessibility modifier	return type	method name	comma-separated list of formal parameters, enclosed in parentheses (parentheses *may* be left empty)

> There is actually one more aspect to a method's header, having to do with what are referred to as **modifiers on individual parameters**, that is beyond the scope of this book to address.

Accessing Private Features from Client Code

If private features can't be accessed outside of an object's own methods, how does client code ever manipulate them? Through *public* features, of course! Good OO programming practice calls for providing public **accessors** by which clients of an object can effectively manipulate selected private attributes to read or modify their values. Why is this? *So that we may empower an object to have the "final say" in whether or not what client code is trying to do to its attributes is "okay."* That is, letting an object determine whether or not any of the business rules defined by its class are being violated. Before we go into an in-depth discussion of why this is so important, we'd like to first discuss the "mechanics" of how we create accessors.

Two General Approaches

There are two general approaches to providing accessors:

- The *generic OOPL approach* is to provide what are known informally as **"get"** and **"set" methods** (or, collectively, **accessor methods**) for reading/modifying attributes, respectively.

- The *C# preferred approach* is to use a language construct called a **property** for accessing (reading/modifying) attributes. A property defines what are known as **get** and **set accessors** (note that these are *not* methods, despite the similarity of their names) that can return the value of an attribute to client code or modify the value of an attribute value at the request of client code, respectively.

Because our goals in this book are twofold—namely, to introduce you to general object concepts as well as to teach you basic C# syntax—and because ***both*** of these goals are equally important in our opinion, we're going to cover both of these approaches—conventional OOPL "get"/"set" methods and properties—in this section. Please realize, however, that the .NET programming community favors the use of properties over "get"/"set" methods for reasons that will become clear a bit later.

Sorting Out Terminology

*Throughout the book, whenever we're talking generically and collectively about **all** of the various **OOPL** ways of accessing an attribute value—whether via "get"/"set" methods or properties—in the "loosest" sense, to mean "accessing an attribute," we'll use the informal generic term "accessor."*

*If we wish to refer informally about "getting" the value of an attribute via either a "get" method or a property's get accessor, we'll use the informal term **"getter."***

*If we wish to refer informally about "setting" the value of an attribute via either a "set" method or a property's set accessor, we'll use the informal term **"setter."***

Otherwise, we'll use the more precise terminology "get method," "set method," "get accessor," or "set accessor," as appropriate.

All of these various terms and their interrelationships are illustrated in Figure 4-7.

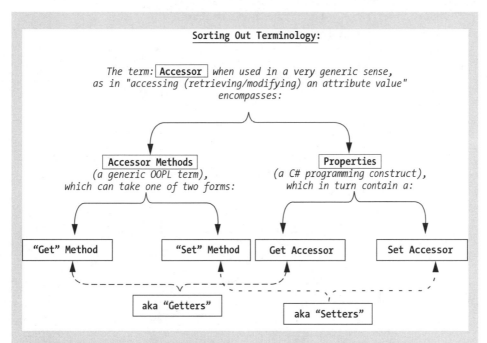

Figure 4-7. Sorting out terminology

Note, however, that by **collectively** *referring to both accessor* **methods** *and* **property** *accessors as simply "accessors," we do* **not** *mean to imply that they are equivalent constructs, just as referring to apples and oranges collectively as "fruit" does not imply that apples and oranges are equivalent.*

"Get"/"Set" Methods

The following code, excerpted from the Student class, illustrates the conventional "get" and "set" methods that we might write for a private attribute called name:

```
public class Student
{
  // Attributes are typically declared to be private.
  private string name;
  // other attributes omitted ...

  // Provide public accessor methods for reading/modifying
  // the private "name" attribute from client code.

  // Read ("get") the value of the name attribute.
  public string GetName() {
    return name;
  }
}
```

```
// Modify ("set") the value of the name attribute.
public void SetName(string newName) {
    name = newName;
}


// etc.
}
```

The nomenclature "get" and "set" is stated from the standpoint of ***client code:*** think of a "set" method as the way that ***client code*** stuffs a value ***into*** an object's attribute (see Figure 4-8) . . .

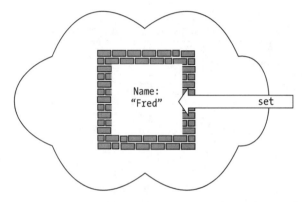

*Figure 4-8. A "set" method is used to pass data **into** an object*

. . . and the "get" method as the way that ***client code*** retrieves an attribute value ***out of*** an object (see Figure 4-9).

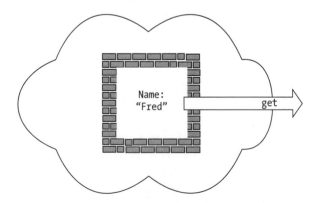

*Figure 4-9. A "get" method is used to retrieve data **out of** an object.*

Declaring "Get"/"Set" Methods

For an attribute declaration of the form

accessibility * *attribute-type* attributeName;   * typically private

e.g.,

private string majorField;

the recommended accessor method headers are as follows:

- **"get" method:** public *attribute-type* GetAttributeName()

  For example, public string GetMajorField()

  Note that we don't pass any arguments into a "get" method, because all we want an object to do is to hand us back the value of one of its attributes; we don't typically need to tell the object anything more for it to know how to do this.

  Also, because we're expecting an object to hand back the value of a specific attribute, the return type of the "get" method must match the type of the attribute of interest. If we're "getting" the value of an int attribute, then the return type of the method must be int; if we're "getting" the value of a string attribute, then the return type of the method must be string; and so forth.

- **"set" method:** public void SetAttributeName(*attribute-type parameterName*)

  For example, public void SetMajorField(string major)

  In the case of a "set" method, we must pass in the value that we want the object to use when setting its corresponding attribute value, and the type of the value that we're passing in must match the type of the attribute being set. If we're "setting" the value of an int attribute, then the argument that is passed in must be an int; if we're "setting" the value of a string attribute, then the argument that is passed in must be a string; and so forth.

  However, since most "set" methods perform their mission silently, without returning a value to the client, we typically declare "set" methods to have a return type of void.

Note that we devise the names for both types of method by capitalizing the first letter of the attribute name and sticking either Get or Set in front of it. There is one exception to this method naming convention: when an attribute is of type bool, it's recommended that we name the "get" method starting with the verb "Is" instead of with "Get". The "set" method for a bool attribute would still follow the standard naming convention. For example:

```
public class Student
{
  private bool honorsStudent;
  // other attributes omitted ...

  // Get method.
  public bool IsHonorsStudent() {
    return honorsStudent;
  }

  // Set method.
  public void SetHonorsStudent(bool x) {
    honorsStudent = x;
  }

// etc.
}
```

All of the "get"/"set" method bodies that we've seen thus far are simple "one liners": we're either returning the value of the attribute of interest with a simple return statement in a "get" method, or copying the value of the passed-in argument to the internal attribute in a "set" method so as to store it. This isn't to imply that all "get"/"set" methods need be this simple; in fact, there are endless possibilities for what actually gets coded in accessor methods, because as we discussed earlier, methods must implement business rules, not only about how an object behaves, but also what valid states its data can assume.

Utilizing "Get"/"Set" Methods from Client Code

We already know how to utilize dot notation to invoke methods on objects from client code:

```
Student s = new Student();

// Modify ("set") the attribute value.
s.SetName("Joe");

// Read ("get") the attribute value.
Console.WriteLine("Name: " +  s.GetName());
```

Properties

As mentioned earlier, C# also provides a programming construct for accessing attributes called a **property.** In a nutshell, a property is a way of "disguising" accessor logic so that, from the perspective of client code, it appears that we're accessing a public attribute:

```
// Client code for setting Student s's name via a property it APPEARS as though
// we're accessing a public attribute, but we are not!
s.Name = "Melbito";
```

```
// or, for getting s's name via a property:
Console.WriteLine(s.Name);
```

when in fact we are invoking ***behind-the-scenes*** accessor code, albeit not in the explicit "get"/"set" method-calling sense.

Let's learn how to declare and use properties.

Declaring Properties

We use the following general syntax for declaring a property:

```
access-modifier-keyword type propertyName {
  get {
    // code body of get accessor
  }

  set {
    // code body of set accessor
  }
}
```

For example, if we wish to declare a property associated with the private attribute name in lieu of "get"/"set" methods in our Student class, we might write the following code:

```
public class Student
{
  // We're still declaring the name attribute in the same way as we did before.
  private string name;
  // etc.

  // However, we're now defining a property called "Name" in lieu of writing
  // "get"/"set" methods for the "name" attribute.
```

133

```
            public string Name {
              // This takes the place of a "get" method.
              get {
                return name;
              }

              // This takes the place of a "set" method.
              set {
                // "value" is an implicit input parameter that is automatically
                // passed to the set accessor.
                name = value;
              }

              // etc.
            }
        }
```

Some noteworthy features about properties:

- The convention for a property name is that it should match the name of its associated attribute, but should begin with a capital letter (property names use the Pascal capitalization style). Recall that, since C# is a case-sensitive language, name and Name are treated as *different* symbols by the compiler.

- The type of a property must match the type of its associated attribute. Our Name property is defined to be of type string, which indeed is the type of the name attribute.

- A property defines **get** and **set accessors,** which work very much like "get"/"set" methods, but which are syntactically quite different, both in terms of how they are declared and how they are invoked from client code (the latter of which we'll see in a moment).

- Analogous to a "get" method, a get accessor is used to return the value of the corresponding attribute to client code.

- Note that there is no need to declare a return type for a get accessor as we must do for a "get" method, because a get accessor *implicitly* returns the same type as the property in which it is defined.

```
            get {
              return name;
            }
```

- Analogous to a "set" method, a set accessor is used to change the value of the corresponding attribute at the request of client code.

- Note that there is no need to declare a parameter list for a set accessor as we must do for a "set" method because a set accessor *implicitly* takes a single parameter, named `value`, which represents the new value being suggested for the attribute by client code:

```
set {
   name = value; // value is implicitly declared
}
```

- Note that there is also no need to declare a return type for a set accessor, as it implicitly has a return type of void.

The preceding example featured a property with simple, "one-liner" get and set accessors. Of course, as we mentioned for "get"/"set" methods earlier, there are endless possibilities for what actually gets coded in get and set accessors because they must implement the appropriate business logic for the attribute that they control. We'll see more complex examples of property accessors later in the chapter.

Let's place the code used in the two different approaches to declaring accessors—"get"/"set" methods vs. properties—side-by-side, to emphasize the differences in their syntax:

Student Version with Get/Set Methods	Equivalent Student Version Using a Property
```public class Student { private string name;```	```public class Student { private string name;```
```public string GetName() { return name; }```	```public string Name { get { return name; }```
```public void SetName(string n) { name = n; }```	```set { name = value; } }```
```}```	```}```

Property syntax is a bit more streamlined, as follows:

- By declaring a type for the property as a whole—string—we don't have to redundantly declare the return type of the get accessor or the type of the value being handed in to the set accessor: they will automatically derive the string type from the property.

- By declaring accessibility of the property—public—we don't have to redundantly declare the accessibility of the get accessor or set accessor: both will derive public accessibility from the property.

Accessing Properties from Client Code

Now, let's take a look at how we access a property from client code. We'll continue our example using the Name property defined earlier:

```
// Client code:
Student s = new Student();

// Modify ("set") the attribute value.
// Note that it LOOKS LIKE we're accessing a public attribute.
s.Name = "Joe";

// Read ("get") the attribute value.
// Again, it LOOKS LIKE we're accessing a public attribute.
Console.WriteLine("Name is " + s.Name);
```

From the standpoint of client code, properties are accessed via dot notation *as if they were declared to be public attributes.* That is, from client code, when we see an expression such as

```
s.Name = "Joe";
```

we can't tell whether Name represents a property or a public attribute! But, behind the scenes, there is quite a difference, in that with public attributes, no code is being executed beyond the direct assignment . . . whereas with property accessors, whatever code we've written is transparently executed behind the scenes. We'll return to this critical distinction later in the chapter.

Let's place the code used in the two different approaches to accessing attributes from client code—"get"/"set" methods vs. properties—side-by-side, to emphasize the differences in their syntax:

Client Code Version Utilizing Get/Set Methods	Equivalent Client Code Utilizing a Property

``
Student s = new Student();
 	
// Modify ('set') the attribute value.
s.SetName("Joe");
 	
// Read ('get') the attribute value.
Console.WriteLine("Name: " +
s.GetName());
``
	``
	Student s = new Student();
	
	// Modify ('set') the attribute value.
	s.Name = "Joe";
	
	// Read ('get') the attribute value.
	Console.WriteLine("Name is " +
	s.Name);
	``

Client code is a bit more streamlined when properties are used.

"Singing the Praises" of Properties

The elegance of property syntax is touted as one of the major advantages of C# (.NET languages as a whole) over other OOPLs. In the .NET world (as in its predecessor Visual Basic and ActiveX worlds), virtually all data is exposed as properties.

Properties are logically equivalent to (and impossible to distinguish from) attributes, but are syntactically easier to use than "get"/"set" methods. In a sense, properties give us the "best of both worlds": the ease of access of a public attribute from client code, but with the programmatic control over data integrity that we get with private attributes and "get"/"set" methods.

> *When working with OO programming languages that don't support the notion of properties—e.g., C++, Java—one **must** be "savvy" in the use of "get"/"set" method syntax to reap all of the benefits of encapsulation and information hiding—benefits that we'll cover in depth a bit later in this chapter. Because of the "favored status" of properties when programming in C#, however, we'll illustrate all remaining OO principles throughout the book in detail using properties, but will remind you that many of the **same** benefits can be achieved in other OOP languages using "get"/"set" method syntax.*

The "Persistence" of Attribute Values

Because we haven't explicitly stated so before, and because it may not be obvious to everyone, let's call attention now to the fact that an object's attribute values persist as long as the object itself persists in memory. That is, once we instantiate a Student object in our application:

```
Student s = new Student();
```

then any values that we assign to s's attributes, whether via "set" methods or properties:

```
s.Name = "Steve";
```

will persist until either (a) such time as the value is explicitly changed:

```
// Renaming Student s.
s.Name = "Mel";
```

or (b) such time as the object is destroyed and its memory is recycled (we'll talk about ways of destroying an object and recycling its memory in Chapter 13). So, as long as the memory allocated to Student object s stays around (or, to return to our analogy from Chapter 3, as long as the "helium balloon" representing s stays "inflated"), whenever we ask s for its name, it will remember whatever value we've *last* assigned to its name attribute.

Exceptions to the Public/Private Rule

Even though it's generally true that

- Attributes are declared to be private;

- Methods are declared to be public; and

- Private attributes are accessed through either public properties or methods

there are numerous exceptions to this rule.

1. ***An attribute may be used by a class strictly for internal housekeeping purposes.*** (Like the dishwashing detergent you keep under the sink, guests needn't know about it!) For such attributes, we needn't bother to provide public accessors. One example for the Student class might be an attribute:

   ```
   private int countOfDsAndFs;
   ```

This attribute might be used to keep track of how many poor grades a student has received in order to determine whether or not the student is on academic probation. We may provide a Student class method as follows:

```
public bool OnAcademicProbation() {
  // If the student received more than three substandard grades,
  // they will be put on academic probation.
  if (countOfDsAndFs > 3) {
    return true;
  }
  else {
    return false;
  }
}
```

This method uses the value of private attribute countOfDsAndFs to determine whether a student is on academic probation, but no ***client code*** need ever know that there is such an attribute as countOfDsAndFs, and so no explicit public accessors are provided for this attribute. Such attributes are instead set as a "side effect" of performing some ***other*** method, as in the following example, also taken from the Student class:

```
public void CompleteCourse(string courseName,
                           int creditHours,
                           char grade) {
  // Updating this private attribute is considered to be a
  // "side effect" of completing a course.
  if (grade == 'D' || grade == 'F') countOfDsAndFs++;

  // Other processing details omitted.
}
```

2. ***Some methods/properties may be used strictly for internal housekeeping, as well, in which case these may also be declared private rather than public.*** An example of such a Student class method might be UpdateGpa, which recomputes the value of the gpa attribute each time a student completes another course and receives a grade. The only time that this method may ever need to be called is perhaps from within another method of Student—for example, the public CompleteCourse method—as follows:

```
public class Student
{
  private double gpa;
```

```
private int totalCoursesTaken;
private int totalQualityPointsEarned;
private int countOfDsAndFs;
// other details omitted ...

public void CompleteCourse(string courseName,
                                  int creditHours,
                                  char grade) {
  if (grade == 'D' || grade == 'F') {
    countOfDsAndFs++;
  }

  // Record grade in transcript.
  // details omitted ...

  // Update an attribute ...
  totalCoursesTaken = totalCoursesTaken + 1;

  // ... and call a PRIVATE housekeeping method from within this
  // public method to adjust the student's GPA accordingly.
  UpdateGpa(creditHours, grade);
}

// The details of HOW the GPA gets updated are a deep, dark
// secret! Even the EXISTENCE of this next method is hidden from
// the "outside world" (i.e., inaccessible from client code) by
// virtue of its having been declared to be PRIVATE.
private void UpdateGpa(int creditHours, char grade) {
  int letterGradeValue = 0;

  if (grade == 'A') letterGradeValue = 4;
  if (grade == 'B') letterGradeValue = 3;
  if (grade == 'C') letterGradeValue = 2;
  if (grade == 'D') letterGradeValue = 1;
  // For an 'F', it remains 0.

  int qualityPoints = creditHours * letterGradeValue;

  // Update two attributes.
  totalQualityPointsEarned =
          totalQualityPointsEarned + qualityPoints;
  gpa = totalQualityPointsEarned/totalCoursesTaken;
}
}
```

Client code shouldn't be able to directly cause a `Student` object's GPA to be updated; this should only occur as a side effect of completing a course. By making the `UpdateGpa` method private, we've prevented any client code from explicitly invoking this method to manipulate this attribute's value out of context.

3. ***We needn't always provide both a "getter" and a "setter" for private attributes.***

   If we provide only a "getter" for an attribute, then that attribute is rendered effectively read-only. We might do so, for example, with a student's ID number, which once set, should remain unchanged.

   ```
   public class Student
   {
     string studentId;
     // details omitted

     // We define a read-only property by only writing a get accessor
     public string ID {
       get {
         return studentId;
       }

       // The set accessor is omitted.
     }
   }
   ```

   *How do we **ever** set such an attribute's value the first time? We've already seen that some attributes' values get modified as a side effect of performing a method (as with* `countOfDsAndFs`*). We'll also see how to explicitly initialize such a "read-only" attribute a bit later in this chapter, when we talk about* ***constructors***.

   By the same token, we can provide only a "setter" for an attribute, in which case the attribute would be write-only.

   If we provide ***neither*** a "getter" or "setter," we've effectively rendered the attribute as a private "housekeeping" data item, as previously discussed.

The Power of Encapsulation

We learned earlier that encapsulation is the mechanism that bundles together the state information (attributes) and behavior (methods) of an object. Now that we've gained some insights into public/private accessibility, encapsulation warrants a more in-depth discussion.

It's useful to think of an object as a "fortress" that "guards" data—namely, the values of all of its attributes. Rather than trying to march straight through the walls of a fortress, which typically results in death and destruction (!), we ideally would approach the guard at the gate to ask permission to enter. Generally speaking, the same is true for objects: we can't directly access the values of an object's privately declared attributes without an object's permission and knowledge, that is, without using one of an object's publicly accessible methods/properties to access the attribute's value.

Assume that you've just met someone for the first time, and wish to know his name. One way to determine his name would be to reach into his pocket, pull out his wallet, and look at his driver's license—essentially, accessing his private attribute values without his permission! The more "socially acceptable" way would be to simply ask him for his name—akin to using his GetName method or Name property—and to allow him to respond accordingly. He may respond with his formal name, or a nickname, or an alias, or may say "It's none of your business!"—but the important point is that you're giving the person (object) control over his response.

By restricting access to an object's private attributes through public accessors, we derive three benefits:

- Preventing unauthorized access to encapsulated data

- Helping to ensure data integrity

- Limiting "ripple effects" that can otherwise occur throughout an application when the private implementation details of a class must change.

Let's discuss each of these benefits in detail.

Preventing Unauthorized Access to Encapsulated Data

Some of the information that a Student object maintains about itself—say, the student's identification number—may be highly confidential. A Student object may choose to selectively pass along this information when necessary—for example, when registering for a course—but may not wish to hand out this information to any object that happens to casually ask for it. Simply by making the attribute private, and intentionally omitting a public "getter" with which to request the attribute's value, there would be no way for another object to request the Student object's identification number.

Helping to Ensure Data Integrity

As mentioned previously, one of the arguments against declaring public attributes is that the object loses control over its data. As we saw earlier, a public attribute's value can be changed by client code without regard to any business rules that the object's class may wish to impose. On the other hand, when an accessor is used to change the value of a private attribute, value checking can be built into the set method or set accessor of a property to ensure that the attribute value won't be set to an "improper" value.

As an example, let's say that we've declared a Student attribute as follows:

```
private string birthDate;
```

Our intention is to record birth dates in the format "mm/dd/yyyy". By providing accessors with which to manipulate the birthDate attribute (instead of permitting direct public access to the attribute), we can provide logic to validate the format of any newly proposed date, and reject those that are invalid. We'll illustrate this concept by declaring a property called BirthDate for the student class as illustrated in the following code; but again, keep in mind that we could accomplish essentially the same "bulletproofing" through the creation of a SetBirthDate method:

```
public class Student
{
    private string birthDate;
    // Details omitted.

    // Properties.

    public string BirthDate {
        get {
            return birthDate;
        }
        set {
            // Perform appropriate validations.
            // Remember, italics represent pseudocode!
            if (date is not in the format mm/dd/yyyy) {
                do not update the birthDate attribute
            }
            else if (mm not in the range 01 to 12) {
```

```
        do not update the birthDate attribute
      }
      else if (the day number isn't valid for the selected month) {
        do not update the birthDate attribute
      }
      else if (the year is NOT a leap year, but 2/29 was specified) {
        // details omitted ...
      }
      // etc. for other validation tests.
      else {
        // All is well with what was passed in as a value to this
        // set accessor, and so we can go ahead and update the value of the
        // birthDate attribute with this value.
        birthDate = value;
      }
    }
  }


  // etc.
}
```

If an attempt is made to pass an invalid birth date to the property from client code, as in

```
s.BirthDate = "foo";
```

the change will be rejected and the value of the birthDate attribute will be unchanged.

On the other hand, if birthDate had been declared to be a ***public*** attribute:

```
public class Student
{
  public string birthDate;
  // etc.
```

then setting the attribute directly, thus bypassing the property (note ***lowercase*** "b") as follows:

```
s.birthDate = "foo";
```

would corrupt the attribute's value.

Limiting "Ripple Effects" When Private Features Change

Despite our best attempts, we often have a need to go back and modify code after an application has been deployed, either when an inevitable change in requirements occurs, or if we unfortunately discover a design flaw that needs attention. Unfortunately, this can often open us up to "ripple effects," wherein dozens, or hundreds, or **thousands** of lines of code throughout an application have to be changed, retested, etc. One of the most dramatic examples of the impact of ripple effects was the notorious "Y2K" problem: when the need to change date formats to accommodate a four-digit year arose, the burden to hunt through **millions** of lines of code in **millions** of applications worldwide to find all such cases—and to *fix* them without **breaking** anything!—was mind boggling.

Perhaps the most dramatic benefit of encapsulation combined with information hiding, therefore, is that the hidden implementation details of a class—i.e., its private data structure and/or its (effectively private) accessor code—can change without affecting how an object belonging to that class gets used in client code. To illustrate this principle, we'll craft an example using properties; but again, realize that the same power of encapsulation can be achieved through the appropriate use of "get"/"set" methods.

Let's say that an attribute is declared in the Student class as follows:

```
private int age;
```

and that we craft a corresponding Age property as follows:

```
public int Age {
  get {
    return age;
  }
  // will be read-only -- no set accessor provided.
}
```

We then proceed to use our Student class in countless applications; so, in thousands of places within the client code of these applications, we write statements such as the following, relying on the get accessor to provide us with a student's age as an int value:

```
if (s.Age <= 21)  { ... }
// or:
int retirementAge = s.Age + 20;
// etc.
```

A few years later, we decide to change the data structure of a Student so that, instead of maintaining an age attribute explicitly, we instead use the student's birthDate attribute to compute a student's age whenever it's needed. We thus modify our Student class code as follows:

The "Before" Code	The "After" Code
```\npublic class Student\n{\n // We have an explicit age attribute.\n private int age;\n\n public int Age {\n get {\n return age;\n }\n }\n\n // etc.\n}\n```	```\npublic class Student\n{\n // We replace age with birthDate.\n private DateTime birthDate;\n\n public int Age {\n get {\n // Compute the age on demand\n // (pseudocode).\n return (system date - birthDate);\n }\n }\n\n // etc.\n}\n```

In the "after" version of Student, we're computing the student's age by subtracting his or her birth date (an attribute) from today's date. This is an example of what we informally refer to as a **"pseudoattribute"**—to client code, the presence of an Age property implies that there is an attribute by the name of age, when in fact there may not be!

> Note that the same effect can be achieved with "get" and "set" methods: i.e., the availability of a getXxx() method signature for a class doesn't guarantee that there is actually an explicit attribute by the name of xxx in that class.

The beauty is that *we don't care* that the *private details* of the Student class design have changed! In all of the thousands of places within the client code of countless applications where we've used an expression such as

```
// This client code is unaffected by the private details of how age is
// computed internally to the Student class. Such details can in fact
// change after this client code is written, and the client code
// won't "break"!
if (s.Age <= 21)  { ... }
```

```
// or:
int retirementAge = s.Age + 20;
```

to retrieve a student's age as an int value, this code will continue to work ***as-is***, ***without any changes being necessary.*** Hence, we've avoided the "dreaded" ripple effect and have ***dramatically*** reduced the amount of effort necessary to accommodate a design change.

Such changes are said to be **encapsulated,** or limited to the internal code of the Student class only.

Of course, all bets are off if the developer of a class changes one of its ***public*** method or property headers, because then all of the client code that passes messages to objects of this type using this method or property header will potentially have to change. For example, if we were to change the Student class design as follows:

```
public class Student
{
  // We've changed the type of the age attribute from int to float ...
  private float age;

  // ... and the type of the Age attribute accordingly.
  public float Age {
    get {
      // details omitted.
    }
  }

  // etc.
}
```

then much our client code would indeed "break," as in the following example:

```
// This will no longer compile!
int currentAge = s.Age;
```

This client code will "break" because we now have a type mismatch: we're getting back a float value, but are trying to assign it to an int variable, which as we learned in Chapter 1 will generate a compiler error as follows:

```
error CS0029: Cannot implicitly convert type 'float' to 'int'
```

We'd have to hunt for all of the thousands of places in our countless applications where we are using the Age get accessor, and modify our code, such as the following:

```
// We're now using a cast.
int currentAge = (int) s.Age;
```

which is indeed a major ripple effect. But again, this ripple effect is due to the fact that we changed a ***public*** feature of our class—a public property header, to be precise. As long as we restrict our changes to private features of a class—private attributes and accessor code bodies, but not public method/property header(s)—ripple effects aren't an issue. Any client code that was previously written to utilize Student accessors will continue to work as intended; the client code will be blissfully ignorant that the internal details of the Student class have changed.

Using Accessors from Within a Class's Own Methods

As we saw earlier in the chapter, there are no restrictions on directly accessing a class's features from within that class's own methods. Both public and private features may be manipulated at will, using simple names, as the following code example illustrates:

```
using System;

public class Student
{
  private string name;
  // etc.

  // Properties.

  public string Name {
    get {
      return name;
    }
    set {
      name = value;
    }
  }

  // etc.

  public void PrintAllAttributes() {
    // We're directly accessing the values of the name attribute, simply
    // because we CAN!  We're not bothering to use the Name property
    // declared above.
    Console.WriteLine(name);
```

```
    // etc.
  }


  // etc.
}
```

However, it's considered a best practice to get into the habit of invoking a class's accessors, when available, even from within that class's ***own*** methods, vs. directly accessing attributes "just because we can," as a convenience. The reason for this is as follows: just because an attribute may be simple today, there's no guarantee that it won't become complicated down the road.

As an example, let's say that after we've programmed the Student class—including the PrintAllAttributes method shown previously—we decide that we want a student's name to always appear with the first name abbreviated as a single letter followed by a period; for example, "John Smith" should always appear as "J. Smith". So, we change the internal logic of the Name property's get accessor to make it a bit more sophisticated, as follows:

```
public class Student
{
  private string name;
  // etc.

  public string Name {
    // This version of the get accessor does more work: it reformats
    // the Student's name as internally stored, e.g.,
    // "Chris Williams" would be returned as "C. Williams".
    get {
      // Declare a few temporary variables.
      string firstInitial;
      string lastName;

      // Extract the first letter of the first name from the "name"
      // attribute, and store the result in variable "firstInitial".
      // (Details omitted.)

      // Extract the last name from the "name" attribute, and store
      // the result in variable "lastName".
      // (Details omitted.)
```

```
        return firstInitial + ". " + lastName;
      }
      set {
        name = value;
      }
    }


    // etc.
  }
```

No longer does the Name get accessor simply return the value of the name attribute unaltered, as it used to. But, if from within our PrintAllAttributes method we're still directly accessing the values of the attributes via dot notation:

```
  public void PrintAllAttributes() {
      // We're still directly accessing the values of the attributes, and
      // so we're losing out on the logic of the newly crafted Name
      // property's get accessor.
      Console.WriteLine(name);
      // etc.
  }


    // etc.
  }
```

we wind up circumventing the Name property, which means that all of our hard work to restructure the student's name in the Name get accessor is being ignored. Hence, client code such as the following:

```
Student s = new Student();
s.Name = "Cynthia Coleman";
// details omitted.
s.PrintAllAttributes();
```

produces incorrect results:

```
Cynthia Coleman
```

On the other hand, if we had recrafted the PrintAllAttributes method to utilize the Name get accessor:

```
  public void PrintAllAttributes() {
      // We're now using our own get accessors.
      Console.WriteLine(Name);
      // etc.
```

then we'd have automatically benefited from the change that we made to Name, and our client code would now produce correct results:

```
Student s = new Student();
s.Name = "Cynthia Coleman";
// details omitted.
s.PrintAllAttributes();
```

This results in the following output:

```
C. Coleman
```

again without having to have modified the client code.

Instance Constructors

When we talked about instantiating objects in the previous chapter, you may have been curious about the interesting syntax involved with the new operator:

```
Student x = new Student();
```

In particular, you may have wondered why there were parentheses tacked onto the end of the statement. It turns out that when we instantiate an object via the new operator, we're actually invoking a special type of function member called an **instance constructor.** An instance constructor literally constructs (instantiates) a brand-new object by allocating enough program memory to house the object's attributes.

Default Instance Constructors

It turns out that if we don't explicitly declare any instance constructors for a class, C# automatically provides a default parameterless instance constructor for that class. The default instance constructor will initialize any attributes of the class to their zero-equivalent values. So, even though we may have designed a class with no constructors whatsoever:

```
public class Student
{
  // Attributes.

  private string name;
  // other details omitted

  // Properties/methods (but NO EXPLICIT CONSTRUCTORS!).
```

```
  public string Name {
    get {
      return name;
    }
    set {
      name = value;
    }
  }

  // etc.
}
```

we are still able to write client code as follows:

```
Student s1 = new Student();  // We're calling the default constructor.
```

because we are using the ***default*** parameterless instance constructor.

Writing Our Own Constructors

We needn't merely rely on C# to provide us with a default constructor; we can also write constructors of our own design. When writing our own constructors, note that the header for a constructor is a bit different from that of methods:

```
    public              Student        ()
  accessibility      constructor name    comma-separated list of formal parameters,
  modifier, but      must match the    enclosed in parentheses
  no return type!    class name        (parentheses may be left empty)
```

Points to note:

- A constructor's name must be exactly the same as the name of the class for which we're writing the constructor—we have no choice in the matter.

- We ***can't*** specify a return type for a constructor, because by definition a constructor returns a reference to a newly created object of the type represented by the class.

- A parameter list, enclosed in parentheses, is provided for a constructor header as with method headers; and, as with method headers, it may be left empty if appropriate.

Another oddity with respect to constructors, as compared with methods, is that invoking them does ***not*** involve dot notation:

```
// We are invoking the Professor class's constructor method from client
// code without using dot notation.

Professor p = new Professor();
```

This is because we aren't requesting a service of a particular object, but rather are requesting that a new object be crafted from "thin air" by the programming environment; the use of the new operator emphasizes this difference syntactically. For this reason, constructors aren't considered to be methods, because as we learned earlier, methods are invoked in the context of a particular object using dot notation.

If we wish, we can *explicitly* program a parameterless instance constructor for our classes to do something more interesting than merely instantiating a "bare bones" object, in which case the default parameterless constructor is *not* automatically created for us:

```
public class Student
{
  // Attributes.
  private string name;
  // etc.

  // We've explicitly programmed a parameterless constructor, thus REPLACING the
  // default constructor.  (Again, note that there is no return type, and that
  // the name of a constructor must match the name of the class.)
  public Student() {
    // Perhaps we wish to initialize the attribute values to something OTHER THAN
    // their zero equivalents.
    name = "?";

    // etc. -- we can do whatever makes sense in constructing a new Student:
    // creating additional objects; accessing a database; communicating with
    // other preexisting objects; whatever is required!
  }
  // Other methods omitted from this example.
}
```

Passing Arguments to Constructors

Constructors may also be used to pass in initial values for an object's attributes at the time that an object is being instantiated. Instead of creating an object whose attributes are all initialized to zero-equivalent values, and then utilizing the accessors provided by that class to initialize attribute values one-by-one, as illustrated by this next snippet:

```
// Create a bare bones Student object.
Student s = new Student();

// Initialize the attributes one-by-one.
s.Name = "Fred Schnurd";
s.Ssn = "123-45-6789";
s.Major = "MATH";
// etc.
```

the initial values for selected attributes can all be passed in as a single step when the constructor is called, if desired:

```
Student s = new Student("Fred Schnurd", "123-45-6789", "MATH");
```

In order to accommodate this, we'd have to define a Student constructor with an appropriate header, as shown here:

```
public class Student
{
  // Attributes.
  private string name;
  private string ssn;
  private string major;
  // etc.

  // We've programmed a constructor with three parameters to accommodate
  // passing in argument values.
  public Student(string s, string n, string m) {
    Name = n;
    Ssn = s;
    Major = m;
  }
}
```

> *Note that we're using the* Name, Ssn, *and* Major *properties in the previous constructor to set the values of the associated* name, ssn, *and* major *attributes. As we discussed earlier in this chapter, using set accessors to set the value of attributes rather than manipulating attribute values directly allows us to make use of whatever value checking or other operations are performed inside the set accessor.*

As with methods, constructor arguments can also be used to provide general "fuel" for controlling how a constructor behaves, as illustrated in the next example:

```
public Student(string name, bool assignDefaults) {
  Name = n;
  // Optional logic to be performed, depending on what value
  // is passed in to the assignDefaults parameter from
  // client code.
  if (assignDefaults) {
    Ssn = "?";
    Major = "undeclared";
  }
}
```

Constructors can be declared with any one of the five previously mentioned C# accessibility types. They are most often given public accessibility so as to enable other classes to freely instantiate objects of the constructor's type.

*We'll revisit constructors twice more in this book—in our discussion of **overloading** in Chapter 5, and again with respect to inheritance in Chapter 13.*

Summary

In this chapter, you've learned

- How to formally specify method headers, the "language" with which services may be requested of an object, and how to formulate messages—using dot notation—to actually get an object to perform such services

- That multiple objects often have to collaborate in carrying out a particular system function, such as registering a student for a course

- That an object A can only communicate with another object B if A has a handle on B, and the various ways that such a handle can be obtained

- How classes designate the public/private accessibility of their features (attributes, properties, methods)

- How powerful a mechanism information hiding is, both in terms of protecting the integrity of an object's data and in preventing "ripple effects" in client code when private implementation details of an application inevitably change

- How to declare and use accessors—either accessor ("get"/"set") methods or properties—to gracefully access private attributes; and, that using properties is the preferred approach with C#

- How to harness the power of encapsulation

- How an instance constructor is specified and used to instantiate new objects

Exercises

1. Given a class `Book` defined as having the following attributes:

   ```
   Author author;
   string title;
   int noOfPages;
   bool fiction;
   ```

   write a set of properties for these attributes with simple, one-line get and set accessors.

   What would the recommended headers be if we were to write "get" and "set" methods, rather than properties, for all of these attributes?

2. It's often possible to discern something about a class's design based on the messages that are getting passed to objects in client code. Consider the following client code "snippet":

   ```
   Student s;
   Professor p;
   bool b;
   string x = "Math";

   s.Major = x;
   if (!s.HasAdvisor()) b = s.DesignateAdvisor(p);
   ```

   What features—attributes, methods, properties—are implied for the `Student` and `Professor` classes by virtue of how this client code is structured? Be as specific as possible with respect to

   - The accessibility of each feature

   - How each feature would be declared: e.g., the details, to the extent that you can "discover" them, of a method or property's header

3. What's wrong with the following code? Point out things that go against OO convention based on what you've learned in this chapter, regardless of whether or not the C# compiler would "complain" about them.

First, an example using "get"/"set" methods:

```
public class Building
{
  private string address;
  public int numberOfFloors;

  void GetnumberOfFloors() {
    return numberOfFloors;
  }

  private void SetNoOfFloors(float n) {
    NumberOfFloors = n;
  }
}
```

Next, an example using properties:

```
public class Building
{
  private string address;
  public int numberOfFloors

  public long NumberOfFloors {
    int get {
      return numberOfFloors;
    }
    private set {
      numberOfFloors = value;
    }
  }
}
```

CHAPTER 5

Relationships Between Objects

As we saw in Chapter 4, any two objects can have a "fleeting relationship" based on the fact that they exchange messages, in the same way that two strangers passing on the street might say "Hello!" to one another. We informally call such relationships between objects **behavioral relationships,** because they arise out of the behaviors, or actions, taken by one object X relative to another object Y. With behavioral relationships, object X is either temporarily handed a reference to object Y as an argument in a method call, or temporarily requests a handle on Y from another object Z. However, the emphasis is on *temporary:* when X is finished communicating with Y, object X often discards the reference to Y.

In the same way that you have significant and more lasting relationships with some people (family members, friends, colleagues, and so forth), there is also the notion of a more permanent relationship between objects. We informally refer to such relationships as **structural relationships** because, in order to keep track of such relationships, an object actually maintains lasting handles on its related objects in the form of attributes, a technique that we discussed in Chapter 3. Hence, the relationship becomes part of the data structure of the object in question.

In this chapter, you'll learn

- The various kinds of structural relationships that may exist between classes and between individual objects, and how we characterize them

- How, through a powerful mechanism called **inheritance,** we can derive new classes by describing only how they differ from existing classes

- The rules for what we can and can't do when deriving classes through inheritance

Associations and Links

The formal name for a structural relationship that exists between classes is an **association.** With respect to the Student Registration System, some sample associations might be as follows:

- A Student *is enrolled in* a Course.

- A Professor *teaches* a Course.

- A Degree Program *requires* a Course.

Whereas an association refers to a relationship between *classes,* the term **link** is used to refer to a structural relationship that exists between two specific *objects* (*instances*). Given the association "A Student *is enrolled in* a Course," we might have the following links:

- Joe Blow (a particular Student object) is enrolled in Math 101 (a particular Course object).

- Fred Schnurd (a particular Student object) is enrolled in Basketweaving 972 (a particular Course object).

- Mary Smith (a particular Student object) is enrolled in Basketweaving 972 (a particular Course object; as it turns out, the *same* Course object that Fred Schnurd is linked to).

In the same way that an object is a specific instance of a class with its attribute values filled in, a link is a specific instance of an association with its member objects filled in, as illustrated in Figure 5-1.

```
Association: _ _ _ _ _ _ _ _ _ _  is enrolled in  _ _ _ _ _ _ _ _ .
                (Some Student)                      (Some Course)

      Link: _ _ _ James Conroy_ _ _  is enrolled in _ Phys ED 311 _ .
              (A Specific Student)                   (A Specific Course)
```

Figure 5-1. An association is a template for creating links.

Another way to think of the difference between an association and a link is that

- An association is a *potential* relationship between objects of a certain type/class.

- A link is an *actual* relationship between objects of those particular types.

Given any Student object X and any Course object Y, there is the ***potential*** for a link of type "is enrolled in" to exist between those two objects ***precisely because*** there is an *is enrolled in* association defined between the two classes that those objects belong to. In other words, associations enable links.

Most of the time, we define associations between two different classes; such associations are known as **binary associations.** The *is enrolled in* association, for example, is a binary association, because it interrelates two different classes—Student and Course. A **unary,** or **reflexive, association,** on the other hand, is between two instances of the same class; for example:

- A Course *is a prerequisite for* (another) Course.

- A Professor *supervises* (other) Professor(s).

Even though the two classes at either end of a reflexive association are the same, the objects are typically different instances of that class:

- Math 101 (a Course object) is a prerequisite for Math 202 (a different Course object).

- Professor Smith (a Professor object) supervises Professors Jones and Green (other Professor objects).

and so forth. However, although somewhat rare, there can be situations in which the same object can serve in both roles of a reflexive relationship.

Higher-order associations are possible, but rare. A **ternary association,** for example, involves three classes; for example, a Student takes a Course from a particular Professor, as shown in Figure 5-2.

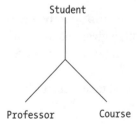

Figure 5-2. A ternary association

When describing associations, however, we usually decompose higher-order associations into an appropriate number of binary associations. We can, for example, represent the preceding three-way association as three binary associations instead (see Figure 5-3):

- A Student *attends* a Course.

- A Professor *teaches* a Course.

- A Professor *instructs* a Student.

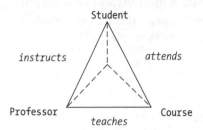

Figure 5-3. An equivalent representation using three binary associations

Within a given association, each participant class is said to have a **role.** In the *advises* association (a Professor *advises* a Student), the role of the Professor might be said to be "advisor," and the role of the Student might be said to be "advisee." We only bother to assign names to the roles at either end of an association if it helps to clarify the model. In the *is enrolled in* association (a Student *is enrolled in* a Course), there is probably no need to invent role names for the Student and Course ends of the association, because they wouldn't add significantly to the clarity of the abstraction of which this association is a part.

Multiplicity

For a given association type *X* between classes A and B, the term **multiplicity** refers to the number of objects of type A that may be associated with a given instance of type B. For example, a Student attends *multiple* Courses, but a Student has *only one* Professor in the role of advisor.

There are three basic categories of multiplicity, which we'll take a closer look at next: **one-to-one, one-to-many,** and **many-to-many.**

One-to-One (1:1)

Exactly one instance of class A is related to exactly one instance of class B, no fewer, no more, and vice versa. For example:

- A Student has *exactly one* Transcript, and a Transcript belongs to *exactly one* Student.

- A Professor chairs *exactly one* Department, and a Department has *exactly one* Professor in the role of chairperson.

We can further constrain an association by stating whether the participation of the class at either end is **optional** or **mandatory**. For example, we can change the preceding association to read as follows:

- A Professor *optionally* chairs exactly one Department, but it's *mandatory* that a Department have exactly one Professor in the role of chairperson.

This revised version of the association is a more realistic portrayal of real-world circumstances than the previous version because, while every department in a university typically does indeed have a chairperson, not every professor is a chairperson of a department — there aren't enough departments to go around! However, it's typically true that, *if* a professor happens to be a chairperson of a department, then they are chairperson of only *one* department.

One-to-Many (1:m)

For a given single instance of class A, there can be many instances of class B related to it in a particular fashion; but, from the perspective of an object of type B, there can only be one instance of class A that is so related. For example:

- A Department employs *many* Professors, but a Professor (usually) works for *exactly one* Department.

- A Professor advises *many* Students, but a given Student has *exactly one* Professor as an advisor.

Note that "many" in this case can be interpreted as either "zero or more (optional)" or as "one or more (mandatory)." To be a bit more specific, we can refine the previous one-to-many associations as follows:

- A Department employs *one or more* ("many"; *mandatory*) Professors, but a Professor (usually) works for exactly one Department.

- A Professor advises *zero or more* ("many"; *optional*) Students, but a given Student has exactly one Professor as an advisor.

The "one" end of a one-to-many association may also be designated as either mandatory or optional. We may, for example, wish to "fine-tune" the previous association as follows if we're modeling a university setting in which students aren't required to select an advisor:

- A Professor advises many (zero or more; *optional*) students, and a given Student may *optionally* have at most one advisor.

Many-to-Many (m:m)

For a given single instance of class A, there can be many instances of class B related to it, and vice versa. For example:

- A Student enrolls in *many* Courses, and a Course has *many* Students enrolled in it.

- A given Course can have *many* prerequisite Courses, and a given Course can in turn be a prerequisite for *many* other Courses. (This is an example of a many-to-many *reflexive* association.)

As with one-to-many associations, "many" can be interpreted as *zero* or more (*optional*) or as *one* or more (*mandatory*); for example:

- A Student enrolls in *zero or more* ("many"; *optional*) Courses, and a Course has *one or more* ("many"; *mandatory*) Students enrolled in it.

Of course, the validity of a particular association—the classes that are involved, its multiplicity, and the optional or mandatory nature of participation in the association—is wholly dependent on the real-world circumstances being modeled. If you were modeling a university in which departments could have more than one chairperson, or where students could have more than one advisor, your choice of multiplicities would differ from those used in our preceding examples.

Multiplicity and Links

Note that the concept of multiplicity pertains to associations, but not to links. *Links always exist in pairwise fashion between two objects* (or, in rare cases, between an object and itself). Therefore, multiplicity in essence defines how many links of a certain association type can originate from a given object. This is best illustrated with an example.

Consider once again the many-to-many association:

A Student *enrolls in* zero or more Courses, and a Course has one or more Students *enrolled* in it.

A ***specific*** Student object X can have zero, one, or more ***links*** to Course objects, but any ***one*** of those links is between exactly ***two*** objects—Student X and a single Course object. In Figure 5-4, for example:

- Student X has one link (to Course A).

- Student Y has four links (to Courses A, B, C, and D).

- Student Z has no links to any Course objects whatsoever. (Z is taking the semester off!)

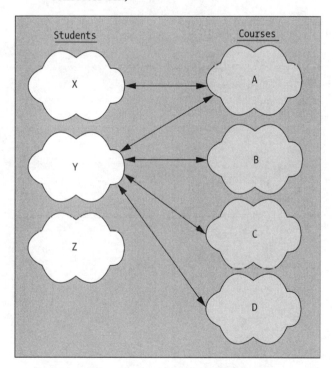

Figure 5-4. A many-to-many assocation between classes; links are always pairwise between objects.

Conversely, a ***specific*** Course object A must have one or more links to Student objects to satisfy the mandatory nature and multiplicity of the association, but again, any ***one*** of those links is between exactly ***two*** objects—Course A and a single Student object. In Figure 5-4, for example:

- Course A has two links (to Students X and Y).

- Courses B, C, and D each have one link (to the same Student, Y).

Note, however, that once again every link is between precisely two objects: a Student and a Course. This example scenario does indeed uphold the many-to-many *is enrolled in* association between Student and Course; it's but one of a vast number of possible scenarios that may exist between objects belonging to the classes in question.

Just to make sure that this concept is clear, let's look at one more example, this time using the one-to-one association:

A Professor ***optionally*** chairs exactly one Department, and it's ***mandatory*** that a Department have exactly one Professor in the role of chairman. As illustrated in Figure 5-5

- Professor objects 1 and 4 each have one link, to Department objects A and B, respectively.

- Professor objects 2 and 3 have no such links.

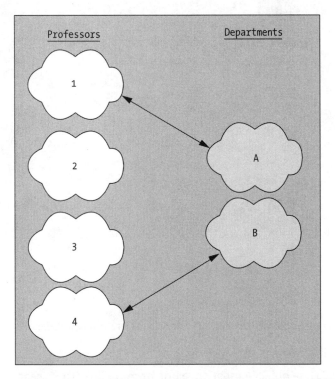

Figure 5-5. A one-to-one assocation between classes; links are always pairwise between objects.

Moreover, from the `Department` objects' perspective, each `Department` does indeed have exactly one link to a `Professor`. Therefore, this example upholds the one-to-one *chairs* association between Professor and Department, while further illustrating the optional nature of the `Professor` class's participation in such links. Again, it's but one of a vast number of possible scenarios that may exist between the classes in question.

Aggregation

Aggregation is a special form of association, alternatively referred to as the "consists of," "is composed of," or "has a" relationship. Like an association, an aggregation is used to represent a relationship between two classes A and B. But, with an aggregation, we're representing more than mere relationship: we're stating that an object belonging to a class A, known as an **aggregate class,** is composed of, or contains, **component objects** belonging to a class B.

For example, a car is composed of an engine, a transmission, four wheels, etc., so if Car, Engine, Transmission, and Wheel were all classes, then we could form the following aggregations:

- A Car *contains* an Engine.

- A Car *contains* a Transmission.

- A Car *is composed of* many (in this case, four) Wheels.

Or, as an example related to the SRS, we can say that

- A University *is composed of* many Schools (the School of Engineering; the School of Law; etc.).

- A School *is composed of* many Departments.

One wouldn't typically say, however, that a Department is *composed of* many Professors; instead, we'd probably state that a Department *employs* many Professors.

Note that these aggregation statements appear awfully similar to associations, where the name of the association just so happens to be "is composed of" or "contains." That's because an aggregation *is* an association! So, why the fuss over trying to differentiate between aggregation and association? Do we even need to recognize that there is such a thing as an aggregation? It turns out that there are some subtle differences between aggregation and association that affect how an abstraction is rendered in code. Therefore, we'll defer further discussion of aggregation for now, but will return to discuss these sub-tleties in Chapter 14.

For now, use this simple rule of thumb: when you detect a relationship between two classes A and B, and the name you're inclined to give that association implies *containment*—"contains," "is composed of," "is comprised of," "consists of," and so forth—then it's probably really an aggregation that you're dealing with.

Inheritance

Let's assume that we've accurately and thoroughly modeled all of the essential features of students via our Student class, and furthermore that we've pro-grammed the class in C#. A simplified version of the Student class is shown here:

```
using System;

public class Student
{
  private string name;
  private string studentId;
  // etc.

  public string Name {
    get {
      return name;
    }
    set {
      name = value;
    }
  }

  public string StudentId {
    get {
      return studentId;
    }
    set {
      studentId = value;
    }
  }

  // etc.
}
```

In fact, let's further assume that our Student class code has been rigorously tested, found to be bug free, and is actually being used in a number of applications: our Student Registration System, for example, as well as perhaps a student billing system and an alumni relations system for the same university.

A new requirement has just arisen for modeling ***graduate students*** as a special type of student. As it turns out, the only features of a graduate student that we need to track above and beyond those that we've already modeled for a "generic" student are

- What undergraduate degree the student previously received before entering their graduate program of study

- What institution they received the undergraduate degree from

All of the other features necessary to describe a graduate student—attributes name, studentId, and so forth, along with properties to access these and the methods modeling a student's behaviors—are the same as those that we've already programmed for the Student class, because a graduate student *is* a student, after all.

How might we approach this new requirement for a GraduateStudent class? If we weren't well versed in object-oriented concepts, we might try one of the following approaches.

Approach #1: Modify the Student Class to Do "Double Duty"

We could add attributes to reflect undergraduate degree information to our definition of a Student, along with properties to access these, and simply leave these attributes empty when they are nonapplicable: that is, for an undergraduate student who hadn't yet graduated.

```
public class Student
{
  private string name;
  private string studentId;
  private string undergraduateDegree;
  private string undergraduateInstitution;
  // etc.
```

Then, to keep track of whether these attributes were supposed to contain values or not for a given Student object, we'd probably also want to add a bool attribute to note whether a particular student is a graduate student:

```
public class Student
{
    private string name;
    private string studentId;
    private string undergraduateDegree;
    private string undergraduateInstitution;
    private bool isGraduateStudent;
    // etc.
```

In any new methods that we subsequently write for this class, we'll have to take the value of this bool attribute into account:

```
public void DisplayAllFields() {
    Console.WriteLine(name);
    Console.WriteLine(studentId);

    // If a particular student is NOT a graduate student, then the values
    // of the attributes "undergraduateDegree" and
    // "undergraduateInstitution" would be undefined, and so we would
    // only wish to print them if we are dealing with a graduate student.
    if (isGraduateStudent) {
        Console.WriteLine(undergraduateDegree);
        Console.WriteLine(undergraduateInstitution);
    }
    // etc.
}
```

This results in convoluted code, which is difficult to debug and maintain.

Approach #2: "Clone" the Student Class

We could instead create a new GraduateStudent class by (a) making a duplicate copy of the Student class, (b) renaming the copy to be the GraduateStudent class, and (c) adding the extra features required of a graduate student to the copy.

```
public class Student {                          public class GraduateStudent {
  // Attributes.                                   // Student attributes DUPLICATED!

  private string name;                            private string name;
  private string studentId;                       private string studentId;
  private string birthDate;                       private string birthDate;
  // etc.                                          // etc.


                                                  // Add the two new attributes.
                                                  private string undergraduateDegree;
                                                  private string
                                                          undergraduateInstitution;


  // Properties.                                   // Student properties DUPLICATED!

  public string Name {                            public string Name {
    get {                                           get {
      return name;                                    return name;
    }                                               }
    set {                                           set {
      name = value;                                   name = value;
    }                                               }
  }                                               }


  // etc.                                          // etc.


                                                  // Add properties for the two
                                                  // new attributes.
                                                  // details omitted ...
```

This would be awfully inefficient, since we'd then have much of the same code in two places, and if we wanted to change how a particular method worked or how an attribute was defined later on—say, a change of the type of the birthDate attribute from string to DateTime, with a corresponding change to the properties for that attribute—then we'd have to make the same changes in both classes.

Strictly speaking, either of the preceding two approaches would work, but the inherent redundancy in the code would make the application difficult to maintain. In addition, where these approaches both really break down is when we have to invent a third, or a fourth, or a fifth type of "special" student. For example, consider how complicated the DisplayAllFields method introduced in approach #1 would become if we wanted to use it to represent a third type of student: namely, continuing education students, who don't seek a degree, but rather are just taking courses for continuing professional enrichment.

- We'd most likely need to add yet another bool flag to keep track of whether or not a degree was being sought:

```
public class Student
{
    private string name;
    private string studentId;
    private string undergraduateDegree;
    private string undergraduateInstitution;
    private string degreeSought;
    private bool isGraduateStudent;
    private bool seekingDegree;
    // etc.
```

- Then, we'd also have to take the value of this bool attribute into account in the DisplayAllFields method:

```
public void DisplayAllFields() {
    Console.WriteLine(name);
    Console.WriteLine(studentId);

    if (isGraduateStudent) {
        Console.WriteLine(undergraduateDegree);
        Console.WriteLine(undergraduateInstitution);
    }

    // If a particular student is NOT seeking a degree, then the value
    // of the attribute 'degreeSought' would be undefined, and so we
    // would only wish to print it if we are dealing with a degree-
    // seeking student.
    if (seekingDegree) {
        Console.WriteLine(degreeSought);
    }
    else {
```

```
        Console.WriteLine("NONE");
      }


      // etc.
    }
```

This ***worsens*** the complexity issue!

We've had to introduce a lot of complexity in the logic of this one method to handle the various types of student; think of how much more "spaghetti-like" the code might become if we had ***dozens*** of different student types to accommodate! Unfortunately, with non-OO languages, these convoluted approaches would typically be our only options for handling the requirement for a new type of object. It's no wonder that applications become so complicated and expensive to maintain as requirements inevitably evolve over time!

Fortunately, we do have yet another alternative!

Approach #3: Inheritance

With an object-oriented programming language, we can solve this problem by taking advantage of **inheritance,** a powerful mechanism for defining a new class by stating only the differences (in terms of features) between the new class and another class that we've already established. Using inheritance, we can declare a new class named GraduateStudent that inherits all of the features of the Student class. The GraduateStudent class would then only have to take care of the two extra attributes associated with a graduate student—undergraduateDegree and undergraduateInstitution. Inheritance is indicated in a C# class declaration using a colon followed by the name of the base class being extended.

```
public class GraduateStudent : Student {
  // Declare two new attributes above and beyond
  // what the Student class declares ...

  private string undergraduateDegree;
  private string undergraduateInstitution;

  // ... and properties for each of these new attributes.

  public string UndergraduateDegree {
    get {
      return undergraduateDegree;
    }
    set {
      undergraduateDegree = value;
    }
```

```
  }

  public string UndergraduateInstitution {
    get {
      return undergraduateInstitution;
    }
    set {
      undergraduateInstitution = value;
    }
  }
}
```

That's all we need to declare in our new GraduateStudent class: two attributes plus their associated properties! There is no need to duplicate any of the features of the Student class, because we're automatically inheriting these. It's as if we had "plagiarized" the code for the attributes, properties, and methods from the Student class, and inserted it into GraduateStudent, but without the fuss of actually having done so.

When we take advantage of inheritance, the original class that we're starting from—Student, in this case—is called the **base class.** The new class—GraduateStudent—is called a **derived class.** A derived class is said to **extend** a base class.

Inheritance is often referred to as the **"is a" relationship** between two classes, because if a class B (GraduateStudent) is derived from a class A (Student), then B truly *is a* special case of A. Anything that we can say about a base class must also be true about all of its derived classes; that is

- A Student attends classes, and so a Graduate Student attends classes.

- A Student has an advisor, and so a Graduate Student has an advisor.

- A Student pursues a degree, and so a Graduate Student pursues a degree.

In fact, an "acid test" for legitimate use of inheritance is as follows: if there is something that can be said about a base class A that *can't* be said about a proposed derived class B, then B really *isn't* a valid derived class of A.

Note, however, that the converse isn't true: because a derived class is a special case of its base class, it's possible to say things about the derived class that can't be said about the base class; for example:

- A GraduateStudent has already attended an undergraduate institution, whereas a "generic" Student may *not* have done so.

- A GraduateStudent has already received an undergraduate degree, whereas a "generic" Student may *not* have done so.

Because derived classes are special cases of their base classes, the term **specialization** is used to refer to the process of deriving one class from another. **Generalization,** on the other hand, is a term used to refer to the opposite process: namely, recognizing the common features of several existing classes and creating a new, common base class for them all. Let's say we now wish to create the Professor class. Students and Professors have some features in common: attributes—name, birthDate, etc., and the properties/methods that manipulate these. Yet, they each have unique features, as well; the Professor class might require the attributes title (a string) and worksFor (a reference to a Department), while the Student class's studentID, degreeSought, and majorField attributes are irrelevant for a Professor. Because each class has attributes that the other would find useless, neither class can be derived from the other. Nonetheless, to duplicate their shared features in two places would be horribly inefficient.

In such a circumstance, we may want to invent a new base class called Person, consolidate the features common to both Students and Professors in that class, and then have Student and Professor inherit these common features from Person. The resultant code in this situation appears here:

```
// Defining the base class:
public class Person
{
  // Attributes common to Students and Professors.
  private string name;       // See note about use of private accessibility
  private string address;    // with inheritance after this code example.
  private string birthDate;

  // Common properties.
  public string Name {
    get {
      return name;
    }
    set {
      name = value;
    }
  }

  // etc.

  // Common methods - details omitted.
}

// Deriving Student from Person ...
public class Student : Person
{
```

```csharp
    // Attributes specific only to a Student.
    private string studentId;
    private string majorField;
    private string degreeSought;

    // Student-specific properties.
    public string StudentId {
      get {
        return studentId;
      }
      set {
        studentId = value;
      }
    }

    // etc.


    // Student-specific methods - details omitted.
}

// Deriving Professor from Person ...
public class Professor : Person
{
    // Attributes specific only to a Professor.
    private string title;
    private Department worksFor;

    // Professor-specific properties.
    public string Title {
      get {
        return title;
      }
      set {
        title = value;
      }
    }

    // etc.

    // Professor-specific methods - details omitted.
}
```

> *You'll learn in Chapter 13 that there are a few extra complexities about inheriting private features, and how another accessibility type—**protected accessibility**—comes into play, which we aren't tackling just yet because we haven't covered enough ground to do them justice at this point.*

The Benefits of Inheritance

Inheritance is perhaps one of the most powerful and unique aspects of an OO programming language because

- *Derived classes are much more succinct than they would be without inheritance.* Derived classes only contain the "essence" of what makes them different from their base classes. We know from looking at the GraduateStudent class definition, for example, that a graduate student is "a student who already holds an undergraduate degree from an educational institution." As a result, the total body of code for a given application is significantly reduced as compared with the traditional non-OO approach to developing the same application.

- *Through inheritance, we can reuse and extend code that has already been thoroughly tested without modifying it.* As we saw, we were able to invent a new class—GraduateStudent—without disturbing the Student class code in any way. So, we can rest assured that any client code that relies on instantiating Student objects and passing messages to them will be unaffected by the creation of derived class GraduateStudent, and thus we avoid having to retest huge portions of our existing application. (Had we used a non-OO approach of "tinkering" with the Student class code to try to accommodate graduate student attributes, we would have had to retest our entire existing application to make sure that nothing had "broken"!)

- *Best of all, we can derive a new derived class from an existing class even if we don't own the source code for the latter!* As long as we have the compiled version of a class, the inheritance mechanism works just fine; we don't need the original source code of a class in order to extend it. This is one of the significant ways to achieve productivity with an object-oriented language: find a class (either written by someone else or one that is built into the language) that does much of what you need, and create a derived class of that class, adding just those features that you need for your own purposes; or buy a third-party library of classes written by someone else, and do the same.

- Finally, as we saw in Chapter 2, *classification is the natural way that humans organize information;* so, it only makes sense that we'd organize our software along the same lines, making it much more intuitive and hence easier to maintain and extend.

Class Hierarchy

Over time, we build up an inverted tree of classes that are interrelated through inheritance; such a tree is called a **class hierarchy.** One such class hierarchy example is shown in Figure 5-6.

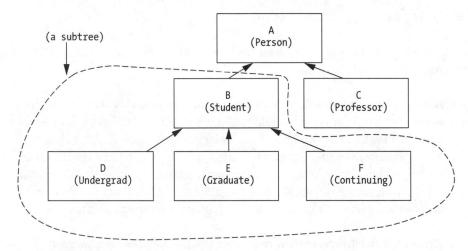

Figure 5-6. A sample class hierarchy

A bit of nomenclature:

- We may refer to each class as a **node** in the hierarchy.

- Any given node in the hierarchy is said to be derived (directly or indirectly) from all of the nodes above it in the hierarchy, known collectively as its **ancestors.**

- The ancestor that is *immediately* above a given node in the hierarchy is considered to be that node's **direct base class.**

- Conversely, all nodes below a given node in the hierarchy are said to be its **descendants.**

- The node that sits at the top of the hierarchy is referred to as the **root node.**

- A **terminal,** or **leaf, node,** is one that has no descendants.

- Two nodes that are derived from the same direct base class are known as **siblings.**

Applying this terminology to the example hierarchy in Figure 5-5

- Class A (Person) is the root node of the entire hierarchy.

- Classes B, C, D, E, and F are all said to be derived from class A, and are thus descendants of A.

- Classes D, E, and F can be said to be derived from class B.

- Classes D, E, and F are siblings; so are classes B and C.

- Class D has two ancestors, A and B.

- Classes C, D, E, and F are terminal nodes, in that they don't have any classes derived from them (as of yet, at any rate).

Note that arrows are used to point **upward** from each derived class to its direct base class.

> In the C# language, the Object *class (of the* System *namespace) serves as the ultimate base class for all other types, both user-defined as well as those built into the language. We'll talk about the* Object *class in more depth in Part Three of the book.*

As with any hierarchy, this one may evolve over time:

- It may **widen** with the addition of new siblings/branches in the tree.

- It may **expand downward** as a result of future specialization.

- It may **expand upward** as a result of future generalization.

Such changes to the hierarchy are made as new requirements emerge, or as our understanding of the existing requirements improves. For example, we may determine the need for MastersStudent and PhDStudent classes (as specializations of GraduateStudent), or for an Administrator class as a sibling to Student and Professor. This would yield the revised hierarchy shown in Figure 5-7.

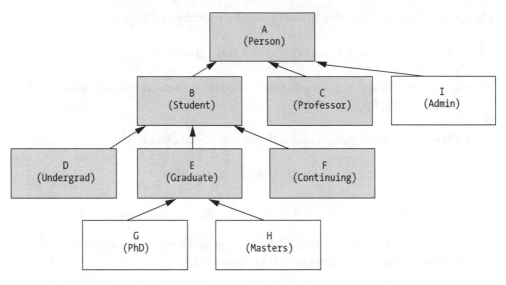

Figure 5-7. Class hierarchies almost always expand over time.

Is Inheritance Really a Relationship?

Association, aggregation, and inheritance are all said to be relationships between *classes.* Where inheritance differs from association and aggregation is at the *object level.*

As we've seen earlier in this chapter, association (and aggregation, as a special form of association) can be said to relate individual objects, in the sense that two different objects are linked to one another by virtue of the existence of an association between their respective classes. Inheritance, on the other hand, is a way of describing the features of a *single* object. With inheritance, an object is *simultaneously* an instance of a derived class and all of its base classes: a GraduateStudent is a Student that is a Person, all wrapped into one!

So, in looking once again at the hierarchy in Figure 5-7, we see that

- *All* classes in the hierarchy—class A (Person) as well as all of its descendants B through I—may be thought of as producing Person objects.

- Class B (Student), along with its descendants D through H, may all be thought of as producing Student objects.

and so forth.

This notion of an object having "multiple identities" is a significant one that we'll revisit several times throughout the book.

Avoiding "Ripple Effects"

Once a class hierarchy is established and an application has been coded, changes to nonleaf classes (i.e., those classes that have descendants) will introduce "ripple effects" down the hierarchy. For example, if after we've established the GraduateStudent class, we go back and add a minorField attribute to the Student class, then GraduateStudent will inherit this new attribute once it has been recompiled. Perhaps this is what we want; on the other hand, we may not have anticipated the derivation of a GraduateStudent class when we first conceived of Student, and so this may ***not*** be what we want!

As the developers of the Student class, it would be ideal if we could speak with the developers of all derived classes—GraduateStudent, MastersStudent, and PhDStudent—to obtain their approval for any proposed changes to Student. But, this isn't an ideal world, and often we may not even know that our class has been extended if, for example, our code is being distributed and reused on other projects or is being sold to clients. This evokes a general rule of thumb:

> ***Whenever possible, avoid adding features to nonleaf classes once they have been established in code in an application to avoid ripple effects throughout an inheritance hierarchy.***

This is easier said than done! However, it reinforces the importance of spending as much time as possible on requirements analysis before diving into the coding stage of an application development project. This won't prevent new requirements from emerging over time, but we should avoid oversights regarding the current requirements.

Rules for Deriving Classes: The "Do's"

When deriving a new class, we can do several things to specialize the base class that we are starting out with.

- We may ***extend*** the base class by ***adding features.*** In our GraduateStudent example, we added four features: two attributes—undergraduateDegree and undergraduateInstitution—and two properties—UndergraduateDegree and UndergraduateInstitution.

- We may ***specialize*** the way that a derived class performs one or more of the ***services*** inherited from its base class. For example, when a "generic" student enrolls for a course, the student may first need to ensure that

  - They have taken the necessary prerequisite courses.

  - The course is required for the degree that the student is seeking.

- When a ***graduate*** student enrolls for a course, on the other hand, they may need to do both of these things as well as to ensure that their graduate committee feels that the course is appropriate.

Specializing the way that a derived class performs a service—that is, how it responds to a given message—as compared with the way that its base class would have responded to the same message, is accomplished via a technique known as **overriding.**

Overriding

Overriding involves "rewiring" how a method or property works internally, without changing the interface to/signature of that method. For example, let's say that we had defined a Print method for the Student class to print out the values of all of a student's attributes:

```
public class Student
{
  // Attributes.
  private string name;
  private string studentId;
  private string majorField;
  private double gpa;
  // etc.

  // Properties for each attribute would also be provided; details omitted.

  public void Print() {
    // Print the values of all of the attributes that the Student class
    // knows about; note use of get accessors.
    Console.WriteLine("Student Name:   " + Name + "\n" +
                "Student No.:   " + StudentId + "\n" +
                "Major Field:   " + MajorField + "\n" +
                "GPA:   " + Gpa);
  }
}
```

The Print method shown in the preceding code example assumes that properties have been created for all of the Student class attributes. The get accessor of each property is used to access the value of the associated attribute, rather than accessing the attributes directly.

> *Using* get *accessors within a class's own methods reflects a "best practices" discussion that we had in Chapter 4; doing so allows us to take advantage of any value checking or other operations that the* get *accessor may provide.*

By virtue of inheritance, all of the derived classes of Student will inherit this method. However, there is a problem: we added two new attributes to the GraduateStudent derived class—undergraduateDegree and undergraduateInstitution. If we take the "lazy" approach of just letting GraduateStudent inherit the Print method of Student as is, then whenever we invoke the Print method for a GraduateStudent, all that will be printed are the values of the four attributes inherited from Student—name, studentId, major, and gpa—because these are the only attributes that the Print method has been explicitly programmed to print the values of. Ideally, we would like the Print method, when invoked for a GraduateStudent, to print these same four attributes *plus* the two additional attributes of undergraduateDegree and undergraduateInstitution.

With an object-oriented language, we are able to override, or supersede, the Student version of the Print method that the GraduateStudent class has inherited. In order to override a base class's method in C#, the method to be overridden first has to be declared to be a **virtual** method in the base class using the virtual keyword. Declaring a method to be virtual means that it *may* be (but doesn't *have to* be) overridden by a derived class.

The derived class can then override the method by reimplementing the method with the override keyword in the derived class's method declaration. The overridden method in the derived class must be declared to have the same accessibility, return type, name, and parameter list as the base class method it's overriding.

Let's look at how the GraduateStudent class would go about overriding the Print method of the Student class:

```
public class Student
{
  // Attributes.
  private sring name;
  private string studentId;
  private string majorField;
  private double gpa;
  // etc.

  // Properties for each attribute would also be provided; details omitted.
```

```
// The Student class Print method is declared to be virtual so that it
// may be overridden by derived classes.
public virtual void Print() {
    // Print the values of all the attributes that the Student class
    // knows about; again, note the use of get accessors.
    Console.WriteLine("Student Name:  " + Name + "\n" +
                      "Student No.:  " + StudentId + "\n" +
                      "Major Field:  " + MajorField + "\n" +
                      "GPA:   " + Gpa);
    }
}


public class GraduateStudent : Student
{
    string undergraduateDegree;
    string undergraduateInstitution;

    // Properties for each newly added attribute would also be provided;
    // details omitted.

    // We are overriding the Student class's Print method; note use of the
    // override keyword to signal this intention.
    public override void Print() {
        // We print the values of all the attributes that the
        // GraduateStudent class knows about:  namely, those that it
        // inherited from Student plus those that it explicitly declares.
        Console.WriteLine("Student Name:  " + Name + "\n" +
                          "Student No.:  " + StudentId + "\n" +
                          "Major Field:  " + GMajorField + "\n" +
                          "GPA:   " + Gpa + "\n" +
                          "Undergrad. Deg.:  " + UndergraduateDegree + "\n" +
                          "Undergrad. Inst.:  " + UndergraduateInstitution);
    }
}
```

The GraduateStudent class's version of Print thus overrides, or supersedes, the version that would otherwise have been inherited from the Student class.

The preceding example is less than ideal because the first four lines of the Print method of GraduateStudent duplicate the code from the Student class's version of Print. Redundancy in an application is to be avoided, because redundant code represents a maintenance nightmare: when we have to change code in one place in an application, we don't want to have to remember to change it in countless other places or, worse yet, forget to do so, and wind up with inconsistency in our logic. We like to avoid code duplication and encourage code reuse in an application whenever possible, so our `Print` method for the `GraduateStudent` class would actually be written as follows:

```
public class GraduateStudent : Student
{
  // details omitted ...

  public override void Print() {
    // Reuse code by calling the Print method defined by the Student
    // base class ...
    base.Print();

    // ... and then go on to print this derived class's specific attributes.
    Console.WriteLine("Undergrad. Deg.:  " + UndergraduateDegree + "\n" +
                      "Undergrad. Inst.:  " + UndergraduateInstitution);
  }
}
```

We use a C# keyword, `base`, as the qualifier for a method name:

base.*methodName*(*arguments*);

when we wish to invoke the version of method *methodName* that was defined in a base class. That is, in the preceding example, we're essentially saying to the compiler "First, execute the `Print` method the way that my parent class, `Student`, would have executed it, and then do something extra—namely, print out the values of the new `GraduateStudent` attributes."

Sometimes, in a complex inheritance hierarchy, we have occasion to override a method multiple times. In the hierarchy shown in Figure 5-8

- Root class A (`Person`) declares a method with the header

  ```
  public virtual void Print()
  ```

  that prints out all of the attributes declared for the `Person` class.

- Derived class B (`Student`) overrides this method, changing the internal logic of the method body to print not only the attributes inherited from `Person`, but also those that were added by the `Student` class itself. The overridden method would have the following header:

  ```
  public override void Print()
  ```

- Derived class E (GraduateStudent) overrides this method again, to print not only the attributes inherited from Student (which include those inherited from Person), but also those that were added by the GraduateStudent class itself. The GraduateStudent version of the Print method would also use the override keyword.

```
public override void Print()
```

Note that, in all cases, the accessibility, return type, and method signature *must* remain the same—public void Print()—for overriding to take place.

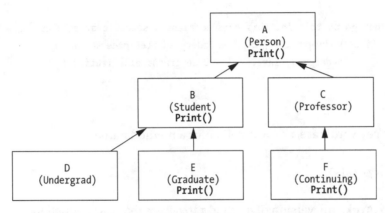

Figure 5-8. A method may be overridden multiple times within a class hierarchy.

Under such circumstances, any class not specifically overriding a given method itself will inherit the definition of that method used by its most immediate ancestor.

Rules for Deriving Classes: The "Don'ts"

When deriving a new class, there are some things that we should *not* attempt to do. (And, as it turns out, OO languages will actually prevent us from successfully compiling programs that attempt to do most of these things.)

We Shouldn't Change the Semantics of a Feature

We shouldn't change the **semantics**—i.e., the intention, or meaning—of a feature. For example:

- If the `Print` method of a base class such as `Student` is intended to display the values of all of an object's attributes on the computer screen, then the `Print` method of a derived class such as `GraduateStudent` shouldn't, for example, be overridden so that it directs all of its output to a file instead.

- If the `name` attribute of a base class such as `Person` is intended to store a person's name in "last name, first name" order, then the `name` attribute of a derived class such as `Student` should be used in the same fashion.

We Can't Eliminate Features

We can't physically eliminate features, nor should we effectively eliminate them by ignoring them. To attempt to do so would break the spirit of the "is a" hierarchy. By definition, inheritance requires that all features of all base classes of a class A must also apply to class A itself in order for A to truly be a proper derived class. If a `GraduateStudent` could eliminate the `degreeSought` attribute that it inherits from `Student`, for example, is a `GraduateStudent` *really* a `Student` after all?

We Can't Change the Type of a Property

A derived class can override a base class property, but the type of the property must remain the same as the base class version of that property. For example, if the `Person` class declared a `BirthDate` property of type `string`:

```
public class Person
{
  // Details omitted.

  // Base class introduces a property.
  public virtual string BirthDate {
    get {
      // details omitted.
    }
  }
}
```

then a `Student` class that derives from `Person` could *not,* in overriding the `BirthDate` property, change its type to, say, `DateTime`:

```
public class Student : Person
{
  // Details omitted.
```

```
// Derived class overrides a property, attempting to modify its type in the
// process.
public override DateTime BirthDate {  // this won't compile
  get {
    // details omitted.
  }
 }
}
```

If we tried to compile the Student class, the following compiler error would occur:

```
error CS0508: 'Student.BirthDate' cannot change return type when overriding
inherited member 'Person.BirthDate'
```

> *It turns out that a derived class can change the type of a base class property by* **hiding,** *rather than overriding, the base class property. We'll discuss property and method hiding in Chapter 13.*

We Shouldn't Attempt to Change a Method Header

For example, if the Print method inherited by the Student class from the Person class has the header public void Print(), then the Student class can't change this method to accept an argument, say, public void Print(int noOfCopies). To do so is to create a different method entirely, due to another C# language feature known as **overloading,** discussed next.

Overloading

Overloading is a language mechanism supported by non-OO languages like C as well as by OO languages like C#. Overloading is sometimes mistakenly confused with overriding because the two mechanisms have similar names, but in reality overloading is a wholly different concept.

Overloading allows two or more ***different*** methods belonging to the ***same*** class to have the ***same*** name as long as they have ***different argument signatures*** (as defined in Chapter 4). For example, the Student class may legitimately define the following five different Print methods:

```
void Print(string fileName) - a single parameter
void Print(int detailLevel) - a different parameter type from above
void Print(int detailLevel, string fileName) - two parameters
```

```
int Print(string reportTitle, int maxPages) - two different parameter types
bool Print() - no parameters
```

and hence the Print method is said to be overloaded. Note that all five of the signatures differ in terms of their argument signatures:

- The first takes a single string as an argument.

- The second takes a single int.

- The third takes two arguments—an int and a string.

- The fourth takes two arguments—a string and an int (although these are the same parameter types as in the previous signature, they are in a different order).

- The fifth takes no arguments at all.

So, all five of these headers represent valid, different methods, and all can coexist happily within the Student class without any complaints from the compiler! We can pick and choose among which of these five "flavors" of Print method we'd like a Student object to perform based on what form of message we send to a Student object:

```
Student s = new Student();

// Calling the version that takes a single string argument.
s.Print("output.rpt");

// Calling the version that takes a single int argument.
s.Print(2);

// Calling the version that takes two arguments, an int and a string.
s.Print(2, "output.rpt");

// etc.
```

The compiler is able to unambiguously match up which version of the Print method is being called in each instance based on the argument signatures.

This example also hints at why only the parameter types and their order, and neither the ***names*** of the parameters nor the ***return type*** of the method, are relevant when determining whether a new method can be added: because these latter aspects of a method aren't evident in a message. This is best illustrated with an example.

We already know that we can't, for example, introduce the following additional method as a sixth method of Student:

```
bool Print(int levelOfDetail)
```

because its argument signature—a single int—duplicates the argument signature of an existing method:

```
int Print(int detailLevel)
```

despite the fact that both the return type (bool vs. int) and the parameter names are different in the two headers.

Let's suppose for a moment that we *were* permitted to introduce the bool Print(int levelOfDetail) header as a sixth "flavor" of Print method for the Student class. If the compiler were to then see a message in client code of the form

```
    s.Print(3);
```

it would be unable to sort out which of these two methods were to be invoked, because all we see in a message like this is (a) the method name and (b) the argument type (an integer literal in this case). So, to make life simple, the compiler prevents this type of ambiguity from arising by preventing classes from declaring methods with identical signatures in the first place.

Constructors, which as we learned in Chapter 4 are a special type of function member used to instantiate objects, are commonly overloaded. Here is an example of a class that provides several overloaded constructors:

```
public class Student
{
  private string name;
  private string ssn;
  private int age;
  // etc.

  // Constructor #1.
  public Student() {
    // Assign default values to selected attributes, if desired.
    ssn = "?";
    // Those which aren't explicitly initialized in the constructor will
    // automatically assume
    // the zero-equivalent value for their respective type.
  }
```

```
// Constructor #2.
public Student(string s) {
   ssn = s;
}

// Constructor #3.
public Student(string s, string n, int i) {
   ssn = s;
   name = n;
   age = i;
}

   // etc. -- other methods omitted from this example
}
```

By providing different "flavors" of constructor, we've made this class more flexible by giving client code a variety of constructors to choose from.

The ability to overload method names allows us to create an entire family of similarly named methods that do essentially the same job, but which accept different types of arguments. Think back to Chapter 1 where we introduced the Write method, which is used to display printed output to the console. As it turns out, there is not one, but rather *many* Write methods; each one accepts a different argument type (Write(int), Write(string), Write(double), etc.). Using a single, overloaded Write method is much simpler and neater than having to use separate methods named WriteString, WriteInt, WriteDouble, and so on.

Note that there is no such thing as "attribute overloading"; that is, if a class tries to declare two attributes with the same name:

```
public class SomeClass
{
   private string foo;
   private int foo;
   // etc.
```

the compiler will generate an error message:

```
   SomeClass.cs(5,15): error CS0102: The class 'SomeClass' already contains
 a definition for 'foo'
```

A Few Words About Multiple Inheritance

So far, the inheritance hierarchies we've looked at are known informally as **"single inheritance"** hierarchies, because any particular class in the hierarchy may only have a single direct base class (immediate ancestor). In the hierarchy shown in Figure 5-9, for example,

- Classes marked B, C, J, and I all have the single direct base class A;

- D, E, and F have the single direct base B; and

- G and H have the single direct base E.

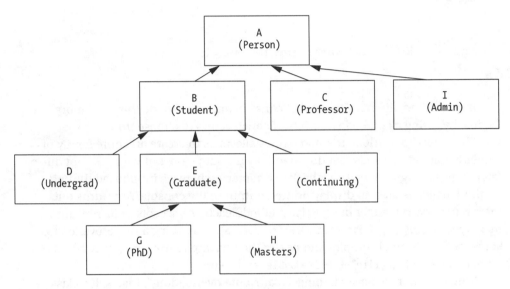

Figure 5-9. A sample single inheritance hierarchy

If we for some reason find ourselves needing to meld together the characteristics of two different base classes to create a hybrid third class, **multiple inheritance** may seem to be the answer. With multiple (as opposed to single) inheritance, any given class in a class hierarchy is permitted to have two or more classes as immediate ancestors.

For example, we have a Professor class representing people who teach classes, and a Student class representing people who take classes. What might we do if we have a professor who wants to enroll in a class via the SRS? Or, a student—most likely a graduate student—who has been asked to teach an undergraduate-level course? In order to accurately represent either of these two people as objects, we would need to be able to combine the features of the Professor class with those of the Student class—a hybrid ProfessorStudent. This might be portrayed in our class hierarchy as shown in Figure 5-10.

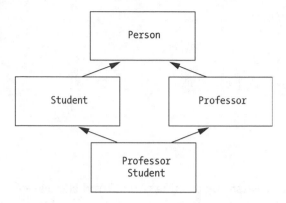

Figure 5-10. Multiple inheritance permits a derived class to have multiple immediate ancestors.

On the surface, this seems quite handy. However, there are many complications inherent with multiple inheritance; so many, in fact, that the C# language designers chose not to support multiple inheritance. Instead, they've provided an alternative mechanism for handling the requirement of creating an object with a "split personality": that is, one that can behave like two or more different real-world entities. This mechanism involves the notion of **interfaces,** and will be explored in detail in Chapter 7. Therefore, if you're primarily interested in object concepts only as they pertain to the C# language, you may wish to skip the rest of this section. If, on the other hand, you're curious as to why multiple inheritance is so tricky, then please read on.

Here's the problem with what we've done in the previous example. We learned that, with inheritance, a derived class automatically inherits the attributes and methods of its base. What about when we have two or more direct base classes? If these base classes have no overlaps in terms of their attribute names or method signatures, then we are fine. But, what if the direct base classes in question

- Have methods with the same signature, but with *different* code body implementations?

- Have *identical attributes* (name and type the same)?

- Have attributes with identical names, but with *different* types?

Let's explore these situations with a simple example.

First, say that we created a trivially simple Person class that declares one attribute, name, and one method, GetDescription, as shown here:

```
public class Person
{
  string name;

  public virtual string GetDescription() {
    return name;
    // e.g., "John Doe"
  }
}
```

Later on, we decide to specialize Person by creating two derived classes—Professor and Student—which each add a few attributes, as well as overriding the GetDescription method to take advantage of their newly added attributes, as follows:

```
public class Student : Person
{
  // We add two attributes, major and id.
  string major;
  int id;  // a unique Student ID number

  // Override this method as inherited from Person.
  public override string GetDescription() {
    return name + " [" + major + "; " + id + "]";
    // e.g., "Mary Smith [Math; 10273]"
  }
}

public class Professor : Person
{
  // We add two attributes, title and id.
  // (Note that id has the same name, but a different
  // data type, as the id attribute of Student.)
  string title;
  string id;  // a unique Employee ID number

  // Override this method as inherited from Person.
  public override string GetDescription() {
    return name + " [" + title + "; " + id + "]";
    // e.g., "Harry Henderson [Chairman; A723]"
  }
}
```

Note that both derived classes happen to have added an attribute named id but that in the case of the Student class, it's declared to be of type int and in

Professor, of type `string`. Also, note that both classes have overridden the `GetDescription` method differently, to take advantage of each class's own unique attributes.

At some future point in the evolution of this system, we determine the need to represent a single object as both a `Student` and a `Professor` simultaneously, and so we create the hybrid class `ProfessorStudent` as a derived class of both `Student` and `Professor`. We don't particularly want to add any attributes or methods; we just want to meld together the characteristics of both base classes, so we'd ideally like to declare `ProfessorStudent` as follows:

```
// * * * Important Note:  this is not permitted in C#!!! * * *
class ProfessorStudent : Professor and Student
{
  // It's OK to leave a class body empty; the class itself is not
  // really 'empty', because it inherits the features of its
  // base classes.
}
```

But, we encounter several roadblocks to doing so.

First of all, we have an attribute name clash. If we were to simple-mindedly inherit all of the attributes of both `Professor` and `Student`, we'd wind up with the items shown in Table 5-1.

Table 5-1. Multiple Inheritance Introduces Many Ambiguities with Respect to Derived Class Features

Attribute	Notes
string name;	Inherited from Student, this in turn inherited it from Person.
string ssn;	Inherited from Student, this in turn inherited it from Person.
string major;	Inherited from Student.
int id;	Inherited from Student; this conflicts with the string id attribute inherited from Professor (the compiler won't allow both to coexist).
string name;	Inherited from Professor, which in turn inherited it from Person; a duplicate! The compiler won't allow this.
string ssn;	Inherited from Professor, which in turn inherited it from Person; another duplicate! The compiler won't allow this.
string title;	Inherited from Professor.
string id;	Inherited from Professor; this conflicts with the int id attribute inherited from Student (the compiler won't allow both to coexist).

Making a compiler intelligent enough to automatically resolve and eliminate true duplicates, such as the second copy of the `name` and `ssn` attributes, wouldn't be too difficult a task; but, what about `int id` vs. `string id`? There's no way for the compiler to know which one to eliminate; and, indeed, we really shouldn't eliminate either, as they represent different information items. Our only choice would be to go back to either the `Student` class or the `Professor` class (or both) and rename their respective `id` attributes to be perhaps `studentId` and/or `employeeId`, to make it clear that the attributes represent different information items. Then, `ProfessorStudent` could inherit both without any problems. If we don't have control over the source code for at least one of these base classes, however, then we're in trouble.

Another problem we face is that the compiler will be confused as to which version of the `GetDescription` method we should inherit. Chances are that we'll want neither, because neither one takes full advantage of the other class's attributes; but even if we did wish to use one of the base class's versions of the method versus the other, we'd have to invent some way of informing the compiler of which one we wanted to inherit, or else we'd be forced to override `GetDescription` in the `ProfessorStudent` class.

This is just a simple example, but it nonetheless illustrates why multiple inheritance can be so cumbersome to take advantage of in an OO programming language.

Three Distinguishing Features of an Object-Oriented Programming Language, Revisited

In Chapter 3, we called out three key mechanisms that are required of a programming language in order to be considered truly object-oriented. We've now defined *two* of the three features required of a true OO language:

- (Programmer creation of) User-defined types—discussed in Chapter 3

- *Inheritance*—discussed in this chapter

- Polymorphism

All that remains is to discuss **polymorphism,** one of the subjects of an upcoming chapter (Chapter 7, to be precise). We're going to take a bit of a detour first, however, to discuss what we can do to gather up and organize groups of objects as we create them through the use of a special type of object called a **collection.**

Summary

In this chapter, you've learned

- That an ***association*** describes a relationship between classes—that is, a potential relationship between objects of two particular types/classes—whereas a ***link*** describes an actual relationship between two objects belonging to these classes.

- That we define the ***multiplicity*** of an association between classes X and Y in terms of how many objects of type X can be linked to a given object of type Y, and vice versa. Possible multiplicities are one-to-one (1:1), one-to-many (1:m), and many-to-many (m:m). In all of these cases, the involvement of the objects at either end of the relationship may be optional or mandatory.

- That an ***aggregation*** is a special type of association that implies containment.

- How to derive new classes based on existing classes through ***inheritance,*** and what the do's and don'ts are when deriving these new classes. Specifically, how we can (a) extend a base class by adding features or (b) specialize a base class by overriding methods.

- How class hierarchies develop over time, and what we can do to try to avoid ripple effects to our application as the class hierarchy changes with evolving requirements.

- How overloading can be used to create multiple methods with the same name but with different argument signatures.

- Why multiple inheritance can be so troublesome to implement in an OO language.

Exercises

1. Given the following pairs of classes, what associations might exist between them from the perspective of the CRRS case study described in Appendix B?

    - Employee—ConferenceRoom

    - Employee—Meeting

2. Go back to your solution for exercise No. 3 at the end of Chapter 2. For all of the classes you suggested, list the pairwise associations that you might envision occurring between them.

3. If the class `FeatureFilm` were defined to have the following methods:

```
public void Update(Actor a, string title);
public void Update(Actor a, Actor b, string title);
public void Update(string topic, string title);
```

which of the following additional headers would be allowed by the compiler?

```
public bool Update(string category, string theater);
public bool Update(string title, Actor a);
public void Update(Actor b, Actor a, string title);
public void Update(Actor a, Actor b);
```

4. Given the following simplistic code, which illustrates overloading, overriding, and straight inheritance of methods:

```
class Vehicle
{
  string name;

  public virtual void Fuel(string fuelType) {
    // details omitted ...
  }

  public virtual bool Fuel(string fuelType, int amount) {
    // details omitted ...
  }
}

class Automobile : Vehicle
{
  public virtual void Fuel(string fuelType, string timeFueled) {
    // details omitted ...
  }

  public override bool Fuel(string fuelType, int amount) {
    // ...
  }
}
```

```
class Truck : Vehicle
{
  public override void Fuel(string fuelType) {
    // ...
  }
}

class SportsCar : Automobile
{
  public override void Fuel(string fuelType) {
    // ...
  }

  public override void Fuel(string fuelType, string timeFueled) {
    // ...
  }
}

// Client code:

Truck t = new Truck();
SportsCar sc = new SportsCar();
```

how many different `Fuel` method signatures would each of the four classes recognize?

5. Given the following simplistic classes:

```
class FarmAnimal
{
  string name;

  public virtual string Name {
    get {
      return name;
    }
    set {
      name = value;
    }
  }

  public virtual void MakeSound() {
    Console.WriteLine(Name + " makes a sound ...");
  }
}
```

```
class Cow : FarmAnimal
{
  public override void MakeSound() {
    Console.WriteLine(Name + " goes Moooooo ...");
  }
}

class Horse : FarmAnimal
{
  public override string Name {
    set {
      base.Name = value + " [a Horse]";
    }
  }
}
```

what would be printed by the following client code?

```
Cow c = new Cow();
Horse h = new Horse();
c.Name = "Elsie";
h.Name = "Mr. Ed";
c.MakeSound();
h.MakeSound();
```

CHAPTER 6
Collections of Objects

You **LEARNED ABOUT** the process of creating objects based on class definitions, a process known as instantiation, in Chapter 3. When we're only creating a few objects, we can afford to declare individualized reference variables for these objects: `Students s1, s2, s3,` perhaps, or `Professors profA, profB, profC.` But, at other times, individualized reference variables are impractical.

- Sometimes, there will be too many objects, as when creating `Course` objects to represent the hundreds of courses in a university's course catalog.

- Worse yet, we may not even **_know_** how many objects of a particular type there will be in advance. With our Student Registration System, for example, we may create a new `Student` object each time a new student logs on for the first time.

Fortunately, OOPLs solve this problem by providing a special category of object called a **collection** that is used to hold and organize other objects. In this chapter, you'll learn about

- The properties and behaviors of some common collection types

- How collections enable us to model very sophisticated real-world concepts or situations

- How we can define our own collection types

What Are Collections?

We'd like a way to gather up objects as they are created so that we can manage them as a group and operate on them collectively, along with referring to them individually when necessary. For example:

- A `Professor` object may need to step through all `Student` objects registered for a particular `Course` that the professor is teaching in order to compute their grades.

- The Student Registration System (SRS) application as a whole may need to step through all of the Course objects in the current schedule of classes to determine which of them don't yet have any students registered for them, possibly to cancel these courses.

We use a special type of object called a **collection** to group other objects. A collection object can hold/contain multiple references to some other type of object. Think of a collection like an egg carton, and the objects it holds like the eggs! Both are objects, but with decidedly different properties.

Because collections are implemented as objects, this implies that

- Collections must be instantiated before they can first be used.

- Collections are defined by classes that in turn define methods for "getting" and "setting" their contents.

- By virtue of being objects, OO collections are encapsulated, and hence take full advantage of information hiding.

Let's discuss each of these three matters in turn.

Collections Must Be Instantiated Before They Can First Be Used

We can't merely declare a collection:

```
CollectionType c;
```

For example:

```
ArrayList c;
```

All this does is to declare a reference variable of type *CollectionType*. Until we "hand" c a *CollectionType* **object** to **refer** to, c is said to have the value null.

> ArrayList *is one of C#'s predefined collection types, defined by the .NET Framework Class Library (FCL). We'll introduce the* ArrayList *class in this chapter, and we'll then go into greater detail about* ArrayLists, *along with several other collection types, in Chapter 13.*

We have to take the distinct step of using the new operator to actually create an empty *CollectionType* object in memory, as follows:

```
c = new CollectionType();
```

For example:

```
c = new ArrayList();
```

Think of the newly created *CollectionType* object as an ***empty*** "egg carton," and the reference variable c as the handle that allows us to locate and access (reference) this egg carton whenever we'd like.

Then, as we instantiate objects ("eggs"), we'll place ***their references*** into the various egg carton compartments:

```
Student s = new Student();
// Pseudocode.
c.Add(s);
```

So, rather than thinking of the objects as eggs that are physically placed inside of the egg carton compartments, we should really think of the objects as balloons whose strings are tied inside the egg carton compartments, as illustrated in Figure 6-1. That is, the objects themselves live physically ***outside*** of the collection, but can be located through their references, which are stored ***within*** the collection.

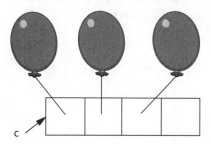

Figure 6-1. A collection organizes object references.

Thus, perhaps a more appropriate analogy than a collection as an egg carton would be that of a collection as an address book: we make an entry in the address book (collection) for each of the persons (objects) that we wish to contact, but the actual persons themselves are physically remote (see Figure 6-2).

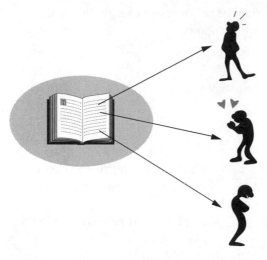

*Figure 6-2. A collection **references** objects, which live separately in memory.*

Note that C# collections can also hold references to value-type variables (int, float, etc.) because in the C# language, value-type variables are actually implemented as objects. This is in contrast to Java, where simple data types— int, float, etc.—are **not** objects, and hence cannot be stored "as is" in Java collections.

Collections Are Defined by Classes

Here is a code snippet that illustrates the use of a collection in C#; we use a bit of pseudocode here to emphasize the common features of collections.

```
// Instantiate a collection object (pseudocode).
CollectionType x = new CollectionType();

// Create a few Student objects.
Student a = new Student();
Student b = new Student();
Student c = new Student();

// Store all three students in the collection by calling the appropriate
// method for adding objects to the collection ...
x.Add(a);
x.Add(b);
x.Add(c);

// ... and then retrieve the first one.
x.Retrieve(0); // we typically start counting at 0.
```

OO Collections Are Encapsulated

We don't need to know the private details of how object references are stored internally to a specific type of collection in order to use the collection properly; we only need to know a collection's public features—in particular, its method headers and properties—in order to choose an appropriate collection type for a particular situation and to use it effectively.

> *This is a tiny bit misleading: in the case of* **huge** *collections, it* **is** *helpful to know a little bit about the inner workings of various collection types so as to choose the one that is most efficient; we'll consider this matter further in Chapter 13.*

Virtually all collections, regardless of type and regardless of the programming language in which they are implemented, provide, at a minimum, methods for

- Adding object (reference)s

- Removing object (reference)s

- Retrieving specific individual object (reference)s

- Iterating through the object (reference)s in some predetermined order

- Getting a count of the number of object (reference)s in the container

- Answering a true/false question as to whether a particular object is referenced by the container or not

> *Throughout this chapter, we'll talk casually about manipulating* **objects** *in collections, but please remember that, with C#, what we really mean is that we're manipulating object* **references.**

Arrays As Simple Collections

One simple type of collection that you may already be familiar with from your work with other programming languages is the **array.** We can think of an array as a series of compartments, with each compartment sized appropriately for whatever data type the array as a whole is intended to hold. Arrays typically hold items of like type: for example, int(eger)s, or char(acter)s, or, in an OO language, object references: Student objects, or Course objects, or Professor objects, etc.

Declaring and Instantiating Arrays

In C#, arrays are objects (as are all C# collections). The Array class of the System namespace is the basis for all C# arrays. The official C# syntax for declaring that a variable x will serve as a reference to an array containing items of a particular data type is as follows:

```
datatype[] x;
```

For example:

```
int[] x;
```

which is to be read "int(eger) array x" (or, alternatively, "x is an array of ints").

Because C# arrays are objects, they must be instantiated using the new operator; we also specify how many items the array is capable of holding, i.e., its size in terms of its number of compartments, when we first instantiate the array. Here is a code snippet that illustrates the somewhat unusual syntax for constructing an array; in this particular example, we're constructing an array designed to hold Student object references, depicted in Figure 6-3:

```
// Here, we are instantiating an array object that will be used to store 20
// Student object references, and are maintaining a handle on the array object
// via reference variable x.
Student[] x = new Student[20];
```

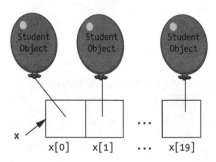

Figure 6-3. Array x *is designed to hold up to 20* Student *references.*

This use of the new operator is unusual, in that we don't see a typical constructor call (with optional arguments being passed in via parentheses) following the new keyword, the way we do when we're constructing other types of objects. Despite its unconventional appearance, however, this line of code is indeed instantiating a new Array object, just the same.

Accessing Individual Array Elements

Individual array elements are accessed by appending square brackets, enclosing the index of the element to be accessed, to the end of the array name. This syntax is known as an **element access expression**. Note that when we refer to individual items in an array based on their position, or **index,** relative to the beginning of the array, we start counting at 0. (As it turns out, the vast majority of collection types in C# as well as in other languages are **zero-based**.) So, the items stored in array Student[ ] x in our previous example would be individually referenced as x[0], x[1], . . . , x[19].

Consider the following code snippet:

```
int[] data = new int[3];
data[0] = 4; // setting an element's value
int temp = data[1]; // getting an element's value
```

In the first line of code, we're declaring and instantiating an int(eger) array of size 3. In the second line of code, we're assigning the int value 4 to the "zeroeth" (*first*) element of the array. In the last line of code, we're obtaining the value of the *second* element of the array (element number 1) and assigning it to an int variable named temp.

In the next snippet, we're populating an array named squareRoot of type double to serve as a look-up table of square root values, where the value stored in cell squareRoot[i] represents the square root of i. (We declare the array to be one element larger than we need it to be so that we may skip over the zeroeth cell; for ease of look-up, we want the square root of 1 to be contained in cell 1 of the array, not in cell 0.)

```
double[] squareRoot = new double[11];  // we'll effectively ignore cell 0

// Note that we're skipping cell 0.
for (int i = 1; i <= 10; i++) {
  squareRoot[i] = Math.Sqrt(i);
}

Console.WriteLine("The square root of 5 is " + squareRoot[5]);
```

> *The* Math.Sqrt() *method computes the square root of a* double *argument passed to the method; we're passing in an* int *in the preceding example, which automatically gets cast to a double. We'll revisit the* Math *class again in Chapter 7.*

Initializing Array Contents

Values can be assigned to individual elements of an array using indexes as shown earlier, or we can initialize an array with a complete set of values when the array is first instantiated. In the latter case, initial values are provided as a comma-separated list enclosed in braces. This syntax replaces the normal right-hand side of the array instantiation statement. For example, the following code instantiates and initializes a three-element string array:

```
string[] names = { "Lisa", "Jackson", "Zachary" };
```

Note that C# automatically counts the number of initial values that we're providing, and sizes the array appropriately. The preceding approach is much more concise than the equivalent alternative shown here:

```
string[] names = new string[3];
names[0] = "Lisa";
names[1] = "Jackson";
names[2] = "Zachary";
```

although the result in both cases is the same: the zeroeth (first) element of the array will reference the string "Lisa", the next element will reference "Jackson", and so on.

Note that it isn't possible to "bulk load" an array in this fashion ***after*** the array has been instantiated, as a separate line of code; that is, the following won't work:

```
string[] names = new string[5];
// This next line won't compile.
names = {"Steve", "Jacquie", "Chloe", "Shylow", "Baby Grode" };
```

If a set of comma-separated initial values aren't provided when an array is first instantiated, the elements of the array are automatically initialized to their zero-equivalent values. For example, int[] data as declared earlier would be initialized to contain 3 integer zeroes (0s), and double[] squareRoot as declared earlier would be initialized to contain 11 floating point zeroes (0.0s). If we declare and instantiate an array intended to hold references to objects, as in

```
Student[] studentBody = new Student[100];
```

then we'd wind up with an Array object containing 100 null values (recall that null, a C# keyword, is the zero equivalent value for an object reference). If we think of an array as a simple type of collection, and we in turn think of a collection as an "egg carton," then we've just created an empty egg carton with 100 egg compartments, but no "eggs."

Manipulating Arrays of Objects

To fill our Student array with values other than null, we'd have to individually store Student object references in each cell of the array. For example, if we wanted to create brand-new Student objects to store in our array, we may write code as follows:

```
studentBody[0] = new Student();
studentBody[1] = new Student();
// etc.
```

or alternatively:

```
Student s = new Student();
studentBody[0] = s;
// Reuse s!
s = new Student();
studentBody[1] = s;
```

In the latter example, note that we're "recycling" the same reference variable, s, to create many different Student objects. This works because, after each instantiation, we store a handle on the newly created object in an array compartment, thus allowing s to let go of *its* handle on that same object, as depicted in Figure 6-4. This technique is used frequently, with ***all*** collection types, in virtually all OO programming languages.

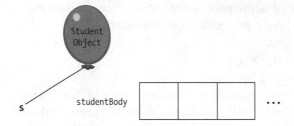

A Student object is created and handed to s ...

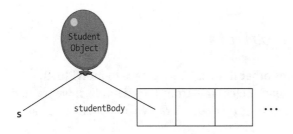

... s hands the object's handle off to the array ...

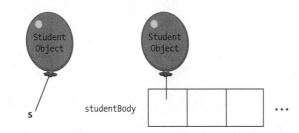

... thus freeing up s to take hold of another new Student!

Figure 6-4. Handing new objects one by one into a collection

When we've created an array to hold objects, as we did for the studentBody array previously, then assuming we've populated the array with object references, an indexed reference to any populated compartment in the array represents an object reference, and can be used accordingly:

```
studentBody[0].GetName();   // We're using dot notation to call a method on
                            // studentBody[0], the first Student object
                            // reference in the array.
```

The syntax of this message may seem a bit peculiar at first, so let's study it a bit more carefully. Since studentBody is declared to be an array capable of holding Student object references, then studentBody[*n*] represents the contents of the *n*th compartment of the array—namely, a reference to a Student object! So, the "dot" in the preceding message is separating an expression representing an object reference from the method call being made on that object, and is no different than any of the other dot notation messages that we've seen up until now.

By using a collection such as an array, we don't have to invent a different variable name for each Student object, which means we can step through them all quite easily using a for loop. Here is the syntax for doing so with an array:

```
// Step through all 100 compartments of the array.
for (int i = 0; i <= 99; i++) {
  // Access the "ith" element of the array -- a Student object (reference) -- so
  // that we may print each student's name in turn; in effect, we're printing
  // a student roster.
  Console.WriteLine(studentBody[i].GetName());
}
```

> *We'll examine a more sophisticated way of stepping through collections in general, using a special type of object called an IEnumerator, in Chapter 13.*

Note that we have to take care when stepping through an array to avoid "land mines" due to empty compartments. That is, if we're executing the preceding for loop, but the array isn't completely filled with Student objects, then our invocation of the GetName method will fail as soon as we hit the first empty/null compartment, because in essence we'd be trying to talk to an object that wasn't there! If we modify our code by inserting an if test to guard against null values, however, we'd be OK:

```
// Step through all 100 compartments of the array.
for (int i = 0; i <= 99; i++) {
  // Avoiding "land mines"!
  if (studentBody[i] != null) {
    Console.WriteLine(studentBody[i].GetName());
  }
}
```

> *We'll learn in Chapter 13 that this type of failure—namely, attempting to talk to a nonexistent object, or **null reference**—results in an **exception** being thrown.*

Other Array Considerations

Some other facts concerning C# arrays:

- ***Once the size of an array has been declared, its size can't be changed.*** This can become an issue in situations where we don't know what the size of an array should be at the time that we're declaring it. For this reason, arrays aren't always the best choice of collection type for a given application, as we'll discuss later in this chapter.

- ***We can't mix and match data types in an array;*** we're constrained to inserting values whose data type matches the type with which the array was first declared. For instance, we can't assign a `string` as an element of an integer array. The only exception is that if we can cast some value of type A into type B, then we can of course make such an assignment. For example, if we wish to assign the value of a `double` variable to an element of a `float` array, we would cast the variable into a `float` and then assign it to the array element as shown here:

```
float[] a = new float[10];
double d = 10.37;
a[0] = (float) d;  // note cast
```

Multidimensional Arrays

So far we've been discussing one-dimensional arrays. It's also possible to declare and use arrays of two or more dimensions. There are two types of **multidimensional arrays—rectangular** and **jagged.**

Rectangular Arrays

A rectangular array is one in which every row has the same number of columns:

3	2	37	8	4
7	4	9	0	3
1	11	99	13	5

This represents a three-row by five-column two-dimensional rectangular integer array.

The syntax for declaring and instantiating a two-dimensional rectangular array is as follows:

```
ArrayType[,] arrayName = new ArrayType[numRows, numCols];
```

For example:

```
double[,] values = new double[3, 5];  // three rows of five columns each
```

We place one comma between the brackets on the left-hand side to signal that the array will have two dimensions, and must then specify the size of each of the two dimensions, separated by a comma, on the right-hand side. For a three-dimensional rectangular array, we would use two commas between the brackets on the left-hand side, and would specify the sizes of three dimensions on the right-hand side:

```
ArrayType[,,] arrayName = new ArrayType[dim1, dim2, dim3];
```

and so forth.

To access the elements of a multidimensional rectangular array, we use indexes, but now must specify an index for each dimension of the element to be accessed. For example, consider the following code snippet, in which we instantiate a two-dimensional array of type double:

```
double[,] data = new double[2, 3];
data[0, 1] = 23.4;  // insert value into the FIRST row, SECOND column
// details omitted ...
double temp = data[1, 2]; // retrieve value from the SECOND row, THIRD column
```

The array has two rows and three columns. In the second line of code, the element in the *first* row and *second* column ([0, 1]—remember that we start counting from 0) of the array is assigned the value 23.4. In the third line, we're accessing the value of the element in the second row and third column of the array, and assigning that value to a double variable named temp.

The elements of a multidimensional rectangular array can be initialized at the time that the array is declared by placing the initial values in braces { ... }, with one set of braces for each dimension of the array. For example, the following syntax would create and initialize a two-row, three-column array of integer values:

```
int[,] data = { {7, 22, 3},
                {48, 5, 10} };
```

Jagged Arrays

A jagged array is one where each row can have a different number of entries:

14	3	85	2
100	11		
3	24	106	

This represents a three-row, two-dimensional jagged integer array.

The syntax for declaring a jagged multidimensional array is different from that of a rectangular array.

- A separate set of empty braces is provided in the declaration for every dimension in the array: for a two-dimensional jagged array, we use two sets of braces; for a three-dimensional jagged array, we use three; etc. For example, the following syntax would declare a two-dimensional jagged string array:

```
string[][] names;  // note two sets of empty braces
```

- In the array instantiation statement, we only specify the size of the first dimension of such an array. For example, the following syntax would instantiate a two-dimensional jagged string array with three rows, allowing for a variable number of columns per row:

```
string[][] names = new string[3][];
```

In effect, when we create a two-dimensional jagged array, we have in essence created an array of one-dimensional arrays of varying sizes, as illustrated in Figure 6-5.

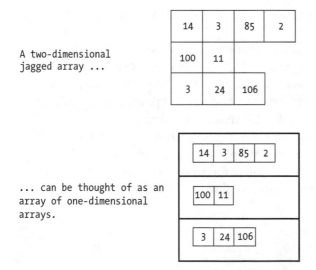

Figure 6-5. A jagged two-dimensional array as an array of one-dimensional arrays

The next step in the process is to initialize the length of each row in the array; for example:

```
names[0] = new string[4];   // first row has 4 columns (numbered 0 ... 3)
names[1] = new string[2];   // second row has 2 columns (numbered 0 ... 1)
names[2] = new string[3];   // third row has 3 columns (numbered 0 ... 2)
```

To access the elements of a multidimensional jagged array, we use indexes with a separate set of brackets to specify each dimension. For example, to assign a value to the element in the second row and second column of the names array, we'd use the following syntax:

```
names[1][1] = "Mel";
```

It's also possible to initialize the elements of a multidimensional jagged array when the array is first declared, but the syntax is a bit complicated. The elements of every one-dimensional array within the multidimensional array can be initialized by placing the initial values inside braces when the one-dimensional array is declared. The new keyword must be used, and the array type must also be specified. For example, the following code creates and initializes a two-dimensional jagged integer array that has three columns in its first row and four columns in the second row:

```
int[][] data = new int[2][];
data[0] = new int[] { 17, 3, 24 };
data[1] = new int[] { 6, 37, 108, 99 };
```

More Sophisticated Collection Types

In an OO language, there are typically many different types of collections available to us as programmers, arrays being arguably the most primitive. There are several problems with using an array to hold a collection of objects:

- It's often hard for us to predict in advance the number of objects that a collection will need to hold—e.g., how many students are going to enroll this semester? However, as mentioned earlier, arrays require that such a determination be made at the time they are first instantiated and, once sized, can't be expanded. So, to use an array in such a situation, we'd have to make it big enough to handle the worst-case scenario, which isn't very efficient. On the other hand, when we do know how many items we're going to need to store—say, the abbreviated names of the 12 months in a year—an array might be a fine choice.

- We also talked earlier about the "land mine" issues inherent in arrays.

Fortunately, OO languages provide a wide variety of collection types besides arrays for us to choose from, each of which has its own unique properties and advantages. Let's talk about the general properties of three basic collection types found in most OO languages:

- Ordered lists

- Sets

- Dictionaries

Then, in Chapter 13, we'll illustrate some specific C# implementations of these collection types.

Ordered Lists

An ordered list is similar to an array, in that items can be placed in the collection in a particular order and later retrieved in that same order. Specific objects can also be retrieved based on their position in the list; e.g., retrieve the second item. One advantage of an ordered list over an array, however, is that its size doesn't have to be specified at the time that the collection object is first created; an ordered list will automatically grow in size as new items are added (see Figure 6-6). (In fact, virtually all collections besides arrays have this advantage!)

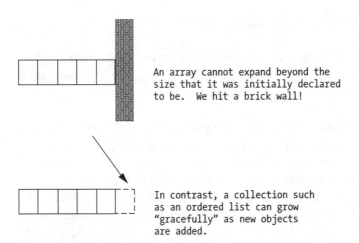

An array cannot expand beyond the size that it was initially declared to be. We hit a brick wall!

In contrast, a collection such as an ordered list can grow "gracefully" as new objects are added.

Figure 6-6. Collections other than arrays grow gracefully as needed.

By default, items are added at the end of an ordered list unless explicit instructions are given to insert a new item somewhere in the middle.

When an item is removed from an ordered list, the "hole" that would have been left behind is automatically closed up as shown in Figure 6-7. This is actually true of most collection types other than arrays, and so we don't generally speaking encounter the "land mine" problem with nonarray collections.

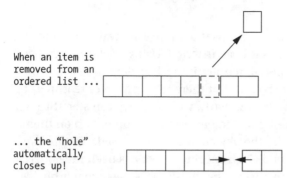

When an item is removed from an ordered list ...

... the "hole" automatically closes up!

Figure 6-7. Collections other than arrays automatically shrink as items are removed.

An example of where we might use an ordered list in building our Student Registration System would be to manage a wait list for a course that had become full. Because the order with which Student objects are added to the list is preserved, we can be fair about selecting students from the wait list in first-come, first-served fashion should seats later become available in the course.

> The C# ArrayList *class is a specific example of an ordered list implementation.*

Sorted Ordered Lists

A **sorted ordered list** is a special ,type of ordered list: when we add an object to a sorted ordered list, the list automatically inserts the object at the appropriate location in the list to maintain sorted order, instead of automatically adding the new object at the end of the list as with a generic ordered list.

With a sorted ordered list, we have to define the basis upon which the objects will be sorted, i.e., we must define a **sort key.** For example, we may wish to maintain a list of Course objects sorted by the value of each Course's courseNo attribute for purposes of displaying the SRS course catalog.

Note that we could accomplish the same goal using a generic ordered list, but then the burden of keeping things sorted properly is on us, the programmers, instead of on the collection object! That is, we'd have to step through the (unsorted) list, comparing a newly added item's value to the value of each object already in the list until we found the correct insertion point, in order to preserve sorted order.

The C# SortedList class is a specific example of a sorted ordered list implementation.

Sets

A set is an ***unordered*** collection, which means that there is no way to ask for a particular item by number once it has been inserted. Using a set is like throwing an assortment of differently colored marbles into a bag: we can reach into the bag to pull the marbles out one by one, but there is no rhyme or reason as to the order with which we pull them out. Similarly, with a set, we can step through the entire collection of objects one-by-one to perform some operation on them; we just can't guarantee in what order the objects will be processed. We can also perform tests to determine whether a given specific object has been previously added to a set or not, just as we can answer the question "Is the blue marble in the bag?" (See Figure 6-8.)

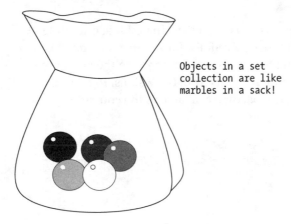

Objects in a set
collection are like
marbles in a sack!

Figure 6-8. A set is an unordered collection.

Note that duplicate object references aren't allowed in a set. If we were to create a set of Student object references, and a particular Student object reference had already been placed in that set, then the same Student object reference couldn't be added to the set a second time; the set would reject it. This isn't true of collections in general, however: if we wanted to, we could add a reference to the same Student object to an ordered list, for example, multiple times (see Figure 6-9).

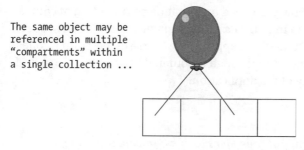

The same object may be referenced in multiple "compartments" within a single collection ...

... UNLESS the collection is a set!

Figure 6-9. Collections other than sets accommodate mutiple references to the same object.

An example of where we might use sets in building our Student Registration System would be to group students according to the academic departments that they are majoring in. Then, if a particular course—say, Biology 216—requires that a student be a Biology major in order to register, it would be a trivial matter to determine if a particular student is a member of the Biology Department set or not.

Dictionaries

A dictionary provides a means for storing each object reference along with a unique look-up key that can later be used to retrieve the object (see Figure 6-10). The key is typically contrived based on one or more of the object's attribute values; for example, in our SRS, a Student object's ID number would make an excellent key, because it's inherently unique for each student. Items in a dictionary can then be quickly retrieved based on this key. Items can typically also be retrieved one by one from a dictionary type collection in ascending key order.

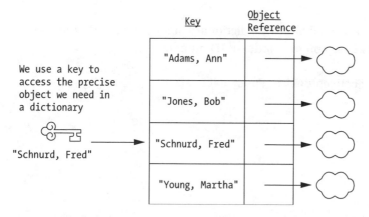

We use a key to access the precise object we need in a dictionary

"Schnurd, Fred"

Figure 6-10. Dictionary collections accommodate direct access by key.

The SRS might use a dictionary, indexed on a unique combination of course number plus section number, to manage its course catalog. With so many courses to keep track of, being able to "pluck" the appropriate Course object from a collection directly (instead of having to step through an ordered list one-by-one to find it) adds greatly to the efficiency of the application.

> *The C# Hashtable class is an example of a specific implementation of a dictionary.*

Referencing the Same Object Simultaneously from Multiple Collections

As we mentioned earlier, when we talk about inserting an object into a collection, what we really mean is that we're inserting a reference to the object, not the object itself. This implies that the same object can be referenced by multiple collections simultaneously. Think of a person as an object, and his or her telephone number as a handle for reaching that person. Now, as we proposed earlier in this chapter, think of an address book as a collection: it's easy to see that the same person's phone number (reference) can be recorded in many different address books (collections) simultaneously.

Now, for an example relevant to the SRS: given the students who are registered to attend a particular course, we may simultaneously maintain the following:

- An ordered list of these students for purposes of knowing who registered first for a follow-on course

- A dictionary that allows us to retrieve a given Student object based on his or her name

- Perhaps even a second SRS-wide dictionary that organizes ***all*** students at the university based on their student ID numbers

This is depicted conceptually in Figure 6-11.

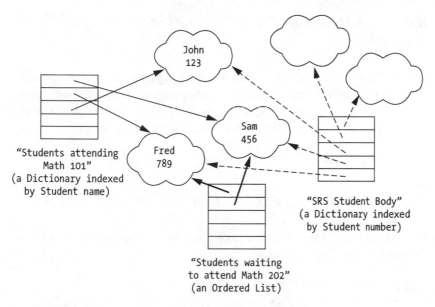

Figure 6-11. A given object may be referenced by multiple collections simultaneously.

Inventing Our Own Collection Types

As mentioned earlier, different types of collections have different properties and behaviors. You must therefore familiarize yourself with the various built-in collection types available for your OO language of choice, and choose the one that is the most appropriate for what you need in a given situation. Or, if none of them suit you, invent your own! This is where we start to get a real sense of the power of an OO language: since we have the ability to invent our own abstract data types, we have free rein to define our own collection types, because these, after all, are merely classes.

There are several ways to create one's own collection type:

- *Approach #1:* We can design a brand-new collection type from scratch.

- *Approach #2:* We can use the techniques that we learned in Chapter 5 to extend a predefined collection class.

- *Approach #3:* We can create a "wrapper" class that encapsulates one of the built-in collection types, to hide some of the details involved with manipulating the collection.

Let's discuss each of these approaches in turn.

Approach #1: Create a Brand-New Collection Type from Scratch

Creating a brand new collection class from scratch is typically quite a bit of work, and since most OO languages provide such a wide range of predefined collection types, it's almost always possible to find a preexisting collection type to use as a starting point, in which case one of the following two approaches would be preferred.

Approach #2: Extend a Predefined Collection Class

In the following example, we extend the built-in ArrayList class to create a collection class called MyStringCollection:

```
using System.Collections;

public class MyStringCollection : ArrayList
{
  // We inherit all of the attributes and methods of a standard ArrayList
  // "as-is," then define a few attributes and methods of our own.
  private string longestStringAddedSoFar;

  // Define a completely new method.
  public void AddAString(string s) {
    // Add the string to the collection using the Add() method that we've
    // inherited from ArrayList.
    Add(s);

    // Pseudocode.
    compare length of s to the length of the longest string inserted so far,
    as recorded by attribute longestStringAddedSoFar;

    // Pseudocode.
    if (s is longer than longestStringAddedSoFar) {
      // Remember this fact!
      longestStringAddedSoFar = s;
    }
  }
}
```

This approach works well if we simply intend to add a few completely ***new*** features (attributes, methods), inheriting the methods and attributes of the parent class "as is." If we plan on ***overriding*** any of the inherited methods, however, we must remember to invoke the parent's version of the code first, via the `base` keyword, as we learned to do in Chapter 5:

```
using System.Collections;

public class MyStringCollection : ArrayList
{
    private string longestStringAddedSoFar;

    // In this case, we choose to override the Add() method of ArrayList.
    public override void Add(Object s) {
        // Add the string to the collection using our parent's version of the
        // Add() method.
        base.Add(s);

        // Pseudocode.
        compare length of s to the length of the longest string inserted so far
        as recorded by attribute longestStringAddedSoFar;

        // Pseudocode.
        if (s is longer than longestStringAddedSoFar) {
            // Remember this fact!
            longestStringAddedSoFar = s;
        }
    }
}
```

By invoking `base.Add()` as the first step in our overridden `Add()` method, we're ensuring that we're doing everything that our parent `ArrayList` class does when adding an item to its internal collection, ***without having to know the details of what is happening behind the scenes,*** before we go on to do something extra: namely, to track the longest such `string` item in this particular case.

Approach #3: Create a "Wrapper" Class to Encapsulate a Predefined Collection Type

By creating such a wrapper class, we are able to hide some of the details involved with manipulating the collection. This is a nice compromise position, and we'll illustrate how one goes about doing this with a specific example.

Let's say we wanted to invent a new type of collection called an `EnrollmentCollection`, to be used by a `Course` object to manage all of its enrolled `Student` objects. We could take advantage of information hiding and encapsulation to "hide" a standard collection object—say, a C# `ArrayList`, which as mentioned

earlier is C#'s implementation of an ordered list collection—inside of our
EnrollmentCollection class, as an attribute. We'd then provide

- Enroll() and Drop() methods for adding or removing a Student from our
  EnrollmentCollection

- An IsEnrolled() method, which will help us to determine if a particular
  Student object is already in the collection (we don't want the same Student
  to enroll twice in the same course)

- A GetTotalEnrollment() method to determine how many students are
  enrolled at any given time

These methods' logic can be as sophisticated as we wish for it to be—the
method bodies are ours to control! The following example uses heavy doses of
pseudocode to give you a sense of what we might actually program these methods to do for us; we'll see plenty of real C# collection manipulation (ArrayLists in
particular) in the SRS code examples in Part Three of the book.

```
public class EnrollmentCollection
{
    // "Hide" a standard C# collection object inside as a private attribute.
    // We'll be storing Student objects in this collection.
    private ArrayList students;

    // Constructor.
    public EnrollmentCollection() {
        // Instantiate the encapsulated ArrayList instance.
        students = new ArrayList();
    }

    // Methods to add a student ...
    public bool Enroll(Student s) {
        // First, make sure that there is room in the class (pseudocode).
        if (adding this student will exceed course capacity) {
            return false;
        }

        // Next, make sure that this student isn't already enrolled
        // in this class (pseudocode).
        if (student is already enrolled) {
            return false;
        }
```

```
  // Verify that the student in question has met
  // all necessary prerequisites (pseudocode).
  if (some prerequisite not satisfied) {
    return false;
  }


  // If we made it to here, all is well!
  // Add the student to the ArrayList by calling its Add() method.
  // (This is an example of delegation, a concept that we discussed
  // in Chapter 4.)
  students.Add(s);
  return true;
}


// ... and to remove a student.
public bool Drop(Student s) {
  // First make sure that the student in question
  // is actually enrolled (pseudocode).
  if (student is not enrolled) {
    return false;
  }


  // Remove the student from the ArrayList by calling the Remove()
  // method.  (Another example of delegation.)
  students.Remove(s);
  return true;
}


public int GetTotalEnrollment() {
  // Access and return the size of the ArrayList.  (Delegation yet again!)
  return students.Count;
}


public bool IsEnrolled(Student s) {
  // More delegation!
  if (students.Contains(s)) {
    return true;
  }
  else {
    return false;
  }
}
}
```

By taking advantage of information hiding to "wrap" a standard collection type inside of one that we've invented, we've allowed for the flexibility to change the internal details of this implementation without disrupting the client code that takes advantage of this collection type. Down the road, we may wish to switch from using an ArrayList to a different predefined collection type, and because we've declared our students collection as a private attribute, we're free to do so, as long as we don't change the headers of our existing public methods.

Now, how do we use this collection class that we've invented? Let's show it in action in the Course class.

```
public class Course
{
    // We declare an attribute to be a collection of type
    // EnrollmentCollection, and will use it to manage
    // all of the students who register for this course.
    private EnrollmentCollection enrolledStudents;

    // Other simple attributes.
    string courseName;
    int credits;
    // etc.

    // Parameterless constructor.
    public Course() {
        enrolledStudents = new EnrollmentCollection();
        // Other details omitted.
    }

    // Other constructors' details omitted.

    public bool Enroll(Student s) {
        // All we have to do is to pass the Student reference
        // in to the collection's enroll method; the collection
        // does all of the hard work! This is another example of
        // delegation.
        enrolledStudents.Enroll(s);
    }

    public bool Drop(Student s) {
        // Ditto!
        enrolledStudents.Drop(s);
    }

    // etc.
}
```

Collections As Method Return Types

Collections provide a way to overcome the limitation that we noted in Chapter 4 about methods only being able to return a single result. If we define a method as having a return type that is a collection type, we can hand back an arbitrary sized collection of object references to the client code that invokes the method.

In the code snippet shown next for the Course class, we provide a GetRegisteredStudents method to enable client code to request a "handle" on the entire collection of Student objects that are registered for a particular course:

```
public class Course
{
  private EnrollmentCollection enrolledStudents;

  // Other details omitted ...

  // The following method returns a reference to an entire collection
  // containing however many students are registered for the course in question.
  EnrollmentCollection GetRegisteredStudents() {
    return enrolledStudents;
  }
}
```

An example of how client code would then use such a method is as follows:

```
// Instantiate a course and several students.
Course c = new Course();
Student s1 = new Student();
Student s2 = new Student();
Student s3 = new Student();

// Enroll the students in the course.
c.Enroll(s1);
c.Enroll(s2);
c.Enroll(s3);

// Now, ask the course to give us a handle on the collection of
// all of its registered students ...
EnrollmentCollection ec = c.GetRegisteredStudents();

// ... and iterate through the collection, printing out a grade report for
// each Student (pseudocode).
for (each Student in EnrollmentCollection) {
  s.PrintGradeReport();
}
```

> Of course, if we return a direct handle on a collection such as enrolledStudents
> to client code, we are giving client code the ability to modify that collection
> (e.g., removing a Student reference). Design considerations may warrant that
> we create a copy of the collection before returning it, so that the original col-
> lection is not modified:

```
public class Course
{
  private EnrollmentCollection enrolledStudents;

  // Other details omitted ...

  // The following method returns a COPY of the Student's enrolledStudents
  // collection, so that client code can't modify the OFFICIAL version.
  EnrollmentCollection GetRegisteredStudents() {
    EnrollmentCollection temp = new EnrollmentCollection();

    // Pseudocode.
    copy contents of enrolledStudents to temp

    return temp;
  }
}
```

> Another way to avoid the problem of allowing client code to modify a collec-
> tion in the previous example would be to have the GetRegisteredStudents
> method return an **enumeration** of the elements contained in the collection.
> We'll discuss how to use enumerators in Chapter 13.

Collections of Supertypes

We said earlier that arrays, as simple collections, contain items that are all of the
same type: all int(egers), for example, or all (references to) Student objects. As it
turns out, this is true of collections in general: we'll typically want to constrain
them to contain similarly typed objects. However, the power of inheritance steps
in to make collections quite versatile.

It turns out that if we declare an array to hold objects of a given type—e.g.,
Person—then we're free to insert objects explicitly declared to be of type Person
or of any types derived from Person—for example, UndergraduateStudent,
GraduateStudent, and Professor. This is due to the "is a" nature of inheritance:

UndergraduateStudent, GraduateStudent, and Professor objects, as subclasses of Person, are simply special cases of Person objects. The C# compiler would therefore be perfectly happy to see code as follows:

```
Person[] people = new Person[100];  // of Person object references

Professor p = new Professor();
UndergraduateStudent s1 = new UndergraduateStudent();
GraduateStudent s2 = new GraduateStudent();

// Add a mixture of professors and students in random order to the array;
// as long as Professor, UndergraduateStudent, and GraduateStudent are
// all derived from Person, the compiler will be happy!
people[0] = s1;
people[1] = p;
people[2] = s2;
// etc.
```

As we'll see when we discuss C# collection types in more detail in Chapter 13, C# collections other than Arrays *actually don't allow us to specify what type of object they will hold when we declare a collection, as illustrated here:*

```
ArrayList list = new ArrayList();  // No type designated!
                                   // ArrayLists hold generic Objects.
```

versus:

```
Student[] s = new Student[100];    // With Arrays, we DO specify a
                                   // type (Student, in this case).
```

Most C# collections are automatically designed to hold objects of type Object, *which as we learned in an earlier chapter is the superclass of all other classes in the C# language, user defined or otherwise. So, from the compiler's perspective we can put whatever types of object we wish into a collection in any combination. But, it's still important that you, as the programmer, know what the intended base type for a collection is going to be from an application design standpoint, so that you discipline yourself to only insert objects of the proper type (including derived types of that type) into the collection. This will be important when we subsequently attempt to iterate through and process all of the objects in the collection: we'll need to know what general class of object they are, so that we'll know what methods they can be called upon to perform. We'll talk about this in more detail when we discuss* polymorphism *in Chapter 7.*

Composite Classes, Revisited

You may recall that when we talked about the attributes of the Student class back in Chapter 3, we held off on assigning types to a few of the attributes, as shown in Table 6-1.

Table 6-1. Proposed Data Structure for the Student Class

Attribute Name	Data Type
name	string
studentID	string
birthdate	System.DateTime
address	string
major	string
gpa	double
advisor	Professor
courseLoad	???
transcript	???

Armed with what we now know about collections, we can go back and assign types to attributes courseLoad and transcript.

courseLoad

The courseLoad attribute is meant to represent a list of all Course objects that the Student is presently enrolled in. So, it makes perfect sense that this attribute be declared to be simply a standard collection of Course objects!

```
public class Student
{
  private string name;
  private string studentId;
  private CollectionType courseLoad; // of Course objects
  // etc.
```

transcript

The transcript attribute is a bit more challenging. What is a transcript, in real-world terms? It's a report of all of the courses that a student has taken since he or she was first admitted to this school, along with the semester in which each course was taken, the number of credit hours that each course was worth, and the letter grade that the student received for the course. If we think of each entry in this list as an object, we can define them via a TranscriptEntry class, representing an abstraction of a single line item on the transcript report, as follows:

```
public class TranscriptEntry
{
  // One TranscriptEntry represents a single line item on a transcript report.
  private Course courseTaken;
  private string semesterTaken;  // e.g., "Spring 2000"
  private string gradeReceived;  // e.g., "B+"

  // Other details omitted ...

  // Note how we "talk to" the courseTaken object via its methods
  // to retrieve some of this information (delegation once again!).
  public void PrintTranscriptEntry() {
    // Reminder:  \t is a tab character.
    Console.WriteLine(courseTaken.CourseNo + "\t" +
        courseTaken.Title + "\t" +
        courseTaken.CreditHours + "\t" +
        gradeReceived);
  }

  // etc.
}
```

Note that we're declaring one of the attributes of TranscriptEntry to be of type Course, which means that each TranscriptEntry object will maintain a handle on its corresponding Course object. By doing this, the TranscriptEntry object can avail itself of the Course object's title, course number, or credit hour value (needed for computing the GPA)—all privately encapsulated in the Course object as attributes—by accessing the appropriate properties on that Course object as needed.

Back in the Student class, we can now define the Student's transcript attribute to be a collection of TranscriptEntry objects. We can then add a PrintTranscript method to the Student class, the code for which is highlighted in the following snippet:

```
public class Student
{
  private string name;
  private string studentId;
  // Pseudocode.
  private CollectionType transcript; // of TranscriptEntry objects
  // etc.

  // Details omitted ...

  public void PrintTranscript() {
    // Pseudocode.
    for (each TranscriptEntry t in transcript) {
      t.PrintTranscriptEntry();
    }
  }
}
```

transcript, Take 2

Alternatively, we could use the technique of creating a wrapper class called
Transcript to encapsulate some standard collection type, as we did with
EnrollmentCollection in an earlier example:

```
public class Transcript
{
    private ArrayList transcriptEntries; // of TranscriptEntry objects
    // other attributes omitted from this example

    // Pseudocode.
    public void AddTranscriptEntry(arglist) {
      insert new entry into the transcriptEntries ArrayList -- details omitted
    }

    // We've transferred the logic of the Student class's PrintTranscript
    // method into THIS class instead.
    public void PrintTranscript() {
      // Pseudocode.
      for (each TranscriptEntry t in transcriptEntries) {
        t.PrintTranscriptEntry();
      }
    }

    // etc.
}
```

We then can go back to the Student class and change our declaration of the transcript attribute from being a standard collection type to being of type Transcript:

```
public class Student
{
  private string name;
  private string studentId;
  // etc.
  private Transcript transcript;   // an ENCAPSULATED collection of
                                   // TranscriptEntry objects

  // etc.
```

We can then turn around and simplify the PrintTranscript method of the Student class accordingly:

```
public class Student
{
  // Details omitted.

  public void PrintTranscript(string filename) {
    // We now delegate the work to the Transcript attribute!
    transcript.Print();
  }

  // etc.
```

This "take 2" approach of introducing *two* new classes/abstractions—TranscriptEntry and Transcript—is a bit more sophisticated than the first approach, where we only introduced TranscriptEntry as an abstraction. Also, this second approach is "truer" to the object paradigm, because the Student class needn't be complicated by the details of how Transcripts are represented or managed internally—those details are hidden inside of the Transcript class, as they should be.

Our Completed Student Data Structure

Table 6-2 illustrates how we've taken full advantage of collections to round out our Student class definition.

Table 6-2. Rounding Out the Student *Class's Data Structure with Collections*

Attribute Name	Data Type
name	string
studentID	string
birthdate	System.DateTime
address	string
major	string
gpa	double
advisor	Professor
courseLoad	Standard type collection of Course objects
transcript	Standard type collection of TranscriptEntry objects or (preferred) Transcript

Summary

In this chapter, you've learned

- That collections are special types of objects used to gather up and manage references to other objects

- That arrays, as simple collections, have some limitations, but that we have other more powerful collection types to draw upon with OO languages, such as

  - Ordered lists

  - Sets

  - Dictionaries

- That it's important to familiarize ourselves with the unique characteristics of whatever collection types are available for a particular OO language so as to make the most intelligent selection of which collection type to use for a particular circumstance

- That we can invent our own collection types by creating "wrapper classes" around any predefined collection classes

- How we can work around the limitation that a method can only return one result by having that result be a collection of objects

- How we can create very sophisticated composite classes through the use of collections as attributes

Exercises

1. Given the following abstraction:

   A book is a collection of chapters, which are each collections of pages.

   sketch out the code for the Book, Chapter, and Page classes.

   - Invent whatever attributes you think would be relevant, taking advantage of collections as attributes where appropriate.

   - Include methods on the Chapter class for adding pages, and for determining how many pages a chapter contains.

   - Include methods on the Book class for adding chapters, for determining how many chapters the book contains, for determining how many pages the book contains (hint: use delegation!), and for printing out a book's table of contents.

2. What generic type(s) of collection(s)—ordered list, sorted ordered list, set, dictionary—might you use to represent each of the following abstractions? Explain your choices.

   - A computer parts catalog

   - A poker hand

   - Trouble calls logged by a technical help desk

3. What collections do you think it would be important to maintain for the SRS, based on the requirements presented in the Introduction to this book?

4. What collections do you think it would be important to maintain for the Prescription Tracking System (PTS) described in Appendix B?

5. What collections do you think it would be important to maintain for the problem area that you described for exercise 3 in Chapter 2?

CHAPTER 7

Some Final
Object Concepts

BY NOW, YOU'VE HOPEFULLY gained a solid appreciation for how powerful object-oriented languages are for modeling complex real-world situations. By way of review:

- We can create our own user-defined types, also known as classes, to model objects of arbitrary complexity, as we discussed in Chapter 3.

- We can arrange these types into class hierarchies to take advantage of the inheritance mechanism of OO languages, as we discussed in Chapter 5.

- Through encapsulation and information hiding, we can shield client code from changes that we make to the private implementation details of our classes, as well as making objects responsible for ensuring the integrity of their own data, as we discussed in Chapter 4.

- Classes can model the most complex of real-world concepts, particularly when we take advantage of collections, as we did when modeling the transcript attribute of the Student class in Chapter 6.

You might wonder how there could possibly be anything more left in our OO bag of tricks! However, as powerful as all of the preceding OO language features are, there is one more essential feature that we haven't yet spoken about, which ties them all together into an unbeatable package: a feature known as **polymorphism.**

Also, as with any technology, there are core concepts and then there are "special topics": things that you don't necessarily need to know when you're first setting out to use the technology, but which are valuable to know as you become adept with the basics. If you buy an expensive, professional-caliber camera, for example, you may initially be able to use it only as a "point-and-shoot" camera, letting the camera do all of the work of automatically determining how to adjust the lens to produce a quality picture. As your familiarity with the camera's features improves, however, you'll find yourself able to command the camera to do some pretty amazing things! Arming yourself with knowledge of such special object technology topics—the "icing" on the object "cake"—will enhance your ability to develop sophisticated OO applications.

In this chapter, you'll learn

- How **polymorphism** allows the same message to be responded to differently by different types of objects

- How programming constructs known as **abstract classes** and **interfaces** can be used to specify *what* an object's mission should be without going to the trouble of specifying the details of *how* the object is to carry out that mission, and also why we'd want to be able to do so

- How an object can have a "split personality" by exhibiting the behaviors of two or more different types of object

- Creative ways for an entire class of objects to easily and efficiently share data without breaking the spirit of encapsulation

- How features can be defined that are associated with a class itself rather than with an instance of a class

- How to define a constant whose value can't be changed once it's initially set

What Is Polymorphism?

Polymorphism refers to the ability of two or more objects belonging to different classes to respond to exactly the same message (method call) in different class-specific ways.

As an example, if we were to instruct three different people—a surgeon, a hair stylist, and an actor—to "cut!", then

- The surgeon would begin to make an incision;

- The hair stylist would begin to cut someone's hair; and

- The actor would abruptly stop acting out the current scene, awaiting directorial guidance.

These three different professionals may be thought of as objects belonging to different professional classes. Each was given the same message—"cut!"—but knew the specific details of what this message meant to him or her by virtue of knowing the profession (class) that he or she is associated with.

Turning to a software example relevant to the SRS, assume that we've defined a Student base class and two derived classes, GraduateStudent and UndergraduateStudent.

In Chapter 5, we discussed the fact that a Print method intended to print the values of all of a Student's attributes wouldn't necessarily suffice for printing the attribute values for a derived class such as GraduateStudent, because the code as written for the Student class wouldn't know about any attributes that may have been added to the derived class. We would therefore override the Print method of Student to create specialized versions of the method for all of its derived classes. The code for doing so, which was first introduced in Chapter 5, is repeated again here for you to review; we've added the UndergraduateStudent class code, and have also made a few minor enhancements to the Print method for the other two classes.

```
// Student.cs

using System;

public class Student
{
    private string name;
    private string studentId;
    private string major;
    private double gpa;

    // Public properties also provided (details omitted) ...

    public virtual void Print() {
        // We can only print the attributes that the Student class
        // knows about.
        Console.WriteLine("Student Name:  " + Name + "\n" +
            "Student No.:  " +  StudentId  + "\n" +
            "Major Field:  " +  Major  + "\n" +
            "GPA:  " + Gpa);
    }
}
```

```
// GraduateStudent.cs

using System;

public class GraduateStudent : Student
{
    // Adding several attributes.
    private string undergraduateDegree;
    private String undergraduateInstitution;
```

```
            // Public properties also provided (details omitted) ...

            // Overriding the Print method.
            public override void Print() {
                // Reuse code by performing the Print method of the
                // Student base class ...
                base.Print();

                // ... and then go on to print this derived class's specific attributes.
                Console.WriteLine("Undergrad. Deg.:   " + UndergraduateDegree +
                    "\n" + "Undergrad. Inst.:   " +
                    UndergraduateInstitution + "\n" +
                    "THIS IS A GRADUATE STUDENT ...");
            }
        }


        // UndergraduateStudent.cs

        using System;

        public class UndergraduateStudent : Student
        {
            // Adding an attribute.
            private string highSchool;

            // Public property also provided (details omitted) ...

            // Overriding the Print method.
            public override void Print() {
                // Reuse code from the Student base class ...
                base.Print();

                // ... and then go on to print this derived class's specific attributes.
                Console.WriteLine("High School Attended:   " + HighSchool +
                    "\n" + "THIS IS AN UNDERGRADUATE STUDENT ...");
            }
        }
```

In our main SRS application, we declare an array called studentBody designed to hold references to Student objects. We then populate the array with Student object references—some graduate students and some undergraduate students, randomly mixed—as shown here:

```
// Declare and instantiate an array.
Student[] studentBody = new Student[20];

// Instantiate various types of Student object.
UndergraduateStudent u1 = new UndergraduateStudent();
UndergraduateStudent u2 = new UndergraduateStudent();
GraduateStudent g1 = new GraduateStudent();
GraduateStudent g2 = new GraduateStudent();
// etc.

// Insert them into the array in random order.
studentBody[0] = u1;
studentBody[1] = g1;
studentBody[2] = g2;
studentBody[3] = u2;
// etc.
```

Since we're storing both GraduateStudent and UndergraduateStudent objects in this array, we've declared the array to be of a base type common to all objects that the array is intended to contain, namely, Student. By virtue of the "is a" nature of inheritance, an UndergraduateStudent object *is a* Student, and a GraduateStudent object *is a* Student, and so the compiler won't complain when we insert either type of object into the array.

> *Note that the compiler* **would** *object, however, if we tried to insert a* Professor *object into the same array, because a* Professor *isn't a* Student, *at least not in terms of the class hierarchy that we've defined for the SRS. If we wanted to include* Professors *in our array along with various types of* Students, *we'd have to declare the array as holding a base type common to* **both** *the* Student *and* Professor *classes, namely,* Person.

Perhaps we'd like to print the attribute values of all of the students in our studentBody array. We'd want each Student object—whether it is a graduate student or an undergraduate student—to use the version of the Print method appropriate for its class. The following code will accomplish this nicely:

```
// Step through the array (collection) ...
for (int i = 0; i < 20; i++) {
  // ... invoking the Print method of the ith student object.
  studentBody[i].Print();
}
```

As we step through this collection of Student objects, processing them one by one, each object will ***automatically*** know which version of the Print method it should execute, based on its own internal knowledge of its type/class (GraduateStudent vs. UndergraduateStudent, in this example). We'd wind up with a report similar to the following, where the highlighted lines emphasize the differences in output between the GraduateStudent and UndergraduateStudent versions of the Print method:

```
Student Name:  John Smith
Student No.:  12345
Major Field:  Biology
GPA:  2.7
High School Attended:  Rocky Mountain High
THIS IS AN UNDERGRADUATE STUDENT ...

Student Name:  Paula Green
Student No.:  34567
Major Field:  Education
GPA:  3.6
Undergrad. Deg.:  B.S. English
Undergrad. Inst.:  UCLA
THIS IS A GRADUATE STUDENT ...

Student Name:  Dinesh Prabhu
Student No.:  98765
Major Field:  Computer Science
GPA:  4.0
Undergrad. Deg.:  B.S. Computer Engineering
Undergrad. Inst.:  Case Western Reserve University
THIS IS A GRADUATE STUDENT ...

Student Name:  James Roberts
Student No.:  82640
Major Field:  Math
GPA:  3.1
High School Attended:  James Ford Rhodes High
THIS IS AN UNDERGRADUATE STUDENT ...
```

The term ***polymorphism*** is defined in Merriam-Webster's dictionary as

The quality or state of being able to assume different forms.

The line of code

```
studentBody[i].Print();
```

is said to be ***polymorphic*** because the method code performed in response to the message can take many different forms, depending on the class identity of the object.

Of course, this approach of iterating through a collection to ask objects one-by-one to each do something in its own class-specific way won't work unless all objects in the collection understand the message being sent. That is, all objects in the studentBody array must have defined a method with the signature: Print(). However, we've ***guaranteed*** that every object in the studentBody array ***will*** have such a method:

- First of all, we declared the array to hold objects of type Student (or derived classes thereof).

- Secondly, we provided the Student base class with a parameterless Print method (had we not done so, then the compiler would have objected to the following line of code:

  ```
  studentBody[i].Print();
  ```

  because it would have checked the Student class for the presence of a Print method).

- Then, by virtue of inheritance, any derived class of Student is ***guaranteed*** to either inherit the Student's version of the Print method or to optionally override it with one of its own, as illustrated in Figure 7-1. As you learned in Chapter 5, there is no way for a derived class to ***"uninherit"*** a method defined for any of its ancestor classes. The bottom line is that all objects declared to be of type Student are ***guaranteed*** to be "Print savvy"!

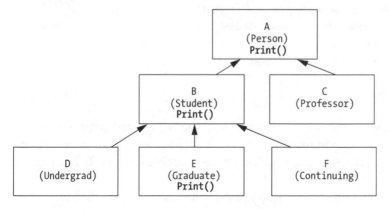

Figure 7-1. The Print *method of* Person *is selectively overridden.*

Reflecting for a moment, you can now see that you've previously learned everything that you need to know about C# objects to facilitate polymorphism—namely, inheritance plus overriding—before this discussion of polymorphism even began. ***Inheritance combined with overriding facilitates polymorphism.***

> *As we discussed in Chapter 6, had we chosen a **different** C# collection type—any type other than* Array—*we would **not** have been able to constrain the type of objects to be inserted when we declared the collection. We must therefore exercise programming discipline when inserting objects into a non-*Array *collection to ensure that they all speak a "common language" in terms of messages that they understand if we wish to take advantage of polymorphism. The C# compiler won't stop us from putting an assortment of objects of literally any type **into** a collection, but the common language runtime may complain when we try to operate on the objects after taking them back **out**. We'll explore this phenomenon in detail in Chapter 13 when we discuss techniques for iterating through collections.*

Polymorphism Simplifies Code Maintenance

To appreciate the power of polymorphism, let's look at how we might have to approach this same challenge—handling different objects in different type-specific ways—with a programming language that doesn't support polymorphism.

In the absence of polymorphism, we'd typically handle scenarios having to do with a variety of different kinds of students using a series of if tests:

```
for (int i = 0; i < 20; i++) {
  // Process the ith student.
  // Pseudocode.
  if (studentBody[i] is an undergraduate student)
    studentBody[i].PrintAsUndergraduateStudent();
  else if (studentBody[i] is a graduate student)
    studentBody[i].PrintAsGraduateStudent();
  else if ...
}
```

As the number of cases grows, so too does the "spaghetti" nature of the resultant code! And, keep in mind that this sort of if test can occur in countless places throughout an application. Maintenance of such code quickly becomes a nightmare.

Let's now contrast this with our polymorphic iteration through the studentBody array:

```
// Step through the array (collection) ...
for (int i = 0; i < 20; i++) {
```

```
// ... invoking the Print method of the ith student object.
studentBody[i].Print();
}
```

Because client code can be written to operate on a variety of objects without knowing what ***specific subtype*** of object is involved, such client code is robust to change. For example, let's say that, long after our SRS application has been coded and tested, we derive classes called PhDStudent and MastersStudent from GraduateStudent, each of which in turn overrides the Print method to provide its own "flavor" of printing as shown in Figure 7-2.

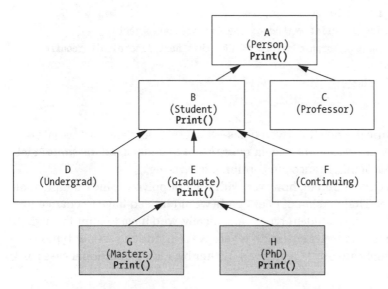

Figure 7-2. Subsequent overriding of Print *by newly derived classes*

We're now free to randomly insert MastersStudent and PhDStudent objects into the mix of GraduateStudents and UndergraduateStudents in the array, and our polymorphic array iteration code ***doesn't have to change!***

```
// Declare and instantiate an array.
Student[] studentBody = new Student[20];

// Instantiate various types of Student object. We're now dealing with four
// different derived types.
UndergraduateStudent u1 = new UndergraduateStudent();
PhDStudent p1 = new PhDStudent();
GraduateStudent g1 = new GraduateStudent();
MastersStudent m1 = new MastersStudent();
// etc.
```

```
// Insert them into the array in random order.
studentBody[0] = u1;
studentBody[1] = p1;
studentBody[2] = g1;
studentBody[3] = m1;
// etc.

// Then, later in our application ...

// This is the exact same code that we've seen before!
// Step through the array (collection) ...
for (int i = 0; i < studentBody.size; i++) {
    // ... and invoke the Print method of the ith student object.
    // Because of the polymorphic nature of C#, this next line didn't require
    // any changes!
    studentBody[i].Print();
}
```

This is because the newly derived types—MastersStudent and PhDStudent—
are, as extensions of Student, once again **_guaranteed_** to understand the **_same_** Print
message by virtue of inheritance plus optional overriding.

The story is quite different, however, with the nonpolymorphic example that
we crafted earlier. That version of client code would indeed have to change to
accommodate these new student types; specifically, we'd have to hunt through
our application to find every situation where we're trying to sort out types of
Student, and complicate our if tests even further by adding additional cases as
shown here:

```
for (int i = 0; i < 20; i++) {
    // Process the ith student.
    // Pseudocode.
    if (studentBody[i] is an undergraduate student)
        studentBody[i].PrintAsUndergraduateStudent();
    else if (studentBody[i] is a masters student)
        studentBody[i].PrintAsMastersStudent();
    else if (studentBody[i] is a PhD student)
        studentBody[i].PrintAsPhDStudent();
    else if (studentBody[i] is a generic graduate student)
        studentBody[i].PrintAsGraduateStudent();
    else if ...
}
```

causing the "spaghetti piles" to grow ever taller.

As we saw with encapsulation and information hiding earlier, polymorphism
is another extremely powerful feature of OOPLs that minimizes "ripple effects" on

existing applications when requirements inevitably change after an application has been deployed.

Three Distinguishing Features of an Object-Oriented Programming Language

We've now defined all three of the features required to make a language truly object-oriented:

- (Programmer creation of) User-defined types

- Inheritance

- *Polymorphism*

By way of review, let's summarize the benefits of each of these three language features.

Programmer creation of user-defined types

- Provides an intuitive way to represent real-world objects, resulting in *easier to verify requirements.*

- Classes are convenient units of reusable code, which means *less code to write when building an application.*

- Through encapsulation, we minimize data redundancy—each item of data is stored once, in the object to which it belongs—and therefore lessen the chance of data integrity errors.

- Through information hiding, we insulate our application against ripple effects if private details of a class must change after deployment, thereby *dramatically reducing maintenance costs.*

- Objects are responsible for ensuring the integrity of their own data, making it *easier to debug data integrity problems.*

Inheritance

- Can extend deployed code without having to change it, resulting in *dramatically reduced maintenance costs.*

- Derived classes are much more succinct, which means *less code overall to write/maintain.*

Polymorphism

- Causes virtually no "ripple effects" on client code when new subclasses are invented, resulting in ***dramatically reduced maintenance costs.***

A common misconception, held by many, is that switching from a non-OO to an OO programming language will dramatically speed up the development time of a given application. Anecdotes abound of managers who have expected that a team utilizing OO approaches should be able to craft an application in a fraction of the time that it would have taken them to build its non-OO counterpart—despite the fact that team in question might be utilizing object-oriented techniques for the first time ever!

*Unfortunately, due to the learning curve involved in switching to the OO paradigm—particularly for software developers who've been entrenched in non-OOPL techniques for many years—it actually can take **longer** for a team to build its first OO application.*

*Where economies of scale **do** come into play, however, is during the **maintenance stage** of an application's life cycle. The maintenance stage of an application—OO or otherwise—is typically much longer/more costly than the development stage, and so by dramatically reducing ripple effects through the thoughtful use of encapsulation/information hiding and inheritance/overriding/polymorphism, we stand to reduce maintenance costs significantly.*

*Once we've become adept with the OO paradigm, we should indeed be able to shorten application **development** time, as well, by virtue of the fact that through reuse via inheritance, we'll have less code to write overall. And, in transitioning from one project to the next, if we embrace the philosophy of code sharing and reuse across projects, we can gain significant productivity during the development stage of the life cycle.*

Abstract Classes

We learned in Chapter 5 how useful it can be to consolidate shared features—attributes and behaviors—of two or more classes into a common base class, a process known as generalization. We did this when we created the Person class as a generalization of Student and Professor and then moved the declarations of all of their common attributes, methods, and properties into this base class. By doing so, the Student- and Professor-derived classes both became simpler, and we eliminated a lot of redundancy that would otherwise have made maintenance of the SRS much more cumbersome.

The preceding example involved a situation where the need for generalization arose after the fact; now let's look at this problem from the opposite perspective. Say that we have the foresight at the very outset of our project that we're going to need various types of Course objects in our SRS: lecture courses, lab courses, independent study courses, etc. We therefore wish to start out on the right foot by designing a Course base class to be as versatile as possible to facilitate *future* specialization.

We might determine up front that all Courses, regardless of type, are going to need to share a few common attributes:

- string courseName;

- string courseNumber;

- int creditValue;

- CollectionType enrolledStudents;

- Professor instructor;

as well as a few common behaviors:

- EstablishCourseSchedule

- EnrollStudent

- AssignInstructor

Some of these behaviors may be generic enough so that we can afford to program them in detail for the Course class, knowing that it's a pretty safe bet that any future derived classes of Course will inherit these methods "as is" without needing to override them; for example:

```
public class Course
{
  string courseName;
  string courseNumber;
  int creditValue;
  Professor instructor;
  // Pseudocode.
  Collection enrolledStudents;

  // Properties provided; details omitted ...

  public bool EnrollStudent(Student s) {
    // Pseudocode.
    if (we haven't exceeded the maximum allowed enrollment yet)
      enrolledStudents.Add(s);
  }
```

```
    public void AssignInstructor(Professor p) {
        Instructor = p;
    }
}
```

However, other of the behaviors may be too specialized for a given derived type to enable us to come up with a useful generic version. For example, the business rules governing how to schedule class meetings may differ for different types of courses:

- A lecture course may only meet once a week for 3 hours at a time.

- A lab course may meet twice a week for 2 hours each time.

- An independent study course may meet on a custom schedule that has been jointly negotiated by a given student and professor.

It would therefore seem to be a waste of time for us to bother trying to program a generic version of the EstablishCourseSchedule method for the Course class, because one size simply can't fit all in this situation; all three types would have to override such logic to make it meaningful for them.

Can we afford to just omit the EstablishCourseSchedule method from the Course class entirely, adding such a method to each of the derived classes of Course as a new feature instead? Part of our decision has to do with whether or not we ever plan on instantiating "generic" Course objects in our application.

- If we do, then the Course class would need an EstablishCourseSchedule method of its own.

- Even if we don't plan on instantiating the Course class directly, however, we still need to define an EstablishCourseSchedule method at the Course class level if we wish to enable polymorphic behavior for this method.

Let's assume that we ***don't*** want to instantiate generic Course objects, but ***do*** wish to take advantage of polymorphism. We're faced with a dilemma! We know that we'll need a type-specific EstablishCourseSchedule method to be programmed for all derived classes of Course, but we don't want to go to the trouble of programming code in the parent class that will never serve a useful purpose. How do we communicate the requirement for such a behavior in all derived classes of Course and, more importantly, ***enforce its future implementation?***

OO languages such as C# come to the rescue with the concept of **abstract classes**. An abstract class is used to enumerate the required behaviors of a class ***without*** having to provide an explicit implementation of each and every such behavior. We program an abstract class in much the same way that we program a nonabstract class (also known informally as a **concrete class**), with one exception: for those behaviors for which we can't (or care not to) devise a generic implementation—e.g., the EstablishCourseSchedule method in our preceding example—we're permitted to specify method ***headers*** without having to program the corresponding method ***bodies***. We refer to a "bodiless," or header-only, method specification as an **abstract method**.

Let's go back to our Course class definition to add an abstract method as highlighted in the following code:

```
public abstract class Course
{
  private string courseName;
  private string courseNumber;
  private int creditValue;
  private ArrayList enrolledStudents;
  private Professor instructor;

  // Other details omitted.

  public bool EnrollStudent(Student s) {
    // Pseudocode.
    if (we haven't exceeded the maximum allowed enrollment yet) {
      enrolledStudents.Add(s);
    }
  }

  public void AssignInstructor(Professor p) {
    Instructor = p;
  }

  // Note the use of the "abstract" keyword and the terminating semicolon.
  public abstract void EstablishCourseSchedule (string startDate,
                                                 string endDate);
}
```

The EstablishCourseSchedule method is declared to be abstract by adding the abstract keyword to its header. Note that the header of an abstract method has no braces following the closing parenthesis of the parameter list. Instead, the header is followed by a semicolon (;)—i.e., it's missing its code body, which normally contains the detailed logic of how the method is to be performed. The method must therefore be explicitly labeled as abstract to notify the compiler that we didn't accidentally forget to program this method, but rather that we knew what we were doing when we intentionally omitted the body.

By specifying an abstract method, we've accomplished several very important goals:

- We've specified a service that objects of various `Course` types must be able to perform.

- We've detailed the means by which we'll ask such objects to perform this service by defining a method header, which as we learned in Chapter 4 controls the format of the message that we'll pass to such objects when we want them to perform the service.

- Furthermore, we've facilitated polymorphism—at least with respect to the method in question—by ensuring that all derived classes of `Course` will indeed recognize a method call involving this method signature.

However, we've done so without pinning down the private details of how the method will accomplish this task—i.e., the business rules that apply for a given derived class. We've in essence specified ***what*** a `Course` type object needs to be able to do without constraining ***how*** it must be done. This gives each derived type of `Course`—`LectureCourse`, `LabCourse`, `IndependentStudyCourse`—the freedom to define the inner workings of the method to reflect the business rules specific to that particular derived type by overriding the abstract method with a concrete version.

Whenever a class contains one or more abstract methods, then the class as a whole must be designated to be an abstract class through inclusion of the `abstract` keyword in the class declaration:

```
public abstract class Course
{
  // details omitted
}
```

Note that it isn't necessary for all methods in an abstract class to be abstract; an abstract class can also contain methods that have a body, known as **concrete methods**.

Abstract Classes and Instantiation

There is one caveat with respect to abstract classes: ***they can't be instantiated.*** That is, if we define `Course` to be an abstract class in the SRS, then we can't ever instantiate generic `Course` objects in our application. This makes intuitive sense, for if we ***could*** create an object of type `Course`, it would then be expected to know how to respond to a message to establish a course schedule, because the `Course` class declares a method header for the `EstablishCourseSchedule` behavior. But because there is no code ***behind*** that method, the `Course` object in question wouldn't know ***how*** to behave in ***response*** to such a message.

The compiler comes to our assistance by preventing us from even writing code to instantiate an abstract class in the first place; if we were to try to compile the following code snippet, for example:

```
Course c = new Course();  // Impossible!  The compiler will generate an error
                          // on this line of code.
// details omitted ...

c.EstablishCourseSchedule('01/10/2001', '05/15/2001');  // Behavior undefined!
```

we'd get the following compilation error on the first line of code:

```
error CS0144: cannot create an instance of the abstract class or
interface 'Course'
```

While we're indeed prevented from instantiating an abstract class, we're nonetheless permitted to **declare reference variables** to be of an abstract type:

```
Course x;  // This is OK.
```

Why would we ever want to declare reference variables of type Course if we can't instantiate objects of type Course? The answer has to do with facilitating polymorphism; you'll learn the importance of being able to define reference variables of an abstract type when we talk about iterating through generic C# collections in more depth in Chapter 13.

Overriding Abstract Methods

When we derive a class from an abstract base class, the derived class will inherit all of the base class's features, including all of its abstract method headers. The derived class may replace an inherited abstract method with a concrete version using the override keyword, as illustrated in the following code:

```
// The abstract base class.
public abstract class Course
{
  private string courseName;
  // etc.

  // Other details omitted.

  public abstract void EstablishCourseSchedule (string startDate,
                                                string endDate);
}
```

```
// Deriving a class from an abstract base class.
public class LectureCourse : Course
{
  // Details omitted.

  // Replace the abstract method with a concrete method.
  public override void EstablishCourseSchedule(string startDate,
                                        string endDate) {
    // Logic specific to the business rules for a LectureCourse ...
    // details omitted.
  }
}
```

We used the override keyword in similar fashion in Chapter 5, when it was used to override a virtual method declared in a base class. Note that in the preceding example, we've dropped the abstract keyword off of the overridden EstablishCourseSchedule method in the LectureCourse derived class, because the method is no longer abstract; we've provided a concrete method body.

Unless a derived class provides a concrete implementation for **all** of the abstract methods that it inherits from an abstract base class, the derived class will automatically be rendered abstract, as well. In such a situation, the derived class of course can't be instantiated, either. Therefore, somewhere in the derivation hierarchy, a class derived from an abstract class must have concrete implementations for all of its ancestors' abstract methods if it wishes to "break the spell of abstractness"— i.e., if we wish to instantiate objects of that derived type (see Figure 7-3).

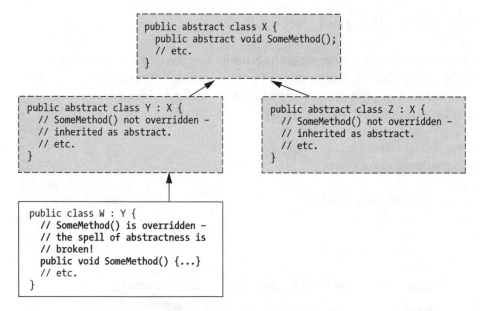

Figure 7-3. "Breaking the spell" of abstractness by overriding abstract methods

"Breaking the Spell" of Abstractness

Let's look at a detailed example. Having intentionally designed Course as an abstract class earlier to serve as a common template for all of the various course types we envision needing for the SRS, we later decide to derive classes LectureCourse, LabCourse, and IndependentStudyCourse. In the following code snippet, we show these three derived classes of Course; of these, only two—LectureCourse and LabCourse—provide implementations for the abstract EstablishCourseSchedule method, and so the third derived class—IndependentStudyCourse—remains abstract and can't be instantiated.

```
public class LectureCourse : Course
{
  // All attributes are inherited from the Course class; no new
  // attributes are added.

  public override void EstablishCourseSchedule (string startDate,
                                                string endDate) {
    // Logic would be provided here for how a lecture course
    // establishes a course schedule; details omitted ...
  }
}


public class LabCourse : Course
{
  // All attributes are inherited from the Course class; no new
  // attributes are added.

  public override void EstablishCourseSchedule (string startDate,
                                                string endDate) {
    // Logic would be provided here for how a lab course establishes a
    // course schedule; details omitted ...
  }
}


public class IndependentStudyCourse : Course
{
  // All attributes are inherited from the Course class; no new
  // attributes are added.

  // We are purposely choosing NOT to implement the
  // EstablishCourseSchedule method in this derived class.
}
```

If we were to try to compile the preceding code, the C# compiler would force us to flag the IndependentStudyCourse class with the abstract keyword; that is, we'd get the following compilation error:

```
error CS0534:  'IndependentStudyCourse' does not implement inherited
abstract member 'Course.EstablishCourseSchedule(string, string)'
```

unless we go back and amend the IndependentStudyCourse class declaration to declare it as abstract:

```
public abstract class IndependentStudyCourse : Course
{
  // details omitted ...
}
```

We've just hit upon how abstract methods serve to enforce implementation requirements! Declaring an abstract method in a base class ultimately *forces* all derived classes to provide type-specific implementations of all inherited abstract methods; otherwise, the derived classes themselves can't be instantiated.

Note that having allowed IndependentStudyCourse to remain an abstract class isn't necessarily a mistake; the only error was subsequently trying to instantiate it. We may plan on deriving another "generation" of classes from IndependentStudyCourse—perhaps IndependentStudy**Graduate**Course and IndependentStudy**Undergraduate**Course—making *them* concrete in lieu of making IndependentStudyCourse concrete. It's perfectly acceptable to have multiple layers of abstract classes in an inheritance hierarchy; we simply need a terminal/leaf class to be concrete in order for it to be useful in creating objects.

We've seen that a derived class of an abstract class can be made concrete by providing nonabstract implementations of all abstract methods declared by the abstract class. It's also possible to go the other direction as well: that is, a derived class can override a nonabstract method declared in a base class with an abstract method. We'll explore examples of this when we discuss the Object class in Chapter 13.

Interfaces

Recall that a class, as a type, is an abstraction of a real-world object from which some of the unessential details have been omitted. We can therefore see that an abstract class is more of an abstraction than a concrete class, because with an abstract class we've omitted the details for how one or more particular behaviors are to be performed.

Now, let's take the notion of abstractness one step further. With an abstract class, we are able to avoid programming the bodies of methods that are declared to be abstract. But what about the *attributes* of such a class? In our Course example, we went ahead and prescribed the data structure (attributes) that we thought would be needed generically by all types of courses:

```
string courseName;
string courseNumber;
int creditValue;
Collection enrolledStudents;
Professor instructor;
```

But, what if we only wanted to specify common **behaviors**, and not even **bother** with declaring **attributes**? Attributes are, after all, typically declared to be private; we simply may not wish to mandate what data structure a future derived class must use in order to achieve the desired public behaviors, instead leaving it up to the designer of that class to ultimately decide.

Say, for example, that we wanted to define what it means to teach at a university. Perhaps, in order to teach, an object would need to be able to perform the following services:

- Agree to teach a particular course.

- Designate a textbook to be used for the course.

- Define a syllabus for the course.

- Approve the enrollment of a particular student in the course.

Each of these behaviors could be formalized by specifying a method header, representing how an object that is **capable of teaching** would be asked to perform each behavior:

```
public bool AgreeToTeach(Course c)
public void DesignateTextbook(TextBook b, Course c)
public Syllabus DefineSyllabus(Course c)
public bool ApproveEnrollment(Student s, Course c)
```

A set of method headers such as these, which collectively define what it means to assume a certain **role** within an application (such as teaching), is known as an **interface.** Interfaces, like classes, are given names; so, let's call this the ITeacher interface. (The C# convention is for interface names to use the Pascal capitalization style; names are prefixed with the letter "I" to indicate that the type is an interface vs. a class.)

To declare an interface, we enclose the method headers that we've defined for the interface, each ending with a semicolon (;), in a set of braces, with the keyword interface and the name of the interface preceding the opening brace, as illustrated here:

```
public interface ITeacher {
    bool AgreeToTeach(Course c);
    void DesignateTextbook(TextBook b, Course c);
    Syllabus DefineSyllabus(Course c);
    bool ApproveEnrollment(Student s, Course c);
}
```

An interface can be given public or internal access and is typically declared to be public. As with classes, each interface typically goes into its own source code file, whose name matches the name of the interface contained within: e.g., the ITeacher interface would go into a file named ITeacher.cs.

All of an interface's method headers are implicitly public and abstract, so we needn't specify either of those two keywords when declaring them; in fact, if we *were* to explicitly try to assign public access to an interface method header:

```
public interface ITeacher {
    public bool AgreeToTeach(Course c);
    // etc.
```

the compiler would generate an error:

```
error CS0106: the modifier 'public' is not valid for this item
```

A similar compiler error is generated if the abstract keyword is applied to an interface method header by mistake.

Implementing an Interface

Once we've defined an interface such as ITeacher, we can set about designating various classes as being teachers—for example, Professors, or Students, or generic Person objects—simply by declaring that the class of interest *implements* the ITeacher interface using the syntax shown here:

```
// Implementing an interface ...
public class Professor : ITeacher
{
    // details omitted ...
}
```

Note that the syntax for declaring that a class is implementing an interface is indistinguishable from the syntax that indicates inheritance—a colon followed by the interface/base class name:

```
// Extending a class via inheritance ...
public class Professor : Person
{
  // details omitted ...
}
```

> *The only way to differentiate an interface* (ITeacher) *from a class* (Person) *when inspecting the derived/implementing class's code* (Professor) *is the fact that an interface name typically begins with an "I" followed by another capital letter: e.g.,* IFoo *or* IBar *would be interfaces, whereas* IceCream *or* Igloo *would be class names.*

Once a class declares that it is implementing an interface:

```
public class Professor : ITeacher { ...
```

the implementing class *must* provide concrete versions of *all* of the (implicitly abstract) methods declared by the interface in question in order to satisfy the compiler. As an example, let's say that we were to code the Professor class as shown in the following code, implementing three of the four methods called for by the ITeacher interface but neglecting to code the fourth method:

```
public class Professor : ITeacher
{
  private string name;
  private string employeeId;
  // etc.

  // Properties defined; details omitted.

  // We implement three of the four methods called for by the
  // ITeacher interface, to provide method bodies.

  public bool AgreeToTeach(Course c) {
    // Logic for the method body goes here; details omitted.
  }

  public void DesignateTextbook(TextBook b, Course c) {
    // Logic for the method body goes here; details omitted.
  }
```

```
public Syllabus DefineSyllabus(Course c) {
  // Logic for the method body goes here; details omitted.
}


// Note that we've failed to provide an implementation of the
// ApproveEnrollment method ...
}
```

If we were to try to compile this class as shown previously, we'd get the following compiler error:

```
error CS0535: 'Professor' does not implement interface
member 'ITeacher.ApproveEnrollment(Student, Course)'
```

Another Form of "Is A" Relationship

You learned in Chapter 5 that inheritance is thought of as the "is a" relationship. As it turns out, implementing an interface is another form of "is a" relationship:

- If the Professor class *extends* the Person *class*, then a professor *is a* person; and

- If the Professor class *implements* the ITeacher *interface*, then a professor *is a* teacher.

Also, when a class A implements an interface X, all of the classes that are derived from A may also be said to implement that same interface. For example, if we derive a class called AdjunctProfessor from Professor, then if Professor implements the ITeacher interface, an adjunct professor is a teacher.

```
public class Professor : ITeacher
{
  // All methods required by ITeacher will be implemented by this class ...
  // details omitted.
}

public class AdjunctProfessor : Professor
{
  // All methods required by ITeacher will be, at a minimum, inherited from
  // Professor ... details omitted.
}
```

This makes intuitive sense, because `AdjunctProfessor` will either inherit all of the methods called for by the `ITeacher` interface from `Professor`, or will override them; but, either way, an `AdjunctProfessor` will be "equipped" to perform all of the services required of an (I)`Teacher`.

Abstract Classes vs. Interfaces

Implementing an interface is conceptually similar to having to "flesh out" abstract methods when extending an abstract class. What are the differences, then, between implementing an interface vs. extending an abstract class? Why might we wish to use one approach over the other when designing an application?

- With an interface, we specify abstract behaviors only, whereas an abstract class often specifies a "concrete" data structure (attributes) as well as a mixture of abstract and concrete behaviors. So, in terms of the "abstractness spectrum," an interface is more abstract than an abstract class (which is in turn more abstract than a concrete class) because an interface leaves even more details to the imagination.

*Note that an abstract class **can** be merely a set of abstract method headers if we wish to design it as such; for example:*

```
public abstract class Person
{
  // We are purposely declaring NO ATTRIBUTES for this class ...

  // ... and ALL of our methods are abstract.
  public abstract void Print();
  public abstract double ComputeSalary();
  // etc.
}
```

However, in such a situation, the preferred approach would be to simply declare an interface instead.

- When a nonabstract class is derived from an abstract class, the derived class provides a concrete implementation of abstract methods declared in the abstract class by overriding them. The derived class method headers therefore must include the `override` keyword.

- When a class implements an interface, the implementing class must once again provide a concrete implementation of all of the methods declared in the interface. However, the implementing class doesn't *override* them. Rather, we're defining the methods *for the first time from scratch,* and so the override keyword isn't included in the implementing class method headers. (If we were to try to apply the override keyword, the compiler would inform us that it has "found no suitable method to override.")

- The syntactical differences in these two approaches are compared side-by-side here:

Example Using an Abstract Class	Example Using an Interface

Declaring the Teacher Type as an Abstract Class:
 	
`public abstract class Teacher`
`{`
`  // Abstract classes may declare`
`  // data structure.`
`  string name;`
`  string employeeId;`
`  // etc.`
 	
`  // We declare abstract methods using`
`  // the "abstract" keyword.`
`  public abstract void AgreeToTeach(`
`    Course c);`
`  public abstract void DesignateTextbook(`
`    TextBook b, Course c);`
 	
`  // etc.`
 	
`  // Abstract classes may declare concrete`
`  // methods.`
`  public void Print() {`
`    Console.WriteLine(name);`
`    // etc.`
`  }`
`}`
	Declaring the Teacher Type as an Interface:
	
	`public interface ITeacher`
	`{`
	`  // Interfaces may not declare`
	`  // attributes.`
	
	`  // We can't use the "public" or`
	`  // "abstract" keywords.`
	`  void AgreeToTeach(Course c);`
	
	`  void DesignateTextbook(`
	`    TextBook b, Course c);`
	
	`  // etc.`
	
	`  // Interfaces may not declare concrete`
	`  // methods.`
	`}`

Deriving Professor from Teacher:	Professor Implements ITeacher:
``public class Professor : Teacher
{
    // Professor inherits attributes, if any,
    // from parent class, and optionally
    // adds additional attributes; details
    // omitted.

    // We override abstract methods inherited
    // from the Teacher class.

    public override void AgreeToTeach(
      Course c) {
      // Logic for the method body goes here;
      // details omitted.
    }

    // etc. for other abstract methods.

    // Additional methods may be added;
    // details omitted.
}``` | ```public class Professor : ITeacher
{
    // Class must provide its own data
    // structure, as an interface
    // cannot provide any.
    string name;
    string employeeId;
    // etc.

    // We implement the methods from the
    // ITeacher interface without using
    // the override keyword.

    public void AgreeToTeach(Course c) {
      // Logic for the method body goes here;
      // details omitted.
    }

    // etc. for other abstract methods.

    // Additional methods may be added;
    // details omitted.
}``` |

- A class that is derived from an abstract class needn't override **all** of the abstract methods it inherits with concrete versions; if one or more of the abstract methods is inherited "as is," then the derived class must also be declared abstract.

- In contrast, a class that implements an interface must provide concrete versions of **all** abstract methods required of the interface; implementing an interface is an "all or nothing" proposition.

- Another important distinction between extending an abstract class vs. implementing an interface is that whereas a given class may only be derived from one immediate base class, a class may implement as *many* interfaces as desired. Because this is such a powerful language feature, we'll illustrate it with an example in the next section.

Implementing Multiple Interfaces

As an example, if we were to invent a second interface called IAdministrator, which in turn specifies the following method headers:

```
public interface IAdministrator
{
  public bool approveNewCourse(Course c);
  public bool hireProfessor(Professor p);
}
```

we could then declare that a class such as Professor implements *both* the ITeacher and IAdministrator interfaces, in which case the class would need to implement all of the methods declared by *both* of these interfaces collectively:

```
public class Professor : ITeacher, IAdministrator
{
  // The Professor class must implement all of the methods called for by
  // the ITeacher interface ... details omitted.

  // The Professor class must implement all of the methods called for by
  // the IAdministrator interface ... details omitted.
}
```

> Note that if a class implements two or more interfaces that call for methods with identical signatures, we need only implement one such method in the implementing class—that method will do "double duty" in satisfying **both** interfaces' implementation requirements as far as the compiler is concerned.

When a class implements more than one interface, its objects are capable of assuming multiple identities or roles in an application; such objects can therefore be "handled" by various types of reference variables. Based on the preceding definition of a Professor as both an ITeacher and an IAdministrator, the following client code would be possible:

```
// Instantiate a Professor object, and store its handle in a reference
// variable of type Professor.
Professor p = new Professor();

// We then declare reference variables of the two types of interfaces that the
// Professor class implements.
ITeacher t;
IAdministrator a;

t = p;  // We store a handle on the Professor in a reference variable of
        // type Teacher; this is possible because a professor IS A teacher!

a = p;  // We store a handle on the Professor in a reference variable of
        // type Administrator; this is possible because a professor IS AN
        // administrator!
```

as illustrated conceptually in Figure 7-4.

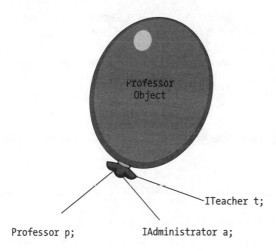

```
A Professor object can be "handled" by Professor,
ITeacher, and IAdministrator references, because a Professor
is a Teacher, and a Professor is an Administrator!
```

Figure 7-4. The Professor object has three different identities.

This is conceptually the same thing as you, as a person, being viewed as having different roles by different people: you're viewed as an employee by your manager, as a son or daughter by your parents, perhaps as a parent by your children, and so forth.

We may then command the *same* object either as a Professor . . .

```
// Department is a property defined for the Professor class ...
p.Department = "Computer Science";
```

or as a Teacher . . .

```
// AgreeToTeach is a method defined for the ITeacher interface ...
t.AgreeToTeach(c);    // Note that p.agreeToTeach(c); also works ...
```

or as an Administrator . . .

```
// ApproveNewCourse is a method defined for the IAdministrator interface ...
a.approveNewCourse(c);  // Note that p.approveNewCourse(c); also works ...
```

because it's all three, rolled into one!

> *Note that not all OO languages embrace the notion of interfaces. For example, both C# and Java do, but C++ does not. C++ does, however, support multiple inheritance; C#'s provision for a class to be able to implement multiple inter-faces enabled the C# language designers to avoid multiple inheritance, as we discussed in Chapter 5.*

A class may simultaneously extend a *single* base class and implement *one or more* interfaces, as follows:

```
public class Professor : Person, ITeacher, IAdministrator { ... }
```

Under such circumstances, the name of the base class will always come first in the list, followed by the names of all interfaces to be implemented. As we discussed in Chapter 5, C# doesn't support multiple inheritance, and so it isn't possible to list more than one class name after the colon; assuming that Professor and Student are both classes, the following wouldn't compile:

```
// This would not compile.
public class StudentTeacher : Professor, Student, ITeacher
{
  // details omitted
}
```

The preceding code would produce the following compilation error:

```
error CS0527: 'Student' type in interface list is not an interface
```

In other words, the compiler will only consider the first entry after the colon as a base class and everything else in the list is assumed to be an interface.

Interfaces and Instantiation

Interfaces can't be instantiated, because there is no such thing as a constructor for an interface. That is, if we define ITeacher to be an interface, we may not try to instantiate it directly:

```
ITeacher t = new ITeacher();  // Impossible!  The compiler will generate an error
                              // on this line of code.
```

We'd get the following compilation error on the preceding line of code:

```
error CS0144: Cannot create an instance of the abstract class or
interface 'ITeacher'
```

While we're indeed prevented from instantiating an interface, we're nonetheless permitted to declare reference variables to be of an interface type, as we saw earlier:

```
ITeacher t;  // This is OK.
```

We could, therefore, do the following:

```
ITeacher t = new Professor();
```

Why is this permitted? The compiler allows assignments to occur if the type of the expression to the right of the equal sign (=) is a type that is compatible with the variable to the left of the equal sign. Since Professor implements ITeacher, a professor *is a* teacher, and so this assignment is permitted.

The Importance of Interfaces

Interfaces are one of the most poorly understood, and hence underutilized, features of the OOPLs that support them. This is quite unfortunate, as interfaces are extremely powerful if utilized properly.

Whenever possible/feasible, design the public aspects of your classes using interface types instead of specific class types to allow for greater flexibility/utility of your methods, to include

- Formal parameters to methods

- Method return types

Let's use two different examples to illustrate the power of interfaces.

Example #1

In this example, assume that

- Professor is a derived class of Person.

- Student is a derived class of Person.

- Professor and Student are sibling classes—neither derives from the other.

- Person implements the ITeacher interface, and thus both Professor and Student indirectly implement the ITeacher interface, as we discussed earlier in this chapter.

We'll start by designing a class called Course with a private attribute of type Professor called teachingAssistant, and a property for accessing this attribute:

```
public class Course
{
  private Professor teachingAssistant;

  // Other features omitted ...

  public Professor TeachingAssistant {
    get {
      return teachingAssistant;
    }
    set {
      teachingAssistant = value;
    }
  }

  // Other features omitted ...
}
```

Then, we'd perhaps utilize this class from client code as follows:

```
// Client code.
Course c = new Course("Math 101");
Professor p = new Professor("John Smith");
c.TeachingAssistant = p;
```

If, later on, we'd prefer to change the type of the private teachingAssistant attribute from Professor to Student, we'd also have to change the type of the public TeachingAssistant property to match:

```
public class Course
{
  // Change type from Professor to Student here ...
  private Student teachingAssistant;

  // ... and here.
  public Student TeachingAssistant {
    // Details omitted ...
  }

  // etc.
}
```

Our client code as originally written would no longer work—the highlighted line in the following code will no longer compile—because the TeachingAssistant property as modified is expecting to be assigned a Student reference now, and a Professor is *not* a Student:

```
// Client code.
Course c = new Course("Math 101");
Professor p = new Professor("John Smith");
c.TeachingAssistant = p;  // This line of code will no longer compile.
```

Now, let's look at an alteration to our original Course class design. Let's say that we had originally taken advantage of the fact that the Professor class implements the ITeacher interface to declare the TeachingAssistant property to be of type ITeacher from the outset:

```
public class Course
{
  private ITeacher teachingAssistant;
  // details omitted ...
```

```
    public ITeacher TeachingAssistant {
      // details omitted ...
    }


    // etc.
  }
```

We're thus opening up more possibilities for client code: we can assign a Professor as a teaching assistant:

```
// Client code
Course c = new Course("Math 101");
Professor p = new Professor("John Smith");
c.TeachingAssistant = p;
```

or a Student as a teaching assistant:

```
// Client code
Course c = new Course("Math 101");
Student s = new Student("George Jones");
c.TeachingAssistant = s;
```

or a reference to any other type of object that implements the ITeacher interface.

Example #2

An example of a commonly used ***predefined*** C# interface is the IList interface. The IList interface enforces implementation of the following method headers:

```
int Add(object value)
void Clear()
bool Contains(object value)
int IndexOf(object value)
void Insert(int index, object value)
void Remove(object value)
void RemoveAt(int index)
```

and is implemented by several of the predefined C# collection types, including the Array and ArrayList classes.

If we write a method that is to operate on a collection so that it accepts a generic IList reference versus a specific type of collection—say, an ArrayList—then the method is much more versatile; client code is free to pass in whatever collection type it wishes.

```
public class SomeClass
{
  // details omitted ...

  public void SomeMethod(IList list) {
    // Within this method, we can manipulate the list argument with any of the
    // methods defined by the IList interface ...
  }
}
```

Static Features

Up until this point, all of the methods, attributes, and properties that we've discussed have been associated with an instance of a class. Every object has its own copy of the feature and can manipulate it independently of what other objects are doing. But there may be times when we'll wish to make a feature common to all instances of a class. In other words, instead of having each object have its own copy of an attribute, there may be an attribute whose value will be shared by all objects of a given class. The C# language satisfies this need through *static* features that are associated with classes as a whole rather than with individual objects.

Static Attributes

We've learned previously that whenever we create an object, we're creating an instance of the appropriate class whose attributes subsequently get "filled" with values specific to that object (see Figure 7-5).

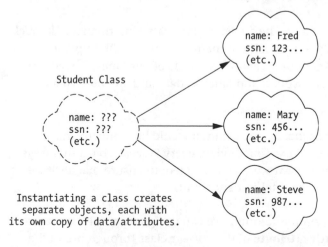

Figure 7-5. Objects "fill in" their individual attribute values.

Suppose there were some piece of general information—say, the count of the total number of students enrolled at the university—that we wanted ***all*** Student objects to have shared access to. We could implement this as a simple attribute of the Student class, int totalStudents, along with code for manipulating the attribute as shown here:

```
using System;

public class Student
{
  private int totalStudents;
  // etc.

  // Property.
  public int TotalStudents {
    // accessor details omitted ...
  }

  public int ReportTotalEnrollment() {
    Console.WriteLine("Total Enrollment:   " + TotalStudents);
  }

  public void IncrementEnrollment() {
    TotalStudents = TotalStudents + 1;
  }

  // etc.
}
```

This would be inefficient for two reasons:

- First of all, each object would be duplicating the same information. Although an int(eger) doesn't take up a lot of memory, this is still, in principle, a waste of storage. And, storage space aside, one of our "quests" in adopting object technology is to avoid redundancy of data and/or code whenever possible.

- Secondly, and perhaps more significantly, it would be cumbersome to have to call the IncrementEnrollment method on every Student object in the system each time a new Student were to be created, to ensure that all Students were in agreement on the total student count.

Fortunately, there is a simple solution! We can designate totalStudents to be what is known as a **static attribute** of the Student class through use of the static keyword:

```
public class Student
{
  // totalStudents is declared to be a static attribute.
  private static int totalStudents;

  // details omitted ...

  public int ReportTotalEnrollment() {
    Console.WriteLine("Total Enrollment:  " + TotalStudents);
  }

  public void IncrementEnrollment() {
    totalStudents = totalStudents + 1;
  }
}
```

The C# naming convention calls for using Pascal casing for all static attribute names **regardless of their accessibility** *(public or nonpublic). Doing so causes conflicts if we later decide to declare a property for such attributes, as we'll then want to capitalize the property's name, as well.*

```
public class Example
{
  private static int ImportantValue;  // This attribute name is
                                       // rendered in Pascal casing ...

  // ... as is this property name! The compiler won't approve.
  public static int ImportantValue {
    // accessor details omitted.
  }
}
```

To resolve this conflict, we're going to "break from tradition" by using **Camel casing** *to name nonpublic static attributes, reserving the use of Pascal casing for* **public** *static attributes only.*

We'll revisit this matter a bit later in this chapter.

A static attribute is one whose value is shared by all instances of a class; its value conceptually belongs to the class as a whole instead of belonging to any one instance/object of that class (see Figure 7-6).

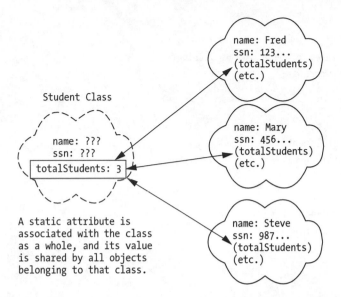

Figure 7-6. The value of a static attribute conceptually belongs to the class as a whole.

Each Student object can access and modify the shared totalStudents attribute just as if it were a nonstatic attribute; in our earlier code example, the ReportTotalEnrollment and IncrementEnrollment methods look no different than any other Student method in terms of how they manipulate the totalStudents attribute. The difference is that the value of a static attribute is shared, so if we were to execute the following client code:

```
Student s1 = new Student();
s1.Name = "Fred";
s1.IncrementEnrollment();

Student s2 = new Student();
s2.Name = "Mary";
s2.IncrementEnrollment();

Student s3 = new Student();
s3.Name = "Steve";
s3.IncrementEnrollment();
```

then the resultant value of totalStudents would be affected as follows (assuming that it starts with a value of 0):

- When s1 is passed the message s1.IncrementEnrollment(), the shared value of totalStudents is incremented by 1 (from 0 to 1).

- When s2 is passed the message s2.IncrementEnrollment(), the shared value of totalStudents is incremented by 1 (from 1 to 2).

- When s3 is passed the message s3.IncrementEnrollment(), the shared value of totalStudents is incremented by 1 (from 2 to 3).

At any time thereafter, if any one of the three objects inspects the value of totalStudents, it will be equal to 3. That is, if we were to invoke the ReportTotalEnrollment method on either s1, or s2, or s3, the result would be the same: the information printed by the method call would be the same in every case. Expanding upon our previous example:

```
Student s1 = new Student();
s1.Name = "Fred";
s1.IncrementEnrollment();

Student s2 = new Student();
s2.Name = "Mary";
s2.IncrementEnrollment();

Student s3 = new Student();
s3.Name = "Steve";
s3.IncrementEnrollment();

s1.ReportTotalEnrollment());
s2.ReportTotalEnrollment());
s3.ReportTotalEnrollment());
```

Here's the output for the preceding code:

```
Total Enrollment:   3
Total Enrollment:   3
Total Enrollment:   3
```

Static Properties

We would most likely declare the static totalStudents attribute to be private (like virtually all attributes), in which case we'd perhaps want to code public accessors for it. The preferred way to access the value of a static attribute in C# is to declare a **static property.** Other than the obvious use of the static keyword, a static property is indistinguishable from a nonstatic property:

```
public class Student
{
  private static int totalStudents;

  // Other details omitted.

  // We've declared a public static property to access our static attribute.
  public static int TotalStudents {
    get {
      return totalStudents;
    }
    set {
      totalStudents = value;
    }
  }

  // Details omitted.

  public void IncrementEnrollment() {
    // We're now taking advantage of our get/set accessors (note use of capital
    // "T" in the following code).
    TotalStudents = TotalStudents + 1;
  }
}
```

> As mentioned earlier, the official C# naming conventions call for us to use
> Pascal casing (a) for all static attributes regardless of their accessibility and
> (b) for the names of all public properties. If we were to follow **both** of these
> naming conventions, the TotalStudents attribute and the TotalStudents
> property would have exactly the same name, which the compiler won't allow.
>
> To avoid such a conflict, one of these two naming conventions must be vio-
> lated, and so as mentioned earlier, we've elected to use Camel casing to name
> **nonpublic** static attributes.

The get and set accessors for a static property are defined in the same manner as they are for a nonstatic property: the return type of the get accessor is
implicitly the same as the property type, and the set accessor implicitly has
a return type of void and is passed a parameter named value.

Static properties can't be invoked on an individual object, but are instead
invoked on a class as a whole using dot notation:

```
Console.WriteLine("Total Enrollment = " + Student.TotalStudents);
```

If we were to try to invoke a static property on an object by mistake:

```
Student s1 = new Student();
Console.WriteLine("Total Enrollment = " + s1.TotalStudents);
```

the compiler would generate the following error:

```
Error CS0176: Static member 'Student.TotalStudents' cannot be accessed
with an instance reference; qualify it with a type name instead
```

Let's rework the client code from the previous example to make use of the static property:

```
Student s1 = new Student();
s1.Name = "Fred";
s1.IncrementEnrollment();

Student s2 = new Student();
s2.Name = "Mary";
s2.IncrementEnrollment();

Student s3 = new Student();
s3.Name = "Steve";
s3.IncrementEnrollment();

Console.WriteLine("Total Enrollment = " + Student.TotalStudents);
```

This results in the following output:

```
Total Enrollment = 3
```

Static Methods

Just as static attributes/properties are associated with a class as a whole versus relating to a specific individual object, **static methods** are in turn methods that may be invoked on a class as a whole.

Let's declare both the IncrementEnrollment and ReportTotalEnrollment methods to be static:

```
public class Student
{
  private static int totalStudents;

  // Other details omitted.
```

```
public static int TotalStudents {
  get {
    return totalStudents;
  }
  set {
    totalStudents = value;
  }
}

// These two methods are now static methods.

public static void IncrementEnrollment() {
  // The method body is unchanged from when this was a nonstatic method.
  TotalStudents = TotalStudents + 1;
}

public static int ReportTotalEnrollment() {
  // Ditto!
  Console.WriteLine("Total Enrollment:  " + TotalStudents);
}

  // etc.
}
```

As with static properties, static methods can *only* be invoked on a class as a whole:

```
Student.IncrementEnrollment();
```

We can't invoke static methods on individual object references; if we were to attempt to invoke the IncrementEnrollement method on a Student object by mistake:

```
Student s1 = new Student();
s1.IncrementEnrollment(); // This won't compile; IncrementEnrollment is static
```

the compiler would produce the following error message:

```
Error: cs0176:  Static member 'Student.IncrementEnrollment()' cannot be
accessed with an instance reference; qualify it with a type name instead
```

Reworking our client code example yet again to take into account the fact that IncrementEnrollment and ReportTotalEnrollment methods are now static methods, we'd have the following:

```
Student s1 = new Student();
s1.Name = "Fred";
Student.IncrementEnrollment();

Student s2 = new Student();
s2.Name = "Mary";
Student.IncrementEnrollment();

Student s3 = new Student();
s3.Name = "Steve";
Student.IncrementEnrollment();

Student.ReportEnrollment();
```

Here's the output that we'd get:

```
Total Enrollment = 3
```

Restrictions on Static Methods

Note that there is an important restriction on static methods with respect to how they may access attributes of the class in which they are declared: namely, they can't access ***nonstatic*** attributes of that class. If we were to attempt to write a static method such as Print, as in the following code example, that tried to access the value of a nonstatic attribute such as name, the compiler would prevent us from doing so.

```
public class Student
{
  // Two attributes -- one static, one nonstatic.
  private string name;
  private static int totalStudents;
  // etc.

  // Assume that public properties Name and TotalStudents have been defined for
  // both attributes (details omitted).
```

```
    public static void Print() {
      // A static method may NOT access NON-static attributes
      // such as 'name' -- the following line won't compile.
      Console.WriteLine(Name + " is one of " + TotalStudents +
                    "students.");
  }
}
```

The compiler would generate the following error message regarding the WriteLine statement:

```
error cs0120: An object reference is required for the non-static field,
method, or property 'Student.name"
```

Why is this? As we learned in Chapter 3, classes are empty templates as far as nonstatic attributes are concerned; it's not until we instantiate an object that its (nonstatic) attribute values get filled in (see Figures 7-7 and 7-8).

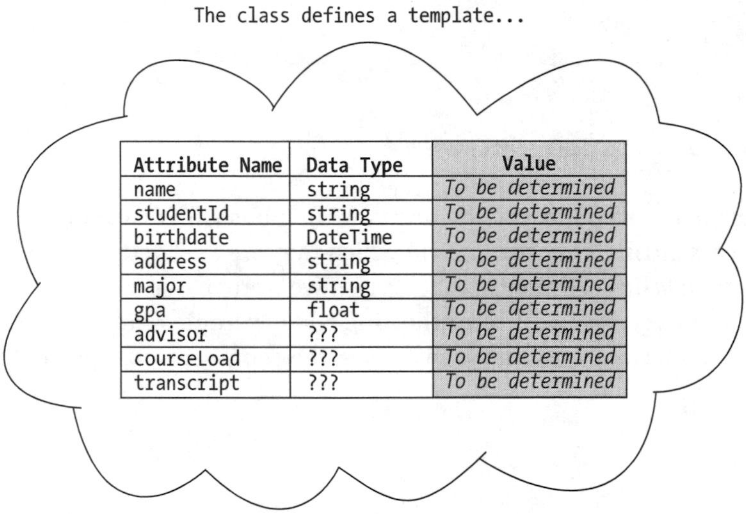

The class defines a template...

Attribute Name	Data Type	Value
name	string	To be determined
studentId	string	To be determined
birthdate	DateTime	To be determined
address	string	To be determined
major	string	To be determined
gpa	float	To be determined
advisor	???	To be determined
courseLoad	???	To be determined
transcript	???	To be determined

Figure 7-7. A class serves as a template for creating objects.

... and each object subsequently
fills in its own unique attribute values.

Attribute Name	Data Type	Value
name	string	John Smith
studentId	string	123456
birthdate	DateTime	November 6, 1980
address	string	123 Main Street, ...
major	string	Computer Science
gpa	float	3.5
advisor	???	(etc.)
courseLoad	???	(etc.)
transcript	???	(etc.)

Figure 7-8. Objects then fill in the values of their **nonstatic** *attributes.*

If a static method is invoked on a class as a whole, and that method were in turn to try to access the value of a nonstatic attribute, the value of that attribute would be undefined for the class, as illustrated conceptually in Figure 7-9.

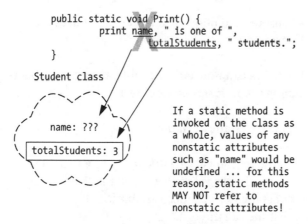

```
public static void Print() {
        print name, " is one of ",
                totalStudents, " students.";
}
```
Student class

name: ???

totalStudents: 3

If a static method is
invoked on the class as
a whole, values of any
nonstatic attributes
such as "name" would be
undefined ... for this
reason, static methods
MAY NOT refer to
nonstatic attributes!

Figure 7-9. Nonstatic attribute values are undefined in the class context.

Two other restrictions on static methods:

- They can't be overridden by derived classes, and so the virtual keyword can't be applied to a static method when it's declared:

```
// This won't compile.
public virtual static void IncrementEnrollment() {
  // details omitted ...
}
```

- Static methods may not be declared to be abstract either:

```
// This won't compile either.
public abstract static void IncrementEnrollment();
```

If we were to try to compile either of the previous code snippets in the context of the Student class, the following compiler error would be generated:

```
error CS0112: A static member 'Student.IncrementEnrollment' cannot be
marked as override, virtual, or abstract
```

C#-Specific Terminology

To differentiate between static attributes and nonstatic attributes, C# uses the following alternative (preferred) terminology:

- The term **instance variable** refers to a nonstatic attribute, because such an attribute has value or meaning for an *instance,* or object.

- The term **static variable** refers to a static attribute.

To round out this terminology, the term **local variable** refers to a variable that is declared inside of a method, and hence is locally scoped relative to that method. Local variables are neither static nor instance variables.

Here is a code snippet that illustrates all three:

```
public class Student
{
  // Attributes.
  private string name;                  // an instance variable
  private static int totalStudentCount; // a static variable
```

```
  // Methods.
  public void SomeMethod(int x) {        // x is a local variable ...
    bool y;                              // ... as is y.
    // etc.
  }


  // etc.
}
```

Utility Classes

As we've just seen, static methods are used to provide generic functionality that is independent of any particular object. For example, we've been using the syntax

```
Console.WriteLine(string expression);
```

throughout the book to display messages to the console. As it turns out, Console is a class predefined in the .NET Framework Class Library (in the System namespace), and WriteLine is a static method on that class. We therefore needn't ever instantiate a Console object to print messages to the screen; we simply call the WriteLine method on the Console class as a whole.

Another example of a predefined class that is comprised wholly of static methods and public static attributes is the Math class (also in the System namespace).

- The Math class declares a variety of static methods to compute trigonometric, exponential, logarithmic, and power functions, to round numeric values, and to generate random numbers. We saw the use of one such method—Math.Sqrt()—in an example in Chapter 6:

  ```
  squareRoot[i] = Math.Sqrt(i);
  ```

- The mathematical constants e and π are declared as public static attributes of the Math class, named Math.E and Math.PI, respectively:

  ```
  Console.WriteLine("The value of pi = " + Math.PI);
  ```

We informally refer to such classes as **utility classes.**

User-Defined Utility Classes

We can use this same technique to create our own *custom* utility classes. For example, suppose that we were going to have a frequent need to do temperature conversions from degrees Fahrenheit to degrees Centigrade and vice versa. We could invent a utility class as follows:

```
// A utility class to provide F=>C and C=>F conversions.

public class Temperature {
  public static double FahrenheitToCentigrade(double tempF) {
    double tempC = (tempF - 32.0) * (5.0/9.0);
    return tempC;
  }

  public static double CentigradeToFahrenheit(double tempC) {
    double tempF = tempC * (9.0/5.0) + 32.0;
    return tempF;
  }
}
```

Then, to use this class, we'd simply write client code as follows:

```
double temp1 = 212.0;   // Boiling point on the Fahrenheit scale

// Calling our own static method.
double temp2 = Temperature.FahrenheitToCentigrade(temp);
Console.WriteLine("" + temp + " degrees F = " + temp2 + "degrees C");
```

This would give us the following output:

```
212.0 degrees F = 100.0 degrees C
```

We might even wish to include some commonly used constants—say, the boiling and freezing points of water in both F and C terms—as public static attributes in our utility class:

```
// A utility class to provide F=>C and C=>F conversions.

public class Temperature {
  // We've added some public static attributes.
  public static double FahrenheitFreezing = 32.0;
  public static double CentigradeFreezing = 0.0;
  public static double FahrenheitBoiling = 212.0;
  public static double CentigradeBoiling = 100.0;

  public static double FahrenheitToCentigrade(double tempF) {
    double tempC = (tempF - 32.0) * (5.0/9.0);
    return tempC;
  }

  public static double CentigradeToFahrenheit(double tempC) {
    double tempF = tempC * (9.0/5.0) + 32.0;
    return tempF;
  }
}
```

We could then take advantage of these constants in our client code, as well:

```
double soupTemperature;
// The value of soupTemperature is established ... details omitted.
if (soupTemperature >= Temperature.FahrenheitBoiling) { ... }
```

There is only one minor problem: we want these "constant" values to ***truly be*** constants, but as we've declared them previously—as public (static) attributes—there is nothing to prevent client code from altering their values:

```
Temperature.FahrenheitBoiling = 98.6;   // Whoops!
```

Fortunately, we can take advantage of a special type of variable known as a **constant** to remedy this problem.

Constants

A constant is a variable whose value can't be changed once it has been given an initial value. We declare a constant with the const keyword, as follows:

```
public const double FahrenheitFreezing = 32.0;
```

- Constants are implicitly static, and so the `static` keyword shouldn't be used in declaring them; if we try to do so:

```
// The following line won't compile.

public static const double FahrenheitFreezing = 32.0;
```

the compiler will generate the following error:

```
error CS0504: 'Temperature.FahrenheitFreezing' cannot be marked static
```

- Constants must be given a value when they are declared; that is, we can't declare a `const` in one part of a program and assign it a value somewhere else. If we try to declare an uninitialized `const`:

```
public const double FahrenheitFreezing;
```

the compiler will generate the following error:

```
error CS0145: a const field requires a value to be provided
```

- The convention when naming constants is to use the Pascal capitalization style.

Let's retrofit our `Temperature` class with `constant` attributes:

```
// A utility class to provide F=>C and C=>F conversions.

public class Temperature
{
    // We've added the const keyword to these declarations.
    public const double FahrenheitFreezing = 32.0;
    public const double CentigradeFreezing = 0.0;
    public const double FahrenheitBoiling = 212.0;
    public const double CentigradeBoiling = 100.0;

    public static double FahrenheitToCentigrade(double tempF) {
        double tempC = (tempF - 32.0) * (5.0/9.0);
        return tempC;
    }
```

```
public static double CentigradeToFahrenheit(double tempC) {
    double tempF = tempC * (9.0/5.0) + 32.0;
    return tempF;
  }
}
```

Now, if we attempt to alter the value of one of these ***truly constant*** constants from client code:

```
Temperature.FahrenheitBoiling = 98.6;   // This won't compile!
```

we'd get the following (admittedly somewhat cryptic) compilation error:

```
error CS0219: The left-hand side of an assignment must be a variable,
property, or indexer
```

Of course, even ***within*** our Temperature class, this same prohibition exists: after the first assignment of a value to any const variable, that value is unchangeable.

Other facts about consts:

- The initial value assigned to a const must be an expression that is computable at ***compile*** time:

  ```
  public class MyUtilityClass
  {
    // This will compile ...
    public const int ImportantConstant = 123 + 456;
    // This will NOT ...
    public const double AnotherConstant = Math.Sqrt(2.0);
  ```

  In the preceding snippet, the second const declaration won't compile, because Math.Sqrt is a ***method*** and hence can only be invoked at ***run time.***

- The type of a const can only be one of the predefined numerical types (char, int, double, byte, etc.) or a string.

- We may declare consts locally to a method, as well:

  ```
  public class SomeClass
  {
    // Details omitted.
  ```

```
public void SomeMethod() {
  int x;
  const int y = 7;
  // etc.
}
}
```

Summary

Hooray—you did it! You've made it through all of the major object technology concepts that you'll need to know for the rest of the book, learning a great deal of C# syntax in the process.

Please make sure that you're comfortable with these concepts before proceeding to Part Two, as they will form the foundation of the rest of your object learning experience:

- These same concepts will be reinforced when you learn how to model a problem in Part Two.

- They will be reinforced yet again when you learn how to render a model as C# code in Part Three.

In this chapter, you've learned that

- Different objects can respond to the same exact message in different class-specific ways, thanks to an OO language feature known as polymorphism.

- Abstract classes are useful if we want to prescribe common behaviors among a group of (derived) classes without having to go into details about those behaviors. We specify the *"what"* that an object must do (the messages that an object must be able to respond to, also known as method signatures) without specifying the *"how"* (the method bodies) in the base class.

- Interfaces are an even more abstract way to prescribe behaviors; by implementing multiple interfaces, a class of objects make take on multiple roles in an application.

- Static attributes/properties may be used to enable an entire class of objects to share data, and static methods enable us to provide services that are available to the application through a class as a whole.

- How we may take advantage of static features along with constant attributes to create custom utility classes.

Reflecting back on our home construction example from the Introduction to this book, you now know all about the unique properties of "blue stars" (objects), and why they are superior construction materials. But, you still need to learn how to lay out a blueprint for how to use them effectively in building an application—we'll teach you how to do so in Part Two!

Exercises

1. Test yourself: run through the following list of OO terms—some formal, some informal—and see if you can define each in your own words without referring back to the text:

Abstract class	Constant	Leaf node
Abstract method	Constructor	Link
Abstraction	Delegation	Member
Accessor (of a property)	Derived class	Message
Accessor method	Dictionary	Method
Aggregation	Encapsulation	Method header
Ancestor class	Feature	Method signature
Association	Field	Modeling
Attribute	Generalization	Multiple inheritance
Base class	get accessor	Multiplicity
Behavioral relationship	"Get" method	Object (in the software sense)
Binary association	Getter	
Class	Handle	Operation
Class hierarchy	Information hiding	Ordered list
Class variable	Inheritance	Overloading
Classification	Instance	Overriding
Client (object)	Instance variable	Parent class
Client code	Instantiation	Polymorphism
Collection class	Interface	Predefined type
Composite class	Local variable	Private accessibility

Public accessibility	set accessor	Static attribute
Reference	"Set" method	Static method
Reference variable	Setter	Static variable
Reflexive association	Sibling class	Structural relationship
Root (of a class hierarchy)	Simple type	Supplier (object)
	Sorted ordered list	Unary association
Service	Specialization	User-defined type
Set (as a collection type)	State	

2. Which attributes, belonging to which SRS classes, might be well suited to being declared as static?

3. Which attributes, belonging to which Prescription Tracking System classes (as described in Appendix B), might be well suited to being declared as static?

4. It has been argued that the ability to declare and implement interfaces in the C# language eliminates the need for multiple inheritance support. Do you agree or disagree? Why? Can you think of any ways in which implementing multiple interfaces "falls short" as compared with true multiple inheritance?

5. The following client code scenarios would each cause compilation errors—can you explain why this is so in each case? Be as precise as possible as to the reasons—they may not be as obvious as first meets the eye!

    Assume that Professor and Student are both classes that implement the ITeacher interface.

    Scenario #1:

    ```
    Professor p;
    Student s = new Student();
    ITeacher t;

    t = s;
    p = t;
    ```

Scenario #2:

```
Professor p = new Professor();
Student s;
ITeacher t = new Student();

s = t;
```

Scenario #3:

```
Professor p = new Professor();
Student s = new Student();
ITeacher t;

p = t;
```

Part Two

Object Modeling 101

CHAPTER 8

The Object Modeling Process in a Nutshell

Let's look in on the homebuilder whom we met in the Introduction to this book. He's just returned from a seminar titled "Blue Stars: A Builder's Dream Come True." He now knows all about the unique properties of blue stars, and appreciates why they are superior construction materials—just as you've learned about the unique properties of software objects as application "construction materials" earlier in the book. But, he is still inexperienced with actually *using* blue stars in a construction project: in particular, he doesn't yet know how to develop a blueprint suitable for a home that is to be built from blue stars. And, *we* still need to discuss how to develop a "blueprint" for a software system that is to be constructed from objects. This is the focus of Part Two of this book.

In this chapter, you'll learn

- The goals and philosophy behind object modeling

- How much flexibility we have in terms of selecting or devising a modeling methodology

- The pros and cons of object modeling software tools

The "Big Picture" Goal of Object Modeling

Our goal in object modeling is to render a precise, concise, understandable object-oriented model, or "blueprint," of the system to be automated. This model will serve as an important tool for communication:

- ***To the future users of the system that we are about to build, an object model communicates our understanding of the system requirements.*** Having the users review and "bless" the model will ensure that we get off on the right foot with a project, for a mistake in judgment at the requirements analysis stage can prove much more costly to fix—by orders of magnitude—than if such a misunderstanding is found and corrected when the system is still just a "gleam in the user's eye."

- **To the software development team, an object model communicates the structure and function of the software that needs to be built in order to satisfy those requirements.** This benefits not only the software engineers themselves, but also the folks who are responsible for quality assurance, testing, and documentation.

- Long after the application is operational, an object model lives on as a "schematic diagram" to help the myriad folks responsible for supporting and maintaining an application understand its structure and function.

> *Of course, this last point is true only if the object model accurately reflects the system as it was actually built, not just as it was originally conceived. The design of complex systems invariably changes during their construction, so care should be taken to keep the object model up-to-date as the system is built.*

Modeling Methodology = Process + Notation + Tool

According to Webster's dictionary, a **methodology** is

> *A set of systematic procedures used by a discipline [to achieve a particular desired outcome].*

A modeling methodology, OO or otherwise, ideally involves three components:

- A **process:** The "how to" steps for gathering the requirements and determining the abstraction to be modeled

- A **notation:** A graphical "language" for communicating the model

- A **tool:** An automated way of rendering the notation, typically in "drag-and-drop" fashion

Although these constitute the ideal components of a modeling methodology, they are not all of equal importance.

- Adhering to a sound *process* is certainly critical.

- However, we can sometimes get by with a narrative text description of an abstraction without having to resort to portraying it with formal graphical *notation.*

- And, when we *do* choose to depict an abstraction formally via a graphical notation, it isn't mandatory that we use a specialized *tool* for doing so.

In other words, following an organized process is the most critical aspect of object modeling; using a particular notation is important, but less so; and our choice of a particular tool for rendering the model is the least important aspect of the three (see Figure 8-1).

Process + Notation + Tool

Figure 8-1. Of the three aspects of a methodology, a sound process is by far the most important.

Many important contributions in the form of new processes, notations, and tools have been made in the OO methodology arena over the years by numerous well-known methodologists. In some sense, if you're just getting into objects for the first time now, you're fortunate, because you managed to avoid the "methodology wars" that raged for many years as methodologists and their followers argued about what were in some cases seemingly esoteric details.

Here is a partial list of contributions made in the object methodology arena over the past few decades; the list is in no particular order.

- *James Rumbaugh et al.:* The Object Modeling Technique (OMT)

- *Grady Booch:* The Booch Method

- *Sally Schlaer and Stephen Mellor:* Emphasis on state diagrams

- *Rebecca Wirfs-Brock et al.:* Responsibility-driven design; "Classes—Responsibilities—Collaborations" (CRC) cards

- *Bertrand Meyer:* The Eiffel programming language; the notion of programming by contract

- *James Martin/James Odell:* Retooling of their functional decomposition methodologies for use with object-oriented systems

- *Peter Coad/Edward Yourdon:* As in the preceding entry

- *Ivar Jacobson:* Use cases as a means of formalizing requirements

- *Derek Coleman et al. (HP):* The Fusion Method

- *Erich Gamma, Richard Helm, Ralph Johnson, John Vlissides (the "Gang of Four"):* Design pattern reuse

In recent years, there has been a major push in the industry to meld the best ideas of competing methodologies into a single approach, with particular emphasis being placed on coming up with a universal modeling notation. The resultant notation, known as the **Unified Modeling Language (UML),** represents the collaborative efforts of three of the leaders in the OO methodology field—James Rumbaugh, Grady Booch, and Ivar Jacobson—and has become the industry standard object modeling notation. (You'll learn the basics of UML in Chapters 10 and 11.)

Along with the UML, these three gentlemen—known affectionately in the industry as the "Three Amigos"—have also contributed heavily to the evolution of an overall methodology known as the Rational Unified Process (RUP), a full-blown software development methodology encompassing modeling, project management, and configuration management workflows. But we aren't going to dwell on the details of this particular methodology in this book, because as we mentioned in the Introduction, it isn't our intention to teach you any one specific methodology in great detail. By learning a sound, *generic* process for object modeling, you'll be armed with the knowledge you need to read about, evaluate, and select a specific methodology such as RUP, or to craft your own hybrid approach by mixing and matching the processes, notation, and tool(s) from various methodologies that make the most sense for your organization.

As for modeling tools, you don't need one, strictly speaking, to appreciate the material presented in this book. But, we've anticipated that you'll likely want to get your "hands dirty" with a modeling tool. Because of this, we include a general discussion of tool pros and cons a bit later in this chapter.

It's important to keep in mind that a methodology is but a means to an end, and it's the *end*—a usable, flexible, maintainable, reliable, and functionally correct software system, along with thorough, clear supporting documentation—that we care most about when all is said and done.

To help illustrate this point, let's use a simple analogy. Say that our goal is to cheer people up. We decide to hand draw (process) a smiley face (an abstraction of the desired behavior, rendered with a graphical notation) with a pencil (tool), as shown in Figure 8-2.

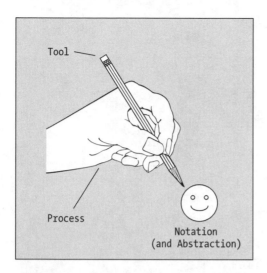

Figure 8-2. A methodology encompasses process, notation, and tools.

After we're done, we put our pencil away, hang our smiley face picture on the wall, and go about our business. A few days go by, and we note that people are indeed cheered up by our picture, and so our original goal has been achieved. In hindsight, we could have accomplished this same goal using

- A variety of different "processes"—hand drawing, rubber stamping, cutting pictures from a magazine

- A variety of different "notations"—the graphical notation of a smiley face, or a cartoon, or the narrative text of a joke or sign

- A variety of different "tools"—a pen, a pencil, a paintbrush, a crayon

Now, back to our homebuilding analogy. Long after the architect and construction crew have left a building site, taking their equipment and tools with them, the house that they have built will remain standing as a testimonial to the quality of the materials they used, how sound a construction approach was employed, and how elegant a blueprint they had to start with. The blueprint will come in handy later on when the time comes to remodel or maintain the home, so we certainly won't throw it away; but, the "livability" and ease/affordability of maintaining the home will be the primary measure of success.

The same is true for software development: the real legacy of a software development project is the resultant software system, which is, after all, the reason for using a methodology to produce a model in the first place. We must take care to avoid getting so caught up in debating the relative merits of one methodology versus another that we fail to produce useful software; as you can see in Figure 8-3, there are ***many*** paths to the same destination.

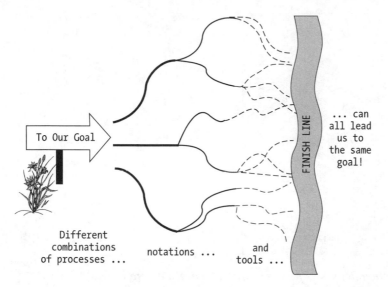

Figure 8-3. Many different approaches can serve us well when building software.

Our Object Modeling Process, in a Nutshell

We present here a basic preview of the modeling process that we advocate, and which we're going to illustrate in depth throughout the remainder of Part Two of the book.

- Begin by obtaining or writing a narrative problem statement, similar to the Student Registration System (SRS) problem statement presented in the Introduction, or the alternative case study problem statements included as Appendix B. Think about the different categories of users that will be interacting with the system, and the various situations in which they'll each use it, to make sure that you uncover any not-so-obvious requirements that may have been missed. (We'll discuss a technique for doing this—known as **use case modeling**—in Chapter 9.)

- Handle the data side of the application by identifying the different classes of "real-world" objects that your application will need to be concerned with, and determine how these interrelate. (We'll illustrate the process of creating a **class diagram** in Chapter 10.)

- Handle the functional side of the application by studying how objects need to collaborate to accomplish the system's mission, determining what behaviors/responsibilities will be required of each class. (We'll illustrate the process of modeling the ***behavioral aspects*** of an OO system in Chapter 11.)

- Test the model to ensure that it does indeed meet all of the original requirements. (We'll discuss testing in Chapter 12.)

You'll see plenty of examples of each of these techniques in the chapters to follow, and will get an opportunity to practice these techniques based on the "hands-on" exercises suggested at the end of each chapter. Armed with a solid model of the SRS, you'll then be ready to render the model into C# code, which is the subject of Part Three of the book.

Note that these process steps need not be performed in strictly sequential fashion. In fact, as you become comfortable with each of the steps, you may find yourself carrying some of them out in parallel, or in "shuffled" order. For example, contemplating the behavioral aspects of a model may bring to light new data requirements. In fact, for all but the most trivial models, it's commonplace to iterate through these steps multiple times, "dialing in" increased levels of understanding, hence more detail in the model and supporting documentation, with each iteration.

It's also important to note that the formality of the process should be adjusted to the size of the project team and the complexity of the requirements. If we separate the *form* of using a methodology from the *substance* of what that methodology produces in the way of **artifacts**—models, documentation, code, and so on—then a good rule of thumb is that a project team should spend no more than 10 to 20 percent of its time on form, 80 to 90 percent on substance. If the team finds itself spending so much time on form that little or no progress is being made on substance, it's time to reevaluate the methodology and its various components, to see where simplifying adjustments or improvements to efficiency may be made.

Thoughts Regarding Object Modeling Software Tools

It's worthwhile to spend a little bit of time talking about the pros and cons of using an object modeling software tool. For purposes of learning how to produce models, a generic drawing tool such as Microsoft PowerPoint may be good enough; for that matter, you may simply want to sketch your models using paper and pencil. But, getting some hands-on experience with using a tool specifically designed for object modeling will better prepare you for your first "industrial-strength" project, and so you may wish to acquire one before embarking upon the next chapter. You'll find information about various object modeling software tools, including links to free or evaluation copies of software, at http://objectstart.com.

> *We make it a practice not to mention specific tools, vendors, versions, etc., in this book, as they change much too rapidly. As soon as a software product is mentioned in print, we're virtually guaranteed that it will either change names, change vendors who market it, or disappear completely!*

Object modeling tools fall under the general heading of **Computer-Aided Software Engineering,** or **CASE, tools.** CASE tools afford us with many advantages, but aren't without their drawbacks.

The Advantages of Using CASE Tools

There are many arguments in favor of using CASE tools; several of the more compelling are as follows.

Ease of Use

CASE tools provide a quick drag-and-drop way to create visual models. Rather than trying to render a given notation with a generic drawing tool, where your basic drawing components are simple lines, arrows, text, boxes, and other geometric shapes, CASE tools provide one or more palettes of prefabricated graphical components specific to the supported notation. For example, you can drag and drop the graphical representation for a class rather than having to painstakingly fabricate it from simpler drawing components.

Added Information Content

CASE tools produce "intelligent" drawings that enforce the syntax rules of a particular notation. This is in contrast to a generic drawing package, which will pretty much let you draw whatever you like, whether it adheres to the notational syntax or not.

The controls imposed by a CASE tool can be a mixed blessing: on the plus side, they will prevent you from making syntactic errors, but as we discuss a little later, they may also prevent you from making desired adjustments to the notation.

Also, information about the classes reflected in a diagram—their names, attributes, methods, and relationships—is typically stored in a repository that underlies the diagram. Most CASE tools provide documentation generation features based upon this repository, enabling you to automatically generate project documentation such as a **data dictionary report,** a type of report that we'll discuss in Chapter 10. Some tools even allow you to tap into this repository programmatically, should you find a need to do so.

Automated Code Generation

Most CASE tools provide code generation capabilities, enabling you to transition from a diagram to skeletal C# (or other) code with the push of a button. You may or may not wish to avail yourself of this feature, however, for the following reasons:

- Depending on how much control the CASE tool gives you as to the structure that the generated code takes, the code that is generated will potentially not meet team/corporate standards.

- With most tools, you're unable to edit the generated code externally to the tool, because the tool will then be "unaware" of the changes that you've made, meaning that the next time the code is generated, your changes will be overwritten and obliterated.

- This has implications for reusing code from other projects, as well: make sure that your tool of choice allows you to import and introduce software components that didn't originate within the tool.

It's sometimes better in the end to write your code from scratch, for even though it may take a bit longer at the outset, it often is much easier to manage such code over the lifetime of the project, and you avoid becoming "enslaved" to a particular modeling tool for ongoing code maintenance. In the worst-case scenario, the tool vendor goes out of business, and you're left with an unsupported product and perhaps unsupportable project.

Project Management Aids

Many CASE tools provide some sort of version control, enabling you to maintain different generations of the same model. If you make a change to your model, but then after reviewing the change with your users decide that you'd prefer to return to the way things were previously, it's trivial to do if version control is in place.

CASE tools also often provide configuration management/team collaboration capabilities, to enable a group of modelers to easily share in the creation of a single model.

Flexibility

Some CASE tools support multiple graphical notations, enabling you to initially create a diagram in one notation but to then convert the diagram to another notation quickly and effortlessly.

This doesn't always occur flawlessly, however; things can get lost in the translation if the two notations don't have a one-for-one match in terms of notational components; it's not unusual to have to do some minor cleanup after the fact.

Some tools even support customizable or "do it yourself" notational paradigms, should you wish to either embellish a standard notation such as UML or to invent a new notation from scratch.

Some Drawbacks of CASE Tools

CASE tools aren't without their drawbacks, however:

- ***CASE tools can be expensive;*** it's not unusual for a high-end CASE tool to cost hundreds or even thousands of dollars per "seat."

- ***CASE tools can sometimes be inflexible***—we talk about adapting processes, notations, and tools to suit your own needs throughout Part Two of the book, but tools don't always cooperate! We'll point out in upcoming chapters some specific examples of situations where you might want to bend the notation a little bit, if your CASE tool will accommodate it.

- You run the risk of ***getting "locked into" a particular vendor's product*** if the CASE tool in question can't export your model in a vendor-neutral fashion (e.g., as XML).

- ***It's easy to get caught up with form over substance!*** This is true of any automated tool—even a word processor tends to lure people into spending more time on the cosmetics of a document than is warranted, long after the substantive content is rock solid.

Generally speaking, however, the pros of using an OO CASE tool significantly outweigh the cons—consider the cons as "words to the wise" on how to successfully apply a tool to your modeling efforts.

A Reminder

Although we've said it several times already in this book, it's important to remind you that the process of object modeling is language neutral. We presented C# syntax in Part One of the book because our ultimate goal is to make you comfortable with both object modeling and C# programming. In Part Two of the book, however, we're going to drift away from C#, because we truly are at a point where the concepts you'll be learning are just as applicable to C# as they are to Java , or C++, or any other OO programming language. But, never fear—we'll return to C# "big time" in Part Three!

Summary

By far, the most important lesson to take away from this chapter is the following:
Don't get caught up in form over substance! The model that you produce is only a means to an end . . . and the process, notation, and tools that you use to produce the model are but a ***means*** to the means to this end. If you get too hung

up on which notation to use, or which process to use, or which tool to use, you may wind up spinning your wheels in "analysis paralysis." Don't lose sight of your ultimate goal: ***to build usable, flexible, maintainable, reliable, functionally correct software systems.***

Exercises

1. Briefly describe the methodology—process, notation, and tool(s)—that you used on a recent software development project. What aspects of this methodology worked well for you and your teammates, and what, in hindsight, do you think could have been approached more effectively?

2. Research one of the object modeling technologies/techniques mentioned in the "Modeling Methodology = Process + Notation + Tool" section earlier in this chapter, and report briefly on the process, notation, and tools involved.

Formalizing Requirements Through Use Cases

WHEN YOU GET READY to leave on a vacation, you may run through a mental or written checklist: Did you pack everything you need to take? Did you pack too much? Did you arrange to have the appropriate services (newspaper, mail delivery, etc.) stopped? Did you arrange for someone to water the plants and feed your pet rat? Once you depart on your trip, you want to enjoy yourself and know that when you arrive home again, you won't find any disasters waiting for you.

This isn't unlike a software development project: we need to organize a checklist of the things that must be provided for by the system before we embark on its development, so that the project runs smoothly and so that we don't create a disaster (in the form of unmet requirements and dissatisfied customers/users) when the system is delivered.

The art and science of requirements analysis—for it truly is both!—is so extensive a topic that we could devote an entire book to this subject alone. There is one technique in particular for discovering and rounding out requirements known as **use case modeling** that is a cornerstone of the Rational Unified Process (RUP), and which warrants your consideration. Use cases aren't strictly an artifact of OO methodologies; they can be prepared for any software system, regardless of the development methodology to be used. However, they made their debut within the software development community in the context of object systems, and have gained widespread popularity in that context.

In this chapter, you'll learn

- How we must anticipate all of the different roles that users will play when interacting with our future system

- That we must assume each of their viewpoints in describing the services that a software application as a whole is to provide

- How to prepare use cases as a means of documenting all of the preceding requirements

We'll also give you enough general background about requirements analysis to provide an appropriate context for use case modeling.

What Are Use Cases?

In determining what the desired functionality of a system is to be, we must seek answers to the following questions:

- ***Who*** will want to use our system?

- What ***services*** will the system need to provide in order to be of value to them?

- When users interact with the system for a particular purpose, what is their expectation as to the ***desired outcome?***

Use cases are a natural way to express the answers to these questions. Each use case is a simple statement, narrative or graphical in fashion, that describes a particular goal or outcome of the system, and by whom that outcome is expected. For example, one goal of the SRS is to "enable a student user to register for a course," and thus we've just expressed our first use case! (Yes, use cases really are that straightforward. In fact, we ***need*** for them to be that straightforward, so that they are understandable by the users/sponsors of the system, as we'll discuss further in a moment.)

Functional vs. Technical Requirements

The purpose of thinking through all of the use cases for a system is to explore the system's functional requirements thoroughly, so as to make sure that a particular category of user, or potential purpose for the system, isn't overlooked. We differentiate between functional requirements and technical requirements as follows.

Functional requirements are those aspects of a system that have to do with how it is to operate or function from the perspective of someone using the system. Functional requirements may in turn be subdivided into

- ***"Goal oriented" functional requirements:*** These provide a statement of a system's purpose without regard to how the requirement will "play out" from the user's vantage point—e.g., "The system must be able to produce tailorable reports." Avoid discussing implementation details when specifying goal-oriented requirements.

- **"Look and feel" requirements:** These requirements get a bit more specific in terms of what the user expects the system to look like externally (e.g., how the graphical user interface will be presented), and how he or she expects it to behave, again from the user's perspective. For example, we might have as a requirement "The user will click a button on the main GUI, and a confirmation message will appear. . . ." A good practice is to write a **concept of operations** document to serve as a "paper prototype" describing how you envision the future system will look and behave, to stimulate discussion with intended users of the as-yet-to-be-built system before you even begin modeling.

> *We present a sample concept of operations for the SRS application in Chapter 16.*

We emphasize *goal-oriented* functional requirements when preparing **use cases.**

Technical requirements, on the other hand, have more to do with *how* a system is to be built internally in order to *meet* the functional requirements; for instance: "The system will use the TCP/IP protocol . . ." or "We will use a dictionary collection as the means for tracking students. . . ." One can think of these as requirements for how programmers should tackle the *solution,* in contrast to functional require-ments, which are a statement of what the *problem* to be tackled actually is. Technical requirements such as these don't play a role in use case analysis.

Although it's certainly conceivable that the users of our system may be tech-nically sophisticated, it's best to express functional requirements in such a way that even a user who knows nothing about the inner workings of a computer will understand them. This helps to ensure that technical requirements don't "creep into" the functional requirements statement, a common mistake made by many inexperienced software developers. When we allow technical requirements to color the functional requirements, they artificially constrain the solution to a problem too early in the development life cycle.

Involving the Users

Because the intended users of a system are the ultimate experts in what they need the system to do, it's essential that they be involved in the use case defi-nition process. If the intended users haven't (as individuals) been specifically defined or recruited, as with a software product that is to be sold commercially, their anticipated needs nonetheless need to be taken into account by identifying people with comparable experience to serve as "user surrogates." Ideally, the users or user surrogates will write some or all of the use cases themselves; at a minimum, you'll interview such people, write the use cases on their behalf, and then get their confirmation that what you've written is indeed accurate.

Use cases are one of the first deliverables/artifacts to emerge in a software development project's life cycle, but also one of the last things to be put to good use in making sure that the system is a success.

They turn out to be quite useful as a basis for writing testing scripts, to ensure that all functional threads are exercised during system and user acceptance testing.

They also lend themselves to the preparation of a **requirements traceability matrix**—that is, a final checklist against which the users can verify that all of their initial requirements have indeed been met when the system is delivered. (Of course, a requirements traceability matrix must take into account all of the requirements for a system—functional as well as technical—of which use cases represent only a subset.)

Returning to the questions that we posed at the outset of this section, let's answer the first question—namely, "Who will want to use our system?"—which in use case nomenclature is known as identifying **actors.**

Actors

Actors represent anybody or anything that will interact with the system after it's built; actors drive use cases. Actors generally fall into two broad categories:

- Human users

- Other computer systems

"Interaction" is generally defined to mean using the system to achieve some result, but can also be thought of as simply (a) providing/contributing information to the system and/or (b) receiving/consuming information from the system.

By *providing* information, we mean whether or not the actor inputs substantive information that adds to the residual data stored by the system: for example, a department chairperson defining a new course offering, or a student registering his or her plan of study. This doesn't include the relatively trivial information that users have to provide to look things up: for example, typing in a student ID to request their transcript.

By *consuming* information, we mean whether or not the actor uses the system to obtain information: for example, a faculty user printing out a student roster for a course that he or she will be teaching, or a student viewing his or her course schedule online.

Identifying Actors and Determining Their Roles

We must create an actor for every different role that will be assumed by various categories of user relative to the system. To identify such roles, we typically turn first to the **narrative requirements specification,** if one exists: that is, a statement of the functional requirements, such as the Student Registration System specification. The only category of user explicitly mentioned by that specification is a student user. So, we would definitely consider Student to be one of the actor types for the SRS.

If we think beyond the specification, however, it isn't difficult to come up with other potential categories of user who might also benefit from using the SRS:

- Faculty may wish to get a headcount of how many students are registered for one of the upcoming classes that they are going to be teaching, or may use the system to post final grades, which in turn are reflected by a student's transcript.

- Department chairs may wish to see how popular various courses are or, conversely, whether or not a course ought to be cancelled due to lack of interest on the part of the student body.

- Personnel in the Registrar's Office may wish to use the SRS to verify that a particular student is projected to have met the requirements to graduate in a given semester.

- Alumni may wish to use the SRS to request copies of their transcripts.

- Prospective students—i.e., those who are thinking about applying for admission but who haven't yet done so—may wish to browse the courses that are going to be offered in an upcoming semester to help them determine whether or not the university has a curriculum that meets their interests.

and so on. Similarly, since we said that other computer systems can be actors, we might have to build interfaces between the SRS and other existing automated systems at the university, such as

- The Billing System, so that students can be billed accurately based on their current course load

- The Classroom Scheduling System, to ensure that classes to be taught are assigned to rooms of adequate capacity based on the student headcount

- The Admissions System, so that the SRS can be notified when a new student has been admitted and is eligible to register for courses

Of course, we have to make a decision early on as to what the scope of the system we're going to build should be, to avoid "requirements inflation" or "scope creep." To try and accommodate all of the actors hypothesized earlier would result in a massive undertaking that may simply be too costly for the sponsors of the system. For example, does it make sense to provide for potential students to use the SRS to preview what the university offers in the way of courses, or is there a different system—say, an online course catalog of some sort—that is better suited to this purpose? Through in-depth interviews with all of the intended user groups, the scope of the system can be appropriately bounded, and some of the actors that we conceived of may be eliminated as a result.

In our particular case, we'll assume that the sponsors of the SRS have decided that we needn't accommodate the needs of alumni or prospective students in building the system; that is, that we needn't recognize alumni or prospective students as actors. A key point here is that the sponsors decide such things, ***not the programmers!*** One responsibility of a software engineer is indeed to identify requirements, and certainly part of that responsibility may include suggesting functional enhancements that the software engineer feels will be of benefit to the user. But, the sponsors of the system rightfully have the final say in what actually gets built.

> *Many software engineers get into trouble because they assume that they "know better" than their clients as to what the users really need. You may indeed have a brilliant idea to suggest, but think of it simply as that—a sug-gestion—and consider your task as one of either convincing the sponsors/ users of its merit, or of graciously accepting their decision to decline your suggestion.*

Note that the same user may interact with the system on different occasions in different roles. That is, a professor who chairs a department may assume the role of a Department Chair actor when he or she is trying to determine whether or not a course should be cancelled. Alternatively, the same professor may assume the role of a Faculty user when he or she wishes to query the SRS for the student headcount for a particular course that he or she is teaching.

Diagramming a System and Its Actors

Once we've settled on the actors for our system, we may wish to optionally diagram them. UML notation calls for representing all actors—whether a human user or a computer system—as stick figures, and then connecting these via straight lines to a rectangle representing the system as you see in Figure 9-1.

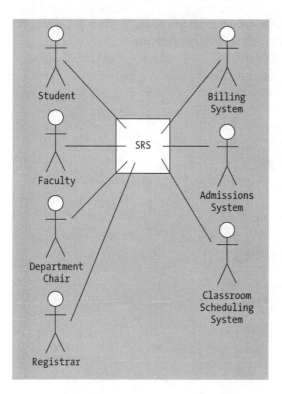

Figure 9-1. A "proper" UML use case diagram

This figure appears rather simplistic, and yet, this is a legitimate diagram that might be produced for a project such as the SRS development effort.

We prefer to use a slightly modified version of the UML notation, as follows:

- We've extended the use of a rectangle to represent not only the core system but also all actors that are external systems, rather than representing the latter as human stick figures.

- We find that using arrowheads to reflect a directional flow of information—i.e., whether an actor provides or consumes information—is a bit more communicative. For example, in our amended version of the notation as follows, we represent a student as both providing and consuming information, whereas a registrar only consumes information.

> Note that the registrar does indeed provide information, but not to the SRS directly. He or she provides information to the Admissions System as to which students are registered at the university; this information then gets fed into the SRS by the Admissions System. So, the Admissions System is shown as providing information as an actor to the SRS; but, from the standpoint of the SRS, the registrar is but a consumer.

With these slight changes in notation, as reflected in Figure 9-2, the UML diagram becomes a much more communicative instrument.

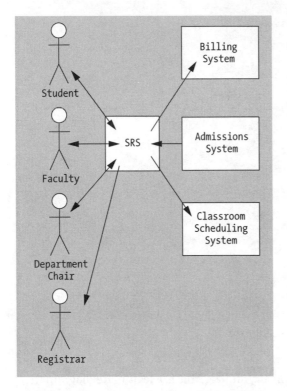

Figure 9-2. Our customized version of use case notation

Of course, if you do decide to deviate from a widely understood notational standard such as UML, you'll need to follow these steps:

1. Reach consensus among your fellow software developers, to ensure that the team as a whole is speaking the same language.

2. Document and communicate such deviations (along with the notation as a whole) to your customers/users, so that they, too, understand your particular "dialect."

3. Make sure that such documentation is incorporated into the full documentation set for the project, so that future reviewers of the documentation will immediately understand your notational "embellishments."

If you make these enhancements intuitive enough, however, they may just speak for themselves!

Of course, as we pointed out in Chapter 8, you'll also need to consider whether the CASE tool you're using, if any, will support such alterations.

Time and again throughout Part Two of this book, we'll remind you that it's perfectly acceptable to adapt or extend any process, notation, or tool that you care to adopt to best suit your company's or project's purposes; none of these methodology components is "sacred."

Specifying Use Cases

Having made a first cut at what the SRS actors are, we'll next enumerate in what ways the system will be used by these actors: in other words, the use cases themselves.

A use case represents a logical "thread," or a series of cause-and-effect events, beginning with an actor's first contact with the system and ending with the achievement of that actor's goal for using the system in the first place. Note that an actor always initiates a use case; actions initiated by a system on its own behalf don't warrant the development of a use case (although they do warrant expression as either a functional or technical requirement, as defined earlier in the chapter).

Use cases emphasize "what" the system is to do—functional requirements—without concern for "how" such things will be accomplished internally, and aren't unlike method signatures in this regard. In fact, you can think of a use case as a "behavioral signature" for the system as a whole.

Some example high-level use cases for the Student Registration System might be

- Register for a course.

- Drop a course.

- Determine a student's course load.

- Choose a faculty advisor.

- Establish a plan of study.

- View the schedule of classes.

- Request a student roster for a given course.

- Request a transcript for a given student.

- Maintain course information (for example, change the course description, reflect a different instructor for the course, and so on).

- Determine a student's eligibility for graduation.

- Post final semester grades for a given course.

Remember that a use case is initiated by an actor, which is why we didn't list other functionality called out by the SRS requirements specification, such as "Notify student by email," as use cases.

We may decompose any one of the use cases into steps, each step representing a more detailed use case; for example, "Register for a course . . ." may be decomposed into these steps:

1. Verify that a student has met the prerequisites.

2. Check student's plan of study to ensure that this course is required.

3. Check for availability of a seat in the course.

4. (Optionally) Place student on a wait list.

and so forth. Use cases may be interrelated in parent-child fashion, with more detailed use cases being shared by more than one general use case; for example, the "Request a student roster . . ." and "Post final semester grades . . ." general use cases may both involve the more detailed "Verify that professor is teaching the course in question" use case.

Unfortunately, as is true of all requirements analysis, there is no magical formula to apply in order to determine whether or not you've identified all of the important use cases or all of the actors, and/or whether you've gone into sufficient depth in terms of sub use cases. The process of use case development is iterative; when subsequent iterations fail to yield substantial changes, you're probably finished! Copious interviews and reviews with users, along with periodic team walkthroughs of the use case set as a whole, go a long way in ensuring that nothing important has been missed.

Matching Up Use Cases with Actors

Another important step is to match up use cases with actors. The relationship between actors and use cases is potentially many-to-many, in that the same actor may initiate many different use cases, and a single use case may be relevant to many different actors. By cross-referencing actors with use cases, we ensure that

- We didn't identify an actor who, in the final analysis, really has no use for the system after all.

- Conversely, that we didn't specify a use case that nobody really cares about after all.

For each use case–actor combination, it's useful to determine whether the actor consumes information and/or provides information. Another way to view this aspect of a system is whether actors need write access to the system's information resources (providing) versus having read-only access (consuming).

If the number of actors and/or use cases isn't prohibitive, a simple table such as Table 9-1 can be used to summarize all of the preceding.

Table 9-1. A Simple Actor/Use Case Cross-Referencing Technique

Initiating Actor ➤ Use Cases (Below)	Student	Faculty	Billing System	(Etc.)
Register for a course	Provides info	N/A	N/A	
Post final grades	Consumes info	Provides info	N/A	
Request a transcript	Consumes info	Consumes info	N/A	
Determine a student's course load	Consumes info	Consumes info	Consumes info	
(Etc.)				

To Diagram or Not to Diagram?

The use case concept is fairly straightforward, and hence simple narrative text as we've seen thus far in the chapter is often sufficient for expressing use cases. The UML does, however, provide a formal means for diagramming use cases and their interactions with actors. As mentioned earlier, actors (whether people or systems) are represented as stick figures; use cases are represented as ovals labeled underneath with a brief phrase describing the use case; and the box surrounding the oval(s) represent the system boundaries. Figure 9-3 shows a sample UML use case diagram; here, we depict three actors—Student, Faculty, and Registrar—as having occasion to participate individually in the Request Transcript use case.

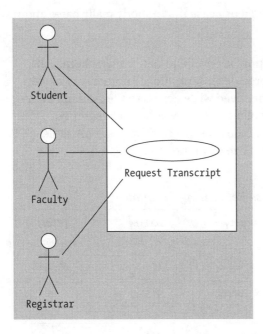

Figure 9-3. A sample UML use case diagram

When deciding whether or not to go to the trouble of diagramming your use cases rather than merely expressing them in narrative form, think back to the rationale for producing use cases in the first place: namely, to think through, and to then communicate, the software development team's understanding of the system requirements to the users/sponsors in order to obtain consensus. It's up to you, your project team, and your users/sponsors to determine whether diagrams enhance this process or not. If they do, use them; if they don't, go with narrative use case documentation instead.

Once you've documented a system's actors and use cases, whether in text alone or with accompanying diagrams, these become part of the core documentation set defining the problem to be automated. In the next chapter, we'll examine how to use such documentation as a starting point for determining what classes we'll need to create and instantiate as our system "building blocks."

The UML spells out some additional formalism with regard to use case modeling; for more details on use case diagrams, including advanced diagramming techniques, please see our recommended reading list in Chapter 17.

Summary

In this chapter, we've seen that

- Use case analysis is a simple yet powerful technique for specifying the requirements for a system more precisely and completely.

- Use cases are based upon the goal-oriented functional requirements for a system.

- Use cases are used to describe

  - The desired behavior/functionality of the system to be built

  - The external users or systems (known as actors) who avail themselves of these services

  - The interactions between the two

Exercises

1. Determine the actors that might be appropriate for the Prescription Tracking System (PTS) case study discussed in Appendix B.

2. For the problem area whose requirements you defined for exercise 3 in Chapter 2, determine what the appropriate actors might be.

3. Based on the PTS specification in Appendix B, list (a) the use cases that are explicitly called for by the specification, and (b) any additional use cases that you suspect might be worth exploring with the future users of the system.

4. Repeat exercise 3, but in the context of the problem area whose requirements you defined for exercise 3 in Chapter 2.

5. Create a table mapping the actors you identified in exercise 1 to the use cases you listed in exercise 3, indicating whether a particular actor's participation in a use case is as an information provider or consumer.

6. Create a table mapping the actors you identified in exercise 2 to the use cases you listed in exercise 4, indicating whether a particular actor's participation in a use case is as an information provider or consumer.

Modeling the Static/Data Aspects of the System

HAVING EMPLOYED USE CASE analysis techniques in Chapter 9 to round out the Student Registration System (SRS) requirements specification, we're ready to tackle the next stage of modeling, which is determining how we're going to meet those requirements in an object-oriented fashion.

We saw in Part One of the book that objects form the building blocks of an OO system, and that classes are the templates used to define and instantiate objects. An OO model, then, must specify the following:

- ***What types of objects we're going to need to create and instantiate in order to represent the proper abstraction:*** In particular, their attributes, methods, and structural relationships with one another. Because these elements of an object-oriented system, once established, are fairly static—in the same way that a house, once built, has a specific layout, a given number of rooms, a particular roofline, and so forth—we often refer to this process as preparing the **static model**.

  We can certainly change the static structure of a house over time by undertaking remodeling projects, just as we can change the static structure of an OO software system as new requirements emerge by deriving new subclasses, inventing new methods for existing classes, and so forth. However, if a structure—whether a home or a software system—is properly designed from the outset, then the need for such changes should arise relatively infrequently over its lifetime and shouldn't be overly difficult to accommodate.

- *How these objects will need to collaborate in carrying out the overall requirements, or "mission," of the system:* The ways in which objects interact can change literally from one moment to the next based upon the circumstances that are in effect. One moment, a Course object may be registering a Student object, and the next, it might be responding to a query by a Professor object as to the current student headcount. We refer to the process of detailing object collaborations as preparing the **dynamic model**. Think of this as all of the different day-to-day activities that go on in a home: same structure, different functions.

The static and dynamic models are simply two different sides of the same coin: they jointly comprise the object-oriented "blueprint" that we'll work from in implementing an object-oriented Student Registration System application in Part Three of the book.

In this chapter, we'll focus on building the static model for the SRS, leaving a discussion of the dynamic model for Chapter 11. You'll learn

- A technique for identifying the appropriate classes and their attributes

- How to determine the structural relationships that exist among these classes

- How to graphically portray this information as a **class diagram** using the Unified Modeling Language (UML) notation

Identifying Appropriate Classes

Our first challenge in object modeling is to determine what classes we're going to need as our system building blocks. Unfortunately, the process of class identification is rather "fuzzy"; it relies heavily on intuition, prior modeling experience, and familiarity with the subject area, or **domain**, of the system to be developed. So, how does an object-modeling novice *ever* get started? One tried and true (but somewhat tedious) procedure for identifying candidate classes is to use the "hunt and gather" method: that is, to hunt for and gather a list of all nouns/noun phrases from the project documentation set and to then use a process of elimination to whittle this list down into a set of appropriate classes.

In the case of the SRS, our documentation set thus far consists of the following:

- The requirements specification

- The use case model that we prepared in Chapter 9

Noun Phrase Analysis

Let's perform noun phrase analysis on the SRS requirements specification first, which was originally presented in the Introduction, a copy of which is provided in the following sidebar. We've highlighted all noun phrases.

Highlighting Noun Phrases in the SRS Specification

We have been asked to develop an *automated Student Registration System* (*SRS*) for the *university*. This *system* will enable *students* to register online for *courses* each *semester*, as well as track their *progress* toward *completion* of their *degree*.

When a *student* first enrolls at the *university*, he/she uses the *SRS* to set forth a *plan of study* as to which *courses* he/she plans on taking to satisfy a particular *degree program,* and chooses a *faculty advisor.* The *SRS* will verify whether or not the proposed *plan of study* satisfies the *requirements of the degree* that the *student* is seeking.

Once a *plan of study* has been established, then, during the *registration period* preceding each *semester, students* are able to view the *schedule of classes* online, and choose whichever *classes* they wish to attend, indicating the *preferred section* (*day of the week* and *time of day*) if the *class* is offered by more than one *professor*. The *SRS* will verify whether or not the *student* has satisfied the necessary *prerequisites* for each *requested course* by referring to the *student*'s online *transcript* of *courses completed* and *grades received* (the *student* may review his/her *transcript* online at any time).

Assuming that (a) the *prerequisites* for the *requested course(s)* are satisfied, (b) the *course(s)* meet(s) one of the *student*'s *plan of study requirements,* and (c) there is *room* available in each of the *class(es),* the *student* is enrolled in the *class(es)*.

If (a) and (b) are satisfied, but (c) is not, the *student* is placed on a *first-come, first-served wait list*. If a *class/section that he/she was previously waitlisted for* becomes available (either because some other *student* has dropped the *class* or because the *seating capacity* for the *class* has been increased), the *student* is automatically enrolled in the *waitlisted class,* and an *email message* to that effect is sent to the *student*. It is his/her *responsibility* to drop the *class* if it is no longer desired; otherwise, he/she will be billed for the *course*.

Students may drop a *class* up to the *end* of the *first week of the semester in which the class is being taught.*

A simple spreadsheet serves as an ideal tool for recording our initial find-
ings; just enter noun phrases as a single-column list in the order in which they
occur in the specification. Don't worry about trying to eliminate duplicates or
consolidating synonyms just yet; we'll do that in a moment. The resultant
spreadsheet is shown in part in Figure 10-1.

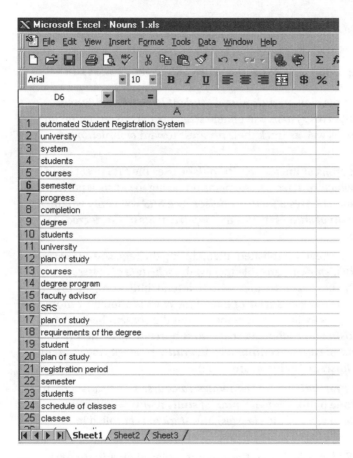

Figure 10-1. Noun phrases found in the SRS specification

We're working with a very concise requirements specification (approxi-
mately 350 words in length), and yet this process is already proving to be very
tedious! It would be impossible to carry out an exhaustive noun phrase analysis
for anything but a trivially simple specification. If you're faced with a volumi-
nous requirements specification, start by writing an "executive summary" of no
more than a few pages to paraphrase the system's mission, and then use your
summary version of the specification as the starting point for your noun survey.
Paraphrasing a specification in this fashion provides the added benefit of ensuring that you have read through the system requirements and understand the
"big picture." Of course, you'll need to review your summary narrative with your
customers/users to ensure that you've accurately captured all key points.

After you've typed all of the nouns/noun phrases into the spreadsheet, sort the spreadsheet and eliminate duplicates; this includes eliminating plural forms of singular terms (e.g., eliminate "students" in favor of "student"). We want all of our class names to be singular in the final analysis, so if any plural forms remain in the list after eliminating duplicates (e.g., "prerequisites"), make these singular, as well. In so doing, our SRS list shrinks to 38 items in length, as shown in Figure 10-2.

	A
1	automated Student Registration System
2	class
3	class that he/she was previously waitlisted for
4	completion
5	course
6	courses completed
7	day of the week
8	degree
9	degree program
10	email message
11	end
12	faculty advisor
13	first week of the semester in which the class is being taught
14	first-come, first-served wait list
15	grades received
16	plan of study
17	plan of study requirements
18	preferred section
19	prerequisites
20	professor
21	progress
22	registration period
23	requested course
24	requirements of the degree
25	responsibility
26	room
27	schedule of classes
28	seating capacity
29	section
30	section that he/she was previously waitlisted for
31	semester
32	SRS
33	student
34	system
35	time of day
36	transcript
37	university
38	waitlisted class

Sheet1 / Sheet2 / Sheet3 /

Figure 10-2. Removing duplicates streamlines the noun phrase list.

Remember, we're trying to identify both physical and conceptual objects: as stated in Chapter 3, ***"something mental or physical toward which thought, feeling, or action is directed."*** Let's now make another pass to eliminate the following:

- References to the system itself ("automated Student Registration System," "SRS," "system").

- References to the university. Because we're building the SRS within the context of a single university, the university in some senses "sits outside" and "surrounds" the SRS; we don't need to manipulate information about the university within the SRS, and so we may eliminate the term "university" from our candidate class list.

  Note, however, that if we were building a system that needed to span multiple universities—say, a system that compared graduate programs of study in information technology across the top 100 universities in the country—then we would indeed need to model each university as a separate object, in which case we'd keep "university" on our candidate class list.

- Other miscellaneous terms that don't seem to fit the definition of an object are "completion," "end," "progress," "responsibility," "registration period," and "requirements of the degree." Admittedly, some of these are debatable, particularly the last two; to play it safe, you may wish to create a list of rejected terms to be revisited later on in the modeling life cycle.

The list shrinks to 27 items as a result, as shown in Figure 10-3—it's starting to get manageable now!

	A
1	class
2	class that he/she was previously waitlisted for
3	course
4	courses completed
5	day of week
6	degree
7	degree program
8	email message
9	faculty advisor
10	first-come, first-served wait list
11	grades received
12	plan of study
13	plan of study requirements
14	preferred section
15	prerequisites
16	professor
17	requested course
18	room
19	schedule of classes
20	seating capacity
21	section
22	section that he/she was previously waitlisted for
23	semester
24	student
25	time of day
26	transcript
27	waitlisted class

`|◄ ◄ ► ►|` \ **Sheet1** / Sheet2 / Sheet3 /

Figure 10-3. Further streamlining the SRS noun phrase list

The next pass is a bit trickier. We need to group apparent synonyms, to choose the one designation from among each group of synonyms that is best suited to serve as a class name. Having a subject matter expert on your modeling team is important for this step, because determining the subtle shades of meaning of some of these terms so as to group them properly isn't always easy.

We've grouped together terms that seem to be synonyms in Figure 10-4, **bolding** the term in each synonym group that we're inclined to choose above the rest; *italicized* words represent those terms for which no synonyms have been identified.

	A
1	**class <==**
2	**course <==**
3	waitlisted class
4	class that he/she was previously waitlisted for
5	section that he/she was previously waitlisted for
6	preferred section
7	requested course
8	**section <==**
9	prerequisites
10	courses completed
11	grades received
12	**transcript <==**
13	*day of week*
14	**degree <==**
15	degree program
16	*email message*
17	faculty advisor
18	**professor <==**
19	*first-come, first-served wait list*
20	**plan of study <==**
21	plan of study requirements
22	*room*
23	*schedule of classes*
24	*seating capacity*
25	*semester*
26	*student*
27	*time of day*

|◀ ◀ ▶ ▶| \ **Sheet1** / Sheet2 / Sheet3 /

Figure 10-4. Grouping synonyms

Let's now review the rationale for our choices.

We choose the shorter form of equivalent expressions whenever possible—"degree" instead of "degree program" and "plan of study" instead of "plan of study requirements"—to make our model more concise.

Although they aren't synonyms as such, the notion of a **transcript** implies a record of "courses completed" and "grades received," so we'll opt to drop the latter two noun phrases for now.

When choosing candidate class names, we should avoid choosing nouns that imply **roles** between objects. As you learned in Chapter 5, a role is something that an object belonging to class A possesses by virtue of its relationship to/association with an object belonging to class B. For example, a professor holds the role of "faculty advisor" when that professor is associated with a student via an *advises* association. Even if a professor were to lose all of his or her advisees, thus losing the role of faculty advisor, he or she would still be a professor by virtue of being employed by the university—it's inherent in the person's nature relative to the SRS.

> *If a professor were to lose his or her job with the university, one might argue that he or she is no longer a professor; but then, this person would have no dealings with the SRS, either, so it's a moot point.*

For this reason, we prefer "Professor" to "Faculty Advisor" as a candidate class name, but make a mental note to ourselves that faculty advisor would make a good potential association when we get to considering such things later on.

Regarding the notion of a course, we see that we've collected numerous noun phrases that all refer to a course in one form or another: "class," "course," "preferred section," "requested course," "section," "prerequisite," "waitlisted class," "class that they were previously waitlisted for," "section that they were previously waitlisted for." Within this grouping, several roles are implied:

- "Waitlisted class" in its several different forms implies a role in an association between a Student and a Course.

- "Prerequisite" implies a role in an association between two Courses.

- "Requested course" implies a role in an association between a Student and a Course.

- "Preferred section" implies a role in an association between a Student and a Course.

Eliminating all of these role designations, we're left with only three terms: "class," "course," and "section." Before we hastily eliminate all but one of these as synonyms, let's think carefully about what real-world concepts we're trying to represent.

- The notion that we typically associate with the term "course" is that of a semester-long series of lectures, assignments, exams, etc., that all relate to a particular subject area, and which are a unit of education toward earning a degree. For example, Beginning Math is a course.

- The terms "class" and "section," on the other hand, generally refer to the offering of a *particular* course in a *given* semester on a given day of the week and at a given time of day. For example, the course Math 101 is being offered this coming Spring semester as three classes/sections:

  - Section 1, which meets Tuesdays from 4 to 6 p.m.

  - Section 2, which meets Wednesdays from 6 to 8 p.m.

  - Section 3, which meets Thursdays from 3 to 5 p.m.

  There is thus a one-to-many association between Course and Class/Section. The same course is offered potentially many times in a given semester and over many semesters during the "lifetime" of the course.

Therefore, "course" and "class/section" truly represent different abstractions, and we'll keep ***both*** concepts in our candidate class list. Since "class" and "section" appear to be synonyms, however, we need to choose one term and discard the other. Our initial inclination would be to keep "class" and discard "section," but in order to avoid confusion when referring to a class named `Class` (!) we'll opt for "section" instead.

Refining the Candidate Class List

A list of candidate classes has begun to emerge from the fog! Here is our remaining "short list" (please disregard the trailing symbols [*, +] for the moment—we'll explain their significance shortly):

- Course

- Day of week*

- Degree*

- Email message+

- Plan of study

- Professor

- Room*

- Schedule of classes+

- Seating capacity*

- Section

- Semester*

- Student

- Time of day*

- Transcript

- (First-come, first-served) Wait list

Not all of these will necessarily survive to the final model, however, as we're going to scrutinize each one very closely before deeming it worthy of implementation as a class. One classic test for determining whether or not an item can stand on its own as a class is to ask these questions:

- Can we think of any *attributes* for this class?

- Can we think of any *services* that would be expected of objects belonging to this class?

One example is the term "room": we could invent a Room class as follows:

```
public class Room {
  // Attributes.
  int roomNo;
  string building;
  int seatingCapacity;
  // etc.
}
```

or we could simply represent a room location as a string attribute of the Section class:

```
public class Section {
  // Attributes.
  Course offeringOf;
  string semester;
  char dayOfWeek;  // 'M', 'T', 'W', 'R', 'F'
  string timeOfDay;
  string classroomLocation; // building name and room name:  e.g.,
                            // "Government Hall Room 105"
  // etc.
}
```

Which approach to representing a room is preferred? It all depends on whether or not a room needs to be a focal point of our application. If the SRS were meant to also do "double duty" as a Classroom Scheduling System, then we may indeed wish to instantiate Room objects so as to be able to ask them to perform such services as printing out their weekly usage schedules or telling us their seating capacities. However, since these services weren't mentioned as requirements in the SRS specification, we'll opt for making a room designation a simple string attribute of the Section class. We reserve the right, however, to change our minds about this later on; it's not unusual for some items to "flip flop" over the life cycle of a modeling exercise between being classes on their own versus being represented as simple attributes of other classes.

Following a similar train of thought for all of the items marked with an asterisk (*) in the preceding candidate class list, we'll opt to treat them all as attributes rather than making them classes of their own:

- "Day of week" will be incorporated as either a `string` or `char` attribute of the `Section` class.

- "Degree" will be incorporated as a `string` attribute of the `Student` class.

- "Seating capacity" will be incorporated as an `int` attribute of the `Section` class.

- "Semester" will be incorporated as a `string` attribute of the `Section` class.

- "Time of day" will be incorporated as a `string` attribute of the `Section` class.

When we're first modeling an application, we want to focus exclusively on functional requirements at the exclusion of technical requirements, as defined in Chapter 9; this means that we need to avoid getting into the technical details of how the system is going to function behind the scenes. Ideally, we want to focus solely on what are known as **domain classes**—that is, abstractions that an end user will recognize, and which represent "real-world" entities—and to avoid introducing any extra classes that are used solely as behind-the-scenes "scaffolding" to hold the application together, known alternatively as **implementation classes** or **solution space classes**. Examples of the latter would be the creation of a collection object to organize and maintain references to all of the `Professor` objects in the system, or the use of a dictionary to provide a way to quickly find a particular `Student` object based on the associated student ID number. We'll talk more about solution space objects in Part Three of the book; for the time being, the items flagged with a plus sign (+) in the candidate class list earlier—"email message", "schedule of classes"—seem arguably more like implementation classes than domain classes.

- An email message is typically a ***transient*** piece of data, not unlike a pop-up message that appears on the screen while using an application: it gets sent ***out*** of the SRS system, and after it's read by the recipient, we have no control over whether the email is retained or deleted. It's unlikely that the SRS is going to archive copies of all email messages that have been sent—there certainly was no requirement to do so—so we won't worry about modeling them as objects at this stage in our analysis.

Email messages will resurface in Chapter 11, when we talk about the behaviors of the SRS application, because *sending* an email message is definitely an important *behavior;* but, emails don't constitute an important *structural* piece of the application, so we don't want to introduce a class for them at this stage in the modeling process. When we actually get to programming the system, we might indeed create an EmailMessage class in C#, but it needn't be modeled as a domain class. (If, on the other hand, we were modeling an email messaging system in anticipation of building one, then EmailMessage would indeed be a key domain class in our model.)

- We could go either way with the schedule of classes—include it as a candidate class, or drop it from our list. The schedule of classes, as a single object, may not be something that the user will manipulate directly, but there will be some notion behind the scenes of a schedule of classes *collection* controlling which Section objects should be presented to the user as a GUI pick list when he or she registers in a given semester. We'll omit ScheduleOfClasses from our candidate class list for now, but can certainly revisit our decision as the model evolves.

Determining whether or not a class constitutes a domain class instead of an implementation class is admittedly a gray area, and either of the preceding candidate class "rejects" could be successfully argued into or out of the list of core domain classes for the SRS. In fact, this entire exercise of identifying classes hopefully illustrates a concept that was first introduced in Chapter 2; because of its importance, we'll repeat it again in the following sidebar.

Object Modeling Isn't Easy!

. . . Developing an appropriate model for a software system is perhaps the most difficult aspect of software engineering, because:

There are an unlimited number of possibilities. Abstraction is to a certain extent in the eye of the beholder: several different observers working independently are almost guaranteed to arrive at different models. Whose is the best? Passionate arguments have ensued!

To further complicate matters, *there is virtually never only one "best" or "correct" model*, only "better" or "worse" models relative to the problem to be solved. The same situation can be modeled in a variety of different, equally valid ways. . . .

. . . There is no "acid test" to determine if a model has adequately captured all of a user's requirements.

As we continue along with our SRS modeling exercise, and particularly as we move from modeling to implementation in Part Three of the book, we'll have many opportunities to rethink the decisions that we've made here. The key point to remember is that the model isn't "cast in stone" until we actually begin programming, and even then, if we've used objects wisely, the model can be fairly painlessly modified to handle most new requirements. Think of a model as being formed out of modeling clay: we'll continue to reshape it over the course of the analysis and design phases of our project until we're satisfied with the result.

Meanwhile, back to the task of coming up with a list of candidate classes for the SRS. The terms that have survived our latest round of scrutiny are as follows:

- Course

- PlanOfStudy

- Professor

- Section

- Student

- Transcript

- WaitList

Let's examine WaitList one last time. There is indeed a requirement for the SRS to maintain a student's position on a first-come, first-served wait list. But, it turns out that this requirement can actually be handled through a combination of an association between the Student and Section classes, plus something known as an **association class**, which you'll learn about later in this chapter. This would not be immediately obvious to a beginning modeler, and so we'd fully expect that the WaitList class might make the final cut as a suggested SRS class. But, we're going to assume that we have an experienced object modeler on the team, who convinces us to eliminate the class; we'll see that this was a suitable move when we complete the SRS class diagram at the end of the chapter.

So, we'll settle on the following list of classes, based on our noun phrase analysis of the SRS specification:

- Course

- PlanOfStudy

- Professor

- Section

- Student

- Transcript

Revisiting the Use Cases

One more thing that we need to do before we deem our class list good to go is to revisit our use cases—in particular, the actors—to see if any of them ought to be added as classes. You may recall that we identified seven potential actors for the SRS in Chapter 9:

- Student

- Faculty

- Department Chair

- Registrar

- Billing System

- Admissions System

- Classroom Scheduling System

Do any of ***these*** deserve to be modeled as classes in the SRS? Here's how to make that determination: if any user associated with any actor type A is going to need to manipulate (access or modify) information concerning an actor type B when A is logged onto the SRS, then B needs to be included as a class in our model. This is best illustrated with a few examples.

- When a student logs onto the SRS, might he or she need to manipulate information about faculty? Yes; when a student selects an advisor, for example, he or she might need to view information about a variety of faculty members in order to choose an appropriate advisor. So, the Faculty actor role must be represented as a class in the SRS; indeed, we have already designated a Professor class, so we're covered there. But, student users are not concerned with department chairs per se.

- Following the same logic, we'd need to represent the Student actor role as a class because when professors log onto the SRS, they will be manipulating Student objects when printing out a course roster or assigning grades to students, for example. Since Student already appears in our candidate class list, we're covered there, as well.

- When *any* of the actors—Faculty, Students, the Registrar, the Billing System, the Admissions System, or the Classroom Scheduling System—access the SRS, will there be a need for any of them to manipulate information about the registrar? No, at least not according to the SRS requirements that we've seen so far. Therefore, we needn't model the Registrar actor role as a class.

- The same holds true for the Billing, Admissions, and Classroom Scheduling Systems: they require "behind the scenes" access to information managed by the SRS, but nobody logging on to the SRS expects to be able to manipulate any of these three systems directly, so they needn't be represented by domain classes in the SRS.

Again, when we get to implementing the SRS in code, we may indeed find it appropriate to create "solution space" C# classes to represent interfaces to these other automated systems; but, such classes don't belong in a **domain** *model of the SRS.*

Therefore, our proposed candidate class list remains unchanged after revisiting all actor roles:

- Course

- PlanOfStudy

- Professor

- Section

- Student

- Transcript

Is this a "perfect" list? No—there is no such thing! In fact, before all is said and done, the list may—and in fact probably will—evolve in the following ways:

- We may add classes later on: terms we eliminated from the specification, or terms that don't even appear in the specification, but which we'll unearth through continued investigation.

- We may see an opportunity to generalize—that is, we may see enough commonality between two or more classes' respective attributes, methods, or relationships with other classes to warrant the creation of a common base class.

- In addition, as we mentioned earlier, we may rethink our decisions regarding representing some concepts as simple attributes (semester, room, etc.) instead of as full-blown classes, and vice versa.

The development of a candidate class list is, as we've tried to illustrate, fraught with uncertainty. For this reason, it's important to have someone experienced with object modeling available to your team when embarking on your first object modeling effort. Most experienced modelers don't use the rote method of noun phrase analysis to derive a candidate class list; such folks can pretty much review a specification and directly pick out significant classes, in the same way that a professional jeweler can easily choose a genuine diamond from among a pile of fake gemstones. Nevertheless, what does "significant" really mean? That's where the "fuzziness" comes in! It's impossible to define precisely what makes one concept significant and another less so. We've tried to illustrate some rules of thumb by working through the SRS example, but you ultimately need a qualified mentor to guide you until you develop—and trust—your own intuitive sense for such things.

The bottom line, however, is that even expert modelers can't really confirm the appropriateness of a given candidate class until they see its proposed use in the full context of a class diagram that also reflects associations, attributes, and methods, which we'll explore later in this chapter as well as in Chapter 11.

Producing a Data Dictionary

Early on in our analysis efforts, it's important that we clarify and begin to document our use of terminology. A **data dictionary** is ideal for this purpose. For each candidate class, the data dictionary should include a simple definition of what this item means in the context of the model/system as a whole; include an example if it helps to illustrate the definition.

The following sidebar shows our complete SRS data dictionary so far.

The SRS Data Dictionary, Take 1: Class Definitions

Course: A semester-long series of lectures, assignments, exams, etc., that all relate to a particular subject area, and which are typically associated with a particular number of credit hours; a unit of study toward a degree. For example, Beginning Objects is a required **course** for the Master of Science degree in Information Systems Technology.

PlanOfStudy: A list of the **courses** that a student intends to take to fulfill the **course** requirements for a particular degree.

Professor: A member of the faculty who teaches **sections** or advises **students**.

Section: The offering of a particular **course** during a particular semester on a particular day of the week and at a particular time of day (for example, **course** Beginning Objects as taught in the Spring 2004 semester on Mondays from 1:00 to 3:00 p.m.).

Student: A person who is currently enrolled at the university and who is eligible to register for one or more **sections**.

Transcript: A record of all of the **courses** taken to date by a particular **student** at this university, including which semester each **course** was taken in, the grade received, and the credits granted for the **course,** as well as a reflection of an overall total number of credits earned and the **student's** grade point average (GPA).

Note that it's permissible, and in fact encouraged, for the definition of one term to include one or more of the other terms; when we do so, we highlight the latter in **bold text**.

The data dictionary joins the set of other SRS narrative documents as a subsequent source of information about the model. As our model evolves, we'll expand the dictionary to include definitions of attributes, associations, and methods.

> *It's a good idea to also include the dictionary definition of a class as a header comment in the C# code representing that class. Make sure to keep this inline documentation in sync with the external dictionary definition, however.*

Determining Associations Between Classes

Once we've settled on an initial candidate class list, the next step is to determine how these classes are interrelated. To do this, we go back to our narrative documentation set (which has grown to consist of the SRS requirements specification, use cases, and data dictionary) and study *verb* phrases this time. Our goal in looking at verb phrases is to choose those that suggest structural relationships, as were defined in Chapter 5—associations, aggregations, and inheritance—but to eliminate or ignore those that represent (transient) actions or behaviors. (We'll focus on behaviors, but from the standpoint of use cases, in Chapter 11.)

For example, the specification states that a student "chooses a faculty advisor." This is indeed an action, but the result of this action is a lasting structural relationship between a professor and a student, which can be modeled via the association "a Professor *advises* a Student."

As a student's advisor, a professor also meets with the student, answers the student's questions, recommends courses for the student to take, approves his or her plan of study, etc.—these are behaviors on the part of a professor acting in the role of an advisor, but don't directly result in any new relationships being formed between objects.

Let's try the verb phrase analysis approach on the requirements specification. We've highlighted all relevant verb phrases in the sidebar that follows (note that we omitted such obviously irrelevant verb phrases as "We've been asked to develop an automated SRS . . .").

Highlighting Verb Phrases in the SRS Specification

We have been asked to develop an automated Student Registration System (SRS) for the university. This system will **enable students to register** online **for courses** each semester, as well as **track their progress toward completion of their degree**.

When a student first **enrolls at the university,** he/she uses the SRS to **set forth a plan of study** as to which **courses he/she plans on taking** to **satisfy a particular degree program,** and **chooses a faculty advisor**. The SRS will **verify whether or not the proposed plan of study satisfies the requirements of the degree that the student is seeking**.

Once a **plan of study has been established,** then, during the registration period preceding each semester, students are able to **view the schedule of classes** online, and **choose whichever classes he/she wishes to attend, indicating the preferred section** (day of the week and time of day) if the **class is offered by more than one professor.** The SRS will **verify whether or not the student has satisfied the necessary prerequisites** for each requested course by **referring to the student's online transcript** of courses completed and grades received (the **student may review his/her transcript** online at any time).

Assuming that (a) the **prerequisites for the requested course(s) are satisfied,** (b) the **course(s) meet(s) one of the student's plan of study requirements,** and (c) **there is room available** in each of the class(es), the **student is enrolled in the class(es).**

If (a) and (b) are satisfied, but (c) is not, the **student is placed on a first-come, first-served wait list.** If a **class/section that he/she was previously waitlisted for becomes available** (either because some other **student has dropped the class** or because the **seating capacity for the class has been increased**), the **student is automatically enrolled in the waitlisted class,** and an **email message** to that effect **is sent** to the student. It is his/her responsibility to **drop the class** if it is no longer desired; otherwise, **he/she will be billed for the course.**

Students may drop a class up to the end of the first week of the semester in which the **class is being taught.**

Let's scrutinize a few of these:

- *"Students [. . .] register [. . .] for courses":* Although the act of registering is a behavior, the end result is that a static relationship is created between a Student and a Section, as represented by the association "a Student *registers* for a Section." (Note that the specification mentions registering for "courses," not "sections," but as we stated in our data dictionary, a Student registers for concrete Sections as embodiments of Courses. Keep in mind when reviewing a specification that natural language is often imprecise, and that as a result we have to read between the lines as to what the author really meant in every case. (If we're going to be the ones to write the specification, here is an incentive to keep the language as clear and concise as possible!)

- *"[Students track] their progress toward completion of their degree":* Again, this is a behavior, but it nonetheless implies a structural relationship between a Student and a Degree. However, recall that we didn't elect to represent Degree as a class—we opted to reflect it as a simple string attribute of the Student class—and so this suggested relationship is immaterial with respect to the candidate class list that we've developed.

- **"Student first enrolls at the university":** This is a behavior that results in a static relationship between a Student and the University; but, we deemed the notion of "university" to be external to the system and so chose not to create a University class in our model. So, we disregard this verb phrase, as well.

- **"[Student] sets forth a plan of study":** This is a behavior that results in the static relationship "a Student *pursues/observes* a Plan of Study."

- **"Students are able to view the schedule of classes online":** This is strictly a transient behavior of the SRS; no lasting relationship results from this action, so we disregard this verb phrase.

and so on.

Association Matrices

Another complementary technique for both determining and recording what the relationships between classes should be is to create an $n \times n$ **association matrix,** where n represents the number of candidate classes that we've identified. Label the rows and the columns with the names of the classes, as shown for the empty matrix represented by Table 10-1.

Table 10-1. An "Empty" Association Matrix for the SRS

	Section	Course	PlanOfStudy	Professor	Student	Transcript
Section						
Course						
PlanOfStudy						
Professor						
Student						
Transcript						

Then, complete the matrix as follows.

In each cell of the matrix, list all of the associations that you can identify between the class named at the head of the row and the class named at the head of the column. For example, in the cell highlighted in Table 10-2 at the intersection of the Student "row" and the Section "column," we have listed three potential associations:

- A Student *is waitlisted for* a Section.

- A Student *is registered for* a Section (this could be alternatively phrased as "a Student *is currently attending* a Section").

- A Student *has previously taken* a Section: This third association is important if we plan on maintaining a history of all of the classes that a student has ever taken in his or her career as a student, which we must do if we are to prepare a student's transcript online. (As it turns out, we'll be able to get by with a single association that does "double duty" for the latter two of these, as we'll see later on in this chapter.)

Mark a cell with an × if there are no known relationships between the classes in question, or if the potential relationships between the classes are irrelevant. For example, we've marked the cells representing the intersection between Professor and Course with an ×, even though there is an association possible—"a Professor *is qualified to teach* a Course"—because it isn't relevant to the mission of the SRS.

We mentioned in Chapter 4 that all associations are inherently bidirectional. This implies that if a cell in row j, column k indicates one or more associations, then the cell in row k, column j should reflect the reciprocal of these relationships. For example, since the intersection of the PlanOfStudy "row" and the Course "column" indicates that "a PlanOfStudy *calls for* a Course," then the intersection of the Course "row" and the PlanOfStudy "column" must indicate that "a Course *is called for by* a PlanOfStudy."

It's not always practical to state the reciprocal of an association; for example, our association matrix shows that "a Student *plans to take* a Course," but trying to state its reciprocal—"a Course *is planned to be taken by* a Student"—is quite awkward. In such cases where a reciprocal association would be awkward to phrase, simply indicate its presence with the symbol ✔.

Table 10-2. Our Completed Association Matrix

	Section	Course	PlanOfStudy	Professor	Student	Transcript
Section	×	*instance of*	×	*is taught by*	✔	*included in*
Course	✔	*prerequisite for*	*is called for by*	×	✔	×
PlanOfStudy	×	*calls for*	×	×	*observed by*	×
Professor	*teaches*	×	×	×	*advises; teaches*	×
Student	*registered for; waitlisted for*	*plans to take; has previously taken*	*observes*	*is advised by; studies under*		*owns* ×
Transcript	*includes*	×	×	×	*belongs to*	×

We'll be portraying these associations in graphical form shortly! For now, we'd want to go back and extend our data dictionary to explain what each of these associations means; here's one such example:

Additions to the SRS Data Dictionary

Calls for (a Plan of Study calls for a Course): In order to demonstrate that a **student** will satisfy the requirements for his or her chosen degree program, the **student** must formulate a **plan of study**. This **plan of study** lays out all of the **courses** that a **student** intends to take, and possibly specifies in which semester the **student** hopes to complete each **course**.

Identifying Attributes

To determine what the attributes for each of our domain classes should be, we make yet another pass through the requirements specification looking for clues. We already stumbled upon a few attributes earlier, when we weeded out some nouns/noun phrases from our candidate class list:

- For the Section class, we identified "day of week", "room", "seating capacity", "semester", and "time of day" as attributes.

- For the Student class, we identified "degree" as an attribute.

We can also bring any prior knowledge that we have about the domain into play when assigning attributes to classes. Our knowledge of the way that universities operate, for example, suggests that all students will need some sort of student ID number as an attribute, even though this isn't mentioned anywhere in the SRS specification. We can't be sure whether this particular university assigns an arbitrary student ID number, or whether the policy is to use a student's social security number (SSN) as his or her ID; these are details that we'd have to go back to our end users for clarification on.

Finally, we can also look at how similar information has been represented in existing legacy systems for clues as to what a class's attributes should be. For example, if a Student Billing System already exists at the university based on a relational database design, we might wish to study the structure of the relational database table housing student information. The columns that have been provided in that table—name, address, birthdate, etc.—are logical attribute choices.

UML Notation: Modeling the Static Aspects of an Abstraction

Now that we have a much better understanding about the static aspects of our model, we're ready to portray these in graphical fashion to complement the narrative documentation that we've developed for the SRS. We'll be using UML to produce a **class diagram.** Here are the rules for how various aspects of the model are to be portrayed.

Classes, Attributes, and Operations

We represent classes as rectangles. When we first conceive of a class—before we know what any of its attributes or methods are going to be—we simply place the class name in the rectangle, as illustrated in Figure 10-5.

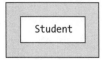

Figure 10-5. UML depiction of the Student *class*

An ***abstract*** class is denoted by presenting the class name in *italics*, as shown in Figure 10-6.

Figure 10-6. UML depiction of an abstract class

When we're ready to reflect the attributes and operations of a class, we divide the class rectangle into three **compartments**—the class name compartment, the attributes compartment, and the operations compartment—as shown in Figure 10-7. Note that the UML favors the nomenclature of "operations" versus "methods" to reinforce the notion that the diagram is intended to be programming language independent.

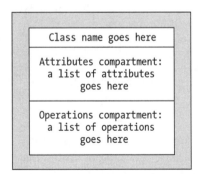

Figure 10-7. Class rectangles are divided into three compartments.

Some CASE tools automatically portray all three (empty) compartments when a class is first created, even if we haven't specified any attributes or operations yet, as shown in Figure 10-8.

Figure 10-8. Alternative UML class depiction as rendered by some CASE tools

As we begin to identify what the attributes and/or operations need to be for a particular class, we can add these to the diagram in as much or as little detail as we care to.

We may choose simply to list attribute names (see Figure 10-9), or we may specify their names along with their types (see Figure 10-10).

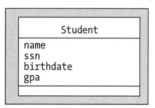

Figure 10-9. Sometimes just attribute names are presented.

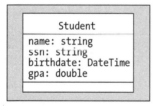

Figure 10-10. Sometimes both attribute names and types are shown.

We may even wish to specify an initial starting value for an attribute, as in gpa : double = 0.0, although this is less common.

Static attributes are identified as such by underlining their names (see Figure 10-11).

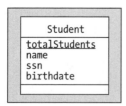

Figure 10-11. Identifying static attributes by underlining

We may choose simply to list operation names in the operations compartment of a class rectangle, as shown in Figure 10-12, or we may optionally choose to use an expanded form of operation definition as we have for the `RegisterForCourse` operation in Figure 10-13.

Figure 10-12. Sometimes just method names are presented.

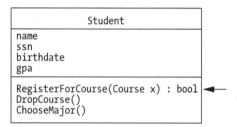

Figure 10-13. Sometimes argument signatures and return types are also reflected.

Note that the formal syntax for operation specifications in a UML class diagram:

[*visibility*] *name* [*(parameter list)*] [*: return type*]

for example,

```
RegisterForCourse(Course x) : bool
```

differs from the syntax that we're used to seeing for C# method signatures:

```
returnType MethodName(parameter list)
```

for example,

```
bool RegisterForCourse(Course x)
```

Note in particular that the UML refers to the combination of operation name, parameters, and return type as the **operation signature,** but that in C# the return type is *not* part of the *method signature*.

> *The rationale for making these operation signatures generic versus language specific is so that the same model may be rendered in any of a variety of target programming languages. It can be argued, however, that there is nothing inherently better or clearer about the first form versus the second. Therefore, if you know that you're going to be programming in C#, it might make sense to reflect standard C# method signatures in your class diagram, if your object modeling tool will accommodate this.*

It's often impractical to show all of the attributes and operations of every class in a class diagram, because the diagram will get so cluttered that it will lose its "punch" as a communications tool. Consider the data dictionary to be the official, complete source of information concerning the model, and only reflect in the diagram those attributes and operations that are particularly important in describing the mission of each class. In particular, "get" and "set" operations (whether implemented through methods or, in the case of C#, accessed as properties) are implied for all attributes, and shouldn't be explicitly shown.

Also, just because the attribute or operation compartment of a class is empty, don't assume that there are no features of that type associated with a class; it may simply mean that the model is still evolving.

Relationships Between Classes

In Chapter 4, we defined several different types of structural relationship that may exist between classes—associations, aggregations (a specific type of association), and inheritance. Let's explore how each of these relationship types is represented graphically.

Binary associations—in other words, relationships between two different classes—are indicated by drawing a line between the rectangles representing the participating classes, and labeling the line with the name of the association. Role names can be reflected at either end of the association line if they add value to the model, but should otherwise be omitted.

We also mark each end of the line with the appropriate **multiplicity designator,** to reflect whether the relationship is one-to-one, one-to-many, or many-to-many (see Figure 10-14); we'll talk about how to do this a bit later in the chapter.

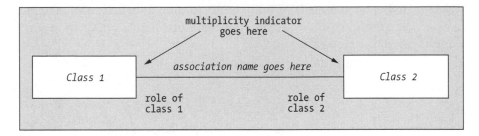

Figure 10-14. *Representing associations between classes*

All associations are assumed to be bidirectional at this stage in the modeling effort, and it doesn't matter in which order the participating classes are arranged in a class diagram. So, to depict the association "a Professor *advises* a Student," the graphical notations in Figure 10-15 are all considered equivalent.

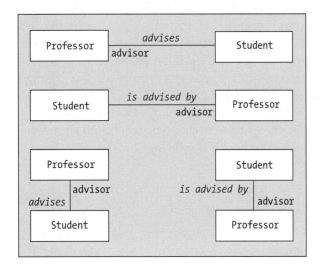

Figure 10-15. *Equivalent depictions of the* advises *association between the* Professor *and* Student *classes*

With OMT notation, a precursor notation to UML, we were instructed to label associations so that their names made sense when reading a diagram from left to right, top to bottom. There was thus an incentive to arrange classes in our diagram in whatever way would make association names less "awkward." In the preceding examples, placing the Professor class above or to the left of Student simplifies the association name. Achieving an optimal placement of classes for purposes of simplifying all of the association names in a diagram is often not possible in an elaborate diagram, however. Therefore, the UML has introduced the simple convention of using a small arrowhead (▶) to reflect the direction in which the association name is to be interpreted, giving us a lot more freedom in how we place our class rectangles in a diagram, as shown in Figure 10-16.

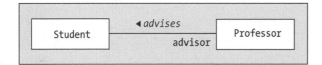

Figure 10-16. Using an arrowhead to indicate the direction of an association label

With the UML, no matter how the preceding two rectangles are situated, we can still always label the association "*advises*".

> *It's easy to get caught up in the trap of trying to make diagrams "perfect" in terms of how classes are positioned, to minimize crossed lines, etc. Try to resist the urge to do so early on, because the diagram will inevitably get changed many times before the modeling effort is finished.*

Unary (reflexive) associations—i.e., relationships between two different objects belonging to the same class—are drawn with an association line that loops back to the same class rectangle from which it originates. For example, to depict the association "a Course *is a prerequisite for* a (different) Course," we'd use the notation shown in Figure 10-17.

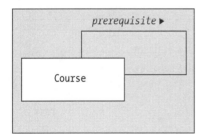

Figure 10-17. A reflexive association involving the Course class

Aggregation, which as we learned in Chapter 5 is a specialized form of association that happens to imply containment, is differentiated from a "normal" association by placing a diamond at the end of the association line that touches the "containing" class. For example, to portray the fact that a university is comprised of schools—the School of Engineering, School of Law, School of Medicine, etc.—we'd use the notation shown in Figure 10-18.

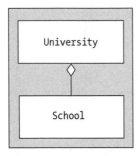

Figure 10-18. Indicating aggregation with a diamond

An aggregation relationship can actually be oriented in any direction, as long as the diamond is properly anchored on the "containing" class as shown in Figure 10-19.

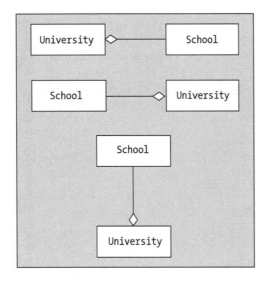

Figure 10-19. Aggregations can be oriented in any direction.

As we mentioned when we first introduced aggregation in Chapter 5, however, you can get by without ever using aggregation! To represent the preceding concept, we could have just created a simple association between the University and School classes, and labeled it "*is composed of*" as shown in Figure 10-20.

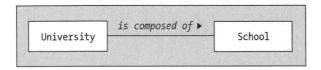

Figure 10-20. A simple association as an alternative to an aggregation

The decision of whether to use aggregation versus plain association is subtle, because it turns out that both can be rendered in code in essentially the same way, as we'll see in Part Three of the book.

Unlike association lines, which should always be labeled with the name of the association that they represent, aggregation lines are typically not labeled, since an aggregation by definition implies containment. However, if you wish to optionally label an aggregation line with a phrase such as "consists of," "is composed of," "contains," etc., it is permissible to do so.

When two or more different classes represent "parts" of some other "whole," each "part" is involved in a separate aggregation with the "whole," as shown in Figure 10-21.

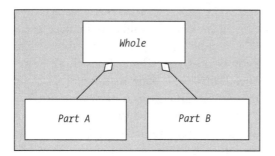

Figure 10-21. Two aggregations, drawn using two diamonds

However, we often join such aggregation lines into a single structure that looks something like an organization chart, as shown in Figure 10-22.

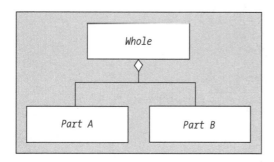

Figure 10-22. Two aggregations involving the same "whole" class, drawn using a single diamond

Doing so is not meant to imply anything about the relationship of Part A to Part B; it's simply a way to clean up the diagram.

Inheritance (generalization/specialization) is illustrated by connecting a derived class to its base class with a line, and then marking the line with a triangle that touches the base class (see Figure 10-23).

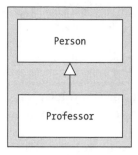

Figure 10-23. Inheritance is indicated with a triangle.

As with aggregation, the classes involved in an inheritance relationship can be portrayed with any orientation, as long as the triangle points to the base class.

Unlike association lines, which must always be labeled, and aggregation lines, which needn't be labeled (but can be if you desire), inheritance lines should **not** be labeled, as they unambiguously represent the "is a" relationship.

As with aggregation, when two or more different classes represent derived classes of the same parent class, each derived class is involved in a separate inheritance relationship with the parent, as shown in Figure 10-24, but we often join the inheritance lines into a single structure, as illustrated in Figure 10-25.

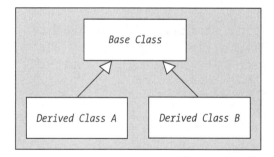

Figure 10-24. Depicting two derived classes with two different triangles

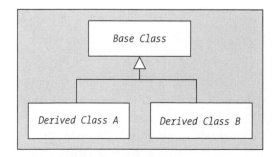

Figure 10-25. Depicting two derived classes with a single triangle

Doing so isn't meant to imply anything different about the relationship of derived class A to derived class B as compared with the previous depiction—these classes are considered to be sibling classes with a common parent class in both cases. It's simply a way to clean up the diagram.

Reflecting Multiplicity

You learned in Chapter 5 that for a given association type X between classes A and B, the term "multiplicity" refers to the number of instances of objects of type A that must/may be associated with a given instance of type B, and vice versa. When preparing a class diagram, we mark each end of an association line to indicate what its multiplicity should be from the perspective of an object belonging to the class at the other end of the line: in other words

- We mark the number of instances of B that can relate to a single instance of A at *B*'s end of the line.

- We mark the number of instances of A that can relate to a single instance of B at *A*'s end of the line.

This is depicted in Figure 10-26.

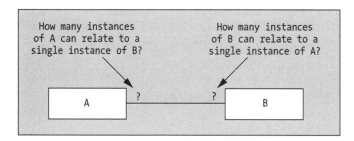

Figure 10-26. Indicating multiplicity between classes

By way of review, given a single object belonging to class A, there are four different scenarios for how object(s) of type B may be related to it:

- The A type object may be related to ***exactly one*** instance of a B type object, as in the situation "a Student (A) *has* a Transcript (B)." Here, the existence of an instance of B for every instance of A is ***mandatory***.

- The A type object may be related to ***at most one*** instance of a B type object, as in the situation "a Professor (A) *chairs* a Department (B)." Here, the existence of an instance of B for every instance of A is ***optional***.

- The A type object may be related to ***one or more*** instances of a B type object, as in the situation "a Department (A) *employs **many*** Professors (B)." Here, the existence of at least one instance of B for every instance of A is ***mandatory***.

- The A type object may be related to ***zero or more*** instances of a "B" type object, as in the situation "a Student (A) *is attending **many*** Sections (B)." (At our hypothetical university, a Student is permitted to take a semester off.) Here, the existence of at least one instance of B for every instance of A is ***optional***.

With UML notation, multiplicity symbols are as follows:

- "Exactly one" is represented by the notation "1".

- "At most one" is represented by the notation "0..1", which is alternatively read as "zero or one."

- "One or more" is represented by the notation "1..*".

- "Zero or more" is represented by the notation "0..*".

- We use the notation "*" when we know that the multiplicity should be "many" but we aren't certain (or we don't care to specify) whether it should be "zero or more" or "one or more."

- It's even possible to represent an arbitrary range of explicit numerical values *x..y*, such as using "3..7" to indicate, for example, that "a Department employs no fewer than three, and no more than seven, Professors."

Here are some UML examples:

"A Student *has* exactly one Transcript, and a Transcript *belongs to* exactly one Student." (See Figure 10-27.)

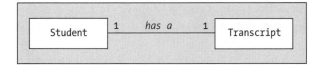

Figure 10-27. An example of mandatory one-to-one multiplicity

"A Professor *works for* exactly one Department, but a Department *has* many (one or more) Professors as employees." (See Figure 10-28.)

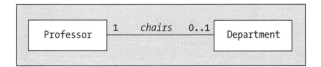

Figure 10-28. An example of mandatory one-to-many multiplicity

"A Professor optionally *chairs* at most one Department, while a Department *has* exactly one Professor in the role of chairman." (See Figure 10-29.)

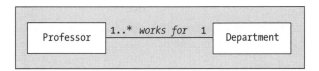

Figure 10-29. An example of optional one-to-many multiplicity

"A Student *attends* many (zero or more) Sections, and a Section *is attended by* many (zero or more) Students." (See Figure 10-30.)

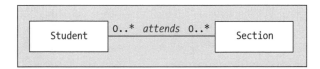

Figure 10-30. An example of optional many-to-many multiplicity

A Section that continues to have zero Students signed up to attend will most likely be cancelled; nonetheless, there is a period of time after a Section is first made available for enrollment via the SRS that it will have zero Students enrolled.

"A Course *is a prerequisite for* many (zero or more) Courses, and a Course *can have* many (zero or more) *prerequisite* Courses." (See Figure 10-31.)

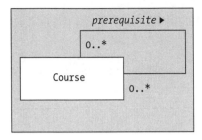

Figure 10-31. An example of optional many-to-many multiplicity on a reflexive association

We reflect multiplicity on aggregations as well as on simple associations. For example, the UML notation shown in Figure 10-32 would be interpreted as follows: "A (Student's) Plan of Study *is comprised of* many Courses; any given Course *can be included in* many different (Students') Plans of Study."

Figure 10-32. Reflecting multiplicity on an aggregation

It makes no sense to reflect multiplicity on inheritance relationships, however, because as we discussed in Chapter 4, inheritance implies a relationship between **classes,** but **not** between **objects.** That is, the notation shown in Figure 10-33 implies that any object belonging to *Derived Class B* is also simultaneously an instance of *Base Class A* by virtue of the "is a" relationship.

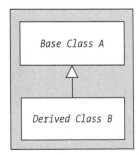

Figure 10-33. Multiplicity adornments are inappropriate for inheritance relationships.

If we wanted to illustrate some sort of relationship between different objects of types A and B, e.g., "a Person *is married to* a Student," we'd need to introduce a separate association between these classes independent of their inheritance relationship, as shown in Figure 10-34.

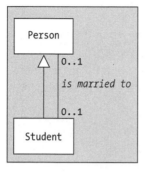

Figure 10-34. Indicating both inheritance and an association between the Person *and* Student *classes*

Object Diagrams

When describing how objects can interact, we sometimes find it helpful to sketch out a scenario of specific objects and their linkages, and for that we create an **object diagram.** An instance, or object, looks much the same as a class in UML notation, the main differences being that

- We typically provide both the name of the object and its type, separated by a colon. We underline the text to emphasize that this is an object, not a class (see Figure 10-35).

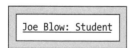

Figure 10-35. Representing an object

- The object's type may be omitted if it's obvious from the object's name; for example, the name "student x" implies that the object in question belongs to the Student class (see Figure 10-36).

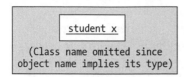

Figure 10-36. We omit the class name if it's otherwise obvious.

- Alternatively, the object's name may be omitted if we want to refer to a "generic" object of a given type; such an object is known as an **anonymous object.** Note that we must precede the class name with a colon (:) in such a situation (see Figure 10-37).

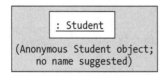

Figure 10-37. Representing an anonymous object

Therefore, if we wanted to indicate that Dr. Brown, a Professor, is the advisor for three Students, we could create the object diagram shown in Figure 10-38.

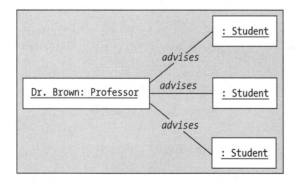

Figure 10-38. Dr. Brown advises three students.

To reflect that a Student by the name of Joe Blow is attending two Sections this semester, one of which is also attended by a Student named Mary Green, we could create the diagram in Figure 10-39.

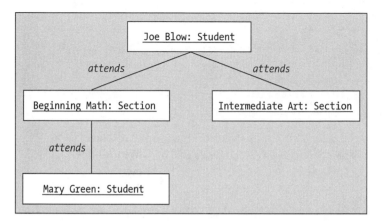

Figure 10-39. An instance diagram involving numerous objects

Associations As Attributes

Given Figure 10-40, which shows the association "a Course *is offered as* a Section," we see that a Course object can be related to many different Section objects, but that any one Section object can only be related to a single Course object.

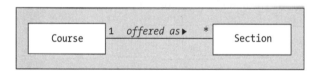

Figure 10-40. A one-to-many association between the Course *and* Section *classes*

By way of review, what does it mean for two objects to be related? It means that they maintain "handles" on one another so that they can easily find one another to communicate and collaborate, a concept that we talked about in detail in Chapter 4. If we were to sketch out the attributes of the Course and Section classes based solely on the diagram in Figure 10-40, we'd need to allow for these handles as reference variables, as follows:

```
public class Section {
  // Attributes.
  private Course represents;   // A "handle" on a single related Course
                               // object.

  // etc.
}
```

```
public class Course {
  // Attributes.
  private Collection offeredAs;        // A collection of related Section
                                       // object "handles."

  // etc.
}
```

So we see that the presence of an association between two classes A and B in a class diagram implies that class A ***potentially*** has an attribute declared to be either

- A reference to a ***single*** instance/object of type B

- A ***collection*** of references to ***many*** objects of type B

depending on the multiplicity involved, and vice versa. We say "potentially" because, when we get to the point of actually programming this application, we may or may not wish to code this relationship bidirectionally, even though at the analysis stage all associations are presumed to be bidirectional. We'll talk about the pros and cons of coding bidirectional relationships in Chapter 14.

Because the presence of an association line implies attributes as handles in both related classes, it's inappropriate to additionally list such attributes in the attribute compartment of the respective classes (see Figure 10-41).

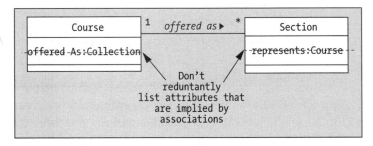

Figure 10-41. Redundantly reflecting references as attributes is incorrect; the presence of an association implies these.

This is a mistake commonly made by beginners. The biggest resultant problem with doing so arises when using the code generation capability of a CASE tool: if the attribute is listed explicitly in a class's attributes compartment, and also implied by an association, it may appear in the generated code twice, as shown in the following snippet representing code that might be generated from the erroneous UML diagram shown in Figure 10-41:

```
public class Course {
  Collection offeredAs;   // by virtue of an explicit attribute
  Collection offered_as;  // by virtue of the association
  // etc.
}
```

Information "Flows" Along the Association "Pipeline"

Beginning modelers also tend to make the mistake of introducing undesired redundancy when it comes to attributes in general. In the association portrayed in Figure 10-42, we see that the name attribute of the Professor class is inappropriately mirrored by the chairmanName attribute of the Department class.

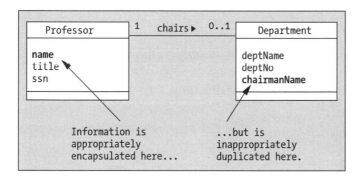

Figure 10-42. The name *and* chairmanName *attributes are redundant.*

While it's true that a Department object needs to know the name of the Professor object that chairs that Department, it's inappropriate to explicitly create a chairmanName attribute to reflect this information. Because the Department object maintains a reference to its associated Professor object as an attribute, the Department has ready access to this information any time it needs it, simply by invoking the Professor object's GetName method (or accessing the Name property, in the case of C#). This piece of information is rightfully encapsulated in the Professor class, where it belongs, and shouldn't be duplicated anywhere else. A corrected version of the preceding diagram is shown in Figure 10-43, with the redundancy eliminated.

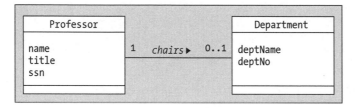

Figure 10-43. The redundancy of Figure 10-42 has been eliminated.

In essence, whenever we see an association/aggregation line in a diagram, we can think of this as a conceptual "pipeline" across which information can "flow" between related objects as needed.

> *At the analysis stage, we don't worry about the accessibility (public, private) of attributes, or of the directionality of associations; we'll assume that the values of all of the attributes reflected in a diagram are obtainable by calling the appropriate "get" methods on an object, or by alternatively accessing C# properties.*

Sometimes, this "pipeline" extends across **multiple** objects, as illustrated by the next example.

In Figure 10-44, we have a diagram involving three classes.

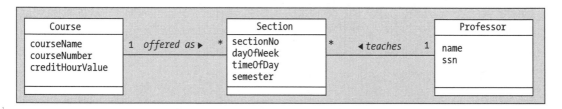

Figure 10-44. An association "pipeline" between the Course, Section, *and* Professor *classes.*

Let's say that someone wishes to obtain a list of all of the Professors who have ever taught the Course titled "Beginning Objects." Because each Course object maintains a handle on all of its Section objects, past and present, the Course object representing Beginning Objects can ask each of its Section objects the name of the Professor who previously taught, or is currently teaching, that Section. The Section objects, in turn, each maintain a handle on the Professor object who taught/teaches the Section, and can use the Professor object's GetName method (or can access the Name property, in the case of C#) to retrieve the name. So, information flows along the association "pipeline" from the Professor objects to their associated Section objects and from there back to the Course object that we started with (see Figure 10-45).

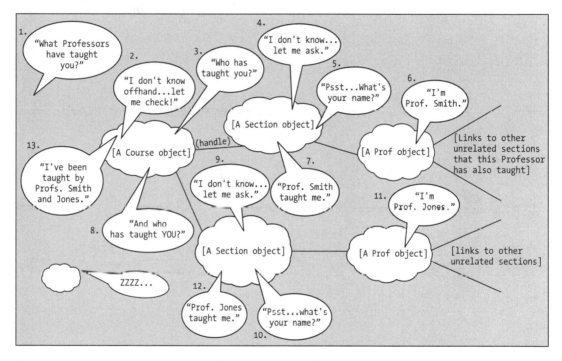

Figure 10-45. Association "pipelines" can be quite elaborate!

You'll learn a formal, UML-appropriate way to analyze and depict such "object conversations" in Chapter 11.

We've modeled these three classes' attributes in the code that follows, high-lighting all of the association-driven attributes:

```
public class Course {
  // Attributes.
  // Pseudocode.
```

```
        private Collection offeredAs;        // a collection of Section object
                                             // "handles"
        private string courseName;
        private int courseNumber;
        private double creditHourValue;
        // etc.
    }


public class Section {
    // Attributes.
    private Course represents;    // a "handle" on the related Course
                                  // object
    private int sectionNo;
    private string dayOfWeek;
    private string timeOfDay;
    private string semester;
    private Professor taughtBy;   // a "handle" on the related Prof. object

    // etc.
}

public class Professor {
    // Pseudocode.
    private Collection sectionsTaught; // a collection of Section obj.
                                       // "handles"
    private string name;
    private string ssn;

    // etc.
}
```

If we knew that the Course class was going to regularly need to know who all the Professors were that had ever taught the Course, we might decide to introduce the redundant association "a Professor *has taught* a *Course*" into our diagram, as illustrated in Figure 10-46.

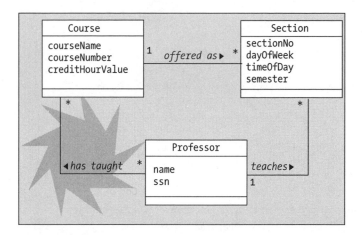

Figure 10-46. We add redundant associations when objects frequently need a more direct "pipeline" for communication.

This has the advantage of improving the speed with which a Course object can determine who has ever taught it: with the addition of the redundant association in Figure 10-46, Course objects can now talk ***directly*** to Professor objects without using Section objects as "go-betweens"—but the cost of this performance improvement is that we've just introduced additional complexity to our application, reflected by the highlighted additions to the following code:

```
public class Course {
  // Attributes.
  // Pseudocode.
  private Collection offeredAs;        // a collection of Section object
                                       // "handles"
  private string courseName;
  private int courseNumber;
  private float creditHourValue;
  // Pseudocode.
  private Collection professors;       // a collection of Professor obj.
                                       // "handles"
  // etc.
}

public class Section {
  // Attributes.
  private Course represents;   // a "handle" on the related Course
                               // object
```

```
        private int sectionNo;
        private string dayOfWeek;
        private string timeOfDay;
        private string semester;
        private Professor taughtBy;  // a "handle" on the related Prof. object

        // etc.
    }

    public class Professor {
        // Pseudocode.
        private Collection coursesTaught;       // a collection of Course obj.
                                                // "handles"
        private Collection sectionsTaught;      // a collection of Section obj.
                                                // "handles"
        private string name;
        private string ssn;

        // etc.
    }
```

By adding the redundant association, we now have extra work to do in terms of maintaining referential integrity. That is, if a different Professor is assigned to teach a particular Section, we have two links to update rather than one: the link between the Professor and the Section, and the link between the Professor and the related Course.

We'll talk more in Part Three of the book about the implications, from a coding standpoint, of making such trade-offs. The bottom line, however, is that deciding which associations to include, and which to eliminate as derivable from others, is similar to the decision of which web pages you might wish to create a bookmark for in your web browser: you bookmark those that you visit frequently, and type out the URL longhand, or alternatively traverse a chain of links, for those that you only occasionally need to access. The same is true for object linkages: the decisions of which to implement in code depends on which "communication pathways" through the application we're going to want to use most frequently. We'll get a much better sense of what these communication patterns are when we move on to modeling behaviors in Chapter 11.

"Mixing and Matching" Relationship Notations

It's possible to intertwine the various relationship types in some rather sophisticated ways. To appreciate this fact, let's study the model in Figure 10-47 to see what it's telling us.

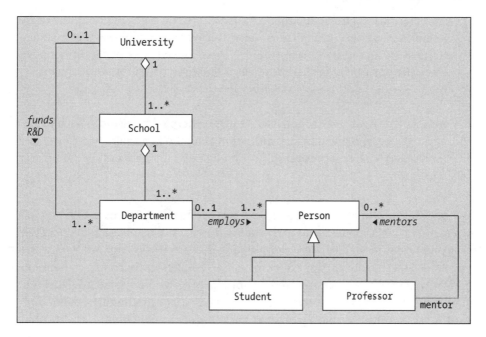

Figure 10-47. A sample UML model

First of all, we see some familiar uses of aggregation and inheritance.

The use of aggregation in the upper-left corner of the diagram—a two-tier aggregation—communicates the facts that a University is comprised of one or more Schools, and that a School is comprised of one or more Departments, but that any one Department is only associated with a single School and any one School is only associated with a single University.

The use of inheritance in the lower-right corner of the diagram indicates that Person is the common base class for both Student and Professor. Alternatively, stated another way: a Student *is a* Person, and a Professor *is a* Person.

The first interesting use of the notation that we observe is that an association can be used to relate classes at differing levels in an aggregation, as in the use of the *funds R&D (Research & Development)* association used to relate the University and Department classes. This indicates that the University funds one or more Departments for research and development purposes, but that a given Department may or may not be funded for R&D.

Next, we note the use of the *employs* association to relate the Department and Person classes, indicating that a Department *employs* one or more Persons, but that a given Person *may work for* only one Department, if indeed they work for **any** Department at all.

Because Person is a base class of both the Student and Professor derived classes, then by virtue of the "is a" relationship, anything we can say about a Person must also be true of its derived classes. Therefore:

- Associations/aggregations that a base class participates in are inherited by its derived classes. (This makes sense, because we now know that associations are really rendered as attributes.) Thus, a given Student may optionally *work for* one Department, perhaps as a teaching assistant, and a given Professor may optionally *work for* one Department.

- Also, because we can deduce (via the aggregation relationship) which School and University a given Department belongs to, the fact that a Person *works for* a given Department also implies which School and University the Person *works for*.

Finally, we note that an association can be used to relate classes at differing levels in an inheritance hierarchy, as in the use of the *mentors* association to relate the Person and Professor classes. Here, we're stating that a Professor optionally *mentors* many Persons—Students and/or Professors—and conversely that a Person—either a Student or a Professor—is mentored by optionally many Professors. We label the end of the association line closest to the Professor class with the role designation "mentor" to emphasize that Professors are mentors at the University, but that Persons in general (i.e., Students) are not.

What if we instead wanted to reflect the fact that both Students and Professors may hold the role of mentor? We could substitute a reflexive association on the Person class, as shown in Figure 10-48, which, by virtue of inheritance, actually implies four relationship possibilities:

- A Professor mentoring a Student

- A Professor mentoring another Professor

- A Student mentoring another Student

- A Student mentoring a Professor (which is not very likely!)

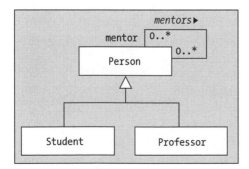

Figure 10-48. Various possible "mentorship" associations are implied.

If we wanted to reflect that only the first three of these are possible, we'd have to resort to the rather more complex version shown in Figure 10-49, where the three relationships of interest are all reflected as separate association lines (two reflexive, one binary).

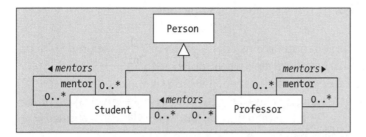

Figure 10-49. Specific mentor associations are deliniated.

As cumbersome as it is to change the diagram to reflect these refinements in our understanding, it would be orders of magnitude more painful to change the software once the application has been coded.

Association Classes

We sometimes find ourselves in a situation where we identify an attribute that is critical to our model, but which doesn't seem to fit nicely into any one class. As an example, let's revisit the association "a Student *attends* a Section," as shown in Figure 10-50. (Note that we're using the "generic" ***many*** multiplicity symbol this time, a single asterisk (*), at each end of the association line.)

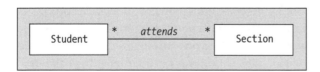

Figure 10-50. A many-to-many association between Student and Section

At the end of every semester, a student receives a letter grade for every section that he or she attended during that semester. We decide that the grade should be represented as a string attribute (e.g., "A-", "C+"). However, where does the "grade" attribute belong?

- It's not an attribute of the Student class, because a student doesn't get a single overall grade for all of his or her coursework, but rather a different grade for each course attended.

- It's not an attribute of the Section class, either, because not all students attending a section typically receive the same letter grade.

If we think about this situation for a moment, we realize that the grade is actually an attribute of the *pairing* of a given Student object with a given Section; that is, it's an attribute of the *link* that exists between these two objects.

With UML, we create a separate class, known as an **association class,** to house attribute(s) belonging to the link between objects, and attach it with a ***dashed*** line to the association line, as shown in Figure 10-51.

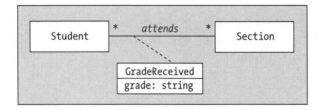

Figure 10-51. Placing an association class on a many-to-many association

Any time you see an association class in a class diagram, realize that there is an alternative equivalent way to represent the same situation ***without*** using an association class.

- In the case of a ***many-to-many association*** involving an association class, you may split the many-to-many association into two one-to-many associations, inserting what was formerly the association class as a "normal" class between the other two classes. Doing this for the preceding *attends* association, we wind up with the alternative equivalent representation in Figure 10-52.

  One important point to note is that the "many" ends of these two new associations reside with the newly inserted class, because a Student *receives* many grades and a Section *issues* many grades.

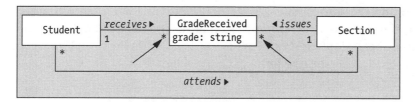

Figure 10-52. An alternative representation for Figure 10-51

- If we happen to have an association class for a ***one-to-many association***, as in the *works for* association between `Professor` and `Department` in Figure 10-53, then the association class's attribute(s) can, in theory, be "folded into" the class at the "many" end of the association instead, and we can do away with the association class completely as shown in Figure 10-54.

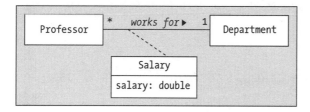

Figure 10-53. Placing an association class on a one-to-many association

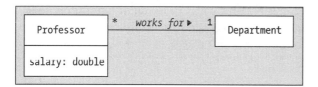

Figure 10-54. An alternative representation for Figure 10-53

- With a ***one-to-one association,*** we can fold the association class's attributes into either class.

That being said, this practice of folding in association class attributes into one end of a one-to-many or one-to-one association is discouraged, however, because it reduces the amount of information communicated by the model. In the preceding example, the only reason that a `Professor` has a `salary` attribute is because he or she *works for* a `Department`; knowledge of this "cause and effect" connection between employment and salary is lost if the association class is eliminated as such from the model.

Note that association classes are "normal" classes that may themselves participate in relationships with other classes. In the diagram in Figure 10-55, for example, we show the association class Role participating in a one-to-many association with the class USPresident; an example illustrating this model would be "Film Star Anthony Hopkins starred in the movie *Nixon* in the role of Richard M. Nixon, thus portraying the ***real*** former U.S. President Richard M. Nixon."

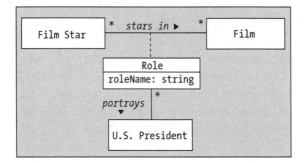

Figure 10-55. Association classes themselves can participate in associations with other classes.

Our "Completed" Student Registration System Class Diagram

Applying all that we've learned in this chapter about static modeling, we've produced the UML class diagram for the SRS shown in Figure 10-56. Of course, as we've said repeatedly, this isn't the only correct way to model the requirements, nor is it necessarily the "best" model that we could have produced; but it is an accurate, concise, and correct model of the static aspects of the problem to be automated.

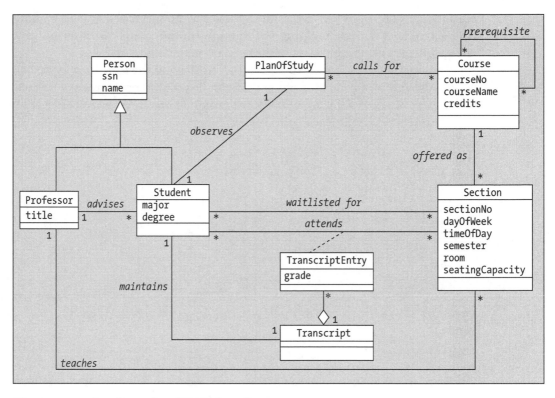

Figure 10-56. Our "completed" SRS class diagram

A few things worth noting:

We opted to use the "generic" ***many*** notation (* for UML) rather than specifying 0..* or 1..*; this is often adequate during the initial modeling stages of
a project.

Note that we've reflected two separate many-to-many associations
between the Student and Section classes: *waitlisted for* and *attends*. A given
Student may be waitlisted for many different Sections, and he or she may be
registered for/attending many ***other*** Sections. What this model doesn't reflect
is the fact that a Student is ***not*** permitted to simultaneously be attending and
waitlisted for the ***same*** Section. Constraints such as these can be reflected as
textual notes on the diagram, enclosed in curly braces, or can be omitted from
the diagram but spelled out in the data dictionary. In the diagram excerpt in
Figure 10-57, we use the annotation [xor] to represent an "exclusive or" situation between the two associations: a Student can either be *waitlisted for* or
attending a given Section, but not both.

As mentioned earlier in this chapter, we're able to get by with a single *attends*
association to handle both the Sections that a Student is currently attending, as well
as those that he or she has attended in the past. The date of attendance—past or

present—is reflected by the "semester" attribute of the Section class; also, for any courses that are currently in progress, the value of the "grade" attribute of the TranscriptEntry association class would be as of yet undetermined.

We could have also reflected an association class on the *waitlisted for* association representing a given Student's position in the wait list for a particular Section, and then could have gone on to model the notion of a WaitList as an aggregation of WaitListEntry objects (see Figure 10-57).

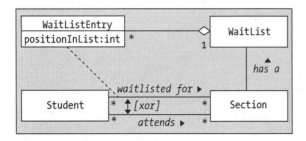

Figure 10-57. A WaitList *can be modeled as an aggregation of* WaitListEntry *objects.*

Since we're going to want to use the object model to gain user confirmation that we understand his or her primary requirements, we needn't clutter the diagram with such behind-the-scenes implementation details just yet, however.

We also renamed the association class for the *attends* relationship; it was introduced earlier in this chapter as GradeReceived, but is now called TranscriptEntry. We've also introduced an aggregation relationship between the TranscriptEntry class and another new class called Transcript (see Figure 10-58).

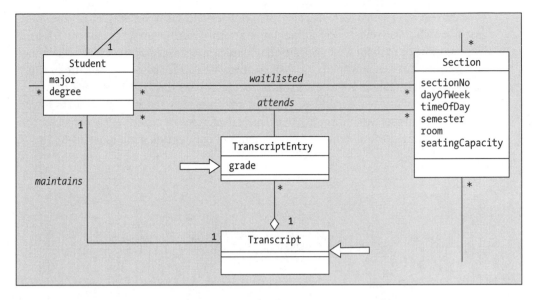

Figure 10-58. A Transcript *is an aggregation of* TranscriptEntry *objects.*

Let's explore how all of this evolved.

When we first introduced the *attends* association earlier in this chapter, we portrayed it as shown in Figure 10-59.

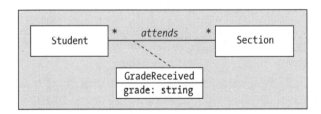

Figure 10-59. Initial portrayal of the attends *association*

We then learned that it could equivalently be represented as a pair of one-to-many associations *issues* and *receives* (see Figure 10-60).

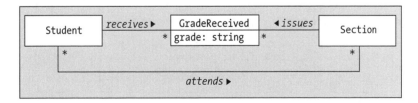

Figure 10-60. The attends *association may be portrayed alternatively as* issues *and* receives.

In this alternative form, it's clear that any individual GradeReceived object maintains one handle on a Student object and another handle on a Section object, and can ask either of them for information whenever necessary. The Section object, in turn, maintains a handle on the Course object that it represents by virtue of the *offered as* association. It's a trivial matter, therefore, for the GradeReceived object to request the values of attributes semester, courseNo, courseName, and credits from the Section object (which would in turn have to ask its associated Course object for the last three of these four values); this is illustrated conceptually in Figure 10-61.

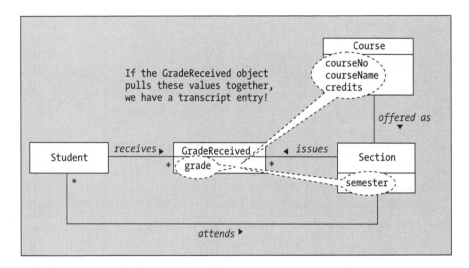

Figure 10-61. GradeReceived *has access to all of the makings of a* TranscriptEntry.

If the GradeReceived object pulls these values together, we have everything that we need for a line item entry on a student's transcript, as shown in Figure 10-62.

```
Transcript For: Joe Blow                              Semester: Spring 2004


Course No.      Credits        Course Name      Grade Received    Credits Earned*
MATH 101          3          Beginning Math          B                 9
OBJECTS 101       3          Intro to Objects        A                12
ART 200           3          Clay Modeling           A                12

* 'Credits Earned' is computed by multiplying the credit value of a course—
  say, 3—by 4 if student earned an A grade, 3 if he/she earned a B, and so forth.
```

Figure 10-62. A sample transcript report

Therefore, we see that renaming the association class from GradeReceived to TranscriptEntry makes good sense. It was then a natural step to aggregate these into a Transcript class.

Our SRS diagram is a little "light" in terms of attributes; we've only reflected those that we'll minimally need when we build an automated SRS in Part Three.

Of course, we now need to go back to the data dictionary to capture definitions of all of the new attributes, relationships, and classes that we've identified in putting together this model. The following sidebar shows our revised SRS data dictionary.

The Revised SRS Data Dictionary

Classes

Course: A semester-long series of lectures, assignments, exams, etc., that all relate to a particular subject area, and which are typically associated with a particular number of credit hours; a unit of study toward a degree. For example, Beginning Objects is a required **course** for the Master of Science degree in Information Systems Technology.

Person: A human being associated with the university.

PlanOfStudy: A list of the **courses** that a student intends to take to fulfill the **course** requirements for a particular degree.

Professor: A member of the faculty who teaches **sections** or advises **students**.

Section: The offering of a particular **course** during a particular semester on a particular day of the week and at a particular time of day. (For example, **course** Beginning Objects is taught in the Spring 2004 semester on Mondays from 1:00 to 3:00 p.m.).

Student: A person who is currently enrolled at the university and who is eligible to register for one or more **sections**.

Transcript: A record of all of the **courses** taken to date by a particular **student** at this university, including which semester each **course** was taken in, the grade received, and the credits granted for the **course,** as well as reflecting an overall total number of credits earned and the **student's** grade point average (GPA).

TranscriptEntry: One-line item entry from a **transcript,** reflecting the **course** number and name, semester taken, value in credit hours, and grade received.

Relationships

Advises: a professor advises a student: A professor is assigned to oversee a student's academic pursuits for the student's entire academic career, leading up to his or her attainment of a degree. An advisor counsels his or her advisees regarding course selection, professional opportunities, and any academic problems the student might be having.

Attends: a student attends a section: A student registers for a section, attends class meetings for a semester, and participates in all assignments and examinations, culminating in the award of a letter grade representing the student's mastery of the subject matter.

Calls for: a plan of study calls for a course: A student may only take a course if it's called out by his or her plan of study. The plan of study may be amended, with a student's advisor's approval.

Maintains: a student maintains a transcript: Each time a student completes a course, a record of the course and the grade received is added to the student's transcript.

Observes: a student observes a plan of study: See notes for the *calls for* association.

Offered as: a course is offered as a section: The same course can be taught numerous times in a given semester, and of course over numerous semesters for the "lifetime" of a course—that is, until such time as the subject matter is no longer considered to be of value to the student body, or there is no qualified faculty to teach the course.

Prerequisite: a course is a prerequisite for another course: If it's determined that the subject matter of a course A is necessary background to understanding the subject matter of a course B, then course A is said to be a prerequisite of course B. A student typically may not take course B unless he or she has either successfully completed course A, or can otherwise demonstrate mastery of the subject matter of course A.

Teaches: a professor teaches a section: A professor is responsible for delivering lectures, assigning thoughtful homework assignments, examining students, and otherwise ensuring that a quality treatment of the subject matter of a course is made available to students.

Waitlisted for: a student is waitlisted for a section: If a section is "full"—for example, the maximum number of students have signed up for the course based on either the classroom capacity or the student group size deemed effective for teaching—then interested students may be placed on a wait list, to be given consideration should seats in the course subsequently become available.

(aggregation between Transcript and TranscriptEntry)

(specialization of Person as Professor)

(specialization of Person as Student)

Attributes

Person.ssn: The unique social security number (SSN) assigned to an individual

Person.name: The person's name, in "last name, first name" order

Professor.title: The rank attained by the professor, e.g., "Adjunct Professor"

Student.major: A reflection of the department in which a student's primary studies lie—for example, Mathematics (We assume that a student may only designate a single major.)

Student.degree: The degree that a student is pursuing, e.g., Master of Science degree

TranscriptEntry.grade: A letter grade of A, B, C, D, or F, with an optional +/- suffix, such as A+ or C-

Course.courseNo: A unique ID assigned to a course, consisting of the department designation plus a unique numeric ID within the department, for example, MATH 101

Course.courseName: A full name describing the subject matter of a course, for example, Beginning Objects

Course.credits: The number of units or credit hours a course is worth, roughly equating to the number of hours spent in the classroom in a single week (typically, 3 credits for a full semester lecture course)

Section.sectionNo: A unique number assigned to distinguish one section/offering of a particular course from another offering of the same course in the same semester, for example, MATH 101 section no. 1

Section.dayOfWeek: The day of the week on which the lecture course meets

Section.timeOfDay: The time (range) during which the course meets, for example 2–4 p.m.

Section.semester: An indication of the scholastic semester in which a section is offered—for example, Spring 2004

Section.room: The building and room number where the section will be meeting—for example, Government Hall, Room 105

Section.seatingCapacity: The maximum number of students permitted to register for a section

---

Metadata

One question that is often raised by beginning modelers is why we don't use an inheritance relationship to relate the Course and Section classes, rather than using a simple association as we've chosen to do. On the surface, it does indeed seem tempting to want Section to be a derived class of Course, because all of the attributes listed for a Course—courseNo, courseName, and credits—also pertain to a Section; so, why wouldn't we want Section to *inherit* these, in the same way that Student and Professor inherit all of the attributes of Person? A simple example should quickly illustrate why inheritance isn't appropriate.

Let's say that, because Beginning Object Concepts is such a popular course, the university is offering three sections of the course for the Spring 2004 semester. So, we instantiate one Course object and three Section objects. If Section were a derived class of Course, then all *four* objects would carry courseNo, courseName, and credits attributes. Filling in the attribute values for these four objects, as shown in Table 10-3, we see that there is quite a bit of repetition in the attribute values across these four objects: we've repeated the same courseName, courseNumber, and creditValue attribute values four times! That's because the information contained within a Course object is common to, and hence describes, *numerous* Section objects.

Table 10-3. Duplication of Data Across Four Object Instances

Attribute Name	Attribute Values for the Course Object		
courseName	Beginning Object Concepts		
courseNumber	OBJECTS 101		
creditValue	3		

Attribute Name	Attr. Values for Section Object #1	Attr. Values for Section Object #2	Attr. Values for Section Object #3
courseName	**Beginning Object Concepts**	**Beginning Object Concepts**	**Beginning Object Concepts**
courseNumber	**OBJECTS 101**	**OBJECTS 101**	**OBJECTS 101**
creditValue	**3**	**3**	**3**
students Registered	(To be determined)	(To be determined)	(To be determined)
instructor	Reference to professor X	Reference to professor Y	Reference to professor Z
semester Offered	Spring 2004	Spring 2004	Spring 2004
dayOfWeek	Monday	Tuesday	Thursday
timeOfDay	7:00 p.m.	4:00 p.m.	6:00 p.m.
classroom	Hall A, Room 123	Hall B, Room 234	Hall A, Room 345

To reduce redundancy and to promote encapsulation, we should eliminate *inheritance* of these attributes, and instead create only one instance of a Course object for *n* instances of its related Section objects. We can then have each Section object maintain a handle on the common Course object so as to retrieve these shared values whenever necessary. This is precisely what we've modeled via the one-to-many *offered as* association.

Whenever an instance of some class A encapsulates information that describes numerous instances of some other class B (such as Course does for Section), we refer to the information contained by the A object (Course) as **metadata** relative to the B objects (Sections).

Summary

Our object model has started to take shape! We have a good idea of what the static structure needs to be for the SRS—the classes, and their attributes and relationships with one another—and are able to communicate this knowledge in a concise, graphical form. There are many more embellishments to the UML notation that we haven't covered in this chapter, but we've presented the core concepts that will suffice for most "industrial-strength" modeling projects. Once you've mastered these, you can explore the Recommended Reading section in Chapter 17 of the book if you'd like to learn more about these notations.

There is an obvious "hole" in our class diagram, however: all of our classes have empty operations compartments. We'll address this deficiency by learning some complementary modeling techniques for determining the dynamic behavior of our intended system in Chapter 11.

In this chapter, you've learned

- The noun phrase analysis technique for identifying candidate domain classes

- The verb phrase analysis technique for determining potential relationships among these classes

- That coming up with candidate classes is a bit subjective, and hence that we have to remain flexible, and willing to revisit our model, through many iterations until we—and our users—are satisfied with the outcome

- The importance of producing a data dictionary as part of a project's documentation set

- How to graphically portray the static structure of our model as a class diagram using UML

- How important it is to have an experienced object modeling mentor available to a project team

Exercises

1. Come up with a list of candidate classes for the Prescription Tracking System (PTS) case study presented in Appendix B, as well as an association matrix.

2. Develop a class diagram for the Prescription Tracking System (PTS) case study, using UML notation. Reflect all significant attributes and relationships among classes, including the appropriate multiplicity. Ideally, you should use an object modeling software tool if you have one available to you.

3. Prepare a data dictionary for the PTS, to include definitions of all classes, attributes, and associations.

4. Devise a list of candidate classes for the problem area whose requirements you defined for exercise 3 in Chapter 2, as well as an association matrix.

5. Develop a class diagram for the problem area whose requirements you defined for exercise 3 in Chapter 2, using UML notation. Reflect all significant attributes and relationships among classes, including the appropriate multiplicity. Ideally, you should use an object modeling software tool if you have one available to you.

6. Prepare a data dictionary for the problem area whose requirements you defined for exercise 3 in Chapter 2 to include definitions of all classes, attributes, and associations.

Modeling the Dynamic/Behavioral Aspects of the System

THUS FAR, we've been focused on the **static structure** of the problem being modeled—the floor plan for our custom home, as it were. As we learned in Chapter 10, this static structure is communicated via a class diagram plus supporting documentation. The building blocks of a class diagram are

- Classes.

- Associations/aggregations.

- Attributes.

- Generalization/specialization hierarchies (also known as inheritance relationships).

- Operations/methods. ***These are conspicuously absent from our class diagram.*** Why? Because they aren't part of the static structure, so we haven't discussed how to determine these yet; this will be the focus of this chapter.

As we've said many times already, an OO software system is a set of collaborating objects, each with a "life" of its own. If each object went about its own business without regard to what any other object needed it to do, however, utter chaos would reign! The only way that objects can collaborate to perform some overall system mission, such as registering a student for a course, is if each class defines the appropriate methods—*services*—that will enable its instances to fulfill their respective roles in the collaboration.

In order to determine what these methods/services must be, we must complement our knowledge of the static structure of the system to be built by also modeling the **dynamic** aspects of the situation: that is, the ways in which concurrently active objects interact over time, and how these interactions affect each object's state. Producing a dynamic model to complement the static model will not only enable us to determine the methods required for each class, but also give us new insights into ways to improve upon the static structure.

In this chapter, you'll learn about the building blocks of a **dynamic model:**

- Events

- Scenarios

- Sequence diagrams

- Collaboration diagrams

and how to use the knowledge gleaned from these to identify the operations/methods that are needed to complete our class diagram.

How Behavior Affects State

Back in Chapter 3, we defined the *state* of an object as the collective set of all of the object's attribute values at a given point in time; this includes

- The values of all of the "simple" attributes for that object—in other words, attributes that don't represent other domain objects

- The values of all of the reference variable attributes representing links to other domain objects

In Table 11-1, we've repeated the list of the Student class attributes from Chapter 6, adding a column to indicate which category each attribute falls into.

Table 11-1. Student *Class Attributes*

Attribute Name	Data Type	Represents Link(s) to an SRS Domain Object?
name	string	No
studentID	string	No
birthdate	DateTime	No
address	string	No
major	string	No
gpa	double	No
advisor	Professor	Yes

Table 11-1. Student Class Attributes (continued)

Attribute Name	Data Type	Represents Link(s) to an SRS Domain Object?
courseLoad	Collection of Course objects	Yes
transcript	Collection of TranscriptEntry objects, or Transcript	Yes

In Chapter 10, we learned about UML object diagrams as a way of portraying a "snapshot" of the links between specific individual objects. Let's use an object diagram to reflect the state of a few hypothetical objects within the SRS domain.

In Figure 11-1, we see that Dr. Smith (a Professor) works for the Math Department, Dr. Green (another Professor) works for the Science Department, and that Bill and Mary, both Students, are majoring in Math and Science, respectively.

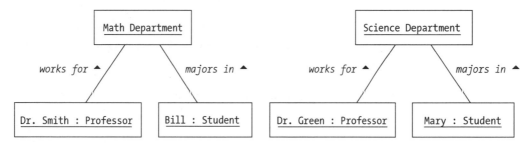

Figure 11-1. The state of an object includes the links it maintains with other objects.

Bill is dissatisfied with his choice of majors, and calls Dr. Green, a professor whom he admires, to make an appointment. Bill wants to discuss the possibility of transferring to the Science Department. After meeting with Dr. Green and discussing his situation, Bill indeed decides to switch majors. We've informally reflected these object interactions using arrows on the object diagram in Figure 11-2; as this chapter progresses, you'll learn the "official" way to portray object interactions in UML notation.

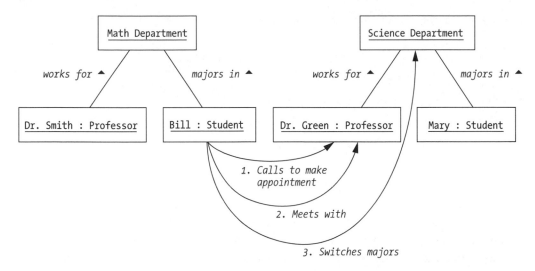

Figure 11-2. Objects' interactions can affect their state.

When the dust settles from all of this activity, we see that the resultant state of the system has changed, as reflected in the revised object diagram "snapshot" in Figure 11-3. In particular

- Bill's state has changed, because his link to the Math Department object has been replaced with a link to the Science Department object.

- The Math Department object's state has changed, because it no longer has a link to Bill.

- The Science Department's state has changed, because it now has an additional link (to Bill) that wasn't previously there.

Note, however, that although Dr. Green collaborated with Bill in helping him to make his decision to switch majors, the state of the "Dr. Green" (Professor) object **has not changed** as a result of the collaboration.

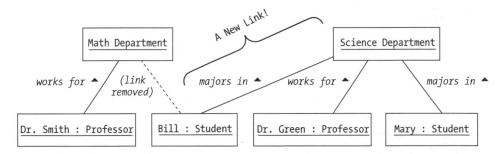

Figure 11-3. Some interacting objects experience a change of state, others don't.

So, we see that

- Objects' dynamic activities can result in changes to the **static structure of a system**—that is, the states of all of its objects taken collectively.

- However, such activities needn't affect the state of ***all*** objects involved in a collaboration.

Events

We saw in Chapter 4 that object collaborations are triggered by events. By way of review, an *event* is an external stimulus to an object, signaled to the object in the form of a *message* (method call). An event can be

- ***User initiated*** (for example, the result of clicking a "button" on a GUI)

- ***Initiated by another computer system*** (such as the arrival of information being transferred from the Student Billing System to the Student Registration System)

- ***Initiated by another object within the same system*** (a Course object requesting some service of a Transcript object, for example)

When an object receives notification of an event via a message, it may react in one or more of the following ways:

- An object may change its state.

- An object may direct an event (message) toward another object.

- An object may return a value.

- An object may react with the external boundaries of its system.

- An object may seemingly ignore an event.

Let's discuss these five types of reaction in detail, one-by-one.

An Object May Change Its State

An object may change its state (the values of its "simple" attributes and/or links to other objects), as in the case of a Professor object receiving a message to take on a new Student advisee, illustrated by the following code snippet:

```
Professor p = new Professor();
Student s = new Student();
// details omitted
p.AddAdvisee(s);
```

Let's look at the code for the Professor class's AddAdvisee method to see how the Professor will respond to this message. We see that the Professor object is inserting the reference to Student object s that it is being handed as an argument into a Collection of Student object references called advisees:

```
public class Professor {
  // Attributes.
  // (pseudocode)
  Collection advisees;  // Holds Student object references.

  // Other details omitted.

  public void AddAdvisee(Student s) {
    // Insert s into the advisees collection.
    // (pseudocode)
    advisees.Insert(s);
  }
}
```

In so doing, Professor object p will have formed a new link of type *advises* with Student object s (see Figure 11-4). Typical "set" methods fall into this category of event response.

Figure 11-4. Revisiting the UML diagram for the advises *association.*

An Object May Direct an Event (Message) Toward Another Object

An object may direct an event (message) toward another object (including, perhaps, the sender of the original message), as in the case of a Section object receiving a message to register a Student, illustrated by the following code snippet:

```
Section x = new Section();
Student s = new Student();
// details omitted
x.Register(s);
```

If we next look at the method code for the `Section` class's `Register` method to see how it will respond to this message, we see that the `Section` object in turn sends a message to the `Student` to be enrolled, to verify that the `Student` has completed a necessary prerequisite course:

```
public class Section {
  // details omitted

  bool Register(Student s) {
    // Verify that the student has completed a necessary
    // prerequisite course. (We are delegating part
    // of the work to another object, Student s.)
    // (pseudocode)
    bool completed = s.SuccessfullyCompleted(some prerequisite);
    if (completed) {
      register the student and return a value of true;
    }
    else {
      return a value of false to signal that the registration
        request has been rejected;
    }
  ]
}
```

This happens to be an example of ***delegation***, which we discussed in Chapter 4: namely, another object (a `Student`, in this case) helping to fulfill a service request originally made of the `Section` object.

An Object May Return a Value

An object may return a value; the returned value may be one of the following:

- The value of one of the object's private attributes

- Some computed value (that is, a "pseudoattribute," as we discussed in Chapter 4)

- A value that was obtained from some ***other*** object through delegation

- A status code (as in `true`/`false` responses, signaling success or failure of Boolean methods)

Typical "get" methods fall into this category of event response.

An Object May React with the External Boundaries of a System

An object may react with the external boundaries of a system: that is, it may display some information on a GUI, or cause information to be printed to a printer. As you'll learn in Chapters 15 and 16, however, what appears to be an external system boundary is often implemented in C# as yet another object.

An Object May Seemingly Ignore an Event

Finally, an object may seemingly ignore an event, as would be the case if a Professor object received the message to add an advisee, but determined that the Student whom it was being asked to take on as an advisee was ***already*** an advisee:

```
Student s = new Student();
Professor p = new Professor();
// details omitted
// Professor p will seemingly "ignore" this next message.
p.AddAdvisee(s);
```

Let's look at a slightly different version of the AddAdvisee method than what we saw previously:

```
public class Professor {
  // (pseudocode)
  Collection advisees;  // Holds Student object references.
  // details omitted

  public void AddAdvisee(Student s) {
    // ONLY insert s into the 'advisees' collection IF IT
    // ISN'T ALREADY IN THERE.
    // (pseudocode)
    if (s is already in collection) return;  // do nothing
    else advisees.Insert(s);
  }
}
```

Actually, to say that the Professor object is doing nothing is an oversimplification: at a minimum, the object is executing the appropriate method code, which is performing some internal state checks ("Is this student already one of my advisees?"). It's just that, when the dust settles, the Professor object has neither changed state nor fired off any messages to other objects, so it ***appears*** as if nothing has happened.

Scenarios

Events originating externally to a system occur randomly: we can't predict, for example, when a user is going to click a button on a GUI. In order for a system to perform useful functions, however, the ***internal*** events that arise in ***response*** to these external events—in other words, the messages that objects exchange in carrying out some system function—can't be left to occur randomly. Rather, they must be orchestrated in such as way as to lead, in cause-and-effect fashion, to some desired result. In the same way that a musical score indicates which notes must be played by various instruments to produce a melody, a **scenario** prescribes the sequence of internal messages (events) that must occur in carrying out some system function from beginning to end.

We introduced use cases in Chapter 9 as a way to specify all of the goals for a system from the standpoint of external actors—users or other computer systems. *Merriam-Webster's Collegiate Dictionary, Eleventh Edition* defines the term scenario as

> *A sequence of events esp. when imagined; esp : an account or synopsis of a possible course of action or events.*

which is precisely how the term is used in the object modeling sense.

A scenario is one hypothetical instance of how a particular use case might play out. Just as an object is an instance of a class, and a link is an instance of an association, ***a scenario may be thought of as an instance of a use case***. Or, stated another way, just as a class is a template for creating objects, and an association is a template for creating links, ***a use case is a template for creating scenarios***. A single use case thus inspires many different scenarios, in the same way that planning a driving trip from one city to another can involve many different routes.

We describe scenarios in narrative fashion, as a series of steps observed from the standpoint of a hypothetical observer who is able to see not only what is happening outwardly as the system carries out a particular request, but also what is going on behind the scenes, internally to the system. (Note, however, that even though we're now concerned with internal system processes, we're still only interested in ***functional*** requirements as defined in Chapter 9, not in the "bits and bytes" of how the computer works.)

The following is a sample scenario representing the "Register for a Course" use case, one of several use cases that we identified for the SRS in Chapter 9.

Scenario #1 for the "Register for a Course" Use Case

In this first scenario, a student by the name of Fred successfully registers for a course. The specific sequence of events is as follows:

1. Fred, a student, logs on to the SRS.

2. He views the schedule of classes for the current semester to determine which section(s) he wishes to register for.

3. Fred requests a seat in a particular section of a course titled "Beginning Objects," course number OBJ101, section 1.

4. Fred's plan of study is checked to ensure that the requested course is appropriate for his overall degree goals. (We assume that students are not permitted to take courses outside of their plans of study.)

5. His transcript is checked to ensure that he has satisfied all of the prerequisites for the requested course, if there are any.

6. Seating availability in the section is confirmed.

7. The section is added to Fred's current course load.

From Fred's vantage point (sitting in front of a computer screen!), here's what he perceives to be occurring: after logging on to the SRS, he indicates that he wishes to register for OBJ101, section 1 by choosing it from the available course list, and then clicks the Add button (see Figure 11-5).

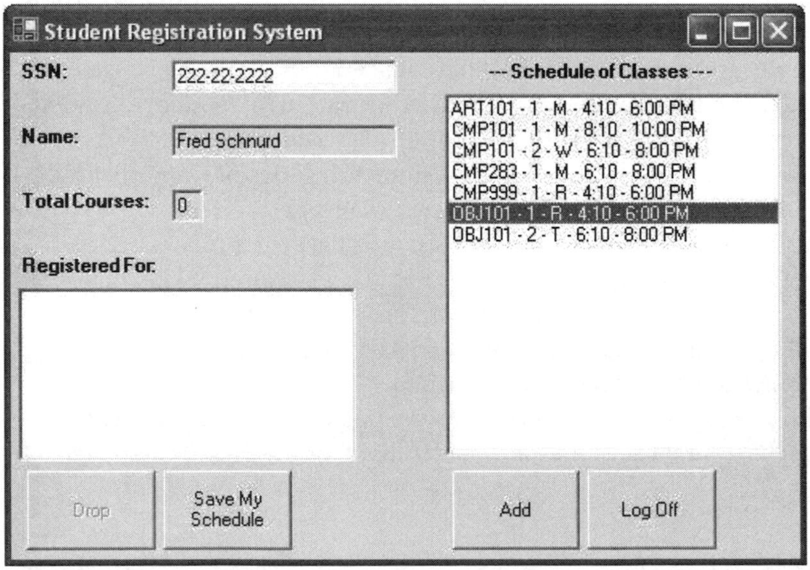

Figure 11-5. Fred's view of things, part 1

A few moments later, Fred receives a confirmation message, as shown in Figure 11-6.

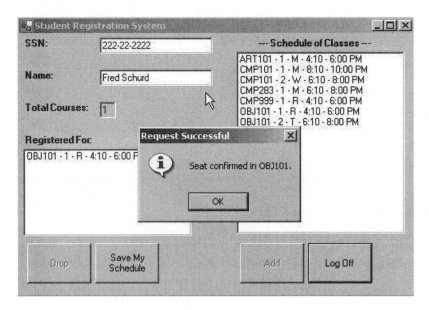

Figure 11-6. Fred's view of things, part 2

Fred's unaware (for the most part) of all of the "behind the scenes" processing steps that are taking place on his behalf!

The preceding scenario represents a "best case" scenario, where everything goes smoothly and Fred ends up being successfully registered for the requested course. But, as we know all too well, things don't always work out this smoothly, as evidenced by the following alternative scenario for the *same* use case. Everything is the same between Scenarios #1 and #2 except for the steps that are shown in *bold*.

Scenario #2 for the "Register for a Course" Use Case

In this scenario, Fred once again attempts to register for a course; while he meets all of the requirements, the requested section is unfortunately full. The SRS offers Fred the option of putting his name on a wait list. The specific sequence of events is as follows:

1. Fred, a student, logs on to the SRS.

2. Fred views the schedule of classes for the current semester to determine which section(s) he wishes to register for.

3. Fred requests a seat in a particular section of a course titled "Beginning Objects," course number OBJ101, section 1.

4. Fred's plan of study is checked to ensure that the requested course is appropriate for his overall degree goals.

5. His transcript is checked to ensure that he has satisfied all of the prerequisites for the requested course, if any.

6. ***Seating availability in the section is checked, but the section is found to be full.***

7. ***Fred is asked if he wishes to be put on a first come, first served wait list.***

8. ***Fred elects to be placed on the wait list.***

With a little imagination, you can undoubtedly think of numerous other scenarios for this use case, involving such circumstances as Fred having requested a course that isn't called for by his plan of study, or a course for which he hasn't met the prerequisites. And, there are many other ***use cases*** to be considered, as well, as were discussed in Chapter 9.

> *Are there practical limits to the number of alternative scenarios that one should consider for a given use case? As with all requirements analysis, the criteria for when to stop are somewhat subjective: we stop when it appears that we can no longer generate* **significantly different** *scenarios; trivial variations are to be avoided.*

When devising scenarios, it's often helpful to observe the future users of the system that we're modeling as they go about performing the same business functions today. In the case of student registration, for example, what manual or automated steps does a student have to go through presently to register for a course? What steps does the university take before deeming a student eligible to register? Whether the registration process is 100 percent manual at present, or is based on an automated system that you're going to be replacing or augmenting, observing the steps that are involved today in carrying out a particular business goal can serve as the basis for one or more useful scenarios.

Scenarios, once written, should be added to our project's use case documentation; generally, we pair all scenarios with their associated use cases in that document.

Why are scenarios so important? Because they are the means by which we start to gain insight into the ***behaviors*** that will be required of our objects. We'll need a way to formalize these scenarios so that the actual methods needed for each of our classes become apparent; UML **sequence diagrams** are the means by which we do so, so let's now discuss how to prepare these.

Sequence Diagrams

Sequence diagrams are one of two types of UML **interaction diagrams** (we'll explore the second type, **collaboration diagrams**, a bit later in this chapter). Sequence diagrams are a way of graphically portraying how messages should flow from one object to another in carrying out a given scenario.

We'll illustrate the process of creating a sequence diagram by creating one for Scenario #1 of the "Register for a Course" use case, which was presented in Chapter 9.

Determining Objects and External Actors for Scenario #1

To prepare a sequence diagram, we must first determine

- Which classes of objects (from among those that we specified in our static model [class diagram] in Chapter 10) are involved in carrying out a particular scenario

- Which external actors are involved

Looking back at Scenario #1 for the "Register for a Course" use case, we determine that the following objects are involved:

- One Student object (representing Fred)

- One Section object (representing the course titled "Beginning Objects," course number OBJ101, section number 1)

- One PlanOfStudy object, belonging to Fred

- One Transcript object, also belonging to Fred

The scenario also mentions that the student "views the schedule of classes for the current semester to determine which section(s) he wishes to register for." You may recall that when we were determining what our candidate classes should be back in Chapter 10, we debated whether or not to add ScheduleOfClasses as a candidate class to our model, and elected to leave it out at that time. In order to fully represent the details of Scenario #1, we're going to reverse that decision, and retrofit ScheduleOfClasses into our UML class diagram now as follows:

- We'll show ScheduleOfClasses participating in a one-to-many aggregation with the Section class because one ScheduleOfClasses object will be instantiated per semester to represent all of the sections that are being taught that semester. (It's an abstraction of the paper booklet or online schedule that students look at in choosing which classes they wish to register for in a given semester.)

- We'll also transfer the semester attribute from the Section class to ScheduleOfClasses. Since each Section object will now be maintaining a handle on its associated ScheduleOfClasses object by virtue of the aggregation relationship between them, a Section object will be able to request semester information whenever it is needed.

The results of these changes to our class diagram are highlighted in Figure 11-7.

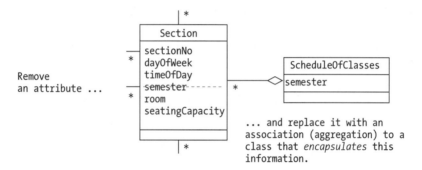

Figure 11-7. Fine-tuning the UML diagram

Acknowledging ScheduleOfClasses as a class in our model allows us to now reference a ScheduleOfClasses object in our sequence diagram, as we'll see in a moment. Scenarios often unearth new classes, attributes, and relationships, thus contributing to our structural "picture" of the system; this is a common occurrence, and is a ***desirable*** side effect of dynamic modeling.

Of course, we must remember to add a definition of ScheduleOfClasses to our data dictionary!

> **Schedule of Classes:** *A list of all classes/**sections** that are being offered for a particular semester; **students** review the **schedule of classes** to determine which **sections** they wish to register for.*

Finally, since the scenario explicitly mentions interactions between the student user and the system, we'll reflect Fred the ***actor*** separately from Fred the ***object.*** Doing so will allow us to represent the SRS interacting externally with the user, as well as showing the system's internal object-to-object interactions. We refer to an object that represents an abstraction of an actor as an instance of a **boundary class.**

Our adjusted list of object/actor participants is now as follows:

- One Student object (representing Fred)

- One Section object (representing the course titled "Beginning Objects," course number OBJ101, section number 1)

- One PlanOfStudy object, belonging to Fred

- One Transcript object, also belonging to Fred

- One ScheduleOfClasses object

- One Student actor (Fred again!)

Preparing the Sequence Diagram

To prepare a sequence diagram for Scenario #1, we do the following:

- We draw vertical dashed lines, one per object or actor that participates in the scenario; these are referred to as the objects' **lifelines.** Note that the objects/actors can be listed in any order from left to right in a diagram, although it's common practice to place the external user/actor at the far left.

- At the top of each lifeline, as appropriate, we place either an **instance icon**—that is, a box containing the (optional) name and class of an object participant—or a stick figure symbol to designate an actor. (For rules governing how an instance icon is to be formed, please refer back to the section on creating object diagrams in Chapter 10.)

- Then, for each event called out by our scenario, we reflect its corresponding message as a horizontal *solid-line* arrow drawn from the lifeline of the sender to the lifeline of the receiver.

- Responses back from messages (in other words, return values from methods, or simple return; statements in the case of methods declared to have a void return type) are shown as horizontal *dashed-line* arrows drawn from the lifeline of the **receiver** of the original message *back to* the lifeline for the **sender** of the message.

- Message arrows appear in chronological order from top to bottom in the diagram.

The completed sequence diagram for Scenario #1 is shown in Figure 11-8.

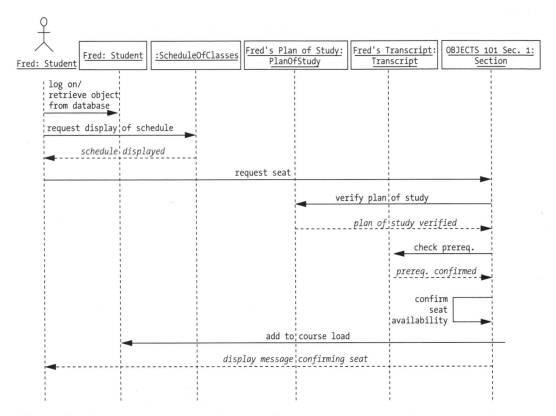

Figure 11-8. Sequence diagram for Scenario #1

> *Note that we've intentionally omitted one element of sequence diagram nota-*
> *tion from this example: namely, the use of **focus of control bars** to illustrate*
> *the period of time over an object's lifeline that the object is actually engaged*
> *in processing a request. For more details on sequence diagram notation,*
> *please see the recommended reading suggestions in Chapter 17.*

Let's step through the diagram to make sure that we understand all of the activities that are reflected in the diagram.

1. When Fred logs on to the system, his "alter ego" as an object is activated (see Figure 11-9).

Presumably, information representing each Student—in other words, the Student *object's attribute values—is maintained offline in persistent storage, such as a DBMS or file, until such time as he or she logs on, at which time the information is used to instantiate a* Student *object in memory, mirroring the user who has just logged on. We'll talk about reconstituting objects from persistent storage in Chapter 15.*

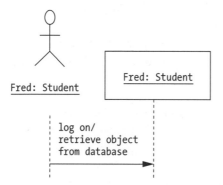

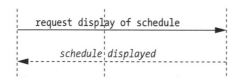

Figure 11-9. When Fred logs on, a Student *object is created.*

2. When Fred the user/actor requests that the semester class schedule be displayed, we reflect the message "request display of schedule" being sent to an anonymous ScheduleOfClasses object. The dashed-line-arrow response from the ScheduleOfClasses object indicates that the schedule is being displayed to the user, strictly speaking, via a GUI (see Figure 11-10).

Figure 11-10. As requested, a schedule of classes is displayed.

We've chosen to label our response arrows with italic *instead of regular font, a slight departure from official UML notation.*

3. The next message shown in our diagram is a message from the user to the Section object, requesting a seat in the class.

This message is shown originating from the user; in reality, it originates from a graphical user interface (GUI) component object of the SRS GUI, but we aren't worrying about such implementation details at this stage in the analysis effort. We'll talk about the object-oriented aspects of graphical user interface design and event processing in depth in Chapter 16.

Note that there is no immediate reply to this message; that's because the Section object has a few other objects that it needs to consult with before it can grant a seat to this student, namely

- The Section sends a message to the object representing Fred's plan of study, asking that object to confirm that the course that Fred has requested is one of the courses required of Fred in completing his degree program.

- The Section next sends a message to the object representing Fred's transcript, asking that object to confirm that a prerequisite course—say COMP 001—has been satisfactorily completed by this student.

4. Assuming that both of these other objects respond favorably, as they are expected to do by virtue of how this scenario was written, the Section object then performs some internal processing to verify that there is indeed room for Fred in this section. We reflect internal processing within a single object as an arrow that loops back to the same lifeline that it starts with, as shown in Figure 11-11.

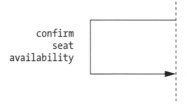

Figure 11-11. Availability of the requested section is confirmed.

Of course, if we were to reflect **all** of the internal processing that is performed by every one of the objects in our sequence diagram, it would be **flooded** with such loops! The only reason that we've chosen to show this particular loop is because it's explicitly called out as a step in Scenario #1; if we had omitted it from our diagram, it might appear that we had accidentally overlooked this step.

5. Finally, with all checks having been satisfied, the Section object has two remaining responsibilities:

    - First, it sends a new message to the "Fred" Student object, requesting that the Student object add this Section to Fred's course load.

    - Next, the Section object sends a response back to Fred the ***user/actor*** (via the GUI) confirming his seat in the section. ***This is the response to the original "request seat" message that was sent by the user toward the beginning of the scenario!*** All of the extra "behind the scenes" processing necessary to fulfill the request—involving a Section object collaborating with a PlanOfStudy object, a Transcript object, and a Student object—is transparent to the user. As we saw earlier in the chapter, Fred merely selected a section from the schedule of classes that was displayed on the SRS GUI, clicked the Add button, and, a few moments later, saw a confirmation message appear on his screen.

Of course, as with all modeling, this particular sequence diagram isn't necessarily the best, or only, way to portray the selected scenario. And, for that matter, one can argue the relative merits of one scenario as compared with another. It's important to keep in mind that preparing sequence diagrams is but a means to an end: namely, discovering the dynamic aspects of the system to be built—that is, the methods—to complement our static/structural knowledge of the system. Recall that our ***ultimate*** goal for Part Two of the book is to produce an object-oriented blueprint that we can use as the basis for coding the SRS as a C# application in Part Three. But, as we've already pointed out, the class diagram that we created in Chapter 10 had a noticeable deficiency: all of its classes' operations compartments were empty. Fortunately, sequence diagrams provide us with the missing pieces of information.

Using Sequence Diagrams to Determine Methods

Now that we've prepared a sequence diagram, how do we put the information that it contains to good use? In particular, how do we "harvest" information from such diagrams concerning the methods that the various classes need to implement?

The process is actually quite simple. We step through the diagram, one lifeline at a time, and study all arrows pointing into that line.

- Arrows representing a new request being made of an object—solid-line arrows—signal methods that the receiving object must be able to perform. For example, we see a solid line arrow labeled "check prerequisite" pointing into the lifeline representing a `Transcript` object. This tells us that the `Transcript` class needs to define a method that will allow some client object to pass in a particular course object reference, and receive back a response indicating whether or not the `Transcript` contains evidence that the course was successfully completed.

We're free to name our methods in whatever intuitive way makes the most sense, consistent with the method naming conventions discussed in Chapter 4. We're using the method in this particular scenario to check completion of a prerequisite course, so we could declare the method as follows:

```
bool CheckPrerequisite(Course c)
```

but this name is unnecessarily restrictive; what we're ***really*** doing with this method is checking the successful completion of some `Course c`; the fact that it happens to be a prerequisite of some other course is immaterial to how this method will perform. So, by naming the method

```
bool VerifyCompletion(Course c)
```

instead, we'll be able to use it anywhere in our application that we need to verify successful completion of a course—for example, when we check whether a student has met all of the course requirements necessary to graduate. (Of course, we could have still used the method in this fashion even if it had been named `CheckPrerequisite`, but then our code would be less accurately self-documenting.)

- Arrows representing responses from an operation that some other object has performed—dashed-line arrows—don't get modeled as methods/operations. These do, however, hint at the return type of the method from which this response is being issued. For example, since the response to the "verify plan of study" message is "plan of study verified," this would imply that the method is returning a `bool` result, hence we'd declare a method header as follows:

```
bool VerifyPlan(Course c)
```

- Loops also represent method calls, performed by an object on itself; these may either represent private "housekeeping" methods or public methods that other client objects may avail themselves of.

In looking at our sequence diagram for Scenario #1 from a few pages back, we note the arrows in Table 11-2.

Table 11-2. Determining the Methods Implied by Scenario #1

Arrow Labeled	Drawn Pointing into Class X	A New Request or a Response to a Previous Request?	Method to be Added to Class X
log on	Student	Request	(A method to reconstitute this object from persistent storage, such as a file or database; perhaps a special form of constructor—we'll discuss this in Part 3 of the book.)
request display of schedule	ScheduleOfClasses	Request	void Display()
schedule displayed	Student	Response	N/A
request seat	Section	Request	bool Enroll(Student s)
verify plan of study	PlanOfStudy	Request	bool VerifyPlan(Course c)
plan of study verified	Section	Response	N/A
check prerequisite	Transcript	Request	bool VerifyCompletion (Course c)
prerequisite confirmed	Section	Response	N/A
confirm seat availability	Section	Request	bool ConfirmSeatAvailability() (perhaps a private housekeeping method)
add to course load	Student	Request	void AddSection(Section s)
display message confirming seat	*(actor/user)*	*Response*	*N/A (will eventually involve calling upon some method of a user interface object—we'll worry about this in Part Three of the book)*

Thus we have identified six new "standard" methods plus one constructor that will need to be added to our class diagram; we'll do so shortly.

Repeating this process of sequence diagram production and analysis for various other use case/scenario combinations will flush out most of the methods that we'll need to implement for the SRS. Despite our best efforts, however, a few methods may not surface until we've begun to program our classes; *this is to be expected*.

Collaboration Diagrams

The UML notation introduced a second type of interaction diagram, called a **collaboration diagram,** as an alternative to sequence diagrams; both types of diagram present more or less the same information, but portrayed in a different manner.

In a collaboration diagram, we eliminate the lifelines used to portray objects and actors. Rather, we lay out instance icons representing objects and stick figures representing actors in whatever configuration is most visually appealing. We then use lines and arrows to represent the flow of messages and responses back and forth between these objects/actors. Because we lose the top-to-bottom chronological sense of message flow that we had with the sequence diagrams, we compensate by numbering the arrows in the order that they would occur during execution of a particular scenario.

The collaboration diagram in Figure 11-12 is equivalent to the sequence diagram that we produced for Scenario #1.

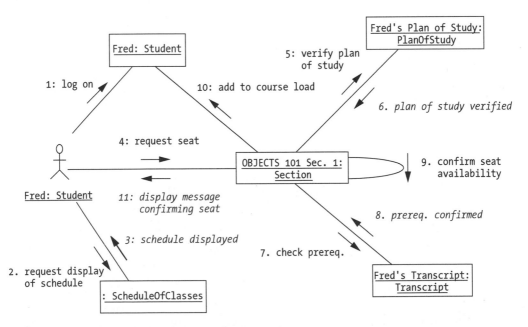

Figure 11-12. Collaboration diagram for Scenario #1

Again, from Fred's vantage point, he observes only a few of these actions, as shown in Figure 11-13.

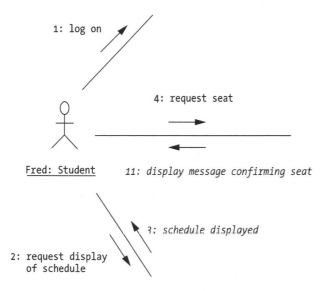

Figure 11-13. Fred sees only a small subset of the SRS collaborations.

Because the sequence and collaboration diagrams reflect essentially the same information, many object modeling software tools automatically enable us to produce one diagram from the other with the push of a button.

Revised SRS Class Diagram

Going back to the SRS class diagram that we produced in Chapter 10, let's reflect all of the new insights—some behavioral, some structural—that we've gained from analyzing one scenario/sequence diagram (see Figure 11-14).

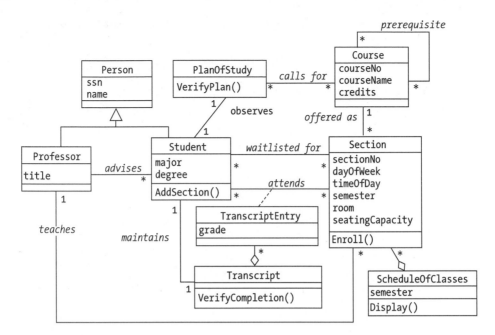

Figure 11-14. Revised SRS class diagram

Note that we've decided not to reflect the ConfirmSeatAvailability() "house-keeping" method at this time, as we suspect that it will be a private method, and therefore don't wish to clutter our diagram. The decision of whether to reflect private methods on a class diagram—or, for that matter, to reflect ***any*** feature of a class—is up to the modeler, because again, the purpose of the diagram is to communicate, and too much detail can actually lessen a diagram's effectiveness in this regard.

We must remember to update the SRS data dictionary any time we add classes, attributes, relationships, or methods to our model. Here's a suggested format for how we might wish to describe a method in the dictionary:

Method: Enroll

Defined for class: Section

Header: bool Enroll(Student s)

Description: This method enrolls the designated person in the section, unless (a) the section is already full, (b) the student's plan of study doesn't call for this course, or (c) the student hasn't met the prerequisites. It returns a bool value to indicate success (true) or failure (false) of the enrollment.

Summary

In this chapter, we've seen how the process of dynamic modeling is a complementary technique to static modeling that enriches our overall understanding of the problem to be automated, hence enabling us to improve our object "blueprint," also known as a class diagram. In particular, we've seen

- How events trigger state changes

- How to develop scenarios, based on use cases

- How to represent these as UML interaction diagrams: sequence diagrams or, alternatively, collaboration diagrams

- How to glean information from sequence diagrams concerning the behaviors expected of objects—that is, the methods that our classes will need to implement—so as to round out our class diagram

- How sequence diagrams can also yield additional knowledge about the structural aspects of a system

Exercises

1. Prepare a sequence diagram for Scenario #2 as presented earlier in this chapter.

2. Prepare a sequence diagram to represent the following scenario for the SRS case study:

   - Mary, a student, logs on to the SRS.

   - She indicates that she wishes to drop ART 222, Section 1.

   - ART 222, Section 1 is removed from Mary's course load.

   - The system determines that Joe, another student, is waitlisted for this section.

   - The section is added to Joe's current course load.

   - An email is sent to Joe notifying him that ART 222 has been added to his course load.

3. Provide a list of all of the method headers that you would add to each of your classes based on the sequence diagram that you prepared for exercise 2. Also, note any new classes, attributes, or relationships that would be needed.

4. Prepare a second sequence diagram for the SRS case study, representing a scenario of your own choosing based upon any of the SRS use cases identified in Chapter 9. This scenario should be significantly different from those presented in this chapter and from the scenario in exercise 2. You must also narrate the scenario as was done for exercise 2.

5. Provide a list of all of the method headers that you would add to each of your classes based on the sequence diagram that you prepared for exercise 4. Also, note any new classes, attributes, or relationships that would be needed.

6. Prepare a sequence diagram to represent the following scenario for the Prescription Tracking System (PTS) case study presented in Appendix B:

   - Mary Jones, an existing customer of the pharmacy, brings in a prescription for eye drops to have it filled.

   - The pharmacist checks to see if Ms. Jones has previously had a prescription filled for this item.

   - He discovers that she has, and furthermore that the last time it was refilled was less than a month ago.

   - Knowing that her insurance won't authorize payment for this same prescription so soon, the pharmacist informs Ms. Jones, and she decides to wait to have it filled at a later date.

7. Devise an "interesting" scenario, and prepare the corresponding sequence diagram, for the problem area whose requirements you defined for exercise 3 in Chapter 2.

8. Provide a list of all of the method headers that you would add to each of your classes based on the sequence diagram that you prepared for exercise 7. Also, note any new classes, attributes, or relationships that would be needed.

CHAPTER 12

Wrapping Up Our Modeling Efforts

HAVING USED THE TECHNIQUES for static and dynamic modeling presented in Chapters 10 and 11, respectively, we've arrived at a fairly thorough object model of the SRS—or so it seems! Before we embark upon implementing our class diagram as C# code in Part Three of the book, however, we need to make sure that our model is as accurate and representative of the goal system as possible.

In this chapter, we'll

- Explore some simple techniques for testing our model.

- Talk about the notion of reusing models.

Testing Your Model

Testing a model doesn't involve "rocket science"; rather, it calls for some commonsense measures designed to identify errors and/or omissions.

- First of all, revisit all requirements-related project documentation—the original problem statement and the supporting use cases—to ensure that no requirements were overlooked. We'll do so for our SRS model in a moment.

- Conduct a minimum of two separate formal walk-throughs of the model: one with the development team members, and a second with the future users of the system. Prior to each walk-through, make sure to distribute copies of the following documentation to each of the participants far enough in advance to allow them adequate time to review these, if they so desire (but be prepared to discuss significant aspects of these at the meeting in case they haven't reviewed them):

  - "Executive summary" problem statement, if available

  - Class diagram

  - Data dictionary

  - Use case documentation

  - Significant scenarios and corresponding message trace diagrams

By this stage in the project, you'll have hopefully already educated your users on how to read UML diagrams, and they'll have informally seen numerous iterations of the evolving models. If any of the participants in the upcoming walk-throughs aren't familiar with any of the notation, however, take time in advance to tutor them in this regard. (The information contained in Chapters 10 and 11 of this book should be more than adequate as the basis for such a tutorial.)

When conducting the walk-through, designate someone to be the narrator and discussion leader, and a different person to be responsible for recording significant discussion content, particularly changes that need to be made. Having one person trying to do both is too distracting, and important notes may be missed as a result. If appropriate, you may even arrange to tape record the discussion.

Remain open-minded throughout the review process. It's human nature to want to defend something that we've worked hard on putting together, but remember that it's far better to find and correct shortcomings now, when the SRS is still a paper skeleton, than after it has been rendered into code.

Revisiting Requirements

In revisiting the SRS case study problem statement, we find that we've indeed *missed* one requirement, namely

> *"The SRS will verify whether or not the proposed plan of study satisfies the requirements of the degree that the student is seeking."*

We didn't model Degree as a class—recall that we debated whether or not to do so back in Chapter 10, and ultimately decided against it. Nor, for that matter, do we reflect the requirements of a particular degree program in our model. Let's look at what it would take to do so properly at this time.

Researching the way in which our university specifies degree program requirements, we learn the following:

- Every degree program specifies five "core" courses—that is, courses that a student *must* take. For example, for the degree of Master of Science in Information Technology (MSIT), students are required to complete the following five core courses:

  - Analysis of Algorithms

  - Application Programming Design

- Computer Systems Architecture

- Data Structures

- Information Systems Project Management

- Secondly, students are expected to select an area of specialization within their degree program known as a concentration. For the MSIT degree, our university offers three different concentrations:

  - Object Technology

  - Database Management Systems

  - Networking and Communications

- Each concentration in turn specifies three mandatory, concentration-specific courses; for the MSIT degree with a concentration in Object Technology, the required concentration-specific courses are

  - Object Methods for Software Development

  - Advanced C# Programming

  - Object Database Management Systems

- Finally, the student must take two additional electives to bring his or her course total to 10.

Phew! To model all of these interdependencies would require a fairly complex class diagram structure, as shown in Figure 12-1.

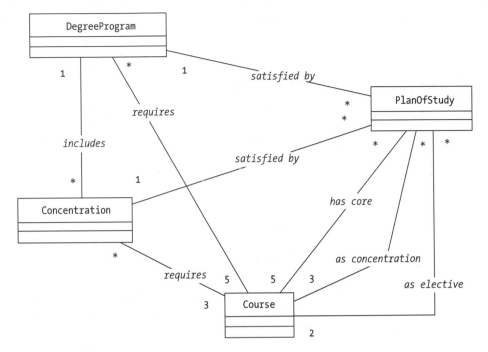

Figure 12-1. Modeling degree program requirements proves to be rather complicated

We go back to our project sponsors—the future users of the SRS—and break the news to them that we've just uncovered a previously missed requirement that is going to significantly increase the complexity and cost of our automation effort. The sponsors decide that having the SRS verify the correctness of a student's plan of study is too ambitious a goal; they instead decide that a student will use the SRS to submit a ***proposed*** plan of study, but that his or her advisor will then be responsible for ***manually*** verifying and approving it. So, all we wind up having to do to correct our SRS class diagram as last presented is to add one attribute to the PlanOfStudy class, reflecting the date on which it was approved, and a new *approves* association connecting the Professor class to the PlanOfStudy class, and we're good to go!

Note that we don't need to add an ApprovePlan method to the PlanOfStudy class, because as discussed in Chapter 10 we may assume the presence of "set" methods for all attributes; the SetDateApproved method would suffice for marking a plan as approved. And, the *approves* association between the PlanOfStudy and Professor classes (see the diagram excerpt in Figure 12-2) ensures us that each PlanOfStudy object will maintain a handle on the Professor object who actually approved the plan on the date indicated.

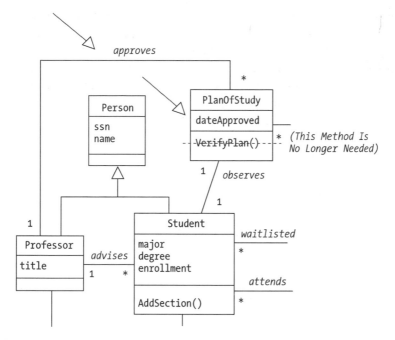

Figure 12-2. Making minor adjustments to the SRS class diagram

Reusing Models: A Word About Design Patterns

As we discussed in Chapter 2, when learning about something new, we automatically search our "mental archive" for other abstractions/models that we've previously built and mastered, to look for similarities that we can build upon. This technique of comparing features to find an abstraction that is similar enough to be reused effectively is known as **pattern reuse**. As it turns out, pattern reuse is an important technique for object-oriented software development.

Let's say that after we finish up our SRS class diagram, we're called upon to model a system for a small travel agency, Wild Blue Yonder (WBY). As a brand-new travel agency, WBY wishes to offer a level of customer service above and beyond their well-established competitors, and so they decide to enable their customers to make travel reservations online via the Web (most of WBY's competitors take such requests over the phone).

For any given travel package—let's say a 10-day trip to Ireland—WBY offers numerous trips throughout the year. Each trip has a maximum client capacity, so if a client can't get a confirmed seat for one of the trips, he or she may request a position on a first-come, first-served wait list.

In order to keep track of each client's overall experience with WBY, the travel agency plans on following up with each client after a trip to conduct a satisfaction survey, and will ask the client to rate his or her experience for that trip on a scale of 1 to 10, with 10 being outstanding. By doing so, WBY can determine which trips are the most successful, so as to offer them more frequently in the future, as well as perhaps eliminating those that are less popular. WBY will also be able to make more informed recommendations for future trips that a given client is likely to enjoy by studying that client's travel satisfaction history.

In reflecting on the requirements for this system, we experience déjà vu! We recognize that many aspects of the WBY system requirements are similar to those of the SRS. In fact, we're able to reuse the overall structure, or ***pattern,*** of the SRS object model by making the following class substitutions:

- Substitute `TravelPackage` for `Course`

- Substitute `Trip` for `Section`

- Substitute `Client` for `Student`

- Substitute `TripRecord` for `TranscriptEntry`

- Substitute `TravelHistory` for `Transcript`

Note that all of the relationships among these classes—their names, types, and even their multiplicities—remain unchanged from the SRS class diagram (see Figure 12-3).

> *Such an exact match is exceptionally rare when reusing design patterns; don't hesitate to change some things (eliminate classes or associations, change multiplicities, and so forth) in order to facilitate reuse.*

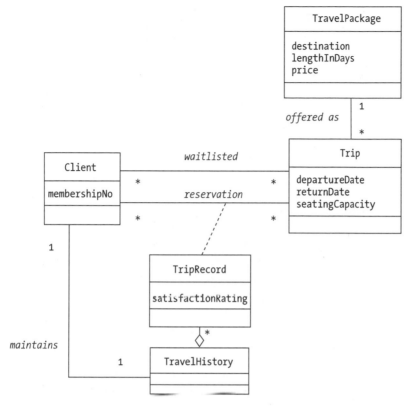

Figure 12-3. Reusing the SRS design pattern for WBY

Having recognized the similarities between these two designs, we're poised to take advantage of quite a bit of reuse with regard to the code of these two systems, as well. In fact, had we anticipated the need for developing these two systems prior to developing either one, we could have taken steps up front to develop a ***generic*** pattern that could have been used as the basis for both systems, as well as any future reservation systems we might be called upon to model, as illustrated in Figure 12-4.

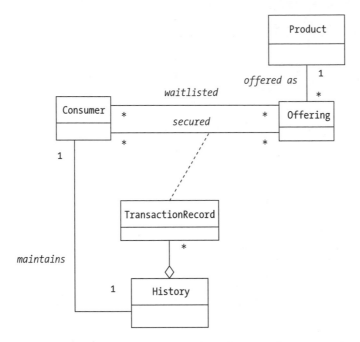

Figure 12-4. A general-purpose class diagram for reservation systems

Many useful, reusable patterns have been studied and documented; before embarking on a new object modeling project, it's worth exploring whether any of these may be a suitable starting point. Our "Recommended Reading" section in Chapter 17 suggests some references that you might wish to explore on this topic.

Summary

Learning to model a problem from the perspective of objects is a bit like learning to ride a bicycle. You can read all the books ever published on the subject of successful bicycle riding, but until you actually sit on the seat, grab the handlebars, and start pedaling, you won't get a real sense of what it means to ride. You'll probably wobble at first, but with a bit of a boost from training wheels or a friendly hand to steady you, you'll be riding off on your own with time. The same is true of object modeling: with practice, you'll get an intuitive feel for what makes a good candidate class, a useful scenario, and so on.

In this chapter, we

- Discussed techniques for verifying the accuracy and completeness of a class diagram

- Looked at how object models can be reused/adapted to other problems with similar requirements

Exercises

1. Conduct a walk-through of one of the class diagrams that you prepared as an exercise for Chapter 10—either the Prescription Tracking System (PTS) case study presented in Appendix B or the problem area whose requirements you defined for exercise 3 in Chapter 2—with a classmate or coworker. Report on any insights that you gained as a result of doing so.

2. Think of two other problem areas where the Reservation pattern that we identified for the Wild Blue Yonder travel agency might also apply. What adjustments, if any, would you need to make to the Reservation pattern in order to use it in those situations?

Part Three

Translating a UML "Blueprint" into C# Code

A Deeper Look at C#

WE'RE ALMOST READY to develop the Student Registration System (SRS) application in C#, based on the UML model that we've created in Part Two. Before we dive into the specifics of coding the SRS, however, there are a number of additional C# language features that we'd like to cover, many of which we'll put to use in building the SRS.

Realize that we can't do justice to all of the remaining features of the C# language in just one chapter; C# is an extremely rich language, and most good C# references are many hundreds of pages long. Our goal isn't to duplicate the hard work that has gone into existing C# reference books, but rather to complement them by showing you how to bridge the gap between producing an object model and turning it into C# code, something that few, if any, other books do.

With that in mind, we're going to be selective in terms of which aspects of the C# language we introduce in this chapter: namely, those that are most critical to understanding the Student Registration System coding examples that follow in Chapters 14 through 16. Nonetheless, you'll have a very respectable working knowledge of C# by the time that we've finished.

> *Even if you've already been programming in C# for a while, and thus feel that you have a fairly good grasp of the language syntax, we encourage you to at least skim this chapter before moving on to Chapter 14, because we mention a few things along the way with regard to how we'll be approaching the SRS.*

In this chapter, you'll learn about

- How to set up a C# programming environment on your machine

- C# source files, including naming and content conventions

- How to compile and run C# programs

- The C# notion of **namespaces**—how to define them, and why we use them

- How C# runtime errors, called **exceptions**, arise, and how to gracefully handle them when they do

- How to read input from the command line when a C# application is invoked, as well as how to prompt the user for keyboard input, useful techniques when testing an application from the command line

- The Object class, a predefined class that is the ultimate base class of every C# type

- The object nature of strings, and some of the methods/properties provided to manipulate them

- The object nature of arrays, and some of the methods/properties provided to manipulate them

- The Hashtable class, one of the .NET Framework collection classes

- The nature of object identities in C#; how to discover the true class that an object belongs to; and how to test the equality of two C# objects

- Using a special keyword, this, to "self-reference" an object from within one of its own methods

- How dynamically created objects are deleted so as to recycle their memory, and the role that the common language runtime **garbage collector** plays in this recycling

- A .NET Framework language construct called an **attribute** (not to be confused with "attributes" in the generic OO sense as we've used the term thus far)

We'll also revisit some of the topics that we introduced in earlier chapters to provide you with additional insights.

Sorting Out Terminology

Up until this point in the book, we've intentionally favored generic object terminology over C#/.NET-specific nomenclature whenever the two diverged. Our purpose in doing so was to familiarize you with object concepts in a language-neutral fashion. For the remainder of the book, we're going to "shift gears" by adopting C#/.NET-specific terminology, to help you get equally accustomed to the unique .NET way of describing and doing things.

By way of review, we've prepared Table 13-1 to relate important generic OO terms to their C#/.NET preferred counterparts. In those cases where the matches aren't 100 percent exact, we've provided comments as to the subtle differences.

Table 13-1. Comparing Generic OO and C#/.NET Terminology

Generic OO Term	C#/.NET Preferred Term(s)	Comments
Feature	**Member**	When used in a general sense, these two terms are identical, in that they both relate to the building blocks comprising a class definition. In a detailed sense, however, the term "member" is a bit broader than "feature": "feature" includes attributes, methods, and constructors; "member" includes attributes, methods, constructors, and properties (among others).
Method	**Method**	Used in identical ways.
N/A	**Function member**	A "function member" is a programming element that contains executable code. Methods, properties, and constructors are all considered to be function members.
Attribute	**Field, data member**	"Field" is preferred over "attribute" to refer to the data elements of a class when discussing C# code. The use of the generic OOPL term "attribute" to describe a C# field/data member is discouraged because of possible confusion with the .NET-specific programming construct known as an "attribute," which we'll explore later in this chapter. The term "data member" is also sometimes used to describe fields.
"Get" method (aka accessor method)	**Get accessor**	Not exactly equivalent—a "get" method is a true method, whereas a get accessor is a component of a property; see Chapter 4 for a detailed explanation of properties in general and get accessors specifically.
"Set" method (aka accessor method)	**Set accessor**	Not exactly equivalent—a "set" method is a true method, whereas a set accessor is a component of a property; see Chapter 4 for a detailed explanation of properties in general and set accessors specifically.
N/A	**Property**	A function member that allows client code to access the value of a field using dot notation while maintaining control over the access to the field; see Chapter 4 for a detailed explanation.
N/A	(.NET-specific) **Attribute**	A programming construct used to assign metadata tags to types, methods, and fields; we'll explore this construct later in this chapter.

Throughout the remainder of the book, we'll use C#/.NET-specific terminology in lieu of generic OO terminology. The first few times that we use the C#/.NET-specific term for something, we'll remind you of the generic OO term in parentheses: e.g., "A field (*attribute*) is a data element of a class."

Setting Up a C# Programming Environment

As we embark upon our in-depth studies of the C# language, it's important that you have access to a C# programming environment so that you can get hands-on experience with the concepts and code that we'll be presenting throughout the remainder of this book.

The best way to get C# up and running on your machine is to download and install the Microsoft .NET Software Development Kit (SDK). The download is free, and can be found on Microsoft's MSDN web site at the following URL:

```
http://msdn.microsoft.com/library/default.asp?url=/downloads/
list/netdevframework.asp
```

Please see Appendix C for helpful tips on what you'll need to do to get the .NET Framework SDK downloaded and installed properly on your computer.

Note that the .NET Framework SDK is a command line–driven toolkit, which means that you'll be doing all of your work in an MS-DOS Prompt window.

*Of course, you can use an **integrated development environment** (IDE) tool to develop your C# applications, the standard C# IDE being **Microsoft's Visual Studio .NET (VS .NET)**. It's the authors' personal bias, however, that if you first learn C# by writing all of your code from scratch using only the .NET Framework SDK and your favorite text editor, you'll gain a much better understanding of C# language fundamentals than if you rely too heavily on an IDE, particularly those that provide drag-and-drop GUI building capabilities and automated code generation. You can always "graduate" to an IDE after you've mastered the basics of objects and the C# language, to take advantage of IDE debugging and code/project management features.*

Compiling and Running C# Programs

As with all other programming languages, C# source code must be compiled before the program can be run. In this section, we'll present the basics of compiling and running C# programs.

C# Source Code Files

The C# language gives us a fair amount of flexibility in naming C# source code files.

- The recommended convention is to end source code file names with the extension .cs, but there is no requirement to do so; a source file could conceivably be named Person.boo, for example.

- Similarly, the name of a C# source file doesn't have to match the name of the class or interface defined within that file. For example, the code defining the Professor class could be placed in a file named Blah.cs, but it's considered good practice for a source file name to match the name of the class or interface declared within the file.

- The code for two or more class or interface definitions can be placed in the same source file; we don't generally do so, however, for it's much easier to manage C# source code when there is a one-to-one correspondence between the external file name and the internal C# class name. Classes and interfaces are also much easier to share/reuse when they are individually packaged one to a .cs file.

When we develop the SRS, we'll create one source code file for every class that we create. Specifically

- We'll create one .cs file for each of the domain classes that we defined in our object model: for the SRS application, for example, we'll have eight:

    Course.cs
    Person.cs
    Professor.cs
    ScheduleOfClasses.cs
    Section.cs
    Student.cs
    Transcript.cs
    TranscriptEntry.cs

- We'll also typically have a separate .cs file for each of the primary windows comprising the graphical user interface of our application, if any. For the SRS application, we'll eventually create two such classes:

    MainForm.cs
    PasswordForm.cs

    (We'll talk about graphical user interfaces in depth in Chapter 16.)

- We'll typically have a separate .cs file that declares the application's driver class, containing the "official" Main method as illustrated in Figure 13-1.

  - One of the primary responsibilities of this driver class's Main method is to instantiate the core objects needed to fulfill a system's mission. Actions taken by these objects, as well as by users as they interact with the application, will cause additional objects to be instantiated as the application executes.

  - The Main method is also responsible for displaying the startup window of the graphical user interface of an application, if any.

  We'll name the driver class for our Student Registration System application SRS, contained in the file SRS.cs.

- Finally, we often create other "helper" classes necessary for behind-the-scenes application support; with the SRS, we'll have a need for three such classes:

  ```
  CollectionWrapper.cs
  CourseCatalog.cs
  Faculty.cs
  ```

All told, by the time we reach the end of Chapter 16, we'll have programmed a total of 14 classes, integrating them into a single SRS application with a GUI front-end and a way to persist data from one SRS application session to the next.

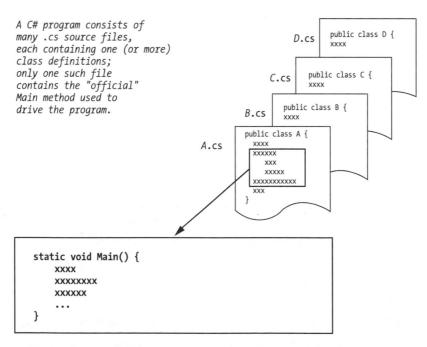

Figure 13-1. One "official" Main *method will drive the SRS.*

The Simple Mechanics of C# Compilation

To illustrate the mechanics of compiling and running C# programs, we'll start with a very simple program. Assume that the following source code is stored in a file named `SimpleProgram.cs`:

```
// SimpleProgram.cs

using System;

public class SimpleProgram
{
  static void Main() {
    Console.WriteLine("Hello");
  }
}
```

Assuming that the .NET Framework SDK is properly installed as discussed in Appendix C, we can compile the `SimpleProgram.cs` source code file by opening a **Command Prompt** window from within Windows, using the DOS `cd` command to change our working directory to the directory in which our source code file is located; e.g.,

```
cd C:\MyCode
```

and then typing the following at the command line:

```
csc SimpleProgram.cs
```

This command invokes the C# compiler (its executable is named `csc.exe`). Assuming that the compiler is properly installed, and that no compiler errors arise from our code, this command produces an **executable file** named `SimpleProgram.exe`. The executable file will by default be placed in the same directory from which the compiler was invoked (which, in this example, will cause it to be collocated with the `SimpleProgram.cs` source code file).

To execute our program, we then type the name of the executable file (the `.exe` suffix is optional) at the command line:

```
SimpleProgram
```

Compiling Multiclass Applications

There are several different ways to compile an application involving **multiple** source code files (i.e., multiple class/interface definitions):

- We can compile all of the source code (.cs) files simultaneously into an executable (.exe) file/application.

- We can compile individual source code (.cs) files into an intermediate form called a **dynamic-link library** (.dll) file for later inclusion into an application.

- We can combine the two preceding approaches.

We'll illustrate each of these scenarios in turn using the following simple multiclass application.

- First, we'll rewrite the SimpleProgram application so that it instantiates a Person object and accesses a property on this object. The source code for the revised SimpleProgram2 class is contained in a file named SimpleProgram2.cs.

```
// SimpleProgram2.cs

using System;

public class SimpleProgram2
{
  static void Main() {
    Person p = new Person("Steve");
    Console.WriteLine("Our person's name is " + p.Name);
  }
}
```

- To support this program, we'll create a very simple Person class definition that has only one field (*attribute*), name; a constructor to initialize the name field; and a Name property with which to access the value of the field from client code. The source code for the Person class is contained in a separate file named Person.cs.

```
// Person.cs

public class Person
{
  // Field.
```

```
      private string name;

      // Constructor.
      public Person(string n) {
        name = n;
      }

      // Property.
      public string Name {
        get {
          return name;
        }
        set {
          name = value;
        }
      }
  }
```

Let's now explore the various ways for producing an executable application (.exe file).

Scenario #1: Compiling from .cs to .exe Files Directly

Let's assume that neither the SimpleProgram2.cs nor the Person.cs file has previously been compiled. If we were to try to compile the SimpleProgram2 class by itself, using the command

```
csc SimpleProgram2.cs
```

the following compiler error message would arise:

```
  error CS0246: The type or namespace name "Person" could not be found
```

This error arises because the C# compiler doesn't automatically search for other files that it needs in order to compile those that we've explicitly directed it to compile. Since Person isn't a predefined C# type, the compiler will complain that it doesn't recognize the name "Person".

One simple solution for this problem is to introduce the Person.cs source file into the syntax of the compilation command:

```
csc SimpleProgram2.cs Person.cs
```

thereby compiling the entire application in a single step to produce an executable file named SimpleProgram2.exe (the default name for an .exe file matches the name of the *first* source (.cs) file specified by a compilation command).

This command syntax can be extended to include any number of source files. Wildcards can also be used; for example, the syntax

```
csc *.cs
```

will compile all of the `.cs` files in the working directory.

The previous compiler command

```
csc SimpleProgram2.cs Person.cs
```

is actually shorthand for the following slightly more complex command:

```
csc /t:exe SimpleProgram2.cs Person.cs
```

The `/t` (or alternatively, `/target`) **compiler option** specifies what type of output the compilation will produce. `/t:exe` indicates that the target for the compilation is a **console application,** i.e., one that will be run from the command line. As it turns out, `/t:exe` is a default compiler option, and thus doesn't have to be specified.

> *It's possible to produce several other types of output, but we'll be sticking with console applications throughout the remainder of the book.*

In order to successfully compile one or more C# source code (`.cs`) files directly into an executable (`.exe`) application file, one of the source code files in the compile statement *must* contain a class that defines a proper `Main` method. If none of the `.cs` files contain such a method, a compilation error will arise; for example, if we were to try to compile the `Person.cs` file by itself with the following command:

```
csc Person.cs
```

the compiler would generate the following error message:

```
error CS5001:  Program 'Person.exe' does not have an entry point defined.
```

There is indeed a way to compile stand-alone class files incrementally, however, which brings us to scenario #2.

Scenario #2: Compiling from .cs to .dll Form

An individual source code file such as `Person.cs` can optionally be compiled into an intermediate, nonexecutable form known as a **dynamic-link library file**

(.dll)—a file that is intended for use as a shared library file, and which can be **dynamically linked** into one or more applications by the .NET runtime.

We produce a .dll file using the /t:library compiler option; for example, the compilation command

```
csc /t:library Person.cs
```

will produce a file named Person.dll.

We can also use the wildcard character, *, to assemble all of the local source code files into a single DLL (in this case, the name of the resulting DLL file will match that of the first source file compiled):

```
csc /t:library *.cs
```

Compiling a class or interface into a .dll file form is useful when the class in question is going to be used in multiple applications: we can compile it once as a .dll, and then link it into as many applications as desired without having to recompile it over and over again. The process of integrating .dll files into an application is discussed as scenario #3 in the next section.

Another advantage of creating a .dll version of a class or interface is to protect proprietary source code. DLL files may be shared with other programmers, who can in turn link them into their applications *without* being able to see how the code was written.

Scenario #3: Combining .cs and .dll Files in a Single Compilation

To make use of a previously compiled DLL file in the compilation of another C# program, the /r (or alternatively the /reference) compiler option can be specified. Returning to scenario #1, where we had run into a "roadblock" because we were trying to compile the SimpleProgram2.cs file by itself, let's now assume that the Person.cs file had been previously compiled into a Person.dll file. We could then use the /r compiler option, as illustrated in the following command, to compile the SimpleProgram2 source file and the Person.dll DLL file into a single executable named SimpleProgram2.exe:

```
csc SimpleProgram2.cs /r: Person.dll
```

To incorporate **multiple** *DLL files into an executable, separate the names of the files with semicolons:*

```
csc filename.cs /r:file1.dll;file2.dll;file3.dll
```

Different Paths from Source to Executable

Figures 13-2 and 13-3 summarize the different paths that a source file can take as it is compiled into an executable program.

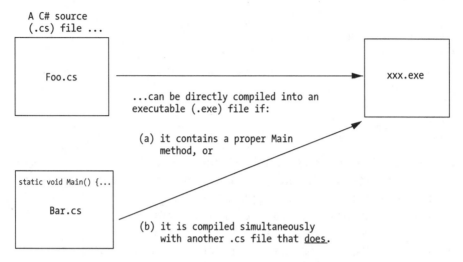

Figure 13-2. Source files can be compiled directly into an executable file ...

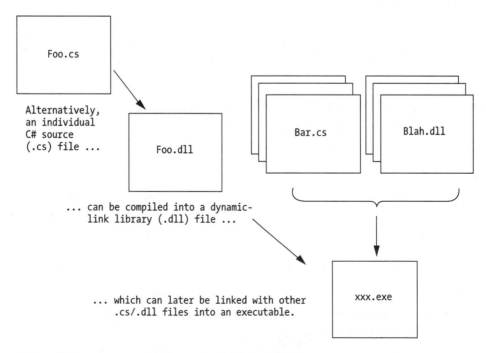

Figure 13-3. ... or can first be compiled into DLL form.

Naming the Resultant Executable

The /out compiler option is used to specify what the name of the resulting .exe or .dll file will be. For example, the following command:

```
csc /out:MyApp.exe SimpleProgram2.cs Person.cs
```

would produce an executable file named MyApp.exe.

   If the /out option isn't used, the default .exe or .dll file name will match the name of the first source (.cs) file specified by the compilation command, as mentioned previously. For example, if the compile command were to omit the /out option as follows:

```
csc Person.cs SimpleProgram2.cs
```

then the resulting executable file would be named Person.exe; or, if a wildcard character is used:

```
csc *.cs
```

then the resulting executable file name will match the name of the *first* .cs file of those that are compiled.

Applications with Multiple Main Methods

We know that every application must define at least one Main method to serve as the entry point/driver for program execution. However, it's also possible for an application to contain *more than one* Main method. One such circumstance might be that we've added a Main method to an arbitrary class so that we may test the features of that class in stand-alone fashion. As an example, let's modify the Person class introduced at the beginning of this section to include a Main method as illustrated here:

```
// Person.cs

using System;

public class Person
{
  // Field.
  private string name;
```

```
// Constructor.
public Person(string n) {
  name = n;
}

// Property.
public string Name {
  get {
    return name;
  }
  set {
    name = value;
  }
}

// We're providing the Person class with its own Main method so that this class
// can be unit tested in isolation from the application as a whole.
static void Main() {
  // Instantiate a Person object ...
  Person p = new Person("Lisa");

  // ... and then display its name.
  Console.WriteLine("Name:  " + p.Name);
}
}
```

We could now compile the Person.cs file by itself into an executable file named Person.exe using the following command:

```
csc Person.cs
```

and could in turn execute the Person class's Main method by typing

```
Person
```

which would produce the output

```
Name:  Lisa
```

However, if we now try to compile the SimpleProgram2.cs and modified Person.cs source files together using the compile command

```
csc SimpleProgram2.cs Person.cs
```

the compiler will generate the following error message:

```
error CS0017: Program 'SimpleProgram2.exe' has more than one entry
point defined.
```

because we've defined Main methods in ***both*** the SimpleProgram2 and Person classes, and hence the compiler doesn't know which one is intended to serve as the entry point for our application.

To solve this problem, we can use the /main compiler option to indicate which class is to serve as the application driver:

```
csc SimpleProgram2.cs Person.cs /main:SimpleProgram2
```

In this case, we've indicated that the Main method in SimpleProgram2 is to be the entry point for the application.

We'll use the /main compiler option in Chapters 15 and 16 because the SRS application developed in those chapters will define more than one Main method to test the features of various individual classes.

Behind the Scenes: Microsoft Intermediate Language vs. Conventional Compilation

To appreciate how the "behind the scenes" mechanism for compiling and running C# programs differs from that of conventionally compiled programs, let's start with a review of the latter.

Conventional Compilation

In order to execute a program written in a conventionally compiled language like C or C++, the source code of the program must first be compiled into an executable form known as **binary code** or **machine code**. Binary code, in essence, is a pattern of 1s and 0s understandable by the underlying **hardware architecture** of the computer on which the program is intended to run.

Even if the original (C, C++) source code is written to be **platform-independent**—that is, the program doesn't take advantage of any operating system–specific language extensions—the resultant executable version will nonetheless still be tied to a particular hardware architecture, and can therefore only be run on that architecture. That is, a version of a (C, C++) program compiled for a Sun workstation won't run on a Windows PC; a version compiled for Windows XP won't run on a Mac; and so forth (see Figure 13-4).

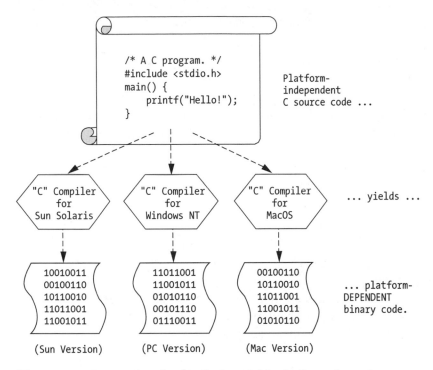

Figure 13-4. *Conventional compilation yields platform-dependent executable code.*

Microsoft Intermediate Language

In contrast, the C# compiler doesn't produce machine code. Instead, C# programs are compiled into an intermediate form called **Microsoft Intermediate Language (MSIL)**. MSIL is **platform-independent** code that contains instructions for a "virtual" processor. When a compiled C# program is actually executed, the .NET runtime environment converts the MSIL code "just in time" into machine code that is honed to the specific platform that the program is being run on, and then executes that machine code (see Figure 13-5). Thus, the *same* MSIL code can be executed on any platform that supports the common language runtime (see Figure 13-6).

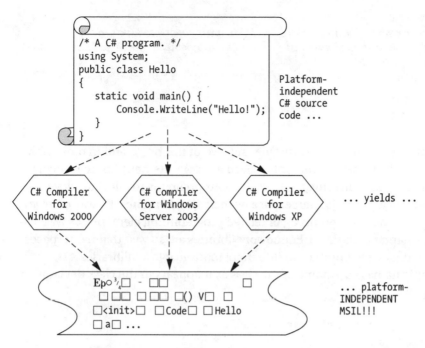

Figure 13-5. .NET compilation yields platform-independent MSIL code.

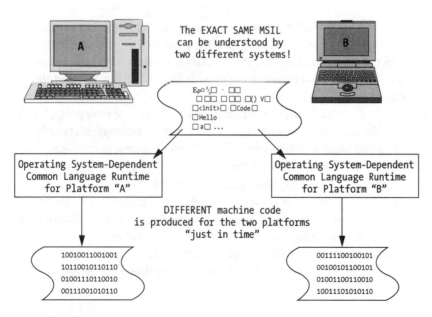

Figure 13-6. Different common language runtimes can understand the same MSIL file.

> *For those readers familiar with Java, MSIL is analogous to Java's byte code, and the .NET common language runtime is analogous to the Java Runtime Environment (JRE).*

Namespaces

Throughout the examples in Parts One and Two of this book, and in most of the examples to follow, we've commonly placed a using statement (more formally referred to as a using directive) at the top of our programs to allow us to access the elements of a particular **namespace** by their **simple names**. By way of review, a namespace is a logical grouping of related programming elements, as was discussed in Chapter 1; the .NET Framework libraries are so vast that namespaces are used to divide the libraries up into more manageable sublibraries.

A simple name is the name of the class as it appears in the class declaration; for example:

```
// This class has the simple name "Student".
public class Student {
  // Details omitted.
}
```

When a class is placed inside a namespace, its name "changes" in that it acquires its namespace as part of its **fully qualified name**. For example, as discussed earlier in the book, because the String class is contained in the System namespace, the *fully qualified name* of the class is System.String; the *simple name* of the class remains String.

It's conceivable that two classes, belonging to two different namespaces A and B, could be given the same simple name X, just as, by way of analogy, it's possible to create two different Microsoft Word documents with the same name—e.g., xyz.doc—as long as they are located in different Windows folders—e.g., C:\MyDocs and D:\Stuff. When we fully qualify the names of such like-named classes—A.X and B.X—these names are guaranteed to be unique, just as in the Word document analogy, the two like-named documents in our example would have different fully qualified file names, e.g., C:\MyDocs\xyz.doc and D:\Stuff\xyz.doc.

To be absolutely certain that the compiler knows which class we wish to use in any given situation, we could always use fully qualified class names in our program:

```
// Note that we've provided no "using" directives
// with this program.

public class SimpleProgram3
{
```

```
   static void Main() {
     System.String name = "Jackson";
     System.Console.WriteLine("The name is " + name);
   }
}
```

Having to type the fully qualified name of every namespace member that we're using in a program is cumbersome, however, and makes for less readable code. Fortunately, the C# language provides the using directive to afford us the convenience of accessing the members of a namespace using the members' simple names.

As we've seen numerous times before, a using directive is placed at the top of a source code file for every namespace whose members are to be accessed within that file; we're then free to refer to the classes of interest by their simple names throughout the code in this source file:

```
// We plan on using the "Console" class from the System namespace.
using System;

// We plan on using the "Foo" class from a DIFFERENT namespace
// named "BarStuff".
using BarStuff;

public class SimpleProgram3
{
   static void Main() {
     // We may now refer to Foo and Console by their simple names.
     Foo x = new Foo();
     Console.WriteLine("A Foo is born every minute!");
   }
}
```

The compiler will search each of the specified namespaces in turn to ensure that it can find declarations of Console and Foo in one or the other of them.

A small problem arises if a class name that we're referring to in our code exists in ***more than one*** of the namespaces that we've specified in using directives. As an example, let's assume that we wish to use two different versions of a class called Course in the same program, one that is defined by the SRS namespace and another that is defined by the ObjectStart namespace. Even if we were to provide using directives for these two namespaces, we would still have to fully qualify each use of the Course class names to disambiguate the situation:

```
// Example.cs

using ObjectStart;
using SRS;
```

```
public class Example
{
  static void Main() {
    // Use the SRS version of Course here ...
    SRS.Course math = new SRS.Course();

    // ... and the ObjectStart version here.
    ObjectStart.Course english = new ObjectStart.Course();
    // etc.
  }
}
```

Thus, there is no point in providing using directives for namespaces SRS or ObjectStart in this particular case.

Of course, if we wanted to use additional ***uniquely named*** classes from either the SRS or ObjectStart namespaces that we ***weren't*** planning on fully qualifying, then such using directives would be helpful. Say, for example, that we were not only using the two versions of Course as discussed previously, but also using a class named Student that exists in the SRS namespace but not in ObjectStart, and conversely, a class named Professor that exists in the ObjectStart namespace but not in SRS, as illustrated in Figure 13-7.

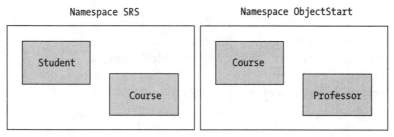

Both namespaces contain versions of a class named Course, but Student exists only in SRS, and Professor exists only in ObjectStart.

Figure 13-7. Course exists in two namespaces; Professor *and* Student *do not.*

We'll need to fully qualify references to the name Course once again, but won't have to fully qualify Student or Professor if we include using directives in our program as illustrated in the following code:

```
using SRS;
using ObjectStart;
```

```
public class Example
{
  static void Main() {
    // We are still qualifying Course wherever we use it in
    // this program ...
    SRS.Course math = new SRS.Course();
    ObjectStart.Course english = new ObjectStart.Course();

    // ... but simple name Professor is OK because of the using directive
    // at the top of the code listing.
    Professor p = new Professor();
    math.AssignProfessor(p);

    // Ditto for Student.
    Student s = new Student();

    // etc.
  }
}
```

We'll use predefined classes from five of the .NET FCL namespaces in developing the SRS application in Chapters 14 through 16:

- The System namespace, which includes the String, Console, and Array classes

- The System.Collections namespace, which includes the ArrayList and Hashtable collection classes

- The System.IO namespace, which includes the FileStream, StreamReader, and StreamWriter classes that we'll use to save and restore the data used by the SRS to/from files in Chapter 15

- The System.Windows.Forms and System.Drawing namespaces, which include the GUI classes and support classes that we'll use in creating a GUI front-end for the SRS in Chapter 16

Programmer-Defined Namespaces

The C# language also gives us the ability to create our own namespaces. The reasons we might want to do so are the same reasons that were used by Microsoft in creating/designing the .NET FCL:

- ***To logically partition our classes so as to facilitate their reuse.*** For example, a rocket scientist might want to put all of the classes she designed relating to planets into a Planets namespace for reuse by astronomers, and all of the classes she designed relating to rocket design in a Rockets namespace for reuse by rocket manufacturers.

- ***To ensure unique fully qualified names for our user-defined classes.*** For example, if we were to want to design a class with the same simple name as a class found in one of the .NET namespaces—say, perhaps a class called Console—then by putting it into a namespace of our own creation—say, perhaps ObjectStart—we'd facilitate use of both the System.Console and ObjectStart.Console classes in the same program.

To assign a particular programming element (e.g., class, interface) to a namespace, we place the namespace keyword followed by the name that we're inventing for the namespace (observing Pascal casing conventions) at the top of the code listing, followed by a pair of braces {...} enclosing the declarations of one or more programming elements that are to be included in that particular namespace.

For example, if we wanted to create a namespace called PetStore that is to include classes representing different types of pets, we might create a source code file named PetRat.cs as follows:

```
// PetRat.cs

// Simply by using "PetStore" in a namespace declaration, the PetStore
// namespace is born!
namespace PetStore
{
  // Every class or interface declared within this namespace code block
  // becomes part of the PetStore namespace.

  // "using" directives for any OTHER namespaces required by the code
  // that follows are inserted here. In this example, we are using two such
  // classes -- Console and Seed -- which come from the System and AnimalFood
  // namespaces, respectively.
  using System;        // a Framework Class Library (FCL) namespace
  using AnimalFood;    // a different user-defined namespace,
                       // defined elsewhere

  // The PetRat class now becomes part of the PetStore namespace; its fully
  // qualified name is "PetStore.PetRat".
  public class PetRat
  {
    // Fields.
```

```
    string name;
    string coatColor;

    // Seed is a class in the AnimalFood namespace, but since we've
    // included a "using AnimalFood" directive above, we may
    // reference the Seed class by its simple name.
    Seed favoriteSeedType;

    // Properties for all three fields are assumed to exist, but
    // are omitted from this example.

    public void DisplayRatInfo() {
      // The "using System" directive above enables us to refer to the
      // Console class by its simple name.
      Console.WriteLine("Rat's Name:   " + Name)
      Console.WriteLine("Coat Color:   " + CoatColor);
      Console.WriteLine("Favorite Seed Type:   " +
            FavoriteSeedType.Name);
      // etc.
    }
  }

  // Other classes/interfaces to be inserted into PetStore could be defined
  // here, if desired, or in separate source files (preferred).
} // end of namespace declaration
```

The PetRat class would thus be assigned to the PetStore namespace.

Then, if we had a second class—say, Tarantula—that we also wanted to include in the same PetStore namespace, we could do so in the same file or, preferably, in a separate file named Tarantula.cs, as shown here:

```
// Tarantula.cs

// We're inserting the Tarantula class into the SAME namespace
// as the PetRat class.
namespace PetStore
{
  // "using" directives for any OTHER namespaces required by the Tarantula
  // class code are inserted here; details omitted.

  // The Tarantula class now becomes part of the PetStore namespace; its fully
  // qualified name is "PetStore.Tarantula".
  public class Tarantula
  {
```

```
        // Details omitted.
    }
}
```

Then, if we wish to access either the PetRat or Tarantula class by its simple name from client code, we'd insert a using PetStore; directive at the top of *that* code:

```
// Example.cs

using PetStore;
// Any other using directives required by the Example program would
// be inserted here, as well ...

public class Example
{
  static void Main() {
    // We're able to use the simple name "PetRat" here ...
    PetRat r = new PetRat();
    r.Name = "Baby Grode";

    // ... and the simple name "Tarantula" here.
    Tarantula t = new Tarantula();
    t.Name = "Fuzzy";

    // etc.
  }
}
```

Having provided the using PetStore directive, the compiler will be able to find the definitions of the PetRat and Tarantula classes in the PetStore namespace.

The Global Namespace

One final point about namespaces is that if we don't include an explicit namespace directive in a source file, the class or interface that we're defining in that source file will be assigned to the "nameless" **global namespace.** As long as the source code (.cs) files for two classes A and B reside in the same working directory

- A can make references to B using B's simple name, and

- B can make references to A using A's simple name, and

- **Both** classes will compile properly

all without either class having to include a using directive to find the other, because they are both coresident in the global namespace.

Given that

- *All* of the code that we write for the SRS application will be housed in the same working directory, and

- *None* of the SRS-related classes—Student, Professor, SRS, etc.,—includes a namespace directive in their respective definitions so as to "insert themselves" into a particular *named* namespace,

then *all* of the SRS-related classes will fall within the global namespace. This is what enables us to write code such as

```
public class SRS
{
  static void Main() {
    Student s = new Student();    // Using a simple name.
    Course c = new Course();      // Ditto.
    // etc.
  }
}
```

without having to include using directives to qualify the simple names Student and Course for the compiler.

Strings As Objects

In Chapter 1, we introduced a number of predefined C# types, including the string type. What we hinted at, but didn't make explicitly clear at the time, is that strings are objects. We went over some of the basics of creating and using strings in Chapter 1; we'll now review some of what we've learned before, as well as provide additional insights about strings' object nature in this section.

The "string" Alias

The keyword string is really an alias for the String class defined in the System namespace. When we declare a string variable and assign it a value as follows:

```
string name = "Jackson";
```

we're in actuality instantiating an object/instance of the System.String class.

- The expressions string and System.String are syntactically equivalent as far as the C# compiler is concerned; a string object has access to the methods, properties, and constructors declared in the System.String class.

- Despite the fact that we don't see the use of the new operator to explicitly invoke a constructor of the System.String class, we're doing so nonetheless in "shorthand" fashion.

To reference the string type in our programs, we thus have several choices:

- We can refer to the simple name of the class, String (uppercase "S"), if we include a using System; directive at the top of the program:

```
using System;

public class Foo
{
  static void Main() {
    String s = "Whee!";
  }
}
```

- The fully qualified name System.String can be used, in which case it isn't necessary to provide the using System; directive at the top of the program:

```
// No "using" directive needed!

public class Foo
{
  static void Main() {
    System.String s = "Whee!";
  }
}
```

> *Of course, the* using System; *directive is still necessary if we wish to access* **other** System *namespace elements, such as the* Console *class, by* **their** *simple names.*

- The *preferred* method in C# is to use the alias string (lowercase "s"). It provides a simpler syntax than System.String, but again enables us to omit a using System; directive at the top of the program:

```
                // No "using" directive needed!

                public class Foo
                {
                  static void Main() {
                    string s = "Whee!";
                  }
                }
```

Given the convenience of the string alias, we virtually never use either the simple or fully qualified *capitalized* forms of String in a C# application.

> *As it turns out,* **all** *of the predefined simple types discussed in Chapter 1—* bool, float, int, double, long, char, *etc.—are in actuality aliases for elements defined in the* System *namespace.*

Creating String Instances

As we learned in Chapter 1, we create a string instance by declaring a reference variable of type string and assigning it any valid string expression as a value:

```
string name = "Chen";
```

or

```
string name = student.Name;
```

or

```
string name = department.FindChairperson().Name;
```

etc.

A string can also be created using one of the overloaded String class constructors in conjunction with the new operator; the headers for some of the more commonly used String constructors are as follows:

```
public String(char[] characters)
public String(char c, int count)
public String(char[] characters, int start, int end)
```

As an example of using one of the String class constructors, we could do the following:

```
char[] chars = { 'C', 'h', 'e', 'n' };
string name = new String(chars);
```

> *Note that, unlike Java, there is no constructor with a header that takes a single* String *argument:*
>
> ```
> public String(String s)
> ```
>
> *e.g.,*
>
> ```
> string s = new String("Fred");  // This doesn't exist in C#!
> ```

The @ Character

We learned in Chapter 1 that certain **escape characters** can be used to represent special characters such as tabs (\t) or newlines (\n) within a string literal. For example, if we wanted to output the following text to the console:

```
This line should break here:
and can contain backslashes (\), etc.
```

we could do so through the use of \n (newline) and \\ (backslash) escape characters as follows:

```
String str = "This line should break here:\n"+
             "and can contain backslashes (\\), etc.";
Console.WriteLine(str);
```

C# provides us with an alternative way of declaring such string literals without having to resort to the use of escape characters. If we precede the opening double quote mark of a string literal with @, the literal will be read "verbatim" from the source code file, allowing the literal to span multiple lines and leaving all newlines, tabs, backslashes, etc. intact.

Using the @ character, the previous code example could be rewritten exactly as follows:

```
String str = @"This line should break here:
and can contain backslashes (\), etc.";
Console.WriteLine(str);
```

If the previous code snippet were executed, the desired output would be displayed to the console:

```
This line should break here:
and can contain backslashes (\), etc.
```

Special String Operators

As we learned in Chapter 1, the plus sign operator (+) concatenates string values:

```
string x = "foo";
string y = "bar";
string z = x + y + "!";   // z now has the value "foobar!"
```

The String class also provides specially defined versions of the == and != operators that can be used to compare the values of two strings for equality or inequality, respectively. The following code snippet demonstrates how these operators can be used:

```
string name = "Mary Jones";
if (name == "Cynthia Coleman") {
  Console.WriteLine("This is Cynthia Coleman");
}
else {
  Console.WriteLine("Hey!  What happened to Cynthia?");
}
```

The previous code snippet would generate the following output:

```
Hey!  What happened to Cynthia?
```

> *We'll discover a bit later in this chapter that when we use the == and != operators to compare object references in general, the outcome is somewhat different.*

String Properties

The String class also defines two useful properties.

The Length property returns the number of characters in the associated String, including white space characters:

```
string sentence = "How long am I?";
Console.WriteLine("Length = " + sentence.Length);
```

The output for the previous code snippet would be

```
Length = 14
```

Another useful feature of the String class is a special property called an **indexer** that allows the individual characters of a String to be accessed according to a character's position, or **index,** in the String. The use of an indexer is indicated by placing a pair of brackets around the desired index—any legitimate integer expression—thus mimicking the syntax of arrays:

```
String str = "Tom Servo";
Console.WriteLine("The first character is " + str[0]);
```

This code snippet would generate the following output:

```
The first character is T
```

String Methods

In addition to the operators and properties we've discussed so far, every string object has access to the methods declared by the String class. We'll discuss a few of the more useful methods in this section; for a complete description of all of the methods defined by the String class, please consult the FCL Reference on the MSDN web site.

- `public bool StartsWith(string str)`: Returns true if the string to which this method is applied starts with the value of the string expression provided as an argument, false otherwise.

  ```
  string s = "foobar";
  string t = "foo";

  // This will evaluate to true.
  if (s.StartsWith(t)) ...
  ```

- `public bool EndsWith(string str)`: Returns true if the string to which this method is applied ends with the value of the string expression provided as an argument, false otherwise.

  ```
  string s = "foobar";

  // This will evaluate to true.
  if (s.EndsWith("bar")) ...
  ```

- `public int IndexOf(string str)`: Returns a nonnegative integer indicating the starting character position (counting from 0) at which the value of the string expression provided as an argument is found within the string to which this method is applied, or a negative value if it isn't found.

```
string s = "foobar";
int i = s.IndexOf("bar");   // i will equal 3

string t = "cat";
int j = s.IndexOf(t);   // j will be less than 0, because the
                        // value of the argument -- "cat" --
                        // is not found in "foobar".
```

- `public string Replace(char old, char new)`: Creates a new `string` object in which all instances of the old character are replaced with the new character—the original string remains unaffected.

```
string s = "o1o2o3o4";
// Note use of single quotes around character literals.
string p = s.Replace('o', 'x');   // p now equals "x1x2x3x4",
                                  // while s remains "o1o2o3o4"
```

- `public string Replace(string old, string new)`: An overloaded version of the `Replace` method that allows us to replace one substring with another substring; note that the substrings need not be of equal length.

```
string t = "foobar";
string p = t.Replace("foo", "candy");   // p now equals "candybar"
```

- `public string Substring(int startIndex)`: Creates a new string whose value is based on a substring of an existing string, starting at the position in the existing string indicated by the `int` expression passed as an argument (counting from 0) and continuing through the end of the existing string:

```
string s = "foobar";
int i = 3;
string p = s.Substring(i); // p now equals "bar"
```

- `public string Substring(int startIndex, int length)`: An overloaded form of the `Substring` method that creates a new string by taking a substring of an existing string, starting at the position indicated by the *first* `int` expression passed as an argument, and stopping just *before* the position indicated by the *second* `int` expression argument; again, we begin counting with 0 as the first character position.

```
string s = "foobar";
string p = s.Substring(1, 5);  // p now equals "ooba"
```

- `public string ToLower()`: Returns a copy of the string on which this method is applied, changing all of the characters to lowercase.

```
string s = "Jose Cruz";
string p = s.ToLower();      //  p now equals "jose cruz"
```

- `public string ToUpper()`: Returns a copy of the string on which this method is applied, changing all of the characters to uppercase.

```
string s = "Jose Cruz";
string p = s.ToUpper();      //  p now equals "JOSE CRUZ"
```

C# Exception Handling

Exceptions are a way for the .NET runtime to signal that a serious error condition has arisen during program execution, one that could potentially cause a program to abort. One such situation would be trying to access a nonexistent object, as in the following example:

```
Student s1 = new Student();
Student s2 = null;

s1.Name = "Fred";  // this line is fine
s2.Name = "Mary";  // this line throws an exception
```

Let's explore what is happening in the preceding code:

We declare two `Student` object references, but only instantiate *one* `Student` object; `s2` is assigned the value `null`, indicating that it isn't presently holding onto any object:

```
Student s1 = new Student();
Student s2 = null;
```

When we subsequently attempt to assign a value to the `Name` property of `s1`, all is well:

```
s1.Name = "Fred";  // this line is fine
```

However, this next line of code throws a `NullReferenceException` at run time, because we are trying to access a property of a nonexistent object:

```
s2.Name = "Mary"; // throws an exception
```

Exception handling enables a programmer to gracefully anticipate and handle such exceptions by providing a way for a program to automatically transfer control from within the block of code where the exception arose—known as a try block—into a special error-handling code block known as a **catch block**.

The Mechanics of Exception Handling

The mechanics of exception handling are as follows:

- We place code that is likely to throw an exception inside of a pair of braces { ... }, then place the keyword try just ahead of the opening brace for that block to signal the fact that we intend to catch exceptions thrown within that block:

```
try {
    code likely to cause problems goes in here ...
}
```

This is known as a **try** block.

- A try block must also be accompanied by either: (a) one (or more) **catch** blocks, (b) a **finally** block, or (c) a combination of (a) and (b).

- Each catch block begins with a **catch** clause of the form

```
catch (exception_type variable_name)
```

that declares which category of exception it will catch, along with providing a reference variable name to represent the exception object being thrown so that we may manipulate the exception object from within the catch block if desired. The contents of the catch block represent the "recovery" code that is to be automatically executed upon occurrence of that exception:

```
try {
    code likely to cause problems goes in here ...
}
catch (exception_type_1 variable_name_1) {
    recovery code for the first exception type goes here ...
}
catch (exception_type_2 variable_name_2) {
    recovery code for the second exception type goes here ...
}
// etc.
```

- We can also optionally specify a block of code that will ***always*** execute regardless of whether an exception has occurred in the try block or not. Known as a `finally` block, this block of code is preceded by the `finally` keyword, and follows the last `catch` block (if any are present). A `finally` block is typically used to perform any necessary cleanup operations, such as perhaps closing either a file or a connection to a database.

```
try {
    code likely to cause problems goes in here ...
}
catch (exception_type_1 variable_name) {
    recovery code for the first exception type goes here ...
}
catch (exception_type_2 variable_name) {
    recovery code for the second exception type goes here ...
}
finally {
    perform cleanup operations ...
}
```

Alternative paths through a try-catch block ***without*** an optional `finally` block are illustrated in Figure 13-8, and alternative paths through a try-catch block ***with*** an optional `finally` block are illustrated in Figure 13-9.

If no exceptions arise, the try block executes to completion ...

If an exception arises, and a *matching* catch clause exists, control jumps to the catch block ...

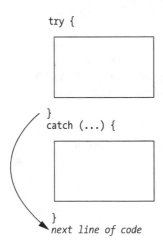
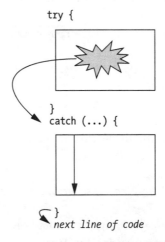

... and then execution transfers to the line of code immediately following the ***last*** of the catch block(s).

... and after the catch block executes to completion, control transfers to the line of code immediately following the last of the catch block(s).

Figure 13-8. Execution sequence for try-catch *blocks*

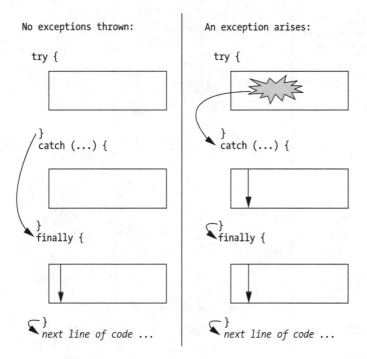

Figure 13-9. Execution sequence for try-catch-finally *blocks*

If **none** of the catch blocks match when an exception is thrown, responsibility for handling the exception is transferred to the client code that invoked the "offensive" code to begin with (see Figure 13-10).

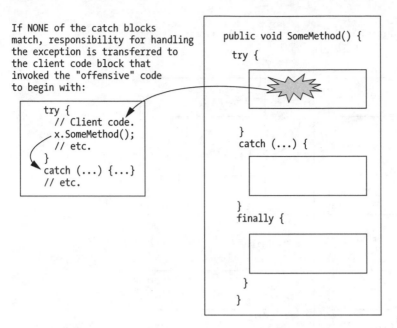

Figure 13-10. If no catch *blocks match, the exception is "thrown" to the client code.*

Going back to our previous example involving Student objects, here's an enhanced version of the code that employs exception handling:

```
// We declare two Student object references, but only instantiate one
// Student object; s2 is given a value of null, indicating that it
// isn't presently holding onto any object.
Student s1 = new Student();
Student s2 = null;

// Exception handling is now in place.
try {
  Console.WriteLine("Initializing students ...");

  // This line executes without throwing an exception.
  s1.Name = "Fred";

  // This next line of code throws a NullReferenceException at run time because
  // s2 was never initialized to refer to an actual Student object ...
  s2.Name = "Mary";
  // ... and as soon as the exception is detected by the runtime, execution
  // jumps out of the try block -- none of the remaining code in
  // this try block will be executed -- and into the first catch block
  // below that is found to match a NullReferenceException, if any.
```

```
    s1.Major = "MATH";
    s2.Major = "SCIENCE";

    Console.WriteLine("Initialization successfully completed.");
} // end of try block
// Pseudocode.
catch (UnrelatedExceptionType e1) {
    exception handling code for this type of (hypothetical) exception
    goes here ... but, since our example doesn't involve throwing this
    particular type of exception at run time, this catch block will be
    skipped over without being executed.
    Console.WriteLine("UnrelatedExceptionType was detected ...");
}
catch (NullReferenceException e2) {
    // Here's where we place the code for what the program should do if
    // a null reference was detected at run time.
    Console.WriteLine("Whoops -- we forgot to initialize all of the students!");
}
finally {
    // This code gets executed whether or not an exception occurred:  that is,
    // whether we made it through the try block without any exceptions being
    // thrown, or whether one of the catch blocks was triggered.
    Console.WriteLine("Finally!!!");
}

// After the finally block executes, control transfers to the
// line of code immediately following the finally block.
System.out.println("Continuing along our merry way ...");
```

When the previous code is executed, the following output would result:

```
Initializing students ...
Whoops -- we forgot to initialize all of the students!
Finally!!!
Continuing along our merry way ...
```

because both the second catch block and the finally block will have executed.

Note that nothing needs to be done from a programming perspective to *explicitly* transfer control from the try block to the appropriate catch block—that is, there is no "jump" type statement required; the runtime handles this transfer automatically as needed.

The Exception Class Hierarchy

The System.Exception class is the base class of all exceptions in the C# language. For example, the System.IO.IOException class is derived from System.Exception and collectively represents any of the things that can go wrong when performing IO operations; the System.IO.FileNotFoundException class is in turn a derived class of System.IO.IOException, and represents a *specific* IO problem.

By virtue of the "is a" nature of inheritance, a FileNotFoundException is also both an IOException and a generic Exception, all rolled into one, and so we can catch it as any one of these three exception types.

Sequential Evaluation of "catch" Clauses

The catch clauses for a given try block are examined in order from top to bottom. The runtime compares the type of exception that has been thrown with the exception type declared to be caught for each catch clause until it finds a match—either an exact match or a match with a supertype—and then executes the code enclosed in the braces immediately following the matching catch clause; note that only the *first* such match is executed.

```
try {
    // File IO operations are being performed here ... details omitted.
}
catch (FileNotFoundException e1) {
    Console.WriteLine("FileNotFoundException detected!");

    // Pseudocode.
    recovery code would go here ...
}
catch (IOException e2) {
    Console.WriteLine("IOException detected!");

    // Pseudocode.
    recovery code would go here ...
}
catch (Exception e3) {
    // Note: "Exception" is the base class for all exception types, and hence
    // a "catch (Exception e)" block is a "catch-all" for any exceptions that
    // weren't a match for any of the preceding catch clauses.
    Console.WriteLine("Exception detected!");

    // Pseudocode.
    recovery code would go here ...
}
```

Let's examine the output that would occur if various types of exceptions arise while the `try` block of this example is executing:

- If a `FileNotFoundException` is thrown, this code would print the output:

```
FileNotFoundException detected!
```

- If some other type of `IOException` is thrown while the `try` block is executing, this code would print the output:

```
IOException detected!
```

(Of course, catching an `IOException` could in theory take care of any `FileNotFoundExceptions` that arise, except for the fact that this `catch` clause occurs *after* an explicit catch of `FileNotFoundException`.)

- And if any type of exception other than an `IOException` were to be thrown—say, a `NullReferenceException`—then the output would be

```
Exception detected!
```

Hence, the generic `Exception` type can be used in the last `catch` block of a try block (as shown in the preceding code) to literally serve as a "catch-all" if desired.

Proper Ordering of Catch Blocks

The preceding example illustrates the fact that `catch` blocks for derived types should precede `catch` blocks for base types; otherwise, the derived types' `catch` blocks will never get executed. For example, if we were to place an `IOException` catch block before a `FileNotFoundException` catch block as shown in the following code, any instances of `FileNotFoundException` would always be caught by the `IOException` catch block. We may have provided some really nifty exception-handling code in the `FileNotFoundException` catch block, but it will never get invoked.

```
try {
  // File IO operations are being performed here ... details omitted.
}
catch (IOException e2) {
  // This block will catch all types of IOExceptions, INCLUDING
  // FileNotFoundExceptions specifically.
```

```
    //Pseudocode.
    recovery code for handling IOExceptions generally ...
}
catch (FileNotFoundException e1) {
    // This block will never be executed because FileNotFoundException is a
    // derived class of IOException.

    //Pseudocode.
    recovery code for handling FileNotFoundExceptions specifically ...
}
```

Nesting "try" Statements

It's often necessary to nest one try statement within another, if the recovery code that we propose to execute in a catch block may itself be prone to generating exceptions.

For example, returning to our file IO example, let's assume that our application is going to require the user to provide the name of a file to be opened by interacting with the application's GUI. It's possible that the user-provided file name may be incorrect, such that the named file doesn't actually exist, in which case attempting to open the file will throw a FileNotFoundException. We decide to provide a default file behind the scenes, to be opened by our application in such an event.

```
// Pseudocode.
string filename = the name of a file provided by a user via a GUI;

try {
    // Pseudocode.
    attempt to open the filename file
}
catch (FileNotFoundException e1) {
    // Since the user-provided filename is not valid, let's open a default
    // file instead.
    // Pseudocode.
    attempt to open a file named "default.dat";
}
```

However, it's certainly possible that something may have happened to our default file—for example, it may have accidentally been deleted by a system administrator. So, to be completely rock-solid, we must also provide exception handling for code that attempts to open the default file; in the modified version that follows, we've nested an ***inner*** try–catch construct within the catch block of the ***outer*** try statement:

```
// Pseudocode.
string filename = the name of a file provided by a user via a GUI;

try {
  // Pseudocode.
  attempt to open the filename file
}
catch (FileNotFoundException e1) {
  // Since the user's filename is not valid, let's open a default file instead.
  try {
    // Pseudocode.
    attempt to open the file named "default.dat";
  }
  catch (IOException e2) {
    // This code will execute if the default.dat cannot be opened, either.
    Console.WriteLine("Unrecoverable error ...");
    // etc.
  } // end of inner try-catch
} // end of outer try-catch
```

Referencing the Thrown Exception Object

Exception classes are like any other classes in that they define properties and methods with which to manipulate exception objects. As we've previously seen, a reference to the exception object being caught is included in the declaration of a catch clause. This reference is locally scoped to/available inside of the catch block, and provides us with a handle with which to call methods on or invoke properties of the exception object. For example, we may wish to access an exception's type-specific message via the Message property:

```
catch (IOException e) {
  Console.WriteLine(e.Message);
}
```

In the preceding code snippet, an instance of the IOException class named e is declared in a catch clause. Inside the catch block, the Message property is invoked on reference variable e to write a message to the console explaining the nature of the exception; an example of such a message is

```
Could not find file "C:/MyDocs/default.dat"
```

> *Another useful* Exception *class property is the* Source *property, used to determine the application or object that triggered the exception. For a complete listing of methods/properties available for each of the derived exception types, please consult the FCL Reference on the MSDN web site.*

User-Defined Exceptions

In addition to the exception classes provided by the FCL, it's also possible in C# to declare user-defined, application-specific exception types by extending the System.Exception class or any of its derived classes. We then may explicitly instantiate and throw such exceptions to signal problems when they arise. This is analogous to shooting off a signal flare if you're lost in the wilderness and wish to call out for help! Defining and then subsequently throwing custom exception types is a popular technique for signaling that something has gone awry in an application.

As an example of creating a user-defined exception, let's define a class called InvalidStudentIdException, derived from the Exception class, to signal a problem when an attempt is made to instantiate a Student object with an invalid student ID. In deriving InvalidStudentIdException from Exception, we've added one feature—a field that represents the invalid student ID—and overridden the Message property in order to provide a class-specific message.

The code for our InvalidStudentIdException class is as follows:

```
// InvalidStudentIdException.cs

using System;

public class InvalidStudentIdException : Exception {
  // Declare a field representing the student ID.
  string id;

  // A constructor that sets the value of the id field.
  public InvalidStudentIdException(string id) {
    this.id = id;
  }

  // A read-only property associated with the id field.
  public string Id {
    get {
      return id;
    }
  }
```

```
    // Override the Message property.
    public override string Message {
      get {
        return "Error: Invalid student ID: "+ Id;
      }
    }
  }
}
```

Next, we'll take advantage of our user-defined exception in the constructor of the Student class, to enforce the fact that we want a student's ID to be 11 characters long. (There are most likely other considerations that we'd also check, such as ensuring that the ID consists of only numeric characters and hyphens arranged in a certain sequence, but for this simple example we'll only test for the number of characters.) If the number of characters in the string passed as an argument to the Student constructor doesn't equal 11, we'll want the Student constructor to "send up a signal flare": i.e., to throw a new instance of an InvalidStudentIdException object using the throw keyword.

Here is the code listing of the Student class; once again, we've kept this example simple by having the Student class declare a single field named studentId and a single property to access this field.

```
// Student.cs

public class Student {
  // Declare a field representing a student ID.
  private string studentId;

  // Property.
  public string StudentId {
    // Accessor details omitted.
  }

  // Constructor.
  public Student(string id) {
    // Test to see if the string passed to the constructor
    // contains exactly 11 characters. If it doesn't, then
    // we want to signal a problem by throwing an
    // InvalidStudentIdException.  Note that we pass in
    // the value of the invalid id.
    if (id.Length != 11) {
      throw new InvalidStudentIdException(id);
      // Execution of the constructor halts at this point, and control is
      // transferred back to the client code that invoked the constructor.
    }
```

```
        // If we got this far in our constructor code, then the string passed
        // to the constructor DOES contain 11 characters, and so we'll
        // accept the proposed value.
        StudentId = id;
    } // end of constructor
}
```

We must now add the necessary exception-handling logic to our application to **detect** such exceptions. Because the Student constructor can now throw an InvalidStudentIdException, we place all client code logic for instantiating Student objects inside a try-catch block; the catch clause will specify the InvalidStudentIdException type.

In this first example, a valid 11-character string is passed to the Student constructor.

```
// Code is excerpted from an application's Main() method.

Student s;

try {
    // Assign a valid student ID.
    s = new Student("123-45-6789");
}
catch (InvalidStudentIdException ex) {
    // Access our "customized" message.
    Console.WriteLine(ex.Message);

    // Create a student using a "dummy" id value instead.
    s = new Student("???-??-????");
}

// Display the student's ID.
Console.WriteLine("Student ID = " + s.Id);
```

When this code snippet is run, an InvalidStudentIdException is **not** thrown, and so the output will be as follows:

```
Student ID = 123-45-6789
```

However, if we change the code snippet such that an invalid student ID is passed as an argument to the Student constructor:

```
Student s;

try {
  s = new Student("123-45-");  // Oh-oh, an invalid student ID!
}
catch (InvalidStudentIdException ex) {
  // Access our "customized" message.
  Console.WriteLine(ex.Message);

  // Create a student using a "dummy" id value instead.
  s = new Student("???-??-????");
}

// Display the student's ID.
Console.WriteLine("Student ID = " + s.Id);
```

an InvalidStudentIdException *is* thrown, the catch block is executed, and the out
put is instead as follows:

```
Error: Invalid student ID: 123-45-
Student ID = ???-??-????
```

> *While we chose not to take advantage of user-defined exceptions in building
> the SRS, this is nonetheless an important technique to be aware of.*

Compiler-Mandated Exception Handling

Many programming languages support the notion of exception handling. In
some of these languages—Java, for example—the compiler will mandate try
statements in certain situations. That is, in Java, if we were to try to write the following logic without an enclosing try statement:

```
// Pseudocode.
string filename = the name of a file provided by a user via a GUI;
attempt to open the filename file;
```

the Java compiler would generate an error message forcing us to deal with the
potential for an exception in some fashion.

In contrast, the C# compiler doesn't mandate exception handling; if we
choose to write code such as that just shown in C#, it will indeed compile, but of
course if an IOException arises at run time that we haven't provided recovery
code for, the runtime will abruptly terminate the program's execution. So, while
the use of try statements for code that can throw exceptions isn't mandatory in

C#, inclusion of explicit exception-handling code is nonetheless highly desirable because it's the only mechanism with which to gracefully anticipate and handle run-time issues.

The Object Class

In addition to the String class, there are several other classes that deserve special mention in the C# language—one such class is the Object class. The Object class is at the very root of the .NET class hierarchy. Every other .NET type, from the simple predefined value types, to strings, to arrays, to predefined reference types, to user-defined types, ultimately derives from the Object class.

Inheritance from the Object class is implicit; there is no need to include the syntax

```
: Object
```

in a class definition; that is, the class definition syntax

```
public class Student { ... }
```

is equivalent to the more explicit

```
public class Student : Object { ... }
```

The Object class is contained in the System namespace, but as with the String class, there is an alias for the Object class—the keyword object (all lowercase)—which allows us to declare Object references without having to insert a using System; directive at the top of our program; the following two lines of code are thus equivalent:

```
System.Object x = y;
```

and

```
object x = y;
```

The Object class declares five public methods that are inherited by, and hence available to, any object of any type. We'll discuss the two most commonly used Object methods in detail in the following sections: Equals and ToString.

The Equals Method

The Equals method determines whether two object references are "equal": that is, whether the two references are referring to the exact same object in memory. There are two versions of this method:

- public virtual bool Equals(object obj): This method can be called on any object, passing in a second object as an argument: if (x.Equals(y)) { ... }

- public static bool Equals(object objA, object objB): This static method is called on the Object class, and the two references to be compared are both passed in as arguments to the method:
  if (Object.Equals(x, y)) { ... }

For example, let's create a Student object and maintain two handles on it:

```
Student s1 = new Student("Fred");
Student s2 = s1;
```

Reference variables s1 and s2 thus reference the same object in memory. Now, let's create a second Student object with the same data values as the first:

```
Student s3 = new Student("Fred");
```

Using the "object as helium balloon" analogy, we've created the situation portrayed in Figure 13-11.

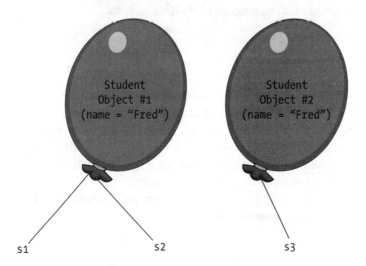

Figure 13-11. Object #2 has the same data values as Object #1 but is a separate, distinct object in memory.

If we test for equality of s1 and s2 using the Equals method:

```
if (s1.Equals(s2)) {  // or, equivalently:    Object.Equals(s1, s2);
  Console.WriteLine("s1 equals s2");
}
else {
  Console.WriteLine("s1 does not equal s2");
}
```

the output of this code would be as follows:

```
s1 equals s2
```

because s1 and s2 are indeed referencing the same object, whereas testing s1 and s3 for equality:

```
if (s1.Equals(s3)) {  // or, equivalently:    Object.Equals(s1, s3);
  Console.WriteLine("s1 equals s3");
}
else {
  Console.WriteLine("s1 does not equal s3");
}
```

would generate the following output:

```
s1 does not equal s3
```

because despite the fact that s1 and s3 have the same data values (name is "Fred" in both cases), they are nonetheless references to ***distinct*** objects.

Overriding the Equals Method

The nonstatic version of the Object class's Equals method is declared to be virtual, allowing us to override its behavior in a derived class. We often override the Equals method to define a different interpretation of what it means for two objects to be equal: for example, in the Student class, we may wish to deem two ***physically distinct*** Student objects as nonetheless being "equal" if they have the same value for their respective student ID numbers.

Because the code involved in doing so is a bit complex, we'll present it in its entirety first, and will then explain it step by step:

```csharp
using System;

public class Student
{
  // Field.
  private string studentId;

  // Property.
  public string StudentId {
    // Accessor details omitted.
  }

  // Overriding the Equals method.
  public override bool Equals(object obj) {
    // Initialize a flag.
    bool isEqual = false;

    try {
      // Start by attempting to cast the generic object reference,
      // "obj", as a Student; if an InvalidCastException arises
      // at run time, we KNOW that the object in question is NOT
      // a Student, and so by definition cannot be equal to THIS
      // Student!
      Student s = (Student) obj;

      // If we make it this far in the Equals method without
      // throwing an InvalidCastException, we know that we are
      // indeed dealing with two Student instances.  Next,
      // we'll compare their ID numbers.
      if (this.StudentID == s.StudentID) {
        // Eureka!  They're equal, according to our new
        // definition of Student equality.
        isEqual = true;
      }
      else {
        isEqual = false;
      }
    }
    catch (InvalidCastException e) {
      // As mentioned above, if "obj" cannot be cast as a Student,
      // we know it doesn't equal THIS Student!
      isEqual = false;
    }
```

```
            return isEqual;
        }
    }
```

Let's now discuss key aspects of this code.

First, note that the *Object* class's version of the Equals method:

```
public virtual bool Equals(object obj)
```

takes a generic *object* reference as an argument. In our overridden Equals method for the Student class, however, we're interested in establishing the equality/inequality of two *Student* objects, so we first attempt to cast the obj argument into a Student object reference.

```
        Student s = (Student) obj;
```

Two possible outcomes can arise:

- If the object reference being passed in is indeed a Student reference, the cast proceeds without exception at run time, and we then proceed to compare the two students' ID numbers. If they are found to be identical, we set the isEqual flag to true to indicate that they are "equal" according to our business rules for Student equality; otherwise, we set the flag to false.

```
        if (this.StudentID == s.StudentID) {
            isEqual = true;
        }
        else {
            isEqual = false;
        }
```

- On the other hand, if the object being passed in is *not* a Student, an InvalidCastException is thrown, transferring control to the catch block of our example. Here, we automatically set the isEqual flag to false: if the object being compared to *this* Student isn't even a Student, then they are obviously unequal!

```
        catch (InvalidCastException e) {
            // If obj cannot be cast to a Student, we know it doesn't equal
            // THIS Student!
            isEqual = false;
        }
```

Let's put our new overridden method to work in our client code:

```
public class Example
{
  static void Main() {
    Professor p = new Professor();

    Student s1 = new Student(); // first object ...
    s1.StudentID = "123-45-6789";

    Student s2 = new Student(); // second object ...
    s2.StudentID = "123-45-6789"; // same ID as s1

    Student s3 = new Student(); // third object!
    s3.StudentID = "987-65-4321"; // different ID as s1 and s2

    Console.WriteLine("Is s1 equal to s2?  " + s1.Equals(s2));
    Console.WriteLine("Is s1 equal to s3?  " + s1.Equals(s3));
    Console.WriteLine("Is s1 equal to p?  " + s1.Equals(p));
  }
}
```

The preceding code would generate the following output:

```
Is s1 equal to s2?  true
Is s1 equal to s3?  false
Is s1 equal to p?  false
```

> *Note that when we instead use the == operator to test two references for equality*
>
> ```
> if (x == y) { ... }
> ```
>
> *the nature of the equality test is again class-dependent; if x and y are generic* **object** *references, then == tests to see if the two references are referring to the* **same physical object in memory***; if x and y are* **string** *references, then as we learned earlier, == tests to see if the two strings have the same* **values***, regardless of whether they are referring to the same or different physical string objects.*
>
> *For a user-defined class such as* Student *that has overridden the* Equals *method, there is also a way to override the == operator, but the means of doing so is beyond the scope of this book to address.*

The ToString Method

The most commonly used (and most commonly overridden) Object class method is ToString. It's used to return a string representation of the object on which the method is called, and has the following header:

```
public virtual string ToString()
```

The Object class implementation of ToString simply returns the fully qualified name of the type of the object on which it's called. For example, if the Student class belongs in the SRS namespace and we were to call the ToString method on a Student object as it's inherited from the Object class:

```
Student s = new Student();
s.Name = "Dianne Bolden";
s.StudentId = "999999";
Console.WriteLine(s.ToString());
```

the following output would result:

```
  SRS.Student
```

However, simply printing out the name of the class that an object belongs to isn't very informative. Fortunately, as was the case with the Equals method, the Object class version of the ToString method is declared to be virtual, which enables us to override its behavior for a derived class.

Overriding the ToString Method

In the preceding example, we'd prefer that the ToString method for a Student return a more informative result, such as perhaps the label "Student:" followed by a given student's name and student ID number, formatted as shown here:

```
  Student:   Dianne Bolden [999999]
```

To achieve this result, we'd simply need to override the ToString method in the Student class as follows:

```
public class Student {
  // Fields.
  private string name;
  private string studentId;
  // Other details omitted ...
```

```
public override string ToString() {
  return "Student:  " + Name + " [" + StudentId + "]";
}
```

Now, the snippet shown earlier:

```
Student s = new Student();
s.Name = "Dianne Bolden";
s.StudentId = "999999";
Console.WriteLine(s.ToString());
```

would output the desired result when executed:

```
Student:  Dianne Bolden [999999]
```

by virtue of our overridden ToString method.

"Behind the Scenes" Use of ToString

As it turns out, the ToString method is often called "behind the scenes"—for example, by the Console.WriteLine method. The Console.WriteLine method, which we normally think of as accepting string arguments, is overloaded such that an arbitrary object reference can be passed as an argument to the method. It's therefore perfectly acceptable to write code as follows:

```
Student s = new Student();
s.Name = "Cheryl Richter";
s.StudentId = "123456";
Console.WriteLine(s);
```

When an arbitrary object reference is passed to the WriteLine method, the WriteLine method automatically calls the object's ToString method to obtain its class-specific string representation, which is then printed to the console. Given the way in which we'd overridden the ToString method for the Student class earlier, the result of running the preceding code snippet would produce the following output:

```
Student:  Cheryl Richter [123456]
```

Many of the predefined classes in the .NET Framework libraries have overridden the ToString method. What's more, it's a good idea to get into the habit of overriding the ToString method for all user-defined classes, to ensure that whenever ToString is called "behind the scenes" on an instance of such a class, a meaningful result is returned.

Other Object Class Methods

There are three other public methods defined by the Object class:

- The GetType method allows us to determine the type of an arbitrary object at run time, and will be discussed in detail later in this chapter in the section titled "Object Identities."

- GetHashCode and ReferenceEquals are less frequently used, and won't be covered in detail in this book. Please consult the FCL Reference on the MSDN web site if you'd like more information on these methods.

C#'s Collection Classes

Back in Chapter 6, we discussed the need for a convenient way to collect references to objects as we create them, so that we may iterate over them, retrieve a particular object on demand, and so forth. We learned that the way to do so in an OOPL is to create a special type of object called a ***collection,*** and that one of the simplest collection types in C# is the fixed-size array. When we introduced arrays in Chapter 6, we alluded to the fact that they are objects in the C# language; as it turns out, the System.Array class is the basis for all arrays. We'll revisit arrays in this section to learn about some of the more interesting features of the System.Array class.

As we discussed in Chapter 6, it's often impossible to anticipate how many of a given object type we're going to have to create as an application is running, and so using fixed-size arrays to store varying numbers of objects is often inefficient. The System.Collections namespace of the .NET FCL defines a number of alternative collection classes that can be used to store object collections. In this section, we'll discuss two of the most commonly used collection classes that we plan on using in building the SRS—the ArrayList and Hashtable classes.

> *Note that the* System.Array *class isn't part of the* System.Collections *namespace; nonetheless, all C# collection classes—*System.Array *as well as the various* System.Collections *classes—implement the* ICollection *interface, which is defined in the* System.Collections *namespace, and hence share a common set of behaviors.*

Arrays, Revisited

The System.Array class defines a variety of useful methods and properties that can be used to do such things as search, sort, modify, and determine the length of arrays.

Array Length Property

The most commonly used Array property is the Length property. It's of type int and represents the total number of elements in an array across all of its dimensions. The following snippet shows the Length property in use for a one-dimensional array:

```
int[] x = new int[20];

// details of array content initialization omitted ...

// Step through the array.
// Stop BEFORE i equals x.Length!!!!
for (int i = 0; i < x.Length; i++) {
  Console.WriteLine(x[i]);
}
```

Because arrays are zero-based, we always need to stop just one short of the length when using it as an upper bound in a for loop, as the preceding example illustrates.

Note that the length of an array doesn't reflect how many elements have been explicitly assigned values because, technically speaking, even if nothing is stored explicitly in an array, its elements will be automatically filled with zero-equivalent values suitable for the array's type, as was discussed in Chapter 6. Rather, the length of an array simply represents the total capacity of the array in terms of the total number of items that it can hold; the capacity is fixed when an array is first declared, and can't be changed thereafter.

> In Chapter 6 we introduced the ArrayList *class that represents a collection whose size can "grow gracefully" as needed. We'll talk more about* ArrayLists *later in this section.*

Array Methods

The Array class declares a variety of useful static and instance methods that can be used to examine or manipulate arrays; we'll discuss a few of the more commonly used methods here. A complete description of all of the Array class methods can be found in the FCL Reference on the MSDN web site.

The first three methods are static methods, meaning that they must be invoked on the Array class as a whole, passing in the array instance to be affected as an argument:

- `public static void Clear(Array array, int startIndex, int length):` Resets the contents of all or part of an array to zero-equivalent values. The arguments include the array to be cleared, the starting index (counting from 0), and the number of elements to clear.

```
int[] x = new int[5];

// Clear the entire array.
Array.Clear(x, 0, x.Length);
```

- `public static void Reverse(Array array):` Reverses the order of the elements of a one-dimensional array.

```
int[] x = {1, 2, 3};
Array.Reverse(x);
// x now contains the values:  {3, 2, 1}
```

There is also an overloaded version of this method in which the starting index and number of elements to reverse can be specified:

```
public static void Reverse(Array array, int startIndex, int length)
```

- `public static void Sort(Array array):` Sorts the elements of a one-dimensional array. The default sorting criterion is alphabetically, for string elements; or smallest-to-largest, for numerical elements.

```
string[] names = {"Vijay", "Tiger", "Phil"};
Array.Sort(names);
// the order of the elements is now "Phil", "Tiger", "Vijay"
```

There is also an overloaded version of this method in which the starting index and number of elements to sort can be specified:

```
public static void Sort(Array array, int startIndex, int length)
```

> *Yet another overloaded version of this method enables user-defined sorting criteria to be specified for arbitrary object types, but is beyond the scope of this book to address.*

The next three methods are instance methods, meaning that they can be invoked on an individual array instance directly:

- `public object GetValue(int index)`: Returns the element at the specified index of a one-dimensional array as a generic object. If we happen to know what the specific type of that object is, we can cast it:

```
String[] names = {"Chris", "Sandi", "Brennan"};
// Cast the returned object as a string.
string name = (string) names.GetValue(0);
```

  or:

```
int[] numbers = {11, 17, 85};
// Cast the returned object as an int.
string number = (int) numbers.GetValue(0);
```

  There are also overloaded versions of this method for returning an element of a 2- or 3-dimensional array:

```
public object GetValue(int index1, int index2)
public object GetValue(int index1, int index2, int index3)
```

- `public void SetValue(object value, int index)`: Changes the element at the specified index of a one-dimensional array.

  There are also overloaded versions for changing an element of a two- or three-dimensional array:

```
public void SetValue(object value, int index1, int index2)
public void SetValue(object value, int index1, int index2, int index3)
```

Even though `GetValue` *and* `SetValue` *methods are provided by the* `Array` *class, the indexer notation is easier and more convenient to use. The syntax*

```
string name = names[0];
```

is easier to write and understand than the equivalent syntax

```
string name = (string) names.GetValue(0);
```

- `public int GetLength(int dimension)`: Returns the length of the specified dimension in an array of any number of dimensions. For example, to obtain the length of the first dimension of a two-dimensional array, we would use `GetLength(0)`. (For a one-dimensional array, we may simply use the `Length` property to determine the length of the array.)

The ArrayList Class

We first learned about the `ArrayList` class in Chapter 6. It represents a simple, dynamically resizable, one-dimensional ordered list that allows us to store a varying number of object references without having to worry about properly sizing the container in advance. It's the logical equivalent of a one-dimensional Array, but whose size is automatically increased or decreased as needed.

ArrayLists can contain elements of any type (since all types in C# represent objects) and indeed it's possible to mix-and-match types within an `ArrayList` if it makes sense to do so in a given application.

The `ArrayList` class is defined within the `System.Collections` namespace. To refer to the `ArrayList` class by its simple name, a `using` directive can be included at the top of the code:

```
using System.Collections;
```

or an `ArrayList` can be referred to by its fully qualified name:

```
System.Collections.ArrayList.
```

Creating an ArrayList

An `ArrayList` object can be instantiated by using one of three constructors provided by the `ArrayList` class.

- The simplest form of constructor is the parameterless constructor:

```
ArrayList coursesTaken = new ArrayList();
```

This constructor will create an empty `ArrayList` with an initial default capacity of 16. When the number of elements in the `ArrayList` reaches the current capacity of the `ArrayList`, its capacity is automatically doubled.

- The second form of `ArrayList` constructor takes an integer argument representing the initial capacity of the `ArrayList`; e.g.,

```
ArrayList students = new ArrayList(400);
```

We might use this form of constructor if we knew that we would be adding a large number of object references to the ArrayList. Starting with a capacity greater than the default of 16 can increase performance by reducing the number of times the ArrayList would need to resize itself as it grows.

- The third constructor takes as its argument any proper C# collection object—that is, any object belonging to one of the classes that implements the ICollection interface, which as we mentioned earlier includes all of the System.Collections classes along with the System.Array class—and copies the contents of the passed-in collection to populate the newly constructed ArrayList:

```
// Create an array of Course objects ...
Course[] courses = new Course[3];
courses[0] = new Course("Math 101");
courses[1] = new Course("Physics 250");
courses[2] - new Course("Management 283");

// Intervening details omitted.

// ... and, later in the program, use it to initialize
// an ArrayList.
ArrayList coursesTaken = new ArrayList(courses);
```

In the previous code snippet, we initialized an ArrayList with the contents of a Course array; note that both collections are now referencing the same objects, as illustrated conceptually in Figure 13-12.

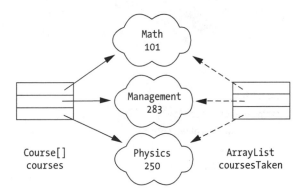

Figure 13-12. An ArrayList *can be initialized with the contents of another collection.*

ArrayList Properties

The ArrayList class declares a number of properties that return information about the ArrayList.

- The Capacity property is used to get or set the capacity of the ArrayList. (If we programmatically attempt to resize an ArrayList to be smaller than the number of items it holds at any given time, an ArgumentOutOfRangeException is thrown.)

- The Count property returns the current number of elements actually contained in the ArrayList.

- To access an element stored inside an ArrayList, the ArrayList class defines a special indexer property that allows us to get or set an element of an ArrayList just as we would access an element of a standard array—with an integer expression representing the desired index, surrounded by brackets. When the indexer returns an ArrayList element, it's returned as a generic object, and the element is then typically cast to its original type.

Here is an example illustrating all of these properties:

```
Course c1 = new Course("Math 101");
Course c2 = new Course("Physics 250");
Course c3 = new Course("Management 283");

// Using the ArrayList indexer property.  (Note that it looks as
// if we are accessing an Array!)
coursesTaken[0] = c1;
coursesTaken[1] = c2;
coursesTaken[2] = c3;

// Access the Capacity and Count properties.
Console.WriteLine("capacity = " + coursesTaken.Capacity);
Console.WriteLine("no. of elements = " + coursesTaken.Count);

// Let's now pull the ArrayList elements back out, again
// using the indexer.
for (int i = 0; i < coursesTaken.Count; i++) {
   // Use the indexer to retrieve each element of the ArrayList.
   // Cast a generic object reference back into a Course reference.
   Course c = (Course) coursesTaken[i];
```

```
  // We now can invoke the methods of a Course on c.
  Console.WriteLine(c.Name);
}
```

The previous example highlights why it can be dangerous to mix and match types in an ArrayList. The ArrayList elements are accessed one-by-one and cast into a Course object. The Name property is then invoked on each Course object. This process works fine if all of the ArrayList elements are Course objects (or objects that derive from Course). If there happened to be an element of a disparate type—say, a double—mixed in with the Course objects, the cast wouldn't work—an InvalidCastException would be thrown because there is no way to cast a double into a Course. We'll see a more complete example of how mixing types can be a problem in the "Collections and Casting" section later in the chapter.

ArrayList Methods

Some of the more commonly used ArrayList class methods are as follows:

- public virtual int Add(object value): Adds an object reference to the end of the ArrayList by default, automatically expanding the ArrayList if need be to accommodate the reference. The provision of the virtual keyword allows derived classes to override this method as desired. The return value of the method is an int representing the index position in the ArrayList at which the argument was placed.

- public void Add(ICollection c): Appends the contents of the specified collection to the end of the ArrayList.

- public void SetRange(int startIndex, ICollection c): Replaces the current elements of an ArrayList with the contents of a different ICollection object, beginning at the specified starting index in the target ArrayList. If "c" contains more elements than the segment of the ArrayList that it is replacing, the ArrayList automatically gets extended in size as needed.

- public IEnumerator GetEnumerator(): Retrieves an instance of a special type of object called an IEnumerator that can be used to iterate through the elements of an ArrayList. We'll discuss IEnumerators later in this chapter.

- public int IndexOf(object obj): Hunts for the existence of a specific object reference and, if found, returns an integer indicating the (first) index location at which this reference was found (counting from 0). If the specified object isn't found, the value –1 is returned.

- `public bool Contains(object obj)`: Hunts for existence of the object reference in question and, if found, returns the value `true`, otherwise `false`.

- `public void RemoveAt(int index)`: Takes out the element at the specified index and "closes up"/"collapses" the resultant "hole." The value of the `Count` property decreases by one, but the `Capacity` remains the same. An `ArgumentOutOfRangeException` is thrown if the specified index exceeds the `Count` or is less than zero.

- `public void Remove(object obj)`: Hunts for existence of a specific object reference in question and, if found, removes the (first) occurrence of that reference from the `ArrayList`, again closing up the "hole." The `Count` decreases by one, but the `Capacity` remains the same. If the specified object isn't found, the `ArrayList` is unchanged. To remove all instances of `obj`, use a combination of the `Contains` and `Remove` methods in conjunction with a `while` loop:

```
while (arraylist.Contains(x)) {
  arraylist.Remove(x)
}
```

- `public void Sort()`: Sorts the elements of the `ArrayList`. The default is to sort `string` elements alphabetically and numerical elements smallest-to-largest.

> *There is an overloaded version of this method that enables us to customize the sorting algorithm for arbitrary object types, but discussing user-defined sorting algorithms is beyond the scope of this book.*

- `public void Clear()`: Empties out the `ArrayList`. The `Count` property is set to zero. The `Capacity` is unchanged.

- `public object[] ToArray()`: Creates an instance of an `object` array, and copies the elements of the `ArrayList` into the array.

and there are more! Please consult the FCL Reference on the MSDN web site for a complete description of all of the `ArrayList` methods.

The Hashtable Class

The Hashtable class provides us with another way to manage collections of object references in C#. A Hashtable is a bit more sophisticated than an ArrayList because it gives us direct access to a given object based on a unique key value; it's an implementation of the dictionary collection type that we defined in Chapter 6. Both the key and the object itself can be of any object type; keys are often, but not always, strings.

Like the ArrayList class, the Hashtable class can be found in the System.Collections namespace. To refer to a Hashtable by its simple name, a using System.Collections; directive can be placed at the top of a source code file, or a Hashtable can be referred to by its fully qualified name—System.Collections.Hashtable.

Creating a Hashtable

A Hashtable object can be created using any one of the various constructors declared by the Hashtable class. The simplest way to instantiate a Hashtable is with the parameterless constructor, which creates an empty Hashtable. We then insert objects as desired using the Add method, whose header is as follows:

```
public void Add(object key, object value)
```

Note that we must specify a key value for each item as we add it to the Hashtable, to be used to retrieve the item later on; we'll use simple string objects for the keys in this example—in particular, the students' social security numbers:

```
// Create a Hashtable instance (the "egg carton").
Hashtable students = new Hashtable();

// Create several Student objects ("eggs").
Student s1 = new Student("123-45-6789", "John Smith");
Student s2 = new Student("987-65-4321", "Mary Jones");
Student s3 = new Student("654-32-1987", "Jim Green");

// Store their handles in the Hashtable, using the value of the Ssn property
// (which happens to be declared as type string) as the key for each.
students.Add(s1.Ssn, s1);
students.Add(s2.Ssn, s2);
students.Add(s3.Ssn, s3);
```

The Hashtable class defines an indexer that can be used to get or set an element of the Hashtable. As with the ArrayList, the indexer is denoted by a pair of brackets; with Hashtables, however, the brackets surround the key value of the element to be accessed:

```
// Note that we have to recast the object when we retrieve it,
// just as we must do with ArrayLists.
Student s = (Student) students["123-45-6789"];  // retrieves the object
                                                // reference representing
                                                // Student John Smith
Console.WriteLine("name is " + s.Name);
```

or, by way of another example:

```
// Pseudocode.
string id = retrieve student ID number from a GUI;
Student s = (Student) students[id];
```

Note that we have to cast an object when we retrieve it from a Hashtable if we wish to manipulate it as an instance of its original type (in this case, a Student), just as we do when retrieving an object from an ArrayList.

Hashtable Properties

In addition to Count and indexer properties, which work the same for a Hashtable as they do for an ArrayList, the Hashtable class declares a number of other properties to return information about the Hashtable.

- The Keys property returns an ICollection object whose elements are the keys contained in the Hashtable.

- The Values property returns an ICollection object whose elements are the keys contained in the Hashtable.

> We'll learn how to iterate through generic ICollection *collections later in this chapter.*

and there are others. For a complete list of all Hashtable properties, consult the FCL reference on the MSDN web site.

Hashtable Methods

Some of the more commonly used methods from the Hashtable class are as follows:

- `public void Add(object key, object value)`: As already discussed, this method inserts the second object reference (value) into the table with a retrieval key represented by the first object reference (key). This method will throw an ArgumentException if there already was a previously stored object at that key location, so it's important to first verify that the key we're about to use isn't already in use in the table, using the ContainsKey method discussed next.

- `public bool ContainsKey(object key)`: Returns true if an entry with the designated key value is found in the Hashtable, otherwise returns false.

    Here's how we'd use the ContainsKey method in concert with the Add method to make sure we weren't trying to overwrite an existing entry in the Hashtable:

    ```
    Student s = new Student("111-11-1111", "Arnold Brown");
    if (students.ContainsKey(s.Ssn)) {
      // Whoops! This is a duplicate; we need to decide what to do!
      // details omitted ...
    }
    else {
      students.Add(s.Ssn, s);  // OK, because no duplicate was detected.
    }
    ```

- `public bool ContainsValue(object value)`: Looks for the designated ***value*** without the aid of its associated key, and returns true if the value is found, otherwise returns false.

- `public void Remove(object key)`: Removes the ***reference*** to the object represented by the given key from the Hashtable; note that the object itself, as it exists outside of the Hashtable, is unaffected.

- `public IDictionaryEnumerator GetEnumerator()`: Returns an IDictionaryEnumerator object that can be used to examine the key-object pairs currently stored in the Hashtable. We'll talk about enumerators in the next section.

- `public void Clear()`: Empties out the Hashtable, as if it had just been newly instantiated. The Count property is set to zero.

Collections and Casting

As we learned in Chapter 6, the only C# collection type that allows us to constrain the types of objects that we insert is the Array. That is, when we declare an Array, we must declare the type of entities that we plan on inserting:

```
int[] x = new int[20];   // We're constraining x to hold int(eger)s.
```

With all other formal collection types in C#, however, we *can't* constrain the type of objects to be inserted when we declare the collection; as mentioned in Chapter 6, C# collections other than Arrays are designed to hold *generic* objects. We must therefore exercise programming discipline when inserting objects into such a collection to ensure that they all speak a "common language" in terms of messages that they understand if we wish to take advantage of polymorphism, because the C# compiler won't stop us from putting an odd assortment of objects *into* a collection, but the C# compiler or runtime may complain if we try to operate on the objects "inappropriately" after taking them back *out.*

To illustrate this notion, let's look at a simple example. We'll use an ArrayList as the collection type, but the concepts presented in this section apply to all of the C# System.Collections classes. Suppose we define a Student class that, among other things, declares a CalculateGPA method:

```
public class Student
{
  // Details omitted.

  public void CalculateGPA() {
    // Details omitted.
  }
}
```

Let's also declare a Professor class that does *not* declare a CalculateGPA method:

```
public class Professor {
  // Details omitted -- but, NO CalculateGPA method is declared.
}
```

We're permitted by the compiler to add an assortment of Student and Professor objects to the same ArrayList, because as we learned in Chapter 6, non-Array collections can't be constrained as to the type of object that they hold:

```
Student s = new Student();
Student t = new Student();
Professor p = new Professor();
Professor q = new Professor();
```

```
// We cannot declare an ArrayList as holding a particular type
// of object.
ArrayList people = new ArrayList();

// Add a mixture of Professors and Students to the collection.
people.Add(s);
people.Add(p);
people.Add(q);
people.Add(t);
```

As the programmers who wrote this code, we ***know*** that the zeroeth element of the ArrayList is a Student, and so let's use the indexer to retrieve that element and invoke the CalculateGPA method on it:

```
people[0].CalculateGPA();
```

This seems reasonable to do; however, when we try to compile the previous line of code, an error is generated:

```
Error CS0117: 'object' does not contain a definition for 'CalculateGPA'
```

Even though the zeroeth element of the ArrayList is indeed a Student object at *run time,* the *compiler* "knows" that an indexer returns generic object references. Since people[0] therefore is a generic object in the compiler's "eyes," and since the Object class doesn't declare a CalculateGPA method—only the Student class does—this line of code won't compile.

The solution to this compilation problem would be to cast the return value from the ArrayList indexer back into a Student before invoking the CalculateGPA method:

```
// Note addition of cast.
Student s2 = (Student) people[0];
s2.CalculateGPA();
```

or, collapsing this into a single line of code by chaining expressions:

```
 ((Student) people[0]).CalculateGPA();
```

Either way, the compiler will now be "happy," because by casting, we're effectively asking the compiler to "trust us" that, at run time, the object reference in question will indeed be referencing a Student object; and, since the compiler knows that the Student class defines a CalculateGPA method, all is well!

There is still one potential issue, however: if the ArrayList collection indeed contains a mixture of Student and Professor object references, and we want to iterate through the entire collection, we can't cast them as Students so as to call the CalculateGPA method because, at run time, some of the objects in the collection will be Professors for which CalculateGPA is undefined:

```
for (int i = 0; i < people.Count; i++) {
  Student x = (Student) people[i];  // The ith object may NOT be a Student!
  x.CalculateGPA();
}
```

The previous code snippet will **compile,** because once again we're asking the compiler to "trust us" that the objects in this collection will all be Student objects; but at **run time,** when we actually try to execute this code, an InvalidCastException will be thrown and the program will terminate as soon as the first Professor reference is encountered, because there is no valid way to cast a Professor object into a Student object.

If we want to iterate through our people collection using a looping construct, our only choices, having mixed Professors and Students into the same collection, are to

- Treat them as **generic** Objects.

- Cast them into a **common supertype.**

Let's look at the implications of these two choices.

If we treat all the objects in our people collection as generic objects, then the only methods that the compiler will allow us to call on each object reference are the handful of methods defined by the Object class:

```
for (int i = 0; i < people.Count; i++) {
  // We're NOT casting the references.
  object x = people[i];

  // Therefore, the only methods we can invoke on x
  // are methods defined by the Object class.
  Console.WriteLine(x.ToString());
}
```

However, if the various types in question all have some common supertype other than object—say, for example, that both Student and Professor derive from a common base class called Person—then we may cast all of the object references in the people collection to Person object references, since by virtue of the "is a" nature of inheritance, a Student is a Person, and a Professor is a Person. Under these circumstances, we may call any methods on the objects that are common to the Person class:

```
for (int i = 0; i < people.Count; i++) {
  Person x = (Person) people[i];   // Casting to a common supertype.
  x.printAddress();   // A method defined in the Person class.
}
```

Because a System.Collections collection such as an ArrayList or Hashtable treats everything that is inserted as a generic object reference, we as programmers must remember what class of object reference we're storing in a given collection so that we may cast these references back to the correct (common base) class when we retrieve them. One way to help remember what types are going to be stored in such a collection is to add a comment to the collection declaration to help us remember what sort of object references we intend to store within the collection:

```
ArrayList coursesTaken; // of Course object references
```

Stepping Through Collections with Enumerators

When we create collections of objects, we often have a need to step through the entire collection to process it in some fashion; for example, we may want to iterate through an ArrayList of Student object references to compute final grades for the semester. One way that we've already seen for stepping through an ArrayList is to use a for loop:

```
ArrayList enrollment = new ArrayList();   // of Student references

// Populate the ArrayList ... details omitted.

// Step through the ArrayList, and process all Students' grades.
for (int i = 0; i < enrollment.Count; i++) {
  Student s = (Student) enrollment[i];
  s.ComputeFinalGrade();
}
```

Processing all items in an ArrayList in this fashion is possible because we have a means for referring to a particular element in the ArrayList by its index: e.g., enrollment[i].

There is an alternative way of stepping through all of the elements in a System.Collections collection using a special type of object called an **enumerator.** An enumerator is a mechanism for iterating through a collection. When we obtain an enumerator for a collection—say, for an ArrayList—we can think of this conceptually as making a copy of the original collection's contents, similar in concept to making a photocopy of someone's address book (a collection of Person references) in preparation for conducting a tele-marketing campaign (see Figure 13-13).

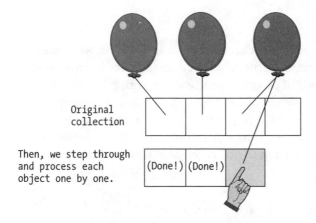

Figure 13-13. An enumerator can step through the elements of a collection.

We then step through the "photocopy" (enumerator) one by one, "crossing off each phone number" (processing each object reference) until we reach the end of the enumeration.

The IEnumerator Interface

As mentioned previously, the ArrayList class (and some of the other System.Collections classes, as well) defines a GetEnumerator method with the following header:

```
public virtual IEnumerator GetEnumerator()
```

The return type of this method, IEnumerator, is an interface defined in the System.Collections namespace. An IEnumerator object represents a temporary copy of the ArrayList for which it has been acquired, and has the following methods:

- bool MoveNext(): Advances the enumerator to the next element in the collection. The method returns true if another element is successfully reached, or false if the end of the collection has been reached.

- void Reset(): Moves the enumerator back to its original position *before* the first item in the collection, such that the *next* call to MoveNext will advance the cursor to the *first* element in the collection.

The IEnumerator interface also declares a read-only property (i.e., one that has a get but not a set accessor) named Current that accesses the element currently being pointed to by the cursor as a generic object reference.

Here's a simple example to illustrate how to put all of this IEnumerator functionality to use. We'll use this simple version of the Course class:

```
public class Course
{
  // Field.
  private string name;

  // Constructor.
  public Course(string n) {
    name = n;
  }

  // Property.
  public string Name {
    // Accessor details omitted.
  }
}
```

This next program will serve as the driver:

```
using System.Collections;

public class EnumDemo
{
  static void Main() {
    ArrayList coursesTaken = new ArrayList();

    Course c1 = ncw Course("Math 101");
    Course c2 = new Course("Physics 250");
    Course c3 = new Course("Management 283");

    // Insert Course object references into the ArrayList.
    coursesTaken.Add(c1);
    coursesTaken.Add(c2);
    coursesTaken.Add(c3);

    // Obtain an enumerator for the ArrayList.
    IEnumerator enum = coursesTaken.GetEnumerator();

    // Iterate through the collection using the enumerator.
    while (enum.MoveNext()) {
      // Use the Current property to retrieve the current element;
      // cast a generic object reference back into a Course reference.
      Course c = (Course) enum.Current;
```

```
        // We now can manipulate c as a Course object.
        Console.WriteLine(c.Name);
      }
    }
}
```

This program, when run, produces the following output:

```
Math 101
Physics 250
Management 283
```

The IDictionaryEnumerator Interface

As we now know, a Hashtable is a collection that stores data in the form of key-value pairs. A specialized type of enumerator is used with Hashtables —specifically, an IDictionaryEnumerator. As mentioned previously, the Hashtable class declares the following method to retrieve an IDictionaryEnumerator for a given Hashtable:

```
public virtual IDictionaryEnumerator GetEnumerator()
```

The IDictionaryEnumerator interface derives from IEnumerator and inherits the MoveNext and Reset methods, which were previously discussed. The IDictionaryEnumerator interface declares several additional properties; of particular interest are Key and Value, which can be used to return the key and value of the current element of the enumeration, respectively.

Here is an example of using an IDictionaryEnumerator to iterate through the elements of a Hashtable. We'll start with a simplified version of the Student class:

```
public class Student
{
  private string name;
  private string ssn;

  // Constructor.
  public Student(string s, string n) {
    ssn = s;
    name = n;
  }

  // Properties.
  public string Name {
    // Accessor details omitted.
  }
```

```
  public string Ssn {
    // Accessor details omitted.
  }
}
```

Here is the driver code for our IDictionaryEnumerator example:

```
using System;
using System.Collections;

public class EnumDemo2
{
  static void Main() {
    // Create an instance of a Hashtable.
    Hashtable students = new Hashtable();

    // Instantiate several Student objects.
    Student s1 = new Student("123-45-6789", "Chris Williams");
    Student s2 = new Student("987-65-4321", "Yukio Koyari");
    Student s3 = new Student("654-32-1987", "Maria Lopez");

    // Store their handles in the Hashtable, using the Ssn value as the key.
    students.Add(s1.Ssn, s1);
    students.Add(s2.Ssn, s2);
    students.Add(s3.Ssn, s3);

    // Obtain an IDictionaryEnumerator for the Hashtable.
    IDictionaryEnumerator enum = students.GetEnumerator();

    // Iterate through the collection using the IDictionaryEnumerator.
    while (enum.MoveNext()) {
      // Obtain the next Student object from the collection as the VALUE in
      // a key-value pair.
      Student s = (Student) enum.Value;
      Console.WriteLine(s.Name + ": " + s.Ssn);
    }
  }
}
```

When this program is run, the following output is produced:

```
Maria Lopez: 654-32-1987
Yukio Koyari: 987-65-4321
Chris Williams: 123-45-6789
```

Note that the student information has been printed out in a different order from the order in which the students were originally added to the Hashtable. Entries in a Hashtable aren't retrieved in any particular order by an IDictionaryEnumerator; we're simply guaranteed that we'll have iterated through all the items.

Iterating Through Generic ICollections

Recall that when we were talking earlier about Hashtables, we mentioned that they have two properties—Keys and Values—of type ICollection. Let's look at a way to iterate through the elements of a generic ICollection.

An ICollection object only has access to one method named CopyTo that has the following header:

```
void CopyTo(Array array, int index)
```

The CopyTo method is used to copy the contents of an ICollection into an Array object. If you recall from Chapter 6, the Array class is the parent of all C# arrays. The index parameter is the index of the array at which to begin copying the ICollection elements. Once the keys and/or values are transferred into an Array, the elements of the array can be accessed in the normal fashion.

As an example of iterating through the keys and values of a Hashtable, we'll use the same Student class as defined previously, but different driver code:

```
using System;
using System.Collections;

public class EnumDemo3
{
  static void Main() {
    // Create an instance of a Hashtable.
    Hashtable students = new Hashtable();

    // Instantiate several Student objects.
    Student s1 = new Student("123-45-6789", "John Smith");
    Student s2 = new Student("987-65-4321", "Yukio Koyari");
    Student s3 = new Student("654-32-1987", "Maria Lopez");

    // Store their handles in the Hashtable, using the Ssn value as the key.
    students.Add(s1.Ssn, s1);
    students.Add(s2.Ssn, s2);
    students.Add(s3.Ssn, s3);
```

```
    // Obtain two ICollections for the Hashtable, using the Keys
    // and Values properties.
    ICollection keys = students.Keys;
    ICollection values = students.Values;

    // Create string and Student arrays that will hold
    // the keys and values.
    string[] studentIDs = new string[students.Count];
    Student[] studentObjects = new Student[students.Count];

    // Copy the contents of the ICollections into the arrays.
    keys.CopyTo(studentIDs, 0);
    values.CopyTo(studentObjects, 0);

    // Iterate through both.

    Console.WriteLine("Student IDs (Keys):");
    for(int i = 0; i < studentIDs.Length; ++i) {
      Console.WriteLine("Student ID: " + studentIDs[i]);
    }

    Console.WriteLine("Students (Values):");
    for(int i=0; i < studentObjects.Length; ++i) {
      Console.WriteLine(s.Name + ": " + s.Ssn);
    }
  }
}
```

When this program is run, the following output is produced:

```
Student IDs (Keys):
Student ID: 654-32-1987
Student ID: 987-65-4321
Student ID: 123-45-6789

Students (Values):
Maria Lopez: 654-32-1987
Yukio Koyari: 987-65-4321
John Smith: 123-45-6789
```

foreach Loop

The foreach loop is a C# flow of control structure beyond those that we discussed in Chapter 1. A foreach loop provides yet another way to iterate through the elements of an Array or other type of ICollection.

The general syntax of the foreach loop is as follows:

```
foreach (type variable_name in collection_name) {
    // code to be executed
}
```

Inside the parentheses following the foreach keyword, we find

- The type of items in the collection being processed—items retrieved from the collection being processed are automatically cast to this type.

- A local reference variable that refers one-by-one to each of the items in the collection in turn.

- The name of the collection to be searched, preceded by the keyword in.

For example:

```
// An int array.
int[] numbers = { 1, 3, 5, 7, 9 };
int sum = 0;

foreach (int x in numbers) {
    // Do whatever we wish to do with x; note that no cast is required;
    // x will automatically refer to an int.
    Console.WriteLine("Adding " + x + " to sum ...");
    sum += x;
}

Console.WriteLine("Sum = " + sum);
```

The preceding code snippet produces the following output:

```
Adding 1 to sum ...
Adding 3 to sum ...
Adding 5 to sum ...
Adding 7 to sum ...
Adding 9 to sum ...
Sum = 25
```

As another example:

```
// A collection of Student references.
ArrayList studentBody = new ArrayList();
// Details of populating the studentBody collection are omitted.

foreach (Student s in studentBody) {
  // Do whatever we wish with s; note that no cast is required;
  // s will automatically refer to a Student.
  s.ComputeGPA();
}
```

The block of code provided as part of the foreach statement is executed every time another element of the specified type is retrieved by the foreach loop.

Note that once we begin iterating within a foreach block, we can't change where the foreach reference variable is "pointing" by attempting to assign a new value to the variable; that is, the following won't compile:

```
foreach (Student s in studentBody) {
  // This will not compile!  Reference s is read-only.
  s = (Student) studentBody[0];
}
error CS1604: cannot assign to 's' because it is read-only
```

Of course, the object *referred to* by s is accessible/*modifiable* the same way that *any* object is once we have a reference to it:

```
foreach (Student s in studentBody) {
  // This is perfectly OK to do.
  s.Name = "?";
}
```

Here is one final example of using a foreach loop to iterate through the elements of an ArrayList that contains a mixture of Professor and Student objects. Assuming that both the Professor and Student classes are derived from the Person class, we'll use the common supertype Person as the type being searched for in the ArrayList. The name of each Person in the ArrayList is displayed.

```
using System;
using System.Collections;

public class ForeachDemo
{
  static void Main() {
    //  Create an ArrayList and fill it with a mix of Student
    //  and Professor objects.
```

```
ArrayList people = new ArrayList();
people.Add(new Professor("Jacquie Barker"));
people.Add(new Student("Maria Vasquez"));
people.Add(new Professor("John Carson"));
people.Add(new Professor("Mike Vito"));
people.Add(new Student("Jackson Palmer"));

// Use a foreach loop to retrieve Person object references from the
// ArrayList, and print out their names.
foreach (Person p in people) {
  Console.WriteLine(p.Name);
}
}
}
```

This results in the following output:

```
Jacquie Barker
Maria Vasquez
John Carson
Mike Vito
Jackson Palmer
```

Of course, if we try to do an implicit cast via a foreach statement to a type that is invalid for some item in the collection as of run time, an InvalidCastException will be thrown, just as when we attempt an invalid *explicit* cast.

Initialization of Variables, Revisited

We said back in Chapter 1 that trying to access variables without explicitly initializing them will result in a compilation error. For example, this next bit of code

```
public class Example
{
  static void Main() {
      // Declare several local variables within the Main() method.
      int i;  // not automatically initialized
      int j;  // ditto
      j = i;  // compilation error!
  }
}
```

was shown to produce the following compilation error on the line that is highlighted in the snippet:

```
error CS0165: Use of unassigned local variable 'i'
```

We also stated in Chapter 3 that variables are implicitly assigned their zero-equivalent value in some situations, if we haven't explicitly assigned them a value.

Both of these statements regarding initialization of variables were a bit oversimplified, however, and we'd like to correct the oversimplification now.

To properly understand the notion of initialization in C#, we must differentiate between *local variables*—that is, variables declared *within a method,* and whose scope is therefore limited to that method (recall our discussion of the scope of a variable in Chapter 1)—and *fields* of a class (whether instance or static variables), which are declared at the class scope level. As it turns out:

- All local variables, of any type, are considered by the compiler to be uninitialized until they have been ***explicitly initialized*** within a program.

- ***All fields,*** on the other hand, of any type, are ***automatically initialized*** to their zero-equivalent values—that is, bools are initialized to false, numerics to either 0 or 0.0, reference types to null, and so forth.

Here is an example illustrating all of these points:

```
public class Student
{
  // Fields ARE automatically initialized.
  private int age;                    // initialized to 0
  private double gpa;                 // initialized to 0.0
  private bool isHonorsStudent;       // initialized to false
  private Professor myAdvisor;        // initialized to null
  // This includes STATIC variables.
  private static int studentCount;    // initialized to 0
  // etc.

  // Methods.
  public void UpdateGPA() {
    // Local variables are NOT automatically initialized.
    double val;    // NOT initialized -- value is undefined.
    Course c;      // NOT initialized -- value is undefined.
    // etc.
  }
}
```

More About the Main Method

In Chapter 1, we introduced the Main method as the initial point of execution for a C# program. We'd now like to go into a little more detail on some features and nuances of the Main method.

Main Method Variants

It turns out that there are actually four variations of the Main method header:

- The first is the version we introduced in Chapter 1—a parameterless method with a return type of void:

```
static void Main()
```

- The next version returns a result of type int instead:

```
static int Main()
```

Returning an int value is a way to signal to the execution environment (operating system) the status of how the program terminated:

```
public class Foo
{
  static int Main() {
    if (something goes awry) {
      return -1;
    }
    else {
      // All is well!
      return 0;
    }
  }
}
```

(A return value of 0 is typically used to indicate that the program executed normally.)

- Then, we have two forms of Main that take an array of strings as an argument, representing command-line arguments that can be passed in to the Main method when the program is invoked. Note that the name given to this array, typically "args", can in actuality be any valid array name:

```
static void Main(string[] args)
static int Main(string[] args)
```

We'll talk about passing command-line arguments into a C# program in more detail later in this chapter.

Note that none of the four Main method headers includes an access modifier (e.g., public). If we were to include one, the runtime will ignore it. The C# convention is to omit the access modifier from the Main method.

Static Main

Why must the Main method of an application be declared to be static? At the moment that the .NET runtime launches an application by calling its Main method, no objects exist yet, because it's the Main method that will **start** the process of instantiating our application's objects. Thus, we're faced with a "chicken vs. egg" dilemma: how can we invoke the Main method to initiate object creation if we don't have an initial object to invoke it upon?

As we learned in Chapter 7, a static method is a type of method that can be invoked on a class as a whole, even if we don't have an instance of that class handy. So, before any objects have yet been created, the best option for the designers of C# was to mandate that the Main method be designed as a static method, so that it could be called on the class that serves as the "wrapper" for that method.

Developing Command Line-Driven Applications

We occasionally have a need to develop a command line–driven application—i.e., an application that doesn't have a formal GUI front-end for either soliciting input from the user or for displaying output to the user. When building such applications, we need to be able to

- Accept input, either by

  - Reading data from the command line, in the form of command-line arguments, or

  - Accepting keyboard input as typed by the user

- Display textual messages to the user, including both prompts for input as well as feedback on operations that have been performed.

Reading Command-Line Arguments

As mentioned earlier, the Main method can accept command-line arguments. Such arguments are typically used to either pass in small amounts of data, or to control some aspect of the program's execution.

Command-line arguments are included as part of the command to execute a C# application, following the name of the driver class on the command line. For example, if we wanted to provide an executable named SimpleProgram.exe with the command-line arguments Jackson, ABC, and 123, we would type the following command to run the program:

```
SimpleProgram Jackson ABC 123
```

Such data gets passed to the Main method of the C# program as a string array called args (or whatever else we wish to name it, as indicated by the Main method's parameter list). To accept command-line arguments, therefore, a program must use one of the two forms of the Main method that takes a string array as a parameter:

```
static void Main(string[] args)
static int Main(string[] args)
```

The args array is automatically sized to hold however many arguments are provided on the command line when the program is invoked. In the SimpleProgram invocation at the beginning of this section, the args array would contain three entries: the string "Jackson" would be placed as the zeroeth element of the args array, the string "ABC" would be the next element of args, and the string "123" would be the last element.

Inside the Main method, we can do with args whatever we'd do with any other array; for example, determine its length, manipulate individual string items within the array, and so forth. The program that follows illustrates some of the things that we might wish to do with command-line arguments:

```
// FruitExample.cs

// This nonsensical program is intended to illustrate command line argument
// passing.

using System;

public class FruitExample {
    // The signature of the Main method can declare as an
    // argument a string array named 'args'. (We can name the
    // array whatever we'd like, but 'args' is the standard
```

```
// name that most people use.)
//
// This array is automatically initialized when the program is run
// from the command prompt with whatever (space-separated)
// values ('arguments') we've typed on the command line
// after the program name.
//
// For example, if this compiled program is run from the
// command prompt as follows:
//
//      FruitExample apple banana cherry
//
// then the args array will be automatically initialized with
// three string objects "apple", "banana", and "cherry" which
// will be stored in array elements args[0], args[1], and
// args[2], respectively.

static void Main(string[] args) {
  // Let's print out a few things.
  Console.WriteLine("The args array contains " + args.Length +
                    " entries." );

  // Only execute this next block of code if the array isn't empty.
  // The Length property returns the number of elements in the array.
  if (args.Length > 0) {
    int last = args.Length - 1;
    Console.WriteLine("The last array entry is: " + args[last]);

    // Every string has a Length property, as well, that contains
    // the number of characters in the string.
    Console.WriteLine("The last array entry is " + args[last].Length +
                      " characters long.");
  }
  else {
    Console.WriteLine("No command line arguments detected.");
  }
 }
}
```

When this program is run from the command line as follows:

```
FruitExample apple banana cherry
```

it produces the following output:

```
The args array contains 3 entries.
The last array entry is: cherry
The last array entry is 6 characters long.
```

Command-Line Arguments As Control Flags

In addition to passing data in via the command line, command-line arguments are also a convenient way to control a program's operation through the use of **control flags.** In the following example, valid ways to invoke the FlagExample program would be as follows:

```
FlagExample -b
FlagExample -f
```

whereas failure to provide a command-line control flag, or providing an invalid flag, causes appropriate error messages to be printed (please refer to in-line comments):

```csharp
using System;

public class FlagExample
{
  static void Main(string[] args) {
    // If the user hasn't provided a control flag, report an error.
    if (args.Length != 1) {
      Console.WriteLine("Usage:  FlagExample -x    where x may be f or b");
    }
    else {
      if (args[0] == "-f") {
        Console.WriteLine("FOO!");
      }
      else if (args[0] == "-b") {
        Console.WriteLine("BAR ...");
      }
      else {
        Console.WriteLine("Incorrect control flag:  " + args[0]);
      }
    }
  }
}
```

Invoking the program properly as follows:

```
FlagExample -f
```

would produce as output

```
FOO!
```

because –f is a "legal" command-line flag, whereas invoking the program without providing a flag, as follows:

```
FlagExample
```

would produce as output

```
Usage:  FlagExample -x      where x may be f or b
```

Providing an invalid flag as follows:

```
FlagExample -a
```

would produce as output

```
Incorrect control flag:  -a
```

Accepting Keyboard Input

Most applications receive information either directly from users via an application's graphical user interface, or by reading information from a file or database. But, until you've learned how to program such things in C# in Chapters 15 and 16, it's handy to know how to prompt for textual input from the command-line window.

To read keyboard input, we'll turn once again to the Console class from the System namespace. The Console class declares a ReadLine method that can be used to read keyboard input.

```
public static string ReadLine()
```

Data is read character by character but is buffered internally by this method until the Enter key is pressed, at which point an entire line of input is returned by the method as a string.

The ReadLine method reads data from the standard input I/O stream, which in most cases is associated with the keyboard. The ReadLine method can generate an IOException, so calls to the method should be enclosed in a try block.

Here is a simple example that illustrates reading data from the keyboard using the ReadLine method; we'll present the program in its entirety first, then will narrate it in step-by-step fashion.

```
using System;
using System.IO;

public class KeyboardDemo
{
  static void Main() {
    string name = "";

    try {
      // Prompt the user for input; note the use of
      // Write() vs. WriteLine(), so that the prompt will
      // be displayed on the same line as the text entered
      // by the user.
      Console.Write("Enter your name: ");

      // Read their response from the keyboard.
      name = Console.ReadLine();
    }
    catch (IOException ioe) {
      Console.WriteLine("IO Exception occurred: " + ioe);
    }

    // Display the input back as a test.
    Console.WriteLine("Name entered was " + name);
  }
}
```

Stepping through the code:

- When the KeyboardDemo program is run, the user is prompted to enter his or her name via a call to the Console.Write method:

  ```
  Console.Write("Enter your name: ");
  ```

  Note our use of Write vs. WriteLine, so that the prompt will be displayed on the same line as the text entered by the user.

- The value of a local string variable called name is set to the string value returned by the ReadLine method:

```
name = Console.ReadLine();
```

This operation is performed inside a try block.

- A catch clause is provided to catch IOExceptions. In a real-life application, we might want to provide a more extensive response to the exception, but in this simple example we just print out a message that an exception has occurred. The IOException class is from the System.IO namespace, so the appropriate using directive is placed at the top of the code.

Running this program would produce the following results (**bolded text** reflects input by the user):

```
Enter your name: Jackie Chan
Name entered was Jackie Chan
```

Printing to the Screen, Revisited

As we saw in Chapter 1, we invoke one of two methods—Console.WriteLine() or Console.Write()—to print text messages to the command-line window as follows:

```
Console.WriteLine(expression to be printed);
Console.Write(expression to be printed);
```

We glossed over the syntax of this particular operation when this capability was first introduced; now that we know much more about objects, let's revisit this syntax in more depth.

Console is a class provided by the CLR Base Class Library (part of the Framework Class Library) within the System namespace. The Console class defines numerous overloaded static Write and WriteLine methods; the various versions each accept a different argument type—string, the various predefined value types, or arbitrary object references:

```
public static void WriteLine(string s)
public static void WriteLine(int i)
public static void WriteLine(double d)
public static void WriteLine(bool b)
public static void WriteLine(object obj)
```

and so forth (the same is true for Write).

The Write and WriteLine methods can accept expressions of arbitrary complexity, and do their best to ultimately render these into a single string value, which then gets displayed to the standard output window—i.e., the command-line window from which we invoked the program. This is accomplished by calling the ToString method "behind the scenes" on ***nonstring*** arguments to render a string representation of the argument, as discussed earlier in this chapter.

The following code snippet illustrates several complex invocations of Console.Write. The expression being passed in as an argument to the first call to Write ultimately evaluates to a string value, and the expression being passed in as an argument to the second call to Write evaluates to a double value; thus, two different (overloaded) versions of the Write method are being called in this example:

```
Professor p = new Professor();
// Details omitted.
Console.Write("Professor " + p.Name + " has an advisee named " +
              p.Advisee.Name + " with a GPA of ");
Console.Write(p.Advisee.ComputeGPA());
Console.WriteLine(".");
```

Here's some simulated output:

```
Professor Jacquie Barker has an advisee named Sandy Tucker with a GPA of 4.0.
```

Object Self-Referencing with "this"

In client code, such as the Main method of a program, we declare reference variables with which to store handles on objects:

```
Student s = new Student();  // s is a reference variable of type Student.
```

and can then conveniently access the objects that these reference variables refer to by manipulating the reference variables themselves:

```
s.Name = "Fred";
```

When we're executing the code that comprises the body of one of an object's own methods, we sometimes need the object to be able to refer to itself—i.e., to **self-reference,** as in this next bit of code:

```
public class Student
{
  Professor facultyAdvisor;
  // other details omitted
```

```
public void SelectAdvisor(Professor p) {
    // We're down in the "bowels" of the SelectAdvisor() method,
    // executing this method for a particular Student object.

    // We save the handle on our new advisor as one of our fields ...
    facultyAdvisor = p;

    // ... and now we want to turn around and tell this Professor object to
    // add us as one of its (Student) advisees. The Professor class has a
    // method with signature:
    //
    //          public void AddAdvisee(Student s);
    //
    // so, all we need to do is call this method on our advisor object
    // and pass in a reference to ourselves; but who the heck are we?
    // That is, how do we refer to ourself?
    p.AddAdvisee(???);
  }
}
```

Within the body of a method, when we need a way to refer to the object whose method we're executing, we use the reserved word this to "self-reference." So, in our preceding example, the following line of code would do the trick:

```
p.AddAdvisee(this);
```

Specifically, it would pass a reference to *this* Student—the Student object whose method we're executing at this very moment—as an argument of the AddAdvisee method, to Professor p.

We mentioned back in Chapter 4 that we may invoke one method/feature of a class from within another method of the *same* class without using dot notation:

```
public class Student
{
    // details omitted

    public void MethodA() {
        // We can call MethodB from within MethodA without
        // using dot notation.
        MethodB();
        // other details omitted ...
    }
```

```
  public void MethodB() {
    // details omitted ...
  }
}
```

As it turns out, this is shorthand for the following equivalent dot notation:

```
public void MethodA() {
  // Calling MethodB from within MethodA.
  this.MethodB();
  // other details omitted ...
}
```

Since the `this.` prefix is implied, we needn't include it, but are free to do so if we wish.

We'll see yet another use for the `this` keyword, having to do with constructors, in a moment.

Constructors, Revisited

We learned in Chapter 4 that when we instantiate a brand-new object with the `new` operator, we're creating a "bare bones" object with essentially empty fields (each field will be initialized to 0, `null`, or whatever is appropriate for a given field type, as we discussed earlier). We also learned that if we want to create an object in a more intelligent fashion—that is, to do more elaborate things when the object is first created—we need to declare a constructor. By way of review, a constructor

- Has the same name as the class

- Has no explicit return type, because it really has a ***default*** return type matching the class that it's defined for—a constructor returns a brand-new object/instance of that type

- Can take any number or variety of arguments

Here's one simple example of a constructor for the `Student` class:

```
public class Student
{
  // Fields.
  private string name;
  // other details omitted
```

```
// A constructor. (Note: no return type!)
// This constructor passes in a string value representing the name that is
// to be assigned to the Student object when it is first instantiated.
public Student(string n) {
    name = n;
}

// etc.
}
```

We'll now provide some new insights regarding constructors.

Constructor Overloading

We can create many different constructors for the same class that take different combinations of arguments—this is known as *overloading,* a concept that we discussed in Chapter 5. As long as each constructor has a different argument signature, it's considered to be a different constructor:

```
// One argument, a string.
public Student(string name) {
    // details omitted ...
}

// Two string arguments; this is OK!
public Student(string name, string ssn) {
    // details omitted ...
}

// One int, one string; this is also OK!
public Student(string name, int id) {
    // details omitted ...
}
```

If we tried to add the following *fourth* constructor to the Student class, it would be *rejected* by the compiler, since there is already another constructor with two string arguments—the fact that the parameter names are different is immaterial.

```
public Student(string firstName, string lastName) {
    // details omitted ...
}
```

Replacing the Default Parameterless Constructor

We learned in Chapter 4 that if we don't declare any constructors for a class, a default parameterless constructor is provided by the system that will initialize any fields to their zero-equivalent values. There is one very important caveat about default constructors in C#: if we invent ***any*** of our own constructors for a class, with any argument signature, then the default parameterless constructor is ***not*** automatically provided. This is by design, because it's assumed that if we've gone to the trouble to program any constructors whatsoever, then we must have some special initialization requirements for our class that the C# default constructor couldn't possibly anticipate.

If we want or need a parameterless constructor for a particular class ***along with*** other versions of constructors that ***do*** take arguments, we must explicitly program a parameterless constructor ourselves. Generally speaking, it's considered good practice to always explicitly provide a parameterless constructor if we're explicitly providing any other constructors at all.

Here is another version of a Student class, this time with multiple constructors provided; note that here we're indeed replacing the "lost" parameterless constructor (please read in-line comments):

```
// Student.cs

using System;

public class Student
{
  private string name;
  private string ssn;
  private Professor facultyAdvisor;

  // Constructors.

  // This version takes three arguments.
  public Student(string n, string s, Professor p) {
    name = n;
    ssn = s;
    facultyAdvisor = p;
  }

  // This "flavor" takes two arguments.
  public Student(string n, string s) {
    name = n;
    ssn = s;
```

```
      // Since we aren't getting a Professor object handed in to us in
      // this version, we set the facultyAdvisor field to null for the
      // time being.  (Strictly speaking, we don't need to do this, as it
      // will automatically be initialized to null anyway -- but, this makes it
      // clear to anyone reading the code.)
      facultyAdvisor = null;
   }


   // We must explicitly provide a parameterless constructor (if we want
   // to be able to use such a constructor) if we have created ANY other
   // constructors.
   public Student() {
      // Note here that we've decided to invent some "placeholder"
      // values for the name and ssn fields in the case where
      // specific values are not being passed in.

      name = "???";
      ssn = "???-??-????";
      facultyAdvisor = null;
   }


   public string Name {
      // Accessor details omitted.
   }


   // etc. for other properties

   public string GetFacultyAdvisorName() {
      // Note: since some of our constructors initialize facultyAdvisor with
      // a Professor object, and others do not, we cannot assume that the
      // field has been initialized to a Professor "handle" when the
      // GetFacultyAdvisorName() method is invoked. To avoid the possibility
      // of throwing a NullReferenceException, we check to make sure that the
      // facultyAdvisor field is NOT null before proceeding.
      if (facultyAdvisor != null) {
         return facultyAdvisor.Name;
      }
      else {
         return "TBD";
      }
   }
}
```

Here is a simplistic version of a `Professor` class to use in testing:

```
// Professor.cs

public class Professor {
  private string name;

  public string Name {
    get {
      return name;
    }
    set {
      name = value;
    }
  }
}
```

and, here is a main program that exercises the various forms of constructor:

```
public class MyProgram
{
  static void Main() {
    Student[] students = new Student[3];
    Professor p;

    p = new Professor();
    p.SetName("Dr. Oompah");

    // We'll try out the various Student constructor signatures.
    students[0] = new Student("Joe", "123-45-6789", p);
    students[1] = new Student("Bob", "987-65-4321");
    students[2] = new Student();

    Console.WriteLine("Advisor Information\n");
    for (int i = 0; i < students.Length; i++) {
      Console.WriteLine("Name:   " + students[i].Name +
        "\tAdvisor:   " +
        students[i].GetFacultyAdvisorName());
    }
  }
}
```

The preceding program produces the following output when run at the command line:

```
Advisor Information

Name:  Joe    Advisor:  Dr. Oompah
Name:  Bob    Advisor:  TBD
Name:  ???    Advisor:  TBD
```

There are some additional complexities that you need to be aware of when it comes to constructors of derived classes and inheritance—we'll discuss these later in this chapter, in the section titled "More About Inheritance and C#."

Reusing Constructor Code Within a Class

We talked about the use of the this keyword for object self-referencing earlier in this chapter; another noteworthy use of the this keyword has to do with reusing constructor code.

If we have a class that declares more than one form of constructor, and we wish to reuse the code from one constructor in the body of another constructor, we can use the expression

```
: this(optional arguments)
```

in the declaration of a constructor as a shorthand way of running one constructor from within another. This is best illustrated by a short example.

```
// Student.cs

using System;

public class Student
{
  private string name;
  private string ssn;
  private Transcript transcript;

  // Constructors.

  // This version takes one argument.
  public Student(string n) {
    name = n;
    transcript = new Transcript();
    // do some other complicated things ...
  }
```

```
// This version takes two arguments.  We want to reuse the logic
// from the preceding constructor without having to repeat the
// same code in both constructors. We can invoke the one-argument
// constructor from this two-argument version by using the
// "this" keyword in the manner shown below:
public Student(string n, string s) : this(n) {
    // Now, we can go on to do other "extra" things that this version
    // of the constructor needs to take care of.
    ssn = s;
}


// etc.
}
```

By using the syntax : this(n) in this fashion, it's as if we've written the code for the second constructor as follows:

```
public Student(string n, string s) {
    // Duplicate the code from the first constructor ...
    name = n;
    transcript = new Transcript();
    // do some other complicated things ...

    // ... then go on to do other "extra" things that this version
    // of the constructor needs to take care of.
    ssn = s;
}
```

but *without* having to duplicate code from the first constructor. Thus, by using the : this(...) syntax to reuse constructor code from one version to another, if the logic of the first constructor changes down the road, the second constructor will also benefit.

Because each overloaded version of a constructor in a class is guaranteed to have a unique parameter list, the argument signature being passed into the this(...) expression will unambiguously select the alternative constructor that is to be invoked.

Note that if constructor version 1 invokes constructor version 2 in this manner, the invocation of constructor version 2 is the *first* operation performed when the constructor version 1 is invoked. That is, by the time the first explicit line of code of constructor 1 is executed, all of the code of constructor 2 may be assumed to have already executed, as illustrated here:

```
public Student(string n, string s) : this(n) {
    // The single argument constructor has already run to completion
    // by the time we reach this first line of code ...
    // details omitted.
}
```

More About Inheritance and C#

From our discussion of inheritance in Chapter 5, we learned that

- Inheritance is used to derive a new class definition from an existing class when the new class is perceived to be a special case of the existing class.

- The derived class automatically inherits the data structure and behaviors of the base class.

- C# uses a colon followed by a class name in a class declaration to signal that one class is derived from another:

```
public class Person
{
    string name;

    public string Name {
        get {
            return name;
        }
        set {
            name = value;
        }
    }
}
```

```
// We derive the Student class from Person.
public class Student : Person
{
    // If we define nothing in the body of this class, it will still have
    // one field -- name -- and one property -- Name -- because these are
    // inherited from Person.  (Actually, we have more features than that,
    // because Person in turn inherits features from Object!)
}
```

Although we mastered the basics of inheritance in that chapter, it turns out that there are a lot of important subtleties about inheritance in C# that we haven't yet discussed; we'll do so now.

Accessibility of Inherited Components

By virtue of inheritance, everything defined in a base class is automatically present in a derived class—inheritance is an "all-or-nothing" proposition. However, some inherited features (fields, methods, properties, and so on) may not be directly accessible by the derived class, depending on their access permissions as assigned in the base class.

Consider the following base class:

```
public class Person
{
  // Field.
  accessibility_modifier int age;

  // Other details of this class omitted.
}
```

Accessibility for a feature, as we learned in Chapter 4, can be one of the following:

- private

- public

- protected

- internal

- protected internal

- Unspecified, which for features defaults to private

We learned in Chapter 4 about public and private accessibility; a feature given protected accessibility is in scope and hence publicly available to derived classes but private to everything else. The other two accessibilities, internal and protected internal, are less frequently used and a discussion of them is beyond the scope of this book.

Suppose that we derive the Student class from Person as follows:

```
public class Student : Person
{
  // The age field is inherited from the base class ...
  // here, we add a method that directly manipulates this field
  // by name.
  public bool IsOver65( ) {
    if (age > 65) {
      return true;
    }
    else {
      return false;
    }
  }
}
```

What will happen when we try to compile the Student class? The answer to this question depends on how access has been defined for the age field of Person.

- If we declared age to be either protected or public in Person, then the age field is both inherited and directly accessible to the Student class by its simple name, and the Student class shown earlier will compile without error.

- If, on the other hand, age is declared to be private in Person, then we'll get a compilation error on following line of Student code:

```
if (age > 65) {
```

The error message will be

```
error CS0122: 'Person.age' is inaccessible due to its protection level
```

That's because the age field is indeed inherited—it's part of the data structure comprising a Student object—but it's nonetheless "invisible" to the Student class! It's analogous to an internal organ in our body: e.g., our heart is part of our physical body, but we can't see or access it directly.

If our inclination is to make all fields private, how can a subclass *ever* manipulate its privately inherited fields? The answer is quite simple: through the public (or protected) accessor methods or properties that it has also inherited from its parent class. We've revised the previous example program to illustrate this technique.

First, we make sure that the parent Person class provides a public Age property (good programming practice would always call for this anyway):

```
public class Person
{
  private int age;
  // details omitted

  // We provide a property for subclasses to inherit.
  // (The property could be given protected access if
  // we ONLY want subclasses to access it.)
  public int Age {
    get {
      return age;
    }
    set {
      age = value;
    }
  }
}
```

Then, we use the ***inherited*** Age property from within the Student's IsOver65 method, and we're back in business: Student compiles without error.

```
public class Student : Person
{
  // other details omitted.

  public bool IsOver65( ) {
    // Even though the age field per se is inaccessible,
    // the Age property that we inherit from Person
    // allows us to access the value of the age attribute.
    if (Age > 65) return true;
    else return false;
  }
}
```

As we mentioned back in Chapter 4, it's generally considered good practice to always use properties to access the values of fields, even from within a class's own methods, so as to take advantage of any special processing that the property accessors might provide relative to that field.

Reusing Base Class Behaviors: The "base" Keyword

As we learned in Chapter 5, if we provide a method in a derived class whose signature matches that of a base class method (identical method name and parameter list) then we're said to have ***overridden*** the base class method. When would we want/need to do this? When the derived class needs to do something slightly more specialized in response to a message than its base class did, as in the following example:

```
public class Person
{
  private string name;
  private string ssn;

  public string Name {
    // Accessor details omitted.
  }

  // etc. for Ssn

  // Have a Person object describe itself.
  public virtual string GetDescription() {
    return Name + " (" + Ssn + ")";
    // e.g., "John Doe (123-45-6789)"
  }
}

public class Student : Person
{
  private string major;

  public string Major {
    // Accessor details omitted.
  }

  // We want a Student object to return a description of itself
  // differently from the way its parent class (Person) does so.
  // So, we equip this subclass with a method having the exact
  // same signature as was defined for its parent class; this
  // version of the method overrides (masks) the inherited version.
  public override string GetDescription() {
    return Name + " (" + Ssn + ") [" + Major + "]";
    // e.g., "Mary Smith (987-65-4321) [Math]"
  }
}
```

As we learned in Chapter 5, a derived class method can call a base class version of the same method using the base keyword. This feature allows us to reduce code redundancy because we can reuse the work done by the base class method and then add in whatever additional code the derived class method needs.

Let's streamline the GetDescription method of the Student class such that it first calls the Person class version of the same method.

```
public class Student : Person
{
  string major;

  // etc.

  // Exact same method signature as was defined for Person -- so, this
  // method overrides (masks) the inherited version.
  public override string GetDescription() {
    // Notice, however, that we are now calling the parent class's version
    // of the method so as to reuse that code.
    return base.GetDescription() + " [" + Major + "]";
    // e.g., "Mary Smith (123-45-6789) [Math]"
  }
}
```

Just as the this keyword is used to generically refer to an object from within one of its methods, base is used when we want to generically refer to the parent class's version of a feature from within one of its methods.

Another important use of the base keyword has to do with constructors and inheritance, which we'll discuss next.

Inheritance and Constructors

Constructors aren't inherited in the same manner that methods are. This raises some interesting complications that are best illustrated via an example.

Let's start by declaring a constructor for the Person class that takes two arguments:

```
public class Person
{
  string name;
  string ssn;

  // Public properties Name and Ssn are declared; details omitted.

  // Only one constructor is explicitly declared.
  public Person(string n, string s) {
    Name = n;
```

```
    Ssn = s;
  }


  // etc.
}
```

We know from an earlier discussion that the Person class now only recognizes one constructor signature—one that takes two arguments—because the default parameterless constructor for Person has been eliminated.

Now, say that we derive the Student class from Person, and furthermore that we want the Student class to define two constructors—one that takes two arguments and one that takes three arguments. Because constructors aren't inherited, we won't automatically benefit from the fact that the Person class has already gone to the trouble to define a constructor that takes two arguments; we have to recode one explicitly for Student, as follows:

```
public class Student : Person
{
  string major;

  // Major property provided; details omitted.

  // Constructor that takes two arguments.
  public Student(string n, string s) {
    // Note the redundancy of logic between this constructor and
    // the parent constructor -- we'll come back and fix this in a
    // moment.
    Name = n;  // redundant
    Ssn = s;   // redundant
    Major = null;
  }

  // Constructor that takes three arguments.
  public Student(string n, string s, string m) {
    // MORE redundancy!
    Name = n;  // redundant
    Ssn = s;   // redundant
    Major = m;
  }

  // No other constructors are explicitly declared.
}
```

Fortunately, there is a way to reuse a parent class's constructor code without having to duplicate its logic in the derived class's constructor(s). We accomplish this via the same base keyword we discussed a moment ago for the reuse of methods. To explicitly reuse a particular parent class's constructor, we refer to it as : base(*optional arguments*), and pass in whatever arguments it needs, as the following revised version of the Student class illustrates:

```
public class Student : Person
{
    string major;

    // Constructor that takes two arguments.
    // We'll explicitly invoke the Person constructor with two
    // arguments, passing in the values of n and s.
    public Student(string n, string s) : base(n, s) {
        // We can now concentrate on only those things that need be done
        // uniquely for a Student.
        major = null;
    }

    // Constructor that takes three arguments.
    // See above comments.
    public Student(string n, string s, string m) : base(n, s) {
        major = m;
    }
}
```

Similar to the situation in which we used the syntax : this(...) to reuse constructor code within the *same* class, if a *derived* class constructor calls a *base* class constructor, that call is the *first* operation performed when the derived class constructor is invoked.

Implied Invocations of base()

Whether we *explicitly* invoke a base class constructor from a derived class constructor using the : base(...) construct or not, the fact is that C# will always attempt to execute constructors for all of the ancestor classes for a given class, from most general to most specific in the class hierarchy, before launching into a given class's constructor code.

For example, when we create a Student object, we're in reality simultaneously creating an Object, a Person, and a Student, for a Student is all three! So, when we invoke a Student constructor, then an Object constructor will be executed first, followed by a Person constructor, followed by a Student constructor. So, if we were to write a Student constructor without taking advantage of the base(...) syntax, as shown here:

```
public class Student : Person
{
  string major;

  // Constructor that takes two arguments.
  // Here, we're not calling any particular base constructor.
  public Student(string n, string s) {
    // We can now concentrate on only those things that need be done
    // uniquely for a Student.
    major = null;
  }
}
```

it's as if we've written the following code instead (note **bolding**):

```
public class Student : Person
{
  string major;

  // Constructor that takes two arguments.
  public Student(string n, string s) : base() {
    // We can now concentrate on only those things that need be done
    // uniquely for a Student.
    major = null;
  }
}
```

thereby explicitly calling the parameterless Person constructor.

This makes intuitive sense, because we said that inheritance represents the "is a" relationship—a Student is a Person, and a Person is an Object—so whatever we have to do when we create an object and a Person will also be required when we create a Student. The question is, *which* base class constructor will be called if we've defined more than one?

There are several different scenarios that we must explore in answering this question.

Case #1: A Derived Class Declares No Constructors of Its Own

We already know that if we derive a class such as Student, but don't bother to define any constructors for the derived class, then C# will attempt to provide us with a default parameterless constructor for that derived class. When we create a new object of the derived class, the parameterless constructor for each of the ancestor class(es) automatically will get called in top-down fashion, with the default constructor of the derived class being called last. The implication of this phenomenon is that if we've derived a class B from class A, and expect to use B's default parameterless constructor, then the ***base class*** A must also have a para-meterless constructor available for B's constructor to call, either explicitly programmed or by default.

The following example won't compile (we'll explain why in a moment):

```
public class Person
{
  string name;

  // A constructor that takes one argument - by having created this,
  // we've lost Person's default (parameterless) constructor.
  public Person(string n) {
    name = n;
  }

  // The parameterless constructor is not being replaced in this example.
}

public class Student : Person
{
  string major;

  // NO constructors are explicitly defined for Student!  So, all
  // we get for Student is the default parameterless constructor.
}
```

When we try to compile Student, we'll get the following (rather cryptic) error message:

```
error CS1501: No overload for method 'Person' takes '0' arguments
```

This is because the C# compiler is trying to create a default constructor that takes no arguments for the Student class but, in order to do so, it knows that it's going to need to be able to call a parameterless constructor for a Person from within the Student default constructor—but, no such constructor for Person exists! The compiler is, in essence, trying to generate the following default constructor for Student:

```
public Student() : base() {
  // Initialize a "bare bones" Student -- details omitted.
}
```

The only way around this dilemma is to either

- Explicitly program a parameterless constructor for the Person class, to replace the "lost" default Person constructor, for the compiler to take advantage of when creating a default Student class constructor (this is the ***preferred*** approach); or

- Always use a constructor for the Student class that ***explicitly*** invokes a ***particular*** version of Person constructor through use of the base keyword.

This latter option is explored in the next case.

Case #2: The Derived Class Explicitly Declares One or More Constructors

This can actually be split into two subcases:

Subcase #2A: Derived Class Constructor Does Not Explicitly Invoke a Base Class Constructor

If a base class constructor isn't explicitly called from the derived class constructor via the base : (...) construct, a base class parameterless constructor will still be called, as in Case #1. The following code won't compile, for the same reasons cited earlier:

```
public class Person
{
  // Details omitted.

  // A constructor that takes one argument - by having created this,
  // we've lost Person's default parameterless constructor.
  public Person(string n) {
    Name = n;
  }
}


public class Student : Person {
  // Details omitted.

  // We declare a Student constructor, but don't explicitly invoke a
  // particular Person constructor from within it.
  public Student(string n, string m) {
    Name = n;
    Major = m;
  }
}
```

When we try to compile `Student`, we'll get the compiler error message

```
No constructor matching Person() found in class Person
```

Subcase #2B: Derived Class Constructor Does Explicitly Invoke a Base Class Constructor

Let's repair the problem in Subcase #2A by having the derived class constructor explicitly call a particular parent class constructor that we know to exist via the base(...) construct:

```
public class Person
{
  string name;

  // A constructor that takes one argument - by having created this,
  // we've lost Person's default parameterless constructor.
  public Person(string n) {
    name = n;
  }

  // No additional constructors are provided for Person.
}

public class Student : Person
{
  string major;

  // Constructor.
  // We'll explicitly invoke the Person constructor with one
  // argument, passing through the value of n.
  public Student(string n, string m) : base(n) {
    major = m;
  }
}
```

All is well when this code is compiled!

More on Methods

We've discussed methods in a fair amount of detail in this chapter and in Part One of this book. Now it's time to round out the discussion with a few more important observations about methods.

Message Chaining

In object-oriented programming languages like C#, it's quite commonplace to form complex expressions by concatenating one method call onto another via dot notation, a mechanism known as **message chaining.** Here's one hypothetical example:

```
Student s = new Student();
s.Name = "Fred";

Professor p = new Professor();
p.Name = "John";

Course c = new Course();
c.Name = "Math";

s.setFacultyAdvisor(p);
p.setCourseTaught(c);

Course c2 = new Course();
// A message "chain".
c2.Name = "Beginning " + (s.GetFacultyAdvisor().GetCourseTaught().Name);
```

As we saw in Chapter 1, we evaluate expressions from innermost to outermost parentheses, left to right, so let's evaluate the expression in the last line of this snippet:

1. Looking for the deepest level of nested parentheses, we see that part of the expression is two sets of parentheses deep, so we evaluate the left-most deepest subexpression first:

    ```
    s.GetFacultyAdvisor()
    ```

    which returns a reference to Professor p.

2. Next, we apply the GetCourseTaught() method to this Professor:

    ```
    p.GetCourseTaught()
    ```

    which returns a reference to Course c.

3. Next, we access the Name property of this Course:

    ```
    c.Name
    ```

    which returns the string value "Math".

4. We've now completed evaluating the expression enclosed within the innermost set of parentheses, effectively giving us the equivalent expression

```
c2.Name = "Beginning " + "Math";
```

So, we see in the final analysis that the outcome of the complex expression is to assign the name "Beginning Math" to Course object c2.

We'll see many such method chains in the SRS code.

Method Hiding

In Chapter 5, we learned that a derived class can override a method that has been declared as virtual in a base class: the derived class declares a new version of the base class method with the same signature, and includes the override keyword in the method declaration.

There is also a second way to replace the logic of a base class method, even one that hasn't been declared virtual in the base class, via a technique known as **method hiding.**

To "hide" a base class method, the derived class must define a method with the same signature using the new keyword in the method declaration in lieu of the override keyword. Here is a simple example in which the derived Student class hides the PrintDescription method first declared by the Person base class:

```
public class Person
{
  // details omitted

  // Note:  no virtual keyword -- no provision for overriding was made
  // by the designers of the Person class.
  public void PrintDescription() {
    // details omitted
  }
}

public class Student : Person
{
  // The Student class HIDES the PrintDescription()
  // method from the Person class via the use of the
  // new keyword.
  public new void PrintDescription() {
    // details omitted
  }
}
```

Any base class method—whether virtual or not—can be hidden; thus, we have a work-around (of sorts) if we find ourselves in a position of wanting to modify the behavior of a method derived from a base class that wasn't "prepped" for overriding by the original designer of the base class via the inclusion of the virtual keyword in the base class's method signature. Note, however, that hiding a nonvirtual base class method differs from truly overriding a virtual base class method in one ***very significant way,*** having to do with the notion of polymorphism that we discussed in Chapter 7. Let's explore this issue.

Method Hiding and Polymorphism

We learned in Chapter 7 that, by virtue of inheritance plus overriding, the run-time identity of an object controls what version of a method will be executed for a given object, a phenomenon known as ***polymorphism.*** For example, assuming that ChooseMajor is a virtual method in the Student class that has been overridden by both the GraduateStudent and UndergraduateStudent derived classes, the version of ChooseMajor invoked on s in the following code will depend on what type of Student s is:

```
// Iterating through an ArrayList of Students.
for (int i = 0; i < students.size(); i++) {
  Student s = (Student) students[i];

  // This next line of code is said to be polymorphic:
  // If s refers to a GraduateStudent at run time, the GraduateStudent version
  // of the ChooseMajor method will be executed; and, if s refers to an
  // UndergraduateStudent at run time, the UndergraduateStudent version of
  // ChooseMajor will be executed.
  s.ChooseMajor();
}
```

By contrast, the version of a ***hidden*** method that is run for a given object is "locked in" at ***compile time.*** Let's now assume that ChooseMajor is a ***nonvirtual*** method in the Student class, and is ***hidden*** (not overridden) by both the GraduateStudent and UndergraduateStudent derived classes. While the following two invocations of ChooseMajor will indeed be of the derived classes' respective versions, because we're invoking that method on reference variables explicitly declared to be a GraduateStudent and an UndergraduateStudent, respectively:

```
GraduateStudent g = new GraduateStudent();
g.ChooseMajor(); // GraduateStudent version of this method will execute

UndergraduateStudent s = new UndergraduateStudent();
s.ChooseMajor(); // UndergraduateStudent version of this method will execute
```

polymorphism will ***not*** be enabled in the ***next*** example—the Student base class's version of the ChooseMajor method will be invoked for ***both*** GraduateStudents and UndergraduateStudents because s is declared to be of type Student at compile time:

```
// Iterating through an ArrayList of Students.
for (int i = 0; i < students.size(); i++) {
  Student s = (Student) students[i];

  // This next line of code is NOT polymorphic:
  // Regardless of whether s refers to a GraduateStudent at run time or to
  // an Undergraduate student, the Student version of the ChooseMajor method
  // will be executed.
  s.ChooseMajor();
}
```

We mentioned earlier that any method, virtual or not, can be hidden. Why might we want to hide a ***virtual*** base class method vs. overriding it if we lose the benefit of polymorphism? Because hidden methods yield better performance (they run faster) than virtual methods.

Final Notes Regarding Method Hiding

A few final points:

- The original base class version of a hidden method can be called from within the "new" derived/hidden method using the base keyword, just as when overriding.

- A derived class's "hidden" method can have a different return type than the base class version it's hiding.

- An abstract method can't be hidden.

Overriding and Abstract Classes, Revisited

We learned in Chapter 7 that a class derived from an abstract class can be made concrete by providing ***nonabstract*** implementations of all of the abstract methods declared by the abstract base class. As it turns out, it's also possible to go the other direction as well: that is, a derived class can override a ***nonabstract*** method declared in a base class with an ***abstract*** method. Let's look at an example using predefined C# classes.

We know that every C# class implicitly derives from the Object class of the System namespace. One of the methods declared by the Object class is ToString, a nonabstract, virtual method that we discussed earlier in this chapter. It's perfectly acceptable to define a Person class that implicitly derives from Object (as all classes do), but which overrides the nonabstract ToString method it inherits from Object with an abstract version:

```
// Derives from Object implicitly.
public abstract class Person
{
  // We're overriding the nonabstract Object class's ToString method
  // with an ABSTRACT version.
  public abstract override string ToString();

  // Other Person class details omitted.
}
```

There are several things to note about the Person class:

- As discussed earlier in this chapter, derivation from the Object class is implicit, so we don't need the syntax : Object in the Person class declaration.

- Second, because the ToString method as defined in the Person class is abstract, the Person class itself is declared to be abstract.

- Finally, because the Person's ToString method is overriding the Object class's version of that method, the override keyword is used in the method declaration.

Why might we wish to override a nonabstract method with an abstract one? The answer is to *force* derived classes of Person to implement their own class-specific versions of the ToString method. That is, we don't want any of the future classes derived from Person to be "lazy" by simply inheriting the default behavior of the Object class's ToString method—we want to effectively "erase" the details of how this behavior is carried out. We'll in fact do this very thing when we create the Person class in Chapter 14 that will be used in conjunction with the SRS application. The Person class will declare an abstract ToString method that will be overridden by its derived classes.

Object Identities

When we discussed two of the C# collection classes—ArrayList and Hashtable—earlier, we spoke about the need to cast an object reference back into the appropriate reference type when extracting an object from one of these collections. This may lead one to believe that an object somehow "forgets" what class it belongs to, but this isn't true. An object always retains its class identity; it's simply that we can **refer** to an object with various different reference variables, which may be declared to be of different types, and it's this phenomenon that affects what messages the compiler believes that an object is capable of responding to. To help illustrate this point, let's use an example.

A Professor Is a Person and an Object, Rolled Into One

If we instantiate a Professor object, which is a type of Person, and therefore, as we saw earlier, is also a type of Object, we can think of the Professor object as being allocated in memory as demonstrated in Figure 13-14.

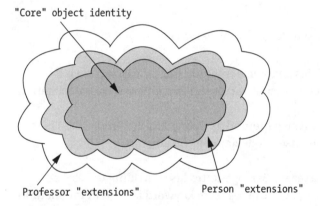

Figure 13-14. A Professor *object is simultaneously a* Person *object and an* Object *object, all rolled into one!*

We can then create reference variables of varying types (namely, any of the types in this object's derivation chain) to store handles on this Object/Person/Professor; each reference refers to a different "rendition" of the object:

```
// Create a Professor object, and maintain three handles on it of varying types.
Professor pr = new Professor();
Person p = pr;
object o = pr;
```

If we refer to this Professor object by its object reference o, then, as far as the compiler is concerned, the only aspects of the object that exist are its Object "core"; the "Person-ness" and "Professor-ness" of the object is in question (see

Figure 13-15). So, the compiler will reject any attempts to access the Professor- or Person-defined features of o:

```
// The compiler would reject this attempt to invoke the AddAdvisee() method,
// declared for the Professor class, on this object, because even though WE
// know from the code above that it is really a Professor whose handle is
// stored as an object, the compiler cannot be certain of this.
o.AddAdvisee();  // compiler error

// However, we can invoke any of the methods that this Professor inherited
// from the Object class:
o.ToString();
```

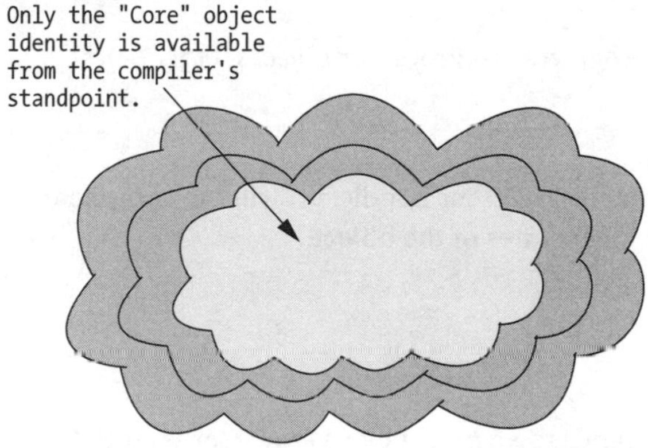

Only the "Core" object identity is available from the compiler's standpoint.

Figure 13-15. The compiler only knows about this Professor *object's "*Object-ness.*"*

If we instead refer to the Professor object by its Person reference p, then, as far as the compiler is concerned, the only aspects of the object that exist are its Object "core" and its Person "extensions"; the "Professor-ness" of the object is in question (see Figure 13-16):

```
// The compiler would again reject this attempt to invoke the AddAdvisee()
// method, declared for the Professor class, on this object, because even
// though WE know from the code above that it is really a Professor whose
// handle is stored as a Person at run time, the compiler cannot be certain
// of this at COMPILE time.
p.AddAdvisee();  // compiler error

// However, we can invoke any of the methods that this Professor inherited
// from EITHER the Object class ...
p.ToString();

// ... OR the Person class:
p.Name;
```

The compiler now
recognizes both the "core"
object identity of this
Professor object ...

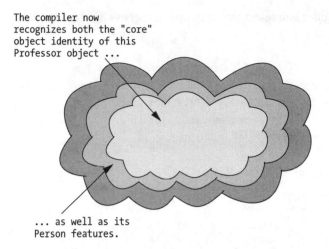

... as well as its
Person features.

Figure 13-16. The compiler now recognizes this Professor *object's "*Object-*ness"*
*and "*Person-*ness."*

Only if we refer to the object by its Professor handle, pr, will the compiler allow us to access Professor-specific features of the object.

Casting, Revisited

Now, back to casting: when a reference to an object like a Professor is stored in an ArrayList, it gets stored in the ArrayList as a generic object reference. When this reference is subsequently retrieved from the ArrayList, the compiler has no way to be certain that the object referred to by the reference is anything but a generic object. Because we, as programmers, know that the object is in reality a Professor, we can inform the compiler that it's so by performing a cast:

```
Professor p1 = new Professor();
Professor p2 = new Professor();

ArrayList list = new ArrayList();
list.Add(p1);
list.Add(p2);

for (int i = 0; i < list.Count; i++) {
  // Cast the object reference that was stored in the
  // ArrayList back into a Professor reference.
  Professor pr = (Professor) list[i];
```

```
    // We may now manipulate the reference as a true Professor.
    pr.ListAdvisees();

    // etc.
}
```

What would happen if we tried to cast the retrieved object to an inappropriate type? For example, if we placed a reference to a Professor object in the ArrayList, but then tried to cast it to be a Student reference when we retrieved it from the ArrayList? The compiler would trust that we knew what we were doing, and wouldn't produce an error; however, at ***run time,*** an exception would be thrown, for there is no way to "morph" a Professor object into a Student object via a simple cast.

Fortunately, there are ways for us to programmatically determine the type of an object reference at run time, as we'll now discuss.

Determining the Class That an Object Belongs To

There are several ways to ask an object what class it belongs to at run time; we can take advantage of

- The GetType method defined by the Object class

- The typeof operator

The GetType Method

As mentioned earlier, by virtue of being derived from the Object class, every object inherits a method with the header:

```
public Type GetType()
```

When invoked on an object, this method returns an object of type Type, representing the type of the object on which the GetType method has been invoked. For example, if the Person class is defined to belong to the SRS namespace, then the following invocation of GetType:

```
Person p = new Person();
Type t = p.GetType();
```

would yield a Type object representing the class SRS.Person. The Type class, in turn, defines a string property named FullName that can be used to access the fully qualified name of the type:

```
Person p = new Person();
Type t = p.GetType();
String s = t.FullName; // s now equals "SRS.Person".
```

Chaining the method call and property invocation together, we can ask any object reference to identify which class the object it refers to belongs to, as follows:

```
reference.GetType().FullName;
```

For example:

```
using System;
using System.Collections;

public class CastingExample
{
  static void Main() {
    Student s = new Student();
    Professor p = new Professor();

    ArrayList list = new ArrayList();
    list.Add(s);
    list.Add(p);

    for (int i = 0; i < list.Count; i++) {
      // Note that we are not casting the objects here!
      // We're pulling them out as generic objects.
      object o = list[i];
      Console.WriteLine(o.GetType().FullName);
    }
  }
}
```

This program produces as output (assuming that neither Student nor Professor belong to a named namespace):

```
Student
Professor
```

This demonstrates that the objects themselves really do remember their "roots"!

The typeof Operator

Another way to test whether a given object reference belongs to a particular class is via the typeof operator. This operator takes as its argument the name of a type (note: the type name is ***not*** quoted) and returns the corresponding Type object. Here is a simple code snippet to illustrate how the typeof operator can be used to see if a reference is of a certain type. (The == operator works in this case because there is only one System.Type object for each type in the C# language, whether user-defined or predefined.)

```
Student s = new Student();

// Determine if the type of the s reference variable is
// is equal to the Student type.
if (s.GetType() == typeof(Student)) {
  Console.WriteLine("s is a Student");
}
```

The preceding code would produce the following as output:

```
s is a Student
```

Note that if we wish to refer to the name of a class that belongs to an ***explicitly named*** namespace, and we haven't included the appropriate using statement with our code, we must fully qualify the class name when using typeof:

```
// Assume that Bar is a class in the Foo namespace.
if (x.GetType() == typeOf(Foo.Bar) { ... }
```

> *While the use of parentheses to surround the name of a class—* typeof(Student)—*makes it look as if* typeof *is a method, it's indeed an* **operator.**

Object Deletion and Garbage Collection

In the C++ language, there is a delete operator that allows the programmer to explicitly control when a dynamically allocated object is no longer needed, and its memory can therefore be recycled. This is both a blessing and a curse! It's a blessing, because it gives a C++ programmer very tight control over his/her memory resources in a program. But, if a C++ programmer forgets to recycle his/her objects, the program can literally run out of memory—this is known as a "memory leak."

With C#, however, there is no delete operator: anything dynamically created—i.e., everything but simple data types—is a candidate for C# garbage collection when all references to it (handles) have been eliminated. Like the "object as a helium balloon" example that we discussed in Chapter 3, when we let go of all strings on a balloon, it essentially floats away. Garbage collection is an automatic function performed by the C# runtime; when an object is garbage collected, the memory that was allocated to that object is recycled and added back to the pool of memory that is available to the runtime for new object creation.

By way of review, there are several ways to release handles on objects in C# so as to make them candidates for garbage collection, as the following example illustrates:

```
// Declare two reference variables to hold on to future
// (as of yet to be created) Student objects.
Student s1;
Student s2;

// Instantiate a Student object, and store a handle on this object in s1.
s1 = new Student();

// Copy the handle into s2, so that we now have two handles on the same object.
s2 = s1;

// Let's now look at two different ways to "drop" an object reference.

// We can reset a variable previously holding a handle to the value null ...
s1 = null;  // (We still have one of two handles left on the object.)

// ... or we can hand a variable some OTHER object's handle,
// causing it to drop the first handle. Here, by creating a
// second Student object and handing it to s2, s2 drops the
// only remaining handle on the first Student object.
s2 = new Student( );  // No more handles on the original student remain!
```

We've eliminated all obvious references to the original instance of a Student; if there are no remaining references to an object, it becomes a **_candidate_** for garbage collection. We emphasize the word "candidate" in the previous sentence, however, because the garbage collector doesn't immediately recycle the object. Rather, the garbage collector runs whenever the runtime determines that there is a need for some recycling to be done, e.g., when the application is getting low on free memory necessary to allocate new objects. So, for some period of time, the "orphaned" Student object will still exist in memory—we merely won't have any handles with which to reach it.

The inclusion of garbage collection in C# has virtually eliminated memory leaks. Note that it's still possible for the runtime to run out of memory, however, if too many handles are maintained on too many objects; so, a C# programmer can't be totally oblivious to memory management—but it's far less error prone than with C/C++.

The "Other" Kind of Attribute

Throughout most of this book we've been using the term "attribute" in the generic OO sense to represent a state-describing data element of a class, also known in C# as a "field." We mentioned back in Chapter 3 that there is also a *.NET-specific* programming element called an **attribute**. Although we don't make use of this .NET attribute in building the SRS, we'd like to at least provide a brief description of this "other" kind of attribute.

A (.NET) attribute is a reference type that derives from the System.Attribute class, and is used to assign **metadata tags** to *other* programming elements—that is, descriptive information about such elements.

An attribute can be applied to any code element (class, constructor, delegate, method, field, etc.) by placing the name of the attribute in brackets before the code element. For example, the System.Array class has an associated attribute named SerializableAttribute as shown here:

```
[SerializableAttribute]
public abstract class Array : ICloneable, IList, ICollection, IEnumerable { ... }
```

The application of this attribute to the Array class indicates that Array objects are **serializable**, meaning that they can be stored to or restored from disk in binary form.

As programmers, we could certainly determine that Arrays are serializable from inspecting the C# language documentation; so, what does an attribute buy us? The "knowledge" that is imparted through the application of an attribute can be *programmatically "discovered"* at run time, through a mechanism known as **reflection**. (Going into the full details of how reflection works is beyond the scope of a beginning-level book such as this to address.)

We can apply any of the predefined attributes provided by the FCL to our own code. For example, we can place the predefined Obsolete attribute before the header of a method that we wish to flag as obsolete, to indicate that this method is perhaps going to be phased out at some later date so as to discourage its use:

```
public class MyClass
{
  // We're adding an attribute to Foo().
  [Obsolete]
  public void Foo() {
    // Method details omitted ...
  }

  // Other details omitted.
}
```

If client code subsequently attempts to invoke the Foo method on an instance of MyClass:

```
public class AttrDemo {
  static void Main() {
    MyClass x = new MyClass();

    // We're trying to call a method that has been
    // tagged as obsolete.
    x.Foo();
  }
}
```

then when the AttrDemo class is compiled, the compiler will detect that a method that has been tagged as obsolete is being called on an object, and will generate the following warning:

```
warning CS0612:  'MyClass.Foo()' is obsolete
```

The program can still be executed, but the programmer has been "warned" that using the Foo method may not be advisable.

> *We can also create user-defined attributes for whatever specific metadata needs we might have, but this topic is beyond the scope of this book to address.*

Summary

We've just been on a whirlwind tour of the C# language! Although there is much more that can be said about C#, you've been "armed" with all of the essential information that you'll need in order to understand—and experiment with—the sample SRS application that we'll build in the remaining chapters of the book.

In particular, we discussed

- The differences between generic OO terminology and C#/.NET-specific terms

- The anatomy of a real-world C# program, consisting of many separate classes driven by one "official" `Main` method

- The C# notion of namespaces and how they are used to divide classes and interfaces into logical units

- The object nature of `strings`, and some of the methods provided to manipulate them

- How C# exceptions arise, and how to gracefully handle them

- The parent of all C# types—the `Object` class

- The object nature of `Arrays` in a bit more depth

- How to use two of C#'s collection classes, `ArrayList` and `Hashtable`, the need for casting objects retrieved from a collection, and the use of `IEnumerator` to iterate through the contents of a collection

- Some subtleties of variable initialization

- Additional insights regarding the `Main` method

- How to read input from the command line when a C# application is invoked, as well as how to prompt the user for keyboard inputs, useful techniques when running a command line–driven application testing program

- Using constructors to initialize an object's fields at the time that the object first comes into being

- Inheritance in the C# language: in particular, how the visibility of a feature affects the way in which a derived class can utilize that feature, how to reuse base class behaviors via the `base` keyword, and complexities concerning constructors and inheritance

- The nature of object identities in C#, how to discover the true class that an object belongs to, and how to test the equality of two C# objects

- How we delete dynamically created objects so as to recycle their memory at run time, and the role that the C# garbage collector plays in this recycling

With all of this C# knowledge at our fingertips, we're now ready to proceed to building the SRS application.

> *This is **a great** time to download the code associated with the remaining chapters from the Apress web site, if you haven't already done so! Please see Appendix D for instructions.*

Exercises

1. Follow the instructions included in Appendix C to get the latest version of Microsoft's .NET Framework SDK running on your computer.

2. Write a C# program that will print out the integers from 1 to 10 in reverse order.

3. Write a C# program that will accept a series of individual characters, separated by one or more spaces, as command-line input, and will then "glue" them together to form a word. For example, if we were to invoke the executable Glue.exe as follows:

    ```
    Glue B A    N A   N    A
    ```

    then the program should output

    ```
    BANANA
    ```

    with no spaces.

4. *Advanced exercise:* Write a C# program that accepts a sentence as command-line input, and outputs statistics about this sentence. For example, if we were to invoke the program as follows:

    ```
    SentenceStatistics this is my sample sentence
    ```

    then the program should output the following results:

    ```
    number of words:            5
    longest word(s):            sentence
    length of longest word(s):  8
    shortest word(s):           is my
    length of shortest word(s): 2
    ```

    (To keep things simple, don't use any punctuation in your sentence.)

Hint: See the section titled "Reading Command-Line Arguments" for ideas on how to approach this.

5. ***Advanced Exercise:*** Write a C# program that accepts strings as command-line arguments, and outputs these strings in sorted order. For example, if we were to invoke the program as follows:

StringSorter dog cat bird fish

then the program should output the following results:

```
bird
cat
dog
fish
```

In writing this program, use the bubble sort algorithm, which is a simple way to sort a list of items by comparing them in pairwise fashion.

- Start by comparing the first string to the second and, if the second is less than the first, swap their positions; then, compare the second to the third, etc.

- Keep making passes through the entire list from beginning to end, comparing them in pairwise fashion, until you are able to get through the list without having to make any "swaps."

- Then, have your program print out the results.

Transforming Our UML Model into C# Code

IT'S NOW TIME to turn our attention back to the class diagram that we produced in Part Two of the book in order to develop a C# application based on that object-oriented blueprint. We'll step through all of the C# code necessary to automate a simple command-line version of the SRS application first, so that we may focus solely on what it takes to accurately model the SRS domain information in an OO programming language. Then, in the next two chapters, we'll round out our application by adding a means of persisting data from one session to another and a graphical user interface, respectively.

In this chapter, you'll learn how to represent all of the following object-oriented constructs in C# code:

- Associations of varying multiplicities (one-to-one, one-to-many, and many-to-many), including aggregations

- Inheritance relationships

- Association classes

- Reflexive associations

- Abstract classes

- Metadata

- Static fields and methods

along with practical guidelines as to when to use these various constructs. We also cover a technique for testing your core classes via a command-line driven application.

> As we discussed in Chapter 13, the formal C#-specific term for what we've been calling an "attribute" in Parts One and Two of the book is "field." Because we're now developing a real-life C# application, we'll be using the term "field" in the descriptive text throughout this chapter as well as in Chapters 15 and 16.

Suggestions for Getting the Maximum Value out of This and Subsequent Chapters

Our primary goal for this book is to show you how to take the same Student Registration System case study through a complete object life cycle, from requirements definition via use cases, to object modeling, and from there into C# code as a working application. To do so, however, required us to develop a nontrivial application that was complex enough to be able to demonstrate as many "real-world" issues surrounding OO development as possible within the scope of a single book.

The code that we've written for the SRS application is sizeable; to have included the full listings for each and every C# class intact in every chapter would have been prohibitive. So, to make this as effective a learning experience as possible for you, we've chosen to feature just those portions of code in each chapter that are particularly critical to your understanding of object concepts as they translate into the C# language.

Of course, we realize that you'll need access to the complete source code to round out your understanding of the SRS application as we've implemented it, so we're making an electronic softcopy of the SRS source code files available for download from the Apress web site, `http://www.apress.com/book/download.html`.

One of the best ways to master a language is to start with code that works, and to experiment with it. We'd like you to get some hands-on experience with C# by actually compiling and running the SRS application; studying it, so as to familiarize yourself with the techniques that we've used; and finally, modifying it yourself. Exercises provided at the end of each chapter provide specific suggestions for experiments that you may wish to try. Therefore, before you dive into this chapter, *we encourage you to download the C# source code for this chapter from the Apress web site if you haven't already done so;* instructions for doing so are included in Appendix D. You'll also want to install Microsoft's free C# software development kit (SDK) if you haven't already done so; please see Appendix C for details.

The SRS Class Diagram, Revisited

Let's turn our attention back to the SRS class diagram that we produced in Part Two the book. In speaking with our sponsors for the SRS system, we learn that they've decided to cut back on a few features in the interest of reducing development costs:

- First of all, they've decided not to automate students' Plans of Study via the SRS. Instead, it will be up to each student to make sure that the courses that he or she registers for are appropriate for the degree that he or she is seeking.

- Since automated plans of study are being eliminated, there will no longer be a need to track who a student's faculty advisor is. The only reason for modeling the *advises* relationship between the Professor and Student classes in the first place was so that a student's advisor could be called upon to approve a tentative Plan of Study when a student had first posted it via the SRS.

- Finally, our sponsors have decided that maintaining a wait list for a section once it becomes full is a luxury that they can live without, since most students, upon learning that a section is full, immediately choose an alternative course anyway.

Therefore, we've pared down the SRS class diagram accordingly, to eliminate these unnecessary features; also, to keep the diagram from getting too cluttered, we didn't reflect field types or full method headers. The resultant diagram is shown in Figure 14-1.

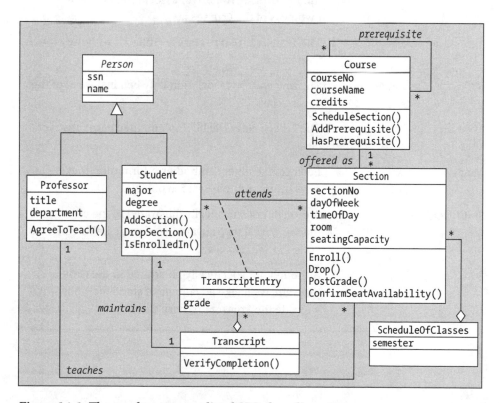

Figure 14-1. The resultant streamlined SRS class diagram

Fortunately for us, the resultant model still provides examples of all of the key object-oriented elements that we need to learn how to program, as listed in Table 14-1.

Table 14-1. OO Features Illustrated by the SRS Class Diagram

OO Feature	Embodied in the SRS Class Diagram As Follows
Inheritance	The Person class serves as the base class for the Student and Professor classes.
Aggregation	We have two examples of this: the Transcript class represents an aggregation of TranscriptEntry objects, and the ScheduleOfClasses class represents an aggregation of Section objects.
One-to-one association	The *maintains* association between the Student and Transcript classes.
One-to-many association	The *teaches* association between Professor and Section; the *offered as* association between Course and Section.
Many-to-many association	The *attends* association between Student and Section; the *prerequisite* (reflexive) association between instances of the Course class.
Association Class	The TranscriptEntry class is affiliated with the *attends* association.
Reflexive association	The *prerequisite* association between instances of the Course class.
Abstract class	The Person class will be implemented as an abstract class.
Metadata	Each Course object embodies information that is relevant to multiple Section objects.
Static fields	Although not specifically illustrated in the class diagram, we'll take advantage of static fields when we code the Section class.
Static methods	Although not specifically illustrated in the class diagram, we'll take advantage of static methods when we code the TranscriptEntry class.

As mentioned earlier, we're going to implement a command-line driven version of the SRS in this chapter; in particular, we're going to code the eight classes illustrated in the class diagram along with a ninth "driver" class that will house the Main method necessary to run the application. In Chapter 16, we'll explain why it was useful to do so.

The Person Class (Specifying Abstract Classes)

The Person class will be the abstract base class for all of the "people" represented by the SRS. The derived classes of Person will include the Student and Professor classes.

Let's start by writing the code for the Person class (see Figure 14-2). We will be using the System.Console class in this class, so we'll include a using directive at the top of the code.

```
using System;
```

Figure 14-2. The Person *class*

The first thing that we notice in the class diagram is that the name of the class is *italicized*, which we learned in Chapter 10 means that Person is to be implemented as an abstract class. By including the keyword "abstract" in the class declaration, we prevent client code from ever being able to instantiate a Person object directly.

```
// We are making this class abstract because we do not wish for it
// to be instantiated.

public abstract class Person {
```

Person Fields

The Person class icon specifies two simple fields; we'll make all of our fields *private* throughout the SRS application unless otherwise stated:

```
//------------
// Fields.
//------------

private string name;
private string ssn;
```

Person Constructors

We'll provide a constructor for the Person class that accepts two arguments, so as to initialize these two fields:

```
//----------------
// Constructor(s).
//----------------

// Initialize the field values using the set
// accessor of the associated property.

public Person(string name, string ssn) {
  this.Name = name;
  this.Ssn = ssn;
}
```

Note that we use the set accessor of the Person class's properties to set the values of the name and ssn fields as was recommended in Chapter 13. Strictly speaking, the this. syntax isn't necessary when referencing a property declared in the same class, but can be included as a reminder that we're talking about a property associated with the *current* object.

And, because the creation of any constructor for a class suppresses the automatic generation of that class's default constructor as we discussed in Chapter 13, we'll program a parameterless constructor to replace it.

```
// We're replacing the default constructor that got "wiped out"
// as a result of having created a constructor previously. We reuse
// the two-argument constructor with dummy values.
```

```
public Person() : this("?", "???-??-????")  {
    // Because this constructor needn't do anything more than what the parent's
    // constructor is going to do, the body of this constructor is empty.
}
```

taking advantage of the : this(...) construct to reuse the code from the first constructor.

Person Properties

Next, we provide read/write properties for all of the fields, observing the proper property syntax as presented in Chapter 4:

```
//------------------
// Properties.
//-----------------

public string Name {
  get {
    return name;
  }
  set {
    name = value;
  }
}

public string Ssn {
  get {
    return ssn;
  }
  set {
    ssn = value;
  }
}
```

ToString Method

We'd like for all derived classes of the Person class to implement a ToString method, but we don't want to bother coding the details of such a method for Person; we'd prefer to let each derived class handle the details of how the ToString method will work in its own class-appropriate way. The best way to enforce the requirement for a ToString method is to declare ToString as an ***abstract method*** in Person, as we discussed in Chapters 7 and 13. The override keyword is required because the Object class (the base class of our Person class) also declares a ToString method.

```
//-----------------------------
// Miscellaneous other methods.
//-----------------------------

// We'll let each derived class implement how it wishes to be
// represented as a String value.

public abstract override string ToString();
```

> *The* ToString *method is declared in the* Object *class as a* **nonabstract,** *virtual method. We're overriding that method in the* Person *class with an* **abstract** *method, but it's perfectly acceptable to do so, as we discussed in Chapter 13; making the* Person ToString *method abstract forces derived classes of* Person *to implement their own* ToString *logic.*

Display Method

We also want all derived classes of Person to implement a Display method, to be used for printing the values of all of an object's fields to the command-line window; we'll be using the Display method solely for testing our application, to verify that an object's fields have been properly initialized. But, rather than making this method abstract as well, we'll go ahead and actually program the body of this method, since we know how we'd like the fields of Person to be displayed when these are inherited, at a minimum.

```
// Used for testing purposes.

public virtual void Display() {
  Console.WriteLine("Person Information:");
  Console.WriteLine("\tName:  " + this.Name);
  Console.WriteLine("\tSoc. Security No.:  " + this.Ssn);
}
```

This way, we enable derived classes of Person (Student, Professor) to use the base keyword to recycle this logic in their own Display methods.

> Here is a "preview" excerpt from the Student *class's* Display *method to illustrate how the* base *keyword will be used:*
>
> ```
> public void Display() {
>     // First, let's display the generic Person information inherited by Student.
>     base.display();
>
>
>     // Then, we'll go on to display the Student-specific attribute values.
> ```

Again, note that we're invoking the Person class's ***properties*** from within the WriteLine method calls, versus accessing Person fields directly by name.

That's all there is to programming the Person class—pretty straightforward! We'll tackle the Student and Professor classes derived from Person next.

The Student Class (Reuse Through Inheritance; Extending Abstract Classes; Delegation)

The Student class serves as an abstraction of a student, and is derived from the abstract Person class. In order to be able to instantiate Student objects within the SRS, we must implement all of Person's abstract methods concretely within the Student class, thus "breaking the spell" of abstractness, as we discussed in Chapter 7.

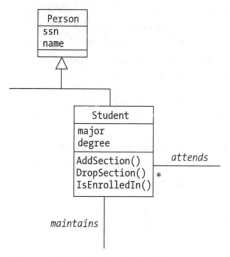

Figure 14-3. The Student *class*

We indicate that Student is a derived class of Person (see Figure 14-3) with the following syntax:

```
public class Student : Person {
```

Student Fields

There are two fields indicated for the Student class in our class diagram—major and degree—but we learned in Chapter 10 that we must also encode associations as fields. Student participates in two associations:

- *attends*, a many-to-many association with the Section class

- *maintains*, a one-to-one association with the Transcript class

and so we must allow for each Student to maintain handles on **one** Transcript object and on **many** Section objects. Of the C# collection types that we learned about in Chapters 6 and 13—Arrays, ArrayLists, and Hashtables—an ArrayList seems like the best choice for managing multiple Section handles:

- An Array is a bit too rigid; we'd have to size the Array in advance to be large enough to accommodate references to all of the Sections that a Student will ever attend over the course of his or her studies at the university. An ArrayList, on the other hand, can start out small and automatically grow in size as needed.

- The decision of whether to use an ArrayList versus a Hashtable to manage a collection comes down to whether or not we'll need to retrieve an object reference from the collection based on some key value. We don't anticipate the need for such a lookup capability as it pertains to the Sections that a Student has attended; we'll need the ability to verify if a Student has taken a particular Section or not, but this can be accomplished by using the ArrayList class's Contains method: that is, if attends is declared to be of type ArrayList, then we can use the statement

  ```
  if (attends.Contains(someSection)) { ... }
  ```

  For most other uses of the attends collection, we'll need to step through the entire collection anyway, as when printing out the Student's course schedule. So, an ArrayList should serve our purposes just fine.

The fields for the Student class thus turn out as follows:

```
//------------
// Fields.
//------------
```

```
private string major;
private string degree;
private Transcript transcript;
private ArrayList attends; // of Sections
```

Student Constructors

We'll provide a constructor for convenience of initializing fields; note, though, that we aren't trying to initialize the attends ArrayList via the constructor, because a Student object will most likely come into existence before we know which Sections they will be attending. Nonetheless, we ideally prefer to instantiate collection fields such as the attends ArrayList so that we have an empty "egg carton" ready for us when it is time to add "eggs."

```
//----------------
// Constructor(s).
//----------------

// Reuse the code of the parent's constructor.
// Initialize the field values using the set
// accessor of the associated property.

public Student(string name, string ssn,
               string major, string degree) : base(name, ssn) {

  this.Major = major;
  this.Degree = degree;

  // Create a brand new Transcript.

  this.Transcript = new Transcript(this);

  // Note that we must instantiate an empty ArrayList.

  attends = new ArrayList();
}
```

In the preceding code, note that we create a brand-new Transcript object on the fly by calling the Transcript constructor, passing a reference to ***this*** Student in as the lone argument to the constructor. Since we haven't discussed the structure of the Transcript class yet, the signature of its constructor may seem a bit puzzling to you, but will make sense once we get a chance to review the Transcript class in its entirety later in this chapter.

We choose to overload the Student constructor by providing a second constructor signature, to be used if we wish to create a Student object for whom we don't yet know the major field of study or degree sought. We once again take advantage of the this keyword (introduced in Chapter 13) to reuse the code from the first constructor, passing in the String value "TBD" to serve as a temporary value for both the major and degree fields.

```
// A second form of constructor, used when a Student has not yet
// declared a major or degree.
// Reuse the code of the other Student constructor.

public Student(string name, string ssn) : this(name, ssn, "TBD", "TBD") {
  // Because this constructor needn't do anything more than what the parent's
  // constructor is going to do, the body of this constructor is empty.
}
```

Student Properties

We provide properties for all of the simple (noncollection) fields:

```
//------------------
// Properties.
//------------------

public string Major {
  get {
    return major;
  }
  set {
    major = value;
  }
}

public string Degree {
  get {
    return degree;
  }
  set {
    degree = value;
  }
}
```

```
    public Transcript Transcript {
      get {
        return transcript;
      }
      set {
        transcript = value;
      }
    }
```

The `Transcript` property associated with the `transcript` field returns a `Transcript` object reference; thus, the property's ***name*** is the ***same*** as its ***return type***!

```
public Transcript Transcript {
```

Although this looks a bit strange, it does conform to the C# naming convention that the property name should match the field name, and the compiler won't have a problem with it. If we were to try to access the property with the following client code snippet:

```
Student s1 = new Student("Gerson Lopez", "123456789");
Transcipt t = new Transcript();
s1.Transcript = t;
```

the runtime would understand that the third line of code is accessing the `get` accessor of the `Transcript` property on the `s1` `Student` object.

For the attends collection field, we'll provide methods `AddSection` and `DropSection` in lieu of traditional properties, to be used for adding and removing `Section` objects from the `ArrayList`; we'll talk about these methods momentarily.

Display Method

As we did for `Person`, we choose to provide a `Display` method for `Student` for use in testing our command-line version of the SRS. Because a `Student` is a `Person`, and because we've already gone to the trouble of programming a `Display` method for the fields inherited from `Person`, we'll reuse that method code by making use of the `base` keyword before going on to additionally display field values specific to a `Student` object:

```
public override void Display() {
    // First, let's display the generic Person info.

    base.Display();

    // Then, display Student-specific info.
```

```
Console.WriteLine("Student-Specific Information:");
Console.WriteLine("\tMajor:   " + this.Major);
Console.WriteLine("\tDegree:  " + this.Degree);
DisplayCourseSchedule();
PrintTranscript();
}
```

Note that we're calling two of the Student class's other methods, DisplayCourseSchedule and PrintTranscript, from within the Student's Display method. We chose to program these as separate methods versus incorporating their code into the body of the Display method to keep the Display method from getting too cluttered.

PrintTranscript Method

The PrintTranscript method is a straightforward example of delegation: we use the Student's Transcript property to retrieve a handle on the Transcript object that belongs to this Student, and then invoke the Display method for that Transcript object:

```
public void PrintTranscript() {
  this.Transcript.Display();
}
```

Note that we could have accomplished this with two lines of code instead of one:

```
public void PrintTranscript() {
  Transcript t = this.Transcript;
  t.Display();
}
```

but as we discussed in Chapter 13, it's common to create expressions in C# by "chaining together" one method call after another. When each subsequent method is called in such an expression, it's called on the *object reference* that is returned by the *previous* method call in the chain; this is illustrated in Figure 14-4.

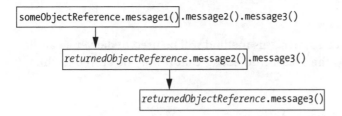

Figure 14-4. The "mechanics" of method chaining

There is no point in going to the trouble of declaring a variable t to serve as a handle on a Transcript object if we're only going to reference the variable one time, and then discard it when it goes out of scope as soon as the method exits.

DisplayCourseSchedule Method

The DisplayCourseSchedule method is a more complex example of delegation; we'll defer a discussion of this method until we've discussed a few more of the SRS classes.

ToString Method

By extending an abstract class, as we did with the Person class when we created the Student-derived class, we implicitly agree to implement any abstract method(s) specified by the parent class with concrete methods. In the case of the Person class, we have one such method, ToString:

```
// We are forced to program this method because it is specified
// as an abstract method in our parent class (Person); failing to
// do so would render the Student class abstract, as well.
//
// For a Student, we wish to return a String as follows:
//    Joe Blow (123-45-6789) [Master of Science - Math]

public override string ToString() {
  return this.Name + " (" + this.Ssn + ") [" + this.Degree +
        " - " + this.Major + "]";
}
```

AddSection Method

When a Student enrolls in a Section, this method will be used to deliver a handle on that Section object to the Student object so that it may be stored in the attends ArrayList:

```
public void AddSection(Section s) {
  attends.Add(s);
}
```

DropSection Method

When a Student withdraws from a Section, this method will be used to pass a handle on that Section object to the Student object, so that it can use the ArrayList class's Remove method to seek and remove that specific Section reference from the attends ArrayList:

```
public void DropSection(Section s) {
  attends.Remove(s);
}
```

IsEnrolledIn Method

This method is used to determine whether a given Student is already enrolled in a particular Section—that is, whether that Student is already maintaining a handle on the Section in question—by taking advantage of the ArrayList class's Contains method:

```
public bool IsEnrolledIn(Section s) {
  if (attends.Contains(s)) {
    return true;
  }
  else {
    return false;
  }
}
```

IsCurrentlyEnrolledInSimilar Method

Although not specified by our model, we've added another version of the IsEnrolledIn method called IsCurrentlyEnrolledInSimilar, because we found a need for such a method when we coded the Section class (coming up later in this chapter). No matter how much thought you put into object modeling, you'll inevitably determine the need for additional fields and methods for your classes once coding is under way, because coding causes you to think at a much more finely grained level of detail about the "mechanics" of your application.

Because this method is so complex, we'll show the method code in its entirety first, followed by an in-depth explanation.

```csharp
// Determine whether the Student is already enrolled in ANOTHER
// Section of this SAME Course.

public bool IsCurrentlyEnrolledInSimilar(Section s1) {
  bool foundMatch = false;
  Course c1 = s1.RepresentedCourse;
  IEnumerator e = GetEnrolledSections();
  while (e.MoveNext()) {
    Section s2 = (Section) e.Current;
    Course c2 = s2.RepresentedCourse;
    if (c1 == c2) {
      // There is indeed a Section in the attends
      // ArrayList representing the same Course.
      // Check to see if the Student is CURRENTLY
      // ENROLLED (i.e., whether or not he/she has
      // yet received a grade). If there is no
      // grade, he/she is currently enrolled; if
      // there is a grade, then he/she completed
      // the course some time in the past.
      if (s2.GetGrade(this) == null) {
        // No grade was assigned!  This means
        // that the Student is currently
        // enrolled in a Section of this
        // same Course.
        foundMatch = true;
        break;
      }
    }
  }

  return foundMatch;
}
```

In coding the Enroll method of the Section class, we realized that we needed a way to determine whether a particular Student is enrolled in any Section of a given Course. That is, if a Student is attempting to enroll for Math 101 Section **1**, we want to reject this request if he or she is already enrolled in Math 101 Section **2**. We chose to pass in a Section object reference as an argument to this method, although we could have alternatively declared the argument to this method to be a Course reference.

```
// Determine whether the Student is already enrolled in another
// Section of this same Course.

public bool IsCurrentlyEnrolledInSimilar(Section s1) {
```

We initialize a flag to false, with the intention of resetting it to true later on if we do indeed discover that the Student is currently enrolled in a Section of the same Course.

```
bool foundMatch = false;
```

We obtain a handle on the Course object that the Section of interest represents, and then step through an IEnumerator of all of the Sections that this Student is either currently enrolled in or has previously enrolled in, using the variable s2 to maintain a temporary handle on each such Section one by one.

```
Course c1 = s1.RepresentedCourse;
IEnumerator e = GetEnrolledSections();
while (e.MoveNext()) {
   Section s2 = (Section) e.Current;
```

We obtain a handle on a second Course object—the Course object that Section s2 is a Section of—and test the equality of the two Course objects. If we find a match, we're not quite done yet, however, because the attends ArrayList for a Student holds onto all Sections that the Student has ever taken. To determine if Section s2 is truly a Section that the Student is currently enrolled in, we must check to see if a grade has been issued for this Section; a missing grade—that is, a grade value of null—indicates that the Section is currently in progress. As soon as we've found the first such situation, we can break out of the enclosing while loop and return a value of true to the caller.

```
    Course c2 = s2.RepresentedCourse;
    if (c1 == c2) {
       // There is indeed a Section in the attends
       // ArrayList representing the same Course.
       // Check to see if the Student is CURRENTLY
       // ENROLLED (i.e., whether or not he/she has
       // yet received a grade).  If there is no
       // grade, he/she is currently enrolled; if
       // there is a grade, then he/she completed
       // the course some time in the past.
       if (s2.GetGrade(this) == null) {
```

```
        // No grade was assigned!  This means
        // that the Student is currently
        // enrolled in a Section of this
        // same Course.
        foundMatch = true;
        break;
      }
    }
  }

  return foundMatch;
} // end of method
```

GetEnrolledSections Method

The GetEnrolledSections method used previously is a simple one-liner:

```
public IEnumerator GetEnrolledSections() {
  return attends.GetEnumerator();
}
```

Recall from Chapter 13 that an IEnumerator instance can be used to step through the elements of a collection; hence, our choice of IEnumerator as the return type of this method. In this case, the collection holds the sections for which a student is registered.

Next, we'll turn our attention to the Professor class.

The Professor Class (Bidirectionality of Relationships)

The Professor class is a derived class of Person that serves as an abstraction a college professor. Because the code that is necessary to implement the Professor class is so similar to that of Student, we'll only comment on those features of Professor that are particularly noteworthy. We encourage you to look at the full code of the Professor class as downloaded from the Apress web site, however, to reinforce your ability to read and interpret C# syntax.

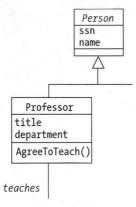

Figure 14-5. The `Professor` *class*

To indicate that the `Professor` is a derived class of `Person` (see Figure 14-5), we use the following syntax:

```
public class Professor : Person {
```

Professor Fields

The `Professor` class is involved in one association—the one-to-many *teaches* association with the `Section` class—and so we must provide a means for a `Professor` object to maintain multiple `Section` handles, which we do by creating a teaches field of type `ArrayList`:

```
//------------
// Fields.
//------------

private string title;
private string department;
private ArrayList teaches; // of Sections
```

AgreeToTeach Method

Our class diagram calls for us to implement an `AgreeToTeach` method. This method accepts a `Section` object reference as an argument, and begins by storing this handle in the teaches `ArrayList`:

```
public void AgreeToTeach(Section s) {
  teaches.Add(s);
```

Associations, as modeled in a class diagram, are assumed to be bidirectional. When implementing associations in code, however, we must think about whether or not bidirectionality is important.

- Can we think of any situations in which a Professor object would need to know which Sections it's responsible for teaching? Yes, as, for example, when we ask a Professor object to print out its teaching assignments.

- How about the reverse: that is, can we think of any situations in which a Section object would need to know who is teaching it? Yes, as, for example, when we print out a Student's course schedule.

So, not only must we store a handle on the Section object in the Professor's teaches ArrayList, but we must also make sure that the Section object is somehow notified that this Professor is going to be its instructor. We accomplish this by accessing the Section object's Instructor property, passing it a handle on the Professor object whose method we are in the midst of executing:

```
public void AgreeToTeach(Section s) {
  teaches.Add(s);

  // We need to link this bidirectionally.
  s.Instructor = this;
}
```

We'll explore the implications of bidirectionality, and the various options for implementing bidirectional relationships, in more depth a bit later in this chapter.

We'll turn our attention next to the Course class.

The Course Class (Reflexive Relationships; Unidirectional Relationships)

The Course class, shown in Figure 14-6, represents an abstraction of a college course. Note that Course participates in the only reflexive association found in our UML diagram.

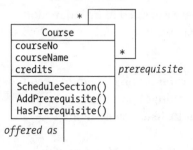

Figure 14-6. The Course *class*

Course Fields

Referring back to the SRS class diagram, we see that Course has three simple fields and participates in two associations:

- *offered as*, a one-to-many association with the Section class, and

- *prerequisite*, a many-to-many reflexive association

for a total of five fields:

```
//------------
// Fields.
//------------

private string courseNo;
private string courseName;
private double credits;
private ArrayList offeredAsSection; // of Section object references
private ArrayList prerequisites;    // of Course object references
```

Note that a reflexive association is handled in exactly the same way that any other association is handled: we provide the Course class with an ArrayList field called prerequisites that enables a given Course object to maintain handles on other Course objects. We've chosen not to encode this reflexive association bidirectionally. That is, a given Course object X knows which other Course objects A, B, C, etc. serve as *its* prerequisites, but doesn't know which Course objects L, M, N, etc. consider X to be one of *their* prerequisites (see Figure 14-7).

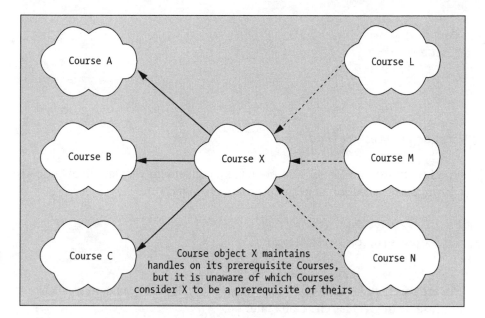

Figure 14-7. The prerequisite *association isn't implemented bidirectionally.*

Had we wanted this association to be bidirectional, we would have had to include a second ArrayList as a field in the Course class:

```
private ArrayList prerequisites;  // of Course object references
private ArrayList prerequisiteOf; // of Course object references
```

so that Course object X could hold onto this latter group of Course objects separately.

Course Methods

Most of the Course class methods use techniques that should already be familiar to you, based on our discussions of the Person, Professor, and Student classes. We'll highlight a few of the more interesting Course methods here, and leave it for you as an exercise to review the rest.

HasPrerequisites Method

This method inspects the size of the prerequisites ArrayList to determine whether or not a given Course has any prerequisite Courses:

```
public bool HasPrerequisites() {
  if (prerequisites.Count > 0) {
    return true;
```

```
    }
    else {
      return false;
    }
  }
```

GetPrerequisites Method

This method returns an IEnumerator object as a convenient way for client code to step through the collection of prerequisite Course objects:

```
public IEnumerator GetPrerequisites() {
  return prerequisites.GetEnumerator();
}
```

We see this method in use within the Course Display method, and we'll also see it in use by the Section class a bit later on.

ScheduleSection Method

This method illustrates several interesting techniques. First, note that this method invokes the Section class constructor to fabricate a new Section object on the fly, storing one handle on this Section object in the offeredAsSection ArrayList before returning a second handle on the object to the client code:

```
public Section ScheduleSection(char day, string time, string room,
                               int capacity) {
  // Create a new Section (note the creative way in
  // which we are assigning a section number) ...
  Section s = new Section(offeredAsSection.Count + 1,
                          day, time, this, room, capacity);

  // ... and then remember it!
  offeredAsSection.Add(s);

  return s;
}
```

Secondly, we're generating the first argument to the Section constructor—representing the Section number to be created—as a "one up" number by adding 1 to the number of elements in the offeredAsSection ArrayList. The first time that we invoke the ScheduleSection method for a given Course object, the ArrayList will be empty, and so the expression

```
offeredAsSection.Count + 1
```

will evaluate to 1, and hence we'll be creating Section number 1. The second time that this method is invoked for the same Course object, the ArrayList will already contain a handle on the first Section object that was created, and so the expression

```
offeredAsSection.Count + 1
```

will evaluate to 2, and hence we'll be creating Section number 2, and so forth.

There is one flaw with this approach: if we were to create, then delete, Section objects, the size of the ArrayList would expand and contract, and we could wind up with duplicate Section numbers. We'll remedy this flaw in Chapter 15.

Now, let's turn our attention to the Section class.

The Section Class (Representing Association Classes; Public Constant Fields)

The Section class represents an abstraction of a particular section of a college course as offered in a given semester, and is illustrated in Figure 14-8.

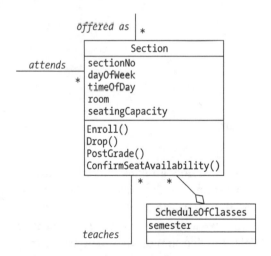

Figure 14-8. The Section *class*

Section Fields

The Section class participates in numerous relationships with other classes:

- *offered as*, a one-to-many association with Course

- An unnamed, one-to-many aggregation with ScheduleOfClasses

- *teaches*, a one-to-many association with Professor

- *attends*, a many-to-many association with Student

The *attends* association is in turn affiliated with an association class, TranscriptEntry. We learned in Chapter 10 that an association class can alternatively be depicted in a class diagram as having direct relationships with the classes at either end of the association, as shown in Figure 14-9, and so we'll encode a fifth relationship for the Section class, namely

- *assigns grade*, a one-to-many association with the TranscriptEntry class

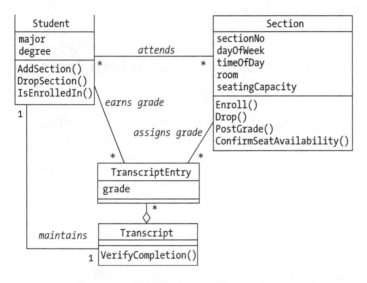

Figure 14-9. Adding the assigns grade *association*

(You may be wondering whether we should now go back and adjust the Student class to reflect the *earns grade* association with the TranscriptEntry class as a Student class field. The decision of whether or not to implement a particular relationship in code depends in part on what we anticipate our usage patterns to be, as we discussed in Chapter 10. We'll defer the decision of what to do with *earns grade* until we talk about the TranscriptEntry class in a bit more depth later in this chapter.)

We'll represent these five relationships in terms of Section fields as follows.

A Section object need only maintain a handle on one other object for those one-to-many relationships in which Section occupies the "many" end, namely

```
private Course representedCourse;
private ScheduleOfClasses offeredIn;
private Professor instructor;
```

For the two situations in which Section needs to maintain handles on ***collections*** of objects—Students and TranscriptEntries—we're going to employ Hashtables instead of ArrayLists this time. We do so because it's conceivable that we'll have a frequent need to "pluck" a given item from the collection directly, and Hashtable provides a key-based lookup mechanism that is ideal for this purpose.

For the Hashtable of Student object references, we'll use a string representing the Student's social security number (ssn) as a key for looking up a Student:

```
// The enrolledStudents Hashtable stores Student object references,
// using each Student's ssn as a string key.

private Hashtable enrolledStudents;
```

but for the Hashtable of TranscriptEntry object references, on the other hand, we'll use a Student object ***as a whole*** as a key for looking up that particular Student's TranscriptEntry as issued by this Section.

```
// The assignedGrades Hashtable stores TranscriptEntry object
// references, using a reference to the Student to whom it belongs
// as the key.

private Hashtable assignedGrades;
```

Public Constant Fields

In the Section class, we encounter our first use of const fields, which as we learned in Chapter 13 are an excellent means of defining constant values. In this particular situation, we want to define some status codes that the Section class can use when signaling the outcome of an enrollment attempt.

```
public const int SUCCESSFULLY_ENROLLED = 0;
public const int SECTION_FULL = 1;
public const int PREREQ_NOT_SATISFIED = 2;
public const int PREVIOUSLY_ENROLLED = 3;
```

Let's look at how these are put to use by studying the Enroll method of Section.

Enroll Method

This is a very complex method; we'll present the code in its entirety first without discussing it, and will then proceed to "dissect" it afterward.

```
public int Enroll(Student s) {
  // First, make sure that this Student is not already
  // enrolled for this Section, has not already enrolled
  // in another section of this class and that he/she has
  // NEVER taken and passed the course before.

  Transcript transcript = s.Transcript;

  if (s.IsEnrolledIn(this) ||
      s.IsCurrentlyEnrolledInSimilar(this) ||
      transcript.VerifyCompletion(this.RepresentedCourse)) {
    return PREVIOUSLY_ENROLLED;
  }

  // If there are any prerequisites for this course,
  // check to ensure that the Student has completed them.

  Course c = this.RepresentedCourse;
  if (c.HasPrerequisites()) {
    IEnumerator e = c.GetPrerequisites();
    while (e.MoveNext()) {
      Course pre = (Course) e.Current;

      // See if the Student's Transcript reflects
      // successful completion of the prerequisite.

      if (!transcript.VerifyCompletion(pre)) {
        return PREREQ_NOT_SATISFIED;
      }
    }
  }

  // If the total enrollment is already at the
  // the capacity for this Section, we reject this
  // enrollment request.

  if (!ConfirmSeatAvailability()) {
    return SECTION_FULL;
  }

  // If we made it to here in the code, we're ready to
  // officially enroll the Student.
```

```
// Note bidirectionality:  this Section holds
// onto the Student via the Hashtable, and then
// the Student is given a handle on this Section.

enrolledStudents.Add(s.Ssn, s);
s.AddSection(this);
return SUCCESSFULLY_ENROLLED;
}
```

We begin by verifying that the Student seeking enrollment (represented by argument s) hasn't already enrolled for this Section, and furthermore that he or she has never taken and successfully completed this Course (any Sections) in the past. To do so, we must obtain a handle on the Student's transcript; we store it in a locally declared reference variable called transcript, because we're going to need to consult with the Transcript object twice in this method:

```
public int Enroll(Student s) {
    // First, make sure that this Student is not already
    // enrolled for this Section, has not already enrolled
    // in another section of this class, and that he/she has
    // NEVER taken and passed the course before.

    Transcript transcript = s.Transcript;
```

We then use an if statement to test for either of two conditions: (a) is the Student currently enrolled in ***this*** Section or ***another*** Section of the ***same*** Course, and/or (b) does his or her Transcript indicate successful ***prior*** completion of the Course that is represented by this Section? Because we only need to use this Course object once in this method, we don't bother to save the handle returned to us by the RepresentedCourse property in a local variable; we just nest the invocation of this method within the call to VerifyCompletion, so that the Course object can be retrieved by the former and immediately passed along as an argument to the latter.

```
if (s.IsEnrolledIn(this) ||
    s.IsCurrentlyEnrolledInSimilar(this) ||
    transcript.VerifyCompletion(this.RepresentedCourse)) {
  return PREVIOUSLY_ENROLLED;
}
```

Whenever we encounter a return statement midway through a method as we have here, the method will immediately terminate execution without running to completion.

Note our use of PREVIOUSLY_ENROLLED, one of the constant fields declared by Section, as a return value. Declaring and using such standardized values is a great way to communicate status back to client code, as this sample pseudocode invocation of the Enroll method illustrates:

```
// Client code (pseudocode).

Section sec = new Section(...);
Student s = new Student(...);
// ...
int status = sec1.Enroll(s1);
if (status == Section.PREVIOUSLY_ENROLLED) {
  // Pseudocode.
  take appropriate action
}
if (status == Section.PREREQ_NOT_SATISFIED) {
  // Pseudocode.
  take appropriate action
}
else if (status == Section.SECTION_FULL) {
  // Pseudocode.
  take appropriate action
}
// etc.
```

Thus, both the client code and the Section object's method code are using the same symbolic names to communicate.

Next, we check to see if the Student has satisfied the prerequisites for this Section, if there are any. We use the Section's RepresentedCourse property to obtain a handle on the Course object that this Section represents, and then invoke the HasPrerequisites method on that Course object; if the result returned is true, then we know that there are prerequisites to be checked.

```
// If there are any prerequisites for this course,
// check to ensure that the Student has completed them.

Course c = this.RepresentedCourse;
if (c.HasPrerequisites()) {
```

If there are indeed prerequisites for this Course, we use the GetPrerequisites method defined by the Course class to obtain an IEnumerator object of all prerequisite Courses.

```
IEnumerator e = c.GetPrerequisites();
```

Then, we iterate through the IEnumerator; for each Course object reference pre that we extract from the IEnumerator, we invoke the VerifyCompletion method on the Student's Transcript object, passing in the prerequisite Course object reference pre. We haven't taken a look at the inner workings of the Transcript class yet, so for now, all we need to know about VerifyCompletion is that it will return a value of true if the Student has indeed successfully taken and passed the Course in question, or a value of false otherwise. We want to take action in situations where a prerequisite was *not* satisfied, so we use the unary negation operator (!) in front of the expression to indicate that we want the if test to succeed if the method call returns a value of false:

```
while (e.MoveNext()) {
  Course pre = (Course) e.Current;

  // See if the Student's Transcript reflects
  // successful completion of the prerequisite.

  if (!transcript.VerifyCompletion(pre)) {
    return PREREQ_NOT_SATISFIED;
  }
} // end if
```

If we make it through the prerequisite check without triggering the return statement, the next step in this method is to verify that there is still available seating in the Section; we return the status value SECTION_FULL value if there is not.

```
// If the total enrollment is already at the
// the capacity for this Section, we reject this
// enrollment request.

if (!ConfirmSeatAvailability()) {
  return SECTION_FULL;
}
```

Finally, if we've made it through both of the preceding tests unscathed, we're ready to officially enroll the Student. We use the Hashtable class's Add method to insert the Student reference into the enrolledStudents Hashtable, accessing the Ssn property on the Student to retrieve the string value of its ssn field, which we pass in as the key value. To achieve bidirectionality of the link between a Student and a Section, we then turn around and invoke the AddSection method on the Student object reference, passing it a handle on this Section.

```
    // Note bidirectionality: this Section holds
    // onto the Student via the Hashtable, and then
    // the Student is given a handle on this Section.

    enrolledStudents.Add(s.Ssn, s);
    s.AddSection(this);
    return SUCCESSFULLY_ENROLLED;
  }
```

Drop Method

The Drop method of Section performs the reverse operation of the Enroll method. We start by verifying that the Student in question is indeed enrolled in this Section, since we can't drop a Student who isn't enrolled in the first place:

```
public bool Drop(Student s) {
    // We may only drop a student if he/she is enrolled.

    if (!s.IsEnrolledIn(this)) {
      return false;
    }
```

and, if he or she truly is enrolled, then we use the Hashtable class's Remove method to locate and delete the Student reference, again via its ssn field value. In the interest of bidirectionality, we invoke the DropSection method on the Student, as well, to get rid of the handles at *both* ends of the link.

```
    else {
      // Find the student in our Hashtable, and remove it.

      enrolledStudents.Remove(s.Ssn);

      // Note bidirectionality.

      s.DropSection(this);
      return true;
    }
  }
```

PostGrade Method

The PostGrade method is used to assign a grade to a Student by creating a TranscriptEntry object to link the two. To ensure that we aren't inadvertently trying to assign a grade to a given Student more than once, we first check the assignedGrades Hashtable to see if it already contains an entry for this Student. If the Hashtable search returns anything but null, then we know a grade has already been posted for this Student, and we terminate execution of the method.

```
public bool PostGrade(Student s, string grade) {
    // Make sure that we haven't previously assigned a
    // grade to this Student by looking in the Hashtable
    // for an entry using this Student as the key.  If
    // we discover that a grade has already been assigned,
    // we return a value of false to indicate that
    // we are at risk of overwriting an existing grade.
    // (A different method, EraseGrade, can then be written
    // to allow a Professor to change his/her mind.)

    if (assignedGrades[s] != null) {
      return false;
    }
```

Assuming that a grade wasn't previously assigned, we invoke the appropriate constructor to create a new TranscriptEntry object. As we'll see when we study the inner workings of the TranscriptEntry class, this object will maintain handles on both the Student to whom a grade has been assigned and on the Section for which the grade was assigned. To enable this latter link to be bidirectional, we also store a handle on the TranscriptEntry object in the Section's Hashtable for this purpose.

```
    // First, we create a new TranscriptEntry object.  Note
    // that we are passing in a reference to THIS Section,
    // because we want the TranscriptEntry object,
    // as an association class ..., to maintain
    // "handles" on the Section as well as on the Student.
    // (We'll let the TranscriptEntry constructor take care of
    // "hooking" this T.E. to the correct Transcript.)

    TranscriptEntry te = new TranscriptEntry(s, grade, this);

    // Then, we "remember" this grade because we wish for
    // the connection between a T.E. and a Section to be
    // bidirectional.

    assignedGrades.Add(s, te);

    return true;
}
```

ConfirmAvailability Method

The `ConfirmSeatAvailability` method called from within `Enroll` is an internal housekeeping method; by declaring it to have private versus public visibility, we restrict its use so that only other methods of the `Section` class may invoke it.

```
private bool ConfirmSeatAvailability() {
  if (enrolledStudents.Count < GetSeatingCapacity()) {
    return true;
  }
  else {
    return false;
  }
}
```

Delegation, Revisited

In discussing the `Student` class, we briefly mentioned the `DisplayCourseSchedule` method as a complex example of delegation, and promised to come back and discuss it further.

What are the "raw materials"—data—available for an object to use when it's responding to a service request by executing one of its methods? By way of review, an object has at its disposal the following data sources:

- Simple data and/or object references that have been *encapsulated as fields* within the object itself

- Simple data and/or object references that are *passed in as arguments* in the method signature

- Data that is made available *globally* to the application as public static fields of some *other* class (We saw this technique demonstrated earlier in the chapter when we defined various status codes for the `Section` class, and will see this technique used again several more times within the SRS.)

- Data that can be *requested* from any of the objects that this object has a handle on, a process that we learned in Chapter 3 is known as *delegation*

It's this last source of data—data available by collaborating with other objects and delegating part of a task to them—that is going to play a particularly signifi-cant role in implementing the `DisplayCourseSchedule` method for the `Student` class.

Let's say we want the DisplayCourseSchedule method to display the following information for each Section that a Student is currently enrolled in:

```
Course No.:
Section No.:
Course Name:
Meeting Day and Time:
Room Location:
Professor's Name:
```

For example:

```
Course Schedule for Fred Schnurd
    Course No.:  CMP101
    Section No.:  2
    Course Name:  Beginning Computer Technology
    Meeting Day and Time Held:  W - 6:10 - 8:00 PM
    Room Location:  GOVT202
    Professor's Name:  John Carson
    -----
    Course No.:  ART101
    Section No.:  1
    Course Name:  Beginning Basketweaving
    Meeting Day and Time Held:  M - 4:10 - 6:00 PM
    Room Location:  ARTS25
    Professor's Name:  Snidely Whiplash
    -----
```

Let's start by looking at the fields of the Student class, to see which of this information is readily available to us. Student inherits from Person:

```
private string name;
private string ssn;
```

and adds

```
private string major;
private string degree;
private Transcript transcript;
private ArrayList attends; // of Sections
```

Let's begin to write the method; by stepping through the attends ArrayList, we can gain access to Section objects one by one:

```
public void DisplayCourseSchedule() {
  // Display a title first.

  Console.WriteLine("Course Schedule for " + this.Name);

  // Step through the ArrayList of Section objects,
  // processing these one by one.

  for (int i = 0; i < attends.Count; i++) {
    Section s = (Section) attends[i];

    // Now what goes here????
    // We must create the rest of the method ...
  }
}
```

Now that we have the beginnings of the method, let's determine how to fill in the gap (highlighted) in the preceding code.

Looking at all of the method and property headers declared for the Section class as evidence of the services that a Section object can perform, we see that several of these can immediately provide us with useful pieces of information relative to our mission of displaying a Student's course schedule:

Properties:

```
public int SectionNo(get; set;)
public char DayOfWeek(get; set;)
public string TimeOfDay(get; set;)
public Professor Instructor(get; set;)
public Course RepresentedCourse(get; set;)
public string Room(get; set;)
public int SeatingCapacity(get; set;)
public ScheduleOfClasses OfferedIn(get; set;)
```

Methods:

```
public override string ToString()
public int Enroll(Student s)
public bool Drop(Student s)
public int GetTotalEnrollment()
public override void Display()
public void DisplayStudentRoster()
public string GetGrade(Student s)
public bool PostGrade(Student s, string grade)
public bool SuccessfulCompletion(Student s)
public bool IsSectionOf(Course c)
```

Let's put the four highlighted Section class properties to use, and where we can't yet fill the gap completely, we'll insert "???" as a placeholder:

```csharp
public void DisplayCourseSchedule() {
  // Display a title first.

  Console.WriteLine("Course Schedule for " + this.Name);

  // Step through the ArrayList of Section objects,
  // processing these one by one.

  for (int i = 0; i < attends.Count; i++) {
    Section s = (Section) attends[i];

    // Since the attends ArrayList contains Sections that the
    // Student took in the past as well as those for which
    // the Student is currently enrolled, we only want to
    // report on those for which a grade has not yet been
    // assigned.

    if (s.GetGrade(this) == null) {
      Console.WriteLine("\tCourse No.:  " + ???);
      Console.WriteLine("\tSection No.:  " + s.SectionNo);
      Console.WriteLine("\tCourse Name:  " + ???);
      Console.WriteLine("\tMeeting Day and Time Held:  " +
              s.DayOfWeek + " - " + s.TimeOfDay);
      Console.WriteLine("\tRoom Location:  " + s.Room);
      Console.WriteLine("\tProfessor's Name:  " + ???);
      Console.WriteLine("\t-----");
    }
  }
}
```

Now what about the remaining "holes"?

The following two Section class properties:

```csharp
public Professor Instructor(get; set;)
public Course RepresentedCourse(get; set;)
```

will each hand us yet another object that we can "talk to": the Professor who teaches this Section, and the Course that this Section represents. Let's now look at what these objects can perform in the way of services.

A Professor object provides the following properties/methods (those marked with an asterisk comment (// *) are inherited from Person):

```
public string Name(get; set;)          // *
public string Ssn(get; set;)           // *
public string Title(get; set;)
public string Department(get; set;)
public override void Display()
public override string ToString()
public void DisplayTeachingAssignments()
public void AgreeToTeach(Section s)
```

and a Course object provides the following properties/methods:

```
public string CourseNo(get; set;)
public string CourseName(get; set;)
public double Credits(get; set;)
public void Display()
public override string ToString()
public void AddPrerequisite(Course c)
public bool HasPrerequisites()
public IEnumerator GetPrerequisites()
public Section ScheduleSection(char day, string time, string room,
    int capacity)
```

If we bring all of the highlighted properties to bear, we can wrap up the DisplayCourseSchedule method of the Student class as follows:

```
public void DisplayCourseSchedule() {
  // Display a title first.

  Console.WriteLine("Course Schedule for " + this.Name);

  // Step through the ArrayList of Section objects,
  // processing these one by one.

  for (int i = 0; i < attends.Count; i++) {
    Section s = (Section) attends[i];

    // Since the attends ArrayList contains Sections that the
    // Student took in the past as well as those for which
    // the Student is currently enrolled, we only want to
    // report on those for which a grade has not yet been
    // assigned.
```

```
    if (s.GetGrade(this) == null) {
      Console.WriteLine("\tCourse No.:   " +
                            s.RepresentedCourse.CourseNo);
      Console.WriteLine("\tSection No.:  " + s.SectionNo);
      Console.WriteLine("\tCourse Name:   " +
                            s.RepresentedCourse.CourseName);
      Console.WriteLine("\tMeeting Day and Time Held:   " +
                            s.DayOfWeek + " - " +
                            s.TimeOfDay);
      Console.WriteLine("\tRoom Location:   " + s.Room);
      Console.WriteLine("\tProfessor's Name:   " +
                            s.Instructor.Name);
      Console.WriteLine("\t-----");
    }
  }
}
```

Note that we're accessing the `RepresentedCourse` property of each `Section` object twice; we could instead access this property once, retrieving a `Course` object reference and holding on to it with reference variable `c`, as shown in the next snippet (and, while we're at it, we'll retrieve the `Professor` object representing the instructor for this section, and will hold onto with reference variable `p`):

```
for (int i = 0; i < attends.Count; i++) {
  Section s = (Section) attends[i];
  Course c = s.RepresentedCourse;
  Professor p = s.Instructor;

  // ...

  if (s.GetGrade(this) == null) {
    Console.WriteLine("\tCourse No.:   " + c.CourseNo);
    Console.WriteLine("\tSection No.:   " + s.SectionNo);
    Console.WriteLine("\tCourse Name:   " + c.CourseName);
    Console.WriteLine("\tMeeting Day and Time Held:   " +
                        s.DayOfWeek + " - " +
                        s.TimeOfDay);
    Console.WriteLine("\tRoom Location:   " + s.Room);
    Console.WriteLine("\tProfessor's Name:   " + p.Name);
    Console.WriteLine("\t-----");
  }
}
}
```

This method is a classic example of delegation:

- We start out asking a Student object to do something for us—namely, to display the Student's course schedule.

- The Student object in turn has to talk to the Section objects representing sections that the student is enrolled in, asking each of them to perform some of their services (methods).

- The Student object also has to ask those Section objects to hand over references to the Professor and Course objects that the Section objects know about, in turn asking *those* objects to perform some of *their* services.

This multitiered collaboration is depicted conceptually in Figure 14-10.

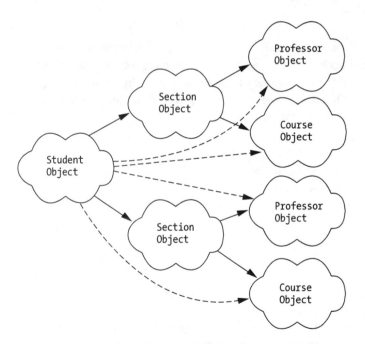

Figure 14-10. Many objects collaborate to accomplish a single method.

The ScheduleOfClasses Class

The ScheduleOfClasses class is a fairly simple class that serves as an example of how we can encapsulate a "standard" collection object within another class (see Figure 14-11), a design technique that we discussed in Chapter 6.

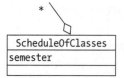

Figure 14-11. The ScheduleOfClasses *class*

ScheduleOfClasses Fields

The ScheduleOfClasses class consists of only two fields: a simple string representing the semester for which the schedule is valid (for example, "SP2004" for the Spring 2004 semester), and a Hashtable used to maintain handles on all of the Sections that are being offered that semester.

```
private string semester;

// This Hashtable stores Section object references, using
// a String concatenation of course no. and section no. as the
// key, for example, "MATH101 - 1".

private Hashtable sectionsOffered;
```

AddSection Method

Aside from a simple constructor, a Display method, and a property for the semester field, the only other feature that this class provides is a method for adding a Section object to the Hashtable, and then bidirectionally connecting the ScheduleOfClasses object back to the Section:

```
public void AddSection(Section s) {
    // We formulate a key by concatenating the course no.
    // and section no., separated by a hyphen.

    string key = s.RepresentedCourse.CourseNo +
                    " - " + s.SectionNo;
    sectionsOffered.Add(key, s);

    // Bidirectionally hook the ScheduleOfClasses back to the Section.

    s.OfferedIn = this;
}
```

587

The TranscriptEntry Association Class (Static Methods)

As we discussed in Chapter 6, the TranscriptEntry class (depicted in Figure 14-12) represents a single line item on a student's transcript.

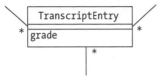

Figure 14-12. The TranscriptEntry *class*

TranscriptEntry Fields

As we saw earlier in this chapter, the TranscriptEntry class has one simple field, grade, and maintains associations with three other classes (see Figure 14-13):

- *earns grade*, a one-to-many association with Student

- *assigns grade*, a one-to-many association with Section

- An unnamed, one-to-many aggregation with the Transcript class

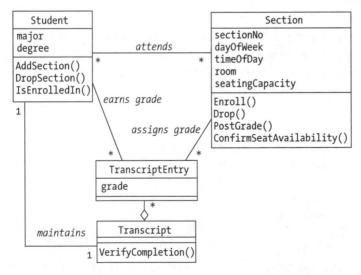

Figure 14-13. The TranscriptEntry *class has relationships with many other classes.*

TranscriptEntry is at the "many" end of all of these associations, and so it only needs to maintain a ***single*** handle on each type of object; no collection fields are required:

```
private string grade;
private Student student;
private Section section;
private Transcript transcript;
```

TranscriptEntry Constructor

The constructor for this class does most of the work of maintaining all of these relationships.

Using the set accessor of the Student property, we store the associated Student object's handle in the appropriate field.

```
//----------------
// Constructor(s).
//----------------

// Initialize the field values using the set accessor of the
// associated property.

public TranscriptEntry(Student s, string grade, Section se) {
  this.Student = s;
```

Note that we have chosen ***not*** to maintain the *earns grade* association bidirectionally; that is, we've provided no code in either this or the Student class to provide the Student object with a handle on this TranscriptEntry object. We've made this decision based upon the fact that we don't expect a Student to ever have to manipulate TranscriptEntry objects directly. Every Student object has an indirect means of reaching all of its TranscriptEntry objects, via the handle that a Student object maintains on its Transcript object, and the handles that the Transcript object in turn maintains on its TranscriptEntry objects. One might think that giving a Student object the ability to directly pull a given TranscriptEntry might be useful when wishing to determine the grade that the Student earned for a particular Section, but we've provided an alternative means of doing so, via the Section class's GetGrade method.

Even though it may not appear so, we are maintaining the ***assigns grade*** association with Section bidirectionally. We only see half of the "handshake" in the TranscriptEntry constructor:

```
this.Section = se;
```

but recall that when we looked at the PostGrade method of the Section class, we discussed the fact that Section was responsible for maintaining the bidirectionality of this association. When the Section's PostGrade method invokes the TranscriptEntry constructor, the Section object is returned a handle on this TranscriptEntry object, which it stores in the appropriate field. So, we only need worry about the second half of this "handshake" in TranscriptEntry.

On the other hand, the TranscriptEntry object has full responsibility for maintaining the bidirectionality of the association between it and the Transcript object:

```
// Obtain the Student's transcript ...

Transcript t = s.Transcript;

// ... and then hook the Transcript and the TranscriptEntry
// together bidirectionally.

this.Transcript = t;
t.AddTranscriptEntry(this);
}
```

ValidateGrade and *PassingGrade* Methods

The TranscriptEntry class provides our first SRS example of public static methods: it declares two methods, ValidateGrade and PassingGrade, that may be invoked as utility methods on the TranscriptEntry class from anywhere in the SRS application.

The first method is used to validate whether or not a particular string—say, "B+"—is formatted properly to represent a grade: namely, whether it starts with a capital letter "A," "B," "C," "D," "F," or "I" (for "Incomplete"), followed by an optional + or - character:

```
//  These next two methods are declared to be static, so that they
// may be used as utility methods.
public static bool ValidateGrade(string grade) {
  bool outcome = false;

  if (grade.Equals("F") || grade.Equals("I")) {
    outcome = true;
  }

  if (grade.StartsWith("A") || grade.StartsWith("B") ||
      grade.StartsWith("C") || grade.StartsWith("D")) {
    if (grade.Length == 1) {
      outcome = true;
    }
```

```
    else {
      if (grade.Length > 2) {
        outcome = false;
      }
      else {
        if (grade.EndsWith("+") || grade.EndsWith("-")) {
          outcome = true;
        }
        else {
          outcome = false;
        }
      }
    }
  }


  return outcome;
}
```

The second method is used to determine whether or not a particular string—say "D+"—represents a *passing* grade.

```
public static bool PassingGrade(string grade) {
  // First, make sure it is a valid grade.

  if (!ValidateGrade(grade)) {
    return false;
  }

  // Next, make sure that the grade is a D or better.

  if (grade.StartsWith("A") || grade.StartsWith("B") ||
      grade.StartsWith("C") || grade.StartsWith("D")) {
    return true;
  }
  else {
    return false;
  }
}
```

As we discussed in Chapters 7 and 13, public static methods are invoked on the hosting class as a whole—in other words, an object needn't be instantiated in order to use these methods.

We'll see actual use of the PassingGrade method in a moment, when we discuss the Transcript class.

The Transcript Class

The Transcript class, shown in Figure 14-14, serves as an abstraction of a student's transcript; i.e., a collection of TranscriptEntry references.

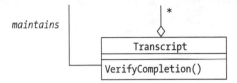

Figure 14-14. The Transcript *class*

Transcript Fields

The Transcript class participates in two relationships:

- *maintains*, a one-to-one association with Student

- An unnamed, one-to-many aggregation with TranscriptEntry

The SRS class diagram doesn't call out any other fields for the Transcript class, so we only encode these two:

```
private ArrayList transcriptEntries; // of TranscriptEntry object references
private Student studentOwner;
```

VerifyCompletion Method

The Transcript class has one particularly interesting method, VerifyCompletion, which is used to determine whether or not the Transcript contains evidence that a particular Course requirement has been satisfied. This method steps through the ArrayList of TranscriptEntries maintained by the Transcript object:

```
public bool VerifyCompletion(Course c) {
  bool outcome = false;

  // Step through all TranscriptEntries, looking for one
  // that reflects a Section of the Course of interest.

  for (int i = 0; i < transcriptEntries.Count; i++) {
    TranscriptEntry te = (TranscriptEntry) transcriptEntries[i];
```

For each entry, the method obtains a handle on the Section object represented by this entry, and then invokes the IsSectionOf method on that object to determine whether or not that Section represents the Course of interest.

```
Section s = te.Section;

if (s.IsSectionOf(c)) {
```

Assuming that the Section is indeed relevant, the method next uses the static PassingGrade method of the TranscriptEntry class to determine whether the grade earned in this Section was a passing grade or not. If it was a passing grade, we can terminate the loop immediately, since we only need to find *one* example of a passing grade for the Course of interest in order to ensure that the student whose Transcript we are inspecting contains evidence of successful course completion.

```
    // Ensure that the grade was high enough.

    if (TranscriptEntry.PassingGrade(te.Grade)) {
       outcome = true;

       // We've found one, so we can afford to
       // terminate the loop now.

       break;
    }
  }
}

return outcome;
}
```

The SRS Driver Program

Now that we've coded all of the classes called for by our model of the SRS, we need a way to test these. We could wait to put our application through its paces until we've built a GUI front-end; however, it would be nice to know sooner rather than later that our core classes are working properly. One very helpful technique for doing so is to write a command-line–driven program to instantiate objects of varying types and to invoke their critical methods, displaying the results to the command-line window for us to inspect.

We've developed just such a program by creating a class called SRS with a Main method that will serve as our test driver.

Public Static Fields

We're going to instantiate some Professor, Student, Course, and Section objects in this program, so we need a way to organize handles on these objects; we'll create collection objects as fields of the SRS class to hold each of these different object types. While we're at it, we'll declare them to be public static fields, which means that we're making these main object collections globally available to the entire application.

```
// We can effectively create "global" data by declaring
// public static fields in the main class.

// Entry points/"roots" for getting at objects.

public static ScheduleOfClasses scheduleOfClasses =
  new ScheduleOfClasses("SP2004");
public static ArrayList faculty; // of Professors
public static ArrayList studentBody; // of Students
public static ArrayList courseCatalog; // of Courses
```

The SRS ScheduleOfClasses class serves as a collection point for Section objects; for the other types of objects, we use simple ArrayLists, although we could go ahead and design classes comparable to ScheduleOfClasses to serve as encapsulated collections, perhaps named Faculty, StudentBody, and CourseCatalog, respectively. (In fact, we'll actually do so in Chapter 15, for reasons that will become clear at that time.) We don't need a collection for Transcript objects—we'll get to these via the handles that Student objects maintain—nor do we need one for TranscriptEntry objects—we'll get to these via the Transcript objects themselves.

Main Method

We'll now dive into the Main method for the SRS class. We'll start by declaring reference variables for each of the four main object types:

```
static void Main(string[] args) {
  Professor p1, p2, p3;
  Student s1, s2, s3;
  Course c1, c2, c3, c4, c5;
  Section sec1, sec2, sec3, sec4, sec5, sec6, sec7;
```

and we'll then use their various constructors to fabricate object instances, storing handles in the appropriate collections. (In Chapter 15, we'll explore how we can instantiate objects by reading data from a file instead of "hard coding" field values as we have here.)

```
// -----------
// Professors.
// -----------


p1 = new Professor("Jacquie Barker", "123-45-6789",
                    "Adjunct Professor", "Information Technology");
p2 = new Professor("John Carson", "567-81-2345",
                    "Full Professor", "Information Technology");
p3 = new Professor("Jackie Chan", "987-65-4321",
                    "Full Professor", "Information Technology");


// Add these to the appropriate ArrayList.

faculty = new ArrayList();
faculty.Add(p1);
faculty.Add(p2);
faculty.Add(p3);


// ---------
// Students.
// ---------


s1 = new Student("Joe Blow", "111-11-1111", "Math", "M.S.");
s2 = new Student("Gerson Lopez", "222-22-2222",
                "Information Technology", "Ph. D.");
s3 = new Student("Mary Smith", "333-33-3333", "Physics", "B.S.");


// Add these to the appropriate ArrayList.

studentBody = new ArrayList();
studentBody.Add(s1);
studentBody.Add(s2);
studentBody.Add(s3);


// --------
// Courses.
// --------


c1 = new Course("CMP101","Beginning Computer Technology", 3.0);
c2 = new Course("OBJ101","Object Methods for Software Development", 3.0);
c3 = new Course("CMP283","Higher Level Languages (C#)", 3.0);
c4 = new Course("CMP999","Living Brain Computers", 3.0);
c5 = new Course("ART101","Beginning Basketweaving", 3.0);
```

```
// Add these to the appropriate ArrayList.

courseCatalog = new ArrayList();
courseCatalog.Add(c1);
courseCatalog.Add(c2);
courseCatalog.Add(c3);
courseCatalog.Add(c4);
courseCatalog.Add(c5);
```

We use the AddPrerequisite method of the Course class to interrelate some of the Courses, so that c1 is a prerequisite for c2, c2 for c3, and c3 for c4. The only Courses that we don't specify prerequisites for in our test case are c1 and c5.

```
// Establish some prerequisites (c1 => c2 => c3 => c4).

c2.AddPrerequisite(c1);
c3.AddPrerequisite(c2);
c4.AddPrerequisite(c3);
```

To create Section objects, we take advantage of the Course class's ScheduleSection method, which, as you may recall, contains an embedded call to a Section class constructor. Each invocation of ScheduleSection returns a handle to a newly created Section object, which we store in the appropriate collection.

```
// ---------
// Sections.
// ---------

// Schedule sections of each Course by calling the
// ScheduleSection method of Course (which internally
// invokes the Section constructor).

sec1 = c1.ScheduleSection('M', "8:10 - 10:00 PM", "GOVT101", 30);
sec2 = c1.ScheduleSection('W', "6:10 - 8:00 PM", "GOVT202", 30);
sec3 = c2.ScheduleSection('R', "4:10 - 6:00 PM", "GOVT105", 25);
sec4 = c2.ScheduleSection('T', "6:10 - 8:00 PM", "SCI330", 25);
sec5 = c3.ScheduleSection('M', "6:10 - 8:00 PM", "GOVT101", 20);
sec6 = c4.ScheduleSection('R', "4:10 - 6:00 PM", "SCI241", 15);
sec7 = c5.ScheduleSection('M', "4:10 - 6:00 PM", "ARTS25", 40);

// Add these to the Schedule of Classes.

scheduleOfClasses.AddSection(sec1);
scheduleOfClasses.AddSection(sec2);
scheduleOfClasses.AddSection(sec3);
```

```
scheduleOfClasses.AddSection(sec4);
scheduleOfClasses.AddSection(sec5);
scheduleOfClasses.AddSection(sec6);
scheduleOfClasses.AddSection(sec7);
```

Next, we use the AgreeToTeach method declared for the Professor class to assign Professor objects to Section objects:

```
// Recruit a professor to teach each of the sections.

p3.AgreeToTeach(sec1);
p2.AgreeToTeach(sec2);
p1.AgreeToTeach(sec3);
p3.AgreeToTeach(sec4);
p1.AgreeToTeach(sec5);
p2.AgreeToTeach(sec6);
p3.AgreeToTeach(sec7);
```

We then simulate student registration by having Students enroll in the various Sections using the Enroll method. Recall that this method returns one of a set of predefined status values—either SUCCESSFULLY_ENROLLED, SECTION_FULL, PREREQ_NOT_SATISFIED, or PREVIOUSLY_ENROLLED—and so in order to display which status is returned in each case, we created a ReportStatus method solely for the purpose of formatting an informational message (the ReportStatus method is discussed separately a bit later):

```
Console.WriteLine("Student registration has begun!");
Console.WriteLine("");

// Students drop/add courses.

Console.WriteLine("Student " + s1.Name +
    " is attempting to enroll in " + sec1.ToString());

int status = sec1.Enroll(s1);

// Note the use of a special method to interpret
// and display the outcome of this enrollment request.
// (We could have included the code inline here, but
// since (a) it is rather complex and (b) it will need
// to be repeated for all subsequent enrollment requests
// below, it made sense to turn it into a reusable method
// instead.)
```

```
        ReportStatus(status);

        Console.WriteLine("Student " + s1.Name +
            " is attempting to enroll in " + sec2.ToString());
        status = sec2.Enroll(s1);
        ReportStatus(status);

        Console.WriteLine("Student " + s2.Name +
            " is attempting to enroll in " + sec2.ToString());
        status = sec2.Enroll(s2);
        ReportStatus(status);

        Console.WriteLine("Student " + s2.Name +
            " is attempting to enroll in " + sec3.ToString());
        status = sec3.Enroll(s2);
        ReportStatus(status);

        Console.WriteLine("Student " + s2.Name +
            " is attempting to enroll in " + sec7.ToString());
        status = sec7.Enroll(s2);
        ReportStatus(status);

        Console.WriteLine("Student " + s3.Name +
            " is attempting to enroll in " + sec1.ToString());
        status = sec1.Enroll(s3);
        ReportStatus(status);

        Console.WriteLine("Student " + s3.Name +
            " is attempting to enroll in " + sec5.ToString());
        status = sec5.Enroll(s3);
        ReportStatus(status);

        // Output a blank line.
        Console.WriteLine("");

        // When the dust settles, here's what folks wound up
        // being registered for:
        //    Section sec1:  Students s1, s3
        //    Section sec2:  Student s2
        //    Section sec7:  Student s2
```

Next, we simulate the assignment of grades at the end of the semester by invoking the postGrade method for each Student-Section combination:

```
// Semester is finished (boy, that was quick!).
// Professors assign grades.

sec1.PostGrade(s1, "C+");
sec1.PostGrade(s3, "A");
sec2.PostGrade(s2, "B+");
sec7.PostGrade(s2, "A-");
```

Finally, we put our various `Display` methods to good use by displaying the internal state of the various objects that we created—in essence, an "object dump":

```
// Let's see if everything got set up properly
// by calling various display methods!

Console.WriteLine("====================");
Console.WriteLine("Schedule of Classes:");
Console.WriteLine("====================");
Console.WriteLine("");
scheduleOfClasses.Display();

Console.WriteLine("======================");
Console.WriteLine("Professor Information:");
Console.WriteLine("======================");
Console.WriteLine("");
p1.Display();
Console.WriteLine("");
p2.Display();
Console.WriteLine("");
p3.Display();
Console.WriteLine("");

Console.WriteLine("====================");
Console.WriteLine("Student Information:");
Console.WriteLine("====================");
Console.WriteLine("");
s1.Display();
Console.WriteLine("");
s2.Display();
Console.WriteLine("");
s3.Display();
}
```

Here is the ReportStatus housekeeping method that we mentioned earlier; it simply translates the various constant int values into a printed string message:

```
public static void ReportStatus(int status) {
    if (status == Section.SUCCESSFULLY_ENROLLED) {
      Console.WriteLine("outcome:   SUCCESSFULLY_ENROLLED");
    }
    else if (status == Section.PREREQ_NOT_SATISFIED) {
      Console.WriteLine("outcome:   PREREQ_NOT_SATISFIED");
    }
    else if (status == Section.PREVIOUSLY_ENROLLED) {
      Console.WriteLine("outcome:   PREVIOUSLY_ENROLLED");
    }
    else if (status == Section.SECTION_FULL) {
      Console.WriteLine("outcome:   SECTION_FULL");
    }
}
```

Compiling the SRS

Now that we've written the initial version of the SRS, we can compile it. The simplest way to compile the source code is with the following command:

```
csc *.cs
```

However, if the code is compiled in this manner, the result will be an executable named Course.exe, because as we discussed in Chapter 13 an executable is by default named after the first source code file that is compiled. A file named Course.exe would indeed serve just fine as the SRS application's executable, but it would be more intuitive if the executable were named SRS.exe. To achieve this end, we can either rename the Course.exe file after the fact, or we can use the /out option when the source code is compiled, as follows:

```
csc /out:SRS.exe *.cs
```

As discussed in Chapter 13, the /out option is used to designate an output file name, in this case SRS.exe.

We then execute the SRS program simply by typing

```
SRS
```

at the command line.

When compiled and run, the SRS program produces the following command-line window output:

Student registration has begun!

Student Joe Blow is attempting to enroll in CMP101 - 1 - M - 8:10 - 10:00 PM
outcome: SUCCESSFULLY_ENROLLED
Student Joe Blow is attempting to enroll in CMP101 - 2 - W - 6:10 - 8:00 PM
outcome: PREVIOUSLY_ENROLLED
Student Gerson Lopez is attempting to enroll in CMP101 - 2 - W - 6:10 - 8:00 PM
outcome: SUCCESSFULLY_ENROLLED
Student Gerson Lopez is attempting to enroll in OBJ101 - 1 - R - 4:10 - 6:00 PM
outcome: PREREQ_NOT_SATISFIED
Student Gerson Lopez is attempting to enroll in ART101 - 1 - M - 4:10 - 6:00 PM
outcome: SUCCESSFULLY_ENROLLED
Student Mary Smith is attempting to enroll in CMP101 - 1 - M - 8:10 - 10:00 PM
outcome: SUCCESSFULLY_ENROLLED
Student Mary Smith is attempting to enroll in CMP283 - 1 - M - 6:10 - 8:00 PM
outcome: PREREQ_NOT_SATISFIED

=====================
Schedule of Classes:
=====================

Schedule of Classes for SP2004

Section Information:
  Semester: SP2004
  Course No.: CMP101
  Section No: 2
  Offered: W at 6:10 - 8:00 PM
  In Room: GOVT202
  Professor: John Carson
        Total of 1 student enrolled, as follows:
  Gerson Lopez

Section Information:
  Semester: SP2004
  Course No.: CMP101
  Section No: 1
  Offered: M at 8:10 - 10:00 PM
  In Room: GOVT101
  Professor: Jackie Chan
        Total of 2 students enrolled, as follows:
  Mary Smith
  Joe Blow

```
Section Information:
  Semester:  SP2004
  Course No.:  CMP283
  Section No:  1
  Offered:  M at 6:10 - 8:00 PM
  In Room:  GOVT101
  Professor:  Jacquie Barker
Total of 0 students enrolled.

Section Information:
  Semester:  SP2004
  Course No.:  CMP999
  Section No:  1
  Offered:  R at 4:10 - 6:00 PM
  In Room:  SCI241
  Professor:  John Carson
Total of 0 students enrolled.

Section Information:
  Semester:  SP2004
  Course No.:  OBJ101
  Section No:  2
  Offered:  T at 6:10 - 8:00 PM
  In Room:  SCI330
  Professor:  Jackie Chan
Total of 0 students enrolled.

Section Information:
  Semester:  SP2004
  Course No.:  OBJ101
  Section No:  1
  Offered:  R at 4:10 - 6:00 PM
  In Room:  GOVT105
  Professor:  Jacquie Barker
Total of 0 students enrolled.

Section Information:
  Semester:  SP2004
  Course No.:  ART101
  Section No:  1
  Offered:  M at 4:10 - 6:00 PM
  In Room:  ARTS25
  Professor:  Jackie Chan
        Total of 1 student enrolled, as follows:
  Gerson Lopez
```

```
=======================
Professor Information:
=======================

Person Information:
  Name:  Jacquie Barker
  Soc. Security No.:  123-45-6789
Professor-Specific Information:
  Title:  Adjunct Professor
  Teaches for Dept.:  Information Technology
Teaching Assignments for Jacquie Barker:
  Course No.:  OBJ101
  Section No.:  1
  Course Name:  Object Methods for Software Development
  Day and Time:  R - 4:10 - 6:00 PM
  -----
  Course No.:  CMP283
  Section No.:  1
  Course Name:  Higher Level Languages (C#)
  Day and Time:  M - 6:10 - 8:00 PM
  -----

Person Information:
  Name:  John Carson
  Soc. Security No.:  567-81-2345
Professor-Specific Information:
  Title:  Full Professor
  Teaches for Dept.:  Information Technology
Teaching Assignments for John Carson:
  Course No.:  CMP101
  Section No.:  2
  Course Name:  Beginning Computer Technology
  Day and Time:  W - 6:10 - 8:00 PM
  -----
  Course No.:  CMP999
  Section No.:  1
  Course Name:  Living Brain Computers
  Day and Time:  R - 4:10 - 6:00 PM
  -----

Person Information:
  Name:  Jackie Chan
  Soc. Security No.:  987-65-4321
```

```
Professor-Specific Information:
  Title:  Full Professor
  Teaches for Dept.:  Information Technology
Teaching Assignments for Jackie Chan:
  Course No.:  CMP101
  Section No.:  1
  Course Name:  Beginning Computer Technology
  Day and Time:  M - 8:10 - 10:00 PM
  -----
  Course No.:  OBJ101
  Section No.:  2
  Course Name:  Object Methods for Software Development
  Day and Time:  T - 6:10 - 8:00 PM
  -----
  Course No.:  ART101
  Section No.:  1
  Course Name:  Beginning Basketweaving
  Day and Time:  M - 4:10 - 6:00 PM
  -----


====================
Student Information:
====================


Person Information:
  Name:  Joe Blow
  Soc. Security No.:  111-11-1111
Student-Specific Information:
  Major:  Math
  Degree:  M.S.
Course Schedule for Joe Blow
Transcript for:  Joe Blow (111-11-1111) [M.S. - Math]
  Semester:        SP2004
  Course No.:      CMP101
  Credits:         3.0
  Grade Received:  C+
  -----
Person Information:
  Name:  Gerson Lopez
  Soc. Security No.:  222-22-2222
Student-Specific Information:
  Major:  Information Technology
  Degree:  Ph. D.
```

```
Course Schedule for Gerson Lopez
Transcript for:  Gerson Lopez (222-22-2222) [Ph. D. - Information Technology]
   Semester:        SP2004
   Course No.:      CMP101
   Credits:         3.0
   Grade Received:  B+
   -----
   Semester:        SP2004
   Course No.:      ART101
   Credits:         3.0
   Grade Received:  A-
   -----

Person Information:
   Name:  Mary Smith
   Soc. Security No.:  333-33-3333
Student-Specific Information:
   Major:  Physics
   Degree:  B.S.
Course Schedule for Mary Smith
Transcript for:  Mary Smith (333-33-3333) [B.S. - Physics]
   Semester:        SP2004
   Course No.:      CMP101
   Credits:         3.0
   Grade Received:  A
   -----
```

The preceding output demonstrates that the SRS is working properly! Of course, the SRS driver program could be extended to test various other scenarios; some of the exercises at the end of this chapter suggest ways that you might wish to try doing so.

Debugging Tip

One of the most frequent problems that a new C# programmer encounters when testing an application is a **null reference exception.** This is a runtime error caused when a programmer has forgotten to initialize a reference, but then tries to access it as though it were referencing an actual object.

A Null Reference Exception Example

Let's purposely create a situation where a null reference exception will arise. We'll use the following simplified version of the Section class in our experiment that only declares two fields, representing a section number and an instructor:

```
using System;

public class Section {
  private int sectionNo;
  private Professor instructor;
  // etc.

  // Constructor.
  public Section(int sNo) {
    this.SectionNo = sNo;

    // A specific Professor has not yet been identified to teach this Section;
    // the client application must explicitly call the Instructor property as
    // a separate step later on, to initialize the instructor field. So, by
    // default, the instructor field is initialized to the value null.
  }

  //-----------------
  // Properties.
  //-----------------

  public int SectionNo {
    get {
      return sectionNo;
    }
    set {
      sectionNo = value;
    }
  }

  public Professor Instructor {
    get {
      return instructor;
    }
    set {
      instructor = value;
    }
  }
```

```
public void Display() {
   // This method is written assuming that both the sectionNo and
   // instructor have already been initialized to meaningful values.
   Console.WriteLine("\tSection No.:  " + this.SectionNo);
   Console.WriteLine("\tProfessor:  " + this.Instructor.Name);
 }
}
```

Now, in our main program, we'll try to instantiate, and then display, a Section object:

```
using System;

public class NullReferenceExample {
  static void Main(string[] args) {
    Section s = new Section(1);

    // We've forgotten to set s's Instructor property to refer to
    // a valid Professor object, so when we call s's Display
    // method on the next line, we'll be in trouble at run time!
    s.Display();
  }
}
```

We get the following output from our program, including a runtime error message generated by our call to s.Display():

```
Section No: 1
System.NullReferenceException: Object reference not set to an
instance of an object
    at Section.Display()
    at NullReferenceExample.Main(String[] args)
```

This runtime output is known as an **exception trace**—it indicates that an exception occurred in the Display method of the Section class, which was in turn called from the Main method of the NullReferenceExample class.

If we want to know precisely which line of source code the exception occurred on, we can include the line numbers in an exception trace. To do so, the program must be recompiled with the debugging option turned on:

```
csc /debug  NullReferenceExample.cs Section.cs
```

in which case the exception trace would display line numbers as follows:

```
Section No: 1
System.NullReferenceException: Object reference not set to an
instance of an object
    at Section.Display() in C:\Section.cs : line 24
    at NullReferenceExample.Main(String[] args)
        in C:\NullReferenceExample.cs : line 8
```

A null reference exception indicates that some reference variable, instead of referring to a legitimate object, refers to ***nothing!*** That is, that the value of the reference variable in question was null at the time that the offending line of code was executed. In this case, the exception actually arises in the line of code in the Display method that is highlighted here:

```
public void Display() {
   Console.WriteLine("\tSection No.:  " + this.SectionNo);
   Console.WriteLine("\tProfessor:   " + this.Instructor.Name);
}
```

In this line of code, the Instructor property's get accessor—this.Instructor—is returning the value of the instructor field of the Section object, which was initialized to the value null by the constructor and then never updated. So, the subsequent attempt to invoke the Name property—this.Instructor.Name—is what actually raised the exception—we can't get the name of a nonexistent object! We are, in effect, trying to evaluate the expression null.Name, which makes no sense.

If it's likely that we'll want to display information about a Section object that doesn't have a Professor assigned to teach it, we could "bulletproof" the offending line of code to read as follows:

```
public void Display() {
   Console.WriteLine("\tSection No.:  " + this.SectionNo);
   Professor p = this.Instructor;
   if (p != null) Console.WriteLine("\tProfessor:   " + p.Name);
}
```

Here, we've inserted a test to ensure that p isn't equal to null before we attempt to "talk" to the object referenced by p. If p is indeed null, the second WriteLine call is skipped over. We could be a bit more thorough, adding an else clause to our if statement so that two lines of output are always generated no matter what:

```
public void Display() {
   Console.WriteLine("\tSection No.:  " + this.SectionNo);
   Professor p = this.Instructor;
   if (p != null) {
     Console.WriteLine("\tProfessor:   " + p.Name);
   }
```

```
    else {
      Console.WriteLine("\tProfessor:  TBD");
    }
  }
}
```

Summary

You've now seen C# in action! We've built a command-line driven version of the SRS application; although this isn't typically how most applications are invoked—most "industrial-strength" applications have GUI front-ends—developing such a version is a crucial step in testing your "core" classes to ensure that all methods are working properly. And, aside from the various Display methods that we encoded for testing purposes, all of the code that we've written for the command-line version of the application will carry forward intact when we round the application out in the next two chapters.

Exercises

All of the following exercises involve making modifications/extensions to the SRS code presented in this chapter. If you haven't already done so, please download the code from the Apress web site in preparation for these exercises; see Appendix D for details.

1. Expand the SRS.cs class's Main method to represent a second semester's worth of course registrations. (Hint: this will require a second instantiation of the ScheduleOfClasses class.)

    *   Change the grades received by some Students in the first semester to failing grades, then attempt to register the Student for a course in the second semester requiring successful completion in a previous semester.

    *   Try registering a Student for a course in the second semester that he or she has already successfully completed in the first semester.

2. Improve the logic of the AddPrerequisite method of the Course class to ensure that a Course can't accidentally be assigned as its own prerequisite.

3. Improve the logic of the AgreeToTeach method of the Professor class so that a Professor can't accidentally agree to teach two different Sections that meet at the same day/time.

4. Implement a CancelSection method for the Course class, and then correct the erroneous logic of the ScheduleSection method having to do with the manner in which Section numbers are assigned. (Hint: introduce a static field to the Course class for this purpose.)

5. The Enroll method of the Section class doesn't take into account the fact that a Student may simultaneously be registered for a course and its pre-requisite. Modify this method to allow for this possibility.

6. The PostGrade method of the Section class makes mention of the need for an EraseGrade method, in the event that a Professor wishes to change his or her mind about the grade that has been issued to a Student; create the EraseGrade method.

7. *Advanced exercise:* Modify the ScheduleSection method of the Course class to prevent two Sections from being scheduled for the same classroom at the same day/time.

8. *Advanced exercise:* The Display method of the ScheduleOfClasses class doesn't presently list Sections in alphabetically sorted order by course name; make whatever changes are necessary to do so.

Rounding Out Our Application, Part 1: Adding File Persistence

IN CHAPTER 14, we built our first version of the SRS as a command-line driven application that focused on the domain classes called out by our model: Person, Professor, Student, Course, Section, ScheduleOfClasses, Transcript, and TranscriptEntry. The Main method of the SRS driver class was written simply to instantiate objects of the various types and to put them through their paces, as a means of testing that we've implemented the logic of their methods correctly. But, the SRS application as written isn't useful as an "industrial-strength" application yet because

- It "hard codes" all of its objects/data.

- It provides no means of saving the state of the objects from one invocation of the application to the next, a process known as **persisting data.**

- Most "industrial-strength" information systems requiring significant user interaction rely on a graphical user interface (GUI) for such interaction.

In essence, we've developed the core of our application by creating the classes that represent the domain model. In this chapter, we're going to revise our SRS application to provide a means for reading/writing data to/from files so that we can remedy the first two of these shortcomings; then, in Chapter 16, we'll remedy the third deficiency by adding a graphical user interface front-end as shown in Figure 15-1.

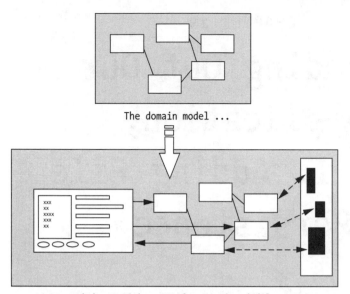

... gets rounded out with a GUI front-end and file persistence.

Figure 15-1. Adding file persistence and a GUI front-end to the SRS

In this chapter, you'll get to apply much of what you've learned about C# in Chapter 13, and to actually see it in action in the SRS. You'll also learn the following techniques:

- How we approach file input/output in C#

- An approach for parsing tab-delimited ASCII records to initialize an object's state, or to initialize a collection of objects

- A means of persisting an object's state in a simple ASCII file

- How to prepare a "test scaffold" Main method for testing isolated classes

- How proper encapsulation streamlines client code (for example, the SRS Main method)

What Is Persistence?

Whenever we run a program such as our SRS application, any objects (or value types, for that matter) that we declare and instantiate "live" in memory. When the program terminates, all of the memory allocated to the program is released back to the operating system, and the internal states of all of the objects created by the application are lost unless they have been saved—**persisted**—in some fashion.

Using various APIs, C# provides a wealth of options with regard to persisting data.

- The programming elements found in the System.Data, System.Data.Odbc, and System.Data.OleDb namespaces allow us to save data to an ODBC- or OLE DB–compliant database.

- We can output whole objects in a special binary form known as a C# **serialized object**, ideal for distributing objects over a network.

- We can also save information in a fairly straightforward, "human readable" ASCII data format, as either of the following:

  - Hierarchically arranged data, such as with the Extensible Markup Language (XML) standard, in which we intersperse information—**"content"**—with **custom tags** that describe how the information is to be interpreted, such as this simple example illustrating a Professor object with two Student advisees:

```
<Professor>
  <name>Dr. Irving Smith</name>
  <ssn>123-45-6789</ssn>
  <title>Associate Professor</title>
  <advisee>
    <type>Student</type>
    <sname>Joe Blow</sname>
    <sssn>987-65-4321</sssn>
  </advisee>
  <advisee>
    <type>Student</type>
    <sname>Mary Jones</sname>
    <sssn>999-88-7777</sssn>
  </advisee>
</Professor>
```

  - Simple tab- or comma-delimited record-oriented data.

We'll be illustrating the most basic form of data persistence—**record-oriented ASCII file persistence**—in our SRS application code; but many of the same design issues are applicable to the other forms of persistence as well, such as

- ***Hiding the details of how we persist an object*** by encapsulating them within an object's methods, so that client code doesn't have to get bogged down with the details.

- Ensuring that whatever approach we take to persisting an object today is ***flexible***, so that we can swap out one approach and swap in another without making dramatic changes to our entire application.

- ***Proper and graceful error handling*** when something goes amiss; since persistence involves interacting with an external file system, database management system, and/or network, there are a lot of potential points of failure that are outside of the immediate program's control.

and so forth.

Of course, there are two "sides" to the file persistence "coin": writing an object's state out to a file, and reading it back in again later. We'll talk briefly about a C# approach for each.

The FileStream Class

A FileStream object is a type of C# object that knows how to open a file and either ***read data from*** the file or ***write data to*** the file, one byte at a time.

The constructor for the FileStream class has the following header:

```
public FileStream(string filename, int mode)
```

e.g.,

```
FileStream fs = new FileStream("data.dat", FileMode.Open);
```

where mode is one of several constants defined by the FileMode class:

- FileMode.Open opens an existing file for either reading or writing; if the file in question doesn't exist or can't be opened, a FileNotFoundException is thrown.

- FileMode.Create opens a brand-new file for writing; if a file by the specified name already exists, or if a file can't be created for some reason—e.g., if the target directory is write-protected—then an IOException is thrown.

- FileMode.Append opens an existing file for writing, so that additional data may be appended to the end of the file; if the specified file isn't found, a FileNotFoundException is thrown.

- FileMode.CreateOrAppend will attempt to open an existing file for writing, if one is found with the specified name; otherwise, it will create a new file for writing. If for some reason a file can't be opened or created—e.g., if the target directory is write-protected—then an IOException is thrown.

The FileStream class is defined in the System.IO namespace.

Reading from a File

The basic C# approach that we're going to use for reading records one-by-one from an ASCII file involves *two* types C# objects—a FileStream object and a StreamReader object (see Figure 15-2).

1. First, we'll create an object of type FileStream, which as we've already mentioned knows how to open a file and read data from the file *one byte at a time.*

2. Next, we'll pass a reference to that FileStream object as an argument to the constructor for a StreamReader, a more sophisticated type of object that is effectively "wrapped around" the FileStream. The StreamReader's ReadLine method knows how to internally collect up, or **buffer,** individual characters as read by the FileStream until an end-of-line character is detected, at which point the StreamReader hands back a *complete line/record of data* to the client code.

The StreamReader class is also defined in the System.IO namespace.

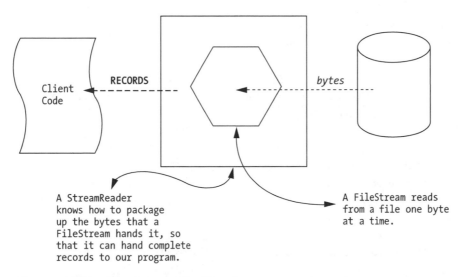

Figure 15-2. Reading from a file, C# style

Here is an example to illustrate the general process of reading from a file; we've left out some details, but will see this process carried out in earnest in the various SRS classes that we'll be reviewing later on in this chapter. We'll present the example in its entirety first, and then we'll highlight some noteworthy points afterward.

```csharp
using System.IO;

public class IOExample
{
  static void Main() {
    // Declare references to the objects that we'll need
    // in order to read from a file.
    FileStream fs;
    StreamReader srIn;

    // Read operations should be placed in a try-catch block.
    try {
      // Create a FileStream ...
      fs = new FileStream("data.dat", FileMode.Open);

      // ... and a StreamReader based on that FileStream.
      srIn = new StreamReader(fs);

      // Read the first line from the file.
      string line = srIn.ReadLine();

      // As long as the line isn't null, keep going!
      while (line != null) {
        // Pseudocode.
        process the most recently read line

        // Read another line (will be set to null when
        // the file has been exhausted).
        line = srIn.ReadLine();
      }

      // Close the StreamReader, which causes the FileStream to
      // also be closed.
      srIn.Close();
    }
    catch (IOException ioe) {
      // Perform exception handling ... details omitted.
    }
  }
}
```

Narrating our example:

- Because so many things can potentially go wrong when attempting to perform file I/O—a file that we're trying to open may not exist, a file that we want to write data to may have read-only protection, and so forth—we must place our code within a try block, and provide code to catch and respond to potential IOExceptions.

- We want to read data from an ***existing*** file, and so the FileMode.Open constant is being passed to the FileStream constructor:

```
fs = new FileStream("data.dat", FileMode.Open);
```

- We then "wrap" the FileStream in a new instance of a StreamReader to allow us to read data from the file a line at a time using the ReadLine method of the StreamReader class:

```
srIn = new StreamReader(fs);
```

- We use the StreamReader's ReadLine method to read one line/record's worth of data at a time:

```
string line = srIn.ReadLine();
```

and as long as this method doesn't return a value of null—null signals that the end of file has been reached—then we know that we've read in a legitimate record from the file:

```
// As long as the line isn't null, keep going!
while (line != null) { ... }
```

- We must remember to read another record's worth of data from within the while loop so that we don't wind up creating an infinite loop:

```
line = srIn.ReadLine();
```

- Finally, we must remember to close the StreamReader, which also closes the FileStream:

```
srIn.Close();
```

It's important to remember to close a StreamReader when we're finished with a file for several reasons:

- So that the file won't remain open/locked to subsequent access

- So that the application as a whole doesn't exceed the (platform-dependent) maximum allowable open file limit

- For the general good of freeing up unused objects so that they will be subject to garbage collection

Writing to a File

The basic C# approach that we'll be using for ***writing*** records to an ASCII file is similar, but of course in reverse, to what it takes to ***read*** from a file (see Figure 15-3).

1. We again create an object of type FileStream; by specifying the appropriate mode to the FileStream constructor, the FileStream can be used to overwrite an existing file (FileMode.Open), append data to an existing file (FileMode.Append), create a new file (FileMode.Create), or combine the previous two approaches (FileMode.OpenOrCreate).

2. Then, we pass that FileStream object as an argument to the constructor for a StreamWriter, a more sophisticated type of object that is "wrapped around" the FileStream. The StreamWriter's WriteLine method knows how to pass an ***entire record/line's worth of data***, one character at a time, to its encapsulated FileStream object, which then outputs the data ***one byte at a time*** to the file.

The StreamWriter class inherits the WriteLine method from the TextWriter class. The method works in a similar fashion to the Console.WriteLine method that you're already familiar with, the only difference being that the former causes text to be written to a file or output stream, whereas the latter causes text to be displayed in the command-line window. StreamWriter also defines a Write method, which works exactly like the Console.Write method.

The StreamWriter class is defined in the System.IO namespace.

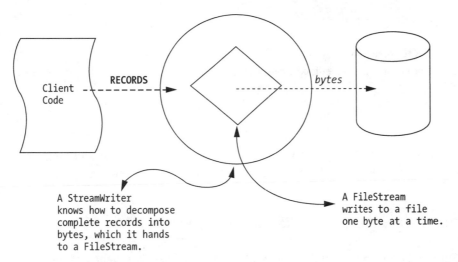

A StreamWriter
knows how to decompose
complete records into
bytes, which it hands
to a FileStream.

A FileStream
writes to a file
one byte at a time.

Figure 15-3. Writing to a file, C# style

We'll see this carried out in earnest in the Student class, which we'll be reviewing in detail later in this chapter, but for now, here's the general approach; because this code is so similar to the previous IOExample, we'll present it without narration here—please refer to the in-line comments:

```
using System.IO;

public class IOExample2
{
  static void Main() {
    FileStream fs;
    StreamWriter sw;

    // Write operations should be placed in a try-catch block.
    try {
      // Create a FileStream ...
      fs = new FileStream("data.dat", FileMode.OpenOrCreate);

      // ... and a StreamWriter based on that FileStream.
      sw = new StreamWriter(fs);

      // Pseudocode.
      while (still want to print more) {
        sw.WriteLine(whatever string data we wish to output);
      }
```

```
      sw.Close();
    }
    catch (IOException ioe) {
      // perform some exception handling
    }
  }
}
```

We'll use this basic approach when we persist the results of a student registration session to a file; this will be discussed in detail toward the end of the chapter.

Populating the Main SRS Collections

In Chapter 14, we introduced the ScheduleOfClasses class as a means of encapsulating a collection of Section objects, but all of the work necessary to populate this collection was performed in the Main method of the SRS class. By way of review, we first instantiated a ScheduleOfClasses object as a public static attribute of the SRS class:

```
public static ScheduleOfClasses scheduleOfClasses =
    new ScheduleOfClasses("SP2004");
```

Next, we called the ScheduleSection method on various Course objects named c1 through to c5 from the SRS Main method to instantiate seven Section objects named sec1 through to sec7, using hard-coded attribute values:

```
// Schedule sections of each Course by calling the
// ScheduleSection method of Course (which internally
// invokes the Section constructor).

sec1 = c1.ScheduleSection('M', "8:10 - 10:00 PM", "GOVT101", 30);
sec2 = c1.ScheduleSection('W', "6:10 - 8:00 PM", "GOVT202", 30);
sec3 = c2.ScheduleSection('R', "4:10 - 6:00 PM", "GOVT105", 25);
sec4 = c2.ScheduleSection('T', "6:10 - 8:00 PM", "SCI330", 25);
sec5 = c3.ScheduleSection('M', "6:10 - 8:00 PM", "GOVT101", 20);
sec6 = c4.ScheduleSection('R', "4:10 - 6:00 PM", "SCI241", 15);
sec7 = c5.ScheduleSection('M', "4:10 - 6:00 PM", "ARTS25", 40);
```

We then invoked the AddSection method on the scheduleOfClasses object numerous times to add these Sections to its encapsulated collection:

```
// Add these to the Schedule of Classes.

scheduleOfClasses.AddSection(sec1);
scheduleOfClasses.AddSection(sec2);
```

```
scheduleOfClasses.AddSection(sec3);
scheduleOfClasses.AddSection(sec4);
scheduleOfClasses.AddSection(sec5);
scheduleOfClasses.AddSection(sec6);
scheduleOfClasses.AddSection(sec7);
```

Ideally, rather than hard-coding the information about these Sections in the Main method of the SRS class, we'd like to acquire this information dynamically from an ASCII file. In fact, while we're at it, it would be preferable to acquire *all* of the data needed to initialize the SRS application's primary object collections from ASCII files. This includes

- The schedule of classes itself

- The course catalog: that is, a list of courses on which the schedule of classes is based, along with information about which course is a prerequisite of which other(s)

- The faculty roster, along with information regarding which professor is scheduled to teach which section(s)

These latter two collections haven't appeared in our object model before, because they weren't necessary for fulfilling the use cases that we came up with for the SRS back in Chapter 9. These collections represent what we've spoken of before as **implementation classes;** looking ahead, we know that we're going to need these when the time comes to build our SRS user interface, so we'll go ahead and implement them now. (We're not worrying about creating a StudentBody collection to house Student objects, for reasons that will become apparent later.)

We'll define five data files to "feed" these three collections, as follows:

- CourseCatalog.dat: This file contains records consisting of three tab-delimited fields: a course number, a course title, and the number of credits that the course is worth, represented as a floating point number.

  In other words, this data file represents the attributes of the Course class in our domain model. It will "feed" the CourseCatalog collection.

  Here are the test data contents of the file that we'll use for all of the work that we'll do in this chapter; <tab> represents the presence of an otherwise invisible tab character.

```
CMP101<tab>Beginning Computer Technology<tab>3.0
OBJ101<tab>Object Methods for Software Development<tab>3.0
CMP283<tab>Higher Level Languages (C#)<tab>3.0
CMP999<tab>Living Brain Computers<tab>3.0
ART101<tab>Beginning Basketweaving<tab>3.0
```

- `Faculty.dat`: This file contains records consisting of four tab-delimited fields, representing a professor's name, SSN, title, and the department that they work for.

  In other words, this file represents the attributes of the `Professor` class in our domain model. It will "feed" the `Faculty` collection.

  Here is the test data that we'll use:

  ```
  Jacquie Barker<tab>123-45-6789<tab>Asst. Professor<tab>Info. Technology
  John Carson<tab>567-81-2345<tab>Full Professor<tab>Info. Technology
  Jackie Chan<tab>987-65-4321<tab>Full Professor<tab>Info. Technology
  ```

- `SoC_SP2004.dat`: This file contains the Schedule of Classes (SoC) information for the Spring 2004 (SP2004) semester; each tab-delimited record consists of six fields representing the course number, section number, day of the week, time of day, room, and seating capacity for the section in question.

  This file represents the attributes of the `Section` class, **combined with** the `courseNo` attribute of `Course`, which the `Section` class is able to "pull" by virtue of its one-to-many association with `Course` (recall our discussion of "data flowing along an association line" from Chapter 10). In other words, it simultaneously represents `Section` objects as a whole as well as **links** that `Section` objects maintain to `Course` objects.Here is the test data that we'll use:

  ```
  CMP101<tab>1<tab>M<tab>8:10 - 10:00 PM<tab>GOVT101<tab>30
  CMP101<tab>2<tab>W<tab>6:10 - 8:00 PM<tab>GOVT202<tab>30
  OBJ101<tab>1<tab>R<tab>4:10 - 6:00 PM<tab>GOVT105<tab>25
  OBJ101<tab>2<tab>T<tab>6:10 - 8:00 PM<tab>SCI330<tab>25
  CMP283<tab>1<tab>M<tab>6:10 - 8:00 PM<tab>GOVT101<tab>20
  CMP999<tab>1<tab>R<tab>4:10 - 6:00 PM<tab>SCI241<tab>15
  ART101<tab>1<tab>M<tab>4:10 - 6:00 PM<tab>ARTS25<tab>40
  ```

- `Prerequisites.dat`: This file contains information about which `Course`, listed in the first column, is a prerequisite for which other `Course`, listed in the second column.

  In other words, this file represents the reflexive **prerequisite** association that exists on the `Course` class, and the records themselves represent links between specific `Course` objects.

Here is the test data that we'll use:

```
CMP101<tab>OBJ101
OBJ101<tab>CMP283
CMP283<tab>CMP999
```

- TeachingAssignments.dat: This file pairs up a Professor (whose ssn is reflected in the first column) with the Course/Section number that the professor is going to be teaching (listed in the second column).

  In other words, this file represents the *teaches* association between a Professor and a Section.

  Here is our test data:

  ```
  987-65-4321<tab>CMP101 - 1
  567-81-2345<tab>CMP101 - 2
  123-45-6789<tab>OBJ101 - 1
  987-65-4321<tab>OBJ101 - 2
  123-45-6789<tab>CMP283 - 1
  567-81-2345<tab>CMP999 - 1
  987-65-4321<tab>ART101 - 1
  ```

All five of these data files are provided with the accompanying SRS code for download from the Apress web site (http://www.apress.com).

Persisting Student Data

One key difference between the way that we plan on handling Student data as compared with data for the other classes mentioned previously is that we're going to store each Student object's data in its own separate file, versus lumping all of the data about all Students into a single StudentBody.dat file. This will enable us to retrieve the information for just one student at a time—namely, whichever student is currently logged on to the SRS—and to easily save any changes that occur to that Student object's information during his or her SRS session when he or she logs off. (We'll see how a student logs on in Chapter 16, when we add a GUI to our application.)

- The naming convention for a student's data file will be to use the student's Social Security Number (ssn) with a suffix of .dat; for example, 111-11-1111.dat.

- At a minimum, a student's data file will contain a single ***primary*** record, comprised of four tab-delimited fields representing the student's SSN, name, major department, and degree sought. In other words, this record represents the attributes of the Student class in our object model.

- If the student has already registered for one or more sections in a previous SRS session, then the student's data file will also contain one or more ***secondary*** records, each consisting of a single field representing the full section number (that is, the course number followed by a hyphen, followed by the section number as an integer) of a section that the student is currently enrolled in. In other words, a secondary record represents the *attends* association in our object model, and any one record implies a link between this Student and a Section object.

We'll simulate three students in this fashion:

- 111-11-1111.dat: This student will be simulated as already having enrolled in two sections; the contents of this data file are as follows:

```
111-11-1111<tab>Joe Blow<tab>Math<tab>M.S.
CMP101 - 1
ART101 - 1
```

- 222-22-2222.dat: This student will be simulated as not yet having enrolled in any sections; the contents of this data file are as follows:

```
222-22-2222<tab>Gerson Lopez<tab>Information Technology<tab>Ph. D.
```

- 333-33-3333.dat: This student will also be simulated as not yet having enrolled in any sections; the contents of this data file are as follows:

```
333-33-3333<tab>Mary Smith<tab>Physics<tab>B.S.
```

> *As with the previous data files, all three of these are provided with the accompanying SRS code for download from the Apress web site.*

Why Aren't We Going to Persist Other Object Types?

We're not worried about persisting information about any other object type besides Student, because we assume that the rest of the data is "static": that is, during a particular login session, the user won't be able to alter Professor or Course information. All the student user will be able to do is to choose classes (sections) from the ScheduleOfClasses to register for, and/or to drop classes (sections); this merely changes the status of the **links** between a Student and various Section objects, which are stored as **secondary** records in the **student's** data file. In fact, we aren't even giving student users the ability to change their own **primary** information—name, ssn, etc.—via this application.

CollectionWrapper (Encapsulating Collections; Reading from an ASCII File)

The UML diagram in Figure 15-4 illustrates the design approach that we're going to take with regard to populating the CourseCatalog, Faculty, and ScheduleOfClasses collections.

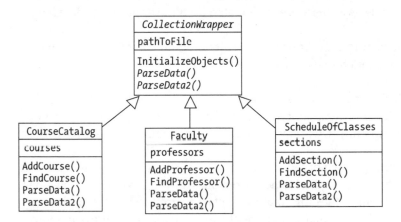

Figure 15-4. UML diagram for the SRS collections

We'll first create an abstract base class called CollectionWrapper. CollectionWrapper will define a single attribute: namely, a string that holds onto the full path to the file that is currently being read, for example: C:\SRS\Faculty.dat.
CollectionWrapper will also prescribe three behaviors:

- The ability to read a generic ASCII file using a combination of a StreamReader and a FileStream.

- Two different flavors of "parse" methods to allow for the fact that at least two of the three subclasses will need to read two separate data files, as we've just discussed.

- As we'll see in a moment, the InitializeObjects method will be a concrete method, whereas the ParseData and ParseData2 method signatures will be abstract.

The three derived classes will each extend this abstract class as follows:

- They will each encapsulate a Collection of their own choosing:

  - The CourseCatalog class will call its collection courses, and will use it to store handles on Course objects as these are instantiated from the appropriate data file.

  - The Faculty class will call its collection professors, and will use it to store handles on Professor objects as these are instantiated from the appropriate data file.

  - The ScheduleOfClasses class already had a collection attribute as of the Chapter 14 version that we built, called sections, used to store handles on Section objects as these are instantiated from the appropriate data file.

- They will all inherit the InitializeObjects method "as is," because it will be generic enough to handle routine file I/O.

- They will all need to override the abstract ParseData and ParseData2 methods in order to provide concrete method bodies; otherwise, as we learned in Chapters 7 and 13, we wouldn't be able to instantiate these three classes.

We'll step through each of these four classes, reviewing significant aspects of their class structure and method logic. We encourage you, however, to download the full set of C# source files for all of these classes from the Apress web site (http://www.apress.com) if you haven't already done so; please refer to Appendix D for the instructions on how to do this.

Since we started out this discussion talking about the CollectionWrapper class, let's proceed with a discussion of its methods.

InitializeObjects Method

We'll declare a method called InitializeObjects that accepts a value for, and initializes, the pathToFile attribute (the file path is determined and handed in to this method from the client code, that is, from the SRS class's Main method). The purpose of this method will be to step through the data file of interest, processing its contents one record at a time until the end of the file is reached.

We'll present the full code of the method first, and then we'll talk through it in detail.

```
public bool InitializeObjects(string pathToFile, bool primary) {
    this.pathToFile = pathToFile;
    string line = null;
```

```
    StreamReader srIn = null;
    bool outcome = true;

    try {
      // Open the file.
      srIn = new StreamReader(new FileStream(pathToFile, FileMode.Open));

      line = srIn.ReadLine();
      while (line != null) {
        if (primary) {
          ParseData(line);
        }
        else  {
          ParseData2(line);
        }
        line = srIn.ReadLine();
      }

      srIn.Close();
    }
    catch (FileNotFoundException f) {
      outcome = false;
    }
    catch (IOException i) {
      outcome = false;
    }

    return outcome;
  }
```

The method expects two arguments; the second of these is a bool flag, to indicate whether we're going to read a primary file or a secondary file—in other words, whether we should invoke ParseData (primary == true) or ParseData2 (primary == false):

```
public bool InitializeObjects(string pathToFile, bool primary) {
```

After initializing a few temporary variables, we attempt to open the file with the technique of using a combination StreamReader/FileStream as discussed earlier in the chapter. Note that we must wrap this code in a try-catch block, because as mentioned earlier, there are many environmental issues that can pose problems when accessing a computer's file system (the file may not exist; it may exist, but be locked against the attempted access; etc.).

```
        this.pathToFile = pathToFile;
        string line = null;
        StreamReader srIn = null;
        bool outcome = true;

        try {
          // Open the file.
          srIn = new StreamReader(new FileStream(pathToFile, FileMode.Open));
```

We use the ReadLine method of the StreamReader class to successively read in one line/record's worth of data at a time. The ReadLine method will set the value of string variable line to null as a signal when the end of the file has been reached, so we use a while loop to check for this condition. Within the while loop, we make a call to one of two "flavors" of Parse method—either ParseData or ParseData2—depending on whether the value of primary, passed in as an argument when the InitializeObjects method was called, is set to true or false. We'll talk about what the ParseData and ParseData2 methods need to do shortly.

```
        line = srIn.ReadLine();
        while (line != null) {
          if (primary) {
            ParseData(line);
          }
          else {
            ParseData2(line);
          }
          line = srIn.ReadLine();
        }
```

After the end of file has been reached, the while loop will automatically terminate. We then close the StreamReader (which closes the FileStream, which closes the file itself) with the command

```
        srIn.close();
      }
```

Our error handling in this example isn't very sophisticated! We simply print out an error message, then set the outcome flag to false to signal that something went wrong, so that we may return this news to whatever client code invoked the InitializeObjects method in the first place. In an industrial-strength application with a GUI, for example, we might pop up a window containing a more elaborate error message; we might record such an error in an error log file; or we might have some alternative means of recovering "gracefully." (An exercise at the end of Chapter 16 will request that you enhance error handling for the GUI version of the SRS application.)

```
catch (FileNotFoundException f) {
  Console.WriteLine("FILE NOT FOUND:  " + pathToFile);
  outcome = false;
}
catch (IOException i) {
  Console.WriteLine("IO EXCEPTION:  " + pathToFile);
  outcome = false;
}
```

Finally, we return a true/false status just prior to exiting. Note that outcome was initialized to the value true when this method first started, and will *still* have a true value unless something went wrong that in turn caused one of the catch blocks to execute.

```
  return outcome;
}
```

ParseData and ParseData2 Methods

Now, back to the ParseData and ParseData2 methods. What do these methods need to do in order to process a record from a data file? Generally speaking, for each record, we'll need to

1. Break apart the record along tab-separated boundaries.

2. Call one or more constructor(s) to construct the appropriate object(s) whose attributes have been parsed from the record.

3. Create links between objects, if appropriate.

4. Finally, insert the newly created object(s) into the appropriate encapsulated collection.

The details of how these steps take place will differ widely from one data file to the next, however:

- In the case of the CourseCatalog.dat file, for example, we need to break each record into three different values—two string values and a double numeric value—along tab boundaries. Then, we'll use those values as inputs to the Course class constructor. Finally, we'll insert the newly created Course object into the courses collection, an attribute of the CourseCatalog class.

We'll then read a *second* file—Prerequisites.dat—to determine how the various Courses that we've created are to be linked together to represent prerequisite interdependencies.

- For the Faculty.dat file, we need to break each record into four different string values. Then, we'll use those values to construct a Professor object. Finally, we'll insert the newly created Professor object into the professors collection of the Faculty class.

  We'll then read a *second* file—TeachingAssignments.dat—to determine how Professor objects should be linked to the Section objects that they are assigned to teach, and vice versa.

and so forth for the remaining files. Since we can't easily write a universal parsing method that can handle all of the different permutations and combinations of record formats and desired outcomes, we'll instead declare two abstract methods with the following signatures:

```
public abstract void ParseData(string line);
public abstract void ParseData2(string line);
```

and leave the job of working out the details of these two methods' respective behaviors to the various classes that extend the abstract CollectionWrapper class. Let's tackle these classes next.

CourseCatalog

We'll start with the CourseCatalog class. As mentioned earlier, we'll treat it as an encapsulated collection by adding one feature, an attribute named courses declared to be of type Hashtable that will be used to hold Course object references.

```
using System;
using System.Collections;
using System.IO;

public class CourseCatalog : CollectionWrapper {
    //------------
    // Attributes.
    //------------
```

```
// This Hashtable stores Course object references, using
// the (string) course no. of the Course as the key.

private Hashtable courses;
```

Constructor

The constructor for this class is fairly trivial:

```
public CourseCatalog() {
  // Instantiate a new Hashtable.

  courses = new Hashtable();
}
```

and no properties are declared in the CourseCatalog class.

Display Method

We create a Display method for testing purposes, which uses an IDictionaryEnumerator object to step through the table, a technique that we discussed in Chapter 13.

```
// Used for testing purposes.

public void Display() {
  Console.WriteLine("Course Catalog:");
  Console.WriteLine("");

  // Step through the Hashtable and display all entries.

  IDictionaryEnumerator e = courses.GetEnumerator();

  while (e.MoveNext()) {
    Course c = (Course) e.Value;
    c.Display();
    Console.WriteLine("");
  }
}
```

AddCourse Method

We also create an AddCourse "housekeeping" method, which is used to insert a Course object reference into the encapsulated collection:

```
public void AddCourse(Course c) {
    // We use the course no. as the key.
    string key = c.CourseNo;
    courses.Add(key, c);
}
```

ParseData Method

In order to be able to instantiate the CourseCatalog class, we must make it concrete by providing a method body for the abstract ParseData and ParseData2 methods that we've inherited from CollectionWrapper. We'll start with ParseData, which will be used to read the CourseCatalog.dat file.

Because this is a fairly complex method, we'll present the code in its entirety first, and will then narrate it after the fact.

```
public override void ParseData(string line) {
    // We're going to parse tab-delimited records into
    // three attributes -- courseNo, courseName, and credits --
    // and then call the Course constructor to fabricate a new
    // course.

    // We'll use the Split method of the System.String class to split
    // the line we read from the file into substrings, using tabs
    // as the delimiter.

    string[] strings = line.Split('\t');

    // Now assign a value to each of three local string variables
    // using the appropriate substring.

    string courseNo = strings[0];
    string courseName = strings[1];
    string creditValue = strings[2];

    // We have to convert the last value into a number,
    // using a static method on the Double class to do so.

    double credits = Convert.ToDouble(creditValue);
```

```
// Finally, we call the Course constructor to create
// an appropriate Course object, and store it in our
// collection.

Course c = new Course(courseNo, courseName, credits);
AddCourse(c);
}
```

We'll now narrate selected portions of the code.

The System.String class defines the Split method, which is used to split a string value into substrings based on a programmer-specified delimiter, storing the resultant substrings in a string array. In our case, we've designated the tab character, '\t', as the delimiter.

```
string[] strings = line.Split('\t');
```

As an example, if we call the Split method on the following line/string (where <tab> indicates the presence of an otherwise invisible tab character):

```
CMP101<tab>Beginning Computer Technology<tab>3.0
```

then the resultant string array would contain three elements, "CMP101", "Beginning Computer Technology", and "3.0". Since we know that the first substring will be the course number, the second will be the course name, and the third will be the number of credits for the course, we can assign the value of each substring to an appropriate local variable:

```
string courseNo = strings[0];
string courseName = strings[1];
string creditValue = strings[2];
```

We now have three string variables—courseNo, courseName, and creditValue— correctly parsed. But, there's one small problem: the Course constructor, shown here:

```
public Course(string cNo, string cName, double credits) { ... }
```

expects to be handed a double value for the credit value of the course, not a string value. We therefore must convert the string stored in variable creditValue into a double value. Fortunately, the Convert class in the System namespace provides a number of static methods for converting one type into another. We'll use the ToDouble method to convert the string into a double:

```
double credits = Convert.ToDouble(creditValue);
```

We're finally ready to call the Course constructor to create an appropriate Course object, and to store it in our collection by calling the AddCourse method:

```
Course c = new Course(courseNo, courseName, credits);
AddCourse(c);
}
```

Please note that we've provided virtually no error checking in the ParseData method. We're assuming that the CourseCatalog.dat file is perfectly formatted, which is a risky assumption in real life! One of the exercises at the end of this chapter will give you a chance to make this code more robust.

FindCourse Method

We also provide a convenience method, FindCourse, to enable client code to easily retrieve a particular Course object from this collection based on its course number. If the requested course number isn't found, the value null will be returned by this method:

```
public Course FindCourse(string courseNo) {
  return (Course) courses[courseNo];
}
```

Providing such a method hides the fact that the collection is implemented as a Hashtable: client code simply invokes the method and gets handed back a Course object, without any idea as to what is happening behind the scenes, as simulated by the following hypothetical client code "snippet":

```
// Sample client code.
CourseCatalog courseCatalog = new CourseCatalog();
// ...
Course c = courseCatalog.FindCourse("ART101");
```

ParseData2 Method

We're not quite done yet. We must read a second file, Prequisites.dat, which defines course prerequisites, so that we may properly link our newly created Course objects together. (We have to do this as a separate second step after all Course objects have been created via the ParseData method so that we don't wind up with a "chicken vs. egg" situation—namely, needing to link together two Courses that don't both exist yet.)

So, let's now provide a body for the abstract `ParseData2` method. Because the logic of the `ParseData2` method is so similar to the `ParseData` method, we won't discuss all of its logic in detail, but **will** point out one interesting "twist":

```
public override void ParseData2(string line) {
    // We're going to parse tab-delimited records into
    // two values, representing the courseNo "A" of
    // a course that serves as a prerequisite for
    // courseNo "B".

    // Once again we'll make use of the Split method to split
    // the line into substrings using tabs as the delimiter

    string[] strings = line.Split('\t');

    // Now assign the value of the substrings to the
    // appropriate local string variables.

    string courseNoA = strings[0];
    string courseNoB = strings[1];
```

Because we wish to link together two preexisting Course objects via the `AddPrerequisite` method of the `Course` class, we have to obtain handles on these objects. We do so by using our `FindCourse` method to look up the two course numbers that we've just parsed. Only if we're successful in finding **both** Courses in our internal `Hashtable`—that is, only if both `Course` references a and b have non-null values—will we invoke the `AddPrerequisite` method on b, passing in a reference to a:

```
    // Look these two courses up in the CourseCatalog.

    Course a = FindCourse(courseNoA);
    Course b = FindCourse(courseNoB);
    if (a != null && b != null) {
      b.AddPrerequisite(a);
    }
}
```

Adding a "Test Scaffold" Main Method

In Chapter 13, we discussed the fact that the C# runtime environment looks for a method with a particular header, e.g., `static void Main()`, when we start up the application. As an example, to run the SRS application we developed in Chapter 14, we'd type the command: SRS, and the C# runtime environment would invoke the Main method declared within the SRS.cs file.

As we've discussed previously in the book, it's permissible to have more than one Main method sprinkled throughout an application's classes; however, only one of these will serve as the official main method for purposes of driving the application. Why would we ever want to declare extra Main methods? That is, what would we use the other Main methods for? As test drivers, or "scaffolds," for putting a single class through its paces. As an example, perhaps after we finish coding the CourseCatalog class, we wish to test it to ensure that it

- Properly parses the CourseCatalog.dat and Prerequisites.dat files

- Instantiates all Course objects correctly

- Links prerequisites appropriately

- Stores them all in the courses Hashtable that is encapsulated within the CourseCatalog class

We **could** run the full-blown SRS application to test this class. However, we'd have to jump ahead and modify the SRS class's Main method to take advantage of the CourseCatalog class and all of its various methods in order to do this. A simpler approach is to provide the CourseCatalog class with its **own** Main method, for use in testing the class in isolation, as follows:

```
// Test scaffold (a Main() method INSIDE OF the CourseCatalog class!).

static void Main() {
    // We instantiate a CourseCatalog object ...

    CourseCatalog cc = new CourseCatalog();

    // ... and cause it to read both the CourseCatalog.dat and
    // Prerequisites.dat files, thereby testing both
    // the ParseData() and ParseData2() methods internally
    // to the InitializeObjects() method ...

    cc.InitializeObjects("CourseCatalog.dat", true);
    cc.InitializeObjects("Prerequisites.dat", false);

    // ... then use its Display() method to demonstrate the
    // results!

    cc.Display();
}
```

With the addition of this Main method to class CourseCatalog, we can now compile the application from the command line using the following command:

```
csc /out:CourseCatalog.exe *.cs /main:CourseCatalog
```

As we've discussed previously, the /out compiler option tells the compiler to name the resulting executable file CourseCatalog.exe. The /main option signifies that the Main method defined in the CourseCatalog class will be used to drive the program. If the CourseCatalog.exe file is run, the following output would be produced as a result of the invocation of cc.Display():

```
Course Catalog:

Course Information:
  Course No.:  CMP101
  Course Name:  Beginning Computer Technology
  Credits:  3.0
  Prerequisite Courses:
    (none)
  Offered As Section(s):

Course Information:
  Course No.:  CMP283
  Course Name:  Higher Level Languages (C#)
  Credits:  3.0
  Prerequisite Courses:
    OBJ101:  Object Methods for Software Development
  Offered As Section(s):

Course Information:
  Course No.:  CMP999
  Course Name:  Living Brain Computers
  Credits:  3.0
  Prerequisite Courses:
    CMP283:  Higher Level Languages (C#)
  Offered As Section(s):

Course Information:
  Course No.:  ART101
  Course Name:  Beginning Basketweaving
  Credits:  3.0
  Prerequisite Courses:
    (none)
  Offered As Section(s):
```

```
Course Information:
  Course No.:  OBJ101
  Course Name:  Object Methods for Software Development
  Credits:  3.0

  Prerequisite Courses:
    CMP101:  Beginning Computer Technology
  Offered As Section(s):
```

thus demonstrating that our code does indeed work!

Note that there is no harm in leaving this Main method in the CourseCatalog class even after our testing is finished—in fact, it's a handy thing to keep around in case we change the details of how any of these methods work later on, and want to retest it.

Faculty

Next, we'll create the Faculty class, which is used to populate a Hashtable with Professor objects by reading their pertinent information from *two* data files:

- Faculty.dat, the primary file used as the basis for creating the Professors

- TeachingAssignments.dat, a secondary file used for linking Professor objects to the Section objects that they are assigned to teach, and vice versa

Since the structure and behaviors of the Faculty class are so similar to those of CourseCatalog, we won't explain the Faculty class in detail, but will point out one interesting nuance regarding its ParseData2 method.

ParseData2 Method

The first part of the ParseData2 method of the Faculty class is similar to the logic that was used in the ParseData2 method of the CourseCatalog class: a line of text is read from a file and split into substrings using the Split method.

```
// This next method is used when reading in the file that defines
// teaching assignments.

public override void ParseData2(string line) {
    // We're going to parse tab-delimited records into
    // two values, representing the professor's SSN
    // and the section number that he/she is going to teach.
```

```
// Once again we'll make use of the Split() method to split
// the line into substrings using a tab as the delimiter.

string[] strings = line.Split('\t');

// Now assign the value of the substring to an appropriate
// local string variable.

string ssn = strings[0];

// The full section number is a concatenation of the
// course no. and section no., separated by a hyphen;
// e.g., "ART101 - 1".

string fullSectionNo = strings[1];
```

Just as we did in the ParseData2 method of CourseCatalog, we're linking together two objects here, and so we need to first verify that both objects do indeed exist, and obtain handles on them. But, unlike the ParseData2 method of CourseCatalog, where both objects were Courses, and hence both objects were stored in the Hashtable internal to the CourseCatalog class, here we have a situation where one of the objects (a Professor) is stored in our own *internal* professors Hashtable, but the other object (a Section) is stored in a collection elsewhere in our application: namely, in the scheduleOfClasses collection that we've defined as an attribute of the main SRS class. However, by declaring the latter collection to be a public static attribute of the SRS class, we have in essence made it globally visible/accessible to the entire application, which enables us to reference it as highlighted in the following code:

```
// Look these two objects up in the appropriate collections.
// Note that having made scheduleOfClasses a public
// static attribute of the SRS class helps!

Professor p = FindProfessor(ssn);
Section s = SRS.scheduleOfClasses.FindSection(fullSectionNo);
if (p != null && s != null) {
  p.AgreeToTeach(s);
  }
}
```

Adding a "Test Scaffold" Main Method

Just as we did for CourseCatalog, we also provide a test scaffold Main method for the Faculty class. We're a bit constrained with regard to testing the full functionality of Faculty in this manner, however: because the ParseData2 method expects to access the SRS.scheduleOfClasses collection object, and because we won't have instantiated that object through our test scaffold, we can't put the ParseData2 method through its paces without running the full-blown SRS application. Nonetheless, we'll go ahead and at least test our code for reading the primary file, Faculty.dat.

```
// Test scaffold.
static void Main() {
  Faculty f = new Faculty();
  f.InitializeObjects("Faculty.dat", true);

  // We cannot test the next feature, because the code
  // of ParseData2() expects the SRS.scheduleOfClasses
  // collection object to have been instantiated; but
  // it will NOT have been if we are running this test
  // scaffold instead; hence, we've commented out the next line.
  // f.InitializeObjects("TeachingAssignments.dat", false);

  f.Display();
}
```

Revamping ScheduleOfClasses

Next, we'll retrofit the ScheduleOfClasses class that we developed in Chapter 14 with this same ability to "self-initialize" from an ASCII file. To do so, we'll start by indicating that we want ScheduleOfClasses to extend our previously defined CollectionWrapper class:

```
public class ScheduleOfClasses : CollectionWrapper {
```

By doing so, we'll inherit the InitializeObjects method of CollectionWrapper, which will give us all of the generic file manipulation capability that we need. Note that we can do so after the fact without disturbing any of the code that we've already written and tested for ScheduleOfClasses from Chapter 14!

ParseData Method

Next, we must provide a method body for the abstract ParseData method that we've inherited; since it's so similar to the ParseData methods of both the Faculty and CourseCatalog classes, we won't discuss it in detail, but simply present its code here.

```
public override void ParseData(string line) {
    // We're going to parse tab-delimited records into
    // six attributes -- courseNo, sectionNo, dayOfWeek,
    // timeOfDay, room, and capacity.  We'll use courseNo to
    // look up the appropriate Course object, and will then
    // call the ScheduleSection() method to fabricate a
    // new Section object.

    // We'll use the Split method of the System.String class to split
    // the line we read from the file into substrings using tabs
    // as the delimiter.

    string[] strings = line.Split('\t');

    // Now assign the value of the substrings to the
    // appropriate local variables.

    string courseNo = strings[0];
    string sectionNumber = strings[1];
    string dayOfWeek = strings[2];
    string timeOfDay = strings[3];
    string room = strings[4];
    string capacityValue = strings[5];

    // We need to convert the sectionNumber and capacityValue
    // strings to ints.

    int sectionNo = Convert.ToInt32(sectionNumber);
    int capacity = Convert.ToInt32(capacityValue);

    // Look up the Course object in the Course Catalog.
    // Having made courseCatalog a public static attribute
    // of the SRS class comes in handy!

    Course c = SRS.courseCatalog.FindCourse(courseNo);

    // Schedule the Section.

    Section s = c.ScheduleSection(sectionNo, dayOfWeek[0],
                                  timeOfDay, room, capacity);
    string key = courseNo + " - " + s.SectionNo;
    AddSection(s);
}
```

ParseData2 Method

There is one minor flaw in our application design. Unlike both the CourseCatalog and Faculty classes, which each required us to read both a primary and a secondary data file when initializing their respective Hashtables, we don't have a need at present to read and parse a secondary file when loading the ScheduleOfClasses Hashtable; all of the information that we need to process is contained within the SoC_SP2004.dat file, which is handled by the ParseData method. So, we really don't have a need for a ParseData2 method in the ScheduleOfClasses class. But, because we've chosen to extend the CollectionWrapper class, we're forced to implement such a method; otherwise, as we learned in Chapter 13, the ScheduleOfClasses class will be deemed abstract by the compiler, and we won't be able to instantiate it in the Main method of the SRS class.

To work around this dilemma, we'll "stub out" a ParseData2 method with an *empty* method body, as follows:

```
public override void ParseData2(string line) { }
```

This makes the compiler happy and, since we have no intention of ever calling this method anyway, no serious harm is done. However, this breaks (or at least severely bends!) the spirit of the "is a" relationship of inheritance. Strictly speaking, if the ScheduleOfClasses class has no need for a ParseData2 method, then we shouldn't declare it to be a subclass of CollectionWrapper. But, if we didn't inherit the methods of CollectionWrapper, we'd then have to code an InitializeObjects method for the ScheduleOfClasses class from scratch to replace the one that it's no longer inheriting from CollectionWrapper, which would complicate our application in a different way by introducing code redundancy. So, doing what we've done by extending CollectionWrapper and "stubbing out" the ParseData2 method seems like a reasonable compromise.

FindSection Method

As we did for the CourseCatalog and Faculty classes, we provide ScheduleOfClasses with a convenience method for looking up a particular Section based upon the full section number, which is defined here as being a concatenation of course number and section number, separated by a hyphen; for example, "ART101 - 1":

```
public Section FindSection(string fullSectionNo) {
  return (Section) sectionsOffered[fullSectionNo];
}
```

Why No Test Scaffolding?

We can't provide a simple test scaffold Main method for the ScheduleOfClasses class as we did for CourseCatalog and Faculty; this is due to the fact that the ParseData method of the ScheduleOfClasses object will attempt to access the SRS.courseCatalog, which will not have been initialized.

Course Modifications

There is only one minor change to be made to the Course class from the way that it was presented in Chapter 14, to accommodate our new file persistence scheme.

Because we're now reading in a ***predetermined*** section number from the SoC_SP2004.dat file, we must modify the ScheduleSection method of the Course class so that it no longer automatically assigns a "one-up" section number to each Section.

Here is the original code for the ScheduleSection method from Chapter 14; the highlighted code shows that we were automatically determining how many sections had already been created and stored in the offeredAsSection collection (an attribute of Course), and bumping that up by one to create a section number on the fly.

```
public Section ScheduleSection(char day, string time, string room,
                               int capacity) {
  // Create a new Section (note the creative way in
  // which we are assigning a section number) ...
  Section s = new Section(offeredAsSection.Count + 1,
                          day, time, this, room, capacity);

  // ... and then remember it!
  offeredAsSection.Add(s);

  return s;
}
```

In our new, modified version of this method, shown in the following code, we've added an argument, secNo, to enable us to simply hand in the section number as read in from the data file.

```
public Section ScheduleSection(int secNo, char day, string time,
                               string room, int capacity) {
  // Create a new Section.
  Section s = new Section(secNo, day, time, this, room, capacity);
```

```
    // ... and then remember it!
    offeredAsSection.Add(s);

    return s;
  }
```

The Student Class (Dynamic Data Retrieval; Persisting Object State)

Aside from making a minor change to the ScheduleSection method of the Course class that we just discussed, and "refurbishing" the ScheduleOfClasses class that we previously discussed, the only other domain class that we wish to enhance among those that we created in Chapter 14 is the Student class. To demonstrate the techniques of dynamic data retrieval and data persistence, we're going to

- Modify the Student class's constructor to read data from a student's data file, to be used in initializing attributes.

- Add a Persist method that can be called from the SRS Main method when a student logs off, to persist the student's state back to his or her data file.

Much of the Student class's code remains unchanged from the way that it was presented in Chapter 14, so we'll only touch upon the significant changes that we've made to the class here.

Initializing a Student's State

The first significant change that we've made is in the Student class constructor. Because this code is fairly involved, we'll present the constructor here in its entirety first, and will then narrate it.

```
//----------------
// Constructor(s).
//----------------

public Student(string ssn) : this() {
    // First, construct a "dummy" Student object.  Then,
    // attempt to pull this Student's information from the
    // appropriate file (ssn.dat:  e.g., 111-11-1111.dat).
    // The file consists of a header record, containing
    // the student's basic info. (ssn, name, etc.), and
    // 0 or more subsequent records representing a list of
    // the sections that he/she is currently registered for.
```

```
string line = null;
StreamReader srIn = null;

// Formulate the file name.

string pathToFile = ssn + ".dat";

try {
  // Open the file.

  srIn = new StreamReader(new FileStream(pathToFile,FileMode.Open));

  // The first line in the file contains the header
  // information, so we use ParseData() to process it.

  line = srIn.ReadLine();
  if (line != null) {
    ParseData(line);
  }

  // Remaining lines (if there are any) contain
  // section references.  Note that we must
  // instantiate an empty vector so that the
  // ParseData2 method may insert
  // items into the ArrayList.

  attends = new ArrayList();

  line = srIn.ReadLine();

  // If there were no secondary records in the file,
  // this "while" loop won't execute at all.

  while (line != null) {
    ParseData2(line);
    line = srIn.ReadLine();
  }

  srIn.Close();
}
catch (FileNotFoundException f) {
  // Since we are encoding a "dummy" Student to begin
  // with, the fact that his/her name will be equal
  // to "???" flags an error.  We have included
```

```
        // a boolean method SuccessfullyInitialized
        // which allows client code to verify the success
        // or failure of this constructor (see code below).
        // So, we needn't do anything special in this
        // "catch" clause!
    }
    catch (IOException i) {
        // See comments for FileNotFoundException above;
        // we needn't do anything special in this
        // "catch" clause, either!
    }


    // Create a brand new Transcript.
    // (Ideally, we'd read in an existing Transcript from
    // a file, but we're not bothering to do so in this
    // example).

    this.Transcript = new Transcript(this);
  }
```

Before we discuss the preceding constructor in depth, let's take a look at a second parameterless constructor that we've created for the Student class, because as we learned in Chapter 13, if we overload the constructor for a class, then the default parameterless constructor is unavailable unless we explicitly replace it.

All of the attributes are set to the value "???" in this constructor; as we'll see later, if these never get overwritten with the proper values from a Student's file, then we'll be able to detect that an error has occurred.

```
    // A second form of constructor, used when a Student's data
    // file cannot be found for some reason.

    public Student() : base("???", "???") {
        // Reuse the code of the parent's (Person) constructor.
        // Question marks indicate that something went wrong!

        this.Major = "???";
        this.Degree = "???";

        // Placeholders for the remaining attributes (this
        // Student is invalid anyway).

        this.Transcript = new Transcript(this);
        attends = new ArrayList();
    }
```

Now, let's go back and walk through the *first* constructor. Rather than simply passing in hard-coded attribute values as constructor arguments, we're going to attempt to read these from the appropriate student data file. Therefore, the constructor now expects only one argument: the Student-to-be-constructed's ssn, which will be used to formulate the data file name (ssn.dat):

```
public Student(string ssn) : this() {
```

The first thing this constructor does is to construct a "dummy" Student object using the parameterless Student constructor. (Recall that the this keyword can be used to call a different constructor declared by the same class, a concept that was discussed in Chapter 13.)

Next, we'll attempt to open and read the appropriate data file, using a technique very similar to the technique used in the InitializeObjects method of CollectionWrapper. (If we were to have made Student a derived class of CollectionWrapper, then we could have simply inherited InitializeObjects; but, such inheritance would truly compromise the "is a" relationship—far more severely than we did with the ScheduleOfClasses class [when we knew it didn't need to parse two files, but extended CollectionWrapper anyway]—because a Student is clearly *not* a collection! So, we resist the urge to "misuse" inheritance, and instead write code that looks remarkably similar to the InitializeObjects method.)

```
string line = null;
StreamReader srIn = null;
bool outcome = true;

// Formulate the file name.

string pathToFile = ssn + ".dat";

try {
  // Open the file.

  srIn = new StreamReader(new FileStream(pathToFile), FileMode.Open);
```

Note that we use two different methods once again—ParseData and ParseData2—but back-to-back in this case, because although we're only reading one student data file, there are two different record formats within a single file: the primary record containing student information, and zero or more secondary records containing section numbers for which the student has registered.

```
// The first line in the file contains the header
// information, so we use ParseData to process it.
```

```
        line = srIn.ReadLine();
        if (line != null) {
          ParseData(line);
        }

        // Remaining lines (if there are any) contain
        // section references.  Note that we must
        // instantiate an empty vector so that the
        // ParseData2 method may insert
        // items into the ArrayList.

        attends = new ArrayList();

        line = srIn.ReadLine();

        // If there were no secondary records in the file,
        // this "while" loop won't execute at all.

        while (line != null) {
          ParseData2(line);
          line = srIn.readLine();
        }

        srIn.close();
      }
```

If anything goes wrong while attempting to read the student's data file (e.g., the file isn't found or can't be accessed, or it contains incorrectly formatted data), then one or the other of the catch clauses will be invoked. But, since we've already gone to the trouble of executing the generic constructor (with no arguments) as the first step of this constructor, then we have a "bare bones" (albeit somewhat useless) Student object full of "???" values.

There really isn't any way for a constructor to return an error flag (say, a bool true/false)—by definition, a constructor returns an object (of type Student, in this case)—so we have to devise an alternative way for the client code to detect whether or not the Student object initialization succeeded or failed. We'll do so by creating a separate method called StudentSuccessfullyInitialized in a moment.

```
    catch (FileNotFoundException f) {
      // Since we are encoding a "dummy" Student to begin
      // with, the fact that his/her name will be equal
      // to "???" flags an error. We have included
```

```
    // a boolean method StudentSuccessfullyInitialized
    // which allows client code to verify the success
    // or failure of this constructor (see code below).
    // So, we needn't do anything special in this catch
    // clause!
  }
  catch (IOException i) {
    // See comments for FileNotFoundException earlier;
    // we needn't do anything special in this catch
    // clause, either!
  }


  // Create a brand new Transcript.
  // (Ideally, we'd read in an existing Transcript from
  // a file, but we're not bothering to do so in this
  // example).

  this.Transcript = new Transcript(this);
}
```

StudentSuccessfullyInitialized Method

We were concerned about how to return failure status from a constructor. This turns out to be a rather simple matter: since we've created a "dummy" Student to begin with, the fact that the student's name will be equal to "???" constitutes an error. So, we provide a Boolean method, StudentSuccessfullyInitialized, to allow client code to verify the success or failure of this constructor after the fact.

```
// Used after the constructor is called to verify whether or not
// there were any file access errors.

public bool StudentSuccessfullyInitialized() {
  if (this.Name.Equals("???")) {
    return false;
  }
  else {
    return true;
  }
}
```

Here is an example of how the preceding method would be used in client code (say, in the Main method of the SRS application):

```
// Excerpt from the Main method of SRS:

string ssn;

// Obtain an ssn value as a user input when he/she logs on (details omitted;
// we'll see how this is done via a GUI in Chapter 16).

// Invoke the new form of Student constructor, which will attempt to read the
// appropriate data file behind the scenes.

Student s = new Student(ssn);

// Now, check to see if the Student's data was successfully retrieved!

if (s.StudentSuccessfullyInitialized()) {
  // Success! Do whatever is appropriate in this case ... details omitted.
}
else {
  // Failure! Do whatever is appropriate in this case ... details omitted.
}
```

> *Another way to indicate that a* Student *object hadn't been properly initialized would be by utilizing a user-defined exception class. If a problem occurred during* Student *initialization, the* Student *constructor could throw an instance of a user-defined exception—for example, a* StudentImproperlyInitializedException. *The client code calling the* Student *constructor would then be placed in a* try-catch *block in order to detect and handle any instances* StudentImproperlyInitializedException. *The concept of user-defined exceptions was mentioned in Chapter 13.*

ParseData and ParseData2 Methods

Because the logic of the ParseData and ParseData2 methods of Student is so similar to the ParseData and ParseData2 methods that we've discussed for these other classes, we won't review them in detail here, but merely present their code. First, here is the ParseData method code listing:

```
public void ParseData(string line) {
    // We're going to parse tab-delimited records into
    // four attributes -- ssn, name, major, and degree.
```

```
// We'll use the Split method of the System.String class to split
// the line we read from the file into substrings using tabs
// as the delimiter.

string[] strings = line.Split('\t');

// Now use the substring values to update the
// appropriate Student properties.

this.Ssn = strings[0];
this.Name = strings[1];
this.Major = strings[2];
this.Degree = strings[3];
}
```

Here is the `ParseData2` method code listing:

```
public void ParseData2(string line) {
    // The full section number is a concatenation of the
    // course no. and section no., separated by a hyphen;
    // e.g., "ART101 - 1".

    string fullSectionNo = line.Trim();
    Section s = SRS.scheduleOfClasses.FindSection(fullSectionNo);

    // Note that we are using the Section class's enroll()
    // method to ensure that bidirectionality is established
    // between the Student and the Section.
    s.Enroll(this);
}
```

We've now provided all of the code necessary to dynamically retrieve a student's information whenever he or she logs on to the SRS. We'll demonstrate how to simulate a logon in order to test this code when we talk about changes to the SRS class's Main method in a few moments. Before we do so, however, there is one more important enhancement that we wish to make to the Student class, having to do with persisting the results of a student's registration session.

Persisting the State of a Student

During the course of an SRS session, the student will presumably be registering for sections and/or dropping sections. The state of the Student object representing that student—namely the attribute values of the Student object and all links maintained by that Student object with other objects (in particular, with Section objects in which the student is enrolled)—is thus likely to change.

We must provide a way for the SRS to "remember" these changes from one logon session to the next; otherwise, the SRS system will be of no practical value. So, we're going to provide a method to persist a Student object's state whenever the student logs off: specifically, we're going to write information about this Student back out to the same data file that we originally used to initialize the Student object's state in the constructor.

```
// This method writes out all of the student's information to
// his/her ssn.dat file when he/she logs off.

public bool Persist() {
```

We use the approach discussed earlier in the chapter of using a FileStream/StreamWriter combination to write to the student's data file.

```
FileStream fs = null;
StreamWriter sw = null;
try {
  // Attempt to create the ssn.dat file.  Note that
  // it will overwrite one if it already exists, which
  // is what we want to have happen.

  string file = this.Ssn + ".dat";
  fs = new FileStream(file, FileMode.OpenOrCreate);
  sw = new StreamWriter(fs);

  // First, we output the header record as a tab-delimited
  // record.

  sw.WriteLine(this.Ssn + "\t" + this.Name + "\t" +
               this.Major + "\t" + this.Degree);

  // Then, we output one record for every Section that
  // the Student is enrolled in.

  for (int i = 0; i < attends.Count; i++) {
    Section s = (Section) attends[i];
    sw.WriteLine(s.GetFullSectionNo());
  }

  sw.Close();
}
```

If anything went wrong during the persistence process (such as the file couldn't be opened or written to), the following catch block is triggered. In this case, we'll return a bool value of false to signal to the client code that something went wrong, and will allow the client code to determine what needs to be done as a result (whether some error message needs to be displayed to the user, or whether some alternative recovery mechanism needs to be engaged):

```
catch (IOException e) {
  // Signal that an error has occurred.

  return false;
}

// All is well!
return true;
}
```

> *Writing out the values of an object's fields to a file in ASCII record format is a "quick and dirty" approach to **object serialization**. The .NET Framework offers a variety of more sophisticated ways to persist objects to files. More detailed information on alternative serialization techniques can be found in the MSDN documentation pages.*

Revisiting the SRS Class

Having encapsulated so much functionality into the ScheduleOfCourses, CourseCatalog, and Faculty classes allows us to **dramatically** simplify the Main method for the SRS "driver" class; let's revisit that class to see how it should be changed to accommodate all that we've done in this chapter.

First, in addition to the public static scheduleOfClasses attribute that we provided in Chapter 14, we now will provide two more such attributes—faculty and courseCatalog:

```
// SRS.cs

// A main driver for the command-line driven version of the SRS, with
// file persistence added.

using System;
using System.Collections;
```

```
public class SRS {
    // We can effectively create "global" data by declaring
    // PUBLIC STATIC attributes in the main class.

    // Entry points/"roots" for getting at objects.

    public static Faculty faculty = new Faculty();

    public static CourseCatalog courseCatalog = new CourseCatalog();

    public static ScheduleOfClasses scheduleOfClasses =
        new ScheduleOfClasses("SP2004");

    // We don't create a collection for Student objects, because
    // we're only going to handle one Student object at a time -- namely,
    // an object representing whichever Student is currently logged on.
```

In the Main method, we take advantage of our InitializeObjects method to read data from the various ASCII files that we've provided, automatically initializing the faculty, courseCatalog, and scheduleOfClasses collections with the appropriate objects.

```
static void Main() {
    // Initialize the key objects by reading data from files.
    // Setting the second argument to true causes the
    // InitializeObjects method to use the ParseData
    // method instead of ParseData2.

    faculty.InitializeObjects("Faculty.dat", true);
    courseCatalog.InitializeObjects("CourseCatalog.dat", true);
    scheduleOfClasses.InitializeObjects("SoC_SP2004.dat", true);
```

We'll handle the students differently: that is, rather than loading them all in at application outset, we'll pull in the data that we need just for one Student when that Student logs on, as we saw when we reviewed the "new and improved" Student class constructor earlier in this chapter. Because we don't yet have a mechanism to allow a user to log on—we'll provide that in Chapter 16—we'll temporarily create a few Student objects by hard-coding calls to the Student constructor, to simulate Students logging on. This enables us to exercise and test the enhanced Student class constructor. Note that only the first of these Students has preregistered for courses based on the content of their ssn.dat file, as discussed earlier.

```
    // Let's temporarily create Students this way as a test,
    // to simulate Students logging on. Note that only the
    // first Student has preregistered for courses based
```

```
// on the content of his/her ssn.dat file (see Student.cs
// for details).

Student s1 = new Student("111-11-1111");
Student s2 = new Student("222-22-2222");
Student s3 = new Student("333-33-3333");
```

We invoke the InitializeObjects method a second time for the CourseCatalog and Faculty classes, respectively, to enable us to read their respective supplemental data files:

```
// Establish some prerequisites (c1 => c2 => c3 => c4).
// Setting the second argument to false causes the
// InitializeObjects method to use the ParseData2
// method instead of ParseData.

courseCatalog.InitializeObjects("Prerequisites.dat", false);

// Recruit a professor to teach each of the sections.
// Setting the second argument to false causes the
// InitializeObjects method to use the ParseData2
// method instead of ParseData.

faculty.InitializeObjects("TeachingAssignments.dat", false);
```

Now, we'll simulate having Student s2 enroll in a Section, so that we may exercise and test the Persist method. We use the FindSection convenience method of the ScheduleOfClasses class to obtain a handle on a Section object based on a particular course and section number, and then use the Enroll method of the Section class to bidirectionally enroll Student s2 in that Section:

```
// Let's have one Student try enrolling in something, so
// that we can simulate their logging off and persisting
// the enrollment data in the ssn.dat file (see Student.cs
// for details).

Section sec = scheduleOfClasses.FindSection("ART101 - 1");
sec.Enroll(s2);
```

Now, we invoke the Persist method on Student object s2.

```
s2.Persist();
```

Before running the SRS application, the contents of the 222-22-2222.dat file consisted of a single record as follows:

```
222-22-2222<tab>Gerson Lopez<tab>Information Technology<tab>Ph. D.
```

because this student wasn't enrolled in any sections. After running the SRS application, if we inspect the contents of the 222-22-2222.dat file, we find that a record has been added to persist the fact that this student is now enrolled in ART101 section 1:

```
222-22-2222<tab>Gerson Lopez<tab>Information Technology<tab>Ph. D.
ART101 - 1
```

and so the Persist method is indeed working!

To round out our testing, we include a few calls to the Display methods of our various collection objects:

```
// Let's see if everything got initialized properly
// by calling various display methods!

Console.WriteLine("=====================");
Console.WriteLine("Course Catalog:");
Console.WriteLine("=====================");
Console.WriteLine("");
courseCatalog.Display();

Console.WriteLine("=====================");
Console.WriteLine("Schedule of Classes:");
Console.WriteLine("=====================");
Console.WriteLine("");
scheduleOfClasses.Display();

Console.WriteLine("========================");
Console.WriteLine("Professor Information:");
Console.WriteLine("========================");
Console.WriteLine("");
faculty.Display();

Console.WriteLine("=====================");
Console.WriteLine("Student Information:");
Console.WriteLine("=====================");
Console.WriteLine("");
s1.Display();
Console.WriteLine("");
s2.Display();
Console.WriteLine("");
s3.Display();
  }
}
```

Because several of the classes that make up the SRS have `Main` methods, we'll have to use the `/main` option when we compile the SRS application. The following command will compile the SRS and name the executable `SRS.exe`:

```
csc /out:SRS.exe *.cs /main:SRS
```

The output produced by running this program is as follows:

```
====================
Course Catalog:
====================

Course Catalog:

Course Information:
  Course No.:  CMP101
  Course Name:  Beginning Computer Technology
  Credits:  3.0
  Prerequisite Courses:
    (none)
  Offered As Section(s):  1 2

Course Information:
  Course No.:  CMP283
  Course Name:  Higher Level Languages (C#)
  Credits:  3.0
  Prerequisite Courses:
    OBJ101:  Object Methods for Software Development
  Offered As Section(s):  1

Course Information:
  Course No.:  CMP999
  Course Name:  Living Brain Computers
  Credits:  3.0
  Prerequisite Courses:
    CMP283:  Higher Level Languages (C#)
  Offered As Section(s):  1

Course Information:
  Course No.:  ART101
  Course Name:  Beginning Basketweaving
  Credits:  3.0
  Prerequisite Courses:
    (none)
  Offered As Section(s):  1
```

```
Course Information:
  Course No.:  OBJ101
  Course Name:  Object Methods for Software Development

  Credits:  3.0
  Prerequisite Courses:
    CMP101:  Beginning Computer Technology
  Offered As Section(s):  1 2


=====================
Schedule of Classes:
=====================


Schedule of Classes for SP2001

Section Information:
  Semester:  SP2001
  Course No.:  CMP101
  Section No:  2
  Offered:  W at 6:10 - 8:00 PM
  In Room:  GOVT202
  Professor:  John Carson
  Total of 0 students enrolled.

Section Information:
  Semester:  SP2001
  Course No.:  CMP101
  Section No:  1
  Offered:  M at 8:10 - 10:00 PM
  In Room:  GOVT101
  Professor:  Jackie Chan
  Total of 1 students enrolled, as follows:
    Joe Blow

Section Information:
  Semester:  SP2001
  Course No.:  CMP283
  Section No:  1
  Offered:  M at 6:10 - 8:00 PM
  In Room:  GOVT101
  Professor:  Jacquie Barker
  Total of 0 students enrolled.
```

```
Section Information:
  Semester:  SP2001
  Course No.:  CMP999
  Section No:  1
  Offered:  R at 4:10 - 6:00 PM
  In Room:  SCI241
  Professor:  John Carson
  Total of 0 students enrolled.

Section Information:
  Semester:  SP2001
  Course No.:  OBJ101
  Section No:  2

  Offered:  T at 6:10 - 8:00 PM
  In Room:  SCI330
  Professor:  Jackie Chan
  Total of 0 students enrolled.

Section Information:
  Semester:  SP2001
  Course No.:  OBJ101
  Section No:  1
  Offered:  R at 4:10 - 6:00 PM
  In Room:  GOVT105
  Professor:  Jacquie Barker
  Total of 0 students enrolled.

Section Information:
  Semester:  SP2001
  Course No.:  ART101
  Section No:  1
  Offered:  M at 4:10 - 6:00 PM
  In Room:  ARTS25
  Professor:  Jackie Chan
  Total of 2 students enrolled, as follows:
    Gerson Lopez
    Joe Blow


======================
Professor Information:
======================
```

Faculty:

Person Information:
  Name: John Carson
  Soc. Security No.: 567-81-2345
Professor-Specific Information:
  Title: Full Professor
  Teaches for Dept.: Info. Technology
Teaching Assignments for John Carson:
  Course No.: CMP101
  Section No.: 2
  Course Name: Beginning Computer Technology
  Day and Time: W - 6:10 - 8:00 PM

  Course No.: CMP999
  Section No.: 1
  Course Name: Living Brain Computers
  Day and Time: R - 4:10 - 6:00 PM

Person Information:
  Name: Jacquie Barker
  Soc. Security No.: 123-45-6789
Professor-Specific Information:

  Title: Asst. Professor
  Teaches for Dept.: Info. Technology
Teaching Assignments for Jacquie Barker:
  Course No.: OBJ101
  Section No.: 1
  Course Name: Object Methods for Software Development
  Day and Time: R - 4:10 - 6:00 PM

  Course No.: CMP283
  Section No.: 1
  Course Name: Higher Level Languages (C#)
  Day and Time: M - 6:10 - 8:00 PM

Person Information:
  Name: Jackie Chan
  Soc. Security No.: 987-65-4321
Professor-Specific Information:
  Title: Full Professor
  Teaches for Dept.: Info. Technology

```
Teaching Assignments for Jackie Chan:
   Course No.:  CMP101
   Section No.:  1
   Course Name:  Beginning Computer Technology
   Day and Time:  M - 8:10 - 10:00 PM
   -----
   Course No.:  OBJ101
   Section No.:  2
   Course Name:  Object Methods for Software Development
   Day and Time:  T - 6:10 - 8:00 PM
   -----
   Course No.:  ART101
   Section No.:  1
   Course Name:  Beginning Basketweaving
   Day and Time:  M - 4:10 - 6:00 PM
   -----


====================
Student Information:
====================


Person Information:
   Name:  Joe Blow
   Soc. Security No.:  111-11-1111
Student-Specific Information:
   Major:  Math
   Degree:  M.S.
Course Schedule for Joe Blow
   Course No.:  CMP101
   Section No.:  1
   Course Name:  Beginning Computer Technology
   Meeting Day and Time Held:  M - 8:10 - 10:00 PM

   Room Location:  GOVT101
   Professor's Name:  Jackie Chan
   -----
   Course No.:  ART101
   Section No.:  1
   Course Name:  Beginning Basketweaving
   Meeting Day and Time Held:  M - 4:10 - 6:00 PM
   Room Location:  ARTS25
   Professor's Name:  Jackie Chan
   -----
```

```
Transcript for:   Joe Blow (111-11-1111) [M.S. - Math]
  (no entries)


Person Information:
  Name:  Gerson Lopez
  Soc. Security No.:  222-22-2222
Student-Specific Information:
  Major:  Information Technology
  Degree:  Ph. D.
Course Schedule for Gerson Lopez
  Course No.:  ART101
  Section No.:  1
  Course Name:  Beginning Basketweaving
  Meeting Day and Time Held:  M - 4:10 - 6:00 PM
  Room Location:  ARTS25
  Professor's Name:  Jackie Chan
  -----
Transcript for:   Gerson Lopez (222-22-2222) [Ph. D. - Information Technology]
  (no entries)


Person Information:
  Name:  Mary Smith
  Soc. Security No.:  333-33-3333
Student-Specific Information:
  Major:  Physics
  Degree:  B.S.
Course Schedule for Mary Smith
  (none)
Transcript for:  Mary Smith (333-33-3333) [B.S. - Physics]
  (no entries)
```

In summary, Table 15-1 shows how our Chapter 14 version of the SRS had to be modified to achieve file persistence.

Table 15-1. Modifications Made to Achieve File Persistence

Class	Modifications?
CollectionWrapper	(New class)
CourseCatalog	(New class)
Course	Yes: we changed the signature of the ScheduleSection method to accept an explicit section number as an argument, because we're now reading it from a file.
Faculty	(New class)
Person	No.
Professor	No.
Section	No.
ScheduleOfClasses	Yes: it now extends the CollectionWrapper class; we implemented the ParseData and ParseData2 methods; and we added a FindSection method.
SRS	Yes: it was revamped—and streamlined!—to take advantage of all of the new collections that we've created.
Student	Yes: we did a lot! We revamped the constructor to do dynamic data loading at logon from a student's private data file by using a version of ParseData and ParseData2 written specifically for Student; we created a StudentSuccessfullyInitialized method; we created a Persist method that will record the state of a student's registration situation when he or she logs off.
Transcript	No.
TranscriptEntry	No.

This concludes the work that we're going to do with respect to persistence in the SRS application. We'll finish rounding out the SRS application by adding a graphical user interface in Chapter 16.

Summary

In this chapter, you've learned

- How we approach file I/O in C#, using the `FileStream`, `StreamReader`, and `StreamWriter` classes of the `System.IO` namespace

- An approach for parsing tab-delimited ASCII records to initialize an object's state, or a collection of objects, using the `String.Split` method

- A means of persisting an object's state in an ASCII file

- How to prepare a "test scaffold" `Main` method for testing isolated classes

- How proper encapsulation streamlines client code (for example, the SRS `Main` method)

We're also getting quite an opportunity to apply the C# language skills that we covered in earlier chapters. We encourage you to work with the SRS code, and to attempt some of the exercises that follow, to reinforce your learning experience.

Exercises

1. Review all of the code associated with the SRS as produced in this chapter, and cite all cases where error handling could be improved.

2. Use the test scaffold provided in the `CourseCatalog` class to test the `ParseData` and `ParseData2` methods of that class against all of the following error situations in either the `CourseCatalog.dat` or `Prerequisites.dat` files (edit these files to introduce the following problems one by one, and then run the code to see what happens):

   a. The course name is missing from one of the records in `CourseCatalog.dat` (i.e., the record only contains two fields instead of three).

   b. The value for credits (third field in a record) in `CourseCatalog.dat` is a nonnumeric value, such as "X".

   c. The `Prerequisites.dat` file refers to a course that wasn't defined in the `CourseCatalog.dat` file.

   d. The `Prerequisites.dat` file is empty.

   e. The `Prerequisites.dat` file contains a record with only one field in it.

Describe what happens in each case, and discuss what coding changes you'd have to make, if any, to handle each of the preceding situations "gracefully."

3. Follow up exercise 2 by actually making the necessary changes to the CourseCatalog.cs file, and then retest. (Hint: This will involve exception handling.)

Rounding Out Our Application, Part 2: Adding a Graphical User Interface

In Chapter 15, we greatly improved the usefulness of the SRS application by providing a means for persisting the state of Student objects—in particular, their enrollment status in various classes—from one SRS invocation to the next. However, we still haven't provided a means by which a student user can interact with the SRS. As it's currently implemented, we launch the application from the command line by running the SRS executable, and from then on the application runs to completion without any further user input, relying solely on ASCII files and/or hard-coded information as its "fuel" (data).

In this chapter, we're going to enhance our latest version of the SRS application once again by retrofitting a graphical user interface (GUI) front-end. With the GUI that we add, we'll provide hypothetical student users with the capability to

- Log on to the SRS.

- View the schedule of sections available for registration in the current semester.

- View and modify their individual course load by dropping and adding sections of courses that they are eligible to attend.

- Save these changes to a file before logging off again.

In this chapter, you'll learn

- The basics of C# GUI composition and event handling

- What the GUI classes in the System.Windows.Forms and System.Drawing namespaces have to offer

- Details about a number of FCL GUI classes

- A recommended architecture for C# GUI applications

- The importance of developing a concept of operations of how the GUI is to look, operate, and "flow" before any code is written

- How to retrofit a GUI to an existing application, using our SRS application from Chapter 15 as an example

It's important to remember when reading this chapter that it's only meant to provide an **introduction** *to C# GUIs. Our goal is to teach you how to create a simple, yet completely functional, GUI front-end for our SRS application. With this goal in mind, we're only going to cover that subset of available GUI classes that we'll need for building the SRS; furthermore, we'll only cover those features of these classes that we'll be taking advantage of in building the SRS. Nonetheless, you'll gain valuable insights into the fundamentals of C# GUI building and event handling.*

After you've finished reading this chapter and mastering the basics of C# GUI development, we suggest that you pay a visit to the .NET Framework SDK documentation and look specifically at the contents of the GUI-related namespaces.

C# GUIs: A Primer

One of the many advantages of C# is that GUI development is supported by the Framework Class Library (FCL). Every aspect of our C# application—the domain classes/objects, persistence of the state of these objects to a file, GUI manipulation of these objects, and so on—can be conveniently programmed using FCL types.

GUI Classes As Objects

The fundamental approach to graphical user interface programming with virtually any programming language, C# or otherwise, is to assemble graphical building blocks generically called **components** (and, in C#, often referred to specifically as **controls**). We assemble them in specific ways to provide the **"look,"** or **presentation**, that we desire for an application, and then program their behind-the-scenes logic to enable them to do useful things. Users interact with GUI objects—buttons, text fields, lists, and so on—to provide information to the system and/or to obtain information from the system, in order to achieve some worthwhile goal: in other words, to fulfill the use cases that we identified in Chapter 9.

Moreover, because objects are responsible for carrying out the mission of an object-oriented system, a GUI enables us to create and interact with objects. In the case of the SRS, we'll be

- ***Instantiating objects:*** for example, when a student user logs on to the system, we'll instantiate a Student object as an abstraction of that user.

- ***Invoking their methods,*** as we do when we invoke the ValidatePassword method on a Student object to ensure that the password a user has typed is valid.

- ***Changing their states,*** by modifying attribute values and/or creating new links between the objects; for example, when a student successfully enrolls in a course, we'll form a link between the appropriate Student and Section objects.

In fact, the GUI *itself* consists of objects! All C# GUI components are created as objects, and hence

- Are described by classes

- Are instantiated via the new operator, using an appropriate constructor

- Have fields (which are typically private), and properties/methods (which are typically public) that we access via dot notation

- Communicate via messages

- Participate in inheritance hierarchies

- Are referenced by reference variables, when we wish to maintain named "handles" on them

- Maintain handles on *other* objects—GUI as well as non-GUI objects

- Collaborate with other objects—GUI as well as non-GUI objects—to accomplish the mission of the overall system

Therefore, all of the techniques that you've learned about creating and communicating with objects in general throughout this book will apply to GUI objects in particular. Through user interactions with the SRS GUI, the GUI's objects will be requested to perform services, which in many cases lead them to collaborate behind the scenes with the domain objects—Students, Professors, Courses, Sections, and so on—to carry out a particular user-requested service such as registering for a course.

Containers

Just as we often use collections to organize object references (e.g., an ArrayList to organize Student references), we assemble C# GUIs by organizing collections of components using a special type of GUI object known as a **container**.

We may depict the relationship between containers, components, and objects via a UML diagram, as shown in Figure 16-1.

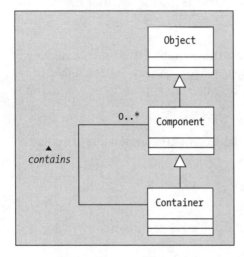

Figure 16-1. Relationship of containers to components

We learn from this diagram that

- Every container *is a* component (by virtue of inheritance), but conversely, every component is *not* necessarily a container.

- Since a container can *contain* components, and a container *is* a component, then a container may contain other containers. In fact, this is the way that we build up complex GUIs—by embedding components in containers, a technique that we'll explore in depth in this chapter.

By way of analogy, a container is like a directory on your computer system, and the objects placed in it are like items placed within that directory.

- Just as any one file has only one "home" directory, any one object can be placed in only one container.

- Conversely, a container may contain many objects—including other containers—just as a directory may contain many files and/or other directories.

Containers available in C# include the Form class of the System.Windows.Forms namespace, which we'll use as our top-level container when we construct our SRS GUI.

GUIs Are Event-Driven

The C# GUI model is an event-driven system, wherein each visual object can generate a number of **events** based on a user's interaction with that object. For example, clicking a graphical button, pressing the Enter key on the keyboard after typing in a text field, or clicking an item within a list to select it all automatically generate events.

Events are the system's way of telling us that the user has interacted with the GUI in some fashion. Events are informational in nature; as application developers, we can choose to either program a response to an event or to ignore it as we see fit. We'll discuss events and **event handling** in more detail later in this chapter.

The System.Windows.Forms and System.Drawing Namespaces

The GUI classes and support classes that we'll discuss in this chapter can be found in the System.Windows.Forms and System.Drawing namespaces of the .NET Framework Class Library. These C# namespaces provide an extensive array of ready-made GUI classes.

- The System.Windows.Forms namespace contains predefined GUI classes that represent buttons, labels, menus, windows, panels, and many other things besides. We can extend the existing GUI classes to create our own custom GUI classes.

- The System.Windows.Forms namespace also contains a variety of delegate types. A **delegate** is a C# class that can be used to respond to events generated by a GUI object. We'll discuss delegates when we discuss C# event handling later in this chapter.

- The System.Drawing namespace contains support classes that can be used for such operations as changing a font, adding color to a GUI object, or defining a geometrical construct such as a point or a rectangle.

Before we dive into the details of the classes defined by the GUI libraries of the .NET FCL, however, let's take a step back and talk about some fundamental concepts of proper GUI design.

Separating the Model from the View

A technique known as **separating the model from the view** is an important design approach when developing a graphically oriented application. This concept relates to the Model-View-Controller (MVC) paradigm, which was popularized as a formal concept with the Smalltalk language, but is equally applicable to all OO languages, including C#.

MVC is a way of thinking of an application as being subdivided into three parts, known as the **model,** the **view,** and the **controller:**

- The *model* embodies the abstract domain knowledge of the application: that is, the objects/classes that represent the real-world items/issues that the users of an application are familiar with, often referred to as the **business logic** or **domain** of the application. Up until this point in the book, we've been focusing almost exclusively on these so-called domain classes: Person, Student, Professor, Course, Section, and the like.

- The *view* is the way in which we present this knowledge to the user—typically, although not exclusively, via a graphical user interface. Note that there can be many different views of the same model, in either the same or different applications. For example, with respect to the SRS GUI, we could represent the Students enrolled in a particular Section as a list of their names and student ID numbers; or as photographs; or in diagram form, as shown in Figures 16-2 through 16-4.

Figure 16-2. Using a list to display Student information

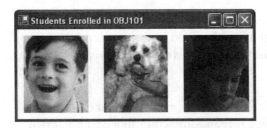

Figure 16-3. Using photographs to display Student information

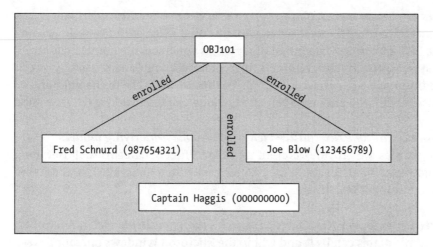

Figure 16-4. Using a diagram to display Student *information*

- The ***controller*** is the automatic mechanism by which the user interface is displayed, and by which events are communicated back and forth between the model and the view; changes to the model are reflected in the view, and user interactions with the view trigger changes to the model. In the case of C#, this is handled by the .NET runtime in conjunction with the underlying windowing mechanism of your particular computer system.

As OO developers, we must

- ***Design and program the model,*** as we did throughout Part Two of the book and in Chapter 14, respectively.

- ***Design and program the view(s);*** in C#, this is accomplished through the use of the Framework Class Library (FCL) GUI namespaces that provide the graphical user interface building blocks we'll focus our attention on for much of this chapter.

- ***Understand how the controller works,*** in order to take advantage of the mechanism for connecting the model and view together. This involves learning C#'s approach to event handling, which we'll discuss later in this chapter as well.

When designing and programming an application, if we take care to cleanly separate and insulate the code for the model from the code for the view, then it becomes much easier to

- ***Add or change a view, if need be, without disturbing the underlying model:*** That, in essence, is what we'll be doing when we add a GUI view to the SRS application later in this chapter. As you'll see, the domain classes that we've already programmed will remain virtually unchanged by our addition of a GUI; and, those changes that we ***do*** make to the domain classes will be to enhance their abstractions, ***not*** to introduce GUI features.

- ***Provide multiple alternative views of the same underlying model:*** Sometimes, we provide different views for different categories of user; for example, a professor using the SRS may see different windows and options than a student would see.

- ***Give a single user the ability to switch among multiple views:*** A familiar example of this can be found within the Microsoft Windows operating system. With Windows, users are able to view the contents of a folder as icons, or as a detailed list, or as an HTML page, or even as a DOS directory listing, as shown in Figures 16-5 through 16-8.

Figure 16-5. Viewing folder contents as icons . . .

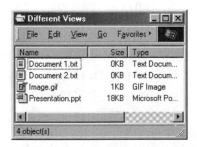

Figure 16-6. . . . or as a detailed list . . .

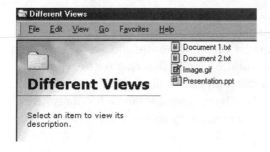

Figure 16-7. . . . or as an HTML page . . .

```
.              <DIR>          06-30-00  7:32p .
..             <DIR>          06-30-00  7:32p ..
DOCUME~1 TXT                0  06-30-00  7:32p Document 1.txt
IMAGE    GIF              796  06-30-00  7:34p Image.gif
DOCUME~2 TXT                0  06-30-00  7:32p Document 2.txt
PRESEN~1 PPT           18,432  04-07-00  1:42p Presentation.ppt
         4 file(s)          19,228 bytes
         2 dir(s)      25,133,056 bytes free
```

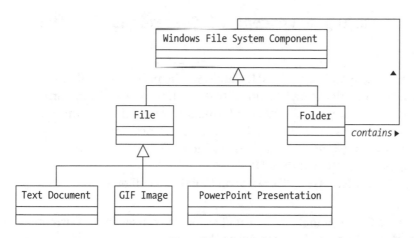

Figure 16-8. . . . or as a DOS directory listing.

Regardless of the view chosen, however, the underlying model in our Windows example is the same: we have a directory titled "Different Views" on our file system, and it contains four files: two text documents, a GIF image, and a PowerPoint presentation, as reflected in the UML diagram in Figure 16-9.

Figure 16-9. The UML model underlying all of our various Windows views

Our model should, in essence, be "view free": just as we can change the appearance of a sofa by adding a slipcover without changing its underlying structure or general functionality, so too should we be able to change the appearance of an application without changing its underlying structure.

One way to help ensure that the model and view are logically separated is to develop the model first, without regard for the view. In theory, if we do a proper job of developing the model, based on the analysis techniques of Part Two, then virtually any view relevant to the original goals (use cases) set forth for the system should be attainable. We'll demonstrate this concept by retroactively adding a GUI to the model that we automated in Chapter 14.

Our Learning "Roadmap"

We'll learn about building C# GUIs in three stages:

- First, we'll learn how to describe the desired "look" and behavior of our GUI by preparing a **concept of operations** document.

- Secondly, we'll learn about the various classes and techniques used in producing the visual appearance of a GUI.

- Finally, we'll learn how to provide behavior to our GUI through **event handling.**

Stage 1: Preparing a Concept of Operations for the SRS GUI

Before we can decide which specific GUI classes will be needed in building the SRS GUI, we must consider what functionality the GUI is to provide. In particular, we must answer the questions "What information should the GUI present to the user?" and "What actions will the GUI allow a user to perform?" Once we've answered these two questions, we can decide which classes are best suited to accomplishing the objectives of the GUI.

In a nutshell, the SRS GUI we'll create will function as follows:

1. When the GUI is launched, the list of available courses in the current semester's schedule of classes will be displayed.

2. Before a student can use the SRS GUI, he or she will have to log in. Logging in will be accomplished by having the user type in his or her student ID number.

3. Once a student has logged in, the student's name will be displayed, along with a list of the courses for which the student is already registered (i.e., the student's current course load/list).

4. After logging on, the SRS GUI should allow a student to take any of the following actions:

   - Adding a course to his or her course list by selecting one from the schedule of classes

   - Dropping a course from his or her course list

   - Saving his or her current course schedule to a file

   - Logging off from the SRS

Sketching out the functional flow of a graphical user interface through pictures and accompanying narrative—a technique informally known as **storyboarding**—is a great way to come to agreement with the future users of a system on how the application should look and behave before development begins. And, if the application truly evolves as we envisioned that it would, then the document that we've prepared to narrate the storyboard *before* developing the application, known as a **concept of operations document,** can be used as the basis for a user's guide and/or online tutorial *after* the application is finished. The "story" that is told by the concept of operations document is presented from the external viewpoint of a user; it is, in essence, a pictorial representation of how the various use cases for the application will be fulfilled.

Because we developed the code for the SRS GUI before this chapter was written, we had the luxury of using actual screen snapshots of the GUI as illustrations for our concept of operations; but, in a real-life situation, we'd start by informally sketching our ideas, perhaps with pen or paper or on a whiteboard, so as to "test drive" the concepts with future users of the system. Once we verified that we were on the right track, then, depending on what tools we have available, we might either render our conceptualized GUI with a conventional drawing tool such as Microsoft PowerPoint, or perhaps even create a GUI "shell" using an IDE.

> **Cautionary note:** *If you use an IDE to mock up the look of a GUI, realize that you've put the cart before the horse if the application's model classes haven't already been designed and built. This, in fact, is a common mistake that many beginning OO programmers make: they build a GUI first using a drag-and-drop IDE, and then try to retrofit the back-end application without having engineered it properly around objects.*
>
> *For this very reason, we don't endorse the use of drag-and-drop IDEs when first learning how to build GUIs. As with the rest of C#, we believe that you'll learn so much more about GUI development if you build them from scratch first. Once you have a good handle on GUI fundamentals, however, the use of an IDE such as Visual Studio .NET does indeed increase productivity.*
>
> *If you do use an IDE to propose a GUI's look early on in the project, be prepared to radically change, if not abandon, your mock-up when you get to coding the application in earnest.*

A Hypothetical Scenario

A concept of operations document helps us to think through and describe how the GUI should look and flow. For the SRS application, our concept of operations begins when Joe Blow, a student user, launches the SRS application. The GUI that first appears, shown in Figure 16-10, presents a list of all sections offered this semester titled Schedule of Classes, along with a number of empty fields labeled SSN, Name, and Total Courses. A number of buttons appear at the bottom of the window labeled Drop, Save My Schedule, Add, and Log Off, but these are all initially grayed out to signal that they are disabled; until a user logs on, none of the functions provided by these buttons is valid. (We recognize that the SSN field can accept user input by its white background, whereas the Name and Total Courses fields are read-only due to their gray backgrounds.)

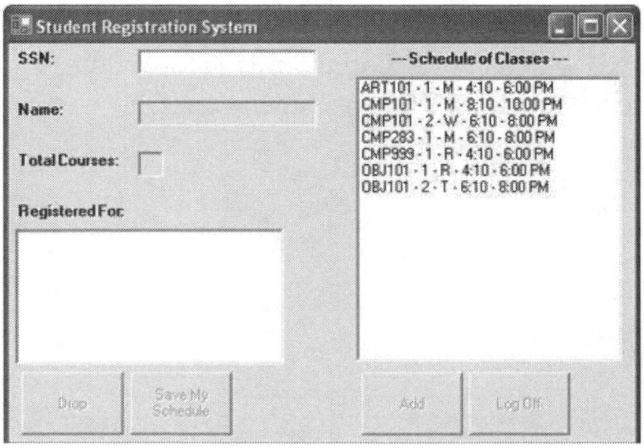

Figure 16-10. The initial view of the SRS GUI

Joe logs on to the SRS by typing his student ID number (which for the SRS is the student's social security number), 111-11-1111, in the field labeled SSN, and then presses the Enter key. A small dialog window, illustrated in Figure 16-11, pops up to request that he enter his password to complete the logon process. As Joe types in his password (which happens to be 111, the first three digits of his social security number), asterisks (*) appear in place of the characters that he types, to ensure his privacy.

Figure 16-11. Joe types his password into the dialog box.

After typing in his password, Joe presses the Enter key. Unfortunately, Joe has mistyped his password, and so the pop-up message in Figure 16-12 appears.

Figure 16-12. If the password is invalid, a warning dialog box appears.

After Joe clicks the OK button on this pop-up dialog box to dismiss it, he must click anywhere in the SSN field to give that field focus, and then press the Enter key again to redisplay the password dialog box a second time (he needn't retype his SSN, however). Assuming that he types his password correctly this time, he receives confirmation of a successful logon (see Figure 16-13).

Figure 16-13. Joe has successfully logged on to the SRS.

After clicking OK on this confirmation pop-up, Joe sees that his current registration information appears in the Name, Total Courses, and Registered For fields in the main GUI window. (Although Joe doesn't know it, this information was read in behind-the-scenes from a data file named 111-11-1111.dat.) We see that

Joe had previously used the SRS to register for section 1 of course number CMP101. Notice that two of the buttons at the bottom of the GUI—Save My Schedule and Log Off—have now become enabled and "clickable." (See Figure 16-14.)

Note that there are three data files supplied with the SRS code download from Apress that support this application, and which represent three different students' data: 111-11-1111.dat, 222-22-2222.dat, and 333-33-3333.dat.

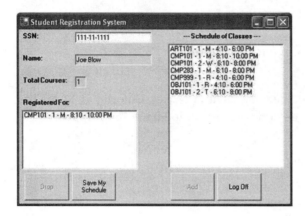

Figure 16-14. Joe's current registration data is displayed.

Joe decides to try to enroll in course CMP101–2. He selects this section from the Schedule of Classes list, which causes the Add button at the bottom of the screen to automatically become active. (Until he had selected a section in the Schedule of Classes list, it made no sense for the Add button to be selectable.)

Joe clicks the Add button, shown in Figure 16-15.

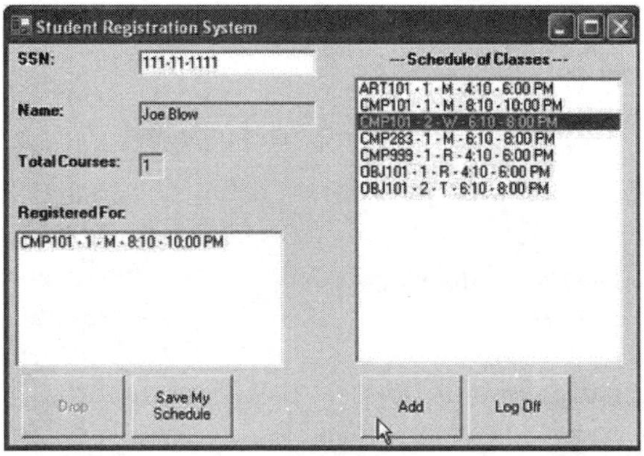

Figure 16-15. Joe tries to register for a course.

But because Joe is already registered for a different section of that same course (CMP101–1), the system notifies him via the pop-up message shown in Figure 16-16 that he may not register for CMP101–2. (Had Joe's transcript reflected successful *prior* completion of any section of CMP101, his request would have also been rejected.)

Figure 16-16. Joe has already enrolled in a different section of CMP101.

Joe clicks OK to dismiss the dialog box. He next selects CMP999–1 from the Schedule of Classes, and again clicks the Add button (see Figure 16-17).

Figure 16-17. Joe attempts to register for CMP999.

Unfortunately, Joe strikes out again! Course CMP999, "Living Brain Computers," requires students to have successfully completed the prerequisite course CMP283, "Higher Level Languages (C#)." Since Joe's transcript (which is being checked behind-the-scenes, unbeknownst to Joe) doesn't show any evidence that he has previously completed CMP283, the system once again rejects his registration request with a pop-up explanation (see Figure 16-18).

Figure 16-18. Joe hasn't satisfied the prerequisites for CMP999.

After clicking OK to dismiss this pop-up dialog box, Joe selects ART101–1 from the Schedule of Classes list, and clicks the Add button yet again (see Figure 16-19).

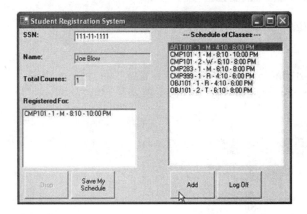

Figure 16-19. Joe tries to register for ART101.

Success at last! ART101 has no prerequisites to satisfy, and Joe is neither currently registered for, nor has ever successfully completed, a section of this course. Joe receives confirmation that he has been registered in ART 101-1, as shown in Figure 16-20.

Figure 16-20. Success at last!

After Joe dismisses the confirmation pop-up by clicking the OK button, he sees the newly added section reflected in the Registered For list on the main SRS window, with the Total Courses field reflecting his correct new total of two (2) registered courses (see Figure 16-21).

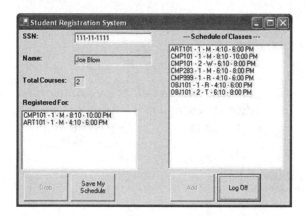

Figure 16-21. Joe is now registered for two courses.

Note that Joe's selection in the Schedule of Classes list has been cleared, and that the Add button is no longer enabled.

Next, Joe decides that he wishes to drop CMP101. He clicks that entry in his Registered For list, at which point the Drop button becomes enabled and selectable.

Joe clicks the Drop button, as shown in Figure 16-22.

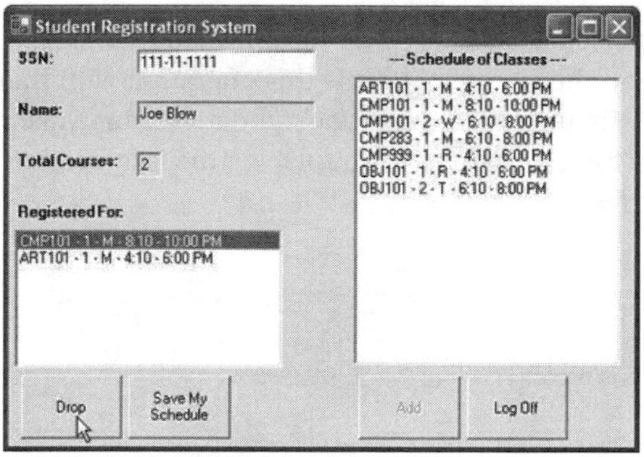

Figure 16-22. Joe drops CMP101.

In response, the SRS displays a confirmation pop-up dialog box, as we can see in Figure 16-23, that the course has been dropped from his course load.

Figure 16-23. The drop request is successful.

When Joe dismisses the pop-up by clicking OK, we see that Joe's course load information has once again been properly updated, and that the Drop button has once again become disabled, as shown in Figure 16-24.

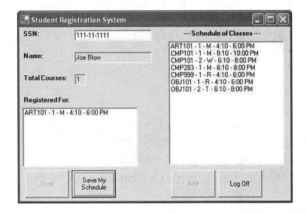

Figure 16-24. Joe is only registered for ART101 now.

Satisfied with his new schedule, Joe decides to save this information by clicking the Save My Schedule button, and the system confirms this operation with the dialog box shown in Figure 16-25. (Behind the scenes, Joe's updated course load information has been persisted to file 111-11-1111.dat, replacing the information that was previously stored in that file.)

Figure 16-25. Joe's schedule is saved to a file.

Joe dismisses the dialog box, and then clicks the Log Off button on the main window; in response, the screen is cleared of all of Joe's student-specific information as shown in Figure 16-26, and is ready for a different student to log on.

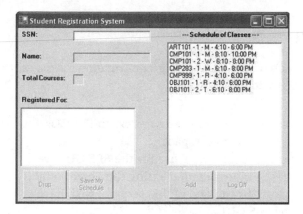

Figure 16-26. Joe has logged off of the SRS system.

Now that we've narrated the concept of operations for our GUI, let's move on to stage 2: programming the look of the GUI through the use of FCL GUI classes.

Stage 2: Creating the Look of Our GUI

Let's look at each of the functional requirements of the GUI as specified by the concept of operations, and identify the GUI class best suited to each.

- To log in to the SRS, the student will need to type his or her SSN into a field. The C# TextBox class will suit this requirement nicely. We can also use noneditable TextBox objects to display the student's name and the number of courses for which he or she is registered.

- To display both the course catalog and the student's course list, we need an object that can display a multiline list of items. The object also has to allow the student to make a selection from the list and keep track of which item is selected. The ListBox class can fulfill all of these requirements.

- One of the best ways to initiate an action is by having the user click a button. We'll use four Button objects to implement the Add, Drop, Save, and Log Off functionality.

- The GUI would be somewhat confusing if we didn't include labels to describe what the various objects were to be used for. We'll use several instances of the Label class to achieve this goal.

- We'll need a container to organize all of these objects into a main window for the GUI; we'll use the Form class for this purpose.

- Finally, we'll need a way to pop up various warning/confirmation messages; we'll use the MessageBox class to do so.

All of these classes—Button, Form, Label, ListBox, MessageBox, and TextBox—are defined within the System.Windows.Forms namespace.

Now that we've proposed the objects that we'll use for the SRS GUI, we'll describe each of the chosen classes in more detail, creating the objects and adding them to our SRS GUI as we go. By the end of this section, we'll have completed building the look of the SRS GUI.

One thing to remember with GUI development is that there are multiple ways to achieve the same functional goals. That is, there is nothing "sacred" about the classes that we've chosen for the SRS GUI. We could have, for example, implemented the Add, Drop, Save, and Log Off actions using menu items rather than buttons.

The Form Class

Earlier in this chapter, we discussed how a container is used to organize, manage, and present other objects in a GUI. We can think of a top-level container as a surface onto which all of the other GUI objects are arranged (see Figure 16-27).

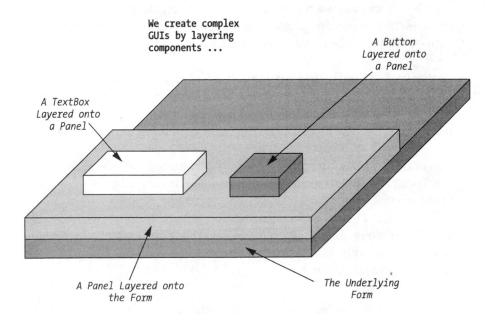

Figure 16-27. GUI components are placed on a container.

In building the SRS GUI, we'll use an instance of the Form class as our main container. A Form object serves as a stand-alone window; note that a Form may **not** be contained in/attached to any other type of GUI object.

A Form has a title bar, and may optionally be equipped with a menu bar (we won't be using a menu bar for the SRS GUI as designed, however). A Form also automatically provides **window control buttons** in its upper right-hand corner; from left to right, the three window control buttons are used to minimize the size of, maximize the size of, or close the Form and optionally exit the application (see Figure 16-28).

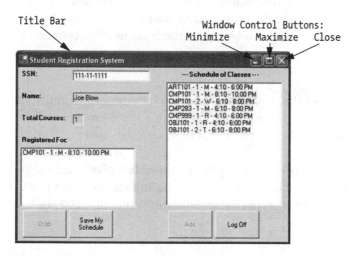

Figure 16-28. Some of the built-in features of a Form

When building a C# GUI application, one main Form is created at a minimum to hold the objects necessary to provide the desired GUI appearance and functionality. Nontrivial GUI applications typically consist of **multiple** separate windows—one main Form and multiple other Form/MessageBox/Dialog objects that can represent such things as transient pop-up windows. (We'll use MessageBox objects when we build the SRS GUI, and will discuss them later in this chapter after we've explored event handling a bit.)

Building a Simple Form

A Form object will serve as the primary container for the SRS GUI, but before we launch into actually building the SRS GUI, let's "get our feet wet" by building a simple Form.

First, we'll create a program/class called TestForm1, and will place using directives at the top of the program so we can refer to the appropriate GUI classes by their simple names.

```
// TestForm1.cs

using System;
using System.Windows.Forms;

public class TestForm1
{
  static void Main() {
```

Within the `Main` method of this class, we'll perform the bare minimum steps necessary to create and display a `Form`: namely, we'll instantiate a `Form` object by using the `Form` class's lone, parameterless constructor, and will maintain a handle on the newly created `Form` object with a reference variable named `simpleForm`:

```
Form simpleForm = new Form();
```

Most of the characteristics that define the state of a `Form` can be manipulated through properties declared by the `Form` class. There are several properties that allow us to specify the size of a `Form`; in this example, we'll use the `Height` and `Width` properties.

The width and height of GUI objects is expressed in **pixels;** a pixel is the smallest addressable graphical unit on a display screen. The default size for a `Form` is 300 pixels high by 300 pixels wide. We'll set the size of our form to be 200 × 200 pixels.

```
simpleForm.Height = 200;
simpleForm.Width = 200;
```

Next, we'll add a title to the `Form` by setting the value of the `Text` property. (The default is for a `Form` to be untitled.) We'll give our `Form` the title "Whee!!!".

```
simpleForm.Text = "Whee!!!";
```

We're now ready to display our simple `Form` on the screen. The `Application` class, also from the `System.Windows.Forms` namespace, defines static methods and properties that are used to manage an application, including methods to start and stop an application. We'll use the static `Run` method from the `Application` class to launch our `Form`.

```
Application.Run(simpleForm);
```

Here is the code for the `TestForm1` class again, in its entirety:

```
// TestForm1.cs

using System;
```

```
using System.Windows.Forms;

public class TestForm1
{
  static void Main() {
    // Create a Form by calling the Form constructor.
    Form simpleForm = new Form();

    // Set the size of the Form using the Height
    // and Width properties.
    simpleForm.Height = 200;
    simpleForm.Width = 200;

    // Add a title to the Form using the Text property.
    simpleForm.Text = "Whee!!!";

    // Use the Application class Run() method to launch
    // the Form.
    Application.Run(simpleForm);
  }
}
```

> **Reminder:** *the complete code for all of the examples in this chapter is available as a download from the Apress web site; see Appendix D for details.*

When we subsequently compile, then run, the program by typing the commands

```
csc TestForm1.cs
TestForm1
```

we see the window (form) shown in Figure 16-29 appear in the upper-left corner of the screen. Our form is blank because we haven't yet attached any objects (labels, buttons, etc.)—we'll do so in due time.

Figure 16-29. A simple Form

To dismiss this form and stop the TestForm1 program from executing, click the window close (X) button in the upper-right corner of the frame.

> *Of course, C# programs may also be launched through other means; one of the most frequently used approaches is to create a Windows desktop shortcut. The shortcut should execute the same command that a user would have typed if launching the program from the command prompt.*

In our simple Form example, we specified the height, width, and title of the Form by setting the value of the Height, Width, and Text properties. The Form class declares a large number of properties that can be used to define the appearance and behavior of a Form. We'll use another one of the Form properties in the next section to center our simple form on the screen.

Centering a Form on the Screen

By default, a Form will appear in the upper-left corner of the computer screen, as shown in Figure 16-30.

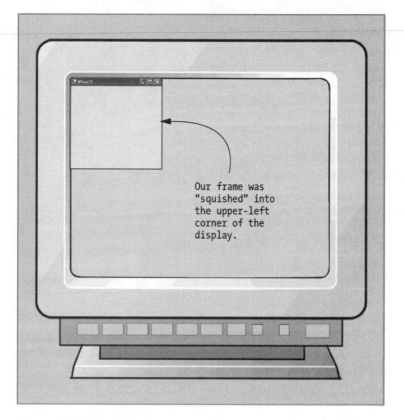

Our frame was "squished" into the upper-left corner of the display.

Figure 16-30. By default, a Form *will appear in the upper-left corner of the display.*

Often, we would like to *center* a new Form in the middle of the screen when it first appears. To center a form, we simply need to set its StartPosition property value to the constant FormStartPosition.CenterScreen, also defined by the Form class.

Let's rewrite the previous example to take advantage of the StartPosition property:

```
// TestForm2.cs

using System;
using System.Windows.Forms;
using System.Drawing;

public class TestForm2
{
  static void Main() {
    // Create a Form by calling the Form constructor.
    Form simpleForm = new Form();
```

```
    // Set the size of the Form using the Height
    // and Width properties.
    simpleForm.Height = 200;
    simpleForm.Width = 200;

    // Add a title to the Form using the Text property
    simpleForm.Text = "Whee!!!";

    // Center the Form on the Desktop.
    simpleForm.StartPosition = FormStartPosition.CenterScreen;

    simpleForm.Visible = true;

    // Use the Application class's Run method to launch
    // the Form.
    Application.Run(simpleForm);
  }
}
```

The Form will now appear in the center of the computer screen, regardless of the size of the monitor in question (see Figure 16-31).

Figure 16-31. A Form *can be centered on the display using the* StartPosition *property.*

Application Architecture with GUIs

The simple GUI examples that we've seen thus far all involve a single class whose Main method instantiates and displays a Form; TestForm1 and TestForm2 were both designed in this fashion. This single-class methodology isn't an appropriate architecture for anything but trivial applications, however.

A better architecture for a GUI application is to create a minimum of two classes:

1. A class, derived from Form, that defines the appearance (and ultimately, the behavior) of the main GUI window:

   - All objects to be attached to the frame become **fields** of this class.

   - The objects are instantiated and attached in the **constructor** for this class.

2. A **separate** application driver class that

   - Instantiates an instance of the main window/Form in its Main method

   - Handles any other application initialization steps—e.g., establishing database connectivity, perhaps with the help of a log-on dialog box

   - Houses any "global data" (as public static fields), constants, or convenience methods (as public static methods) for the application as a whole

If more than one window is needed for the GUI (as will be the case for the SRS GUI), additional classes are created to define the appearance and behavior of each of the other key windows, each of which is derived from an appropriate predefined GUI container class (usually another Form or a different type of container, such as a MessageBox, which we'll discuss later in this chapter).

Let's take another look at the TestForm2.cs example, redesigned as previously suggested.

- First, we'll create a class called TestForm3, derived from the Form class, to represent the main window.

- Secondly, we'll create the driver class, TestForm3Driver, in a separate file called TestForm3Driver.cs.

Let's start with TestForm3; we'll show the complete code listing for TestForm3.cs first, and will then comment on some of the differences between TestForm3 and TestForm2:

```
// TestForm3.cs

using System;
using System.Windows.Forms;
using System.Drawing;

public class TestForm3 : Form {
    // When we add eventually attach objects to the Form --
    // labels, buttons, and so forth -- they will be declared here,
    // as FIELDS of the TestForm4 class.

    // Constructor:  we "assemble" the GUI here.
    public TestForm3() {
        // Set the size of the Form using the Height
        // and Width properties.
        this.Height = 200;
        this.Width = 200;

        // Add a title to the Form using the Text property.
        this.Text = "Whee!!!";

        // Center the Form on the desktop.
        this.StartPosition = FormStartPosition.CenterScreen;
        this.Visible = true;
    }

    // Note that there is no longer a Main method in this class!
}
```

The Form's properties are set as before, except now we're doing so from *within* the TestForm3 class—specifically, from within its *constructor*—rather than setting them *externally* to the Form *instance* from within the Main method. Note the use of the this. prefix when setting the Form property values:

```
this.Height = 200;
this.Width = 200;
```

Strictly speaking, the this. prefix isn't necessary, but can optionally be used as a reminder that we're setting the value of the property on the current object: namely, *this* Form, which we're currently assembling.

Now, let's look at the code for the driver class, TestForm3Driver. For this example, the Main method of the driver class simply calls the Application.Run method, passing the method a call to the TestForm3 constructor. The TestForm3 class constructor that we reviewed previously does all the work of assembling the GUI instance.

```
// TestForm3Driver.cs

using System;
using System.Windows.Forms;

public class TestForm3Driver {
  static void Main() {
    // The Main() method has become quite simple;
    // we simply call the Run() method to display
    // an (unnamed) instance of TestForm3.
    Application.Run(new TestForm3());
  }
}
```

> *In the previous example, we created an unnamed* TestForm3 *object "on the fly," nested inside of the* Run *method call:*
>
> ```
> Application.Run(new TestForm3());
> ```
>
> *We could have accomplished the same result as a two-step process:*
>
> ```
> TestForm3 form3 = new TestForm3();
> Application.Run(form3);
> ```
>
> *However, since we have no reason to maintain a named handle on the* TestForm3 *object—once it's passed as an argument to the* Run *method, we have no further need to address it by name in this application—we've collapsed what would have been two statements into one. This is a commonly used technique throughout the C# language, whenever an object* A *requires us to pass it an instance of a class* B *for its own private use.*

The previous Form example is significant, because the TestForm3 and TestForm3Driver classes will be the starting points for our SRS GUI—we'll rename them MainForm and SRS, respectively, as they evolve.

Now that we have our top-level container, we'll next learn about the various other objects needed to round out our GUI's main window (see Figure 16-32):

- Label

- Button

- ListBox

- TextBox

- MessageBox

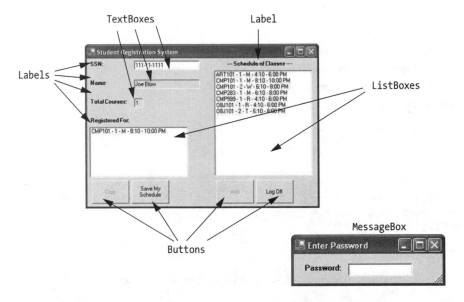

Figure 16-32. The SRS GUI will showcase a variety of GUI objects.

> **Recommendation:** *While reading through the next several sections, it would be helpful to look at the entire* MainForm.cs *and* PasswordForm.cs *code listings. This will give you a sense of the "big picture" of how the GUI objects are incorporated into their underlying Form. You can download the Chapter 16 source code from the Apress web site. Details are provided in Appendix D.*

The Label Class

A GUI wouldn't be very useful if it simply displayed an assortment of GUI objects with no explanation of what the objects were supposed to do or be used for. Virtually every GUI application uses labels to describe the purpose of the various GUI objects that it presents, as well to provide other instructions/status information to the user. We'll define a number of informational labels for the SRS GUI using instances of the Label class.

The Label class represents a simple GUI object that can be used to display a single line of text. (A Label can also be used to display an image, but we won't be using that capability in building the SRS GUI.)

The Label class defines a single, parameterless constructor:

```
public Label()
```

This constructor creates a blank Label with default properties. As with the Form class, the state and appearance of a Label can be specified through properties declared by the Label class. To create the labels for the SRS GUI, we'll make use of the following Label properties:

- public virtual string Text: The Text property is used to access the text that is displayed by the Label. The property defines both get and set accessors, so it can be used to retrieve or change Label text programmatically.

```
Label name = new Label();
name.Text = "Jackson";
Console.WriteLine("name is " + name.Text);
```

Note that Label values can't be modified directly by a user, only indirectly by our application in response to a user's actions on some other object; for example:

```
Label status = new Label();  // Create a blank label.
// Later in the application (pseudocode):
if (user presses the Submit button) {
  // Programmatically set the text on this label.
  status.Text = "Process underway ... please wait";
}
```

- public virtual Font Font: The Font property is used to get or set the font used to display the text of the Label on the screen. It can also be used to specify if the Label will be displayed using **bold** or *italic* font.

The value of the Font property is set by assigning it an instance of the Font class (from the System.Drawing namespace). The Font class defines a wide variety of constructors; the constructor we'll use in building the SRS is used to create a new font style based on an already existing font:

```
public Font(Font existingFont, FontStyle newStyle)
```

For example, to change the style of the student's name Label font to **bold,** we would access the existing (default) Font for the name label, and then set the Font property to a **bolded** version as follows:

```
name.Font = new Font(name.Font, FontStyle.Bold);
```

We could similarly change the font style to *italic* by using

```
name.Font = new Font(name.Font, FontStyle.Italic);
```

We can change the style to be both ***bold and italic*** in a single step using the | operator:

```
name.Font = new Font(name.Font, FontStyle.Bold | FontStyle.Italic);
```

- public virtual bool AutoSize: If the AutoSize property is set to true, the width and height of the Label will be automatically set based on the textual content and font of the Label. The default value is false, meaning that the size of the Label will have to be explicitly changed using its Width and Height properties.

```
name.AutoSize = true;   // the name Label will be automatically sized.
```

- public int Top: The Top property is inherited from the Control class and is used to get or set the vertical position of the object inside its parent container. The value of the property is equal to the distance in pixels between the ***top*** edge of the Label and the ***top*** edge of its parent container.

```
// The Label is positioned 200 pixels below the top of its container.
name.Top = 200;
```

- public int Left: The Left property is inherited from the Control class and is used to get or set the horizontal position of the object inside its parent container. The value of the property is equal to the distance in pixels between the ***left*** edge of the Label and the ***left*** edge of its parent container.

```
// The Label is positioned 200 pixels from the container's left edge.
name.Left = 200;
```

There are many more Label *properties that allow us to customize the look and behavior of a* Label. *For a complete list and description of all of the* Label *class properties, please consult the .NET Framework SDK documentation.*

Adding Labels to a Form

We'll use `Label` objects in the SRS GUI to describe the other `TextBox` and `ListBox` objects comprising the SRS GUI so that the user knows what their intended purposes are. The first set of `Label` objects we'll add to the SRS GUI will be those that describe the `TextBox` objects that will appear on the left side of the `Form`. We'll add `Labels` for the other GUI objects a little later in the chapter.

> **Important note:** *In this section and the other sections that follow, we won't overwhelm you with the entire `MainForm` class listing. Instead, we'll only show excerpts of the code to highlight the particular GUI component that we're discussing. It's therefore important that you download the `MainForm.cs` source code in its entirety from the Apress web site before proceeding, if you haven't already done so, so that you can follow along as you read these sections.*

To include `Labels` as part of the SRS GUI, we'll first declare reference variables for them as attributes of the `MainForm` class:

```
// MainForm.cs

using System;
using System.Windows.Forms;
using System.Drawing;

public class MainForm : Form
{
  // The GUI objects that will be placed on the Form are declared as
  // attributes of the MainForm class.
  private Label ssnLabel;
  private Label nameLabel;
  private Label totalCourseLabel;
  private Label registeredLabel;
```

The `Label` objects are then instantiated inside of the `MainForm` constructor. We'll use the `Label` class properties we previously described to define the appearance of each `Label`. We'll set the text of each `Label` and set the font style to be bold, as well as use the autosize feature to allow the system to size our labels for us. We'll position each `Label` on the `Form` using the `Top` and `Left` properties.

```
  // Constructor.
  public MainForm() {
    // Create left-hand side labels.
    // All labels are offset five pixels from the left-hand edge of the form.
```

```
int labelLeft = 5;
// The vertical spacing between the top edges of adjacent vertical labels
// will be 40 pixels.
int labelVertSpace = 40;

ssnLabel = new Label();
ssnLabel.Text = "SSN:";
// Make this label bold.
ssnLabel.Font = new Font(ssnLabel.Font, FontStyle.Bold);
ssnLabel.AutoSize = true;
ssnLabel.Top = 5;
ssnLabel.Left = labelLeft;
```

and so on for the remaining three labels.

Now that we've created our Label objects and defined their appearance, we're ready to add the Label objects to the Form. The way to add objects to a Form is through the Controls property of the Form class. The Controls property has the following header:

```
public Controls.ControlCollection Controls
```

The Controls.ControlCollection class represents, as the name would suggest, a collection of controls (i.e., GUI objects that accept input or display information) associated with a Form. To add a control to a Form, the Add method is called on the Controls.ControlCollection object associated with the Form. It doesn't matter in which order the Label objects are added to the Form, as their position is determined by the value assigned to their Top and Left properties.

```
// Add the controls to the form using the Controls property.
this.Controls.Add(ssnLabel);
this.Controls.Add(nameLabel);
this.Controls.Add(totalCourseLabel);
this.Controls.Add(registeredLabel);
```

Now it's time to size our Form and to make it visible on the screen. We'll specify the appearance of the SRS GUI form as a whole in a manner similar to that used in our previous TestForm*x* examples, with one exception. When the various TestForm*x* GUIs appeared on the screen, their size could be changed by "grabbing" one corner of the window and dragging the mouse inward or outward.

If the SRS GUI were to be resizable in this fashion, however—in particular, if users were able to *reduce* its size—some of the GUI objects might disappear from view, as illustrated in Figure 16-33.

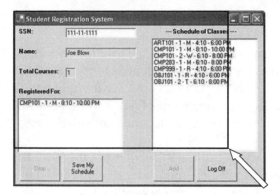

Figure 16-33. If the SRS GUI is resized to be smaller, some of the components won't be visible.

To prevent this from occurring, we can set the MinimumSize property of the Form to be the **current** size of the Form.

```
// Set some appearance properties for the Form.
this.Text = "Student Registration System";
this.Height = 350;
this.Width = 500;
this.MinimumSize = this.Size;
this.StartPosition = FormStartPosition.CenterScreen;
this.Visible = true;
```

Figure 16-34 shows how the SRS GUI looks when the first four Label objects have been added to the Form.

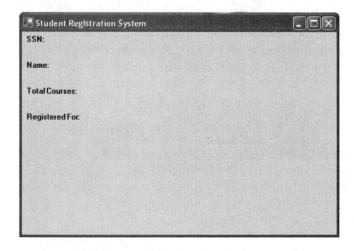

Figure 16-34. We've added four Label objects to the Form.

The TextBox Class

GUIs frequently need to provide components that enable the user to input a line of text. For example, in the case of the SRS GUI, a user will need to type in his or her SSN number to log on to the SRS. A TextBox is a GUI object that is typically used to either accept as input, or to display, a single line of text. It's also possible to create a multiline TextBox, but by default TextBox objects accommodate a single line of text.

In addition to the TextBox used to accept the user's SSN number, the SRS GUI will also use ***read-only*** TextBox objects to display the student's name and the total number of courses in which the student is currently enrolled once he or she has logged on.

Similar to the Label class, the TextBox class declares only a single, parameterless constructor:

```
public TextBox()
```

Once a TextBox object has been instantiated, its state can be defined by setting the value of various properties declared by the TextBox class. In addition to the Top, Left, and AutoSize properties we learned about previously when discussing Labels, we'll also make use of two other properties when we create the TextBox objects.

- `public int Width`: The value of the Width property represents the width of the TextBox in pixels. The AutoSize property works a little differently for TextBox objects than it does for Labels in that only the ***height*** of the TextBox is sized automatically based on the font used for the text; the ***width*** of a TextBox must be explicitly set through its Width property.

- `public bool ReadOnly`: The ReadOnly property controls whether a TextBox will accept user input. If the value of this property is set to `false`, the TextBox will be used for display purposes only.

> *As with the* Label *class, there are many more* TextBox *class properties that allow us to customize the look and behavior of a* TextBox. *For a complete list and description of all of the* TextBox *class properties, please consult the .NET Framework SDK documentation.*

Adding TextBox Objects to the SRS GUI

The process for adding the three TextBox objects to the SRS GUI is similar in many respects to the process for adding the Labels. We'll revisit the MainForm.cs code, highlighting the significant additions made to the MainForm class to accommodate

TextBox objects. The SRS.cs driver code needn't change at all from the previous version that we studied.

To include the TextBox objects as part of the SRS GUI, we'll first declare reference variables to them as attributes of the MainForm class.

```
public class MainForm : Form
{
  // Label declarations go here (omitted from this code listing).

  // Declare three TextBox objects as fields of the MainForm class.
  private TextBox ssnTextBox;
  private TextBox nameTextBox;
  private TextBox totalTextBox;
```

The TextBox objects are created inside the MainForm class constructor. The state of each TextBox is specified by setting the value of some of the TextBox class properties.

- The width of each TextBox is explicitly set through its Width property.

- The value of the AutoSize property is set to be true, so that the height of each TextBox will be set automatically.

- We want the left edges of each TextBox to be aligned with one another vertically, and so we set the value of the Left property for each of the TextBox objects to be 15 pixels to the *right* of the *right* edge of the longest Label, the Total Courses label.

- The position of the top edge of each TextBox is set to be the same as the top edge of its corresponding Label.

- The Total Courses and Name TextBox objects are meant for display purposes only, so the value of their ReadOnly property is set to true.

```
  // Constructor.
  public MainForm() {
    // Create left-hand side labels.
    // Details omitted ... see code for previous example.

    // Create text box objects.
    ssnTextBox = new TextBox();
    ssnTextBox.Width = 140;
    ssnTextBox.AutoSize = true;
    ssnTextBox.Top = ssnLabel.Top;
    ssnTextBox.Left = totalCourseLabel.Right + 15;
```

```
nameTextBox = new TextBox();
nameTextBox.Width = 140;
nameTextBox.AutoSize = true;
nameTextBox.Top = nameLabel.Top;
nameTextBox.Left = totalCourseLabel.Right + 15;

totalTextBox = new TextBox();
totalTextBox.Width = 20;
totalTextBox.AutoSize = true;
totalTextBox.Top = totalCourseLabel.Top;
totalTextBox.Left = totalCourseLabel.Right + 15;
totalTextBox.ReadOnly = true;
```

The TextBox objects are then added to the GUI in the same manner that the Label objects were, by using the Add method on the Controls property of the Form:

```
this.Controls.Add(ssnTextBox);
this.Controls.Add(nameTextBox);
this.Controls.Add(totalTextBox);
```

Figure 16-35 shows how our SRS GUI looks now, with the TextBox objects added to the Form.

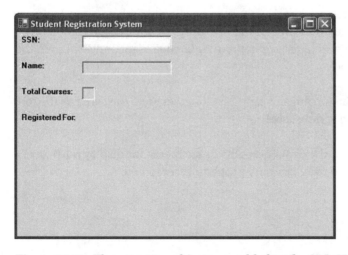

Figure 16-35. Three TextBox *objects are added to the SRS GUI.*

The ListBox Class

The SRS GUI will need to display the schedule of classes for the semester and a list of the courses for which a given student is registered. We'll also want the

user to be able to drop or add a class by selecting one of the classes in the appropriate list. An instance of the ListBox class will satisfy both of these requirements.
A ListBox is a GUI object that displays a list of choices to the user; the user can
select an item from the list simply by clicking it.

Elements of any type can be added to a ListBox. When the ListBox appears on
the screen, the list elements are rendered visually as strings. In the case of the
SRS GUI, Section object references will be added to both of the ListBox objects;
the Section class's ToString method is used to render a string representation of
each Section element. (We talked about overriding the ToString method to provide a meaningful, application-specific string representation of an object's data
values in Chapter 13.)

To create a ListBox object, the ListBox class provides a single, parameterless
constructor:

```
public ListBox()
```

Once a ListBox object has been created, its state can be defined by setting the
value of properties declared by the ListBox class. The only property we'll use that
we haven't seen before for other GUI types is the Height property:

```
public int Height
```

A ListBox object doesn't have an AutoSize property, and so we must explicitly
set both the width and height of a ListBox.

If the list of elements to be displayed by a ListBox is longer than the visible
display area the ListBox can accommodate, a vertical scrollbar will automatically appear on the right-hand side of the ListBox, allowing the user to scroll up
or down so as to access the entire list.

Adding Elements to a ListBox

To add elements to a ListBox, we make use of the Items property of the ListBox
class. This property is of type ListBox.ObjectCollections—a class that is used to
store the elements contained in a ListBox.

To add an element to a ListBox, we use the Add method from the
ListBox.ObjectCollections class, as illustrated in the following example:

```
ListBox aListBox = new ListBox();
aListBox.Items.Add("Sample Entry");
```

As we can see by the Add method header:

```
public int Add(object item)
```

any type of element can be added to a ListBox:

```
ListBox xBox = new ListBox();
Person p = new Person("Steve");
xBox.Items.Add(p); // the ToString method of the Person class will
                   // be used to render a string representation of p
```

In the SRS GUI, the Add method will be used to add Section objects to the ListBox.

Clearing the Elements of a ListBox

To clear all of the elements stored by a ListBox, we again make use of the Items property, invoking the Clear method of the ListBox.ObjectCollections class:

```
public virtual void Clear()
```

For example:

```
ListBox xBox = new ListBox();
// Add items ... details omitted.
xBox.Items.Clear();
```

We'll make use of the Clear method to refresh the SRS GUI display when a user logs off of the SRS.

Adding ListBox Objects to the SRS GUI

We now have enough information to create the two ListBox objects we'll need and to add them to the SRS GUI. We'll also create an additional Label to describe the Schedule of Courses ListBox. As before, we won't display the entire MainForm class code listing, just the segments that we're adding in this iteration.

The first thing we'll do is to add references to the new ListBox and Label objects as private fields of the MainForm class.

```
public class MainForm : Form
{
  // Other GUI component declarations omitted from this example.

  // Declare the ListBox objects and a Label as private fields.
  private Label classScheduleLabel;
  private ListBox scheduleListBox,
  private ListBox registeredListBox;
```

The ListBox and Label objects are instantiated inside the MainForm constructor. The objects' states are defined by setting the value of selected properties.

The properties for the classScheduleLabel object are set in similar fashion to the Label objects that we added earlier. The appearance of the ListBox objects is defined using properties from the ListBox class.

- The top edge of each ListBox object is positioned to be 5 pixels below the bottom edge of its corresponding Label.

- The value of the Width and Height properties are explicitly set. The Height of the registeredListBox is set so that the bottom edges of the two ListBox objects will align visually.

- The left edge of the registeredListBox is set to line up with the left-hand side Labels. The left edge of the scheduleListBox is set to be 30 pixels to the right of the right edge of the SSN TextBox.

```
// Create class schedule ListBox object.
scheduleListBox = new ListBox();
scheduleListBox.Width = 210;
scheduleListBox.Height = 225;
scheduleListBox.Top = classScheduleLabel.Bottom + 5;
scheduleListBox.Left = ssnTextBox.Right + 30;

// Create "Registered For" ListBox Object
registeredListBox = new ListBox();
registeredListBox.Width = 210;
registeredListBox.Height = scheduleListBox.Bottom -
                                registeredListBox.Top + 3;
registeredListBox.Top = registeredLabel.Bottom + 5;
registeredListBox.Left = labelLeft;
```

For now, we'll leave the ListBoxes empty, but will eventually populate them by reading in class schedule and student class list data from local files.

The Label and ListBox objects are then added to the Form:

```
this.Controls.Add(classScheduleLabel);
this.Controls.Add(scheduleListBox);
this.Controls.Add(registeredListBox);
```

and the Form object's visual properties are set as before.

With the ListBox objects included, the SRS Form now looks as shown in Figure 16-36.

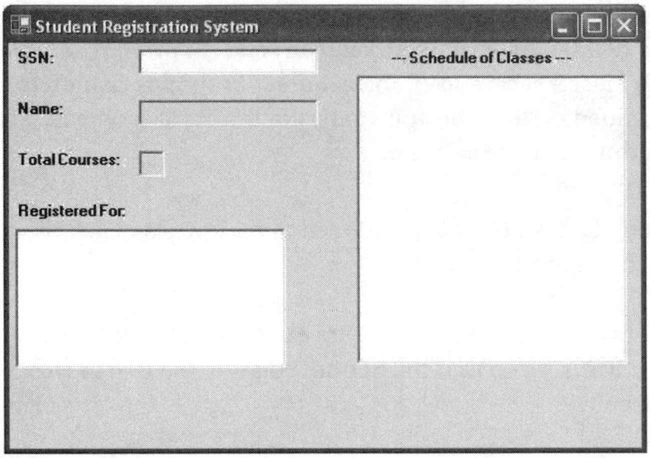

Figure 16-36. Two ListBox *objects are added to the SRS GUI.*

Our SRS GUI is really beginning to take shape! The only objects left to add are the buttons that will initiate the various actions of the GUI.

The Button Class

A Button is a GUI object that allows a user to initiate an action by "clicking" what appears to be a three-dimensional button on the GUI. We have to program an event handler to define what we actually want the button to do when it's clicked (you'll learn about event handlers later in the chapter), but the button is inherently "clickable" just by virtue of creating it—it appears to move in and out of the computer screen.

The Button class declares a single, parameterless constructor:

```
public Button()
```

As with the other objects we've discussed in this chapter, the appearance of a Button can be specified by setting the value of properties declared by the Button class. We've already discussed most of the properties that we'll use for our Button objects before, in the context of other types of object.

- The Text property is used to set the text label that is displayed on the Button.

- The Width and Height properties are used to specify the dimensions of the Button as it will appear on the screen.

- The Top and Left properties are used to position the Button in its underlying container.

The Button class has one more property that we'll take advantage of a little later in the chapter—the Enabled property:

```
public bool Enabled
```

A Button is enabled by default when it's created, meaning that it can respond to user input. There are times, however, when we may want to temporarily disable a Button. For example, it doesn't make sense to allow an SRS user to click the Drop button if that student hasn't yet registered for any classes. A Button can be ***disabled*** by setting the value of its Enabled property to false. The appearance of a Button will change, indicating that it's disabled, and clicking the Button will have no effect.

The TextBox and ListBox classes (and all other C# GUI classes, for that matter) also declare an Enabled property that functions in a similar manner.

Adding Button Objects to the SRS GUI

To add Drop, Save, Add, and Log Off buttons to the SRS GUI, we declare references to them as attributes of the MainForm class:

```
public class MainForm : Form
{
  // Other GUI component declarations omitted from this example.

  //  References to four Button objects are declared as private fields.
  private Button dropButton;
  private Button saveButton;
  private Button addButton;
  private Button logOffButton;
```

In the MainForm constructor, we create the Button objects and define their state by setting the value of some of the Button class properties.

- Each Button is given the same width and height.

- We want the four Button objects to appear aligned horizontally, so the value of the Top property for each Button is set to the same value.

- The left margin of the Drop Button is set to be 10 pixels from the left edge of the Form.

- The left margin of each subsequent Button in the row is set to be a certain distance from the right edge of the Button to its left.

```
// Create buttons; all will be of the same size, and at the same
// vertical distance from the top of the form.
int buttonHeight = 50;
int buttonWidth = 80;
int buttonTop = 260;

dropButton = new Button();
dropButton.Text = "Drop";
dropButton.Height = buttonHeight;
dropButton.Width = buttonWidth;
dropButton.Top = buttonTop;
dropButton.Left = 10;

saveButton = new Button();
saveButton.Text = "Save My Schedule";
saveButton.Height = buttonHeight;
saveButton.Width = buttonWidth;
saveButton.Top = buttonTop;
saveButton.Left = dropButton.Right + 5;

addButton = new Button();
addButton.Text = "Add";
addButton.Height = buttonHeight;
addButton.Width = buttonWidth;
addButton.Top = buttonTop;
addButton.Left = saveButton.Right + 100;

logOffButton = new Button();
logOffButton.Text = "Log Off";
logOffButton.Height = buttonHeight;
logOffButton.Width = buttonWidth;
logOffButton.Top = buttonTop;
logOffButton.Left = addButton.Right + 5;
```

The Button objects are then added to the Form.

```
this.Controls.Add(dropButton);
this.Controls.Add(saveButton);
this.Controls.Add(addButton);
this.Controls.Add(logOffButton);
```

When the new code is compiled and the driver code executed, the GUI shown in Figure 16-37 will appear on the screen.

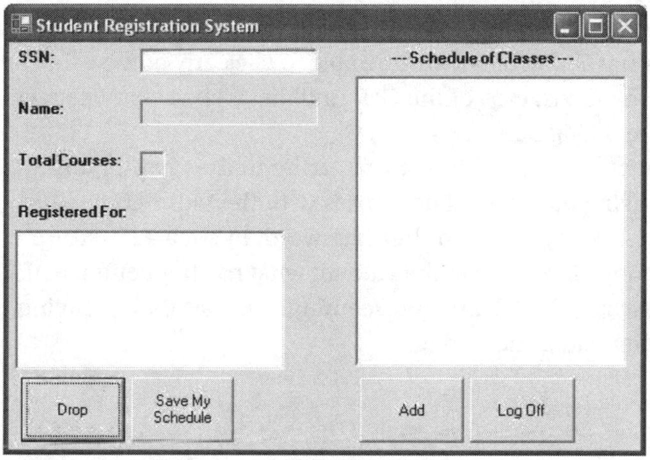

Figure 16-37. The look of our SRS GUI is complete!

Note that the four Button objects are initially enabled, in that each button label appears in black and each button is "clickable." We're going to want the Button objects to initially be **disabled,** until a user successfully logs on; when disabled, the button labels would appear to be grayed out as shown in Figure 16-38, and clicking on them would have no effect. We'll add the logic for programmatically enabling/disabling the buttons a bit later in this chapter.

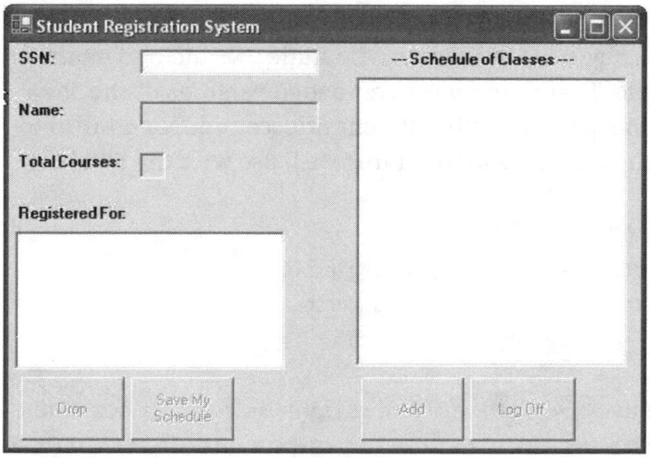

Figure 16-38. The SRS GUI as it would appear with the Button objects disabled

Creating Modal Message Dialog Boxes

The SRS GUI will use **modal** message dialog boxes at certain points in the SRS processing scenario to help guide the user along. The term "modal" means that any other interactions with the GUI are suspended until the message dialog box is dismissed by the user. That is, the user won't be able to click any of the other buttons, type into any of the fields, etc., of the GUI until he or she acknowledges and responds to the modal dialog box.

Recalling our SRS concept of operations from earlier in the chapter, one example of how we'll be using message dialog boxes with the SRS GUI will be to alert the user if he or she mistypes his or her password. In such a situation, a message dialog box will appear to inform the student what has happened; without displaying such a message, the GUI would seemingly just sit there, leaving the user to guess as to what had gone wrong.

> *As an alternative, we could simply display an error message in a read-only* TextBox *field on the main form. Message dialog boxes are a much better way to alert the user to a problem, however, in that while a user can potentially ignore or overlook a message that appears in a field, he or she can't ignore a message dialog box because it must be closed before continuing.*

Modal message dialog boxes are easily implemented in C# using the MessageBox class. A MessageBox is a dialog box that can have a title, display text along with an icon, and include one or more buttons used for responding to the dialog box. We can associate a MessageBox with another GUI object such that the MessageBox will appear automatically centered in front of its associated object.

There are no constructors declared by the MessageBox class. The way to create and display MessageBox objects is by invoking the static Show method on the MessageBox class as a whole. There are many overloaded versions of the Show method, used to create dialog boxes with different title, caption, and button combinations; the version of the Show method that we'll use with the SRS has the following header:

```
public static DialogResult Show(string text, string caption,
                                MessageBoxButtons buttons,
                                MessageBoxIcon icon)
```

- The return value of the Show method is one of eight DialogResult constants that indicate how the MessageBox was closed. By inspecting the returned value from a call to MessageBox.Show, we can ascertain how the user responded to any questions posed by the MessageBox. We won't do anything with the return value of this method for purposes of the SRS GUI.

- The text parameter is the text that will be displayed by the MessageBox.

- The caption serves as the title of the MessageBox.

- We can add one or more buttons to the MessageBox by specifying one of the MessageBoxButtons constants. The one we'll use is the following:

  ```
  MessageBoxButtons.OK
  ```

  Supplying this constant as an argument to the Show method results in a button marked OK being placed inside the MessageBox. When the OK button is subsequently clicked to indicate that the user has acknowledged the message being displayed, the MessageBox closes.

- We'll use two of the various MessageBoxIcon constants to define what icon will be displayed with a given MessageBox instance. The MessageBoxIcon.Information icon is a lowercase "i" inside a circle. It will be used to provide general information to the user. The MessageBoxIcon.Warning icon consists of an exclamation mark inside a triangle. It will be used to warn the user that an issue needs to be addressed.

As a simple example of using a MessageBox, the following code could be used to display an informational MessageBox with the text "You clicked the Drop button":

```
MessageBox.Show("You clicked the Drop button", "Button Clicked",
        MessageBoxButtons.OK, MessageBoxIcon.Information);
```

When the previous line of code is executed, the MessageBox shown in Figure 16-39 appears on the screen.

Figure 16-39. A sample MessageBox

Creating a Password Dialog Box

We've already seen one technique for sharing data throughout the various classes of an application, through the use of public static attributes of the main class/window (or, for that matter, any class/window), as we did with the various collections declared by the SRS driver program in Chapter 14. Another approach to application-wide data sharing is to allow a class/window A to collect data from the user, and to then have that class A provide state retrieval methods/properties for other classes/windows B, C, etc. to use in requesting access to the data that A has collected. We'll use this approach to obtain the user's password when he or she attempts to log on to the SRS.

The first thing a student will do when running the SRS application will be to log on by typing in his or her SSN. When the student finishes typing and presses the Enter key, we want a separate window to appear that will ask the student for his or her password, and which will then "remember" the password until we retrieve it a bit later in our application. The easiest way to accomplish this objective is to declare another class called PasswordForm, derived from Form, to serve as a password dialog box.

The PasswordForm class will be designed using many of the same features that we've already discussed for Forms in general. The PasswordForm class will collect the user's password as it's typed, and will subsequently make the password available to client code (specifically, to methods of the MainForm class in our application) through a public Password property.

One new security feature will be added for the password dialog box. When a user types in his or her password, it's common practice to hide the characters that are being typed using an echo character—a character that will be shown instead of the characters that are actually typed. The TextBox class implements this feature via the PasswordChar property.

```
public char PasswordChar
```

Whatever character is assigned to the PasswordChar property will visibly replace the characters typed into the TextBox. The system will still know what the actual characters are, but passersby won't be able to see them on the computer screen.

Here is the code listing for the PasswordForm class. We'll defer building the event handling capability of the PasswordForm class until a little later in the chapter.

```
// PasswordForm.cs

using System;
using System.Collections;
using System.Windows.Forms;
using System.Drawing;

public class PasswordForm : Form
{
    private TextBox passwordTextBox;
    private Label passwordLabel;
    private string password;
```

```
  public PasswordForm() {
    int componentTop = 15;

    // Create a Label component.
    passwordLabel = new Label();
    passwordLabel.Text = "Password:";
    passwordLabel.Top = componentTop;
    passwordLabel.Left = 15;
    passwordLabel.Width = 70;
    passwordLabel.Font = new Font(passwordLabel.Font, FontStyle.Bold);

    // Create a TextBox component.
    passwordTextBox = new TextBox();
    passwordTextBox.Height = 40;
    passwordTextBox.Width = 100;
    passwordTextBox.Top = componentTop;
    passwordTextBox.Left = passwordLabel.Right;
    // Establish the echo character as an asterisk.
    passwordTextBox.PasswordChar = '*';

    // Add the GUI objects to the form.
    this.Controls.Add(passwordLabel);
    this.Controls.Add(passwordTextBox);

    this.Text = "Enter Password";
    this.Height = 80;
    this.Width = 240;
    this.MinimumSize = this.Size;
    this.StartPosition = FormStartPosition.CenterScreen;
  }

  // Property.
  public string Password {
    get {
      return password;
    }
    // Note:  a set accessor is not necessary, as the
    // student's password is predefined based on his/her
    // student ID number, and is unchangeable.
  }
}
```

The PasswordForm class is quite simple—it consists of a Label and a TextBox placed on a Form. There is a private field named password that, after we've implemented event handling, will store what was typed into the TextBox. The echo

character for the TextBox is set to be an asterisk character (note the use of ***single***
quotes: '*'). The get accessor of the Password property can be used to access the
value of password; a set accessor has been deemed unnecessary, as the value will
always be set by typing into the TextBox field. Later in this chapter we'll provide
the event handling logic necessary for this to occur.

The View Is Complete

We're now finished with constructing the "view" of our SRS GUI. All of the GUI
objects we'll need in order to accomplish the functionality as described in the
SRS concept of operations have been created and placed onto the underlying
Form. There is still some work to be done, however, because while our SRS GUI
looks as it should, it doesn't actually do anything useful yet. Users can click the
buttons or type something into the SSN text box, but nothing useful will happen,
at least as far as student registration is concerned.

To make our GUI fully functional, we need to engage the "controller" aspect
of the Model-View-Controller paradigm to connect our model and view classes
together. Through a process known as event handling, we'll program the logic
necessary to achieve the desired results for various user interactions with the
GUI. In particular

- We'll need the GUI to recognize when a user has typed his or her student
  ID number into the ssnTextBox as a signal that he or she wishes to log on.

- We'll need to program the logic for what is to happen behind the scenes
  when each of the four buttons at the bottom of the GUI—addButton,
  dropButton, saveButton, and logOffButton—is clicked.

- We'll need to recognize when a user has made a selection in either the
  registeredListBox or scheduleListBox.

We'll provide all of these behaviors a bit later in this chapter, after we've
touched on the other C# classes that these behaviors will be reliant upon.

Stage 3: Adding Functionality Through Event Handling

To introduce C# GUI event handling in a gentle, stepwise fashion, we'll do so in
three phases:

- First, we'll talk about the C# event model in general.

- Secondly, we'll illustrate how to tackle event handling with a simple Push
  Me button example.

- Finally, we'll dive in and provide full-blown event handling for the SRS GUI.

The C# Event Model

GUI events are generated whenever a user interacts with an enabled object on the GUI: for example, clicks a button, types in a field, and so on. As with virtually everything else in C#, events themselves are objects! There are many different types of event; we'll learn about several of these shortly.

When we create a GUI object, it ***automatically*** has the ability to generate one or more types of event whenever a user interacts with it—we need do nothing to get this phenomenon to occur (see Figure 16-40).

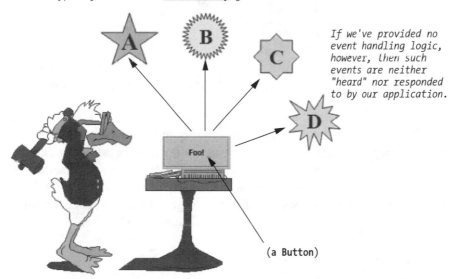

When a user interacts with a GUI component such as a Button, various types of events are <u>automatically</u> generated:

If we've provided no event handling logic, however, then such events are neither "heard" nor responded to by our application.

(a Button)

Figure 16-40. Events are generated automatically in response to user interactions with GUI objects.

What we ***do*** need to explicitly deal with, however, is programming how the GUI should ***react*** to the ***subset*** of events that we're interested in (known as event handling). Otherwise, events are generated but ignored, in the same way that the sound of a tree falling in the woods is ignored if there is nobody there to hear it (see Figure 16-41).

We may only be interested in listening for A and C
type events on the Foo! button, and B type events
on the Bar button.

(Two Buttons)

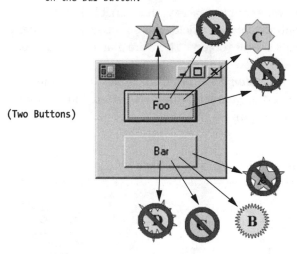

Figure 16-41. We can choose the types of types of events to which we'll respond.

The C# mechanism for "listening for" and responding to *specific* types of events on *specific* GUI objects takes advantage of the C# **delegation model,** and thus involves the use of a special C# type known as a **delegate.** Let's discuss the delegation model in general first, after which we'll return to a discussion of how the delegation model is used specifically in the case of C# GUI event handling.

C# Delegates and the Delegation Model

Recall from our discussion of interfaces in Chapter 7 that an interface is a set of abstract method headers that collectively specify the behaviors that an implementing class must provide. The implementing class, in turn, must program concrete method bodies for each of the methods specified by the interface. By way of review, here's a simple example of an interface, ITeacher, and a class, Professor, that implements the ITeacher interface:

```
// An interface ...
public interface ITeacher {
  // An abstract method header -- no "body" provided.
  void ChooseTextbook();
}
```

```
// ... and a class that implements the interface.
public class Professor : ITeacher {
  // A concrete implementation of the method.
  public void ChooseTextbook() {
    // A concrete method body goes here, to implement the business
    // logic for how this method is to be carried out for a Professor ...
    // details omitted.
  }
}
```

In a certain general sense, we can think of a ***delegate*** as a form of "pseudo-interface" that specifies only ***one*** such abstract method to be programmed by an "implementing" class. However, unlike an interface, which requires that the implementing class (Professor, in our preceding example) provide specific logic for all of the required methods (ChooseTextbook, in our preceding example) at ***compile time***, classes that specify/utilize ***delegates*** can defer a decision on what specific logic is to be performed until ***run time***. Let's look at this conceptually in a bit more detail:

1. As shown in Figure 16-42, at compile time, a class X declares that it requires a delegate "plug-in"–i.e., a method with a header that is ***compatible*** with the delegate header in terms of its return type and argument signature; note that the "plugged in" method needn't have the same ***name*** as the delegate, however.

*At **compile time,** a class "X" declares*
that it requires a delegate "plug-in" ...

```
  public class X
  {
    // Features of the class are declared
    // as always - details omitted.

    ┌───────────────────────────┐
    ┊ delegate void Foo(int x); ┊
    └───────────────────────────┘

    // etc.
  }
```

Figure 16-42. Class X declares a requirement for a delegate "plug-in."

2. Then, at run time, a method with a compatible header is associated with ***a particular object/instance*** of X, serving essentially like a "plug-in" for that object (see Figure 16-43).

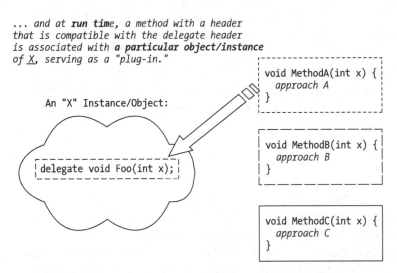

*... and at **run time,** a method with a header*
that is compatible with the delegate header
*is associated with **a particular object/instance***
*of **X**, serving as a "plug-in."*

```
void MethodA(int x) {
    approach A
}
```

An "X" Instance/Object:

```
void MethodB(int x) {
    approach B
}
```

```
delegate void Foo(int x);
```

```
void MethodC(int x) {
    approach C
}
```

Figure 16-43. An appropriate method is associated with an instance of X *at run time.*

As long as the header of the method being handed into the object in question matches the prescribed header of the delegate in terms of its argument signature and return type, all is well. If the headers aren't compatible, the compiler will generate the following error:

```
error CS0123: Method <method_name> does not match delegate <delegate_name>
```

> *For readers who are familiar with the C or C++ programming languages, note that a delegate is, very loosely speaking, conceptually similar in nature to the notion of a function pointer in those languages. However, C# delegates are far more sophisticated than C/C++ function pointers; delegates are true objects, in that they are instantiated at run time using the* new *keyword, and encapsulate both a method and a reference to the target object that the method is to oper-ate upon.*

The actual behind-the-scenes mechanism of delegates is much more complex than what we've conceptualized here, but the net effect—namely, having the ability at run time to "plug in" behavior for a given object—is all we need to understand conceptually about delegates in order to provide event handling for a GUI.

> *We'll be taking advantage of the delegation mechanism that is built into the various C# GUI component classes to plug in behaviors for the various objects comprising the SRS GUI. For an in-depth discussion of how general-purpose delegates can be crafted and used for a variety of purposes beyond GUI event handling, please refer to the recommended reading list in Chapter 17.*

Note that each object/instance of X can be handed a ***different*** behavioral implementation at run time, if desired, as shown in Figure 16-44.

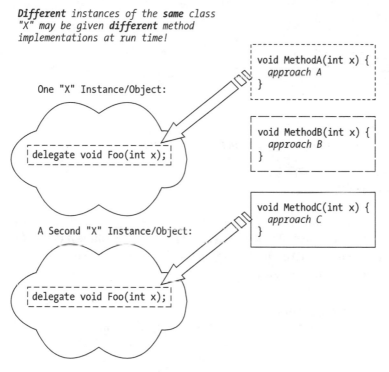

Figure 16-44. Different instances of X can be associated with different methods.

Of course, it's also possible to associate the ***same*** method with more than one object if desired, as we can see in Figure 16-45.

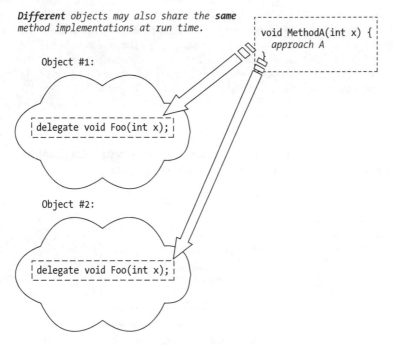

Different objects may also share the *same* method implementations at run time.

```
void MethodA(int x) {
    approach A
}
```

Object #1:

```
delegate void Foo(int x);
```

Object #2:

```
delegate void Foo(int x);
```

Figure 16-45. The same method can be associated with more than one object.

Multicast Delegates

We can actually associate **multiple** behaviors to the **same** delegate if the delegate in question happens to be a special type of delegate known as a **multicast delegate.** As illustrated conceptually in Figure 16-46, a multicast delegate can accept multiple methods as "plug-ins" at run time, and will execute the logic of all of them in turn.

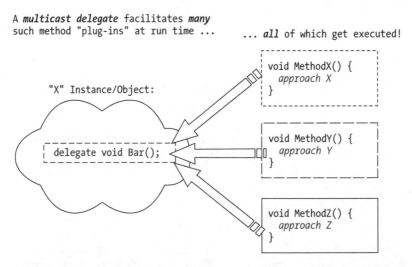

A *multicast delegate* facilitates *many* such method "plug-ins" at run time ...

... *all* of which get executed!

"X" Instance/Object:

```
delegate void Bar();
```

```
void MethodX() {
    approach X
}
```

```
void MethodY() {
    approach Y
}
```

```
void MethodZ() {
    approach Z
}
```

Figure 16-46. More than one method can be associated with a single instance of a multicast delegate.

Again, the actual mechanism of a multicast delegate is much more complex than what we've conceptualized here, but the net effect is the same: namely, having the ability at run time to plug in multiple behaviors for a given object to perform.

GUI Event Handling Using Delegates

The C# language uses the delegation model as described previously to implement **events** and event handling.

Events in C# are represented by instances of a *special* derived type of multicast delegate know as an **event delegate.**

Every FCL GUI class declares or inherits one or more events as public members. Each such event represents a different type of event that a particular type of GUI object can generate in response to user interactions with the object. For example, here are some of the events declared as public members of the Button class:

- MouseDown: Occurs when the mouse pointer is over the Button and the mouse button is pressed.

- MouseUp: Occurs when the mouse pointer is over the Button and the mouse button is released.

- Click: Represents the user's "click" of a button, when the mouse pointer is over the Button and the mouse button is pressed *and* released. (Whenever a user *clicks* a button, therefore, all *three* of these event types–MouseDown, MouseUp, and Click–are generated.)

- BackColorChanged: Occurs when the background color of the Button is programmatically changed.

- SizeChanged: Is generated when the size of the Button is programmatically changed.

and there are more; the Button class declares or inherits over 50 events representing a wide variety of things that can happen to a Button.

To provide event handling for a given object, there are three basic steps that programmers must take:

1. We must first decide which subset of available event types we're interested in handling for that given GUI object.

> A complete list of all event types that are generated for each predefined GUI class can be found in the .NET Framework SDK documentation.

2. We must **write event handler methods** *for every event type that is to be handled for that object*, to define the logic that is to be performed when handling each event of interest. The return type and argument list of the event handling methods have to be the same as those declared by the event delegate.

3. We must provide the logic to "associate" the event handling method(s) to the object's appropriate event delegate(s) at run time.

Before we retrofit event handling into the SRS GUI, we'll use a simple example of a Push Me button to illustrate all three of these steps.

The PushMe Example GUI's Look

The look of our simple Push Me example is achieved via the following code—a Form with a single Button object attached to it—which should be self-explanatory, based on our earlier discussions of assembling the look of a GUI:

```
// PushMe.cs -- Take 1

using System;
using System.Windows.Forms;
using System.Drawing;

public class PushMe : Form
{
  Button pushMeButton;

  public PushMe() {
    // Create the Button.
    pushMeButton = new Button();
    pushMeButton.Text = "Push Me";
    pushMeButton.Height = 60;
    pushMeButton.Width = 80;
```

```
        pushMeButton.Top = 60;
        pushMeButton.Left = 60;

        // Add the Button to the Form.
        this.Controls.Add(pushMeButton);

        // Size the Form and make it visible.
        this.Height = 200;
        this.Width = 200;
        this.StartPosition = FormStartPosition.CenterScreen;
        this.Visible = true;
    }

    // For simplicity, we'll place a Main method inside of the PushMe.cs
    // file, to use as a "test scaffold" driver.
    static void Main() {
        Application.Run(new PushMe());
    }
}
```

When the PushMe.cs file is compiled and the resulting executable run, the GUI in Figure 16-47 should appear on the screen.

Figure 16-47. A Form *with a single* Button

The concept of operations for our Push Me example is quite simple: the button will start out with a label that says "Push Me". When the button is first clicked, its label will change to read "Ouch!!!". When clicked a second time, the button's label will change back to "Push Me"; repeated clicks of the button will toggle its label back and forth.

As the application *currently* stands, however, we can indeed "click" the button, but while various types of events will automatically be generated in response to our clicks (Click events, MouseDown events, MouseUp events, etc.), nothing will change visually on our GUI as a result because we're not yet recognizing and responding to the Click events in particular.

Let's now add event handling to the Push Me button for Click events.

Writing Event Handler Methods

First, let's write an event handler method that will change the label of the Button from "Push Me" to "Ouch!!!", or vice versa, when the Button is clicked. The precise header of an event handler method is mandated by the FCL based on the type of event that we wish to handle; different types of events mandate different event handler signatures.

The Click event of the Button class requires a method with the following header:

```
public void MethodName(object source, EventArgs e)
```

wherein only the method name and parameter names are up to us to specify; the method must have a return type and argument signature as shown.

Two arguments are passed into a method associated with an EventHandler delegate—an object reference representing the event source, and an instance of an EventArgs object, which will contain some additional information about the event, such as where on the screen the event occurred, how many mouse clicks caused the event, and so on.

Arguments are passed automatically by the C# runtime; we needn't concern ourselves with these, just as we didn't have to worry about how the reference to an Exception object gets "handed" to a catch block when performing exception handling.

> *As it turns out, the previous header pattern is known as the **generic** EventHandler **header**. Many event types, belonging to many different classes—for example, the Button class's Click, BackColorChanged, and SizeChanged event types, among many others—**require this same header pattern** when writing event handler methods.*
>
> *Other event types—for example, the MouseUp event type of the Button class—require slightly different header patterns; MouseUp, for example, requires a MouseEventHandler header pattern:*
>
> ```
> public void MethodName(object source, MouseEventArgs e)
> ```
>
> *An exhaustive discussion of all of the various event types and their corresponding handler header syntax is beyond the scope of this book to address; once you've gotten a grasp on the general concepts of C# event handling, however, we encourage you to consult the .NET Framework SDK documentation to study all of the variations that event handling can take for various FCL GUI classes and event types.*

An important consequence of the plug-in nature of the delegation event model used by C# is that an event handling method doesn't have to be declared within the class of the component that generates the event—e.g., a method for handling a button click doesn't have to be declared within the Button class. This is fortunate, as we wouldn't want to have to modify/extend the predefined Button class simply to include an event handling method! Event handling methods can be (and usually are) placed in a different class entirely; for the SRS GUI as well as for our simple PushMe example, all of the event handling methods will be placed in the main Form class to which a given component is attached.

> *Architecturally, we have **several** different options with respect to where we insert the event handling method code—in fact, event handlers can even be declared in a class by themselves. This facilitates reuse of the event handling logic across multiple forms in a given application and, for that matter, across multiple applications. The mechanics of doing so are beyond the scope of this book to address, however.*

Here's a revised version of the PushMe class, expanded to include an appropriate event handler method (**highlighted** in the following code):

```
// PushMe.cs -- Take 2

using System;
using System.Windows.Forms;
using System.Drawing;

public class PushMe : Form
{
  Button pushMeButton;

  public PushMe() {
    // Create the Button.
    pushMeButton = new Button();
    pushMeButton.Text = "Push Me";
    pushMeButton.Height = 60;
    pushMeButton.Width = 80;
    pushMeButton.Top = 60;
    pushMeButton.Left = 60;

    // Add the Button to the Form.
    this.Controls.Add(pushMeButton);

    // Size the Form and make it visible.
    this.Height = 200;
    this.Width = 200;
```

```
    this.StartPosition = FormStartPosition.CenterScreen;
    this.Visible = true;
  }


  // Event handling method for the "Push Me" button's Click events.
  public void ButtonClicked(object source, EventArgs e) {
    // If the button label currently says "Push Me" ...
    if (pushMeButton.Text == "Push Me") {
      // ... switch the label to "Ouch!!!" ...
      pushMeButton.Text = "Ouch!!!";
    }
    // Otherwise, do the reverse!
    else {
      pushMeButton.Text = "Push Me";
    }
  }


  // Test scaffold driver.
  static void Main() {
    Application.Run(new PushMe());
  }
}
```

Note that because the ButtonClicked method is declared at the class scope level of the PushMe class as a method, as is the reference variable pushMeButton as an attribute, we're able to refer to the Button object by reference as pushMeButton within the ButtonClicked method, thereby ignoring the availability of the source parameter that is being passed into the method:

```
// We're ignoring the "source" parameter in this method.
public void ButtonClicked(object source, EventArgs e) {
  // If the button label currently says "Push Me" ...
  if (pushMeButton.Text == "Push Me") {
    // etc.
```

We can rewrite this method to take advantage of the source object reference as shown here:

```
public void ButtonClicked(object source, EventArgs e) {
  // We'll obtain a reference to the Button that generated the event by casting
  // the generic object reference "source" to a Button reference.
  Button b = (Button) source;

  // Everything else about the event handling method is the same, except
  // that we're now referring to "b" rather than "pushMeButton".
```

```
    if (b.Text == "Push Me") {
      b.Text = "Ouch!!!";
    }
    else {
      b.Text = "Push Me";
    }
  }
```

While doing so certainly isn't necessary based on how we've crafted the
PushMe class, if we were to use a different architectural approach to providing
event handling methods (as discussed in an earlier background comment), such
that the pushMeButton reference variable was ***not*** in scope, then this would be the
preferred means of referencing the source object, and so we encourage you to get
into the habit of using the second, more generic approach in all cases.

If we compile and run our "Take 2" version of the program, we ***still*** won't see
the button label change as we click it. Why is this? Because it isn't sufficient to
merely write an event handling method; we must also ***associate*** this event handling
method with the PushMe button specifically, as described in the next section.

Associating an Event Handling Method with a GUI Object via a Delegate

All FCL GUI event delegates, including the Button class's Click delegate, are multicast delegates, which as we explained earlier means that we can associate more
than one event handling method with a given event type for a given component
instance at run time. To associate a ButtonClicked event handling method with the
Click multicast delegate for a particular Button reference, we therefore use the following syntax to ***add*** an event handler to the list of event handlers already acknowledged by the component:

```
// Associate an event handler method with a button.
// Pseudocode.
buttonReference.Click += new EventHandler(methodName);
```

(If no such event handlers have previously been associated with the delegate in
question, the one we're currently attaching becomes the ***first*** such event handler
in the list.)

Specifically, to associate our ButtonClicked event handling method with the
Click multicast delegate for the pushMeButton, we use the following syntax in the
PushMe class constructor:

```
// Associate an event handler method with the button.
pushMeButton.Click += new EventHandler(ButtonClicked);
```

Because event delegates are given public access as members of the associated class (Click is a public member of the Button class), we can access an event delegate of a GUI object from client code via dot notation, as shown earlier.

Our ButtonClicked method is now associated with Click type events for the pushMe button. Whenever this button is clicked, the runtime will automatically invoke every event handler method in the Click event's invocation list—in this case, our ButtonClicked method will be called. All this activity happens automatically "behind the scenes," without us having to worry about any of the invocation details.

Here is the entire listing of the completed PushMe class, with the preceding logic placed in context and **highlighted**:

```
// PushMe.cs -- Take 3

using System;
using System.Windows.Forms;
using System.Drawing;

public class PushMe : Form
{
  Button pushMeButton;

  public PushMe() {
    // Create a Button.
    pushMeButton = new Button();
    pushMeButton.Text = "Push Me";
    pushMeButton.Height = 60;
    pushMeButton.Width = 80;
    pushMeButton.Top = 60;
    pushMeButton.Left = 60;

    // Associate an event handler with the Button.
    pushMeButton.Click += new EventHandler(ButtonClicked);

    // Add the Button to the Form.
    this.Controls.Add(pushMeButton);

    // Size the Form and make it visible
    this.Height = 200;
    this.Width = 200;
    this.StartPosition = FormStartPosition.CenterScreen;
    this.Visible = true;
  }
```

```
// Event handling method for the "Push Me" button.
public void ButtonClicked(object source, EventArgs e) {
  if (pushMeButton.Text == "Push Me") {
    pushMeButton.Text = " Ouch!!!";
  }
  else {
    pushMeButton.Text = "Push Me";
  }
}

static void Main() {
  Application.Run(new PushMe());
}
}
```

Now when the PushMe application is run, the text of the Button will indeed change from "Push Me" to "Ouch!!!" and back again every time the button is clicked.

Simple though it is, the PushMe example nonetheless illustrates how easy it is to take advantage of C# event handling. We'll use the exact same concepts and approach, with only slightly more complexity, in implementing event handling for the SRS GUI. Before we do so, however, let's revisit our model classes.

Revisiting Our SRS Model Classes

Many of the classes used in the Chapter 15 version of the SRS application remain unchanged in the solution to Chapter 16—that's the beauty of separating the model from the view! Because the model is, for the most part, blissfully ignorant that there even is a view (the view knows about the model, but the model doesn't know about the view), the model classes needn't change to accommodate it. So, the following classes (as presented in Chapter 15) are unaltered in the GUI version of the SRS:

- CollectionWrapper.cs

- Course.cs

- CourseCatalog.cs

- Faculty.cs

- Person.cs

- Professor.cs

- Transcript.cs

- TranscriptEntry.cs

and therefore we won't revisit any of these classes' code in this chapter.

The following classes have been modified from the versions used in Chapter 15 so as to add a method or two in support of the GUI; we'll study their code in detail one by one:

- ScheduleOfClasses.cs: We've added a single method, GetSortedSections, to support our use of ListBox objects.

- Student.cs: We've added a single attribute—string password—to handle the requirement for a user to log on to the SRS system, and then made a few changes to the Student methods to recognize this new attribute. We also added a few other data retrieval methods needed to support the GUI; we'll discuss all of these changes in depth shortly.

- Section.cs: We made only one minor change, which as it turns out wasn't related to the GUI at all, but rather was simply an improvement in the logic from that used in Chapter 15.

- And, of course, we had to significantly revamp the main SRS.cs "driver" code to accommodate the newly added GUI. As it turns out, we were able to significantly *streamline* the code of the SRS class, as you'll soon see.

Despite the fact that we did go back to make a few enhancements to the domain classes to accommodate the GUI, these enhancements involved business logic only, and were made in such a way as to keep the model loosely coupled from the view; that is, we could easily swap out the SRS GUI that we're building and add a completely new GUI down the road, and our domain classes would remain intact. In the worst case, our domain classes would contain a few methods (those that we added for use by the first GUI) that would no longer get used.

As we've already discussed in this chapter, we've added two new classes to the SRS application to take care of the GUI "view."

- MainForm.cs, a type of Form, used as our main application window

- PasswordForm.cs, which provides a password dialog box used when logging a student on to the SRS

We'll need to make some minor additional changes to these classes, as well.

The ScheduleOfClasses Class (Harnessing the Power of ListBox Objects)

The only change that we need to make to the ScheduleOfClasses class as originally presented in Chapter 15 is related to our decision to use a ListBox to display the schedule of classes in our SRS GUI.

- We learned earlier in this chapter how to add elements to a ListBox. We would like to add the schedule of classes to the ListBox in alphabetical order.

- However, as originally designed, the ScheduleOfClasses class maintains information on what sections are available for student registration as a Hashtable of Section objects. In the section titled "Stepping Through Collections with Enumerators" in Chapter 13, we learned how to use an IEnumerator object to step one-by-one through all of the objects contained within a collection such as an ArrayList or a Hashtable. But, the Section objects are stored in no particular order in the Hashtable—the nature of Hashtables doesn't guarantee sorted ordering—and so stepping through the Hashtable with an IDictionaryEnumerator wouldn't necessarily yield an *alphabetically sorted* list of Sections. All things being equal, we would prefer to display the schedule of classes sorted in order by course number.

- By adding a single method, GetSortedSections, to return an alphabetically sorted ArrayList of Section objects based on this Hashtable, we're then able to use this method from within MainForm.cs to add an alphabetically sorted list of Section elements to the scheduleListBox.

First, we'll present the new GetSortedSections method in its entirety; then, we'll review what the new method does in depth. (Because the code for the entire ScheduleOfClasses class is rather lengthy, and because you've seen much of the class code in previous chapters, we're only going to present those chunks of code that are new as of the Chapter 16 version. Again, we encourage you to have a printed copy of the complete class available for comparison purposes.)

```
// This next method was added to the ScheduleOfClasses
// class for use with the SRS GUI.
```

```
// Convert the contents of the sectionsOffered Hashtable
// into an ArrayList of Section objects that is sorted in
// alphabetical order.

public ArrayList GetSortedSections() {
  ArrayList sortedKeys = new ArrayList();
  ArrayList sortedSections = new ArrayList();

  // Get an IDictionaryEnumerator of the key-value pairs
  // contained in the sectionsOffered Hashtable. Load the
  // sortedKeys ArrayList with these keys.

  IDictionaryEnumerator e = sectionsOffered.GetEnumerator();

  while (e.MoveNext()) {
    string key = (string) e.Key;
    sortedKeys.Add(key);
  }

  // Sort the keys in the ArrayList alphabetically.

  sortedKeys.Sort();

  // Load the value corresponding to the sorted keys into
  // the sortedSections ArrayList.

  for (int i = 0; i < sortedKeys.Count; i++) {
    string key = (string) sortedKeys[i];
    Section s = (Section) sectionsOffered[key];
    sortedSections.Add(s);
  }

  // Return the ArrayList containing the sorted Sections.

  return sortedSections;
}
```

Let's step through the code for this new method:

We begin by creating two empty ArrayLists, which will be used to store the results of our sorting efforts:

```
public ArrayList GetSortedSections() {
  ArrayList sortedKeys = new ArrayList();
  ArrayList sortedSections = new ArrayList();
```

We'll put IEnumerators to good use now. Using the GetEnumerator method defined for Hashtable objects, we're able to obtain an IDictionaryEnumerator object representing all of the key-value pairs from the sectionsOffered Hashtable as we discussed in Chapter 13. (Recall from Chapter 13 that the keys in our sectionsOffered Hashtable are string objects representing the various course names.)

```
IDictionaryEnumerator e = sectionsOffered.GetEnumerator();
```

Stepping through this IDictionaryEnumerator until it's exhausted, we cast each key as it's retrieved back to its string representation. The unsorted keys are added (still in unsorted order) to the sortedKeys ArrayList.

```
while (e.MoveNext()) {
   string key = (string) e.Key;
   sortedKeys.Add(key);
}
```

The keys are then sorted by calling the Sort method on the sortedKeys ArrayList. As we discussed in Chapter 13, the default behavior for the Sort method is to sort a collection of strings alphabetically.

```
sortedKeys.Sort();
```

Now that sortedKeys ArrayList contains all of the **keys** in alphabetical order, we'll step through this ArrayList and use it to pull the Section objects themselves out of the Hashtable in sorted order! As we pull them out of the Hashtable, we'll stick them into a second ArrayList called sortedSections.

```
for (int i = 0; i < sortedKeys.Count; i++) {
   string key = (string) sortedKeys[i];
   Section s = (Section) sectionsOffered[key];
   sortedSections.Add(s);
}
```

We now have an ArrayList containing all Sections that were originally in the Hashtable, but in alphabetically sorted order.

```
   return sortedSections;
}
```

Retrofitting Attributes in the Student Class

When we first modeled the SRS in Part Two of the book, it didn't occur to us to allow for a Student to have a password field, since this is more of a computer-related artifact than it is a real-world attribute of a student. But, as is frequently the case, we find that we often must expand the features of a class once we begin implementation to accommodate what we often refer to as "solution space" or "implementation space" features. Such is the case with the password attribute of Student.

Because the Student class code is so long (over six pages when printed!), and because you've seen much of the Student class code in previous chapters, we're only going to present those segments of code that are new as of the Chapter 16 version. Again, we encourage you to have a printed copy of the complete class available for comparison purposes.

First, we add the attribute

```
private string password;
```

Next, we acknowledge the existence of this new attribute by adding initialization code to both versions of the Student constructor. Most of the constructor code is unaltered from its Chapter 15 version; we've repeated it all here, but have highlighted only the changes that were necessary:

```
public Student(string ssn) : this() {
    // First, construct a "dummy" Student object.  Then,
    // attempt to pull this Student's information from the
    // appropriate file (ssn.dat:  e.g., 111-11-1111.dat).
    // The file consists of a header record, containing
    // the student's basic info. (ssn, name, etc.), and
    // 0 or more subsequent records representing a list of
    // the sections that he/she is currently registered for.

    string line = null;
    StreamReader srIn = null;

    // Formulate the file name.

    string pathToFile = ssn + ".dat";

    try {
        // Open the file.

        srIn = new StreamReader(new FileStream(pathToFile,FileMode.Open));
```

```
      // The first line in the file contains the header
      // information, so we use ParseData() to process it.

      line = srIn.ReadLine();
      if (line != null) {
        ParseData(line);
      }

      // Remaining lines (if there are any) contain
      // section references.  Note that we must
      // instantiate an empty vector so that the
      // ParseData2() method may insert
      // items into the ArrayList.

      attends = new ArrayList();
      line = srIn.ReadLine();

      // If there were no secondary records in the file,
      // this "while" loop won't execute at all.

      while (line != null) {
        ParseData2(line);
        line = srIn.ReadLine();
      }

      srIn.Close();
    }
    catch (FileNotFoundException f) {
      // Since we are encoding a "dummy" Student to begin
      // with, the fact that his/her name will be equal
      // to "???" flags an error.  We have included
      // a boolean method SuccessfullyInitialized()
      // which allows client code to verify the success
      // or failure of this constructor (see code below).
      // So, we needn't do anything special in this
      // "catch" clause!
    }
    catch (IOException i) {
      // See comments for FileNotFoundException above;
      // we needn't do anything special in this
      // "catch" clause, either!
    }
```

```
    // Initialize the password to be the first three digits
    // of the student's ssn.

    this.Password = this.Ssn.Substring(0,3);  // added for GUI purposes

    // Create a brand new Transcript.
    // (Ideally, we'd read in an existing Transcript from
    // a file, but we're not bothering to do so in this
    // example).

    this.Transcript = new Transcript(this);
}

// A second form of constructor, used when a Student's data
// file cannot be found for some reason.

public Student() : base("???", "???") {
    // Reuse the code of the parent's (Person) constructor.
    // Question marks indicate that something went wrong!

    this.Major = "???";
    this.Degree = "???";

    // Placeholders for the remaining fields (this
    // Student is invalid anyway).

    this.Password = "???";    // added for GUI purposes
    this.Transcript = new Transcript(this);
    attends = new ArrayList();
}
```

Then, we added a property for the password field:

```
// Added for GUI purposes.
public string Password {
  get {
    return password;
  }
  set {
    password = value;
  }
}
```

And, under the heading

```
//----------------------------
// Miscellaneous other methods.
//----------------------------
```

we've added a method that will be used to validate the password that a user types in when logging into the GUI against his or her "official" password. The argument pw represents the value that a user has typed in (we'll see how this is determined when we visit the event handling code of the PasswordForm class), and of course password represents the "authentic" password for this student user.

```
// This next method was added for use with the GUI.
public bool ValidatePassword(string pw) {
  if (pw == null) {
    return false;
  }
  if (pw.Equals(password)) {
    return true;
  }
  else {
    return false;
  }
}
```

As it turns out, there are a few more information retrieval methods that we're going to need in support of the GUI—methods that we didn't anticipate needing when we modeled the SRS in Part Two of the book, but which only surfaced when we designed the SRS GUI.

We want a method that will enable the MainForm to retrieve an ArrayList of all Section objects that the Student is currently enrolled in, so that it may be used to populate the studentCourseList ListBox:

```
// This next method was added for use with the GUI.
public ArrayList GetSectionsEnrolled() {
  return attends;
}
```

We also need a method to use in retrieving the total number of Sections that a Student is registered for, so that we may use this value to update the totalTextBox object on the GUI:

```
// This next method was added for use with the GUI.
public int GetCourseTotal() {
  return attends.Count;
}
```

Again, while we'll add such methods to the class, we won't have compromised our model-view separation in doing so, because they essentially represent business logic only (e.g., what it means for a password to be valid).

Redesigning the Section Class

The Section class for this chapter differs from the version that we presented in Chapter 15 in the way that a section enrolls a student. In the previous version of the SRS, we created a Section object and then called the Enroll method on the Section object, passing a reference to a Student object in as an argument. If all of the "business logic" requirements for enrolling in the section were met, the Student was added to the enrolledStudents Hashtable of the Section object using the value of the Student object's ssn attribute as the Hashtable key.

But now the access to the SRS is through the GUI that we've developed in this chapter. When a student logs on to the SRS, a Student object is created with data read from the student's data file. The GUI will read the sections the student has enrolled in and will call the Enroll method of the corresponding Section object. However, there is a potential problem with this procedure. What happens if a student logs on to the SRS, logs off, and then changes his or her mind and logs on again without ever closing the SRS application? Every time the student logs on, the GUI will have the appropriate Section objects enroll the student. The upshot will be that the student will wind up being enrolled in all of the sections twice! In fact, the student won't even get this far, because an attempt to add a duplicate key to a C# Hashtable causes an exception to be thrown.

This is an example of a bug that managed to make its way undetected through the testing that we performed via the command-line version of the SRS driver as presented in Chapter 14. Despite our best efforts, some usage scenario problems will invariably escape detection when we're using a command line–driven application, because we essentially have to try to simulate all possible permutations and combinations of user interactions as "hardwired" Main method code sequences, which is virtually impossible. Once we have a working GUI connected to the application, on the other hand, we can explore a much broader range of usage patterns.

Nonetheless, the fact that we've only found one such bug in our SRS model code after adding on the GUI speaks highly for the value in using a command line–driven application to flush out many bugs before GUI coding has begun.

Fortunately, the solution to this problem is quite simple. In the Enroll method of the Section class we need to check to see if the Student object is already in the enrolledStudents Hashtable. The ContainsKey method can be used to determine if a Hashtable contains a specified key. We need to change the original Enroll method syntax logic:

```
// If we made it to here in the code, we're ready to
// officially enroll the Student.

// Note bidirectionality:  this Section holds
// onto the Student via the Hashtable, and then
// the Student is given a handle on this Section.

enrolledStudents.Add(s.Ssn, s);
s.AddSection(this);
return SUCCESSFULLY_ENROLLED;
```

to the following:

```
// If we made it to here in the code, we're ready to
// officially enroll the Student.

// Note bidirectionality:  this Section holds
// onto the Student via the Hashtable, and then
// the Student is given a handle on this Section.

// When using the GUI, it's possible for a student to log
// on, log off, and then log on again while the SRS is
// still running. This prevents a student from being
// enrolled in the same class more than one time.

if (!enrolledStudents.ContainsKey(s.Ssn)) {
  enrolledStudents.Add(s.Ssn, s);
}

s.AddSection(this);
return SUCCESSFULLY_ENROLLED;
```

Changes to the MainForm Class

Along with the changes we made to the ScheduleOfClasses and Student classes, several minor changes need to be made to the MainForm class. The first thing we need to add is a reference to the Student currently logged on to the SRS. This reference is declared as an attribute of the MainForm class.

```
// Maintain a handle on the Student who is logged in.
// (Whenever this is set to null, nobody is officially logged on.)
private Student currentUser;
```

We'll use this handle when we retrieve a student's list of registered courses so as to display them, as well as to save a student's data to a file.

Another new attribute of the MainForm class will be a reference to a PasswordForm object:

```
private PasswordForm passwordDialog;
```

When a user tries to log in to the SRS, the passwordDialog object will be displayed; we want to maintain a handle to this object so that we may "talk" to the dialog box to determine what was typed into the passwordDialog TextBox.

The other change to the MainForm class is to load the course catalog into the scheduleListBox object when the SRS is launched. To list the course catalog alphabetically, we make use of GetSortedSections method described earlier in this chapter.

```
// Create "Schedule of Classes" ListBox Object.
scheduleListBox = new ListBox();
scheduleListBox.Width = 210;
scheduleListBox.Height = 225;
scheduleListBox.Top = classScheduleLabel.Bottom + 5;
scheduleListBox.Left = ssnTextBox.Right + 30;

// Display an alphabetically sorted course catalog list
// in the scheduleListBox object.
ArrayList sortedSections = SRS.scheduleOfClasses.GetSortedSections();
for (int i = 0; i < sortedSections.Count; i++) {
  scheduleListBox.Items.Add(sortedSections[i]);
}
```

Once again, we're only showing snippets of the MainForm.cs code listing. Once you've downloaded the source file from the Apress web site, you can review the snippets within the context of the entire code listing.

The SRS Driver Class—Significantly Streamlined

Now that we have a GUI to use in interacting with the SRS, many of the extra steps that we went through in the Chapter 15 version of the SRS driver class to initialize the application are now unnecessary. Let's run through the code segments that we've been able to remove.

We no longer need to create Student objects to simulate logons, since we now have a GUI for this purpose, so we'll remove the code that instantiates Students:

```
// Let's temporarily create Students this way as a test,
// to simulate Students logging on.  Note that only the
// first Student has "preregistered" for courses based
// on the content of his/her ssn.dat file (see Student.cs
// for details).

Student s1 = new Student("111-11-1111");
Student s2 = new Student("222-22-2222");
Student s3 = new Student("333-33-3333");
```

Neither do we need to simulate a student enrolling in a section, since we can perform that function via the GUI now, too, so we'll remove the following:

```
// Let's have one Student try enrolling in something, so
// that we can simulate his/her logging off and persisting
// the enrollment data in the ssn.dat file (see Student.cs
// for details).

Section sec = scheduleOfClasses.FindSection("ART101 - 1");
sec.Enroll(s2);
s2.Persist();  // Check contents of 222-22-2222.dat!
```

And, since we can now verify the outcome of our interactions with the SRS simply by viewing the state of the GUI, we no longer need to use Console.WriteLine() calls to display the internal state of objects (although we may wish to retain this code, and simply comment it out in our SRS program, to help us with debugging the application at a later date).

The only *new* logic that we've had to add to the SRS class was the code needed to create and display an instance of the main GUI window:

```
// Create and display an instance of the main GUI window.
Application.Run(new MainForm());
}
}
```

The resultant streamlined SRS class is as follows:

```
// SRS.cs - Chapter 16 version.
// A main driver for the GUI version of the SRS.
```

```
using System;
using System.Collections;
using System.Windows.Forms;

public class SRS
{
  // We can effectively create "global" data by declaring
  // public static fields in the main class.

  // Entry points/"roots" for getting at objects.
  public static Faculty faculty = new Faculty();
  public static CourseCatalog courseCatalog = new CourseCatalog();
  public static ScheduleOfClasses scheduleOfClasses =
                          new ScheduleOfClasses("SP2004");

  // We don't create a collection for Student objects, because
  // we're only going to handle one Student at a time -- namely,
  // whichever Student is logged on.

  static void Main() {
    // Initialize the key objects by reading data from files.
    // Setting the second argument to true causes the
    // InitializeObjects() method to use the ParseData()
    // method instead of ParseData2().
    faculty.InitializeObjects("Faculty.dat", true);
    courseCatalog.InitializeObjects("CourseCatalog.dat", true);
    scheduleOfClasses.InitializeObjects("SoC_SP2004.dat", true);

    // We'll handle the students differently:  that is,
    // rather than loading them all in at application outset,
    // we'll pull in the data that we need just for one
    // Student when that Student logs on -- see the Student
    // class constructor for the details.

    // Establish prerequisites.
    // Setting the second argument to false causes the
    // InitializeObjects() method to use the ParseData2()
    // method instead of ParseData().
    courseCatalog.InitializeObjects("Prerequisites.dat", false);

    // Recruit a professor to teach each of the sections.
    faculty.InitializeObjects("TeachingAssignments.dat", false);
```

```
    // Create and display an instance of the main GUI window.
    Application.Run(new MainForm());
  }
}
```

The SRS application is compiled as before with the following command:

```
csc /out:SRS.exe *.cs /main:SRS
```

This generates an executable file named SRS.exe that can be run from MS DOS Prompt with the following command:

```
SRS
```

Adding Event Handling to the SRS GUI

We're now ready to complete the development of the SRS GUI. We've already created a GUI view—comprised of the SRS MainForm and PasswordForm classes—of our model—that is, our domain objects Student, Professor, Course, Section, and so on. The last thing that remains to be done, then, is to complete our SRS application by adding event handling, the "controller" aspect, to our GUI.

By way of review, we stated earlier in the chapter that we were going to need to provide listeners for each of the following GUI objects, as these are the objects that the user will be interacting with:

- We'll need the GUI to recognize when a user has typed his or her student ID number into the ssnTextBox as a signal that he or she wishes to log on.

- We'll need to program the logic for what is to happen behind the scenes when each of the four buttons at the bottom of the GUI—addButton, dropButton, saveButton, and logOffButton—is clicked.

- We'll need to recognize when a user has made a selection in either the registeredListBox or scheduleListBox.

Because the MainForm.cs code listing has become so long (10+ pages!), we won't clutter up this chapter by repeating elements we've covered earlier in the chapter, but once again encourage you to download and print the entire file from the Apress web site. We'll provide editorial comments on those segments of code that are most unusual or complex, but please do take the time to read through all of the in-line documentation, as well.

Registering Event Handling Methods with Key GUI Objects

The first thing we'll do is to register event handling methods with various SRS GUI objects. We want to respond to events generated by various ListBox, Button, and TextBox components, and so we'll associate an event handler with the public events of interest for each component using the += operator:

- The ssnTextBox is the object that the user types his or her student ID into, such that the SRS system can recognize that a student wishes to log on. We therefore need to listen for events that are generated when a user presses the Enter key after typing in this field. The KeyUp event of the TextBox class is designed to do just that; as its name suggests, it's an event that is triggered whenever a key is released.

- For the ListBox objects, we'll provide event handling logic to react whenever the element selected by the user inside the ListBox changes. The SelectedIndexChanged event of the ListBox class will serve our purposes.

- For the Button objects, we want event handling to respond when a Button is clicked, and so we'll associate event handling methods with the Click event of the Button class.

To associate event handling methods with the desired type of event as generated by each of our components, we'll add the following code to the MainForm class constructor:

```
// Assign an event handler to the SSN TextBox.
ssnTextBox.KeyUp += new KeyEventHandler(SsnTextBoxKeyUp);

// Add event handlers to the ListBox components.
scheduleListBox.SelectedIndexChanged +=
            new EventHandler(ScheduleSelectionChanged);
registeredListBox.SelectedIndexChanged +=
            new EventHandler(RegisteredSelectionChanged);

// Assign event handlers to the Buttons.
addButton.Click += new EventHandler(AddButtonClicked);
dropButton.Click += new EventHandler(DropButtonClicked);
saveButton.Click += new EventHandler(SaveButtonClicked);
logOffButton.Click += new EventHandler(LogOffButtonClicked);
```

Of course, we haven't written the SsnTextBoxKeyUp, *xxx*SelectionChanged, or *xxx*ButtonClicked event handler methods yet—we'll do so shortly.

The passwordTextBox object of the PasswordForm class will also implement event handling in a similar manner to the ssnTextBox, in that we want to respond to the event that occurs when the Enter key is pressed while typing into the TextBox. Specifically, when the Enter key is pressed, we'll assume that the user has finished typing his or her password. We'll enable our application to respond to KeyUp events in this TextBox by adding the following code to the PasswordForm class constructor:

```
// Assign an event handler to the TextBox.
passwordTextBox.KeyUp += new KeyEventHandler(PasswordKeyUp);
```

Now that we've associated event handling methods with all GUI object events of interest, the next step is to implement those events.

The SsnTextBoxKeyUp Method

The SsnTextBoxKeyUp method is declared as a method in the MainForm class. The method's header syntax is prescribed by the KeyEventHandler delegate that it's associated with, and is as follows:

```
// Event handling method for the ssnTextBox.
public void SsnTextBoxKeyUp(object source, KeyEventArgs e) {
```

Note that the SsnTextBoxKeyUp method will be invoked *every time* a key is released while typing inside the TextBox, including the key presses of each digit in the user's password, but we only want to respond if the Enter key in particular is released. We can determine which key was released for a particular KeyEvent by inspecting the KeyEventArgs argument passed to the SsnTextBoxKeyUp method, as follows:

- Every character on the keyboard has an integer value called a key code associated with it.

- The KeyEventArgs object maintains a property called KeyCode that contains the key code value of whatever keystroke caused the event.

- So, we'll add logic to the SsnTextBoxKeyUp method to first check whether the KeyCode value of the current KeyEvent is equal to the key code of the Enter key. If it is, we'll proceed with the event handling; if not, the if test fails, and we ultimately return from the method without doing any further processing.

```
// We only want to act if the Enter key is pressed
if (e.KeyCode == Keys.Enter) {
```

Next, assuming that the Enter key has indeed been pressed, we want to clear any information left over from a previous student's SRS session. We've created a private "housekeeping" method, ClearFields, which steps through the three objects on the GUI that represent student-specific information—nameTextBox, totalTextBox, and registeredListBox—clearing them of any information that is still being displayed for a previously logged-on student. You'll see the code for this method, along with the code for several other housekeeping methods, later in the chapter.

```
// First, clear the fields reflecting the
// previous student's information.
ClearFields();
```

We use the Text property of the ssnTextBox object to pull whatever string value the user has typed into the field, and attempt to instantiate a new Student object representing the "real" student user (an example of a **boundary class,** as we discussed in Chapter 11):

```
// We'll try to construct a Student based on
// the ssn we read, and if a file containing
// Student's information cannot be found,
// we have a problem.

currentUser = new Student(ssnTextBox.Text);
```

There are three possible outcomes when a user types an SSN number into the ssnTextBox, and we must account for all three.

- A user may type an invalid SSN;

- A user may type a valid SSN, but an invalid password; or

- A user may type a valid SSN and a valid password.

The first possibility is that the user typed in an invalid SSN. To determine whether an SSN is valid, we use the StudentSuccessfullyInitialized method that was added to the Student class in Chapter 15; recall that this method was defined to return a bool value: true if the Student contructor was able to open the associated student's data file (for example, 111-11-1111.dat for a Student with a student ID of 111-11-1111), and false otherwise.

If the result of this method call was `false`, we reset the `currentUser` attribute of the `MainForm` class to `null`, to signify that no user is logged on; this has the added effect of causing reference variable `currentUser` to drop any handle that it might still have been holding on a previously logged-in `Student` object.

```
if (!currentUser.StudentSuccessfullyInitialized()) {
  // Drat! The ID was invalid.
  currentUser = null;
```

Then, we formulate a warning message dialog box to that effect using the `Show` method of the `MessageBox` class, a technique that we discussed earlier in this chapter.

```
  // Let the user know that login failed.
  string message = "Invalid student ID; please try again.";
  MessageBox.Show(message, "Invalid Student ID",
          MessageBoxButtons.OK, MessageBoxIcon.Warning);
}
```

If, on the other hand, the `StudentSuccessfullyInitialized` method returned a value of `true`, then we know that the `Student` class's constructor successfully read in the contents of the student's data file, populating all of the `Student` object's attributes, and that his or her password attribute has been initialized, as well. So, it's time to ask the user to provide a password, for us to check against this student's correct password. (It's conceivable that someone might be trying to impersonate a particular student by typing in his or her ID number, which would indeed retrieve that student's data from a file; but, if this student is an impostor who doesn't know the correct password, we want to find out before revealing/displaying the student's private information.)

```
else {
  // Hooray!  We found one!  Now, we need
  // to request and validate the password.
  passwordDialog = new PasswordForm();
  passwordDialog.ShowDialog(this);
```

The preceding two lines of code are responsible for instantiating and displaying a `PasswordForm` object. We introduced the `PasswordForm` class earlier in this chapter, and will show the event handling code associated with it in the next section.

When the `ShowDialog` method is called on the `passwordDialog` object, the `PasswordForm` is displayed as a modal dialog box, which means that as long as the dialog box is displayed on the screen, the user will be unable to interact with the rest of the SRS GUI. More importantly, though, as long as the dialog box is displayed on the screen, the runtime will be awaiting events from that dialog box, and the code for the `MainForm` method that we're in the middle of executing is also suspended.

By the time we reach the line of code following the call to the ShowDialog method, we know that the password dialog box has been dismissed by the user, so we can use a property that we've declared for the PasswordForm class called Password to retrieve whatever the user has typed into the dialog box.

```
string password = passwordDialog.Password;
```

After we fetch the value of whatever password the user typed in, we can dispose of the dialog box, because we no longer need to "talk" with it to request any of its services:

```
passwordDialog.Dispose();
```

We next attempt to validate the password, and if the attempt succeeds, we display another MessageBox informing the user that the login succeeded. We then use another housekeeping method, SetFields, to populate the various objects on the GUI with this student's information so that he or she can see it. (We'll see that method code in a moment.)

```
if (currentUser.ValidatePassword(password)) {
    // Let the user know that the
    // login succeeded.
    string message =
        "Log in succeeded for " + currentUser.Name + ".";
    MessageBox.Show(message, "Log In Succeeded",
        MessageBoxButtons.OK, MessageBoxIcon.Information);

    // Load the data for the current user into the TextBox and
    // ListBox objects.
    SetFields(currentUser);
}
```

The other possible failure mode of the ssnTextBox "Enter" event is that the student ID was correct, but an invalid password was entered. In this case, the login operation is deemed to have failed, and we notify the user of this as follows:

```
else {
    // The ssn was okay, but the password validation failed;
    // notify the user of this.
    string message = "Invalid password; please try again.";
    MessageBox.Show(message, "Invalid Password",
        MessageBoxButtons.OK, MessageBoxIcon.Warning);
}
}
```

The final thing the event handling method does is to use a third housekeeping method to enable/disable the buttons at the bottom of the screen, as appropriate. (We'll see the code for ResetButtons toward the end of our discussion of the MainForm class.)

```
    // Check states of the various buttons.
    ResetButtons();
  }
}
```

The AddButtonClicked Method

The addButton object is used to add a selected course to a student's registered course list, and the AddButtonClicked method will be called every time the addButton object is clicked to provide this functionality.

The method is declared in the MainForm class; the method's header syntax is prescribed by the EventHandler delegate that it's associated with, and is as follows:

```
// Event handling method for the "Add" Button.
public void AddButtonClicked(object source, EventArgs e) {
```

The first thing the method does is to pull the user-selected item from the scheduleListBox via the SelectedItem property. The get accessor of the SelectedItem property returns a generic object, so we must cast it back into a Section object; we maintain a handle on that Section object via the selected reference variable.

```
    // Determine which section is selected (note that we must
    // cast it, as it is returned as an object reference).
    Section selected = (Section) scheduleListBox.SelectedItem;
```

The AddButtonClicked method now attempts to enroll the student in the selected Section. The return value of the Enroll method, which indicates the success or failure of the enrollment, is saved in a local variable called status.

```
    // Attempt to enroll the student in the section, noting
    // the status code that is returned.
    int status = selected.Enroll(currentUser);
```

There are four possible outcomes when a Section attempts to enroll a Student, as was discussed in Chapter 14, and we need to account for and respond to every possibility. The return value from the Enroll method will be one of the constant variables Section.PREREQ_NOT_SATISFIED, Section.PREVIOUSLY_ENROLLED, Section. SUCCESSFULLY_ENROLLED, or Section.SECTION_FULL. Based on which constant is returned, the appropriate dialog box message is formulated and displayed inside a `MessageBox`.

We'll start with the code for the three failure modes: a section was full, a prerequisite wasn't satisfied, or a student was already enrolled in the current or similar section.

```
// Report the status to the user.
if (status == Section.SECTION_FULL) {
  MessageBox.Show("Sorry - that section is full.", "Request Denied",
          MessageBoxButtons.OK, MessageBoxIcon.Warning);
}
else {
  if (status == Section.PREREQ_NOT_SATISFIED) {
    string message = "You haven't satisfied all " +
            "of the prerequisites for this course.";
    MessageBox.Show(message, "Request Denied",
            MessageBoxButtons.OK, MessageBoxIcon.Warning);
  }
  else {
    if (status == Section.PREVIOUSLY_ENROLLED) {
      string message = "You are enrolled in or have successfully " +
              "completed a section of this course.";
      MessageBox.Show(message, "Request Denied",
              MessageBoxButtons.OK, MessageBoxIcon.Warning);
    }
```

If we make it to this point in the code, we've indeed succeeded in getting this student enrolled in the selected class!

```
    else {  // Success!
      string message = "Seat confirmed in " +
              selected.RepresentedCourse.CourseNo + ".";
      MessageBox.Show(message, "Request Successful",
              MessageBoxButtons.OK, MessageBoxIcon.Information);
```

We must reflect the newly added section to the student's course list on the GUI; it's easy enough to just repopulate the entire list with all of the sections for which this student is enrolled presently. We also update the `TextBox` representing the total enrolled course count.

```
      // Update the list of sections that this
      // student is registered for.
      registeredListBox.Items.Clear();
      IEnumerator ie = currentUser.GetEnrolledSections();
```

```
        while (ie.MoveNext()) {
          registeredListBox.Items.Add((Section) ie.Current);
        }

        // Update the field representing student's course total.
        totalTextBox.Text = "" + currentUser.GetCourseTotal();
```

And, as a housekeeping measure, we clear out the user's "clicked" entry in the scheduleListBox, so that it's ready for another selection to be made:

```
        // Clear the selection in the schedule of classes list.
        scheduleListBox.SelectedItem = null;
      }
    }
  }
```

The ResetButtons method is a housekeeping method that we'll describe in more detail later in this chapter. It ensures that only buttons that ***should*** be enabled given the current state of the application ***are*** enabled. For example, if there are no sections listed in the registeredListBox, then the ResetButtons method will disable the DropButton, since a user can't drop a section if he or she isn't registered for anything.

```
    // Check states of the various buttons.
    ResetButtons();
  }
```

The DropButtonClicked Method

The dropButton object is used by a student to drop a course for which he or she is registered, and the DropButtonClicked method is called every time the dropButton object is clicked. The method is declared in the MainForm class, and its header is as follows:

```
  public void DropButtonClicked(object source, EventArgs e)
```

The code for responding to a press of the Drop button is quite similar to that for the Add button, albeit a bit less elaborate; here, all we need to do is

- Determine which item the user selected in his or her registeredListBox.

- Drop the course.

- Display a confirmation message.

- Refresh the user-related information displayed on the screen.

Because it's so similar to the AddButtonClicked method, we present the dropButtonClicked method code without further discussion; please refer to in-line comments in the code for details.

```
// Event handling method for the "Drop" Button.
public void DropButtonClicked(object source, EventArgs e) {
    // Determine which section is selected (note that we must
    // cast it, as it is returned as an object reference).
    Section selected = (Section) registeredListBox.SelectedItem;

    // Drop the course.
    selected.Drop(currentUser);

    // Display a confirmation message.
    string message = "Course " +
        selected.RepresentedCourse.CourseNo + " dropped.";
    MessageBox.Show(message, "Request Successful",
        MessageBoxButtons.OK, MessageBoxIcon.Information);

    // Update the list of sections that
    // this student is registered for.
    registeredListBox.Items.Clear();
    IEnumerator ie = currentUser.GetEnrolledSections();
    while (ie.MoveNext()) {
      registeredListBox.Items.Add((Section) ie.Current);
    }

    // Update the field representing student's course total.
    totalTextBox.Text = "" + currentUser.GetCourseTotal();

    // Check states of the various buttons.
    ResetButtons();
}
```

The SaveButtonClicked Method

The SaveButtonClicked method is invoked whenever the saveButton object is clicked. The method is a means of invoking the Student class's Persist method on the currentUser Student reference, a method that we studied in depth in Chapter 15. In a nutshell, this method saves all information about the student, including all sections in which he or she is enrolled, to a file by the name of ssn.dat, for example, 111-11-1111.dat. The method is declared in the MainForm class, and its code is as follows:

```
// Event handling method for the "Save" button.
public void SaveButtonClicked(object source, EventArgs e) {
  bool success = currentUser.Persist();

  if (success) {
    // Let the user know that his/her
    // schedule was successfully saved.
    MessageBox.Show("Schedule saved", "Schedule Saved",
          MessageBoxButtons.OK, MessageBoxIcon.Information);
  }
  else {
    // Let the user know that there was a problem.
    string message = "Problem saving your " +
                "schedule; please contact " +
                "SRS Support Staff for assistance.";
    MessageBox.Show(message, "Problem Saving Schedule",
          MessageBoxButtons.OK, MessageBoxIcon.Warning);
  }
}
```

The *LogOffButtonButtonClicked* Method

This method is called whenever the logOffButton object is clicked, to clear out various GUI objects and to reset the value of the currentUser Student reference to null. The LogOffButtonClicked method is implemented in the MainForm class, and its code is as follows:

```
// Event handling method for "Log Off" button.
public void LogOffButtonClicked(object source, EventArgs e) {
  ClearFields();
  ssnTextBox.Text = "";
  currentUser = null;

  // Clear the selection in the
  // schedule of classes list.
  scheduleListBox.SelectedItem = null;

  // Check states of the various buttons.
  ResetButtons();
}
```

The *RegisteredSelectionChanged* and *ScheduleSelectionChanged* Methods

The RegisteredSelectionChanged and ScheduleSelectionChanged methods are called whenever the selected item in either the registeredListBox or scheduleListBox objects changes, respectively. These two objects don't need much in the way of event handling:

- We want them to be mutually exclusive, such that when an element is selected in one of them, the selections in the other one are cleared.

- We also want to reset the enabled state of various buttons when an element is selected. For example, when a student selects a section in the scheduleListBox, the Add button should become enabled and the Drop button should be disabled. The ResetButtons method can be called to reset the enabled state of both buttons.

The ScheduleSelectionChanged and RegisteredSelectionChanged methods are declared in the MainForm class. Their respective code listings are as follows:

```
// Event handling method for the "Schedule of Classes" ListBox.
public void ScheduleSelectionChanged(object source, EventArgs e) {
  // When an item is selected in this list,
  // we clear the selection in the other list.
  if (scheduleListBox.SelectedItem != null)  {
    registeredListBox.SelectedItem = null;
  }

  // Reset the enabled state of the buttons.
  ResetButtons();
}


// Event handling method for the "Registered For:" ListBox.
public void RegisteredSelectionChanged(object source, EventArgs e) {
  // When an item is selected in this list,
  // we clear the selection in the other list.
  if (registeredListBox.SelectedItem != null)  {
    scheduleListBox.SelectedItem = null;
  }

  // Reset the enabled state of the buttons.
  ResetButtons();
}
```

The PasswordKeyUp Method

Unlike the other SRS event handling methods that we've discussed so far, which are all declared in the MainForm class, the PasswordKeyUp method is implemented in the PasswordForm class. It responds to KeyUp events that occur when a key is released inside the passwordTextBox. The PasswordKeyUp method is declared as follows:

```
public void PasswordKeyUp(object source, KeyEventArgs e) {
```

Once again, we want to act if the Enter key is released inside the passwordTextBox. We use the KeyCode property of the KeyEventArgs argument to determine if the Enter key caused the event.

```
if (e.KeyCode == Keys.Enter) {
```

If it was indeed the Enter key, we assign the text inside the passwordTextBox to the password attribute. The Trim method, defined by the String class, is called to remove and leading or trailing white space.

```
password = passwordTextBox.Text.Trim();
```

Finally, the visibility of the PasswordForm is set to be false, so that the password dialog box will "vanish" from the display ***without being garbage collected***; we want to be able to communicate with the PasswordForm to retrieve what was typed inside the passwordTextBox.

```
this.Visible = false;
    }
  }
```

When this method finishes executing, program execution returns to the MainForm class.

Housekeeping Methods

As mentioned throughout this discussion, we've outfitted the MainForm class with a few housekeeping methods; note that these are all declared to be private, meaning that they are only used within MainForm. Note, in particular, our approach to the ResetButtons method (please read in-line comments that follow):

```
// Because there are so many different situations in which one or
// more buttons need to be (de)activated, and because the logic is
// so complex, we centralize it here and then just call this method
```

```
// whenever we need to check the state of one or more of the buttons.
// It is a trade-off of code elegance for execution efficiency:
// we are doing a bit more work each time (because we don't need to
// reset all four buttons every time), but since the execution time
// is minimal, this seems like a reasonable trade-off.
private void ResetButtons() {
  // There are four conditions which collectively govern the
  // state of each button:
  //
  // 1:  Whether a user is logged on or not.
  bool isLoggedOn;
  if (currentUser != null) {
    isLoggedOn = true;
  }
  else {
    isLoggedOn = false;
  }


  // 2:   Whether the user is registered for at least one course.
  bool atLeastOne;
  if (currentUser != null && currentUser.GetCourseTotal() > 0) {
    atLeastOne = true;
  }
  else {
    atLeastOne = false;
  }



  // 3:   Whether a registered course has been selected.
  bool courseSelected;
  if (registeredListBox.SelectedItem == null) {
    courseSelected = false;
  }
  else {
    courseSelected = true;
  }

  // 4:   Whether an item is selected in the Schedule of Classes.
  bool catalogSelected;
  if (scheduleListBox.SelectedItem == null)  {
    catalogSelected = false;
  }
  else {
    catalogSelected = true;
  }
```

```
      // Now, verify the conditions on a button-by-button basis.

      // Drop button:
      if (isLoggedOn && atLeastOne && courseSelected) {
        dropButton.Enabled = true;
      }
      else {
        dropButton.Enabled = false;
      }

      // Add button:
      if (isLoggedOn && catalogSelected) {
        addButton.Enabled = true;
      }
      else {
        addButton.Enabled = false;
      }

      // Save My Schedule button:
      if (isLoggedOn) {
        saveButton.Enabled = true;
      }
      else {
        saveButton.Enabled = false;
      }

      // Log Off button:
      if (isLoggedOn) {
        logOffButton.Enabled = true;
      }
      else {
        logOffButton.Enabled = false;
      }
    }

    // Called whenever a user is logged off.
    private void ClearFields() {
      nameTextBox.Text = "";
      totalTextBox.Text = "";
      registeredListBox.Items.Clear();
    }
```

```
// Set the various fields, lists, etc. to reflect the information
// associated with a particular student.  (Used when logging in.)
private void SetFields(Student theStudent) {
  nameTextBox.Text = theStudent.Name;
  int total = theStudent.GetCourseTotal();
  totalTextBox.Text = "" + total;

  // If the student is registered for any courses, list these, too.
  if (total > 0) {
    // Use the GetEnrolledSections() method to obtain a list
    // of the sections that the student is registered for and
    // add the sections to the registered ListBox.

    IEnumerator e = theStudent.GetEnrolledSections();
    while (e.MoveNext()) {
      registeredListBox.Items.Add((Section) e.Current);
    }
  }
}
```

Summary

We've covered a tremendous amount of ground in this chapter!

- We discussed the two primary FCL GUI namespaces—
  `System.Windows.Forms` and `System.Drawing`.

- We've looked specifically at the following building blocks of GUIs:

  - A top-level container: the `Form` class

  - Other GUI classes: `Label`, `Button`, `ListBox`, `TextBox`

  - How to define the state of the GUI objects by setting property values

  - How to position GUI objects inside a `Form`

  - How to display model message dialog boxes using the `MessageBox` class

- We covered the .NET event handling model; in particular, about how delegates are used to associate event handling methods with an event source.

- We've discussed the philosophy and advantages of model-view separation.

- We talked about the development of a concept of operations, or "story-board," as a means for getting sponsor/client/user buy-in before any code has been written, to ensure that the proposed look and flow of a GUI meets the use case requirements for the system.

- We've discussed state retrieval methods as a data sharing technique.

And, we saw the "pièce de résistance"—adding a GUI front-end to the SRS application! We've now come through the full life cycle of the SRS application, beginning with an expression of requirements via use cases in Chapter 9, to an object model in Chapters 10 and 11, a command line–driven program in Chapter 14, a program with file persistence in Chapter 15, and a GUI-driven application in Chapter 16.

Exercises

1. Modify the event handling in the MainForm class such that the SSN TextBox is disabled once the user has logged in and then reenabled when the user logs out.

2. For all of the catch blocks located in the various SRS classes, introduce a MessageBox to report problems

3. *Advanced exercise:* Modify the SRS application to provide the user with the capability for setting his or her own password. This will involve

   - Displaying an appropriate error message to the user

   - Adding a Set Password button on the MainForm

   - Popping up a dialog box in response to a click of the Set Password button to request that the user enter the old and new password (consider creating a "clone" of the PasswordForm class)

   - Changing the structure of the Student.dat file to accommodate storing a student's password, which will in turn require changing the following methods of the Student class: ParseData, Persist, and the Student constructor

CHAPTER 17

Next Steps

CONGRATULATIONS! You've made it through quite a learning curve, from object concepts, to object modeling, to C# programming. What you do next will depend on what your intentions were for learning this material in the first place:

- *If you're a software developer* primarily interested in building C# applications, you'll want to get some hands-on C# programming experience if you haven't already done so. A good first step is to tackle some of the exercises at the end of each chapter in Part Three of the book; if you've already done so, then you may be ready to try your hand at a full–life cycle object-oriented development project. See the next section in this chapter, "Our 'Tried and True' Approach to Learning C# Properly," for a game plan on how to proceed, and the "Recommended Reading" section later in this chapter for other books in the Apress suite (and beyond) that might be appropriate next steps in your continued professional development.

- *If you're a systems analyst* primarily interested in object modeling, be certain to attempt the exercises at the ends of the chapters in Part Two of the book if you haven't already done so. Then, seek out an opportunity to engage in an object modeling project within your organization, ideally with a senior object modeler to guide and mentor you.

- *If you're a manager* whose goal is to become better versed in these technologies, this may be an appropriate time to conduct a technology review of ongoing projects in your organization to learn how the techniques touched upon in this book are specifically being carried out.

- *If you're an instructor*, please review Appendix A for suggestions on how to use this material as the basis of a beginning object methods/C# curriculum in either an academic or corporate setting.

Whatever your focus, be sure to visit Jacquie's web site, http://objectstart.com, for additional suggestions as well as links to related web sites that you may find of interest.

Our "Tried and True" Approach to Learning C# Properly

Here are our recommendations on how to advance through the C# learning curve as smoothly and effectively as possible.

1. Understand OO analysis and design—hopefully, our book has gone a long way toward helping you to accomplish this, and our recommended reading suggestions later in this chapter will help you to deepen this understanding.

2. Obtain a good reference book on C#—again, our book has hopefully given you a good jump start with the language, and our recommended reading suggestions later in this chapter will serve to complement this.

3. Download and install a free copy of the latest release of the .NET Framework SDK from the MSDN web site as described in Appendix C.

4. Compile and run a simple "Hello, World" program from the command line to ensure that all C# SDK components are installed and working properly.

5. Choose a *simple* first problem to automate: one that (a) you're very familiar with the requirements for—perhaps a small-scale application that you've already built in some other language, or an application based upon some hobby—and (b) that only requires a handful of domain classes when modeled.

6. Produce a UML class diagram for your application based on the object modeling techniques that you learned in Part Two of the book.

7. Write the code for your core model classes, and get the application to work as a command-line application first, as we did for the Student Registration System (SRS) in Chapter 14. (This is your *model,* without a graphical *view.*)

8. Learn more about C# GUI development beyond what we've introduced in Chapter 16, and buy a good reference book about this subject.

9. Add a GUI front-end onto the code that you produced in step 7, as we did for the SRS in Chapter 16. Our personal bias is that you should do so by writing GUI code from scratch the first time around, without using a "drag-and-drop" IDE/GUI building tool, as we believe that you'll learn GUI concepts more thoroughly by doing so.

10. Learn about the various C# database interface options (e.g., ADO.NET), and buy a good reference book about this subject.

11. Acquire the appropriate .NET Framework Data Provider for your particular DBMS, if necessary, and connect your application to a database "back-end" so as to persist your objects. Or, visit `http://objectstart.com` for links regarding free, single-user DBMSs in the public domain that are ideal for educational use.

12. (Optional) If you're inclined to use an integrated development environment (IDE), invest in a commercially available C# IDE such as Microsoft's Visual Studio .NET. A free, open source C# IDE known as SharpDevelop is also available at `http://www.icsharpcode.net/OpenSource/SD`.

13. (Optional) Join a C# special interest group, either online or in person. This is an invaluable way to get informal, ad hoc mentorship from colleagues who are more experienced with C#.

From this point forward, your options are open-ended! For example, you may wish to expand beyond C#-specific matters to further explore the capabilities of the .NET Framework Class Library. Whichever direction you choose to take, you can rest assured that there will be plenty of new C#-related innovations in the months and years to come.

Recommended Reading

Many fine books have been written and published on the subject of OO software development by a variety of publishers, and it would be virtually impossible to do justice to them all here. Consider this list to represent some of our personal recommendations (visit Jacquie's web site, `http://objectstart.com`, for more recommendations), but please do browse the titles available from your favorite technical bookseller, as new titles are being released literally every day.

- Booch, Grady, James Rumbaugh, and Ivar Jacobson, *The Unified Modeling Language User Guide*, Addison-Wesley, 1998.

   A definitive reference on UML, written by its creators; definitely worth adding to your library if you're serious about object modeling.

- Rumbaugh, James, Ivar Jacobson, and Grady Booch, *The Unified Modeling Language Reference Manual*, Addison-Wesley, 1999.

A second definitive reference by the same gentlemen; see our comments for the preceding title.

- Jacobson, Ivar, Grady Booch, and James Rumbaugh, *Unified Software Development Process*, Addison-Wesley, 1999.

And a third!

- Quatrani, Terry, *Visual Modeling with Rational Rose and UML*, Addison-Wesley, 1998.

A practical, step-by-step guide for how to use Rational Rose, one of the industry's leading object modeling CASE tools, to prepare UML models.

- Eriksson, Hans and Magnus Penker, *UML Toolkit*, John Wiley & Sons, Inc., 1998.

Comes with a CD-ROM containing a demo copy of Rational Rose, numerous UML models, and code.

- Taylor, David A., *Object Technology: A Manager's Guide*, Addison-Wesley, 1998.

A classic, high-level review of the direction in which the OO industry as a whole is headed.

- Gamma, Erich, Richard Helm, Ralph Johnson, and John Vlissides, *Design Patterns: Elements of Reusable Object-Oriented Software*, Addison-Wesley, 1994.

An in-depth look at identifying and reusing common design patterns.

- Meyer, Bertrand, *Object-Oriented Software Construction*, Prentice Hall, 1988.

An academic treatment of object-oriented principles, based on the Eiffel programming language.

- Kernighan, Brian W. and Dennis M. Ritchie, *The C Programming Language*, Prentice Hall, 1988.

A solid, classic treatment of C, for those of you who are interested in the most basic of C#'s "roots"!

- Gunnerson, Eric, *A Programmer's Introduction to C#*, Apress, 2001.

A comprehensive reference for the C# language, designed for experienced programmers.

- Palmer, Grant, *C# Programmer's Reference*, Wrox Press, 2002.

A handy quick reference guide to the C# language.

- Troelson, Andrew, *C# and the .NET Platform*, Apress, 2003.

Provides a brief introduction to the C# language and then moves to a discussion of key technical and architectural issues for .NET developers.

- MacDonald, Matthew, *User Interfaces in C#: Windows Forms and Custom Controls*, Apress, 2002.

Covers the Windows Forms namespaces as well as a detailed discussion of good user-interface design principles.

- (**Coming soon!**) Barker, Jacquie, *Taming the Technology Tidalwave*, ObjectStart Press, 2004.

A light-hearted career guide for technical professionals; please visit http://objectstart.com *for details on this upcoming book.*

Your Comments, Please!

In the interest of making this book as useful as possible to our readers, we'd love to hear from you if you have suggestions for how this book could be improved! Please visit Jacquie's web site at http://objectstart.com to contact her, or send Grant an e-mail at grantepalmer@msn.com.

Appendices

Suggestions for Using This Book As a Textbook

IN THIS APPENDIX, we present some ideas for how this book can be used as a textbook for a variety of university-level (or advanced high school–level) beginning object-oriented programming (OOP) courses. The suggestions are equally applicable, however, when applied in a corporate training setting.

Recommended Teaching Approaches

As the basis for a single-semester generic OOP course, focus on the subject matter content in Parts One and Two (Chapters 1 through 12). Make sure to give students ample hands-on experience with both C# programming and object modeling through homework assignments as well as in-class group modeling exercises. The latter is particularly important for giving students an appreciation for how subjective object modeling can be. Time permitting at the end of the semester, cover the material in Chapter 13.

Note from Jacquie: This happens to be the way that I'm currently teaching the material at George Washington University in Washington, DC. When I teach this same material for corporate clients, I do so as a series of six full-day lecture/lab sessions, spread out over several calendar weeks, but follow the same basic outline.

For more information about my instructional approach, or to share in my teaching materials, please contact me via my web site, http://objectstart.com.

As the basis for a single-semester OO methodology course, adapt the approach described for a single-semester generic OOP course so as to emphasize hands-on object modeling and deemphasize actual programming. However, note that exposing students to the way that an object model translates into the syntax of an OO language such as C# really helps to cement object concepts, even for those students who aren't aspiring to be professional programmers. It's therefore important to examine students on the object aspects of the C# language by giving them simple code examples to analyze on paper.

As the basis for a single-semester comprehensive C# language course, devote the first lecture to reviewing UML notation as covered in Chapter 10, using this lecture as an opportunity to refresh students' memories on the basics of key object concepts. Realize, however, that to do justice to C# as an OOP language, students must have previously been exposed to object concepts in depth. Devote the rest of the semester to the C# material in Parts One and Three (Chapters 1–7 and 13–16).

One significant advantage of using our book as a textbook is that it uses a consistent case study as the basis for object concepts, object modeling, and C# programming. Students can actually see how an object model evolves from a requirements specification, and how that same object model translates into a working C# application, something that few other books present.

Suitability of C# As a Teaching Language

As a learning/teaching tool, C# is an ideal language for many of the reasons cited in Chapter 1. By way of review:

- ***C# is an ISO standard and, as such, is consistent across the more recent (2000, XP, Server 2003) Windows-based platforms.*** If you encourage students to use Microsoft's C# Software Development Kit (SDK) as their sole development environment, you will dramatically lessen the "hassle factor" as compared with teaching a language like C++ to a group of students who are using a multitude of different programming environments on their home or work computers.

- ***C# is, in our opinion, a simpler language to grasp than C++***, at least as far as the core language is concerned; C++ pointers have historically sent many a student running for a "course drop" slip! The biggest challenge with learning C# is the phenomenal number of APIs and classes therein, but we believe that we've successfully distilled these down to just those that a beginning student needs to know.

- ***C# is extremely affordable.*** All students need to do programming assignments is Microsoft's C# Software Development Kit (SDK), downloadable for free as detailed in Appendix C, and a text editor.

> *If you prefer to expose students to the use of an integrated development environment (IDE), you might consider Microsoft's Visual Studio .NET. More information about this IDE can be found at* http://msdn.microsoft.com/vstudio/. *Also, please visit* http://objectstart.com *for suggestions of free or low-cost object modeling tools that your students might wish to use.*

Some Final Recommendations

In addition to the Student Registration System case study that is used as the backbone of the book, we recommend using a consistent second case study as the basis for homework assignments and/or in-class group exercises. Either have students devise their own (see suggested exercise 3 at the end of Chapter 2), or use the Prescription Tracking System provided in Appendix B.

Each time a new OO concept or modeling technique is introduced in lectures, a classroom exercise or homework assignment should be assigned to the students so that they may experience that concept or apply that technique.

Spend the beginning of each class for which a homework assignment is due discussing students' and instructor's solutions to the assignment.

> *Note from Jacquie: I often have students submit their homework solutions to me in advance of a class meeting via fax, email, or web posting so that I have time to decide which aspects of their solutions I wish to emphasize; reviewing a student's (possibly flawed) solution for the first time in front of the class can be confusing to classmates.*

For purposes of object modeling, students should be encouraged to work in small teams for both the classroom exercises and the homework assignments. A great deal of the learning that takes place from object modeling comes from "hammering out" differences of opinion among a group, and group projects give students a real taste of the teamwork required in the business world.

It's also enlightening to give the same set of requirements to multiple teams, and to then have the teams review each other's proposed solutions, pointing out what works and what doesn't.

> *Note from Jacquie: Keep an eye on my web site,* http://objectstart.com, *for additional suggestions on how to use this material effectively in an academic setting. And, if you come up with a particularly effective approach or idea, I'd love to hear about it, so that it may be shared with other instructors.*

APPENDIX B

Alternative Case Studies

THIS APPENDIX IS MEANT to be a companion appendix to Appendix A, as well as a supplement to many of the end-of-chapter exercises found throughout the book. In this appendix, we propose some alternative case studies that can be used as the basis of formal course work or personal study applications.

Case Study #1: Prescription Tracking System

This case study is relatively straightforward, and hence can be tackled by most beginning modelers fairly effortlessly.

Background

Drugs For You pharmacy wishes for us to design and develop an automated Prescription Tracking System (PTS). The requirements are as follows:

- The system is to keep track of the following information for each customer:

  - Customer's name

  - Telephone number

  - Date of birth

  - Insurance provider

  - Insurance policy number

  - A prescription history, detailed next

- Each customer's prescription history will record the following information about each prescription:

  - A unique prescription ID number assigned by the pharmacy

  - The medication being prescribed

  - The prescribing physician's name and telephone number

  - The date of issue

  - Expiration date

  - Number of refills authorized

  - Number of "units" per prescription refill, where a "unit" might be a pill, a teaspoon, a milliliter (ml), etc.—see discussion of medications, next

  - Whether or not it's OK to provide the customer with a generic substitute, if one exists

- For each medication stocked by the pharmacy, the system will track

  - Its name

  - The "unit" by which the medication is prescribed (pills, teaspoons, ml, etc.)

  - Which medications can serve as "generic" equivalents of which other medication(s)

  - Any common side effects associated with taking the medication

- The system is required to support the following queries (some will be printed as hardcopy reports, others will be viewed online only):

  - A prescription history—that is, a report of all prescriptions ever issued to a given customer—as requested by a given customer

  - A report of all side effects of a given medication, to be enclosed with each prescription dispensed

  - A list of all generic substitutes available for a given medication

  - Whether a given prescription is refillable: that is, whether any refills remain and whether the prescription has yet to expire

All of the preceding will be accessible via a secure web site to individual customers as well as to the in-store pharmacist.

Simplifying Assumptions

A real-life prescription tracking system would be quite complicated; we suggest the following simplifications to make the PTS problem a bit more tractable for beginning-level object-oriented programmers.

- The system isn't to be concerned with billing matters in any way; that is, we aren't going to worry about computing the price to be paid for a prescription, nor will we be concerned with trying to get a customer's insurance company to reimburse the pharmacy in any way.

- We'll assume that there is only one Drugs For You pharmacy location; that is, it isn't a chain of multiple stores.

- The system isn't responsible for inventory control—that is, we'll assume that "infinite" quantities of all medications are in stock.

- Assume that the prescription is always refilled with the same medication as was issued for that prescription the first time around; that is, we'll never initially fill the prescription with a generic medication, and then refill it with a nongeneric equivalent, or vice versa.

Case Study #2: Conference Room Reservation System

This is an advanced case study that involves scheduling complexities and other elaborate requirements, representative of a real-world modeling challenge. It's best suited to an instructor-led group modeling exercise rather than as an individual exercise for a beginning-level modeler.

Background

We've been asked to develop an automated Conference Room Reservation System (CRRS) for our organization.

- A total of a dozen conference rooms are scattered across the four different buildings that comprise our facility. These rooms differ in terms of their seating capacities as well as what audiovisual (A/V) equipment is permanently installed in each room.

- Each of these rooms is overseen by a different administrative staff member, known as a Conference Room Coordinator.

- Reservations are presently being recorded manually by the various Conference Room Coordinators. The name of the person reserving the room, as well as his or her telephone number, is jotted by hand in an appointment book; the start and stop time of the meeting is also noted.

- A separate, central organization called the A/V Equipment Group provides "loaner" A/V equipment to supplement any equipment that may be permanently installed in a given conference room. Equipment that is available for temporary use through this group includes conventional overhead projectors, televisions, VCRs, LCD projectors for use with PCs, electronic whiteboards, laptop computers, tape recorders, and slide projectors. Personnel from this group deliver equipment directly to the locale where it's needed, and pick it up after the meeting is concluded.

The following problems have been noted regarding the present manual system:

- At present, no supplemental information regarding the number of attendees or planned A/V equipment usage is being noted by the Conference Room Coordinators for a given meeting.

  - If someone planning a meeting involving only 4 people schedules a room with the capacity for 20, the excess capacity in that room will be wasted. Meanwhile, someone truly needing a room for 20 people will be left short.

  - Meeting planners must also be responsible for separately coordinating with the A/V Equipment Group; if they forget to do so, panic often ensues as folks scramble to arrange necessary equipment at the last minute.

- Whenever a given room's Coordinator is away from his or her desk, information about that room's availability is inaccessible, unless the inquirer wishes to walk to the Coordinator's office and inspect the appointment book directly. However, due to the size of the office complex, this isn't practical, so inquirers typically leave a voicemail message or send an email to the Coordinator, who gets back to them at a later point in time.

- People are lax about canceling reservations when a room is no longer needed, so rooms often sit vacant that could otherwise be put to good use. Similarly, they often forget to cancel A/V equipment reservations.

- Pertinent information about the rooms (e.g., their seating capacity, whether or not they have a white board, whether or not they have built-in A/V facilities, whether or not they are "wired" into the company's LAN) isn't presently published anywhere. Someone unfamiliar with the amenities of the various rooms often winds up having to call all 12 of the Conference Room Coordinators in search of an appropriate meeting location.

Goals for the System

We've been asked by management to design a system for providing online, automated conference room and equipment scheduling to remedy the problems of the current manual approach. The goals of this project are to provide the ability for any employee to directly connect into the system to perform the following tasks:

- If the user is interested in scheduling a room for a meeting, he or she will be required to complete an online questionnaire regarding the parameters of the meeting, to include

  - The scheduler's name, title, department, and telephone number

  - The number of attendees anticipated

  - A date range, indicating the earliest and latest acceptable date for the meeting

  - The length of time that the room will be required, in half-hour increments

  - An earliest acceptable start time and latest acceptable stop time

  - A list of all A/V equipment required

- As soon as this questionnaire is completed, the system will present the user with a list of all available suitable room alternatives. The user will be able to select from these options to reserve a room, or change his or her criteria and repeat the search.

> *Note that the system need not "remember" these criteria after the user logs off.*

- When confirming a reservation, the user must designate a subject or purpose for the meeting, such as "Demo of CRRS Prototype."

- After a room has been selected, the system will then determine what "loaner" A/V equipment will be needed to supplement the equipment that is permanently installed in that room, and will automatically arrange for its delivery.

> *For purposes of this case study, we won't worry about running out of equipment—we'll assume an infinite supply of everything—although in real life this would also have to be a consideration.*

- If no rooms meeting the user's requirements are available, the user will be presented with a list of suitable rooms with the number of people waitlisted for each. The user will be able to optionally place his or her name at the end of the waiting list for one of these rooms.

  - When such a request is posted, the system is to send a courtesy email to the person holding that room's reservation, asking that person to rethink his or her need for the room.

  - Should the room on the waiting list become available, it will automatically be temporarily reserved for the first person on the waiting list. An email message is to be sent automatically to the requestor, giving that person 72 hours to confirm his or her selection before the room is either (a) reassigned (again, temporarily) to the next person on the waiting list or (b) becomes generally available if the waiting list has been exhausted.

- A user should be permitted to query the system as to who has a particular room reserved at a given date and time, or to perform a search for a given meeting that the user is to attend based on (a) scheduler or (b) subject.

- The user must be able to cancel a room reservation at any time, whether confirmed or waitlisted.

- The A/V Equipment Group wishes to periodically run a report, sorted by equipment type, indicating how many times a given piece of equipment was used over a 12-month period.

Case Study #3: Blue Skies Airline Reservation System

This is the most complex case study of all; please see our introductory comments for Case Study #2.

Background

Blue Skies Airlines, a new airline, offers services between any two of the following cities: Denver; Washington, DC; Los Angeles; New York City; Atlanta; and Cleveland.

When a customer calls Blue Skies to make a flight reservation, the reservation agent first asks him or her for

- The desired travel dates

- The departure and destination cities

- The seat grade desired (first class, business class, or economy)

The reservation agent then informs the customer of all available flights that meet his or her criteria. For each flight, the flight number, departure date and time, arrival date and time, and round-trip price are communicated to the customer. If the customer finds any of the available flights acceptable, he or she may either pay for the ticket via credit card or request that the seat be held for 24 hours. (A specific seat assignment—row and seat number—isn't issued until the seat is paid for.)

A limited number of seats on each flight are earmarked as frequent flyer seats. A customer who is a frequent flyer member may reserve and "pay for" one of these seats by giving the agent his or her frequent flyer membership number. The agent then verifies that the appropriate balance is available in the customer's account before the seat can be confirmed, at which point those miles are deducted from the account.

The customer has two ticketing options: he or she may request that a conventional "paper" ticket be issued and mailed to his or her home address, or an electronic ticket (E-ticket) may instead be assigned, in which case the customer is simply informed of the E-ticket serial number by telephone. (With an E-ticket, the customer simply reports to the airport at the time of his or her departure, and presents suitable ID to a ticket agent at the gate. No paperwork is exchanged.) In either case, the reservation agent records the serial number of the (conventional or electronic) ticket issued to this customer.

The number of seats available for a given flight in each of the seat grade categories is dependent on the type of aircraft assigned to a given flight.

Other Simplifying Assumptions

As with the PTS case study, there are several simplifying assumptions that can be made as compared with a "real life" airline reservation system to make this case study more tractable.

- Assume that all flights are round-trip between two cities (no three-legged itineraries are permitted).

- Disregard the complication that airlines sometimes have to switch aircraft at the last minute due to mechanical difficulties, thus disrupting the seating assignments.

Setting Up a Basic Object Modeling/C# Environment

IN THIS APPENDIX, we explain the "bare bones" requirements for downloading a trial version of an OO modeling tool and the .NET Framework Software Developer's Kit so that you may experiment with C# while reading our book.

We also provide a number of tips on how to get C# to "behave" under various scenarios. Note that our tips aren't all encompassing; they are simply provided as a professional courtesy, in the hope that you may find something useful among them. For full details on how to properly install and configure a given software tool, please consult the appropriate vendor's instructions.

Object Modeling Tools

Rather than publishing information about the wide variety of object modeling tools that are available at little or no cost, we ask that you visit http://objectstart.com for our latest suggestions on tools that you might wish to download and evaluate. Vendor offerings change regularly; links to these offerings change regularly; and the details for downloading and installing various tools are highly vendor dependent.

The .NET Framework Software Developer's Kit

The .NET Framework Software Developer's Kit (SDK) is available as a free download from Microsoft's web site: http://msdn.microsoft.com/library/default.asp?url=/downloads/list/netdevframework.asp.

> Note: Since URLs and links are continuously changing, the directions for finding the proper location within Microsoft's domain may change after this book is published; please check for updates to these instructions on the Apress web site (http://www.apress.com).

The SDK download includes everything developers need to write, build, test, and deploy C# applications—documentation, samples, and command-line tools and compilers.

Among other things, the SDK comes with

- A command-line C# compiler (`csc.exe`)

- The common language runtime (CLR), the engine that runs compiled C# programs

- A wide variety of utility tools, including a runtime debugger

- Complete documentation for everything in the .NET SDK, including the contents of the .NET Framework Class Libraries

and much more.

You must download two separate sets of software to get C# and .NET running on your machine:

- First, download and install the **.NET Framework Redistributable** package. This package contains the CLR and other .NET Framework components that are needed to *run* .NET Framework applications. The Windows 98, Windows Me, Windows 2000, Windows XP, Windows NT, and Windows Server 2003 operating systems all support the .NET Framework Redistributable package.

- After the .NET Framework Redistributable package is installed on your machine, download and install the **.NET Framework SDK**. The SDK contains everything you will need to *write, compile, test, and deploy* C# applications, including documentation, libraries, compilers, and command-line tools. **You *must* be running one of the "newer" versions of Windows—at least Windows 2000, Windows XP, or Windows Server 2003—to install the .NET Framework SDK. While it's possible to *run* C# applications under "older" versions of Windows—e.g., Windows 98, Windows Me, or Windows NT—you can't *develop* such applications on these platforms.**

Follow the instructions provided by Microsoft for installing both the Redistributable package and the SDK on your particular system.

"Odds and Ends" Tips for Getting C# to Work Properly

After you get the .NET Framework SDK downloaded and installed per the instructions on Microsoft's web site, there are a few additional things you'll need to do to get C# up and running.

> *For the remainder of this appendix, please consider this material to be "help-ful hints," provided merely as a professional courtesy; we don't profess to have all of the answers for all permutations and combinations of platform scenar-ios ... again, for full details on how to properly install and configure C#, please consult the instructions provided on Microsoft's web site.*

If You're Working Under Windows 98, Me, or NT

As mentioned earlier, the .NET Framework SDK only works for the Windows 2000, Windows XP, Windows Server 2003, or newer versions of Windows. If your machine is running an older version of Windows, you'll have to upgrade to a newer operat-ing system before you can install the C# SDK.

If You're Working Under UNIX (Solaris, Linux)

The .NET Framework isn't presently available for the UNIX operating system, although a Linux version is reportedly being considered at the time of publica-tion of this book. Check the Microsoft web site periodically for developments in this regard.

Setting the Path Environment Variable

When the SDK is installed, all associated files will be placed in a specific direc-tory. On machines running Windows XP, for example, the default installation directory will be

```
C:\WINDOWS\Microsoft.NET\Framework
```

To compile C# programs anywhere on your machine, you'll need to add the location of the folder that contains the C# compiler to the Path environment vari-able. The Path variable is a system variable, so you'll most likely need to be logged on with administrator privileges in order to make permanent changes to this vari-able.

To set the path to the C# compiler under Windows XP:

- Click the Start button, select Control Panel, and then select System.

- Select the Advanced tab and then click the Environment Variables button.

- Highlight the Path system variable and click the Edit button.

- Add the path to the directory containing the C# compiler, preceded by a semicolon, onto the end of the Path variable. For example, if the C# compiler (csc.exe) is located in the C:\WINDOWS\Microsoft.NET\Framework\ v1.1.4322 folder, you would add the text

```
;C:\WINDOWS\Microsoft.NET\Framework/v1.1.4322
```

(note the semicolon at the beginning of the string) to the end of the Path variable.

You should now be able to invoke the C# compiler from anywhere on your machine.

> *Note that the manner in which these steps are accomplished will differ for other versions of Windows.*

Once the SDK Is Installed and the Path Variable Is Set

After you have successfully installed the .NET Framework SDK and have set the Path environment variable, you are ready to start developing C# programs! Create a working directory in which you plan to store your various C# experiments, and then download the example code for this book into that directory (see Appendix D for download instructions). ***Important: don't put any of your personal files or folders in the .NET Framework SDK home directory or any of its subdirectories unless specifically instructed to do so.***

Your C# environment should now, hopefully, be up and running. To give it a test drive, type, compile, and run the following trivially simple program:

```
using System;

public class Success
{
  static void Main() {
    Console.WriteLine("Hooray! It works!");
  }
}
```

You must first enter the preceding program text ***exactly*** as shown into a file. The file name can be anything, but the convention is to name the file Success.cs. You can use a variety of methods to enter a C# program into a file:

- Use the Windows Notepad editor.

- Use any other Windows-based text editor that you prefer.

- Use your favorite command-line text editor.

- Use an interactive development environment (IDE) of your choice.

Next, we'll attempt to compile and run this program from the command line. You can open a command prompt window in one of two ways:

- From the Start menu, choose Programs ➤ Accessories ➤ Command Prompt.

- Alternatively, from the Start menu, choose Run, and then type "cmd" (without the quotes).

Once the command prompt window opens, make sure to use the cd command to switch your working directory to be the directory in which your program resides (if you aren't already there), and then type the following command at the prompt to compile the program:

```
csc Success.cs
```

If the program compiles without any errors, an executable Success.exe file will be created in the same directory where the Success.cs file resides. Type the following command at the command prompt to run the program:

```
Success
```

If all goes well, the following should appear as output:

```
Hooray! It works!
```

Troubleshooting Your Installation

The following examples illustrate various problems that might arise when you try to compile a C# program:

- If you get the following error message when attempting to compile:

```
C:\MyDir> csc Success.cs
'csc' is not recognized as an internal or external command, operable
program, or batch file.
```

this means that the C# compiler could not be found; i.e., you've either improperly installed the .NET Framework SDK or not properly updated the Path environment variable.

- If you get the following error message when attempting to compile:

```
C:\MyDir> csc Success.cs
error CS2001: Source file 'Success.cs' could not be found
```

this means that the computer can't find your source code. Make sure that (a) you're in the correct directory where the program source code file resides and (b) you're spelling the name of the file correctly.

- If you get any other compilation errors, for example:

```
C:\MyDir> csc Success.cs
Success.cs (5,23) error CS1010: Newline in constant
        Console.WriteLine("Hooray!);
```

check to make sure that you've typed in the program exactly as shown previously. (In this particular example, we're missing the double quote mark at the end of "Hooray!")

- If you get the following error message when attempting to run a successfully compiled program:

```
C:\MyDir> Success
'Success' is not a recognized internal or external command, operable
program, or batch file
```

this could mean one of several different things: (a) you're spelling the name of the program incorrectly (again, pay attention to upper/lower case); (b) the program didn't compile correctly, thus failing to produce a Success.exe file; (c) you're trying to run the program from the wrong directory.

Using the Online .NET Framework Documentation

Extensive documentation for the .NET Framework SDK can be found at the MSDN website using the following URL: http://msdn.microsoft.com/library/default.asp?url=/library/en-us/netstart/html/cpframeworkref_start.asp

The documentation includes tutorials, code examples, and a complete description of the contents of the .NET Framework libraries. Spend time getting familiar with the online C# documentation—it's tremendously useful!

Some Final Notes

This section contains some final "odds and ends" tips that may make your programming life a little easier.

All Command-Line Environments Aren't Created Equal!

The various different versions of Windows—Windows 2000, Windows XP, and Windows Server 2003—implement command prompts a bit differently. Therefore, rules regarding how "true" command prompts behave won't necessarily apply to your particular version of Windows. You'll have to experiment a bit with your particular "flavor" of command prompt to find out what does or doesn't work well.

Here are some of our experiences with using Windows 2000 and Windows XP specifically.

Capturing Program Output to a File

You can capture program output and compilation error messages to files via the file redirection symbol, >.

For example, running our Success.exe program via the command

```
C:\> Success > somefile
```

captures what would normally appear as output to the screen (e.g., the Hooray! It works! message from our earlier example) in a text file instead; this is known as **redirecting standard output.**

To capture error messages to a file when compiling, the same file redirection symbol should do the trick:

```
C:\> csc Success.cs  > somefile
```

thus taking advantage of a technique known as **standard error redirection**.

> *Note that the technique used for redirecting standard **output** differed from the technique used for redirecting the standard **error** stream with older versions of Windows.*

File Names and the Command Prompt Window

While a command prompt does indeed allow us to manipulate complex Windows file/directory names, such as those that contain white space, we sometimes have to do something extra for this to work out properly.

For example, "C:\Program Files" is the name of a standard directory on most Windows systems; note the blank space between "Program" and "Files" in this directory name. If we were to try to look at the contents of this folder while in the command prompt window via the following command:

```
C:\> dir Program Files
```

the following error message would be displayed:

```
File Not Found
```

This situation arises because the system interprets what we typed as two commands rolled into one: dir Program and dir Files.

The solution is to surround the multiword directory name in double quotes:

```
C:\ dir "Program Files"
```

The system now knows that we're referring to a single, multiple-word directory name.

APPENDIX D

Downloading and Compiling the SRS Source Code

ALL OF THE SOURCE CODE and supporting data files for the key example programs in Chapters 14, 15, and 16 are available for download from the Apress web site, http://www.apress.com/book/download.html, as a single file named 159059360X.zip. To download the file, select the title of this book from the list, click the Submit button, and then click the Download Source Code File link. When downloaded and unzipped, this will create the directory structure shown in Figure D-1; make sure to use your zip utility's provision to "use directory names from the ZIP file" (or equivalent), so that this directory structure is preserved.

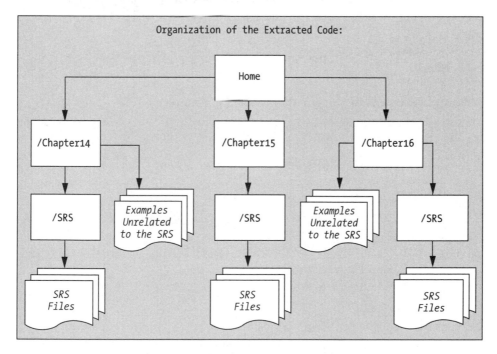

Figure D-1. The source code directory structure

For each of the three chapters, the SRS-specific files will be located in a subdirectory called SRS—for example, *xxx*\Chapter14\SRS. For Chapters 14 and 16, small example programs unrelated to the SRS—for example, the TestForm examples from Chapter 16—will be located in the Chapter14 and Chapter16 "parent" subdirectories, respectively.

To compile the SRS code for a particular chapter, change your default working directory to the appropriate *xxx*\Chapter*nn*\SRS subdirectory—e.g., *xxx*\Chapter14\SRS—and enter the appropriate compile command, which in many cases will simply be

```
csc /out:SRS.exe *.cs
```

In other situations where the compilation command needs to be a bit more complicated—e.g., for selected code in Chapters 15 and 16—you'll be given specific instructions at that point in the chapter text.

Following the procedure that was outlined in Chapter 13, if the SRS source code for a given chapter has been compiled into a file named SRS.exe, the SRS application can be run by typing the command-prompt command:

```
SRS
```

To compile and run individual example files such as TestForm.cs, change your default working directory to the appropriate Chapter subdirectory (*xxx*/Chapter14 or *xxx*/Chapter16), and type

```
csc programName.cs
programName
```

to compile and run the program of interest; for example:

```
csc TestForm.cs
TestForm
```

C# Keywords

As you learned earlier in this book, there are certain reserved words called **keywords** that have special meaning in the C# language. They are used to declare accessibility, control execution flow, define types, and so forth.

For reference purposes, we present in Table E-1 a complete list of the C# keywords, along with a brief description of how each is used and a pointer to that chapter in which we discussed the keyword in depth. Those keywords with an asterisk in the Chapter column are beyond the scope of this book to address in depth, but have been included here in the interest of completeness.

Table E-1. C# Keywords

Keyword	Introduced in Chapter	Description
abstract	7	Indicates a class that can be extended but can't be instantiated or a method that must be implemented.
as	*	A casting operator that returns null if the cast fails.
base	13	Used to access members of a base class hidden by similarly named members in a derived class or struct.
bool	1	A simple type that represents a Boolean value.
break	1	A jump statement used to exit from a loop or switch statement.
byte	1	A simple type that represents an 8-bit unsigned integer.
case	1	Specifies a label in a switch statement. If the constant specified in the label matches the value of the switch expression, the statements associated with the label are executed.
catch	13	Defines a block of code that is executed if a specified type of exception is thrown. Also see try and finally.
char	1	A simple type that represents a single 16-bit Unicode character.
checked	*	Both an operator and statement. Ensures that the compiler and runtime check for overflow in integer-type operations and conversions.
class	1	Designates a declaration as one for a class type.

Table E-1. C# Keywords (continued)

Keyword	Introduced in Chapter	Description
const	13	Indicates that the value of a variable can be computed at compile time, i.e., once assigned, it can't be changed.
continue	1	A jump statement used to return to the top of a loop.
decimal	1	A simple type that represents a 128-bit high-precision decimal value.
default	1	Specifies statements to be executed if none of the preceding case clauses match the expression in a switch statement.
delegate	16	Designates a declaration as one for a delegate type. Delegates encapsulate methods as callable entities that can all be invoked with one invocation of a delegate instance.
do	1	A conditional statement that executes at least once whether or not its condition is satisfied.
double	1	A simple type that represents a 64-bit double-precision floating point value.
else	1	Part of an if conditional statement. The statement following else is executed if the condition isn't true.
enum	*	A value type representing a collection of named constants.
event	16	A member that enables a class or object to provide notifications. It must be of delegate type.
explicit	*	An operator that defines a user-defined cast conversion operator. Generally this will convert a built-in type to a user-defined type or vice versa. Explicit conversion operators must be invoked with a cast.
extern	*	Indicates that a method will be implemented externally, typically in a language other than C#.
false	1	A Boolean literal.
finally	13	Defines a block of code that is always executed when the program control leaves a try block. See also the try and catch keywords.
fixed	*	Assigns a pointer to a variable at a fixed memory location while a block of code executes.
float	1	A simple type that represents a 32-bit single-precision floating point value.
for	1	Defines a loop statement that executes as long as a specified condition holds.
foreach	13	Used to iterate through the elements of a collection.

Table E-1. C# Keywords (continued)

Keyword	Introduced in Chapter	Description
goto	*	A jump statement that redirects program execution to a labeled statement.
if	1	A conditional statement that selects a statement for execution based on the value of a Boolean expression.
implicit	*	An operator that defines a user-defined cast conversion operator. Generally this will convert a predefined type to a user-defined type or vice versa. Implicit conversion operators must be invoked with a cast.
in	13	Part of the iteration syntax in a foreach statement. The in keyword is placed between the variable name and the collection to be iterated over.
int	1	A simple type that represents a 32-bit signed integer value.
interface	7	Designates a declaration as one for an interface type, i.e., a contract that an implementing class or struct must adhere to.
internal	13	An access modifier. A code element with internal access is available to other types in the same assembly. An assembly can be a DLL or EXE file.
is	13	A comparison operator that compares the types of two objects.
lock	*	Used in multithreaded programming to place a mutual exclusion lock (mutex) around a variable.
long	1	A simple type that represents a 64-bit signed integer value.
namespace	1	Defines a logical grouping of types and namespaces.
new	1	An operator used to call a constructor. Also, a modifier used to hide rather than override an inherited method with the same signature.
null	1	A literal that represents the "zero equivalent" value for a reference type.
object	13	A predefined reference type that represents the ultimate base class for all other reference types. It's an alias for the predefined System.Object type.
operator	*	Used when declaring or overloading an operator.
out	*	Indicates that a parameter will affect the value of its argument, but that the argument doesn't have to be initialized before being passed in to the method.

Table E-1. C# Keywords (continued)

Keyword	Introduced in Chapter	Description
override	5	A modifier indicating that a method or operator will override a virtual or abstract method or an operator of the same name defined in a base class.
params	*	Declares a parameter array. If used, it must modify the last parameter specified. Enables optional parameters.
private	1	An access modifier. A member with private access is only available inside the type in which the member is defined.
protected	13	An access modifier. A member with protected access is available to the type in which the member is defined, and to types derived from that type.
public	1	An access modifier. A member with public access is freely available inside or outside of the class or namespace in which the member is defined.
readonly	13	Indicates that the value of a variable can't be changed once it has been initialized.
ref	*	Indicates that a parameter may affect the value of its argument.
return	1	A jump statement used to exit a method. The execution returns to the caller of the method.
sbyte	*	A simple type that represents an 8-bit signed integer.
sealed	13	Prevents types from being derived from and methods and properties from being overridden.
short	1	A simple type that represents a 16-bit signed integer value.
sizeof	*	An operator that returns the size of a value type in bytes.
stackalloc	*	Returns a pointer to a block of memory allocated on the stack.
static	7	A static member is associated with the type in which it's declared rather than with an instance of the type.
string	13	A predefined reference type that represents Unicode character strings. It's an alias for the predefined System.String type.
struct	*	A struct is a value type that can declare constants, fields, methods, properties, indexers, operators, constructors, and nested types.
switch	1	A selection statement that executes a statement list associated with a label that matches the value of an expression.
this	13	References the current instance of a type.

Table E-1. C# Keywords (continued)

Keyword	Introduced in Chapter	Description
throw	*	Causes an exception to be thrown.
true	1	A Boolean literal.
try	13	Part of an exception-handling block of code. The try block contains code that might throw an exception. See also the catch and finally keywords.
typeof	13	An operator that returns the type of the argument passed to it.
uint	*	A simple type that represents a 32-bit unsigned integer value.
ulong	*	A simple type that represents a 64-bit unsigned integer value.
unchecked	*	Suppresses overflow checking.
unsafe	*	Marks a block of code, method, or class that contains pointer operations.
ushort	*	A simple type that represents a 16-bit unsigned integer value.
using	1	When applied to a namespace, the using keyword allows access to the types in a namespace without having to specify the fully qualified type names. Also used for defining finalization scope.
virtual	5	A method modifier indicating that the method can be overridden.
void	1	The return type for methods that don't return a value.
volatile	*	Indicates that an attribute can be modified by the operating system, some type of hardware device, or a concurrently executing thread.
while	1	A while conditional statement executes a statement zero or more times based on a condition. The while part of a do statement specifies the loop termination condition.

Index

Symbols

forums.apress.com

FOR PROFESSIONALS BY PROFESSIONALS™

JOIN THE APRESS FORUMS AND BE PART OF OUR COMMUNITY. You'll find discussions that cover topics of interest to IT professionals, programmers, and enthusiasts just like you. If you post a query to one of our forums, you can expect that some of the best minds in the business—especially Apress authors, who all write with *The Expert's Voice*™—will chime in to help you. Why not aim to become one of our most valuable participants (MVPs) and win cool stuff? Here's a sampling of what you'll find:

DATABASES

Data drives everything.

Share information, exchange ideas, and discuss any database programming or administration issues.

INTERNET TECHNOLOGIES AND NETWORKING

Try living without plumbing (and eventually IPv6).

Talk about networking topics including protocols, design, administration, wireless, wired, storage, backup, certifications, trends, and new technologies.

JAVA

We've come a long way from the old Oak tree.

Hang out and discuss Java in whatever flavor you choose: J2SE, J2EE, J2ME, Jakarta, and so on.

MAC OS X

All about the Zen of OS X.

OS X is both the present and the future for Mac apps. Make suggestions, offer up ideas, or boast about your new hardware.

OPEN SOURCE

Source code is good; understanding (open) source is better.

Discuss open source technologies and related topics such as PHP, MySQL, Linux, Perl, Apache, Python, and more.

PROGRAMMING/BUSINESS

Unfortunately, it is.

Talk about the Apress line of books that cover software methodology, best practices, and how programmers interact with the "suits."

WEB DEVELOPMENT/DESIGN

Ugly doesn't cut it anymore, and CGI is absurd.

Help is in sight for your site. Find design solutions for your projects and get ideas for building an interactive Web site.

SECURITY

Lots of bad guys out there—the good guys need help.

Discuss computer and network security issues here. Just don't let anyone else know the answers!

TECHNOLOGY IN ACTION

Cool things. Fun things.

It's after hours. It's time to play. Whether you're into LEGO® MINDSTORMS™ or turning an old PC into a DVR, this is where technology turns into fun.

WINDOWS

No defenestration here.

Ask questions about all aspects of Windows programming, get help on Microsoft technologies covered in Apress books, or provide feedback on any Apress Windows book.

HOW TO PARTICIPATE:

Go to the Apress Forums site at **http://forums.apress.com/**.
Click the New User link.